USEFUL REFERENCE SERIES NO. 90

Index To Scientists

of the World

from Ancient to Modern Times:

Biographies and Portraits

By

NORMA OLIN IRELAND

BOSTON, MASS.

THE F. W. FAXON COMPANY, INC.

1962

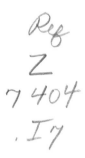

Library of Congress Catalog Card Number 62-13662.

PRINTED IN THE UNITED STATES OF AMERICA

To

My Husband, David E. Ireland,

who, as senior industrial engineer,
has worked with some of the nation's leading
scientists for the past 10 years at Cal Tech's Jet
Propulsion Laboratory in Pasadena, California. First, he
consulted on the production of one of the country's first
missiles, "The Corporal"; next, he purchased all materials for
the country's first successful satellite, "Explorer I"; now he
arranges and plans conferences on "space research" between
representatives of leading research companies and the Lab's
research scientists.

TABLE OF CONTENTS

FOREWORD

We hope this *"Index to Scientists"* will fulfil a timely purpose in today's world: to easily and quickly locate information on world scientists from ancient to modern times — their biographies, portraits, and chief scientific contributions.

With the current emphasis on science in schools and industry, the study of science and scientists has been increasing. According to *Publisher's Weekly,*[1] there were 1494 books on science published by American publishers in 1961, of which number 1193 were new titles, 301 new editions. It is often difficult for the librarian to find sufficient biographical references, however, especially circulating material suitable for large group assignments. For that reason we have analyzed circulating books primarily, altho a few standard reference books have been included.

SCOPE

338 collections, covering all phases of science, have been indexed for this work. If separate volumes of sets are counted, there are 461. We feel that the inclusion of titles is comprehensive, if not complete, as we have based selection on the holdings of three typical public libraries, plus books found in other libraries (including college and university) and borrowed through interlibrary loan.

Altho the books indexed vary greatly in type and amount of information included, this has been purposeful in order to make the Index equally useful for large and small libraries. For instance, we have indexed the large Hammerton's *Concise universal biography* (which was a monumental task in itself), altho probably found only in large libraries, because of its excellent portraits and life-sketches of hard-to-find scientists, especially English. On the other hand, we have indexed several vocational books in which the biographical material was very scanty, but the books are found in most small school libraries.

We have omitted most encyclopedias because of their alphabetical

---

1. *Publisher's Weekly* Jan. 15 '62, p46.

arrangement and comprehensive coverage, also biographical diction-
aries of separate countries and professions. Exceptions are: Hammerton (mentioned above), Chamber's *Dictionary of scientists,* Fitzhugh's
Concise biographical dictionary and a few others which we felt merited
special attention. Neither have we generally indexed magazines, altho
we have included *Current biography,* and a few Memoirs, Proceedings,
etc. of outstanding value. Complete runs have been indexed, whenever
possible, e.g. *Current biography* from its beginning date 1940, especially because the *Biography Index* covers it from 1946 to date, only.

We have indexed many basic juvenile books, both old and new,
which will assemble much biographical data not before correlated.
Altho large lists of references on such personalities as Edison may
seem extraneous, it must be remembered that sometimes 25-50 students
may be assigned the same scientist, for special reports! May we here
express appreciation for the large amount of reference help given by
public libraries to students, especially from schools which do not main-
tain libraries of sufficient size and do not stay open after school hours.
Books for younger readers (as found in juvenile departments) are
indicated by asterisks, but that does not exclude many other titles
which may be equally suitable.

BROAD COVERAGE

More than 7,475 different scientists are listed in this work, exclu-
sive of cross-references. The classification of scientists was broadly
interpreted to include *all* occupations in pure science (biological,
physical), as well as many in applied science but *not* the social science
field. We *have* used a broad coverage, however, to include inventors,
engineers, physicians, aeronautical pioneers, etc. because we felt that
their careers overlapped with pure science. Many "pioneers" are included — in electricity, radio, aviation, and now space. We have used
the term "aero. pioneer", for instance, as we felt that in this recent
scientific field (aeronautical, aerospace) most of the inventors, de-
signers and record-makers were truly "pioneers" in science.

While the material included is, of course, chiefly biographical, in
some instances the chief scientific contribution is all that was available.
Material was not always consistently arranged (even in some of the

most valuable books), but scattered throughout the book, thus making the indexing of it somewhat difficult. In some books, too (such as medicine, entomology, aviation histories), a great many unimportant names were listed, with uneven biographies. In these cases, we attempted to choose the names of most importance, largest coverage, complete dates, etc.

Portraits are a special feature of this Index and we believe their inclusion will extend the usefulness of the work — to artists, research workers, etc. Since the publication of the old *A.L.A. Portrait index,* few attempts have been made to concentrate on portraits. A great many hard-to-find portraits may be found therein.

ARRANGEMENT

Arrangement is strictly alphabetical, by letter, as is usually employed in biographical reference tools. The dates and identification (nationality and occupation) are given for each scientist, followed by the analyzed reference data. We have endeavored to fill in complete dates, whenever possible; we have checked current sources to ascertain dates of death altho sometimes such dates were *not* available in *Who's who* or *New York Times Index.* There was some discrepancy in dates by the various authorities which we tried to correct by checking such sources as *Webster's Biographical dictionary* (latest edition), Hyamson's *Dictionary of universal biography* (revised edition), *Who's who in America,* etc. When authorities disagreed, we have indicated by question marks, and either/or dates. We have excluded *most* names for which no dates at all were available because we felt if they were too obscure to locate, they were not suitable for inclusion.

Any omission of names must be judged by one large factor: the inclusion in the 338 books indexed. Some recent scientists would have been included if they had been listed in current books.

Cross-references, from various forms of the name, have been made in all cases when known. We have tried to follow standard library procedure in regard to foreign names but in some instances popular usage (as adopted by biographical reference books), has been preferred. The variation of some foreign names (especially Arabian) was so great that we have used cross-references most liberally, and only *hope* there has been no duplication.

CONCLUSION AND ACKNOWLEDGMENTS

We wish to thank the following libraries and individuals for their help:

> PASADENA PUBLIC LIBRARY, especially Mrs. Hazel Hammett and others of the Interlibrary Loan staff for their assistance in securing volumes from many California libraries; the Reference and Children's departments.
> LOS ANGELES PUBLIC LIBRARY, especially Miss Gladys Sandifur, Lucile Lipman, and others of the Science department of that library.
> GLENDALE PUBLIC LIBRARY, especially Mrs. Martha Westwood and others of the Reference and Reader's Service department.
> CURRENT BIOGRAPHY STAFF of H. W. Wilson Co., especially for sending us advance notice of recent inclusions.

In conclusion, we wish to say that it has been a real inspiration to read and index books on scientists. We have marveled at the *courage and endurance* of these scientific pioneers in the face of adversity and opposition. Many of them were "controversial" characters of their day because of the ignorance of their contemporaries. We like the following quotations, which are applicable today:

> AGASSIZ: "Every new scientific truth must pass through three stages — first, men say it is not true; then they declare it hostile to religion; finally, they assert that every one has known it always".
> STERNE, EMMA GELDERS, in *Blood brothers; four men of science,* p43:
> "There are those in every age
> who, fearing loss of power
> seek to cut some slender thread.
> It takes a long time
> for the hands of dreamers to splice a cut thread.
> Some say: Stand still. Enough of growing!
> And some: We shall find new ways of knowing. . . .

We have marveled at the developments in science just during our lifetime, in *man's endless searching for truth,* as expressed in the following:

> *"Shape of things to Come," a motion picture*
> *as quoted in Calder, Ritchie's "Science in our lives,"* p94:
> "For Man there can be no rest and no ending. He must go on, conquest beyond conquest. This little planet, its winds and ways and all the laws of mind and matter that restrain him. Then the planets about him and at last out across immensity to the stars. And when he has conquered all the deeps of space and all the mysteries of time — still he will be but beginning".

And over all, we always marvel at the *greatness of GOD,* the greatest of all "scientists", without whom all of man's efforts are in vain. We think this Bible verse expresses our feeling most beautifully of all:

> *Romans 1:20* "Ever since the creation of the world His Invisible nature, namely, His eternal power and deity, has been clearly perceived in the things that have been made".

NORMA OLIN IRELAND

1024 Alpine Villa Drive
Altadena, California

INDEX TO ABBREVIATIONS, ETC.

*	— esp. suitable for younger readers

A

aero.	— aeronautical, aerospace
Afr.	— African
agric.	— agricultural
Alex.	— Alexandrian
Amer.	— American
append.	— appendix
Arab.	— Arabian
Argent.	— Argentinian
Armen.	— Armenian
Assyr.	— Assyrian
Aust.	— Austrian
Austral.	— Australian

B

b.	— born
Babyl.	— Babylonian
Belg.	— Belgian
biol.	— biological
Bohem.	— Bohemian
Bol.	— Bolivian
Brazil.	— Brazilian
Brit.	— British
Byzan.	— Byzantine
Bulg.	— Bulgarian

C

c.	— circa (about)
Can.	— Canadian
cent.	— century
chem.	— chemical
Chile.	— Chilean
Chin.	— Chinese
col.	— column
Czech.	— Czechoslovakian

D

d.	— died
Dan.	— Danish
Dom.R.	— Dominican Republican

E

Egypt.	— Egyptian
elec.	— electrical
Eng.	— English

F

Fin.	— Finnish
fl.	— flourished
Flem.	— Flemish
Fr.	— French
front.	— frontispiece

G

Ger.	— German
Gr.	— Greek

H

Hung.	— Hungarian

I

Ind.	— Indian
isl.	— island
It.	— Italian

J

Japan.	— Japanese

K

Kor.	— Korean

L

Lith.	— Lithuanian

M

math.	— mathematical
mech.	— mechanical
med.	— medical
Mex.	— Mexican
min.	— mining
Morav.	— Moravian

N

N. Afric.	— North African
nat.	— natural
Newfound.	— Newfoundland
New Zeal.	— New Zealander
Norw.	— Norwegian

O

P

p.	— page
Palest.	— Palestinian
path.	— pathological
Pers.	— Persian
Peru.	— Peruvian
phys.	— physical
physiol.	— physiological
pl.	— plate
Pol.	— Polish
Pomer.	— Pomeranian
por.	— portrait
Port.	— Portuguese
pseud.	— pseudonym
pub.	— public

R

Rhod.	— Rhodesian
Rom.	— Romanian
Rus.	— Russian

S.

S.Afr.	— South African
sci.	— scientist
Scot.	— Scottish
Sic.	— Sicilian
Siles.	— Silesian
Slov.	— Slovenian
Sp.	— Spanish
supp.	— supplement
Swed.	— Swedish
Syr.	— Syrian

T

temp.	— temporary
Transyl.	— Transylvanian
Turk.	— Turkish

U

unp.	— unpaged

V

Virgin Isl.	— Virgin Islander
vet.	— veterinarian

W

W.	— West
W.Indies	— West Indian

X,Y,Z

Yugoslav.	— Yugoslavian

LIST OF COLLECTIONS
ANALYZED IN THIS WORK
AND
KEY TO SYMBOLS USED

A.A.A.S.—Proc. (77-81)

    American Academy of Arts and Sciences. *Proceedings*. The Academy, 1949-1952, v.77-82.

Abbot—Great

    Abbot, Charles Greeley. *Great inventions*. (Smithsonian scientific series, v.12). Smithsonian Instit., 1934. 383p.

Abetti—History

    Abetti, Giorgio. *The history of astronomy*. Schuman, 1957. 338p.

Adams—Birth

    Adams, Frank Dawson. *Birth and development of the geological sciences*. Dover pub., Inc., 1938. 506p.

*Adams—Heroines

    Adams, Jean and Margaret Kimball, in collaboration with Jeannette Eaton. *Heroines of the sky*. Doubleday, Doran, 1942. 295p.

Alden—Early

    Alden, Roland H. and John D. Ifft. *Early naturalists in the far West*. Calif. Academy of Sciences, 1943. 59p. (Occasional papers of the Calif. Academy of Sciences, no. XX).

Appleyard—Pioneers

    Appleyard, Rollo. *Pioneers of electrical communication*. Macmillan & Co., 1930. 347p.

Arago—Biog.

    Arago, François. *Biographies of distinguished scientific men*. Ticknor & Fields, 1859. 486p.

Arber—Herbals

    Arber, Agnes. *Herbals, their origin and evolution. A chapter in the history of botany*. Cambridge Univ. Press, 1938. 326p.

Armitage—Cent.
Armitage, Angus. *A century of astronomy.* Sampson Low, 1950. 256p.

Arnold—Airmen
Arnold, Henry H. *Airmen and aircraft.* Ronald Press, 1926. 216p.

Atkinson—Magic
Atkinson, Donald T. *Magic, myth and medicine.* World Pub. Co., 1956. 319p.

*Bachman—Great
Bachman, Frank P. *Great inventors and their inventions.* Amer. Book Co., 1941. 304p.

Ball—Great
Ball, Sir Robert Stawell. *Great astronomers.* Pitman, 1912. 372p.

Ball—Short
Ball, W. W. Rouse. *A short account of the history of mathematics.* Macmillan, 1908. 536p.

*Beard—Foreign
Beard, Annie E. S. *Our foreign-born citizens.* Crowell, 1922. 288p.

Bell—Early
Bell, Whitfield J., Jr. *Early American science, needs and opportunities for study.* Institute of Early Amer. History and Culture, 1955. 85p.

Bell—Men
Bell, Eric Temple. *Men of mathematics.* Simon & Schuster, 1937. 592p.

*Bernays—Outline
Bernays, Edward L. *An outline of careers.* George H. Doran Co., 1927. 431p.

*Bishop—Kite
Bishop, Richard W. *From kite to Kitty Hawk.* Crowell, 1958. 211p.

Bodenheimer—Hist.
Bodenheimer, F. S. *The history of biology.* William Dawson & Sons, Ltd., 1958. 465p.

*Bolton—Famous
Bolton, Sarah K. *Famous men of science.* rev. & enl. Crowell, 1926. 333p.

*Book—Pop. Sci. (1-15)
The book of popular science. Grolier Soc., 1926. v.1-15.

Borth—Pioneers

Borth, Christy. *Pioneers of plenty.* Bobbs Merrill, 1939. 303p.

*Bridges—Master

Bridges, T. C. and H. H. Tiltman. *Master minds of modern science.* Lincoln MacVeagh, 1931. 278p.

Browne—Hist.

Browne, Charles Albert and Mary Elvira Weeks. *A history of the American Chemical Society—seventy-five eventful years.* American Chemical Society, 1952. 526p.

Bulloch—Hist.

Bulloch, William. *The history of bacteriology.* Oxford Univ. Press, 1938. 422p.

Burge—Ency.

Burge, C. G. *Encyclopaedia of aviation.* Pitman & Sons, n.d. 642p.

*Burlingame—Inv.

Burlingame, Roger. *Inventors behind the inventor.* Harcourt, 1947. 211p.

*Burlinghame—Mach.

Burlingame, Roger. *Machines that built America.* Harcourt, 1953. 214p.

*Cajori—Hist.

Cajori, Florian. *A history of mathematics.* Macmillan, 1929. 516p.

Calder—Science

Calder, Ritchie. *Science in our lives.* Michigan State College Press, 1954. 186p.

Carmer—Caval.

Carmer, Carl Lamson. *Cavalcade of America; the deeds and achievements of the men who made our country great.* Crown, 1956. 382p.

Castiglioni—Hist.

Castiglioni, Arturo. *A history of medicine.* 2nd ed., rev. and enl. Knopf, 1947. 1192p.

Ceram—Gods

Ceram, C. W. *Gods, graves and scholars. The story of archaeology.* Translated from the German by E. B. Garside. Knopf, 1951. 426p.

Chalmers—Historic

Chalmers, Thomas Wightman. *Historic researches; chapters in the history of physical and chemical discovery.* Scribner, 1952. 288p.

Chambers—Dict.

Howard, A. V. *Chamber's Dictionary of scientists*. Dutton, 1958. 499p.

*Chandler—Medicine

Chandler, Caroline Auguste. *Famous men of medicine*. (Famous biographies for young people) Dodd, 1950. 140p.

Chem. Ind.

Chemical Industries. *Chemical industry's contribution to nation, 1635-1935*. Chem. Ind., 1935. 176p.

Chymia (1-5)

Chymia. *Annual studies in the history of chemistry*. Univ. of Pa. Press, 1948-date. v.1-5.

Clagett—Greek

Clagett, Marshall. *Greek science in antiquity*. Abelard-Schuman, Inc., 1955. 217p.

Clapesattle—Doctors

Clapesattle, Helen. *The Doctors Mayo*. Univ. of Minn. Press, 1941. 822p.

*Clymer—Modern

Clymer, Eleanor and Lillian Erlich. *Modern American career women*. Dodd Mead, 1959. 178p.

*Cohen—Men

Cohen, Rose N. *The men who gave us wings*. (Aviation readers) Macmillan, 1944. 210p.

*Compton—Conquests

Compton, Ray and Charles H. Nettals, ed. *Conquests of science*. Harcourt, Brace, 1939. 378p.

Coolidge—Six

Coolidge, Julian L. *Six female mathematicians*. Reprint from Scripta Mathematica, v.17, #1-2, Mr.-Je. 1951, p20-31.

*Cooper—Twenty

Cooper, Alice Cecilia and Charles A. Palmer. *Twenty modern Americans*. Harcourt, Brace & Co., 1942. 379p.

Copen.—Prom.

Copenhagen University Library. *Prominent Danish scientists through the ages*. Levin & Munksgaard Pub., 1932. 189p.

*Cottler—Heroes

Cottler, Joseph and Haym Jaffe. *Heroes of civilization.* Little, 1931. 362p.

Crew—Physicists

Crew, Henry. *Portraits of famous physicists, with biographical accounts.* Scripta Mathematica, 1942. unp.

*Crowther—Doctors

Crowther, James Gerald. *Six great doctors.* Hamilton, 1957. 207p.

Crowther—Famous

Crowther, James Gerald. *Famous American men of science.* Norton, 1937. 414p.

Crowther—Founders

Crowther, James Gerald. *Founders of British science.* The Cresset Press, 1960. 296p.

*Crowther—Inventors

Crowther, James Gerald. *Six great inventors.* Hamilton, 1954. 235p.

Crowther—Men

Crowther, James Gerald. *Men of science.* W. W. Norton, 1936. 332p.

*Crowther—Scientists

Crowther, James Gerald. *Six great scientists.* Hamilton, 1955. 269p.

Curr. Biog. ('40 - '61)

Current Biography. H. W. Wilson Co., 1940 - 1960 (annual); 1961, (Jan.-Dec.) (monthly)

Cushing—Medical

Cushing, Harvey. *Medical career.* Little, Brown, 1940. 302p.

Cutright—Great

Cutright, Paul Russell. *The great naturalists explore South America.* Macmillan, 1940. 340p.

Dakin—Perennial

Dakin, Susanna Bryant. *The perennial adventure.* Calif. Academy of Sciences, 1954. 40p.

Daniel Gugg.

The Daniel Guggenheim medal for achievement in aeronautics. Guggenheim, 1936. 62p.

*Eberle—Modern

Eberle, Irmengarde. *Modern medical discoveries.* Crowell, 1948. 183p.

*Elwell—Sci.

Elwell, Felicia Rosemary. *Science and the doctor.* Criterion Books, 1959. 160p.

*Epstein—Real

Epstein, Samuel and Beryl Williams. *Real book about inventions.* Garden City Books, 1951. 191p.

Essig—Hist.

Essig, E. O. *A history of entomology.* Macmillan, 1931. 1029p.

*Everett—When

Everett, Carroll and Charles Francis Reed. *When they were boys.* F. O. Owen, 1922. 192p.

Ewan—Rocky

Ewan, Joseph Andorfer. *Rocky mountain naturalists.* Univ. of Denver Press, 1950. 358p.

Fabricant—Why

Fabricant, Noah D. *Why we became doctors.* Grune & Stratton, 1954. 182p.

Farber—Nobel

Farber, Eduard. *Nobel prize winners in chemistry, 1901-1950.* Schuman, 1953. 219p.

*Faris—Men

Faris, John Thompson. *Men who conquered.* Revell, 1922. 185p.

Farmer—Doctors'

Farmer, Laurence. *Doctors' legacy. A selection of physicians' letters, 1721-1954.* Harper, 1955. 267p.

Fenton—Giants

Fenton, Carroll Lane and Mildred Adams Fenton. *Giants of geology.* Doubleday & Co., Inc., 1952. (rev. & enl. ed. of "The story of the great geologists") 333p.

Findlay—British

Findlay, Alexander and William Holson Mills. *British chemists.* Chemical Soc., 1947. 431p.

Findlay—Hundred

Findlay, Alexander. *A hundred years of chemistry.* Macmillan, 1937. 352p.

Fisher—Amer.
>Fisher, Dorothy Canfield. *American portraits.* Henry Holt, 1946. 318p.

Fitzhugh—Concise
>Fitzhugh, Harriet Lloyd, Percy K. Fitzhugh and William Morris. *Concise biographical dictionary of famous men and women.* Rev. & enl. ed. Grosset, 1949. 830p.

*Fleischman—Careers
>Fleischman, Doris E. *Careers for women.* Garden City Pub., 1928. 514p.

Flexner—Doctors
>Flexner, James T. *Doctors on horseback; pioneers of American medicine.* Viking, 1937. 370p.

Forbes—Fifty
>Forbes, Bertie Charles, ed. *America's 50 foremost business leaders.* Forbes, 1948. 483p.

Forbes—Men
>Forbes, Bertie Charles, ed. *Men who are making America.* Forbes, 1921. 5th ed. 442p.

*Fox—Great
>Fox, Ruth. *Great men of medicine.* Random House, 1947. 240p.

*Fraser—Famous
>Fraser, Chelsea. *Famous American flyers.* Crowell, 1941. 352p.

*Fraser—Heroes
>Fraser, Chelsea. *Heroes of the air.* Crowell, 1939. 846p.

Fülöp—Miller
>Fülöp-Miller, René. *Triumph over pain.* Translated by Eden and Cedar Paul. Literary Guild of Amer., 1938. 438p.

G.S.A.—Proc. ('33 - '57)
>Geological Society of America. *Proceedings, 1933-1957.*

Gartmann—Men
>Gartmann, Heinz. *The men behind the space rockets.* Weidenfeld and Nicolson, 1955. 185p.

Geikie—Founders
>Geikie, Sir Archibald. *The founders of geology.* Macmillan, 1897. 297p.

Geiser—Natural.

Geiser, Samuel Wood. *Naturalists of the frontier.* Southern Methodist Univ., 1948. 296p.

Gibson—Heroes

Gibson, Charles R. *Heroes of the scientific world.* Seeley, Service & Co., 1926. 344p.

Gilmour—British

Gilmour, John. *British botanists.* Collins, 1946. 48p.

Ginzburg—Adven.

Ginzburg, Benjamin. *The adventure of science.* Simon & Schuster, 1930. 487p.

*Glenister—Stories

Glenister, S. H. *Stories of great craftsmen.* George G. Harrap & Co., 1939. 235p.

*Goddard—Eminent

Goddard, Dwight. *Eminent engineers. Brief biographies of 32 of the inventors and engineers who did most to further mechanical progress.* Derry-Collard Co., 1906. 280p.

Goff—Women

Goff, Alice C. *Women can be engineers.* The Author, Youngstown, Ohio, 1946. 277p.

Gordon—Medicine

Gordon, Benjamin Lee. *Medicine throughout antiquity.* F. A. Davis Co., 1949. 818p.

Gordon—Medievel

Gordon, Benjamin Lee. *Medieval and Renaissance medicine.* Philosophical Library, 1959. 843p.

Gordon—Romance

Gordon, Benjamin Lee. *The romance of medicine.* F. A. Davis Co., 1945. 624p.

Grainger—Guide

Grainger, Thomas H., Jr. *A guide to the history of bacteriology.* Ronald Press, 1958. 210p.

Great Names

Great names in neurology . . . by the National Institute of Neurological Diseases and Blindness, National Institute of Health, Bethesda, Maryland. (Public Health Service Publication #554. Public Health Bibl. Series 17) 1957. 80p.

Gregory—British
Gregory, Sir Richard. *British scientists.* William Collins of London, 1931. 48p.

Guinagh—Inspired
Guinagh, Kevin. *Inspired amateurs.* Longmans, Green & Co., 1937. 171p.

Gumpert—Trail
Gumpert, Martin. *Trail-blazers of science. Life stories of some half-forgotten pioneers of modern research.* Funk & Wagnalls, 1936. 306p.

Gunther—Early XI
Gunther, R. T. *Early science in Oxford. vol. XI. Oxford colleges and their men of science.* Oxford (for the Author), 1937. 429p.

Hale-White—Great
Hale-White, Sir William. *Great doctors of the 19th century.* Edward Arnold & Co., 1935. 325p.

Hammerton
Hammerton, Sir J. A. *Concise universal biography.* Amalgamated Press Ltd., n.d. 1452p.

Hammond—Stories
Hammond, Mrs. D. B. *Stories of scientific discovery.* Cambridge Univ. Press, 1923. 199p.

*Harrow—Chemists
Harrow, Benjamin. *Eminent chemists of our time.* D. Van Nostrand Co., 1927. 2d ed. rev. 471p.

Hart—Engineers
Hart, Ivor Blashka. *The great engineers.* Methuen & Co., 1928. 136p.

Hart—Makers
Hart, Ivor Blashka. *Makers of science.* Oxford Univ. Press, 1924. 320p.

Hart—Physicists
Hart, Ivor Blashka. *Great physicists.* Methuen & Co., 1927. 137p.

*Hartman—Mach.
Hartman, Gertrude. *Machines and the men who made the world of industry.* Macmillan, 1939. 278p.

*Hathaway—Partners
Hathaway, Esse V. *Partners in progress.* McGraw-Hill Book Co., 1935. 303p.

Hawks—Pioneers
Hawks, Ellison. *Pioneers of plant study.* Macmillan, 1928. 288p.

Hawks—Wireless
Hawks, Ellison. *Pioneers of wireless.* Methuen & Co., 1927. 304p.

Haynes—Chem. (1)
Haynes, Williams. *Chemical pioneers.* D. Van Nostrand Co., 1939. vol. 1. 288p.

Heath—Amer. (4)
Heath, Monroe. *Great American at a glance. vol. 4 — Great American women.* Pacific Coast Pub., 1957. 32p.

Heathcote—Nobel
Heathcote, N. H. de V. *Nobel prize winners in physics 1901 - 1950.* Schuman, 1953. 473p.

Heinmuller—Man's
Heinmuller, John. *Man's fight to fly.* Funk & Wagnalls, 1944. 366p.

*Hodgins—Behemoth
Hodgins, Eric and F. Alexander Magoun. *Behemoth.* Junior Literary Guild, 1932. 354p.

Hofman—History
Hofman, Joseph Ehrenfried. *The history of mathematics.* Philosophical Library, 1957. 132p.

Holland—Arch.
Holland, Maurice. *Architects of aviation.* Duell, Sloan & Pearce, 1951. 209p.

Holland—Ind.
Holland, Maurice and H. F. Pringle. *Industrial explorers.* Harper, 1928. 347p.

Holmyard—British
Holmyard, Eric John. *British scientists.* Philosophical Library, 1951. 88p.

Holmyard—Chem.
Holmyard, Eric. *Chemistry to the time of Dalton.* Oxford Univ. Press, 1925. 128p.

Holmyard—Great Chem.
Holmyard, Eric. *The great chemists.* Methuen & Co., 1928. 137p.

Holmyard—Makers
Holmyard, Eric. *Makers of chemistry.* Oxford, At the Clarendon Press, 1931. 314p.

Hooper—Makers
Hooper, Alfred. *Makers of mathematics.* Random House, 1948. 402p.

Hubbard—Scientists (2)
Hubbard, Elbert. *Little journeys to the homes of great scientists. vol. 2.* Roycrofters, 1905. 51p.

Huff—Famous (2d)
Huff, Warren and Edna Lenore Webb Huff. *Famous Americans.* (Second series) Charles Webb & Co., 1941. 641p.

*Hughes—Negroes
Hughes, Langston. *Famous American negroes.* Dodd, Mead & Co., 1954. 147p.

*Hyde—Modern
Hyde, Marietta. *Modern biography.* Harcourt, 1926. 345p.

*Hylander—Invent.
Hylander, Clarence J. *American inventors.* Macmillan, 1934. 216p.

*Hylander—Scien.
Hylander, Clarence J. *American scientists.* Macmillan, 1935. 186p.

Iles—Leading
Iles, George. *Leading American inventors.* Henry Holt & Co., 1924. 447p.

*Ivins—Fifty
Ivins, Lester and A. E. Winship. *Fifty famous farmers.* Macmillan, 1924. 407p.

*Jaffe—Crucibles
Jaffe, Bernard. *Crucibles; the story of chemistry.* Simon & Schuster, 1948. rev. ed. 480p.

Jaffe—Men
Jaffe, Bernard. *Men of science in America.* Simon & Schuster, 1958. rev. ed. 715p.

Jaffe—Outposts
Jaffe, Bernard. *Outposts of science.* Simon & Schuster, 1935. 547p.

Lambert—Medical
Lambert, Samuel Waldron. *Medical leaders from Hippocrates to Osler.* Bobbs Merrill, 1929. 330p.

Lambert—Minute
Lambert, Samuel Waldron. *Minute men of life.* Grosset & Dunlap, 1929. 331p.

*Larsen—Men
Larsen, Egon (Lehrburger, Egon). *Men who changed the world. Stories of invention and discovery.* Phoenix House, 1957. 221p.

*Larsen—Prentice
Larsen, Egon (Lehrburger, Egon). *The Prentice-Hall book about invention.* Prentice-Hall, 1954. 184p.

*Larsen—Scrap.
Larsen, Egon (Lehrburger, Egon). *Inventors' scrapbook.* Lindsay Drummond, Ltd., 1947. 216p.

*Larsen—Shaped
Larsen, Egon (Lehrburger, Egon). *Men who shaped the future.* Roy pub., 1954. 223p.

Law—Civiliz.
Law, Frederick Houk. *Civilization builders.* D. Appleton-Century, 1939. 356p.

*Law—Modern
Law, Frederick Houk. *Modern great Americans.* Century Co., 1926. 286p.

Lenard—Great
Lenard, Philip. *Great men of science.* G. Bell & Sons, 1933. 389p.

Leonard—Crus.
Leonard, Jonathan Norton. *Crusaders of chemistry.* Doubleday, Doran, 1930. 307p.

Leonardo—Lives
Leonardo, Richard. *Lives of master surgeons.* Froben, 1948. 469p.

Leonardo—Lives (Supp. 1)
Leonardo, Richard. *Lives of master surgeons. Supplement I.* Froben, 1949. 518p.

*Lewellen—Boy
Lewellen, John Bryan. *Boy scientist.* (Popular Mechanics Book). Simon & Schuster, 1955. 264p.

Lindroth—Swedish
Lindroth, Sten, ed. *Swedish men of science, 1650-1950.* Swedish Institute, 1952. 295p.

*Lockhart—My
Lockhart, E. O. *My vocation, by eminent Americans.* Wilson, 1938. 334p.

Locy—Biology
Locy, William A. *Biology and its makers.* Holt, 1915. 477p.

Lodge—Pioneers
Lodge, Sir Oliver. *Pioneers of science.* Macmillan, 1893. 404p.

*Logie—Careers
Logie, Iona M. R., ed. *Careers in the making. Modern Americans when they were young — and on their way.* Harper, 1935. 381p.

Lovejoy—Women
Lovejoy, Esther Pohl. *Women doctors of the world.* Macmillan Co., 1957. 413p.

Lovejoy—Women Phys.
Lovejoy, Esther Pohl. *Women physicians and surgeons.* Printed by Livingston Press, n.d. 246p.

Ludovici—Nobel
Ludovici, Laurence James. *Nobel prize winners.* Arco, 1957. 226p.

MacFarlane—Lectures
MacFarlane, Alexander. *Lectures on ten British mathematicians.* Wiley, 1916. 148p.

MacFarlane—Ten
MacFarlane, Alexander. *Lectures on Ten British physicists of the nineteenth century.* Wiley & Sons, Inc., 1919. 141p.

MacPherson—Astron.
MacPherson, Hector, Jr. *Astronomers of to-day and their work.* Gall & Inglis, Pub., 1905. 261p.

MacPherson—Makers
MacPherson, Hector, Jr. *Makers of astronomy.* Oxford, At the Clarendon Press, 1933. 244p.

*McSpadden—How
McSpadden, Joseph Walker. *How they blazed the way.* Dodd, 1939. 279p.

Magie—Source
Magie, William Francis. *Source book of physics.* McGraw-Hill, 1935. 620p.

Maitland—Knights
Maitland, Lester J. *Knights of the air.* Doubleday, Doran & Co., 1929. 338p.

Major—History (1)
Major, Ralph H. *A history of medicine.* Charles Thomas, Springfield, Ill., 1954. vol. 1, p1-563.

Major—History (2)
Major, Ralph H. *A history of medicine.* Charles Thomas, Springfield, Ill., 1954. vol. 2, p565-1155.

Makers—Modern
Makers of modern medicine. Charles Darwin . . . Sigmund Freud . . . Albert Einstein. (A 20th Century Library trilogy) Scribners, 1953. 124p;132p; 134p.

Marr—Pioneer
Marr, James Pratt. *Pioneer surgeons of the Woman's Hospital.* F. A. Davis, 1957. 148p.

*Masters—Conquest
Masters, David. *The conquest of disease.* Dodd, Mead, 1925. 353p.

Matschoss—Great
Matschoss, C. *Great engineers.* G. Bell, 1939. 381p.

Mead—Medical
Mead, Kate Campbell Hurd. *Medical women of America.* Froben, 1933. 95p.

Meisen—Prominent.   *See* Copen.—Prom.

*Men—Scien.
Men of science. *15 stories of scientific advances and the men who helped make them.* Westinghouse Electric Corp., 1946. 45p.

Merrill—First
Merrill, George P. *The first one hundred years of American geology.* Yale Univ. Press, 1924. 773p.

Meyer—World
Meyer, Jerome S. *World book of real inventions.* World Pub. Co., 1956. 270p.

Miall—Early

Miall, L. C. *The early naturalists. Their lives and work (1530-1789)*. Macmillan, 1912. 396p.

Milbank—First

Milbank, Jeremiah, Jr. *The first century of flight in America*. Princeton Univ. Press, 1943. 248p.

*Miller—Hist.

Miller, George Abram. *Historical introduction to mathematical literature*. Macmillan, 1916. 302p.

*Milne—Natur.

Milne, Lorus Johnson and Margery Milne. *Famous naturalists*. (Famous biographies for young people). Dodd, Mead, 1952. 178p.

*Montgomery—Invent.

Montgomery, Elizabeth Rider. *The story behind great inventions*. McBride & Co., 1944. 254p.

*Montgomery—Story

Montgomery, Elizabeth Rider. *The story behind great medical discoveries*. Junior Literary Guild, McBride & Co., 1945. 247p.

Morgan—Men

Morgan, Bryan. *Men and discoveries in electricity*. Murray, 1952. 188p.

Morris—Ency.

Morris, Richard B. *Encyclopedia of American history*. Harper, 1953. 776p.

*Morris—Heroes

Morris, Charles. *Heroes of progress in America*. Lippincott Co., 1919. 372p.

Moulton—Auto.

Moulton, Forest Ray and Justus J. Schifferes. *Autobiography of science*. Doubleday, Doran & Co., 1945. 666p.

Mozans—Woman

Mozans, H. J., pseud. (Zahm, John August). *Woman in science*. Appleton, 1913. 452p.

Muir—Men

Muir, Jane. *Of men and numbers. The story of the great mathematicians*. Dodd, Mead, 1961. 249p.

Murray—Science

Murray, Robert H. *Science and scientists in the ninetenth century.* The Sheldon Press, 1925. 450p.

N.A.S.—Biog. (1-35)

National Academy of Sciences. *Biographical memoirs.* The Academy, 1877-date, vol. 1-35.

Newman—Interp.

Newman, George. *Interpreters of nature.* Oxford Univ. Press, 1927. 296p.

Newman—What

Newman, James R. *What is science?* Simon & Schuster, 1955. 493p.

*Nida—Makers

Nida, William Lewis and Stella H. *Makers of progress.* (Science readers, Bk. V.) Heath & Co., 1926. 206p.

*Nisenson—Illus.

Nisenson, Samuel and William A. Dewitt. *Illustrated minute biographies.* rev. ed. Grosset & Dunlap, 1953. 160p.

*Nisenson—More

Nisenson, Samuel and Alfred Parker. *More minute biographies.* Grosset & Dunlap, 1933. 160p.

Oehser—Sons

Oehser, Paul Henry. *Sons of science. The story of the Smithsonian Institution and its leaders.* Henry Schuman, 1949. 220p.

Oliver—Makers

Oliver, F. W., ed. *Makers of British botany.* Cambridge Univ. Press, 1913. 332p.

Oliver—Stalkers

Oliver, Wade W. *Stalkers of pestilence.* Paul B. Hoeber, 1930. 251p.

100 Great

One hundred great lives. Revealing biographies of scientists and inventors . . . edited by John Allen. Greystone Press, 1945. 790p.

Osborn—Fragments

Osborn, Herbert. *Fragments of entomological history.* The Author, Columbus, Ohio, 1937. 394p.

Osborn—Greeks

Osborn, Henry F. *From the Greeks to Darwin.* Scribners, 1929. 398p.

Osborn—Impr.
Osborn, Henry F. *Impressions of great naturalists.* Scribners, 1928. 294p.

*Parkman—Conq.
Parkman, Mary R. *Conquests of invention.* Century, 1921. 413p.

Partington—Short
Partington, J. R. *A short history of chemistry.* 3d ed. Macmillan, 1957. 415p.

*Patterson—Amer.
Patterson, John C. *America's greatest inventors.* Crowell, 1943. 240p.

Peattie—Gather.
Peattie, Donald Culross. *A gathering of birds.* Dodd, Mead, 1929. 379p.

Peattie—Green
Peattie, Donald Culross. *Green laurels; the lives and achievements of the great naturalists.* Simon & Schuster, 1936. 368p.

Peattie—Lives
Peattie, Donald Culross. *Lives of destiny.* Houghton, Mifflin, 1954. 208p.

People
People. Edited by Geoffrey Grigson and Charles Harvard Gibbs-Smith. Hawthorn Books, Inc., (1958 ?) 469p.

*Perry—Four
Perry, Frances Melville. *Four American inventors.* Amer. Book Co., 1901. 260p.

Potter—Flying
Potter, Jean. *The flying North.* Macmillan, 1947. 261p.

*Pratt—Famous
Pratt, Fletcher. *Famous inventors and their inventions.* Random House, 1955. 142p.

Pringle—Great
Pringle, Patrick. *Great discoveries in modern science.* Roy, 1955. 206p.

Progress—Science '40
The progress of science, a review of 1940. Grolier Society, 1941. 442p.

Progress—Science '41
The progress of science, a review of 1941. Grolier Society, 1942. 404p.

R.S.L.—Biog. (1-5)

Royal Society of London. *Biographical memoirs of fellows of Royal Society.* The Society, 1955-date. vol. 1-5.

Radio's 100

Dunlap, Orrin E., Jr. *Radio's 100 men of science.* Harper & Bros., 1944. 294p.

Ramsay—Essays

Ramsay, Sir William. *Essays biographical and chemical.* Archibald Constable & Co., 1909. 247p.

Ratcliffe—Modern

Ratcliff, John Drury. *Modern miracle men.* Dodd, Mead, 1939. 311p.

Raven—English

Raven, Charles E. *English naturalists from Neckham to Ray. A study of the making of the modern world.* Cambridge Univ. Press, 1947. 379p.

Reed—Short

Reed, Howard S. *A short history of the plant sciences.* Chronica Botanica Co., 1942. 320p.

Riedman—Men

Riedman, Sarah R. *Men and women behind the atom.* Abelard-Schuman Ltd., 1958. 228p.

Roberts—Chem.

Roberts, Ethel. *Famous chemists.* George Allen & Co., 1911. 247p.

Robinson—100

Robinson, Donald. *The 100 most important people in the world today.* Little, Brown & Co., 1952. 427p.

Robinson—Path.

Robinson, Victor. *Pathfinders in medicine.* Medical Life Press, 1929. 810p.

Robinson—Victory

Robinson, Victor. *Victory over pain. A history of anesthesia.* Schuman, 1946. 338p.

Rosen—Four

Rosen, George and Beate Caspari-Rosen. *400 years of a doctor's life.* Schuman, 1947. 429p.

Rowntree—Amid

Rowntree, Leonard G. *Amid masters of twentieth century medicine.* Charles C. Thomas, Pub., 1958. 684p.

Sarton—Six

Sarton, George. *Six wings, men of science in the Renaissance.* Indiana Univ. Press, 1957. 318p.

Schuyler—Roeblings

Schuyler, Hamilton. *The Roeblings; a century of engineers, bridge builders, and industrialists.* Princeton Univ. Press, 1931. 425p.

Schwartz—Moments (1)

Schwartz, George and Philip W. Bishop. *Moments of discovery, vol. 1. The origins of science.* Basic Books, Inc., 1958. 497p.

Schwartz—Moments (2)

Schwartz, George and Philip W. Bishop. *Moments of discovery, vol. 2. The development of modern science.* Basic Books, Inc., 1958. 1005p.

Sci. Amer.—Lives

Scientific American. *Lives in science.* Simon & Schuster, 1957. 269p.

*Science Miles.

Science milestone. Windsor Press, 1954. 312p.

Sedgwick—Short

Sedgwick, W. T. and H. W. Tyler. *A short history of science.* Macmillan, 1919. 474p.

Sewell—Brief

Sewell, W. Stuart. *Brief biographies of famous men and women.* Permabooks, 1949. 244p.

Shapley—Astron.

Shapley, Harlow. *A source book in astronomy.* McGraw-Hill Book Co., 1929. 412p.

*Shippen—Bridle

Shippen, Katherine Binney. *A bridle for Pegasus.* Viking Press, 1951. 192p.

*Shippen—Design

Shippen, Katherine Binney. *Bright design.* Viking Press, 1949. 207p.

*Shippen—Men

Shippen, Katherine Binney. *Men of medicine.* Viking Press, 1957. 220p.

*Shippen—Micro.

Shippen, Katherine Binney. *Men, microscopes and living things.* Viking Press, 1955. 192p.

*Shumway—Famous (4th)

Shumway, Harry Irving. *Famous leaders of industry.* Page, 1936. (4th series) 356p.

Sigerist—Great

Sigerist, Henry Ernest. *The great doctors, a biographical history of medicine.* Allen & Unwin, 1933. 436p.

*Simmons—Great

Simmons, Sanford. *Great men of science.* Hart, 1955. 64p.

16 Amer.

16 American health heroes. (vol. XXV of the Health Bulletin for teachers). Metropolitan Life Insurance, (1953?) 75p.

Smith—Chem.

Smith, Edgar F. *Chemistry in America.* D. Appleton & Co., 1929. 356p.

Smith—Hist. I

Smith, David Eugene. *History of mathematics.* Ginn & Co., 1951. 596p. vol. 1
— General survey of the history of elementary mathematics.

Smith—Math.

Smith, David Eugene and Jekuthiel Ginsburg. *A history of mathematics in America before 1900.* Math. Assoc. of Amer., 1934. 209p.

Smith—Portraits (1, 2)

Smith, David Eugene. *Portraits of eminent mathematicians, with brief biographical sketches.* v.1,2. Scripta Mathematica, 1946. unp.

Smith—Torch.

Smith, Henry Monmouth. *Torchbearers of chemistry.* Academic Press, Inc., 1949. 270p.

Smiths.—Misc. (84)

Smithsonian Miscellaneous Collection, v.84. Smithsonian Inst., 1931. 564p.

*Snyder—Biology

Snyder, Emily Eveleth. *Biology in the Making.* McGraw-Hill, 1940. 539p.

*Sootin—Twelve

Sootin, Harry. *Twelve pioneers of science.* Vanguard Press, 1960. 254p.

*Sterling—Polio

    Sterling, Dorothy and Philip. *Polio pioneers.* Doubleday & Co., Inc., 1955. 128p.

*Sterne—Blood

    Sterne, Emma Gelders. *Blood brothers: four men of science.* Knopf, 1959. 174p.

*Stevens—Science

    Stevens, William Oliver. *Famous men of science.* (Famous biographies for young people) Dodd, Mead, 1952. 164p.

Stevenson—Nobel

    Stevenson, Lloyd G. *Nobel prize winners in medicine and physics, 1901-1950.* 291p.

Suter—Gallery

    Suter, Rufus. *A gallery of scientists.* Vantage, 1955. 132p.

Swiss—Prom.

    Swiss-American Historical Society. *Prominent Americans of Swiss origin.* James T. White & Co., 1932. 266p.

*Tappan—Heroes

    Tappan, Eva March. *Heroes of progress. Stories of successful Americans.* Houghton, 1921. 273p.

Taylor—Illus.

    Taylor, F. Sherwood. *An illustrated history of science.* Frederick A. Prager, 1955. 178p.

Thomas—50 Amer.

    Thomas, Henry, pseud., and Dana Lee Thomas, pseud. *50 great Americans.* Doubleday & Co., 1948. 468p.

Thomas—Men

    Thomas, Shirley. *Men of space.* Vol. 1. Chilton Co., 1960. 235p.

Thomas—Men (2)

    Thomas, Shirley. *Men of space.* Vol. 2. Chilton Co., 1961. 238p.

Thomas—Men (3)

    Thomas, Shirley. *Men of space.* Vol. 3. Chilton Co., 1961. 274p.

Thomas—Scien.

    Thomas, Henry, pseud., and Dana Lee Thomas, pseud. *Living biographies of great scientists.* Garden City Pub. Co., 1941. 314p.

Thomson—Great

Thomson, J. Arthur. *Great biologists.* Methuen, 1932. 176p.

Thorwald—Century

Thorwald, Jürgen. *The century of the surgeon.* Pantheon Books, 1957. 432p.

Three—-Amer.

Three American microscope builders. American Optical Co., Scientific Instrument Division, 1945. 77p.

Three Famous

Three famous alchemists. David McKay, n.d. 186p.

Tilden—Famous

Tilden, Sir William A. *Famous chemists, the men and their work.* Dutton, 1921. 296p.

Tobey—Riders

Tobey, James A. *Riders of the plagues. The story of the conquest of disease.* Scribners, 1930. 348p.

*Towers—Beacon

Towers, Walter Kellogg. *From beacon fire to radio.* Harper, 1924. 303p.

Tracy—Amer. Nat.

Tracy, Henry Chester. *American naturalists.* Dutton, 1930. 282p.

Trattner—Arch.

Trattner, Ernest R. *Architects of ideas.* Carrick & Evans, Inc., 1938. 426p.

*Truax—Doctors

Truax, Rhoda. *True adventures of doctors.* Little, Brown & Co., 1954. 216p.

True—Smiths.

True, Webster Prentiss. *The Smithsonian Institution.* (Smithsonian scientific series, v.1) Smithsonian Instit., 1934. 330p.

Turnbull—Great

Turnbull, Herbert W. *Great mathematicians.* Methuen, 1929. 128p.

Tuska—Invent.

Tuska, C. D. *Inventors and inventions.* McGraw-Hill, 1957. 174p.

Untermeyer—Makers
Untermeyer, Louis. *Makers of the modern world.* Simon & Schuster, 1955. 809p.

Van Wagenen—Beacon
Van Wagenen, Theodore F. *Beacon lights of science.* Crowell, 1924. 444p.

Vaucouleurs—Disc.
Vaucouleurs, Gérard De. *Discovery of the universe. An outline of the history of astronomy from the origins to 1956.* Macmillan, 1957. 328p.

Von Hagen—Green
Von Hagen, Victor Wolfgang. *The green world of the naturalists.* Greenberg, 1948. 392p.

Walker—Pioneers
Walker, M. E. M. *Pioneers of public health.* Walker, 1930. 270p.

Walsh—Catholic (2d)
Walsh, James J. *Catholic churchmen in science.* (2nd series) Dolphin Press, 1906. 228p.

Walsh—Makers
Walsh, James J. *Makers of modern medicine.* Fordham Univ. Press, 1907. 362p.

*Watson—Engineers
Watson, Sara Ruth and Emily. *Famous engineers.* (Famous biographies for young people) Dodd, Mead & Co., 1950. 152p.

Webb—Famous
Webb, Mary Griffin and Edna Louise Webb. *Famous living Americans.* Webb Co., 1914. 594p.

Weber—College
Weber, Robert, Marsh W. White and Kenneth V. Manning. *College physics.* McGraw-Hill, 1952. 820p.

Weeks—Discovery
Weeks, Mary Elvira. *Discovery of the elements.* (5th ed., enl. & rev.) Journal of Chemical Education, 1945. 578p.

Welker—Birds
Welker, Robert Henry. *Birds and men. American birds in science, art, literature, and conservation, 1800-1900.* The Belknap Press of Harvard Univ. Press, 1955. 230p.

*White—Famous (3d)

White, Trentwell. *Famous leaders of industry*. (3d series) Page, 1931. 325p.

*Wildman—Famous (1st)

Wildman, Edwin. *Famous leaders of industry*. (1st series) Page, 1920. 357p.

*Wildman—Famous (2d)

Wildman, Edwin. *Famous leaders of industry*. (2d series) Page, 1921. 339p.

*Williams-Ellis

Williams-Ellis, Amabel. *Men who found out. Stories of great scientific discoveries*. Junior Literary Guild, 1930. 259p.

Williams—Great

Williams, Henry Smith. *Great astronomers*. Simon & Schuster, 1930. 618p.

*Williams—Rocket

Williams, Beryl and Samuel Epstein. *Rocket pioneers on the road to space*. Messner, 1955. 241p.

Williams—Story

Williams, Henry Smith. *The story of nineteenth-century science*. Harper, 1900. 475p.

Wilson—Amer.

Wilson, Mitchell. *American science and invention*. Simon & Schuster, 1954. 437p.

Wilson—Human

Wilson, Grove. *The human side of science*. Cosmopolitan Book Corp., 1929. 397p.

Woglom—Discov.

Woglom, William H. *Discoverers for medicine*. Yale Univ. Press, 1949. 229p.

Woodruff—Devel.

Woodruff, L. L., ed. *The development of the sciences*. By Ernest William Brown and others. Yale Univ. Press, 1923. 327p.

*World's Great

The World's great scientists. Home Study Circle Library, ed. by Seymour Eaton. Doubleday & McClure Co., 1900. 399p.

*Wright—Great

Wright, Helen & Samuel Berder Rapport. *Great adventures in science*. Harper, 1956. 338p.

Year—Pic
    Year, Editors of. *A pictorial history of science.* Year, n.d. 257p.

*Yost—Engineers
    Yost, Edna. *Modern American engineers.* Lippincott, 1958. 182p.

Yost—Women Mod.
    Yost, Edna. *Women of modern science.* Dodd, Mead & Co., 1959. 176p.

Yost—Women Sci.
    Yost, Edna. *American women of science.* Lippincott, 1943. 232p.

*Yost—Science
    Yost, Edna. *Modern Americans in science and invention.* Stokes, 1941. 270p.

Youmans—Pioneers
    Youmans, William J. *Pioneers of science in america.* Appleton, 1896. 508p.

Young—Biology
    Young, R. T. *Biology in America.* Richard G. Badger, The Gorham Press, 1922.
        509p.

Young—Scalpel
    Young, Agatha. *Scalpel. Men who made surgery.* Random House, 1956. 311p.

INDEX TO SCIENTISTS

A

Abano, Pietro d' (or Apano, Petrus de; Aponensis) (1250-1316). It. physician.
Gordon—Medieval p333-337   Major—History (1) p331
Hammerton p1

Abauzit, Firmin (1679-1767). Fr. nat. philosopher.
Hammerton p2

Abbadie, Antoine Thomson d' (1810-1897). Irish-Fr. sci. explorer, astronomer.
Hammerton p2

Abbe, Cleveland (1838-1916). Amer. meteorologist, geologist, astronomer.
Chambers—Dict. col.1   N.A.S.—Biog. (8) p469-485 (por.469)
G.S.A.—Proc. '34 p151-153 (por.151)   Van Wagenen—Beacon p380-381
Hammerton p 3

Abbe, Ernst (1840-1905). Ger. physicist, mathematician.
Bulloch—Hist. p349   Hammerton p3 (por.3)
Chambers—Dict. col.1

Abbot, Charles Greeley (b.1872). Amer. astrophysicist, astronomer, meteorologist.
Chambers—Dict. col.1,2   Oehser—Sons p167-181 (por.122)
Hammerton p3 (por.3)   True—Smiths. p67-78,200-201
Jaffe—Outposts p451-484 (por.458)   (por.62)

Abbot, Henry Larcom (1831-1927). Amer. engineer.
N.A.S.—Biog. (13) p1-101 (por.1)

Abbott, Alexander Crever (1860-1935). Amer. bacteriologist.
Bulloch—Hist. p349

Abbott, Maude E. (1869-1940). Can. physician.
Lovejoy—Women p114-116 (por.115)
Mead—Medical p59

Abdallah.   See **Mamun, al-, Caliph Abdallah**

Abd Al-Latif (or Abdul ul Latif; Abu Muhammed Abdul Latif ibn Jusuf) (1162-1231). Arab. physician, anatomist.

Gordon—Medieval p181-182   Major —History (1) p246-247
Hammerton p4

Abderhalden, Emil (1877-1950). Swiss phys. chemist, physiologist.

Abdul ul Latif.   See Abd Al-Latif

Abegg, Richard (1869-1910). Ger. chemist.

Chambers—Dict. col.2   Smith—Torch. p11 (por.11)
Partington—Short p341

Abel, Sir Frederick Augustus (1827-1902). Eng. chemist.

Chambers—Dict. col.2-3   Smith—Torch. p12 (por.12)
Hammerton p6 (por.6)

Abel, John Jacob (1857-1938). Amer. physiol. chemist.

Castiglioni—Hist. p1064   Major—History (2) p916
Chambers—Dict. col.3   N.A.S.—Biog. (24) p231-248
*Darrow—Builders p227-228   (por.231)
Hammerton p6   Rowntree—Amid p94-99 (por.97)
Jaffe—Outposts 161-201 (por.170)

Abel, Niels Henrik (1802-1829). Norw. mathematician.

Ball—Short p461-462   *Miller—Hist. p247-248
Bell—Men p307-326 (por.front.)   Smith—Hist. I p527
Cajori—Hist. p411   Van Wagenen—Beacon p275-277
Chambers—Dict. col.3   Woodruff—Devel. p30,36,261
Hammerton p6

Abel, Rudolf (b.1868). Ger. bacteriologist.

Bulloch—Hist. p349

Abell, Sir Westcott Stile (1877-   ). Eng. engineer.

Hammerton p7

Abenezra (or Ben Ezra, Abraham; Ibn Ezra) (1092/97-1167). Sp. mathematician.

Ball—Short p166
Smith—Hist. I p207-208

Aben-Guefit (or Ibnu'l Wafid) (997-1075). Arab. physician.

Major—History (1) p264-265

Abercrombie, John (1780-1844). Scot. physician.

Hammerton p8

Abercromby, David (d. 1702). Scot. physician.
Hammerton p8

Abercromby, Patrick (1656-c1716). Scot. physician.
Hammerton p8

Abernethy, John (1764-1831). Eng. surgeon.
Hammerton p9 (por.9)   Major—History (2) p704
Leonardo—Lives p1

Abetti, Antonio (1846-1928). It. astronomer.
Chambers—Dict. col.3
Hammerton p9-10

Ab Horto.   See **Horto, Garcia ab**

Abich, Otto Wilhelm Hermann von (1806-1886). Ger.-Rus. geologist.
Chambers—Dict. col.3,4
Hammerton p10

Abildgaard, Peter Christian (1740-1801). Dan. anatomist, zoologist.
Copen.—Prom. p65-67

Abney, Sir William de Wiveleslie (1843-1920). Eng. chemist.
Chambers—Dict. col.4
Hammerton p11 (por.11)

Abraham ibn David (or Halevi, Abraham Ben David) (1110?-1180). Sp.
  biologist.
Bodenheimer—Hist. p199

Abrams, Leroy (b.1874). Amer. botanist.
Hammerton p12

Abt Usaybi'a. See **Ibn abt Usaybi'a**

Abu Kamil (850-930). Egypt. mathematician.
Smith—Hist. I p177

Abu'l Faraj, Juhanna.   See **Bar-Hebraeus**

Abul Kasim (or Abulcasis, Abul Casim of Cordova, Abu L-Qasim uz-Zahrawi) (936-c1013). Arab-Sp. physician, surgeon, chemist).

Atkinson—Magic p57-58
Castiglioni—Hist. p274-275
Gordon—Medicine p693 (por.693)
Gordon—Medieval p201-202
Hammerton p13

Holmyard—Chem. p28
Holmyard—Makers p81
Leonardo—Lives p9-11
Major—History (1) p250

Abu'l Walid Muhammad.   See **Averroes**

Abu'l Wefa (940-998). Pers. mathematician, astronomer.

Cajori—Hist. p105-106

Abu Mansur Muwaffaq (c950). Pers. physician.

Hammerton p13

Abu Ma'shar (805-885). Arab. astronomer.

Hammerton p13

Abu Mervan.   See **Avenzoar**

Abu Sahal Dunash.   See **Ben Tamim, Abu Sahal Dunash**

Abu Yakub ibn Ishaq (c910). Arab. physician.

Gordon—Medieval p148

Abu Ya'quli.   See **Isaac Judaeus**

Accum, Fredrick (1769-1838). Ger.-Eng. chemist.

Chymia v.1 p1-9 (por.2,8)
Hammerton p13 (por.13)

Achard, Franz Karl (1753-1821). Ger. chemist, naturalist.

Chambers—Dict. col.4
Hammerton p13-14

Acharius, Erik (1757-1819). Swed. botanist.

Hammerton p14

Acheson, Albert Robert (1882-1941). Amer engineer.

Curr. Biog. '41 p6

Acheson, Edward Goodrich (1856-1931). Amer. chemist, inventor, engineer.

Chambers—Dict. col.4
Hammerton p14

*Montgomery—Invent. p180-183
*Wildman—Famous (2d) p3-12 (por.3)

Achillini, Alessandro (1463-1512). It. physician.
Castiglioni—Hist. p368-369 (por.371)   Major—History (1) p395 (por.389)
Gordon—Medieval p619-620
    (por.front.)

Ackermann, Johann Christian Gottlieb (1756-1801). Ger. physician.
Hammerton p14

Acland, Sir Henry Wentworth Dyke (1815-1900). Eng. physician.
Gunther—Early XI p162,223-225
    (por.224)
Hammerton p15 (por.15)

Acosta, Cristobal (d.1580). Port. botanist.
Hawks—Pioneers p156

Acosta, Joseph de (1539?-1600). Sp. Naturalist, sci. explorer,
    archaeologist.
Miall—Early p64-70
Von Hagen—Green p56-57

Acquapendente.   See **Fabricius ab Acquapendente, Hieronymus**

Acron (5th cent., B.C.). Sicilian physician.
Gordon—Medicine p493

Actuarius, Johannes (13th cent.). Gr. physician.
Gordon—Medieval p65-68
Major—History (1) p217-218

Adair, Frank Earl (1887-   ). Amer. physician, surgeon.
Curr. Biog '46 p2-4 (por.3)

Adair, Fred Lyman (b.1877). Amer. physician.
Progress—Science '41 p1-2 (por.1)

Adam, Neil Kensington (1891-   ). Eng. phys. chemist.
Chambers—Dict. col.4-5

Adami, John George (1862-1926). Eng. pathologist.
Hammerton p18 (por.18)

Adams, Andrew Leith (1827-1882). Scot. naturalist, surgeon.
Hammerton p18

Adams, Arthur Stanton (1896-   ). Amer. engineer.
Curr. Biog. '51 p3-4 (por.3)

Adams, Charles (1847-1924). Amer. surgeon.
Leonardo—Lives p1-2

Adams, Charles Baker (1814-1853). Amer. geologist, naturalist.
Merrill—First p246-248 (por.247)

Adams, Frank Dawson (1859-1942). Can. geologist.
G.S.A.—Proc.'44 p143-146 (por.143)
Hammerton p18-19

Adams, John Couch (1819-1892). Eng. astronomer, mathematician.
Abetti—History p214-217
Armitage—Cent. p112-113 (por.144)
Ball—Great p354-372 (por.357)
Ball—Short p494-495
Chambers—Dict. col.5 (por.5)
Hammerton p19-20 (por.19)
MacFarlane—Ten p119-130
  (por., front.)
MacPherson—Makers p157-158
Shapley—Astron. p245
*Sootin—Twelve p141-155
Van Wagenen—Beacon p310-311
Williams—Great p309,312,322
  (por.310)
Woodruff—Devel. p162,261 (por.148)
Year—Pic p118 (por.118)

Adams, Joseph Henry (1867-1941). Amer. inventor.
Curr. Biog. '41 p11

Adams, Robert (1791-1875). Irish physician.
Major—History (2) p709-710

Adams, Roger (1889-   ). Amer. chemist.
Browne—Hist. p487-488 (por.149)
Curr. Biog. '47 p1-2 (por.1)
Hammerton p20
Progress—Science '40 p1-2 (por.1)
Robinson—100 p258-260 (por.258)

Adams, Walter Sydney (1876-1956). Amer. astronomer.
Chambers—Dict. col.5,6
Hammerton p20 (por.20)
N.A.S.—Biog.(31) p1-14 (por.1)
Progress—Science '41 p2
R.S.L.—Biog. (2) p1-9 (por.1)

Adams, William Bridges (1797-1872). Eng. inventor.
Hammerton p20

Adanson, Michel (1727-1806). Fr. naturalist.
Chambers—Dict. col.6
Hammerton p21
Reed—Short p110-111

Addenbrooke, John (1680-1719). Eng. physician.
Hammerton p21

Addison, Thomas (1793-1860). Eng. physician.
Atkinson—Magic p222
Castiglioni—Hist. p704-705 (por.709)
Chambers—Dict. col.6-7
Hale-White—Great p106-123
Hammerton p23 (por.23)
Lambert—Medical p219-222
Lambert—Minute p219-220
Major—History (2) p690-691
(por.691)

Adelard of Bath (or Aethelhard) (12th cent.) Eng. biologist.
Bodenheimer—Hist. p209

Ader, Clement (1840/1841-1925). Fr. aero. pioneer, engineer.
*Bishop—Kite p146-152
Burge—Ency. p624
Heinmuller—Man's p252 (por.252)

Adkins, Homer Burton (1892-1949). Amer. chemist.
N.A.S.—Biog.(27) p293-307
(por.293)

Adkins, Walter Scott (1890-1956). Amer. geologist.
G.S.A.—Proc. '56 p97-101 (por.97)

Adkinson, Burton W. (1909-   ). Amer. geographer.
Curr. Biog. '59 p1-2 (por.1)

Adler, Alfred (1870-1937). Amer. psychologist, psychiatrist.
Chambers—Dict. col.7
Hammerton p23 (por.23)
Year—Pic. p224 (por.224)

Adrian, Edgar Douglas (1889-   ). Eng. biologist, neuro-physiologist.
Castiglioni—Hist. p944 (por.944)
Chambers—Dict. col.7,supp.
Curr. Biog. '55 p1-3 (por.1)
Hammerton p25 (por.25)
*Snyder—Biology p406-408 (por.408)
Stevenson—Nobel p155,159-164
(por.150)

Adrian, Robert (1775-1843). Irish-Amer. mathematician.
Smith—Math. p91-92 (por.93)

Aegidius, Pierre Gilles Corbeil de (or Gilles de Corbeil) (c1140-1200).
Fr. physician.
Castiglioni—Hist. p316-317
Major—History (1) p280-283

Aepinus, Franz Elrich Theodor (1724-1802). Ger. physicist.
Magie—Source p406

Aeschylus (525-456 B.C.). Gr. biologist.
Hammerton p26-27 (por.27)
Osborn—Greeks p63-68

Aesculapius (c1300 B.C.). Gr. physician.
Lambert—Medical p7-8 (por.,front.)   Leonardo—Lives p2-3
Lambert—Minute p6-9 (por.,front.)

Aethelhard.   See **Adelard of Bath**

Aëtios   (or Aëtius) **of Amida.** (c502-c550). Gr. physician, surgeon.
Gordon—Medicine p694 (por.694)   Lambert—Minute p63
Gordon—Medieval p50-56   Leonardo—Lives p3-6
Hammerton p27-28   Major—History (1) p211-212
Lambert—Medical p63

af Pontin.   See **Pontin, M. M., af**

Africanus, Sextus Julius (c.150-232?). Afr. sci. explorer.
Chambers—Dict. col.8

Afzelius, Adam (1750-1837). Swed. botanist.
Hammerton p28

Agar, William Macdonough (1894-   ). Amer. geologist.
Curr. Biog. '49 p7-9 (por.8)

Agardh, Karl Adolf (1785-1859). Swed. botanist, mathematician.
Chambers—Dict. col.8
Hammerton p28

Agassiz, Alexander Emanuel (1835-1910). Amer. naturalist,
    oceanographer, zoologist.
Chambers—Dict. col.8-9   N.A.S.—Biog. (7) p289-298 (por.289)
Hammerton p29 (por.29)   Swiss—Prom. p183-185 (por.183)

Agassiz, (Jean) Louis Rodolphe (1807-1873). Swiss-Amer. naturalist.
*Beard—Foreign p1-10   Hammerton p29 (por.29)
*Bolton—Famous p85-119 (por.84)   *Hylander—Scien. p65-76 (por.76)
*Book—Pop. Sci. (1) p143-144   Jaffe—Men p233-257 (por.xxviii)
    (por.142)   Jordan—Leading p147-169 (por.147)
Chambers—Dict. col.8   Locy—Biology p334-337 (por.336)
*Darrow—Masters p198-205 (por.161)   Merrill—First p277 (por.615)
Fenton—Giants p111-123 (por.95)   *Milne—Natur. p57-73 (por.56)
Fitzhugh—Concise p10-12   N.A.S.—Biog (2) p39-73
Geikie—Founders p271-274   Osborn—Fragments p29 (por.340)
(Continued)

Agassiz, (Jean) Louis Rodolphe—*Continued*
  *Snyder—Biology p93-104
    (por.99,102)
  Swiss—Prom. p186-192 (por.186)
  *Tappan—Heroes p79-90
  Thomas—Scien. p167-184 (por.165)
  True—Smiths. p261-263 (por.262)
  Van Wagenen—Beacon p282-284
  Williams—Story p134-136 (por.135)

  Wilson—Amer. p98-99 (por.98)
  Woodruff—Devel. p261 (por.186)
  *World's Great p299-326 (por.312)
  Year—Pic. p135 (por.135)
  Youmans—Pioneers p475-491
    (por.475)
  Young—Biology p38-39 (por.38)

Agatharchides (or Agatharchus) (fl.c.146 B.C.). Gr. naturalist, geographer.
  Adams—Birth p9,21-22

Agathinos of Sparta (90 A.D.). Rom. physician.
  Major—History (1) p219

Agello, Francesco (1902-   ). It. aero. pioneer.
  Hammerton p1445 (n.v.)

Agnesi, Maria Gaetana (1718-1799). It. mathematician.
  Cajori—Hist. p250
  Coolidge—Six p21-23
  Hammerton p30

  Mozans—Woman p143-151
  Smith—Hist. I p519 (por.518)

Agnew, David Hayes (1818-1892). Amer surgeon.
  Hammerton p30
  Leonardo—Lives p6-8

Agnodice (3d cent. B.C.). Gr. physician.
  Mozans—Woman p268-269,290

Agoty, Jacques Gautier d' (1710-1786). Fr. anatomist, physician.
  Major—History (2) p634

Agricola, Georgius (or Georg Bauer) (1490/94-1555). Ger. physician, mineralogist, metallurgist, chemist, geologist, engineer.
  Adams—Birth p183-195,308-309,
    343-345 (por.185)
  *Book—Pop. Sci. (2) p715
  Chambers—Dict. col.9
  Hammerton p31
  Hart—Engineers p47-55
  Holmyard—Chem. p48-50
  Major—History (1) p466-467

  Matschoss—Great p60-70 (por.61)
  Moulton—Auto. p54
  Partington—Short p55
  Sarton—Six p122-127,158-159
  Schwartz—Moments (1) p194-195
  Weeks—Discovery p13,23,30,454
    (por.13)

Agrippa, Cornelius Heinrich (or Agrippa von Nettesheim) (1486-1535). Ger. physician.
  Atkinson—Magic p89-92
  Three Famous p76-134 (por.76)

Ahmes (c 1650 B.C.) Egypt. mathematician.
Smith—Hist. I p47

Aiken, Howard Hathaway (1900-   ). Amer. mathematician, inventor, engineer.
Curr. Biog. '47 p5-7 (por.6)

Ainslee, Charles Nicolas (1856-1939). Amer. entomologist.
Osborn—Fragments p226 (por.378)

Ainslee, George Gooding (1886-1930). Amer. entomologist.
Osborn—Fragments p218 (por.373)

Ainsworth, William Francis (1807-1896). Eng. geographer, geologist, physician.
Hammerton p36

Aird, Sir John (1833-1911). Eng. engineer.
Hamerton p36 (por.36)

Airy, Sir George Biddell (1801-1892). Eng. astronomer.
Ball—Great p289-302 (por.293)   MacFarlane—Ten p106-118
Chambers—Dict. col.9   (port.front.)
Hammerton p37 (por.37)   Shapley—Astron. p202
                                             Woglom—Discov. p109-112

Aitken, John (1839-1919). Scot. physicist, meteorologist.
Chambers—Dict. col.9,10   N.A.S.—Biog. (32) p1-7 (por.1)
Hammerton p37

Aiton, William (1731-1793). Br. botanist.
Hammerton p37

Akeley, Carl Ethan (1864-1926). Amer. naturalist, inventor, sci. explorer.
Tracy—Amer.Nat. p155-163

Akenside, Mark (1721-1770). Eng. physician.
Major—History (2) p635

Akers, Wallace Alan (1888-1954). Eng. phys. chemist.
R.S.L.—Biog. (1) p1-4 (por.1)

Al-Asam.   See **Alhazen**

Alaymo, Marco Antonio (1590-1662). It. physician.
Hammerton p39

Al-Baitar.   See **Ibn al-Baytar**

Al-Bakri (1040-1094). Arab. geographer.
Hammerton p39

Al-Balkhi, Abu Zaid (d934). Arab. geographer.
Hammerton p39

Albarran, Joaquin (1860-1912). Cuban physician-surgeon.
Leonardo—Lives (Supp.1) p471

Albategnius.   See **Battani, Al**

Al-Baytar.   See **Ibn al-Baytar**

Albe.   See **Fournier d'Albe, Edmund Edward**

Albee, Fred Houdlette (1876-1945). Amer. physician, surgeon.
Curr. Biog. '43 p2-4 (por.3); '45 p3
Leonardo—Lives p8-9

Albert, Edouard (1841-1900). Aust. surgeon.
Hammerton p44

Albert, Joseph (1825-1886). Ger. inventor.
Hammerton p44

Alberto (da Motta e Silva), Alvaro (1889-   ). Brazil. chemist.
Curr. Biog. '47 p7-9 (por.8)

Albertus Magnus, Saint, Count von Bollstädt (or Albert of Cologne, Albert the Great, Universal Doctor, or Doctor Universalis) (1193?/1206?-1280). Ger. biologist, botanist, chemist, mineralogist, naturalist, physician.
Adams—Birth p144-145,335
Arber—Herbals p4-6,146-147,163,164
Bodenheimer—Hist. p214
*Book—Pop.Sci. (3) p1064-1065
Castiglioni—Hist. p340-341
Chambers—Dict. col.10
Gordon—Medieval p272-275
Hawks—Pioneers p102-107 (por.102)
Holmyard—Chem. p34-36
Holmyard—Makers p90-92
Major—History (1) p313-314
Partington—Short p36
Reed—Short p57-59
Smith—Hist. I p228
Smith—Torch p13 (por.13)
Walsh—Catholic (2d) p21-58 (por.21)
Weeks—Discovery p20-21 (por.21)

Albe 'thar.   See **Ibn al-Baytar**

Albinus, Bernard Siegfried (1697-1770). Ger. anatomist.
Hammerton p45
Major—History (2) p633

Albright, William Foxwell (1891-   ). Chile.-Amer. archaeologist.
Curr. Biog. '55 p5-6 (por.6)

Albumuazar (c805-885). Arab. astronomer.
Hammerton p45

Albutt.   See **Allbutt, Sir Thomas Clifford**

Albuzjani (or Abul-wafa) (940-998). Pers. mathematician.
Chambers—Dict. col.10

Alchindus (or Al-Kindi, Alkindus) (c813-873). Arab. physician.
Gordon—Medieval p144-145   Major—History (1) p236-262
Hammerton p60-61

Alcmaeon of Crotona (c500 B.C.). Gr. anatomist, physician.
Chambers—Dict. col.10-11   Lambert—Minute p10-11
Gordon—Medicine p486-487
  (por.487)

Alcock, Sir John (1892-1919). Eng. aero. pioneer.
Burge—Ency. p624   Heinmuller—Man's p307 (por.307)
Fraser—Heroes p55-86   La Croix—They p20-40 (por.98)
Hammerton p47 (por.47)

Alcott, William A. (1798-1859). Amer. physician.
Rosen—Four p68-70,168-171

Alcuin of York (735-804). Eng. mathematician.
Ball—Short p134-136   Smith—Hist. I p185-187
Cajori—Hist. p114-115

Al-Damiri (or Kamel Muhammed) (1349-1405). Arab. biologist, zoologist.
Bodenheimer—Hist. p220

Alder, Kurt (1902-1958). Ger. chemist.
Chambers—Dict. supp.
Farber—Nobel p205-207 (por.118)

Alderotti, Thaddeus (or Alderoti, Alderotte, Taddeo) (c1223-c1303).
It. physician.
Gordon—Medieval p327-328
Major—History (1) p292-293

Aldrich, John Merton (1866-1934). Amer. entomologist.
Osborn—Fragments p211-212

Aldrovandi, Ulissi (or Aldrovandus, Ulysse,) (1522-c.1605). It. naturalist,
botanist, biologist.
Adams—Birth p165-168 (por.164)   Sarton—Six p153-155,160
Arber—Herbals p102   Weeks—Discovery p300 (por.300)
Bodenheimer—Hist. p239   Year—Pic p82 (por.82)
Chambers—Dict. col.11

Alembert, Jean Le Rond D' (1717-1783). Fr. mathematician, astronomer.
Abetti—History p155-156   Magie—Source p55
Ball—Short p374-377   Smith—Hist. I p479-480 (por.479)
*Book—Pop. Sci. (9) p2913-2915   Van Wagenen—Beacon p158-159
Cajori—Hist. p241-243   Woodruff—Devel. p21-22,261
Chambers—Dict. col.11   Year—Pic p110

Alexander of Tralles (or Alexander Trallinus) (c525-608). Gr. physician,
surgeon.
Gordon—Medieval p56-59   Leonardo—Lives (supp.1) p471-472
Lambert—Minute p63   Major—History (1) p212-215

Alexander, Archie A. (1888-1958). Virgin Isl. engineer.
Curr. Biog. '55 p911 (por.10); '58
p15

Alexander, Franz (1891-   ). Hung. psychoanalyst.
Curr. Biog. '42 p9-11 por.10),
'60 p4-6 (por.5)
Fabricant—Why p54-58

Alexander, Gustav (1873-1932). Aust. physician.
Kagan—Modern p136 (por.136)

Alexander, Harry Held (1867-1941). Amer. metallurgist.
Curr. Biog. '41 p17

Alexander, Jerome (b.1876). Amer. chemist.
Hammerton p55

Alexander, John H. (1812-1867). Amer. geologist, engineer.
N.A.S.—Biog. (1) p213-225

Alexander, Leo (1905-   ). Aust. psychiatrist.
Fabricant—Why p75-79

Alexander, Stephen (1806-1883). Amer. astronomer.
N.A.S.—Biog. (2) p249-259

Alexander, William (d.1783). Brit. physician.
Hammerton p55

Alexanderson, Ernst Frederik Werner (1878-   ). Swed-Amer. inventor, engineer.
Curr. Biog. '55 p11-13 (por.11)   Morris—Ency. p631
Hammerton p56   Radio's 100 p190-193 (por.140)

Alexandrinos.   See Asclepiodotus

Al-Farghani (c860). Arab. astronomer.
Hammerton p58

Alger, Ellice M. (1870-1945). Amer. ophthalmologist.
Curr. Biolg. '45 p3

Alhazen (or Al-Asam) (965/967?-1038/1039?). Arab. mathematician, astronomer, physician.
Chambers—Dict. col.11-12   Major—History (1) p263
Gordon—Medieval p179-180   Van Wagenen—Beacon p45-46
Hammerton p59   Williams—Great p91-94
Hart—Physicists p17-21

Ali Abbas (or Haly, Filius Abbas, Ali ibn Al Abbas) (d994). Arab. physician, surgeon.
Castiglioni—Hist. p270   Major—History (1) p240 (por.234)
Gordon—Medieval p164-165   Oliver—Stalkers p51-52
Leonardo—Lives(Supp.1) p483

Ali Ben abi Said Abderrahman (or Ibn Junis) (d1009). Egypt. astronomer.
Dreyer—Hist. p247-248

Ali Ben Isa (Ist half, 11th cent.). Arab. physician.
Gordon—Medieval p165-166

Ali-Ibadi.   See Hunain ibn Ishaq

Ali ibn Al Abbas.   See Ali Abbas

Ali ibn-Rodhwan (or Haly-Rodoam) (d.c.1067). Arab. physician.
Castiglioni—Hist. p275
Hammerton p60

Ali-Israeli.   See **Isaac Judaeus**

Alkarismi (or Al-Khwarizmi) (c830). Arab. mathematician.
Ball—Short p155-158
Hammerton p60

Alkarki (or Al-Karkhi) (c1000/1020). Arab. mathematician.
Ball—Short p159-161   Smith—Hist. I p283-284
Cajori—Hist. p106-107

Al Khatīb.   See **Ibn al Khat-īb**

Al-Khowarizmi, Mohammed ibn Mûsâ (or Abd Allah Mohammed ibn
   Musa of Khuwarismi, Al-Khwarizmi). (813?-835/845?). Arab.
   mathematician, astronomer.
Cajori—Hist. p102-104   Smith—Hist. I p170
Hammerton p60   Van Wagenen—Beacon p43-45
Hooper—Makers p82-84

Al-Kindi (or Alkindus).   See **Alchindus**

Allan, John A. (1884-1955). Can. geologist.
G.S.A.—Proc. '55 p89-90 (por.89)

Allan, Sir William (1837-1903). Scot. engineer.
Hammerton p61

Allbutt, Sir Thomas Clifford (1836-1925). Eng. physician, inventor.
Chambers—Dict. col.12   Kagan—Modern p12 (por.12)
Hammerton p61 (por.61)   Major—History (2) p1026 (por.958)
Kagan—Leaders p52-60   *Montgomery—Story p49-51

Allee, Warder Clyde (1885-1955). Amer. biologist, zoologist.
N.A.A.-Biog. (30) p3-40 (por.3)
Newman—What p228-230

Allen, Arthur Augustus (1885-   ). Amer. naturalist, ornithologist.
Curr. Biog. '61 (Jan.) (por.)
*Milne—Natur. p171

Allen, Cecil (1903-   ). Amer. aero. pioneer.
Heinmuller—Man's p344 (por.344)

Allen, Charles Elmer (1872-1954). Amer. botanist.
N.A.S.—Biog. (29) p3-11 (por.3)

Allen, Dudley Peter (1852-1915). Amer. surgeon.
Leonardo—Lives p11-12

Allen, Edgar (1892-1943). Amer. anatomist, endrocinologist.
Curr. Biog. '43 p8

Allen, Edmund Turney (1896-1943). Amer. aero. pioneer.
Daniel—Pioneer. p87-91 (por.86)

Allen, Frederick Madison (1879-   ). Amer. physician.
Hammerton p62

Allen, Sir Harry Brookes (1854-1926). Aust. physician.
Hammerton p62

Allen, Herbert Stanley (1873-1954). Eng. nat. philosopher.
R.S.L.—Biog. (1) p5-9 (por.5)

Allen, Joel Asaph (1838-1921). Amer. zoologist.
N.A.S.—Biog. (11) (XXI Memoirs)
   p1-13 (por.1)

Allen, Raymond Bernard (1902-   ). Amer. physician.
Curr. Biog. '52 p11-13 (por.11)

Allen, Thomas (1542-1632). Eng. astronomer, mathematician.
Gunther—Early XI p285-287
   (por.286)
Hammerton p63

Allen, William (1770-1843). Eng. chemist.
Hammerton p63-64 (por.63)

Allen, William McPherson (1900-   ). Amer. aero. pioneer.
Curr. Biog. '53 p8-10 (por.9)

Allen, Zachariah (1795-1882). Amer. inventor.
Hammerton p64

Allison, Fred (1882-   ). Amer. physicist.
Chambers—Dict. col.12

Allison, Nathaniel (1876-1932). Amer. surgeon.
Leonardo—Lives p12-13

Allman, David Bacharach (1891-   ). Amer. physician, surgeon.
Curr. Biog. '58 p17-18 (por.17)

Allman, George James (1812-1898). Irish botanist, geologist.
Hammerton p65-66

Allman, George Johnston (1824-1904). Irish mathematician.
Hammerton p66

Allmand, Arthur John (1885-   ). Eng. chemist.
Chambers—Dict. col.12-13

Allport, Gordon Willard (1897-   ). Amer. psychologist.
Curr. Biog. '60 p6-8 (por.7)

Allport, Samuel (1816-1897). Eng. geologist.
Hammerton p66

Allyn, Lewis B. (1874-1940). Amer. chemist.
Curr. Biog. '40 p13

Al-Majriti.   See **Maslama al-Majriti of Madrid**

Al Mamun.   See **Mamun, al-, Caliph Abdallah**

Al Mansur.   See **Mansur, al-**

Almeloveen, Theodorus Jannson van (or Janssonius) (1651/1657-1712).
Dutch physician.
Major—History (1) p563

Almenar, Juan (c1502). Sp. physician.
Major—History (1) p464

Al Nafis.   See **Ibn al Nafis**

Alpini, Prospero (or Alpino, Prosper) (1553-1617). It. botanist, physician.
Arber—Herbals p100-102 (por.102)   Major—History (1) p477
Hammerton p70

Al-Quarashi, Annafis (d.1288). Arab. physician.
Castiglioni—Hist. p278-279

Al Rashid,   See **Harun al Rashid**

Al-Razi.   See **Rhazes**

Alsberg, Carl Lucas (1877-1940). Amer. biochemist.
Curr. Biog. '40 p16   Progress—Science '40 p28-29
Hammerton p70

Alstadt, William Robert (1916-   ). Amer. orthodontist.
Curr. Biog. '58 p20-22 (por.21)

Alston, Charles (1683-1760). Scot. botanist.
Oliver—Makers p284-286

Alter, David (1807-1881). Amer. physicist.
Chambers—Dict. col.13
Weeks—Discovery p364-365 (por.365)

Alvarez, Luis Walter (1911-   ). Amer. physicist.
Curr. Biog. '47 p9-10 (por.9)

Alvarez, Walter Clement (1884-   ). Amer. physician.
Curr. Biog. '53 p10-12 (por.11)
Fabricant—Why p66-68

Ames, F. Lothrop (1876-1921). Amer. agriculturist.
*Ivins—Fifty p137-141 (por.138)

Ames, Joseph Sweetman (1864-1943). Amer. physicist, astrophysicist.
Curr. Biog. '43 p12   N.A.S.—Biog. (23) p181-196
Hammerton p76   (por. 181,185)

Ames, Louise Bates (1906?-   ). Amer. psychologist.
Curr. Biog. '56 p299-300 (por.300)

Amici, Giovanni Battista (or Giambattista). (1786?-1863). It. biologist, astronomer, naturalist, mathematician.
Castiglioni—Hist. p678 (por.679)   Dreyer—Hist. p301-304
Chambers—Dict. col.13   Hammerton p77

Amman, Johann Conrad (1669-c1730). Swiss physician.
Hammerton p77

Ammonius (or Lithotomos; Ammonios). (190-244). Gr. physician, surgeon.
Leonardo—Lives p13
Major—History (1) p149

Amontons, Guillaume (1663-1705). Fr. inventor, physicist.

Hammerton p78
Hart—Physicists p90
Magie—Source p128

Ampère, André-Marie (1772-1836). Fr. mathematician, physicist, inventor.

Appleyard—Pioneers p33-53 (por.32,51)
Ball—Short p436
*Book—Pop. Sci. (3) p859-860
Chalmers—Historic p260
Chambers—Dict. col.13-14
Crew—Physicists (#4 folder) (por.)
*Darrow—Masters p326
Dibner—Ten p23-26 (por.24)
*Epstein—Real p54
Hammerton p78 (por.78)
Hart—Makers p199-209
Hart—Physicists p106-108
*Hartman—Mach. p89-90
Hawks—Wireless p27-31
*Hodgins—Behometh p109-113
Law—Civiliz. p205-206
Lenard—Great p223-230 (por.230)
Magie—Source p446-447
Radio's 100 p29-31 (por.140)
*Shippen—Design p62-69
Smith—Torch. p14 (por.14)
Tuska—Invent. p128
Van Wagenen—Beacon p223-225
Weeks—Discovery p456 (ppr.456)
Woodruff—Devel. p56-57,262 (por.52)
Year—Pic p121 (por.121)

Amsden, Charles Avery (1899-1941). Amer. archaeologist.

Curr. Biog. '41 p22

Amundsen, Roald (1872-1928). Norw. sci. explorer, aero. pioneer.

*Book—Pop. Sci. (1) p298-300
*Cottler—Heroes p76-85
*Darrow—Builders p76-84
*Fraser—Heroes p297-334,407-427
Hammerton p78-79 (por.79)
Heinmuller—Man's p321 (por.321)
Maitland—Knights p284-288
*Shippen—Bridle p113-118

Anaxagoras of Clazomenae (498/500?-428 B.C.). Gr. mathematician.

Ball—Short p34
Cajori—Hist. p17
Chambers—Dict. col.14
Gordon—Medicine p470-474
Hammerton p80
Major—History (1) p113
Osborn—Greeks p59-62
Sedgwick—Short p60-61
Smith—Hist. I p78-79
Turnbull—Great p18
Wilson—Human p12-15

Anaximander (610/611?-545/547? B.C.). Gr. mathematician, astronomer, biologist.

*Book—Pop. Sci. (3) p1066
Chambers—Dict. col.14
Gordon—Medicine p461-462
Hammerton p80
Osborn—Greeks p46-49
Sedgwick—Short p47-48
Smith—Hist. I p68-69
Van Wagenen—Beacon p4-5
Year—Pic p27 (por.27)

Anaximenes (c611-546 B.C.). Gr. nat. philosopher.

Gordon—Medicine p462
Hammerton p80
Osborn—Greek p49-50
Sedgwick—Short p48

Anderson, Carl David (1905-   ). Amer. physicist.
Chambers—Dict. col.14-15
(por.105-106)
Curr. Biog. '51 p15-17 (por.16)
Heathcote—Nobel p339,345-352
(por.240)
Morris—Ency. p631
Progress—Science '40 p29-30 (por.29)
Weber—College p604 (por.604)

Anderson, Clinton P. (1895-   ). Amer. agriculturist.
Curr. Biog. '45 p5-8 (por.6)

Anderson, Elizabeth Garrett (1836-1917). Eng. physician.
Chambers—Dict. col.15
Hammerton p82 (por.82)
Lovejoy—Women p134-143,158-161
(por.135)

Anderson, Frank Marion (1863-1945). Amer. geologist.
G.S.A.—Proc. '46 p141-143 (por.141)

Anderson, Frederick Lewis (1905-   ) Amer. aero. pioneer.
Curr. Biog. '44 p11-13 (por.11)

Anderson, Gaylord West (1901-   ). Amer. physician.
Curr. Biog. '53 p12-14 (por.12)

Anderson, George Harold (1893-1956). Amer. geologist.
G.S.A.—Proc. '56 p103 (por.103)

Anderson, Gustavus Edwin (1879-1940). Swed.-Amer. geologist.
G.S.A.—Proc. '42 p149-150 (por.149)

Anderson, James (1739-1808). Scot. agriculturist.
Hammerton p82 (por.82)

Anderson, Sir John Viscount Waverley (1882-1958). Brit. chemist.
R.S.L.—Biog. (4) p307-325 (por.307)

Anderson, Orvil A. (1895-   ). Amer. aero-pioneer.
Heinmuller—Man's p349 (por.349)

Anderson, Robert van Vleck (1884-1949). Amer. geologist.
G.S.A.—Proc. p81-84 (por.81)

Anderson, Thomas (1819-1874). Scot. chemist.
Chambers—Dict. col.15
Partington—Short p270

Anderson, Sir William (1835-1898). Brit. engineer.
Hammerton p84

Andrada e Silva, José Bonifacio de (or José Bonifacio) (1763?-1838).
  Brazil. geologist.
Weeks—Discovery p278-279
  (por.279)

Andrade, Edward Neville da Costa (1887-   ). Eng. physicist.
Chambers—Dict. col.15-16
Hammerton p84 (por.84)

Andral, Gabriel (1797-1876). Fr. physician.
Hammerton p84
Major—History (2) p712

André, Eugene (1861-1922). Trinidad naturalist.
Cutright—Great p38-40

Andree, Karl (1808-1875). Ger. geographer.
Hammerton p85

Andrée, Salomon August (1854-1897). Swed. aero. pioneer.
Hammerton p85
Heinmuller—Man's p256 (por.256)

Andrewes, Frederick William (1859-1932). Eng. bacteriologist, pathologist.
Bulloch—Hist. p349

Andrews, Edmund (1824-1904). Amer. surgeon.
Leonardo—Lives p13-14

Andrews, Ernest Clayton (1870-1948). Aust. geologist.
G.S.A.—Proc. '48 p117-122 (por.117)

Andrews, Frank Maxwell (1884-1943). Amer. aero. pioneer.
Curr. Biog. '42 p21-23 (por.22),
  '43 p14
Heinmuller—Man's p349 (por.349)

Andrews, Roy Chapman (1884-1960). Amer. sci. explorer, naturalist.
Curr. Biog. '41 p26-27 (por.27),   *Hylander—Scien. p174-176
  '53 p24-26 (por.25)   *Snyder—Biology p427-432 (por.433)
Hammerton p87 (por.87)   Tracy—Amer. Nat. p164-172

Andrews, Solomon (1805-1872). Amer. physician, aero. pioneer.
Milbank—First p82-88 (por.54)

Andrews, Thomas (1813-1885). Irish chemist, physicist.
Chambers—Dict. col.16   Partington—Short p339,354
Findlay—Hundred p318   Van Wagenen—Beacon p291-293
Hammerton p87   Woodruff—Devel. p123-124,262
Magie—Source p187

Andrews, Thomas (1847-1907). Eng. metallurgist.
Hammerton p87

Andrews, Thomas Gayleson (1903-1954). Amer. geologist.
G.S.A.—Proc. p105-106 (por.105)

Andromachos of Crete (or Andromachus) (60 A.D.). Gr. physician.
Major—History (1) p161

Andronicus of Cyrrhus (c100 B.C.). Gr. astronomer.
Hammerton p88

Androvandus.   See **Aldrovandi, Ulissi**

Andry, Charles Louis François (1741-1829). Fr. physician.
Hammerton p88

Andry, Nicholas (1658-1742). Fr. physician.
Hammerton p88

Anel, Dominique (1679?--1730?). Fr. surgeon.
Hammerton p88
Leonardo—Lives p14-15

Angell, James Rowland (1869-1949). Amer. psychologist.
Curr. Biog. '40 p20-22) (por.21),
  '49 p9
N.A.S.—Biog. ('26) p191-205
  (por.191)

Anghiera, Pietro Martire de.   See **Peter Martyr**

Angle, Edward H. (1855-1930). Amer. orthodontist.
*Montgomery—Story p180-183

Anglicus.   See **Gilbertus Anglicus**

Anglicus, Johannes.   See **John of Gaddesden**

Ångström, Anders Jonas (1814-1874). Swed. physicist.
Chambers—Dict. col.16   Lindroth—Swedish p193-203
Hammerton p91   Van Wagenen—Beacon p303-306

Ångström, Knut Johan (1857-1910). Swed. physicist.
Chambers—Dict. col.16

Anrep, Gleb (1891-1955). Russ.-Eng. physiologist.
R.S.L.—Biog. (2) p19-31 (por.19)

Anschütz, Richard (1852-1937). Ger. chemist.
A.A.A.S.—Proc. (81) p37-39

Ansted, David Thomas (1814-1867). Eng. geologist.
Hammerton p97

Antipho (or Antiphon) (480?-411 B.C.). Gr. mathematician.
Ball—Short p36
Smith— Hist. 1 p84

Antisell, Thomas (1817-1893). Irish-Amer. geologist.
Merrill—First p313 (por.313)

Antommarchi, Francesco (1780-1838). Fr. physician.
Hammerton p99

Antyllus (or Antyllos) (c150 A.D.). Gr. physician, surgeon.
Gordon—Medicine p692   Major—History (1) p202-204
Leonardo—Lives p15-16

Anville, Jean Baptiste Bourgignon. (1697-1782). Fr. geographer.
Hammerton p100

Aoyama, Tanemichi (1859-1917). Japan. pathologist.
Bulloch—Hist. p349

Aphrodisiensis, Alexander (c200 A.D.). Rom. physician.
Major—History (1) p219

Apinus, Franz Ulrich Theodor (1724-1802). Ger. physicist.
Hammerton p101

Apollodorus of Damascus (98-117). Gr. engineer.
Matschoss—Great p15-16 (por.9)

Apollonia.   See **Diogenes of Apollonia**

Apollonius of Perga (or "The Great Geometer") (c260-200 B.C.). Gr.
   mathematician.
Ball—Short p77-83
Cajori—Hist. p38-41
Chambers—Dict. col.16-17
Clagett—Greek p63,93,94
Hammerton p101-102
Hofman—History p28-30
Hooper—Makers p52-55
*Miller—Hist. p221-224
Sedgwick—Short p108-112
Smith— Hist. I p116-117
Turnbull—Great p40-41
Van Wagenen—Beacon p26-27
Woodruff—Devel. p140,262

Apono, Petrus de.   See **Abano, Pietro d'**

Appert, Francois (1750-1840). Fr. inventor.
Hammerton p102
Meyer—World p236

Appert, Nicolas (c1750-1791). Fr. bacteriologist.
Bulloch—Hist. p349

Appleby, John Francis (1840-1917). Amer. inventor.
*Yost—Science p18-29

Applegarth, Augustus (1790-1870). Eng. inventor.
Hammerton p102-103

Appleton, Sir Edward Victor (1892-   ). Eng. physicist.
Calder—Science p76-77
Chambers—Dict. col.17 (por.17)
Curr. Biog. '45 p8-10 (por.9)
Heathcote—Nobel p431-437 (por.240)
Pringle—Great p38-54 (por.65)
Weber—College p754 (por.754)

Appleyard, Rello (1867-1943). Eng. engineer, physicist, inventor.
Curr. Biog. '43 p14

Aquinas, Saint Thomas (1225-1274). It. chemist, nat. philosopher.
Osborn—Greeks p113
Partington—Short p36

Arago, Dominique François Jean (1786-1853). Fr. physicist, astronomer,
   mathematician.
Abbot—Great p3
Ball—Short p437-438
(Continued)

Arago, Dominique François Jean—*Continued*
*Book—Pop. Sci. (3) p989 (por.989)
Chalmers—Historic p260-261
Chalmers—Dict. col.18
*Darrow—Masters p327
Hammerton p104 (por.104)
Hawks—Wireless p27-35
Magie—Source p324-325
Van Wagenen—Beacon p245-247
Williams—Great p350-351 (por.351)
Williams—Story p202-204 (por.201)
Year—Pic p120 (por.120)

Aranzio, Giulio Cesare (or Julius Caesar) (1530-1589). It. anatomist, physician, surgeon.
Castiglioni—Hist. p427-428
Gordon—Medieval p638
Leonardo—Lives p17
Major—History (1) p473-474

Arban, Francisque (1815-1849). Fr. aero. pioneer.
Heinmuller—Man's p242 (por.242)

Arbuthnot, John (1667-1735). Scot. physician.
Hammerton p106 (por.106)

Arcaeus, Franciscus (or De Arce, Arceo, Francois) (1494-c1575). Sp. physician surgeon.
Leonardo—Lives p18
Major—History (1) p466

Arce, Jose (1881-   ). Argen. physician, surgeon.
Curr. Biog. '47 p10-13 (por.11)

Archagathos (or Archagathus). (c219 B.C.). Gr. physician, surgeon.
Gordon—Medicine p626
Major—History (1) p161
Sigerist—Great p57

Archbold, Richard (1907-   ). Amer. naturalist, sci. explorer, aero. pioneer.
Heinmuller—Man's p356 (por.356)

Archelaus of Miletus (d.428 B.C.) Gr. astronomer, nat. philosopher.
*Book—Pop. Sci. (3) p990
Gordon—Medicine p493

Archiac, Étienne Jules Adolphe Desnier de Saint Simon, Vicomte d' (1802-1868). Fr. geologist.
Hammerton p107

Archigenes (c53-117). Gr. physician.
Gordon—Medicine p681-682
Leonardo—Lives p18-20
Major—History (1) p179,219-220

Archimedes (c287-c212 B.C.). Gr. mathematician, physicist, inventor.

Ball—Short p64-77
Bell—Men p28-34
*Book—Pop. Sci. (2) p433-435
Cajori—Hist. p34-38
Chambers—Dict. col.18-19
Clagett—Greek p59-62,75-76(por.59)
*Darrow—Masters p327
*Darrow—Thinkers p13-17
Ginzburg—Adven. p58-65
Hammerton p107-108
Hart—Makers p38-45 (por.39)
Hart—Physicists p10-13
Hofman—History p25-28
Hooper—Makers p49,55-64,241-249
Leonard—Great p2-3
*McSpadden—How p31-42
Meyer—World p22-24 (por.22)

*Miller—Hist. p219-221
Moulton—Auto. p12-13
Muir—Men p19-25
100 Great p523-531
Schwartz—Moments (1) p142-143
*Science Miles. p12-17 (por.12)
Sedgwick—Short p95-107
*Simmons—Great p9-11 (por.9)
Smith—Hist. I p111-116 (por.112)
Smith—Portraits (1), unp. (por.)
Taylor—Illus. p32
Thomas—Scien. p3-10 (por.1)
Turnbull—Great p34-40
Van Wagenen—Beacon p21-22
Wilson—Human p43-52 (por.44)
Woodruff—Devel. p14,17,47,262
Year—Pic p38 (por.38)

Archytas of Tarentum (c.428-347B.C.). Gr. mathematician.

Ball—Short p28-30
Burge—Ency. p624
Cajori—Hist. p19-20
Chambers—Dict. col.19

Hammerton p108
Sedgwick—Short p75-76
Smith—Hist. I p84-86
Turnbull—Great p20-22

Arco, Georg Wilhelm Alexander Hans Graf von (1869-1940). Ger. engineer.

Curr. Biog. '40 p23

Arcolani, Giovanni (d.1460/1484). It. physician, surgeon.

Leonardo—Lives p20
Major—History (1) p355

Arderne, John.   See **John of Arderne**

Arduino, Giovanni (1713-1795). It. geologist, mineralogist.

Adams—Birth p373-374
Chambers—Dict. col.19

Woodruff—Devel. p206-262

Arends, Leopold (1817-1882). Ger. inventor.

Hammerton p108

Aretaeus of Cappadocia (c 1st to 2nd cent.). Gr. physician.

Castiglioni—Hist. p215
Chambers—Dict. col.19
Gordon—Medicine p685-689

Hammerton p108-109
Major—History (1) p179,181-182
Robinson—Path. p21-30

Arfwedson, Johan August (or Arfvedson) (1792-1841). Swed. chemist. metallurgist, mineralogist.
Chambers—Dict. col.19-20
Weeks—Discovery p279-282,285-292
(por.418)

Argand, Aimé (1775-1803). Swiss chemist.
Chambers—Dict. col.20
Hammerton p109

Argand, Émile (1879-1940). Swiss geologist.
G.S.A.—Proc. '42 p153-161 (por.153)

Argand, Jean Robert (1768-1822). Swiss mathematician.
Ball—Short p471-472
Chambers—Dict. col.20

Argelander, Friedrich Wilhelm August (1799-1875). Ger. astronomer.
Armitage—Cent. p139,147-148,177
(por.144)
Chambers—Dict. col.20
Hammerton p109 (por.109)
MacPherson—Makers p144-146
Shapley—Astron. p229
Vaucouleurs—Disc. p117-119
Williams—Great p297-298 (por.298)
Woodruff—Devel. p262

Argenterio, Giovanni (1513-1572). It. physician.
Major—History (1) p471

Argyll, George John Douglas, Duke of (1823-1900). Eng. aero. pioneer.
Burge—Ency. p624

Aristaeus the Elder (c320 B.C.). Gr. mathematician.
Smith—Hist. I p94-95

Aristarchus of Samos (310-250 B.C.). Gr. astronomer, mathematician.
Abetti—History p37-38
Ball—Short p62-64
*Book—Pop. Sci. (3) p990
Chambers—Dict. col. 20-21
Clagett—Greek p71,90-92
Dreyer—Hist. p135-148
Hammerton p112
Hooper—Makers p109-113
Koestler—Sleep. p48-50
Sedgwick—Short p116-118
Van Wagenen—Beacon p24-26
Vaucouleurs—Disc. p25-26
Woodruff—Devel. p135-136,262

Aristotle (384-322 B.C.). Gr. nat. philosopher, naturalist.
Adams—Birth p12-19,277-279
Ball—Short p48-49
Bodenheimer—Hist. p164 (por.front.)
*Book—Pop. Sci. (3) p1068-1070
Castiglioni—Hist. p180-181
Chambers—Dict. col.21-22
Clagett—Greek p46,64-68 (por.64)
*Darrow—Masters p327
(Continued)

Aristotle—*Continued*

Dreyer—Hist. p108-122
Fenton—Giants p4-11 (por.15)
Fitzhugh—Concise p25-27
Ginzburg—Advent. p24-25
Gordon—Medicine p567-575
   (por.568)
Gordon—Romance p83-88
Hammerton p114-115 (por.114)
Hart—Makers p25-32 (por.25)
Hawks—Pioneers p56-60 (por.56)
Hofman—History p20
Holmyard—Chem. p12-14 (por.13)
Holmyard—Makers p16-21 (por.17)
Lambert—Medical p26-29
Lambert—Minute p27-29
Locy—Biology p9-15 (por.14)
*McSpadden—How p17-28
Moulton—Auto. p10
*Nisenson—Illus. p17 (por.17)

*Nisenson—More p13 (por.13)
Oliver—Stalkers p32-34
100 Great p26-30
Osborn—Greeks p68-76
Reed—Short p32-35
Schwartz—Moments (1) p131-133
Sedgwick—Short p79-84
Sewell—Brief p8-9
*Shippen—Micro. p19-31
Smith—Hist. I p93-94
*Snyder—Biology p5-12 (por.7)
Suter—Gallery p9-12
Taylor—Illus. p19-23,28
Thomson—Great p7-13
Van Wagenen—Beacon p14-17
Wilson—Human p29-42
Woodruff—Devel. p216-218,250-252,
   262 (por.224)
Year—Pic p30,32 (por.31)

Arkell, William Joscelyn (1904-1958). Eng. paleontologist, geologist.

R.S.L.—Biog. (4) p1-7 (por.1)

Arkwright, Sir Joseph Arthur (1864-1944). Eng. bacteriologist, physician.

Bulloch—Hist. p349

Arkwright, Sir Richard (1732-1792). Eng. inventor.

*Book—Pop. Sci. (2) p435-437
   (por.435)
*Burlingame—Mach. p40-43
Chambers—Dict. col.22
*Darrow—Masters p44-47 (por.160)
*Darrow—Thinkers p89-90 (por.88)
*Epstein—Real p150-152
*Glenister—Stories p136-152 (por.136)

*Goddard—Eminent p150-154
   (por.150)
Hammerton p116 (por.116)
*Hartman—Mach. p7-8
*Hathaway—Partners p185-193
*Larsen—Prentice p62-63
Law—Civiliz. p85-88
*Parkman—Conq. p49-53 (por.52)
Year—Pic p139 (por.139)

Arlandes, le Marquis d' (c1783). Fr. aero. pioneer.

*Bishop—Kite p25-34
*Shippen—Bridle p35-42

Arlong, Saturnin (1846-1911). Fr. bacteriologist.

Bulloch—Hist. p350

Armand, Louis (1905-   ). Fr. engineer.

Curr. Biog. '57 p21,22-23 (por.22)

Armour, Allison Vincent (1863-1941). Amer. agriculturist.

Curr. Biog. '41 p30

Armour, Donald John (1869-1933). Brit. surgeon.
Hammerton p117

Armsby, Henry Prentiss (1853-1921). Amer. agriculturist.
*Ivins—Fifty p329-342 (por.331)
N.A.S.—Biog. (19) p271-279
 (por.271)

Armstrong, Charles (1886-   ). Amer. physician.
*Sterling—Polio p65-66 (por.66)

Armstrong, Edwin Howard (1890-1954). Amer. inventor, elec. engineer.
*Bachman—Great p292-293 (por.293)   Radio's 100 p250-254 (por.140)
Curr. Biog. '40 p23-26 (por.25)   *Towers—Beacon p246-256
*Montgomery—Invent. p72-75   Tuska—Invent. p89-91,105-106
*Progress—Science '40 p49-50 (por.49)   Year—Pic p243 (por.243)

Armstrong, George Eli (1855-1933). Can. surgeon.
Leonardo—Lives p24-25

Armstrong, George Ellis (1900-   ). Amer. physician, surgeon.
Curr. Biog. '52 p24-26 (por.25)

Armstrong, Harry George (1899-   ). Amer. physician, surgeon, aero.
 pioneer.
Curr. Biog. '51 p17-19 (por.18)

Armstrong, Henry Edward (1848-1937). Eng. chemist.
Findlay-British p58-95 (por.58)   Partington—Short p321
Hammerton p118   Smith—Torch. p15 (por.15)

Armstrong, John (1709-1779). Scot. physician.
Hammerton p118

Armstrong, John (1784-1829). Eng. physician.
Hammerton p118 (por.118)

Armstrong, William George, Lord (1810-1900). Eng. engineer.
Chambers—Dict. col.22
Hammerton p118

Arnold of Villanova (or Arnaud de Villeneuve, Arnaldus Villanovanus)
 (1235?-1312?). Sp. physician.
Gordon—Medieval p278-282   Major—History (1) p305-308
 (por.211)   (por.306)
Hammerton p119   Partington—Short p39

Arnold, Bion Joseph (1861-1942). Amer. elec. engineer.
Curr. Biog. '42 p33
Hammerton p121

Arnold, Harold deForest (1833-1933). Amer. physicist.
Radio's 100 p216-218 (por.140)

Arnold, Henry Harley (1886-1950). Amer. aero. pioneer.
Curr. Biog. '42 p33-35 (por.34),
   '50 p12
Heinmuller—Man's p293 (por.293)

Arnold, Joseph (1782-1818). Eng. botanist.
Chambers—Dict. col.22-23

Arnon, Daniel Israel (1910-   ). Polish-Amer. plant physiologist.
Curr. Biog. '55 p28-30 (por.28)

Arnott, Neil (1788-1874). Scot. physician.
Chambers—Dict. col.23
Hammerton p123

Aronson, Louis V. (1870-1940). Amer. inventor.
Curr. Biog. '40 p28

Arouet.   See **Voltaire, François Marie Arouet**

Arrhenius, Svante August (1859-1927). Swed. chemist, physicist.
*Book—Pop. Scl. (3) p860
Chambers—Dict. col.23-24 (por.23)
*Darrow—Masters p328
Farber—Nobel p12-16 (por.118)
Findlay—Hundred p318
Hammerton p123-124
*Harrow—Chemists p111-133
   (por.111)
Holmyard—Great Chem. p117-121
Holmyard—Makers p287-289
*Jaffe—Crucibles p219-241
*Kendall—Young p162-174 (por.149)
Lindroth—Swedish p226-238
Moulton—Auto. p287
Partington—Short p334-336,340
   (por.335)
Smith—Torch. p16 (por.16)
Van Wagenen—Beacon p418-420
Weeks—Discovery p417 (por.417)
Williams—Great p467-468 (por.468)
Woodruff—Devel. p119-120,263
   (por.118)

Arrianus, Flavius (c100-180). Gr. geographer, mineralogist.
Adams—Birth p49

Arsonval, Jacques Arsène d' (1851-1940). Fr. physicist, physiologist.
Chambers—Dict. col.24
Curr. Biog. '41 p30

Artedi, Peter (1705-1735). Swed. naturalist.

Hammerton p125

Artemidorus (c100 B.C.). Gr. geographer.

Hammerton p125

Arthur, Joseph Charles (1850-1942). Amer. botanist.

Curr. Biog. '42 p43
Hammerton p126

Aryabhata of Kusumapura (or Pâtaliputra) (c500). Ind. mathematician, astronomer.

Ball—Short p147-148
Dreyer—Hist. p242-243
Hooper—Makers p124-127

Smith—Hist. I p153-156
Van Wagenen—Beacon p41-42

Arzachel (c1029-1087). Arab. astronomer.

Chambers—Dict. col.24
Hammerton p128

Asaph Ha-Ropheh of Syria (or Asaf Judaeus) (6th or 7th cent.). Syr. physician, biologist.

Bodenheimer—Hist. p191
Gordon—Medieval p250-252

Asch, Morris Joseph (1833-1902). Amer. physician.

Kagan—Modern p128 (por.128)

Aschoff, Ludwig (1866-1942). Ger. pathologist, physician.

Castiglioni—Hist. p973,992 (por.973)
Major—History (2) p1026

Rowntree—Amid p161-164 (por.159)

Asclepiades of Prusa (c124 B.C.). Gr. physician.

Castiglioni—Hist. p199-201 (por.198)
Gordon—Medicine p629-634
  (por.630)
Hammerton p129
Lambert—Medical p40-42

Lambert—Minute p40-42
Major—History (1) p164-166
Oliver—Stalkers p35-37
Sigerist—Great p57-60

Asclepiodotus (or Alexandrinos, Askepiodotos). (c470-500) Gr. physician, mathematician.

Major—History (1) p221

Aselli, Gasparo (or Asellio, Gaspari). (1581-1628.). It. anatomist, physician, surgeon.

Chambers—Dict. col.24
Hammerton p129

Major—History (1) p553

Ash, John (1723/1724-1779). Eng. physician.
Hammerton p129

Ashford, Bailey Kelly. (1873-1934). Amer. physician-surgeon.
Fabricant—Why p142-143

Ashhurst, John, Jr. (1839-1900). Amer. surgeon.
Leonardo—Lives p25-26

Ashley, George Hall (1866-1951). Amer. geologist.
G.S.A.—Proc. '51 p85-90 (por.85)

Ashmead, William Harris (1855-1908). Amer. entomologist.
Essig—Hist. p539-542 (por.540)
Osborn—Fragments p187 (por.339)

Askanazy, Max (1865-1940). Ger. pathologist.
Kagan—Modern p163 (por.163)

Askey, (Edwin) Vincent (1895-   ). Amer. physician.
Curr. Biog. '61 (Feb.) (por.)

Asklepiodotos.   See **Asclepiodotus**

Aspdin, Joseph (1779-1855). Eng. inventor.
Hammerton p133
Meyer—World p237

Assolant, Jean (1905-1942). Fr. aero. pioneer.
Heinmuller—Man's p332 (por.332)

Astbury, William Thomas (1898-   ). Eng. physicist.
Chambers—Dict. col.25

Astin, Allen Varley (1904-   ). Amer. physicist.
Curr.Biog. '56 p20-22 (por.21)

Aston, Francis William (1877-1945). Eng. physicist.
Chalmers—Historic p261
Chambers—Dict. col.25 (por.26)
Curr. Biog. '46 p17
Farber—Nobel p86-89 (por.118)
Hammerton p134
Riedman—Men p108-109 (por.89)
Year—Pic p208 (por.208)

Astruc, Jean (1684-1766). Fr. physician.
Gordon—Medieval p715
Major—History (2) p631-632

Atherstone, William Guybon (1813-1898). Brit. geologist.
Hammerton p136

Athy, Lawrence Ferdinand (1898-1955). Amer. geologist.
G.S.A.—Proc. '56 p107-109 (por.107)

Atkins, William Ringrose Gelston (1884-1959). Irish chemist.
*R.S.L.—Biog. (5) p1-14 (por.1)

Atkinson, George Francis (1854-1918). Amer. botanist, zoologist.
N.A.S.—Biog. (29) p17-33 (por.17)

Atkinson, Joseph Hampton (1900-   ). Amer. aero. pioneer.
Curr. Biog. '56 p22-24 (por.23)

Atkinson, Wilmer (1840-1920). Amer. agriculturist.
*Ivins—Fifty p179-185 (por.181)

Atlee, John Light (1799-1885). Amer. physician, surgeon.
Leonardo—Lives (Supp.1) p472

Atlee, Washington Lemuel (1808-1878). Amer. physician, surgeon.
Leonardo—Lives (Supp.1) p473

Atreya (or Atrya) (600-300 B.C.). Ind. surgeon.
Leonardo—Lives p27

Atterbury, William Wallace (1866-1935). Amer. engineer.
*White—Famous (3d) p3-13 (por.1)

Atwater, Wilbur Olin (1844-1907). Amer. agriculturist.
*Ivins—Fifty p245-253 (por.247)
*Snyder—Biology p329-330 (por.329)

Atwell, Wayne Jason (1889-1941). Amer. embryologist, anatomist, biologist.
Curr. Biog. '41 p31
Progress—Science '41 p59

Atwood, George (1746-1807). Eng. mathematician, inventor.
Chambers—Dict. col.25
Hammerton p139

Atwood, Harry N. (1887-   ). Amer. aero. pioneer.
Heinmuller—Man's p289 (por.289)

Atwood, Wallace Walter (1872-1949). Amer. geologist, geographer.
G.S.A.—Proc. '49 p107-111 (por.107)
Hammerton p139

Aub, Joseph (1846-1888). Amer. physician.
Kagan—Modern p145 (por.145)

Audebert, Jean Baptiste (1750/1759-1800). Fr. naturalist.
Hammerton p140

Audemars, Edmond (1882-   ). Fr. aero. pioneer.
Heinmuller—Man's p294 (por.294)

Audouin, Jean Victor (1797-1839/1841). Fr. entomologist, naturalist.
Bulloch—Hist. p350
Hammerton p140

Audubon, John James (1785-1851). Fr. -Amer. ornithologist, naturalist.
*Beard—Foreign p20-29
Bodenheimer—Hist. p350
*Book—Pop. Sci. (1) p144-145
  (por.145)
*Darrow—Masters p328-329
Fitzhugh—Concise p30-31
Geiser—Natural. p79-94
Hammerton p141 (por.141)
*Hylander—Scien. p35-43 (por.29)
Jordan—Leading p71-87 (por.71)
*McSpadden—How p127-142 (por.130)
*Milne—Natur. p43-54 (por.42)
Morris—Ency. p632
*Nisenson—Illus. p16 (por.16)
Peattie—Gather p341-347
Peattie—Green p228-230,238,240-243
  (por.231)
*Tappan—Heroes p2-10
Tracy—Amer. Nat. p52-64
Van Wagenen—Beacon p237-239
Welker—Birds p48-90
Wilson Amer. p96-97 (por.96)
*World's Great p207-237 (por.214)
Youmans—Pioneers p152-166
  (por.152)
Young—Biology p26-32 (por.front)

Auenbrugger (von Auenbrug), Leopold (1722-1809). Aust. physician.
Castiglioni—Hist. p618-619 (por.617)
Chambers—Dict. col.25-26
*Elwell—Sci. p32-33
Hammerton p141
Lambert—Medical p210-213 (por.212)
Lambert—Minute p210-213 (por.225)
Major—History (2) p583-585
  (por.584)
*Montgomery—Story p24-28
*Shippen—Men p99-101
Sigerist—Great p237-242 (por.240)
*Truax—Doctors p31-38
Walsh—Makers p53-85
Year—Pic p109

Auer.   See Wellsbach, Carl Auer, Baron von

Aughinbaugh, William Edmund (1871-1940). Amer. physician, sci. explorer.
Curr. Biog. '41 p31

Augustine, Saint (or Augustinus, Aurelius) (353/354-430). African nat. philosopher.
Hammerton p142-143
Osborn—Greeks p109-112

Aurelianus Caelius.   See **Caelius Aurelianus**

Auriol, Jacqueline Douet (1917-   ). Fr. aero. pioneer.
Curr. Biog. '53 p35-37 (por.36)

Austin, Louis Winslow (1867-1932). Amer. physicist.
Radio's 100 p143-146 (por.140)

Autolycus (c310 B.C.). Gr. astronomer, mathematician.
Hammerton p147
Smith—Hist. I p94

Auwers, Karl Friedrich von (1863-1939). Ger. chemist.
Hammerton p148
Smith—Torch p17 (por.17)

Avebury, John Lubbock, Lord (1834-1913). Eng. naturalist, archaeologist, entomologist.
Chambers—Dict. col.26

Avenzoar (or Ibn Zuhr, or Abu Mervan ul-Malik ibn Zuhr) (1091?-1162). Arab. physician.
Castiglioni—Hist. p276-277
Gordon—Medieval p208-214
(por.front.)
Hammerton p149
Leonardo—Lives p27-28
Major—History (1) p252

Averroes (or Averrhoes, Ibn-Rushd, Abu'l Walid Muhammad) (1126-1198). Arab. physician.
*Book—Pop.Sci. (6) 1891-1892
Gordon—Medieval p214-219
(por.115)
Major—History (1) p254-256

Avery, Oswald Theodore (1877-1955). Can.-Amer. bacteriologist.
N.A.S.-Biog. (32) p31-41 (por.31)
R.S.L.-Biog. (2) p35-44 (por.35)

Avery, Samuel (1865-1936). Amer. chemist.
Hammerton p149

Avicenna (or Ibn Sina, or Abu Ali al Hussein ibn Abdallah . . .) (979/980-1037). Arab. physician.

Castiglioni—Hist. p270-273
Chambers—Dict. col.26-27
*Chandler—Medicine p16-17
Gordon—Medieval p170-174 (por.147)
Gordon—Romance p106
Hammerton p149
Holmyard—Chem. p22-23
Holmyard—Great Chem. p21-25
Holmyard—Makers p68-77

Lambert—Medical p70-71 (por.70)
Lambert—Minute p70-71 (por.32)
Leonardo—Lives p28-30
Major—History (1) p241-246 (por.237)
Oliver—Stalkers p51-52
Partington—Short p28-29
*Shippen—Men p56-57
Sigersit—Great p78-87
Smith—Hist I p285-286

Avinoff, Andrey, (1884-1949). Russ.-Amer. entomologist.

Osborn—Fragments p233 (por.352)

Avogadro, Amedeo, Conte di Quaregna (1776-1856). It. physicist, chemist.

Chalmers—Historic p261
Chambers—Dict. col.27-28
Hammerton p150
Holmyard—Great Chem. p85-89
Holmyard—Makers p248-257 (por.249)
*Jaffe—Crucibles p157-174

Partington—Short p208-209,213-214 (por.208)
Schwartz—Moments (2) p789-791
Smith—Torch. p18 (por.18)
Tilden—Famous p170-173 (por.170)
Van Wagenen—Beacon p225-228
Woodruff—Devel. p100,102,106,263

Ayrton, Hertha (1854-1923). Eng. physicist.

Hammerton p151
Law—Civiliz. p240-241

Mozans—Woman p212,230

Ayrton, William Edward (1847-1908). Eng. physicist, inventor, elec. engineer.

Chambers—Dict. col.28
Hammerton p151

Azara, Felix de (1746-1811?). Sp. naturalist, zoologist.

Von Hagen—Green p131-144

B

Baade, Walter W. (1893-1960). Ger.-Amer. astronomer.

Armitage—Cent. p190

Babbage, Charles (1792-1871). Eng. mathematician.

Ball—Short p441
*Book—Pop. Sci. (2) p437-438 (por.437)
Chambers—Dict. col.29
*Goddard—Eminent p240-253 (por.240)

Hammerton p153 (por.153)
MacFarlane—Ten p71-83 (port.front.)
Sci. Amer.—Lives p229-239 (por.231)
Smith—Hist. I p460
Year—Pic. p117 (por.117)

Babbitt, Isaac (1799-1862). Amer. inventor.
Hammerton p153

Babcock, Ernest Brown (1877-1954). Amer. botanist, naturalist.
N.A.S.—Biog. (32) p50-57 (por.50)

Babcock, Harold Delos (1882-   ). Amer. physicist.
Chambers—Dict. col.29

Babcock, Stephen Moulton (1843-1931). Amer. agriculturist, chemist,
   inventor.
   *Darrow—Builders p183-187   *Ivins—Fifty
   *DeKruif—Hunger p267-297
      (por.266)

Babes, Victor (1854-1926). Aust. pathologist, bacteriologist.
Bulloch—Hist. p350

Babinet, Jacques (1794-1872). Fr. physicist.
Chambers—Dict. col.29

Babington, Benjamin Guy (1794-1866). Eng. physician.
Hammerton p153

Babington, Charles Cardale (1808-1895). Br. botanist.
Hammerton p153

Babington, William (1756-1833). Brit. physician.
Hammerton p154 (por.154)

Babinski, Joseph Jules (1857-1932). Fr. neurologist.
Great Names p3-4 (por.2)
Major—History (2) p965-966,
   1026-1027

Babo, Clemens Heinrich Lambert von (1818-1899). Ger. chemist.
Chambers—Dict. col.29

Babtie, Sir William (1859-1920). Br. surgeon.
Hammerton p154 (por.154)

Baccelli, Guido (1832-1916). It. pathologist.
Castiglioni—Hist. p840 (por.841)
Major—History (2) p971-972

Bache, Alexander Dallas (1806-1867). Amer. chemist, physicist, engineer, mathematician.

*Book—Pop. Sci. (3) 860-861
Hammerton p156
N.A.S.—Biog. (1) p181-205

Smith—Chem. p230
Smith—Math. p99-100
Youmans—Pioneers p436-446
   (por.436)

Bacher, Robert Fox (1905-   ). Amer. physicist.
Curr. Biog. '47 p28-31 (por.29)

Bachet, Claude Gaspard (1581-1638). Swiss mathematician.
Ball—Short p305-306

Bachman, John (1790-1874). Amer. naturalist.
Hammerton p156

Bachmann, Werner Emmanuel (1901-1951). Amer. chemist.
*N.A.S.—Biog. (34) p1-18 (por.1)

Back, Ernest Adna (1880-1959). Amer. entomologist.
Osborn—Fragments p226

Bacon, Francis, Ist Baron Verulam, Viscount St. Albans (1561-1626). Eng. nat. philosopher.

Ball—Short p252
Bodenheimer—Hist. p241
*Book—Pop. Sci. (6) p1892-1893
   (por.1890)
Castiglioni—Hist. p510 (por.507)
Chambers—Dict.col.30-31 (por.30)
Defries—Pioneers p137-160
Fitzhugh—Concise p35-37
Gregory—British p12 (por.13)
Hammerton p156-157 (por.157)
Hart—Physicists p67-70
Major—History (1) p479-480

Moulton—Auto, p118
Osborn—Greeks p135-140
Schwartz—Moments (1) p31-33
*Science Miles. p56 (por.56)
Sewell—Brief p55-56
Smith—Hist. I p379-380
Smith—Torch. p19 (por.19)
*Stevens—Science p31-32 (por.30)
Suter—Gallery p68-75
Tuska—Invent. p113-114
Woodruff—Devel. p263

Bacon, George Preston (1866-1941). Amer. physicist.
Curr. Biog. '41 p34

Bacon, Gertrude (1874-1949). Eng. aero. pioneer.
Hammerton p157-158 (por. 157)

Bacon, John MacKenzie (1846-1904). Eng. aero. pioneer.
Hammerton p158 (por.158)

Bacon, Roger (1214?-1294). Eng. inventor, mathematician, physicist, chemist.

Ball—Short p174-177

*Book—Pop. Sci. (2) p439-440
(*Continued*)

Bacon, Roger—*Continued*
Burge—Ency. p624
Castiglioni—Hist. p350-352
Chambers—Dict. col.31,32 (por.32)
Dreyer—Hist. p233-236
Fitzhugh—Concise p37-38
Gibson—Heroes p39-47
Gordon—Medieval p292-294
  ((por. 243)
Gregory—British p8,9 (por.8)
Hammerton p158-159 (por.159)
Hart—Makers p58-67
Hart—Physicists p23-27
Holmyard—British p5-8 (por.5)
Holmyard—Chem. p36
Holmyard—Great Chem. p26-32
Holmyard—Makers p92-98

Law—Civiliz. p143-144
Leonard—Crus. p17-60
Major—History (1) p324-325
Moulton—Auto. p34
Oliver—Stalkers p58-60
Osborn—Greeks p113-114
Partington—Short p37-39
*Pratt—Famous p4-7
Schwartz—Moments (1) p25-27
Sedgwick—Short p180-181
Smith—Hist. I p222-223
Smith—Torch. p20 (por.20)
Thomas—Scien. p13-20 (por.11)
Van Wagenen—Beacon p48-51
Wilson—Human p72-79
Woodruff—Devel. p15-16,151,225,263

Baden-Powell, Baden Fletcher Smyth (1860-1937). Eng. aero. pioneer, inventor.

Burge—Ency. p624-625

Baeda. See **Bede**

Baehr, George (1887-   ). Amer. physician.

Curr. Biog. '42 p47-48 (por. 48)

Baekeland, Leo Hendrick (1863-1944). Belg.-Amer. chemist, inventor.

Borth—Pioneers p187-199
Browne—Hist. p484 (por.133)
Chambers—Dict. col.32
Curr. Biog. '44 p27
*Darrow—Builders p123-127
Hammerton p160-161
Holland—Ind. p92-112 (por.92)

Killeffer—Eminent p22 (por.22)
Law—Civiliz. p282-285
*Montgomery—Invent. p174-187
N.A.S.—Biog. '47 p281-295 (por.281)
*Patterson—Amer. p207-219
Wilson—Amer. p380-383
  (por.380,382)
*Yost—Science p163-177

Baer, Karl Ernst von (1792-1876). Estonian embryologist, biologist, naturalist.

Bodenheimer—Hist. p367
Chambers—Dict. col.32,33
Gordon—Romance p440 (por.440)
Hammerton p161
Locy—Biology p133-134, 214-222
  (por. 216,217)
Major—History (2) p710-711

Murray—Science p333-334
Rosen—Four p4-6,241-244
*Shippen—Micro. p132-139
Thomson—Great p71-78
Van Wagenen—Beacon p255-257
Woodruff—Devel. p246-247,263
  (por.248)

Baeyer, (Johann Friedrich Wilhelm) Adolph von (1835-1917). Ger. chemist.

Chambers—Dict. col.33
Farber—Nobel p21-24 (por.118)
Findlay—Hundred p318-319
Hammerton p161 (por.161)

Moulton—Auto. p288
Partington—Short p307-310,317
  (por.308)
Smith—Torch. p21 (por.21)

Bagg, Rufus Mather (1869-1946). Amer. geologist, paleontologist.
G.S.A.—Proc. '47 p105-106 (por.105)

Baglivi, Giorgio (1668/1669-1707). It. physician.
Castiglioni—Hist. p548 (por.549)   Major—History (1) p506
Hammerton p161   Sigerist—Great p171-174 (por.168)

Bail, Oscar (1869-1927). Ger. bacteriologist.
Bulloch—Hist. p350

Bailar, John C., Jr. (1904-   ). Amer. chemist.
Curr. Biog. '59 p20-21 (por. 20)

Bailey, Charles P. (1910-   ). Amer. physician.
Rowntree—Amid p474-479 (por.475)

Bailey, Donald Coleman (1902-   ). Eng. engineer.
Curr. Biog. '45 p26-28 (por. 27)

Bailey, Florence Augusta (1863-   ). Amer. ornithologist.
Hammerton p163

Bailey, J. W. (1811-1857). Amer. chemist.
Smith—Chem. p226

Bailey, John (1750-1819). Eng. agriculturist.
Hammerton p163

Bailey, Liberty Hyde (1858-1954). Amer. botanist, argiculturist.
Curr. Biog. '48 p32-34 (por.33),   *Ivins—Fifty p321-324 (por.323)
  '55 p34   Tracy—Amer. Nat. p208-214
Hammerton p163 (por. 163)

Bailey, Lady Mary Westenra (1890-   ). Brit. aero. pioneer.
Burge—Ency. p625
Hammerton p163 (por. 163)

Bailey, Richard William (1885-1957). Eng. engineer.
R.S.L.—Biog. (4) p15-23 (por. 15)

Bailey, Solomon (Solon) Irving (1854-1931). Amer. astronomer.
N.A.S.-Biog. (15) p193-199 (por.193)

Bailey, Vernon (1864-1942). Amer. biologist, naturalist.
Curr. Biog. '42 p48
Hammerton p163

Baillie, Matthew (1761-1823). Scot. pathologist, anatomist, physician.

Castiglioni—Hist. p609 (por.609)   Hammerton p164 (por.164)
Gunther—Early XI p70-72 (por.71)   Major—History (2) p702

Baillon, Henry Ernst (1827-1895). Fr. botanist.

Hammerton p164

Baillou, Guillaume de (or Ballonius) (1538-1616). Fr. physician.

Gordon—Medieval p738-740   Major—History (1) p423 (por.424)
Hammerton p164

Bailly, Jean Sylvain (1736-1793). Fr. astronomer.

*Book—Pop. Sci. (3) p991
Hammerton p164 (por.164)

Bailly, René J. (1909-1954). Belg. geologist.

G.S.A.—Proc. '54 p147

Baily, Francis (1774-1844). Eng. astronomer.

*Book—Pop. Sci. (3) p991   Hammerton p165 (por.165)
Chambers—Dict. col.33

Bain, Alexander (1818-1903). Scot. psychologist.

*Book—Pop. Sci. (6) p1894
Hammerton p165

Bain, Alexander (1810-1877). Scot. inventor.

Hammerton p165

Bain, H. Foster (1817-1948). Amer. geologist.

G.S.A.—Proc. '48 p127-130 (por.127)

Bainbridge, John (1582/1583-1643). Eng. astronomer.

Gunther—Early XI p47
Hammerton p165

Baird, John Logie (1888-1946). Scot. inventor.

*Bridges—Master p15-27 (por.18)   *Larsen—Scrap. p83-92,95,103,178
Chambers—Dict. col.34 (por.35,36)   (por.80)
Hammerton p166 (por.166)   Morgan—Men p138-164 (por.93)
*Larsen—Men p183-197 (por.80)   Pringle—Great p25-37 (por.64)
*Larsen—Prentice p159-163   Radio's 100 p235-236 (por.140)

Baird, Spencer Fullerton (1823-1887). Amer. naturalist, zoologist.

*Book—Pop. Sci. (1) p146-147   Chambers—Dict. col.34
(por.146)   Hammerton p166 (por.166)
(Continued)

Baird, Spencer Fullerton—*Continued*
Jordan— Leading p269-281 (por.269)
N.A.S.—Biog. (3) p141-160
Oehser—Sons p60-91 (por.58)

True—Smiths. p280-286 (por.284)
Welker—Birds p171-173
Young—Biology p44 (por.44)

Baker, Arthur Challen (1885-   ). Amer. entomologist.
Osborn—Fragments p226

Baker, Sir Benjamin (1840-1907). Eng. engineer.
Hammerton p167 (por.167)

Baker, Charles Fuller (1872-1927). Amer. entomologist.
Essig—Hist. p542-548 (por.543)

Baker, Charles Whiting (1865-1941). Amer. engineer.
Curr. Biog. '41 p36

Baker, Frank Collins (1867-1942). Amer. zoologist, geologist.
G.S.A.—Proc. '42 p167-169 (por.167)

Baker, Sir George (1722-1809). Eng. physician.
Major—History (2) p598

Baker, George Theodore (1900-   ). Amer. aero. pioneer.
Curr. Biog. '53 p37-39 (por.38)

Baker, Henry (1698-1774). Eng. inventor, naturalist.
Bulloch—Hist. p350
Hammerton p167

Baker, Henry Frederick (1866-1956). Eng. mathematician.
R.S.L.—Biog. (2) p49-65 (por.49)

Baker, Herbert Brereton (1862-1935). Eng. chemist.
Chambers—Dict. col.34
Findlay—Hundred p319

Hammerton p167 (por.167)
Partington—Short p352

Baker, John Gilbert (1834-1920). Eng. botanist.
Hammerton p167

Baker, John Randal (1900-   ). Eng. zoologist.
Hammerton p167

Baker, Sara Josephine (1873-1945). Amer. physician, pediatrician.
Curr. Biog. '45 p30
Fabricant—Why p129-131
*Fleischman—Careers p78

Rosen—Four p127-130,226-231,291
16 Amer. p65-68

Bakewell, Robert (1725-1795). Eng. agriculturist.
Hammerton p168

Bakewell, Robert (1768-1843). Eng. geologist.
Hammerton p168-169

Bakhtishua family (or Bakhtishwa, Bakhtischu), (George, Gabriel, Johannes). (8-10th cent.) Arab. physicians.
Castiglioni—Hist. p265
Gordon—Medieval p134-137

Balard, Antoine Jerome (1802-1876). Fr. chemist.
A.A.A.S.—Proc. (81) p39-40
Chambers—Dict. col.35
Hammerton p169
Partington—Short p214
Smith—Torch. p22 (por.22)
Weeks—Discovery p450-454 (por.451)

Balbi (or Balbo), Adrian (1782-1848). It. geographer.
Hammerton p169

Balbo, Italo (1896-1940). It. aero. pioneer.
Heinmuller—Man's p345 (por.345)

Balchen, Bernt (1899-   ). Norw. aero. pioneer.
Curr.Biog. '49 p20-22 (por.21)

Balderston, William (1896-   ). Amer. engineer.
Curr. Biog. '49 p22-23 (por.23)

Baldwin, Ernest (1909-   ). Eng. biochemist.
Newman—What p196-197

Baldwin, James Mark (1861-1934). Amer. phychologist.
*Book—Pop. Sci. (6) p1894-1897 (por.1895)
Chambers—Dict. col. 35-36
Hammerton p171

Baldwin, Matthias William (1795-1866). Amer. inventor.
Hammerton p171

Baldwin, Robert T. (1882-   ). Amer. chemist.
Browne—Hist. p494 (por.145)

Baldwin, Thomas Scott (1860-1923). Amer. aero. pioneer.
Heinmuller—Man's p260 (por.260)
Milbank—First p148-149 (por.150)

Balfour, Sr. Andrew, Bart (1630-1694). Scot. physician.
Chambers—Dict. col.36

Balfour, Francis Maitland (1851-1882). Eng. biologist, embryologist, morphologist.
Chambers—Dict. col.36-37   Locy—Biology p226-229 (por.227)
Hammerton p174 (por.174)   Osborn—Impr. p99-108 (por.99)

Balfour, Sir Isaac Bayley (1853-1922). Scot. botanist.
Hammerton p174-175 (por.174)

Balfour, John Hutton (1808-1884). Scot. botanist.
Chambers—Dict. col.37   Oliver—Makers p293-300 (por.front)
Hammerton p175

Balfour, Margaret Ida (d.1945). Eng. physician.
Lovejoy—Women p254

Balk, Robert (1899-1955). Estonian geologist.
G.S.A.—Proc. '55 p93-99 (por.93)

Ball, Albert (1896-1917). Eng. aero. pioneer.
Arnold—Airmen p123-124   Hammerton p175-176 (por.175)
Burge—Ency. p625   Heinmuller—Man's p301 (por.301)

Ball, Elmer Darwin (1870-1943). Amer. entomologist.
Osborn—Fragments p198 (por.366)

Ball, John Rice (1881-1953). Amer. geologist.
G.S.A.—Proc. '52 p87-89 (por.87)

Ball, Sir Robert Stawell (1840-1913). Irish astronomer, mathematician, naturalist.
*Book—Pop. Sci. (3) p991-992   Hammerton p176
Chambers—Dict. col.37   MacPherson—Astron. p99-107
                                   (por.98)

Ball, Sydney Hobart (1877-1949). Amer. geologist, min. engineer.
G.S.A.—Proc. '49 p113-114 (por.113)

Ballatine, Stuart (1897-1944). Amer. engineer, physicist, inventor.
Curr. Biog. '44 p30
Radio's 100 p266-269 (por.140)

Ballantyne, John William (1861-1923). Scot. pathologist.
Hammerton p177

Ballin, Max (1869-1934). Ger.-Amer. surgeon.
Kagan—Modern p102 (por.102)

Balmer, Johann Jakob (1825-1898). Swiss physicist, mathematician.
Chambers—Dict. col.37
Magie—Source p360

Baly, Edward Charles Cyril (1871-1948). Eng. chemist.
Chambers—Dict. col.38

Bamberger, Eugen (1857-1932). Swiss chemist.
Partington—Short p319

Bancroft, Wilder Dwight (1867-1953). Amer. chemist.
Browne—Hist. p481 (por.87)
Killeffer—Eminent p26 (por.26)

Bandelier, Adolph Francis Alphonse (1840-1914). Swiss-Amer.
archaeologist, sci. explorer.
Hammerton p181
Swiss—Prom. p193-197

Bane, Thurman Harrison (1884-   ). Amer. aero. pioneer.
Holland—Arch. p26-44 (por.54)

Banester, John (1533-1610). Eng. physician, surgeon.
Major—History (1) p455-456
(por.456)

Bang, Bernhard Laurits Frederick (1848-1932). Dan. pathologist,
bacteriologist.
Bulloch—Hist. p350
Copen.—Prom. p165-168

Banga, Henry (1848-1913). Swiss physician, surgeon, gynecologist.
Swiss—Prom. p114-118 (por.114)

Banks, Sir Joseph, Bart. (1743-1820). Eng. naturalist, botanist.
*Book—Pop. Sci. (1) p147 (por.147)   Hammerton p182 (por.182)
Chambers—Dict. col.38   Hawks—Pioneers p247,248,251
Gilmour—British p32   Reed—Short p111
Gunther—Early XI p218-219   Weeks—Discovery p84,85 (por.85)
(por.218)

Banks, Nathan (1868-1953). Amer. entomologist.
Essig—Hist. p549-551
Osborn—Fragments p227 (por.368)

Bannister, Roger (1929-   ). Eng. physician.
Curr. Biog. '56 p28-29 (por.28)

Banti, Guido (1852-1925). It. pathologist, physician.
Castiglioni—Hist. p808 (por.808)

Banting, Sir Frederick Grant (1891-1941). Can. physician, surgeon.
Castiglioni—Hist. p996-997 (por.997)
Chambers—Dict. col.38
Curr. Biog '41 p39
*DeKruif—Men p59-87
Hammerton p183
Kagan—Modern p45 (por.45)
Law—Civiliz. p344-346
Major—History (2) p1027 (por.1000)
*Master—Conquest p254-260 (por.258)
*Montgomery—Story p71-77
16 Amer. p37-40
Pringle—Great p123-135 (por.160)
Progress—Science '40 p69-70 (por.69)
Rowntree—Amid p339-354 (por.346)
*Snyder—Biology p386-391 (por.389)
Stevenson—Nobel p109-110,111,112
(por.150)
Thomas—Scien. p283-295 (por.281)
*Truax—Doctors p147-153

Baracca, Francisco (1888-1918). It. aero. pioneer.
Heinmuller—Man's p305 (por.305)

Barany, Robert (1876-1936). Aust. physician.
Chambers—Dict. col.38-39
Kagan—Modern p137 (por.137)
Major—History (2) p1027
Stevenson—Nobel p84-88 (por.150)

Barbaro, Ermolao (1454-1493?). It. naturalist.
Chambers—Dict. col.39

Barbellion, N. P., pseud.   See **Cummings, Bruce Frederick**

Barber, Harry Gardner (1871-1960). Amer. entomologist.
Osborn—Fragments p227-228
(por.353)

Barbour, Erwin Hinckley (1856-1947). Amer. geologist.
G.S.A.—Proc. '47 p109-110 (por.109)

Barbour, Henry Gray (1886-1943). Amer. toxicologist.
Curr. Biog. '43 p27

Barbour, Thomas (1884-1946). Amer. zoologist.
*Milne—Natur. p159-165 (por.158)
N.A.S.—Biog. (27) p13-27 (por.13)

Barclay, John (1758-1826). Scot. anatomist.
Hammerton p186

Barcroft, Sir Joseph (1872-1947). Irish physiologist.
 Castiglioni—Hist. p780,789,937,952   Major—History (2) p961-962,1027
  (por.937)
 Chambers—Dict. col.39

Bard, John (1716-1799). Amer. physician.
 Farmer—Doctors' p25

Bard, Samuel (1742-1821). Amer. physician.
 Major—History (2) p732-733
  (por.732)

Bardeen, John (1908-   ). Amer. elec. engineer, physicist.
 Curr. Biog. '57 p37-39 (por.38)
 Meyer—World p255-256

Barger, George (1878-1939). Eng. chemist.
 Chambers—Dict. col.39
 Findlay—British p419 (por.419)

Bar-Hebraeus (or Barhebraeus, or Abu'l Faraj, Juhanna, or Bar Hebraya)
  (1226-1286). Syr. astronomer.
 Dreyer—Hist. p248

Barigazzi, Jacopo (Berengario, or Berengarius Carpensis, Jacopo da Capri)
  (1470?-1530). It. surgeon.
 Leonardo—Lives p30-33

Barker, Aldred Farrer (b.1868). Eng. textile scientist.
 Hammerton p188

Barker, George F. (1835-1910). Amer. chemist.
 Browne—Hist. p475 (por.35)

Barker, Sir Herbert Atkinson (1869-1950). Eng. surgeon.
 Hammerton p188

Barker, Llewellys Franklin (1867-1943). Amer. physician.
 Curr. Biog. '43 p28
 Major—History (2) p1028

Barker, W. G. (1894-1930). Can. aero. pioneer.
 Burge—Ency. p625

Barkla, Charles Glover (1877-1944). Eng. chemist, physicist.
Chambers—Dict. col.39-40
Hammerton p188-189
Heathcote—Nobel p141-150 (por.240)
Weber—College p273 (por.273)

Barletta, Mariano Santo de (1490-1550). It. surgeon.
Gordon—Medieval p678-679

Barlow, Lester Pence (1887-   ). Amer. inventor, engineer.
Curr. Biog. Jan.-June 1940 only,
   p22-24

Barlow, Peter (1776-1862). Eng. mathematician.
Hammerton p189
Smith—Hist. I p460-461

Barlow, Sir Thomas (1845-1945). Brit. physician.
Castiglioni—Hist. p862,1020-1021
   (por.1021)
Hammerton p189

Barnaby, Ralph Stanton (1893-   ). Amer. aero pioneer.
Heinmuller—Man's p339 (por.339)

Barnard, Edward Emerson (1857-1923). Amer. astronomer.
*Book—Pop. Sci. (3) p993-994
   (por.993)
Chambers—Dict. col.40
Hammerton p189
MacPherson— Astron. p217-224
MacPherson—Makers p205-208
N.A.S.—Biog. (11) (XXI Memoirs)
   p1-17 (por.1)

Barnard, Frederick Augustus Porter (1809-1889). Amer. mathematician.
Hammerton p190
N.A.S.—Biog. (20) p259-267
   (por.259)

Barnard, Harry Everett (1874-1946). Amer. chemist.
Holland—Ind. p282-296 (por.282)

Barnard, John Gross (1815-1882). Amer. engineer.
N.A.S.—Biog. (5) p219-228 (por.219)

Barnard, Joseph Edwin (1870-1949). Eng. physicist.
Chambers—Dict. col.40
Hammerton p190

Barnard, William Stebbins (1847-1887). Amer. entomologist.
Osborn—Fragments p179-180
   (por.351)

Barnes, Albert Coombs (1872-1951). Amer. physiol. chemist.
Curr. Biog. '45 p36-39 (por.37)
   '51 p22

Barnes, Henry A. (1906-   ). Amer. elec. engineer.
Curr. Biog. '55 p37-39 (por.38)

Barnes, Howard Turner (1873-1950). Can. physicist.
Hammerton p191

Barnes, William (1860-1930). Amer. entomologist, surgeon.
Osborn—Fragments p214 (por.349)

Barney, Samuel E. (1859-1940). Amer. engineer.
Curr. Biog. '40 p52

Barnwell, Frank Sowter (1880-   ). Eng. aero. pioneer.
Burge—Ency. p625

Barré de Saint-Venant, A.J.C. (1797-1886.) Fr. mathematician.
Cajori—Hist. p468

Barrell, Joseph (1869-1919). Amer. geologist, engineer.
N.A.S.—Biog. (12) p3-35 (por.3)

Barrett, Sir William Fletcher (1844-1925). Eng. physicist.
Chambers—Dict. col.40-41
Hammerton p194 (por.194)

Barringer, Emily Dunning (b.1876). Amer. physician, surgeon,
   gynecologist.
Curr. Biog. '40 p56
Fabricant—Why p101-103

Barrois, Charles (1851-1939). Fr. geologist.
G.S.A.—Proc. '41 p145-150 (por.145)
Hammerton p196

Barrow, Isaac (1630-1677). Eng. mathematician.
Ball—Short p309-312   Smith—Hist. I p396-398 (por.397)
Cajori—Hist. p188-189   Year—Pic p93 (por.93)

Barry, James (or Miranda) (1795-1865). Scot. physician.
Lovejoy—Women p275-282

Barthez, Paul Joseph (1734-1806). Fr. physician.
Hammerton p199

Bartholinus, Erasmus (or Bartholin) (1625-1698). Dan. physician, physicist.
Chambers—Dict. col.41   Magie—Source p280
Copen.—Prom. p29-32

Bartholinus, Thomas (or Bartholin, Bertelsen) (1616-1680). Dan. anatomist, physician.
Chambers—Dict. col.41   Major—History (1) p555
Copen.—Prom p25-28

Bartholomaeus Anglicus (De Glanvilla) (13th cent.). Eng. physician.
Chambers—Dict. col.41
Major—History (1) p323-324

Bartisch, Georg (1535-1607). Ger. physician, surgeon.
Castiglioni—Hist. p484   Leonard—Lives p33-34
Gordon—Medieval p698-700 (por.83)   Major—History (1) p440-442
                                     (por.441)

Bartlett, Sir Frederick Charles (1886-   ). Eng. psychologist.
Chambers—Dict. col.41

Bartlett, Robert Abram (1875-1946). Newfound. sci. explorer.
Curr. Biog. '46 p31

Bartlett, William H. C. (c.1804-1893). Amer. astronomer.
N.A.S.—Biog. (7) p171-191 (por.171)

Barton, Benjamin Smith (1766-1815). Amer. naturalist, physician, ornithologist.
Bell—Early p45-46   Welker—Birds p16-17
Major—History (2) p767   Youmans—Pioneers p81-89 (por.81)

Barton, Donald C. (1889-1939). Amer. geologist.
G.S.A.—Proc. '39 p153-156 (por.153)

Barton, George H. (1852-1933). Amer. geologist.
G.S.A.—Proc. '34 p161-169 (por.161)

Barton, William Henry, Jr. (1893-1944). Amer. engineer.
Curr. Biog. '44 p32

Bartow, Edward (1870-1958). Amer. chemist.
Browne—Hist. p488 (por. 149)

Bartram, John (1699-1777). Amer. botanist, entomologist, naturalist.
Bell—Early p47-48
Osborn—Fragments p12
Peattie—Green p189-198
Tracy—Amer. Natur. p29-35
Welker—Birds p14
Youmans—Pioneers p24-39

Bartram, John Greer (1893-1955). Amer. geologist.
G.S.A.—Proc. '55 p101-106 (por.101)

Bartram, William (1739-1823). Amer. botanist, entomologist, naturalist.
Bell—Early p47-48
Osborn—Fragments p12
Tracy—Amer. Nat. p36-39
Youmans—Pioneers p24-39 (por.24)

Bartrum, John Arthur (1885-1949). New Zeal. geologist.
G.S.A.—Proc. '49 p115-116 (por.115)

Bartsch, Paul (1871-   ). Ger.-Amer. biologist, zoologist.
Hammerton p201-202 (por.201)

Baruch, Simon (1840-1921). Ger. surgeon.
Kagan—Modern p11 (por.11)

Barus, Carl (1856-1935). Amer. physicist.
N.A.S.—Biog. (22) p171-192
(por.171)

Bary, Heinrich Anton de (1831-1888). Ger. botanist.
Bulloch—Hist. p350-351
Chambers—Dict. col.42
Hammerton p488
Locy—Biology p271-272 (por.272)

Basch, Samuel Siegfried Karl von (1837-1905). Czech. physician.
Major—History (2) p900

Basedow, Carl von (1799-1854). Ger. physician.
Major—History (2) p712

Baseilhac.   See **Saint-Come, Frère Jean de**

Basil Valentine (or Valentinus, Basilius) (c1470.). Ger. physician, chemist.
Atkinson—Magic p128-140
Major—History (1) p457-458
Partington—Short p55-56
Weeks—Discovery p23-24 (por.24)

Bassett, Homer Franklin (1826-1902). Amer. entomologist.
Essig—Hist. p552-553 (por.552)

Bassett, William Hastings (1868-1934). Amer. chemist, metallurgist.
Holland—Ind. p207-223 (por.207)

Bassi, Agostino (1773-1856). It. bacteriologist, micropathologist.
Bulloch—Hist. p351
Castiglioni—Hist. p692-693 (por.692)
Chambers—Dict. col.42
Major—History (2) p827-829 (por.828)

Bassi, Laura Maria Catarina (1711-1778). It. physicist.
Mozans—Woman p202-210

Bassini, Edoardo (1847-1924). It. physician, surgeon.
Castiglioni—Hist. p1013 (por.1012)
Leonardo—Lives p34-36

Bastian, Adolf (1826-1905). Ger. ethnologist.
Hammerton p204

Bastian, Henry Charlton (1837-1915). Eng. neurologist.
Bulloch—Hist. p351

Bastin, Edson Sunderland (1878-1953). Amer. geologist.
G.S.A.—Proc. '54 p87-92 (por.87)

Batani, El.   See Battani, Al

Bateman, Harry (1882-1946). Eng.-Amer. physicist, mathematician.
N.A.S. '49 p241-248 (por.241)

Bates, Henry Walter (1825-1892). Eng. naturalist, entomologist.
*Book—Pop. Sci. (1) p148
Chambers—Dict. col.42
Cutright—Great p27-31
Hammerton p205
Van Wagenen—Beacon p343-345
Von Hagen—Green p223

Bates, Marston (1906-   ). Amer. zoologist.
Curr. Biog. '56 p34-35 (por.34)

Bates, Mary E. (1861-1954). Amer. physician, surgeon.
Lovejoy—Women p93

Bateson, William (1861-1926). Eng. biologist.
Chambers—Dict. col.42
Hammerton p205
*Snyder—Biology p140-143 (por.143)

Bather, Francis Arthur (1863-1934). Eng. geologist, zoologist, morphologist.
G.S.A.—Proc. '34 p173-174
Hammerton p1446

Battani, Al (or Batani, El, or Albategnius, Mohammed Ben Jabir) (c850-929). Arab. astronomer, mathematician.
Abetti—History p48-50
Cajori—Hist. p105
Hammerton p41
Williams—Great p89-90

Batten, Jean (1909-   ). New Zeal. aero. pioneer.
*Fraser—Heroes p717,719,771-775,
    799-803 (por.770)
Hammerton p1446

Baudelocque, Jean Louis (1746/1756-1810). Fr. physician, surgeon, obstetrician.
Major—History (2) p638

Baudens, Jean-Baptiste Luciens (1804-1857). Fr. surgeon.
Leonardo—Lives p36-37

Bauer, Georg.   See **Agricola, Georgius**

Bauer, Louis Hopewell (1888-   ). Amer. physician.
Curr. Biog. '48 p37-38 (por.38)

Bauer, Wilhelm S.V. (1822-1876). Ger. inventor.
Year—Pic. p148 (por.148)

Bauhin, Gaspard (1560-1624). Swiss botanist, anatomist.
Arber—Herbals p114,115,116,159,
    160,168,179,181 (por.114)
Hammerton p207
Hawks—Pioneers p161-162
Major—History (1) p478
Reed—Short p73-74
Year—Pic p82 (por.82)

Bauhin, Jean (1541-1612/1613). Swiss botanist.
Arber—Herbals p113,114
Hawks—Pioneers p160-161

Baumé, Antoine (1728-1804). Fr. chemist.
Chambers—Dict. col.43
Hammerton p207
Weeks—Discovery p242 (por.242)

Baumgarten, Paul von (1848-1928). Ger. pathologist, bacteriologist.
Bulloch—History p351

Baumgartner, Leona (1902-   ). Amer. physician.
Curr. Biog. '50 p22-24 (por.23)

Baxter, Gregory Paul (b.1876). Amer. chemist.
Chambers—Dict. col.43

Bayen, Pierre (1725-1798). Fr. chemist.
Weeks—Discovery p92

Bayer, Johann (1572-1625?). Ger. astronomer.
*Book—Pop. Sci. (3) p994-995   Shapley—Astron. p21,28
Hammerton p209

Bayle, Gaspard Laurent (1774-1816). Fr. physician.
Major—History (2) p659

Bayley, William Shirley (1861-1943). Amer. geologist.
G.S.A.—Proc. '43 p105-108 (por.105)
Hammerton p209

Bayliss, Sir William Maddock (1860-1924). Eng. physiologist, biochemist.
Chambers—Dict. col.43   Major—History (2) p1028
Hammerton p209   *Snyder—Biology p379-381 (por.380)

Bayly, William (1737-1810). Eng. astronomer.
Hammerton p209

Baytar, Ibnu'l   See **Ibn al-Baytar**

Bazalgette, Sir Joseph William (1819-1891). Eng. engineer.
Hammerton p210

Beachey, Lincoln (1887-1915). Amer. aero. pioneer.
Heinmuller—Man's p262 (por.262)
Maitland—Knights p129-135

Beadle, George Wells (1903-   ). Amer. geneticist.
Curr. Biog. '56 p37-39 (por.38)

Beal, Carl Hugh (1889-1946). Amer. geologist.
G.S.A.—Proc. '46 p145-147 (por.145)

Beale, Lionel Smith (1828-1906). Eng. bacteriologist, physiologist.
Bulloch—Hist. p351
Hammerton p212

Beard, Charles Edmund (1900-   ). Amer. aero. pioneer.
Curr. Biog. '56 p39-41 (por.41)

Beard, James Thom (1855-1941). Amer. engineer, inventor.
Curr. Biog. '42 p62

Beau, Lucas Victor (1895-   ). Amer. aero. pioneer.
Curr. Biog. '54 p74-77 (por.75)

Beaulieu, Jacques de (1651-1714?). Fr. physician, surgeon.
Thorwald—Century p49 (por.80)

Beaumont, André. See **Conneau, Jean**

Beaumont, Jean Baptiste Armand Louis Léonce Élie (1798-1874). Fr.
geologist, min. engineer.
Hammerton p216,552   Woodruff—Devel. p186,263
Weeks—Discovery p351 (por.351)

Beaumont, William (1785-1853). Amer. physiologist, physician, surgeon.
Atkinson—Magic p235-240   Lambert—Minute p223-224
Bodenheimer—Hist. p374   Major—History (2) p747-751
Castiglioni—Hist. p686 (por.685)   (por.747)
Chambers—Dict. col.43-44   *Montgomery—Story p34-38
Cushing—Medical p206-224   Morris—Ency. p634
Flexner—Doctors p237-289 (por.237)   Moulton—Auto. p309-310
Hammerton p216   Tuska—Invent. p81-82
Lambert—Medical p223-224   Wilson—Amer. p102-103 (por.102)

Beauperthuy, Louis Daniel (1803-1871). Fr. (W. Indies) physician.
*Book—Pop. Sci. (1) p148-149
Hammerton p216

Beausoleil, Martine, Baroness De (1602-1640). Fr. mineralogist.
Mozans—Woman p238-240

Beauvais. See **Vincent of Beauvais**

Beccaria, Giovanni Battista (1716-1781). It. physicist.
Hammerton p217
Walsh—Catholic (2d) p158-164

Béchamp, Pierre Jacques Antoine (1816-1908). Fr. chemist.
Bulloch—Hist. p352

Becher, Johann Joachim (1635-1682). Ger. chemist, physician.
Chambers—Dict. col.44   Jaffe—Crucibles p34-50
Hammerton p218   Partington—Short p85,148-149
Holmyard—Chem. p57-58   (por.85)
Holmyard—Makers p143-146   Smith—Torch. p23 (por.23)
(por.144)   Weeks—Discovery p82,83 (por.83)

Bechtel, Stephen D. (1900-   ). Amer. engineer.
Curr.Biog. '57 p43-45 (por.43)

Beck, Lewis C. (1798-1853). Amer. chemist, mineralogist.
Smith—Chem. p226

Becker, George Ferdinand (1874-1919). Amer. geologist.
N.A.S.—Biog. (11) (XXI Memoirs)
p1-13 (por.1)

Beckmann, Ernst Otto (1853-1923). Ger. chemist.
Chambers—Dict. col.44   Smith—Torch. p24 (por.24)
Partington—Short p319

Becquerel, Alexandre Edmond (1820-1891). Fr. physicist.
Chambers—Dict. col.45
Hammerton p219-220

Becquerel, Antoine César (1788-1878). Fr. physicist.
*Book—Pop. Sci. (3) p861-862   Hammerton p220 (por.220)
Chambers—Dict. col.44

Becquerel, Antoine Henri (1852-1908). Fr. physicist.
A.A.A.S.—Proc. (81) p40-42   Riedman—Men p17-18 (por.16)
*Book—Pop. Sci. (3) p862   Schwartz—Moments (2) p883-884
Calder—Science p63-64   Smith—Torch. p25 (por.25)
Chambers—Dict. col.45   *Sootin—Twelve p231-246
*Darrow—Masters p329-330   Van Wagenen—Beacon p411-412
Heathcote—Nobel p18-26 (por.240) Weber—College p43 (por.43)
*Lewellen—Boy p215-232 (por.215) Weeks—Discovery p485 (por.485)
Magie—Source p610   Wilson—Amer. p332-333
Moulton—Auto. p490   Year—Pic. p115,207 (por.207)
*Pratt—Famous p129-130

Bedaux, Charles Eugène (1887-1944). Fr.-Amer. engineer.
Curr. Biog. '44 p40

Beddard, Frank Evers (1858-1925). Eng. zoologist, naturalist.
Hammerton p220 (por.220)

Beddoe, John (1826-1911). Eng. anthropologist.
Hammerton p220

Beddoes, Thomas (1760?-1808). Eng. physician.
Fülöp—Miller p58-61 (por.65)   Major—History (2) p701
Gunther—Early XI p277-278   Weeks—Discovery p274-275 (por.275)
Hammerton p220

Beddoes, Thomas Lovell (1803-1849). Eng. physician.
Farmer—Doctors' p109

Bede (or Baeda, Beda the Venerable). (c673-735). Eng. mathematician.
Cajori—Hist. p114   Smith—Hist. I p184-185
Clagett—Greek p160-165

Beebe, Charles William (1877-1962). Amer. naturalist, sci. explorer, ornithologist.
Chambers—Dict. col.45   *Milne—Natur. p171
*Cooper—Twenty p85-100 (por.84)   Peattie—Gather. p189-192
Curr. Biog. '41 p56-58 (por.57)   Progress—Science '40 p70 (por.70)
Cutright—Great p40   *Snyder—Biology p421-427 (por.427)
Hammerton p221   Tracy—Amer. Nat. p215-232
*Hylander—Scien. p171-173   Von Hagen—Green p300-301

Beech, Olive Ann Mellor (1903-   ). Amer. aero pioneer.
Curr. Biog. '56 p41-43 (por.43)

Beecher, Charles Emerson (1856-1904). Amer. paleontologist.
N.A.S.—Biog. (6) p57-66 (por.57)

Beekly, Albert Leon (1883-1952). Amer. geologist.
G.S.A.—Proc. '52 p91-92 (por.91)

Beer, Edwin (1876-1938). Amer. urologist, physician.
Kagan—Modern p107 (por.107)

Begg, Alexander Swanson (1881-1940). Amer. physician.
Curr. Biog. '40 p68 (por.68)

Begg, Colin Luke (1873-1941). Amer. physician.
Curr. Biog. '41 p60

Beguyer de Cancourtois.   See **Chancourtois, Alexandre-Émile Béguyer de**

Behr, Hans Herman (1818-1904). Ger.-Amer. physician, entomologist.
Essig—Hist. p553-556 (por.554)

Behrens, James (1824-1898). Ger.-Amer. entomologist.
Essig—Hist. p556-557 (por.556)

Behring, Emil (Adolph) von (1854-1917). Ger. bacteriologist.
Bodenheimer—Hist. p442   Castiglioni—Hist. p882 (por.821)
Bulloch—Hist. p352 (por.18)   Chambers—Dict. col.45-46
                    (Continued)

Behring, Emil (Adolph) von—*Continued*
   *DeKruif—Microbe p193-206
   Grainger—Guide p145
   Hammerton p225
   Law—Civiliz. p335-336
   Major—History (2) p915

*Montgomery—Story p215-217
Sigerist—Great p372-374 (por.369)
*Snyder—Biology p262-264 (por.268)
Stevenson—Nobel p3-9 (por.150)

Beijerinck, Martinus Willem (1851-1931). Dutch microbiologist.
   Bulloch—Hist. p352
   Grainger—Guide p146

Reed—Short p228,231,296,299

Beilby, Sir George Thomas (1850-1924). Scot. chemist.
   Chambers—Dict. col.46
   Hammerton p225

Beilstein, Friedrich Konrad (1836-1906). Ger. chemist.
   Chambers—Dict. col.46
   Smith—Torch p26 (por.26)

Bekenchons (1293-1225 B.C.). Egypt. engineer.
   Matschoss—Great p8-9 (por.8)

Bekhterev, Vladimir Mikhailovich (1857-1927). Rus. neuropathologist.
   Chambers—Dict. col.46
   Hammerton p226

Belfield, William Thomas (1856-1929). Amer. surgeon.
   Leonardo—Lives p37-38

Belfrage, Gustaf Wilhelm (1834-1882). Swed.-Amer. zoologist, entomologist.
   Geiser—Natural p225-239
   Osborn—Fragments p33

Bell, Alexander Graham (1847-1922). Scot.-Amer. inventor.
   Abbot—Great p99-112 (por.99)
   *Bachman—Great p228-246
   *Beard—Foreign p30-39 (por.32)
   *Book—Pop. Sci. (2) p440-441
      (por. 440)
   Carmer—Caval. p248-250 (por.249)
   Chambers—Dict. col.46-47
   *Cottler—Heroes p211-219
   *Darrow—Builders p271-272 (por.278)
   *Darrow—Masters p281-293 (por.320)
   *Darrow—Thinkers p237-247
      (por.238)
   *Eberle—Invent. p95-100

*Epstein—Real p135-136
*Everett—When p23-29 (por.23)
Fitzhugh—Concise p50-52
Forbes—Men p28-35 (por.1)
*Hartman—Mach. p159-168
*Hathaway—Partners p113-124
Hawks—Wireless p96-112 (por.72)
*Hylander—Invent. p126-139
   (por.146)
Meyer—World p164-172 (por.165,
   180)
*Montgomery—Invent. p54-57
Morris—Ency. p635

(*Continued*)

Bell, Alexander Graham—*Continued*
John Fritz p45-47 (por.44)
*Larsen—Men p9-21 (por.80)
*Larsen—Prentice p49-50
Law—Civiliz. p222-231
Law—Modern p8-21 (por.,front.)
N.A.S.—Biog. (23) p1-19 (por.1)
*Nida—Makers p170-179 (por.171)
*Nisenson—Illus. p24 (por.24)
*Nisenson—More p20 (por.20)
100 Great p648-653 (por.56)
*Parkman—Conq. p379-395
*Patterson—Amer. p110-121
*Pratt—Famous p63-66
Radio's 100 p84-86 (por.140)

*Science Miles p224-231 (por.224)
Sewell—Brief p179-180
*Simmons—Great p33-35 (por. 33)
*Tappan—Heroes p115-121
Thomas—50 Amer. p283-293
*Towers—Beacon p140-187 (por.160)
True—Smiths p270-272 (por.270)
Tuska—Invent. p86-87
Webb—Famous p34-46 (por.35)
*Wildman—Famous (1st) p37-47
(por.35)
Wilson—Amer. p278-285 (por.279)
Year—Pic. p170 (por. 170,173)

Bell, Benjamin (1749-1806). Scot. surgeon.
Leonardo—Lives p38-40

Bell, Sir Charles (1774-1842). Eng. physician, surgeon, anatomist, physiologist.
Atkinson—Magic p219-221
Bodenheimer—Hist. p348
*Book—Pop. Sci. (1) p149-150
(por. 151)
Chambers—Dict. col.47
Farmer—Doctors' p86
Hale-White—Great p42-62

Hammerton p227 (por.227)
Leonardo—Lives p40-41
Locy—Biology p183-184 (por.184)
Major—Hist. (2) p706
Van Wagenen—Beacon p222-223
Williams—Story p401-402 (por.402)

Bell, Henry (1767-1830). Scot. engineer.
Chambers—Dict. col. 47
Hammerton p228

Bell, Jacob (1810-1859). Eng. chemist.
Hammerton p828

Bell, James (1852-1919). Can. surgeon.
Leonardo—Lives p41-43

Bell, James Mackintosh (1877-1934). Can. geologist.
G.S.A.—Proc. '34 p187-189 (por.187)

Bell, John (1763-1820). Scot. surgeon, anatomist.
Hammerton p228 (por.228)   Major—Hist. (2) p702-703
Leonardo—Lives p43-45

Bell, Lawrence Dale (1894-   ). Amer. aero. pioneer.
Curr. Biog. '42 p62-63 (por.63)
Daniel—Pioneer p93-97 (por.92)

Bell, Patrick (1799-1869). Scot. inventor.
Hammerton p228

Bell, Thomas (1792-1880). Eng. zoologist.
Hammerton p229

Bellamy, Frank Arthur (1864-1936). Eng. astronomer.
Gunther—Early XI p323-324
(por.323)

Bellanca, Giuseppe Mario (1886-1961). Amer. aero. pioneer.
Heinmuller—Man's p302. (por.302)

Bellini, (Florentine) Lorenzo (1643-1704). It. physiologist, anatomist.
Castiglioni—Hist. p525,545   Major—History (1) p560
Hammerton p230

Bellonte, Maurice (1893?-   ). Fr. aero. pioneer, engineer.
Hammerton p231
Heinmuller—Man's p340 (por.340)

Bellovacencis, Vicentus.   See **Vincent of Beauvais**

Belon, Pierre (1517/1518-1564). Fr. naturalist.
Bodenheimer—Hist. p234   Miall—Early p40-45
Chambers—Dict. col.47-48   Woodruff—Devel. p223,263
Hawks—Pioneers p153-154

Belopolsky, Aristarch Apolonovich (1854-1934). Rus. astronomer, astrophysicist.
MacPherson—Astron. p201-205

Beltrami, Eugenio (1835-1900). It. mathematician, physicist.
Cajori—Hist. p307
Hammerton p231

Belzoni, Giovanni Battista (1778-1823). It. sc. explorer, archaeologist.
Ceram—Gods p116-120

Ben Abba ha Cohen.   See **Samuel, Mar**

Bender, James Frederick (1905-   ). Amer. psychologist.
Curr. Biog. '49 p35-36 (por.35)

Bender, Lauretta (1897-   ). Amer. physician, psychiatrist.
Knapp—Women p79-93 (por.79)

Bendix, Vincent (1882-1945). Amer. inventor.
Curr. Biog '45 p40

Beneden, Edouard van (1845/1846-1910). Belgian embryologist, zoologist, cytologist.
Bodenheimer—Hist. p425
Chambers—Dict. col.48

Benedetti, Alessandro (1460-1525). It. anatomist, physician.
Castiglioni—Hist. p369-370
Major—History (1) p461

Benedict, Francis Gano (1870-1957). Amer. chemist, biologist, physiologist, inventor.
*Montgomery—Story p66-69
N.A.S.—Biog. (32) p67-78 (por.67)
Ratcliffe—Modern p120-122
*Snyder—Biology p331-332 (por.333)

Benedict, Ruth (1887-1948). Amer. anthropologist.
Curr. Biog. '41 p65-66 (por.65), '48
  p44
Progress—Science '41 p66-67 (por.66)

Benedict, Stanley Rossiter (1884-1936). Amer. chemist.
N.A.S.—Biog. (27) p155-171
  (por.155)

Ben Ezra.   See **Abenezra**

Benioff, Hugo (1899-   ). Amer. geologist.
G.S.A.—Proc. '57 p73 (por.73)

Benivieni, Antonio (c1440/1448-1502). It. physician, surgeon, anatomist.
Castiglioni—Hist. p370
Gordon—Medieval p620-621
Leonardo—Lives p45-48
Major—History (1) p371 (por.372)

Bennet, Abraham (1750-1799). Eng. physicist.
Chambers—Dict. col.48

Bennett, Floyd (1890-1928). Amer. aero. pioneer.
Maitland—Knights p288-291
*Shippen—Bridle p119-124

Bennett, George MacDonald (1892-1959). Eng. chemist.
R.S.L.—Biog. (5) p23-33 (por.23)

Bennett, Hugh Hammond (1881-1960). Amer. agric. chemist.
Curr. Biog. '46 p36-38 (por.37).
'60 p24

Bennett, James Gordon (1841-1918). Amer. aero. pioneer.
Heinmuller—Man's p265 (por.265)

Bennett, John Hughes (1812-1875). Eng. physiologist, physician.
Bulloch—Hist. p352
Major—History (2) p882

Bennett, John Walter Frink (1878-1943). Amer. engineer.
Curr.Biog. '43 p37

Bennett, Rawson, 2d (1905-   ). Amer. elec. engineer.
Curr. Biog. '58 p36-38 (por.37)

Ben Schaprut.   See **Hasdai ibn-Shap-rut**

Ben Shah Rok.   See **Ulugh-Beg, Mirza Mahommed ben Shah Rok**

Ben-Shlomoh.   See **Gershon Ben-Shlomoh**

Bensin, Basil M. (1881-   ). Rus. agriculturist.
Curr. Biog. '48 p44-46 (por.46)

Benson, Francis Colgate, Jr. (1872?-1941). Amer. physician, surgeon.
Curr. Biog. '41 p69

Benson, William Noel (1885-1957). Eng. geologist.
R.S.L.—Biog. (4) p27-31 (por. 27)

Bent, James Theodore (1852-1897). Eng. archaeologist.
Hammerton p235

Ben Tamim, Abu Sahal Dunash (900-960). Arab. physician.
Gordon—Medieval p170

Bentham, George (1800-1884). Eng. botanist.
Chambers—Dict. col. 48   Hammerton p235
Gilmour—British p40 (por.32)

Bentley, Thomas (c1485-1549). Eng. physician.
Gunther—Early XI p136

Benvenutus.   See **Grassus, Benvenutus**

Benz, Carl (or Karl) (1844-1929). Ger. engineer, inventor.
Hammerton p237
*Hodgins—Behemoth   p314-316
*Larsen—Scrap.   p116,118-120
   (por.112)
People p21-22

Bérard, Auguste (1802-1846). Fr. surgeon.
Leonardo—Lives p48

Berengario da Carpi, Jacobus (or Berengarius, Jacobo, Giacomo) (1470-1530). It. physician, anatomist.
Castiglioni—Hist. p417-418
Gordon—Medieval p698 (por.211)
Lambert—Medical p100-101
Lambert—Minute p100-101
Major—Hist. (1) p398-401 (por.399)

Berg, Ernst Julius (1871-1941). Amer. engineer, mathematician, physicist.
Curr. Biog. '41 p70-71

Berg, Hart O. (1865?-1941). Amer. engineer.
Curr. Biog. '42 p72

Berger, Christian Johann (1724-1789). Dan. physician.
Copen.—Prom. p56-59

Berger, Edward William (1869-1944). Amer. entomologist.
Osborn—Fragments p229 (por.342)

Berger, Hans (1873-1941). Ger. physician.
Major—History (2) p1009

Bergius, Friedrich (1884-1949). Ger. chemist.
Chambers—Dict. col. 48-49 (por.50)   Hammerton p238
Farbel—Nobel p124-126 (por.118)

Bergman, Torbern Olof (1735-1784). Swed. physicist, chemist.
Chambers—Dict. col.49
Hammerton p238
Lindroth—Swedish p131-140
Partington—Short p150,153,160
Smith—Torch p27 (por.27)
Weeks—Discovery p69,72,100-101,129
   (por.72,129)

Bergmann, Ernst von (1836-1907). Ger. physician, surgeon.
Hammerton p238
Leonardo—Lives p48-50
Major—History (2) p899

Bergquist, Stanard Gustav (1892-1956). Amer. geologist.
G.S.A.—Proc. '56 p111-115 (por.111)

Berkeley, George (1685-1753). Irish mathematician.
Cajori—Hist. p219

Berkeley, Miles Joseph (1803-1889). Eng. botanist.
Hammerton p239
Oliver—Makers p225-232 (por.225)

Berkey, Charles Peter (1867-1955). Amer. geologist, engineer.
N.A.S.—Biog. (30) p41-51 (por.41)

Berkner, Lloyd Viel (1905-   ). Amer. physicist, elec. engineer.
Curr. Biog. '49 p40-42 (por.41)

Berlandier, Jean Louis (c1805-1851). Fr.-Amer. naturalist.
Geiser—Natural. p30-54

Berliner, Emile (1851-1929). Ger.-Amer. inventor.
A.A.A.S.—Proc. (79) p4-7
Abbot—Great p109-110
*Beard—Foreign p46-51
*Book—Pop. Sci. (2) p441-442
Hammerton p240
*Hylander—Invent. p147-157
   (por.147)
*Montgomery—Invent. p58-61
   Radio's 100 p99-102 (por.140).

Berman, Harry (1902-1944). Amer. geologist.
G.S.A.—Proc. '44 p151-152 (por.151)

Bernard, Charles (1650-1711). Eng. surgeon.
Major—History (1) p562

Bernard, Claude (1813-1878). Fr. physiologist.
Bodenheimer—Hist. p410
*Book—Pop. Sci. (1) p151-153
Bulloch—Hist. p353
Castiglioni—Hist. p682-683
   (por.680)
Chambers—Dict. col.49
Hammerton p240
Lambert—Medical p208-209
Lambert—Minute p208-209
Locy—Biology p190-192 (por. 191)
Major—History (2) p775-778
   (por.776)
Robinson—Path. p579-610
   (por.590,591,594)
Rosen—Four p256-258
Schwartz—Moments (1) p61-63
Schwartz—Moments (2) p622-623
Sigerist—Great p316-321 (por.320)
*Snyder—Biology p381-386
Thomson—Great p93-100
Van Wagenen—Beacon p300-301
Walsh—Makers p269-289
Williams—Story p351-352,405,-406
   (por.351)
Woodruff—Devel. p263-264

Bernard de Gordon (c1285). Fr. physician.
Chambers—Dict. col.49-50

Bernardi, Mario de (1893-1959). It. aero. pioneer.
Hammerton p240

Bernheim, Bertram M. (1880-   ). Amer. physician, surgeon.
Curr. Biog. '43 p38-39 (por.39)

Bernouilli (or Bernoulli) **family.**   See also names of individuals
Bell—Men p131-138   Smith—Hist. I p426-433
Cajori—Hist. p220-224   Turnbull—Great p95-96
Hammerton p242   Woodruff—Devel. p21,264

Bernouilli, (or Bernoulli), **Daniel** (1700-1782). Swiss mathematician,
physicist.
A.A.A.S.—Proc. (78) p7-8   *Lewellen—Boy p103-106 (por.93)
Ball—Short p377-378   Magie—Source p247
Chalmers—Historic p261-262   *Science Miles. p84 (por.94)
Chambers—Dict. col. 51   Van Wagenen—Beacon p146-147
Hooper—Makers p342,347,348,350

Bernouilli, Jacques (or Bernoulli, James, Jakob) (1654-1705). Swiss
mathematician.
Ball—Short p366-367   Hooper—Makers p342,343,346
Cajori—Hist. p220-222   Smith—Hist. I, p427-428 (por.427)
Chambers—Dict. col.50   Woodruff—Devel. p264

Bernouilli, Jean (or Bernoulli, John, Johann) (1667-1748). Swiss
mathematician.
Ball—Short p367-369   Hooper—Makers p262,278,334,344
Cajori—Hist. p222-223   Smith—Hist. I p428-430 (por.249)
Chambers—Dict. col.50-51   Woodruff—Devel. p21, 23, 264
Holmyard—Makers p160 (por.158)   (por.22)

Berosus (or Berossus) (c.3rd cent., B.C.). Chaldean nat. philosopher.
Chambers—Dict. col. 51

Berry, Edward Wilber (1875-1945). Amer. geologist, paleontologist.
Curr. Biog. '45 p47
G.S.A.—Proc. '45 p193-200 (por.193)

Bert, Paul (1833-1886). Fr. physiologist.
Bulloch—Hist. p353
Hammerton p244

Bertapaglia, Leonardo da (c1440-c1460). It. physician.
Major—History (1) p355

Bertelli, Timoteo 1826-1905). It. seismologist.
Davison—Founders p91-93

Bertelsen.   See **Bartholinus, Thomas**

Berthelot, Marcellin Pierre Eugène (1827-1907). Fr. chemist.

Bodenheimer—Hist. p408
*Book—Pop. Sci. (3) p863
Chambers—Dict. col.51-52
Findlay—Hundred p319
Hammerton p244
Partington—Short p283-284,295
   (por.283)

Ramsay—Essays p101-114
Smith—Torch p28 (por.28)
Van Wagenen—Beacon p349-351
Weeks—Discovery p461 (por.461)
Woodruff—Devel. p121,264

Berthollet, Claude Louis, Comte (1748-1822). Fr. chemist.

*Book—Pop. Sci. (3) p864-865
Chambers—Dict. col.52
Hammerton p244
Partington—Short p154-156,177
   (por.155)

Roberts—Chem. p54-62
Smith—Torch. p29 (por. 29)
Van Wagenen—Beacon p193-195
Weeks—Discovery p440 (por.440)

Berthon, Edward Lyon (1813-1899). Eng. inventor.

Hammerton p244

Bertillon, Louis Adolphe (1821-1883). Fr. anthropologist.

Hammerton p244

Bertin, Réné Joseph Hyacinthe (1767-1828). Fr. physician.

Major—History (2) p705

Bertrand, Élie (1712-c1777). Swiss naturalist, geologist.

Davison—Founders p8-11

Bery de St. Venant.   See **Barré de Saint-Venant, A.J.C.**

Berzelius, Jons Jacob, Baron (1779-1848). Swed. chemist.

Adams—Birth p207-208
*Book—Pop. Sci. (3) p865-866
Chambers—Dict. col. 52-53
*Darrow—Masters p113-116 (por.33)
Hammerton p245 (por.245)
Holmyard—Makers p240-248
   (por.241)
*Jaffe—Crucibles p136-156
Lindroth—Swedish p160-171
*Men—Scien. p40-42
Lenard—Great p194-196 (por.195)

Partington—Short p194-208, 212-213,
   295 (por.195)
Roberts—Chem. p88-98
Robinson—Path. p283-307 (por.294)
Smith—Torch. p30 (por.30)
Tilden—Famous p131-151 (por. 131,
   151)
Van Wagenen—Beacon p234-235
Weeks—Discovery p159-167
   (por.158,167)
Williams—Story p256,259,264-268
   (por.261)
Woodruff—Devel. p264 (por.100)

Besredka, Alexander (1870-1940). Rus. bacteriologist, immunologist.

Kagan—Modern p168 (por.168)

Bessel, Friedrich Wilhelm (1784-1846). Ger. astronomer, mathematician.
Abetti—History p177-180
Ball—Short p493-494
*Book—Pop. sci. (3) p995-996
Cajori—Hist. p448-449
Chambers—Dict. col.53
Hammerton p246
Lodge—Pioneers p304-316
MacPherson—Makers p131-134
Shapley—Astron. p216
Van Wagenen—Beacon p241-242
Vaucouleurs—Disc. p110-115
Williams—Great p294-299 (por.300)
Williams—Story p48,66,74 (por.45)
Woodruff—Devel. p264 (por.148)

Bessemer, Sir Henry (1813-1898). Eng. engineer, inventor.
*Bachman—Great p161-185 (por.161)
*Book—Pop. Sci. (2) p442-443 (por.443)
Chambers—Dict. col.54
*Darrow—Masters p174-180 (por.288)
*Darrow—Thinkers p207-212 (por.208)
*Eberle—Invent. p77-84 (por.76)
*Goddard—Eminent p262-269 (por.264)
Gregory—British p28
Hammerton p246 (por.246)
Hart—Engineers p123-129
*Hartman—Mach. p111-116
*Larsen—Shaped p55-65 (por.33)
Law—Civiliz. p259-262
Matschoss—Great p244-259 (por.252)
Meyer—World p254-255
*Nida—Makers p17-25 (por.19)
*Pratt—Famous p93-97
Smith—Torch. p31 (por.31,32)
Year—Pic. p189 (por.189)

Bessey, Charles Edwin (1845-1915). Amer. entomologist, botanist.
Osborn—Fragments p148-149 (por.351)

Bessy. See **Frénicle de Bessy, Bernard**

Best, Charles Herbert (1899-). Amer.-Can. physiologist.
Chambers—Dict. col.54
Curr. Biog. '57 p52-54 (por.53)
Progress—Science '41 p67 (por.67)
Rowntree—Amid p348-354 (por.347,350,351)

Bethe, Hans Albrecht (1906-). Alsace-Lorraine physicist.
Curr. Biog. '40 p81-82 (por.82), '50 p46-48 (por.47)

Bethencourt, Jacques de (fl.1527). Fr. physician.
Major—History (1) p465

Bethune, C.J.S. (1838-1932). Can. entomologist.
Osborn—Fragments p171-172 (por.343)

Beulé, Charles Ernest (1826-1874). Fr. archaeologist.
Hammerton p247

Beutenmueller, William (1864-1919). Amer. entomologist.
Osborn—Fragments p232 (por.356)

Bevan, Arthur Dean (1861-1943). Amer. physician, surgeon.
Curr. Biog. '43 p44

Bevan, Edward John (1856-1921). Eng. chemist.
Chambers—Dict. col.54

Beverage, Harold Henry (1893-   ). Amer. radio engineer.
Radio's 100 p257-261 (por.140)

Bevis (or Bevans), **John** (1693-1771). Eng. physician, astronomer.
Davison—Founders p3-5

Beyrich, Heinrich Ernst von (1815-1896). Ger. geologist.
Hammerton p248

Bézout, Etienne (1730-1783). Fr. mathematician.
Cajori—Hist. p249-250

Bhabha, Homi Jehangir (1909-   ). Ind. physicist.
Chambers—Dict. col.54
Curr. Biog. '56 p49-51 (por.50)

Bhaskara Acharya (c1140). Arab. mathematician, astronomer.
Ball—Short p150-155   Van Wagenen—Beacon p46-48
Smith—Hist. I p275-282   Woodruff—Devel. p13,264

Bianchi, Leonardo (1848-1927). It. psychiatrist.
Castiglioni—Hist. p886 (por.887)

Bichat, Marie Francois Xavier (1771-1802). Fr. physiologist, anatomist,
   pathologist.
Bodenheimer—Hist. p361   Lambert—Minute p201-203 (por.209)
*Book—Pop. Sci. (1) p153-154   Locy—Biology p166-171 (por.169)
   (por.153).   Major—History (2) p650-651
Castiglioni—Hist. p672-673 (por.673)   (por.651)
Chambers—Dict. col.54-55   Oliver—Stalkers p142-144
Gordon—Romance p159 (por.159)   Sigerist—Great p269-271 (por.272)
Hammerton p248 (por.248)   Williams—Story p322-324 (por.323)
Lambert—Medical p201-203
   (por.206)

Bickerton, Alexander William (1842-1929). New Zeal. astronomer.
Armitage—Cent. p38
Hammerton p249

Bidder, George Parker (1806-1878). Br. mathematician.
Hammerton p249 (por.249)

Biddle, Owen (1737-1799). Amer. nat. philosopher.
Bell—Early p48

Bidloo, Gottfried (Govert) (1649-1713). Dutch anatomist.
Major—History (1) p561-562

Biela, Wilhelm von (1782-1856). Aust. astronomer.
Chambers—Dict. col. 55

Bielovucic, Jean (1889-   ). Peru. aero. pioneer.
Heinmuller—Man's p286 (por.286)

Bier, August Karl Gustav (1861-1949). Ger. physician, surgeon.
Hammerton p249
Major—History (2) p1028

Biffen, Sir Rowland (1874-1949). Eng. botanist.
Chambers—Dict. col.55

Bigelow, Erastus Brigham (1814-1879). Amer. inventor.
Hammerton p249

Bigelow, Henry Bryant (b.1879). Amer. zoologist, oceanographer.
Progress—Science '40 p71

Bigelow, Henry Jacob (1818-1890). Amer. surgeon.
Chambers—Dict. col.55   Kagan—Modern p86 (por.86)
Fülöp—Miller p156-160 (por.152)   Leonardo—Lives p50-51

Bigelow, Jacob (1787-1879). Amer. physician.
Hammerton p249

Bigelow, Willard Dell (1866-1939). Amer. chemist.
Holland—Ind. p113-128 (por.113).

Biggs, Herman M. (1859-1923). Amer. bacteriologist, physician.
Farmer—Doctors' p222   Walker—Pioneers p239-251 (por.239)
Grainger—Guide p146

Bignami, Amico (1862-1929). It. physician.
Major—History (2) p919

Bigsby, John Jeremiah (1792-1881). Eng. geologist.
Hammerton p250

Bijl, Hendrick Johnnes van der (1887-   ). S. Afr. physicist.
Radio's 100 p227-229 (por.140)

Bill, Robert (1754-1827). Eng. inventor.
Hammerton p250

Billeter, Otto (1851-1927). Swiss chemist.
A.A.A.S.—Proc. (79) p7-8

Billings, Frank (1854-1932). Amer. physician.
Major—History (2) p950-951, 1028-
  1029 (por.950)
Rowntree—Amid p205-209 (por.210)

Billings, John Shaw (1838-1913). Amer. physician, surgeon.
Castiglioni—Hist. p1128,1129   Major—History (2) p900-901
  (por.1128)   N.A.S.—Biog. (8) p375-416
Kagan—Leaders p72-81   (por.375)

Billings, Martin Hewett (1907-1953). Amer. geologist.
G.S.A.—Proc. '52 p171

Billroth, Christian Albert Theodor (1829-1894). Ger. pathologist,
  physician, surgeon, bacteriologist.
Atkinson—Magic p291-293   Kagan—Modern p90 (por.90)
Bulloch—Hist. p353   Leonardo—Lives p51-52
Castiglioni—Hist. p848 (por.848)   Major—History (2) p894-895
Grainger—Guide p146-147   (por.847)
Hammerton p251 (por.251)   Sigerist—Great p380-383 (por.379)

Binet, Alfred (1857-1911). Fr. psychologist.
*Book—Pop. Sci. (4) p1141-1143   Hammerton p251
  (por.1142)
Chambers—Dict. col.56

Bingham, Eugene Cook (1878-1945). Amer. chemist.
Chambers—Dict. col.56

Bingham, George A. (1860-1922). Can. surgeon.
Leonardo—Lives p52-53

Bingham, Hiram (1875-   ). Amer. sci. explorer, aero. pioneer.
Curr. Biog. '51 p41-44 (por. 42)

Bingham, Millicent Todd (1880-   ). Amer. geographer.
Curr. Biog. '61 (Je.) (por.)

Binney, Edward William (1812-1881). Eng. geologist, botanist.
Hammerton p251
Oliver—Makers p245-246

Binnie, Sir Alexander Richardson (1839-1917). Eng. engineer.
Hammerton p251-252

Binninger, Johann Nikolaus (1628-1692). Fr. physician.
Major—History (1) p557

Biondo, Michelangelo (Blondus) (1497-1565). It. physician, surgeon.
Leonardus—Lives p53-54
Major—History (1) p466

Biot, Jean Baptiste (1774-1862). Fr. mathematician, physicist, astronomer.
*Book—Pop. Sci. (3) p996 (por.996)   Magie—Source p441
Chambers—Dict. col. 56   Williams—Story p158,203 (por.173)
Hammerton p252

Birch, Carroll (1896-   ). Amer. physician.
Lovejoy—Women p227

Birch-Hirschfeld, Felix Victor (1842-1899). Ger. pathologist,
  bacteriologist.
Bulloch—Hist. p353

Birdseye, Clarence (1886-   ). Amer. inventor, naturalist.
Curr. Biog. p44-46 (por.45)
*Pratt—Famous p125-129

Birdseye, Claude Hale (1878-1941). Amer. geographer, sci. explorer.
Curr. Biog. '41 p80

Birge, Raymond Thayer (1887-   ). Amer. physicist.
Curr. Biog. '40 p85

Biringuccio, Vannoccio (c.1480). It. inventor.
Sarton—Six p119-121

Birkeland, Kristian (1867-1917). Norw. physicist.
Chambers—Dict. col. 56-57

Birkhoff, George David (1884-1944). Amer. mathematician.
Fisher—Amer. p183-184 (por.182)
Progress—Science '40 p71-72 (por.71)

Bischof, Karl Gutav Christoph (1792-1870). Ger. chemist, geologist.
Woodruff—Devel. p264

Bischoff, Theodor Ludwig Wilhelm (1807-1882). Ger. biologist, anatomist, physiologist.
Hammerton p254

Bishop, George (1785-1861). Eng. astronomer.
Hammerton p254

Bishop, Hazel (1906-   ). Amer. chemist.
Curr. Biog. '57 p56-58 (por.57)

Bishop, William Avery (1894-1956). Can. aero. pioneer.
Arnold—Airmen p124-125
Burge—Ency. p625
Curr. Biog. '41 p80-82 (por.80)
Heinmuller—Man's p303 (por.303)

Bissell, Clayton L. (1896-   ). Amer. aero. pioneer.
Curr. Biog. '43 (por.51)

Bizzozero, Giulio (1846-1901). It. physician, pathologist.
Castiglioni—Hist. p766 (por.767)

Bjerknes, Vilhelm (1862-1951). Norw. physicist.
Hammerton p257

Black, Arthur Davenport (1870-1937). Amer. dental surgeon.
*Lockhart—My p95 (por.94)

Black, Davidson (1884-1934). Can. anatomist.
G.S.A.—Proc. '34 p193-197 (por.193)

Black, Joseph (1728-1799). Scot. chemist, physicist.
A.A.A.S.—Proc. (77) p54
*Book—Pop. Sci. (3) p866-867
  (por.866)
Chalmers—Historic p262
Chambers—Dict. col. 57 (por.58)
*Darrow—Masters p330
Hammerton p257 (por.257)
Hart—Physicists p92-95
Holmyard—British p31-32 (por.32)
Holmyard—Chem. p79-83 (por.85)
Holmyard—Makers p164-169
  (por.164)
Lenard—Great p126 (por.130)
Magie—Source p134
Major—History (2) p613
Moulton—Auto. p218
(Continued)

Black, Joseph—*Continued*
Partington—Short p93-99 (por.94)
Ramsey—Essays p67-87
Roberts—Chem. p9-12
Schwartz—Moments (1) p430-431
Smith—Torch. p33 (por.33)
Thomson—Great p30

Tilden—Famous p22-31 (por.22)
Van Wagenen—Beacon p162-163
Weeks—Discovery p87-89, 108-116
(por.88)
Woodruff—Devel. p53,264-265
Year—Pic p101 (por.101)

Black, Tom Campbell (1899-   ). Eng. aero. pioneer.
Hammerton p1446

Blackall, John (1771-1860). Eng. physician.
Major—History (2) p705-706

Blackburn, Robert (1885-   ). Eng. aero. pioneer.
Burge—Ency. p625

Blackett, Patrick Maynard Stuart (1897-   ). Eng. physicist.
Chambers—Dict. col.57
Curr. Biog. '49 p56-58 (por.57)

Heathcote—Nobel p438-445
(por.240)
Weber—College p768 (por.768)

Blackfan, Kenneth Daniel (1883-1941). Amer. pediatrician.
Curr. Biog. '42 p84

Blackwell, Elizabeth (1821-1910). Amer. physician.
Carmer—Caval. p204-205 (por.205)
*Chandler—Medicine p53-57 (por.52)
Fabricant—Why p63-65
Hammerton p258
Heath—Amer. (4) p14 (por.14)
Lovejoy—Women p41-70,130
(por.43)

Mead—Medical p21-24 (por.
append.)
Mozans—Woman p300-304,305,307
Robinson—Path. p649-676
(por.662,663)
Rosen—Four p87-92,182-185
16 Amer. p17-20

Blackwell, Emily (1826-1910). Eng.-Amer. physician.
Lovejoy—Women p70-72 (por.71)
Mead—Medical p24-25
(por., append.)

Bladud, Geoffrey of Monmouth (1100-1154). Eng. aero. pioneer.
Burge—Ency. p625-626

Blagonravov, Anatoli Arkadyevich (1894-   ). Rus. technical scientist.
Curr. Biog. '58 p43-44 (por.43)

Blain, Daniel (1898-   ). Amer. psychiatrist.
Curr. Biog. '47 p52-53 (por.53)

Blainville, Henri Marie Ducrotay de (1778-1850). Fr. biologist.
Hammerton p259

Blair, Robert (d.1828). Scot. inventor, astronomer.
Hammerton p259

Blaisdell, Frank Ellsworth (1862-1946). Amer. entomologist.
Osborn—Fragments p182-183

Blake, Francis Gilman (1887-1952). Amer. physician.
Curr. Biog. '43 p53, '52 p53
N.A.S.—Biog. (28) p1-20 (por.1)

Blake, Sophia Jex (1840-1912). Eng. physician.
Mead—Medical p35-37

Blake, William Phipps (1825-1910). Amer. mineralogist, geologist.
Merrill—First p314-315. (por.315).

Blakeslee, Albert Francis (1874-1954). Amer. botanist, geneticist,
   biologist.
Chambers—Dict. col.57-58   Progress—Science '40 p72-73 (por.72)
Curr. Biog. '41 p86-87 (por.86) *Snyder—Biology p157-158 (por.158)
N.A.S.—Biog. (33) p1-23 (por.1)

Blalock, Alfred (1899-   ). Amer. physician, surgeon.
Curr. Biog. '46 p50-53 (por.51) Rowntree—Amid p470-474 (por.466)
Morris—Ency. p636   Truax—Doctors p188-196
Robinson—100 p303-305 (por.303)

Blanchard, Arthur Alphonzo (1876-1956). Amer. chemist.
Chambers—Dict. col. 58

Blanchard, Jean Pierre François (1753-1809). Fr. aero. pioneer, inventor.
*Bishop—Kite p35-45   Heinmuller—Man's p236 (por.236)
Burge—Ency. p625-626   Milbank—First p23-29 (por.23)
Carmer—Caval. p240-243 (por.240) *Shippen—Bridle p57-63
*Epstein—Real p88-89

Blanchard, Thomas (1788-1864). Amer. inventor, engineer.
Goddard—Eminent p70-77 (por.70) *Montgomery—Invent. p121-124
Iles—Leading p104-118 (por.104)

Bland-Sutton, Sir John (1855-1936). Eng. surgeon.
Hammerton p261

Blane, Sir Gilbert (1749-1834). Scot. physician.
Chambers—Dict. col.58-59.
Hammerton p261-262

Blanton, Smiley (1882-   ). Amer. psychiatrist.
Curr. Biog. '56 p55-57 (por.56)

Blatchley, Willis Stanley (1859-1940). Amer. entomologist, naturalist.
Curr. Biog. '40 p88 (por.88)
Osborn—Fragments p173-174
   (por.379)

Blenkinsop, John (1783-1831). Eng. inventor.
Hammerton p262

Blériot, Louis (1872-1936). Fr. aero. pioneer, engineer.
Burge—Ency. p626
*Cohen—Men p139-142
Hammerton p262 (por.262)
Heinmuller—Man's p271 (por.271)

Blichfeldt, Hans Frederik (1873-1945). Dan. mathematician.
N.A.S.—Biog. (26) p181-187 (por.181)

Bliss, Andrew Richard, Jr. (1887-1941). Amer. physician.
Curr. Biog. '41 p87

Bliss, Eleanor Albert (1899-   ). Amer. bacteriologist, physician.
*Montgomery—Story p128-130

Bliss, Gilbert Ames (1876-1951). Amer. mathematician.
N.A.S.—Biog. ('31) p32-45. (por.32)

Bliss, Nathaniel (1700-1764). Eng. astronomer.
Gunther—Early XI p275-277
   (por.276)

Bliss, Raymond Whitcomb (1888-   ). Amer. physician, surgeon.
Curr. Biog. '51 p44-46 (por.45)

Blith, Walter (c1649). Eng. agriculturist.
Hammerton p263

Bloch, Felix (1905-   ). Swiss-Ger.-Amer. physicist.
Chambers—Dict. supp.
Curr. Biog. '54 p93-95 (por.93)

Blodgett, Katharine Burr (1898-   ). Amer. physicist, chemist.
Curr. Biog. '40 p90-91 (por.90)
  '52 p55-57 (por.56)
        Goff—Women p177-182
        Yost—Women Sci. p196-213

Blomstrand, Christian Wilhelm (1826-1897). Ger. chemist.
Partington—Short p294

Bloodgood, Joseph Colt (1867-1935). Amer. surgeon.
Leonardo—Lives p54-55
Major—History (2) p1029

Blumenbach, Johann Friedrich (1752-1840). Ger. physiologist, anthropologist, zoologist.
Bodenheimer-Hist. p236
Chambers—Dict. col.59
        Hammerton p265

Blumer, George Alder (1857-1940). Amer. psychiatrist.
Curr. Biog. '40 p94

Blunt, Katharine (1876-1954). Amer. chemist.
Curr. Biog. '46 p57-59 (por.58)

Boardman, Russell N. (1893-1933). Amer. aero. pioneer.
Fraser—Heroes p597-602
Heinmuller—Man's p150-160,343
  (por.157,159,343)

Boas, Franz (1858-1942). Ger.-Amer. anthropologist.
Curr. Biog. '40 p94-96 (por.94)
  '43 p59
Hammerton p266
        Morris—Ency. p636-637
        N.A.S.—Biog. '47 p303-320 (por.303)
        Trattner—Arch. p351-374 (por.359)

Boas, Ismar (1858-1938). Ger. physician.
Kagan—Modern p19 (por.19)

Bobbs, John S. (1809-1870). Amer. surgeon.
Leonardo—Lives p55-56

Bôcher, Maxime (1867-1918). Amer. mathematician.
Smith—Hist. 1 p533
Smith—Math. p145-146 (por. 147)

Bock, Hieronymus (or Tragus, Jerome) (1498-1554). Ger. botanist, naturalist.
Arber—Herbals p55,58,59,61,151-153,166 (por.58)
Major—History (1) p467
        Miall—Early p20-24
        Sarton—Six p132 (por.131)

Bodansky, Meyer (1896-1941). Amer. biochemist, pathologist.
Curr. Biog. '41 p89

Bode, Johann Elert (1747-1826). Ger. astronomer.
Chambers—Dict. Col.59
Hammerton p267
Shapley—Astron. p180
Van Wagenen—Beacon p190-191

Bodenstein, Ernst August Max (1871-1940). Ger. chemist.
Chambers—Dict. col.59

Bodington, George (1799-1882), Eng. physician.
Major—History (2) p712-713

Bodländer, Guido (1855-1904). Ger. chemist.
Chambers—Dict. col.60

Böe, Franz de la.   See **Sylvius, Franciscus**

Boeckmann, Eduard (1849-1927). Amer. surgeon.
Leonardo—Lives p56

Boeing, William Edward (1881-   ). Amer. aero. pioneer.
Daniel Gugg. p43-49 (por.42)
Daniel—Pioneer p31-35 (por.30)

Boelcke, Oswald Hauptmann (1891-1916). Ger. aero. pioneer.
Burge—Ency. p626
Hammerton p268

Boerhaave, Hermann (1668-1738). Dutch physician.
Book—Pop. Sci. (4) p1143-1145
   (por.1144).
Castiglioni—Hist. p615-617 (por.615)
Chambers—Dict. col.60
Hammerton p268
Holmyard—Chem. p70-74 (por.71)
Holmyard—Makers p161-163
   (por.163)
Lambert—Medical p166-168
   (por.166)
Lambert—Minute p166-168 (por.160)
Major—History (2) p570-573
   (por.572)
Newman—Interp. p73-106
Oliver—Stalkers p134-136 (por.135)
Partington—Short p88,146
Sigerist—Great p185-190 (por.185)
Smith—Torch. p34 (por.34)
Weeks—Discovery p108 (por.108)
Year—Pic p108 (por.108)

Boethius (c.480?-524?). Roman mathematician.
Ball—Short p132-133
Cajori—Hist. p67-68
Clagett—Greek p74,150-153
Sedgwick—Short p148,153
Smith—Hist. I p178-179

Bogardus, James (1800-1874). Amer. inventor.
Chambers—Dict. col.60
Hammerton p268-269

Bogert, Marston Taylor (b.1868). Amer. chemist.
Browne—Hist. p480 (por.73)
Chambers—Dict. col.60

Boggs, Charles Reid (1883-1940). Amer. chemist.
Curr. Biog. '40 p96

Boheman, Carl Heinrich (1796-1868). Swed. entomologist.
Essig.—Hist. p558-559 (por.559)

Bohr, Christian (1855-1911). Dan. physician, physiologist.
Copen.—Prom. p173-176

Bohr, Niels Henrik David (1885-   ). Dan. physicist.
Chambers—Dict. col.61 (por.62)
Curr. Biog. '45 p54-56
Hammerton p269 (por.269)
Heathcote—Nobel p198-205 (por.240)
*Jaffe—Crucibles p322-328,378-383
*Larsen—Scrap. p144,152-153,158
   (por.145)
Moulton—Auto. p540-542
Riedman—Men p116-129 (por.121,
   136,137)
Robinson—100 p243-246 (por.243)
Weber—College p348 (por.348)
Year—Pic. p210,211 (por.211)

Boisbaudran, Paul Émile Lecoq de (or Lecoq de Boisbaudran, Paul Émile
   called François) (1838-1912). Fr. chemist, physicist.
Chambers—Dict. col.61
Findlay—Hundred p319
Smith—Torch. p35 (por.35)
Weeks—Discovery p399-403
   (por.399)

Boisduval, Jean Alphonse (1799-1879). Fr. entomologist.
Essig—Hist. p559-562 (por.560)

Bois-Reymond, Emil du.   See Du Bois-Reymond, Emil Heinrich

Bok, Bart Jan (1906-   ). Dutch-Amer. astrophysicist.
Chambers—Dict. col.61-62

Boll, Jacob (1828-1880). Swiss-Amer. naturalist.
Geiser—Natural. p19-29 (por.10)
Swiss—Prom. p198-201

Bollinger, Otto von (1843-1909). Ger. anatomist, bacteriologist.
Bulloch—Hist. p353

Bollstadt, Albert. See **Albertus Magnus, Saint Count von Bollstädt**

Bolt, Richard Henry (1911-   ). Amer. physicist.
Curr. Biog. '54 p101-103 (por.101)

Boltwood, Bertram Borden (1870-1927). Amer. physicist, chemist.
Chambers—Dict. col.62
Killeffer—Eminent p29 (por.29)
N.A.S.—Biog. (14) p69-94 (por.69,75)
Weeks—Discovery p492-493 (por.493)

Boltzmann, Ludwig (1844-1906). Aust. physicist.
Chambers—Dict. col. 62-63
Lenard—Great p350-358 (por.370)
Magie—Source p262
Van Wagenen—Beacon p394-396
Woodruff—Devel. p40,63,265

Bolyai, Farkas (or De Bloya, Wolfgang) (1775-1856). Hung. mathematician.
Cajori—Hist. p303
Smith—Hist. I p527-529.

Bolyai, Johann (or János) (1802-1860). Hung. mathematician.
Cajori—Hist. p303-304
Chambers—Dict. col.63
Smith—Hist. I p527-529
Woodruff—Devel. p265

Bolzano, Bernard (1781-1848). Czech. mathematician.
Cajori—Hist. p367-368
Murray—Science p344-345

Bombelli, Rafael (c1530-c1560). It. mathematician.
Ball—Short p228
Sarton—Six p42-44
Smith—Hist. I p300-301

Bonaparte, Maria Annunciata, later Carolina (or Murat, Queen Carolina, Caroline Bonaparte) (1782-1839). Fr. archaeologist.
Mozans—Woman p311-312

Bond, George Philips (1825-1865). Amer. astronomer.
Chambers—Dict. col.63
Shapley—Astron. p267

Bond, Thomas (1712-1784). Amer. physician.
Major—History (2) p765

Bond, William Cranch (1789-1859). Amer. astronomer.
*Book—Pop. Sci. (6) p1925
Chambers—Dict. col.63
Youmans—Pioneers p223-233 (por.223)

Bondi, Hermann (1919-   ). Aust. mathematician.
Newman—What p64-65

Bone, William Arthur (1871-1938). Eng. inventor.
Hammerton p274

Bonetus, Theophilus (1620/1628-1689). Swiss physician.
Castiglioni—Hist. p533-534 (por.536)
Major—History (1) p536-537
  (por.536)

Bonine, Frederick N. (1863-1941). Amer. physician.
Curr. Biog. '41 p90

Bonnet, A. (1893-1929). Fr. aero. pioneer.
Heinmuller—Man's p317 (por.317)

Bonnet, Charles (1720-1793). Swiss naturalist.
Bodenheimer—Hist. p295
Hammerton p275
Locy—Biology p211-212 (por.212)
Miall—Early p284-291
Osborn—Greeks p173-177
Woodruff—Devel. p265

Bontius, Jacobus (1592-1631). Dutch physician.
Major—History (1) p537-539

Boole, George (1815-1864). Eng. mathematician.
Ball—Short p474
Bell—Men p433-447 (por.,front.)
MacFarlane—Lectures p50-63
  (por., front)
Smith—Hist. I p462-463

Boone, Joel Thompson (1889-   ). Amer. physician.
Curr. Biog. '51 p48-50 (por.49)

Boorde, Andrew (or Borde) (1490?-1549). Eng. physician.
Gordon—Medieval p759-760

Booth, Hubert Cecil (1871-1955). Eng. inventor, engineer.
*Larsen—Shaped p202-205 (por.193)

Booth, James Curtis (1810-1888). Amer. chemist.
Browne—Hist. p473-474 (por.29)
Killeffer—Eminent p5 (por.5)
Merrill—First p193-194 (por.194)
Smith—Chem. p245-246 (por.246)

Booth, Ralph Sleigh (1895-   ). Brit. aero. pioneer.
Burge—Ency. p626

Borch, Oluf (or Ole) (1626-1690). Dan. physician, chemist.
Copen.—Prom. p33-35
Weeks—Discovery p91-92

Borda, Jean Charles de (1733-1799). Fr. mathematician, astronomer.
Chambers—Dict. col. 63-64

Borde.   See **Boorde, Andrew**

Bordet, Jules (b.1870). Belg. physiologist, bacteriologist.
Bulloch—Hist. p353-354   Grainger—Guide p147
Chambers—Dict. col.64   Hammerton p277
*DeKruif—Men p229-248 (por.237) Stevenson—Nobel p90-95 (por.150)

Bordeu, Théophile (1722-1776). Fr. physician.
Major—History (2) p636

Bordley, John Beale (1727-1804). Amer. argiculturist.
Bell—Early p48-49

Borelli, Giovanni Alfonso (1608-1679). It. physicist, astronomer,
    physician, mathematician, physiologist.
Bodenheimer—Hist. p275   Oliver—Stalkers p106-107
Castiglioni—Hist. p537-539   Sigerist—Great p170-171
Gordon—Medieval p651-654 (por.243) Woodruff—Devel. p237,265
Hammerton p277-278   Year—Pic p90,91 (por.91)
Major—History (1) p505-507 por.505)

Borgognoni, Theodoric.   See **Theodoric, Friar**

Borgognoni, Ugo   See **Hugh of Lucca**

Boring, Edwin G. (1886-   ). Amer. psychologist.
Newman—What p292-293

Born, Ignaz Edler von (1742-1791). Rom. min. engineer, metallurgist,
    mineralogist.
Weeks—Discovery p172 (por.172)

Born, Kendall Eugene (1908-1947). Amer. geologist.
G.S.A.—Proc. '47 p119-122 (por.119)

Born, Max (1882-   ) Ger. physicist.
Chambers—Dict. supp.
Curr. Biog. '55 p53-55 (por.53)

Borst, Lyle Benjamin (1912-   ). Amer. physicist.
Curr. Biog. '54 p112-114 (por.113)

Bortz, Edward Leroy (1896-   ). Amer. physician.
Curr. Biog '47 p55-57 (por.56)

Bory de St. Vincent, Jean Baptiste George Marie (1780-1846). Fr.
naturalist, geographer.
Osborn—Greeks p291-293

Bosanquet, Robert Carr (1871-1935). Eng. archaeologist.
Hammerton p279-280

Bosch, Carl (or Karl) (1874-1940). Ger. chemist.
Chambers—Dict. col.64   Farbel—Nobel p123-124,126-128
Curr. Biog. '40 (por.102)   (por.118)
                                      Hammerton p280

Bosch, Robert August (1861-1942). Ger. inventor, engineer.
Curr. Biog. '42 p100

Boscovich, Ruggiero Giusseppe (or Roger Joseph) (1711-1787). It.
mathematician, astronomer, physicist.
Chambers—Dict. col.64-65   Smith—Hist. I p517
Hammerton p280   Walsh—Catholic (2d) p205-207

Bose, Sir Jagadis Chandra (or Chunder) (1858-1937). **Ind.** physicist,
botanist.
*Bridges—Master p28-36 (por.31)   Hammerton p280 (por.280)
Chambers—Dict. col.65   Radio's 100 p125-126 (por.140)
Defries—Pioneer p23-67

Boss, Lewis (1846-1912). Amer. astronomer.
Armitage—Cent. p141
N.A.S.—Biog. (9) p239-255

Bossoutrot, Lucien (1890-   ). Fr. aero. pioneer.
Heinmuller—Man's p308 (por.308)

Bostock, John (1773-1846). Scot. physician.
Major—History (2) p706. (por.942)

Bostroem, Eugen (1850-1928) Ger. pathologist, bacteriologist.
Bulloch—Hist. p354

Botallo, Leonardo (c1505-c1565) Fr.-It. physician.
Leonardo—Lives p57
Major—History (1) p467-468

Bothe, Walther Wilhelm Georg (1891-1957). Ger. physicist.
Chambers—Dict. Supp.
Curr. Biog. '55 p55-56 (por.56)
    '57 p61

Botta, Paul Émile (or Paolo Emilio) (1802-1870). It. archaeologist, physician.
Alden—Early p31-32   *Science Miles. p160-166 (por.160)
Ceram—Gods p211-215

Bottomley, John T. (1869-1925). Amer. surgeon.
Leonardo—Lives p58

Bouch, Sir Thomas (1822-1880). Eng. engineer.
Hammerton p282

Boucher de Crevecoeur de Perthes, Jacques (1788-1868). Fr. archaeologist.
Hammerton p283 (por.283)

Bouguer, Pierre (1698-1758). Fr. mathematician, astronomer, hydrographer.
Chambers—Dict. col.65

Bouillaud, Jean Baptiste (1796-1881). Fr. physician.
Major—History (2) p669-671
    (por.670)

Boulenger, George Albert (1858-1937). Belg.-Fr. zoologist.
Hammerton p284 (por.284)

Boulliau, Ismael (c.1650). Fr. inventor.
Chambers—Dict. col.66

Boulton, Matthew (1728-1809). Eng. engineer.
Goddard—Eminent p168-172   Hodgins—Behemoth p55-57,64-66
    (por.168)   *Watson—Engineers p13-21 (por.12)
Hammerton p284

Bourgeois, Louise (1563-1636). Fr. physician.
Major—History (1) p551

Boussingault, Jean Baptiste Joseph Dieudonné (1802-1887) Fr. agricultural chemist, engineer.
A.A.A.S.—Proc. (81) p43-44   Smith—Torch. p36 (por.36)
Bodenheim—Hist. p392   *Snyder—Biology p310-311 (por.310)
Chambers—Dict. col.66

Boutelle, Richard Schley (1898-   ). Amer. aero. pioneer.
Curr. Biog. '51 p50-51 (por.51)

Bouveret, Leon (1850-1929). Fr. physician.
Major-History (2) p912

Boveri, Theodor (1862-1915). Ger. zoologist, biologist.
Chambers—Dict. col.66

Bovet, Daniele (1907-   ). Swiss pharmacologist.
Curr. Biog. '58 p55-56 (por.55)

Bowditch, Henry Ingersoll (1808-1892). Amer. physician.
Farmer—Doctors' p180

Bowditch, Henry Pickering (1840-1911). Amer. physiologist.
Kagan—Modern p186 (por.186)   N.A.S.—Biog. (10) p183-194 (por.183)
Major—History (2) p904

Bowditch, Nathaniel (1773-1838). Amer. astronomer, mathematician.
Bell—Early p49-50   Smith—Math. p92-95
*Book—Pop. Sci. (6) p1925-1926   Wilson—Amer. p44-47 (por.44)
Carmer—Caval. p198-200 (por.199)

Bowditch, Richard Lyon (1900-   ). Amer. engineer.
Curr. Biog. '53 p84-85 (por.85)

Bowen, George T. (1803-1828). Amer. mineralogist.
Smith—Chem. p222

Bowen, Ira Sprague (1898-   ). Amer. astrophysicist.
Curr. Biog. '51 p52-54 (por.53)

Bowen, Norman Levi (1887-1956). Can.-Amer. geologist, mineralogist,
  petrologist.
G.S.A.—Proc. '56 p117-119 (por.117)
R.S.L.—Biog. (3) p7-19 (por.7)

Bower, Frederick Orpen (1855-1948). Eng. botanist.
Chambers—Dict. col.66-67

Bowie, Edward Hall (1874-1943). Amer. meteorologist.
Curr. Biog. '43 p62

Bowie, William (1872-1940). Amer. geologist, engineer, geophysicist.
G.S.A.—Proc. '40 p163-165 (por.163)
N.A.S.—Biog. (26) p61-78 (por.61)

Bowman, Isaiah (1878-1950). Can.-Amer. geographer, geologist.
Curr. Biog. '45 p65-68 (por.66), '50   N.A.S.—Biog. (33) p39-54 (por.39)
  p60-61   Progress—Science '40 p82 (por.82)
G.S.A.—Proc. '51 p93-94 (por.93)

Bowman, Sir William (1816-1892). Eng. physician, surgeon, anatomist.
Castiglioni—Hist. p775 (por.775)   Major—History (2) p883
Hale-White—Great p177-188

Bown, Ralph (1891-   ). Amer. physicist, elec. engineer.
Radio's 100 p254-255 (por.140)

Boyce, Rubert William (1863-1911). Irish bacteriologist, pathologist.
Bulloch—Hist. p354

Boyd, J. Errol (1892-   ). Can. aero. pioneer.
Heinmuller—Man's p340 (por.340)

Boyd, James (1904-   ). Austral. geophysicist.
Curr. Biog. '49 p63-65 (por.64)

Boyd, Louise Arner (1887-   ). Amer. sci. explorer, geographer.
Curr. Biog. '60 p48-49 (por.49)

Boyer, Alexis, Baron de (1757-1833). Fr. surgeon.
Hammerton p287
Leonardo—Lives p58-60

Boyer, Harold Raymond (1899-   ). Amer. engineer.
Curr. Biog. '52 p60-62 (por.61)

Boyer, Marion Willard (1901-   ). Amer. chem. engineer.
Curr. Biog. '51 p54-55 (por.54)

Boyle, Robert (1627-1691). Irish chemist, physicist.
Adams—Birth p292-294   Hart—Makers p172-178,186-192
Bodenheimer—Hist. p254   (por.173)
*Book—Pop. Sci. (3) p867-868   Hart—Physicists p63-66
  (por.867)   Holmyard—British p20-22 (por-20)
Chambers—Dict. col.67-68 (por.67)   Holmyard—Chem. p63-66 (por.65)
Chymia (3) p155-168 (por.156)   Holmyard—Great Chem. p40-50
Crowther—Founders p51-93 (por.64)   Holmyard—Makers p132-143
*Darrow—Masters p330   (por.135)
Gordon—Medieval p760   Lenard—Great p62-64 (por.67)
Gregory—British p10 (por.11)   Leonard—Crus. p133-176
Hammerton p288 (por.288)   *Lewellen—Boy p71-92 (por.71)
(Continued)

Boyle, Robert—*Continued*
Magie—Source p84
Major—History (1) p513-515 (por.512)
Partington—Short p66-67,147-148, (por.67)
Ramsay—Essays p23-30
Roberts—Chem. p6-8
Schwartz—Moments (1) p366-367

*Science Miles. p71 (por.71)
Sedgwick—Short p258-259
Smith—Torch. p37 (por.37)
Tilden—Famous p1-21 (por. front.)
Van Wagenen—Beacon p116-118
Weeks—Discovery p35 (por.35)
Woodruff—Devel. p76-79,265 (por.84)
Year—Pic p83,94,102 (por.102)

Boylston, Zabdiel (1679-1766). Amer. physician.
Major—History (2) p765

Boys, Sir Charles Vernon (1855-1944). Eng. physicist.
Chambers—Dict. col.68

Bozzolo, Camillo (1845-1920). It. physician.
Castiglioni—Hist. p841 (por.841)

Bradbury, Norris Edwin (1909-   ). Amer. physicist.
Curr. Biog. '49 p66-68 (por.67)

Bradford, Edward Heckling (1848-1926). Amer. surgeon.
Leonardo—Lives p60-61

Bradley, David John (1915-   ). Amer. physician.
Curr. Biog. '49 p68-69 (por.69)

Bradley, James (1693-1762). Eng. astronomer.
Abetti—History p143-146
Ball—Short p177-178
Chambers—Dict. col.68-69
Gunther—Early XI p65-70 (por.69)
Hammerton p290
Lenard—Great p124-126 (por.125)
Lodge—Pioneers p232,246-253
MacPherson—Makers p82-84
Magie—Source p337
Shapley—Astron. p103
Van Wagenen—Beacon p136-137
Vaucouleurs—Disc. p71-75
Williams—Great p222-234 (por.236)
Woodruff—Devel. p161,265 (por.148)

Bradwardine, Thomas (c1290-1349). Eng. mathematician.
Ball—Great p187-199

Bragg, Sir William Henry (1862-1942). Eng. physicist.
*Bridges—Master p37-47 (por. front.)
Chambers—Dict. col.69 (por.col.70)
Curr. Biog. '42 p105
Gregory—British p16-17 (por.17)
(Continued)

Bragg, Sir William Henry—*Continued*
Hammerton p291 (por.291)
Heathcote—Nobel p125-129,130-139
(por.240)
Smith—Torch. p38 (por.38)

Van Wagenen—Beacon p420-422
Weber—College p235 (por.235)
Woodruff—Devel. p67,265

Bragg, Sir William Lawrence (1890-). Austral. physicist.
Chambers—Dict. col.69
Heathcote—Nobel p125,129-139
(por.240)

*Kendall—Young p175 (por.186)
Weber—College p254 (por.254)

Brahe, Tycho (1546-1601). Dan. astronomer.
Abetti—History p83-89 (por.10,146)
Ball—Great p44-66 (por.47)
*Book—Pop. Sci. (6) p1927-1929
(por.1928)
Chambers—Dict. col.70 (por.71)
Copen.—Prom. p20-24
Dreyer—Hist. p345-371
Gibson—Heroes p56-66
Gumpert—Trail p108-110
Hammerton p291 (por.291)
Hart—Makers p82-83 (por.76)
Hooper—Makers p202-203
Koestler—Sleep p283-312
Lenard—Great p17-20 (por.20)

Lodge—Pioneers p32-55 (por.41)
MacPherson—Makers p7-18
People p46 (por.32)
Sarton—Six p62-69 (por.24)
Schwartz—Moments (1) p232-233
Sedgwick—Short p203-209
Shapley—Astron. p13
Van Wagenen—Beacon p76-81
Vaucouleurs—Disc. p48-51
Williams—Great p128-141 (por.141)
Wilson—Human p105-118
Woodruff—Devel. p144-150, 293-294
(por.138)
Year—Pic. p76,77 (por.76)

Brahmagupta (c640). Arab. mathematician.
Ball—Short p148-150
Smith—Hist. I p157-160

Van Wagenen—Beacon p42-43
Woodruff—Devel. p13,265

Braid, James (1795?-1860). Scot. physician, surgeon.
Fulop—Miller p360-362
Major—History (2) p711

Braille, Louis (1809-1852). Fr. inventor.
*Book—Pop. Sci. (2) p443-444
Hammerton p292

*Science Miles. p167-172 (por.167)

Brainard, Daniel (1812-1866). Amer. surgeon.
Leonardo—Lives p62-63

Braithwaite, John (1797-1870). Eng. engineer.
Hammerton p292

Bramagupta. See **Brahmagupta**

Bramah, Joseph (1748-1814). Eng. engineer, inventor.
Chambers—Dict. col.70-71
Hammerton p292

Brambilla, G. A. (1728-1800). It. physician.
Castiglioni—Hist. p625 (por.626)

Branca (c1450). It. surgeon.
Leonardo—Lives p63-64

Brancker, Sir William Sefton (1877-1930). Eng. aero. pioneer.
Burge—Ency. p626

Brand (or Brandt), **Hennig** (d.c.1692). Ger. chemist.
Chambers—Dict. col.71
Weeks—Discovery p34,41-47

Brande, William Thomas (1788-1866). Eng. chemist, mineralogist.
Weeks—Discovery p208 (por.208)

Brandenberger, Jacques (1872?-1954). Swiss inventor.
Meyer—World p236-237

Brandt, George (1694-1768). Swed. chemist.
Chambers—Dict. col.71
Weeks—Discovery p66-69

Brandt, Hennig.   See **Brand, Hennig**

Branham, Sara (1888-   ). Amer. bacteriologist.
Ratcliffe—Modern p157-162 (por.158)

Braniff, Thomas Elmer (1883-1954). Amer. aero. pioneer.
Curr. Biog. '52 p63-65 (por.64)

Branly, Édouard (1844-1940). Fr. physicist, inventor.
Curr. Biog. '40 p103   Radio's 100 p76-79 (por.140)
Hammerton p293   Year—Pic p178 (por.178)
Hawks—Wireless p191-192 (por.200)

Branner, John Casper (1850-1922). Amer. geologist.
N.A.S.—Biog. (11) (XXI Memoirs).
    p1-7 (por.1)

Branson, Edwin Bayer (1877-1950). Amer. geologist.
G.S.A.—Proc. '50 p85-87 (por.85)

Brasavola, Antonio Musa (1500-1555). It. physician.
Major—History (1) p468

Brasdor, Pierre (1721-1797). Fr. surgeon.
Leonardo—Lives p64

Brashear, John (1840-1920). Amer. astronomer, engineer.
*Men—Scien. p4-6
*Yost—Science p64-84

Brattain, Walter Houser (1902-   ). Amer. physicist, inventor.
Curr. Biog. '57 p68-70 (por.69)
Meyer—World p255-256

Brattle, Thomas (1658-1713). Amer. astronomer.
Smith.—Math. p11-12

Brauell, Friedrich August (1807-1882). Ger. bacteriologist.
Bulloch—Hist. p354

Braun, Joachim Werner (1914-   ). Ger.-Amer. bacteriologist.
Curr. Biog. '58 p70-72 (por.70)

Braun, Karl Ferdinand (1850-1918). Ger. physicist.
A.A.A.S.—Proc. (78) p22-23   Heathcote—Nobel p70,80-86
Chambers—Dict. col. 71-72   Radio's 100 p97-99 (por. 140)
Hammerton p294   Weber—College p157 (por.157)

Braun, Wernher von.   See **Von Braun, Wernher**

Brauner, Bohuslav (1855-1935). Czech. chemist.
Chambers—Dict. col. 72   Weeks—Discovery p393,427,521,524
Partington—Short p354   (por.393,521)

Bravo, Francisco (c1571). Sp. physician.
Gordon—Medieval p740-741
Major—History (1) p551

Bray, William Crowell (1879-1946). Can. chemist.
N.A.S.—Biog. (26) p13-19 (por.13)

Brearey, Frederick William (1816-1896). Eng. aero. pioneer.
Burge—Ency. p626-627

Breasted, James Henry (1865-1935). Amer. archaeologist.
Gordon—Medicine p206 (por.206)   N.A.S.—Biog. (18) p95-114 (por.95)
Hammerton p294 (por.294)

Bréau.   See **Quatrefages de Bréau, Jean Louis Armand de**

Breckenridge, Lester Paige (1858-1940). Amer. engineer.
Curr. Biog. '40 p105 (por.105)

Bredichin, Fëdor Aleksandrovich (1831-1904). Rus. astronomer.
Armitage—Cent. p123-124

Bredig, Georg (1866-1944). Ger. chemist.
Chambers—Dict. col.72
Partington—Short p340

Bredikhine, Theodor (1831-1904). Rus. astronomer.
Shapley—Astron. p358

Brefeld, Oscar (1839-1925). Ger. bacteriologist.
Bulloch—Hist. p354

Breguet, Louis Charles (1880-1955). Fr. aero. pioneer, engineer.
Burge—Ency. p627
Hammerton p295

Brehm, Alfred Edmund (1829-1884). Ger. naturalist.
Hammerton p295

Breislak, Scipio (1748-1826). It. geologist.
Geike—Founders p199-200

Breneman, Abram Adam (1847-1928). Amer. chemist.
Browne—Hist. p494-495 (por.319)

Brennan, Louis (1852-1932). Irish inventor.
*Darrow—Masters p330
Hammerton p295 (por.295)

Brereton, Lewis Hyde (1890-   ). Amer. aero. pioneer.
Curr. Biog. '43 p70-72 (por.71)

Breschet, Gilbert (1784-1845). Fr. surgeon.
Leonardo—Lives p64-65

Bretonneau, Pierre Fidèle (1778-1862). Fr. physician, bacteriologist.
Bulloch—Hist. p354-355
Chambers—Dict. col.72
Hammerton p296
Major—History (2) p667-669
(por.668)

Brett, George Howard (1886-   ). Amer. aero. pioneer.
Curr. Biog. '42 p105-107

Breuer, Josef (1842-1925). Aust. physician, neurologist.
Chambers—Dict. col.72-73

Breuil, Henri Édouard Prosper (1877-   ). Fr. archaeologist.
Hammerton p296
People p46

Brewer, George Emerson (1861-1939). Amer. surgeon.
Leonardo—Lives p65-66

Brewer, Griffith (1867-1948). Eng. aero. pioneer.
Burge-Ency. p627

Brewer, William Henry (1828-1910). Amer. sci. explorer, geographer,
    botanist.
N.A.S.—Biog. (12) p289-315 (por.289)

Brewster, Sir David (1781-1868). Scot. physicist.
*Book—Pop. Sci. (3) p868 (por.868)   Van Wagenen—Beacon p239-241
Chambers—Dict. col.73 (por.74)   Weeks—Discovery p364,365 (por.365)
Hammerton p296 (por.296)

Brialmont, Henri Alexis (1821-1903). Belg. engineer.
Hammerton p296

Brickner, Richard Mex (1896-   ). Amer. neurologist.
Curr. Biog. '43 p76-77

Brickner, Walter M. (1876-1930). Amer. surgeon.
Kagan—Modern p105 (por.105)

Bridge, Josiah (1890-1953). Amer. geologist.
G.S.A.—Proc. '52 p93-95 (por.93)

Bridges, Calvin Blackman (1889-1938). Amer. zoologist, geneticist.
N.A.S.—Biog. (22) p31-40 (por.31)

Bridges, Styles (1898-   ). Amer. space pioneer.
Thomas—Men p.xiv   Thomas—Men (3) p.xv
Thomas—Men (2) p.xiv-xv

Bridgman, Percy Williams (1882-1961). Amer. physicist.

Chambers—Dict. col. 73-74
Curr. Biog. '55 p65-67 (por.65)
    '61 (Nov.)
Heathcote—Nobel p422-430 (por.240)
Progress—Science '40 p83 (por.83)
Weber—College p739 (por.739)

Brieger, Ludwig (1849-1919). Ger. physician, chemist.

Bulloch—Hist. p355

Briggs, Henry (1556?-1631). Eng. mathematician.

Ball—Short p236-237
Cajori—Hist. p150-151
Chambers—Dict. col.74
Gunther—Early XI p46-47
Hammerton p298
Hooper—Makers p187-190
Smith—Hist. I p391-392

Briggs, James E. (1906-   ). Amer. aero. pioneer.

Curr. Biog. '57 p74-76 (por.75)

Briggs, Lyman James (1874-   ). Assyr.-Amer. physicist.

Progress—Science '41 p81 (por.81)

Briggs, Wallace Alvin (1848-1927). Amer. physician.

Jones—Memories p431-435 (por.431)

Brigham, Carl Campbell (1890-1943). Amer. psychologist.

Curr. Biog. '43 p77

Bright, Sir Charles Tilston (1832-1888). Eng. engineer.

Hammerton p298

Bright, Richard (1789-1858). Eng. physician.

Atkinson—Magic p221-222
Castiglioni—Hist. p703-705 (por.704)
Chambers—Dict. col.74-75
Gordon—Romance p155 (por.155)
Hale-White—Great p63-84
Hammerton p299
Lambert—Medical p216-217
Lambert—Minute p218-219
Major—History (2) p689-690
    (por.687)

Bright, Timothy (1550-1615). Eng. physician.

Major—History (1) p476-477

Brill, Nathan Edwin (1860-1925). Amer. physician.

Kagan—Modern p20 (por.20)

Brindley, James (1716-1772). Eng. engineer.

Hammerton p299

Brinell, Johann August (1849-1925). Swed. engineer.

Chambers—Dict. col.75

Brinkley, John (1763-1835). Eng. astronomer.
Ball—Great p233-246
Hammerton p299

Brinkley, John R. (1886-1942). Amer. physician, surgeon.
Curr. Biog. '42 p107

Brinton, Daniel Garrison (1837-1899). Amer. ethnologist.
Hammerton p299-300

Brinton, Howard Haines (1884-   ). Amer. physicist, mathematician.
Curr. Biog. '49 p74-76 (por.75)

Brioschi, Francesco (1824-1897). It. mathematician.
Cajori—Hist. p345-346

Brisbane, Sir Arthur Thomas Makdougall (1773-1860). Scot. astronomer.
Chambers—Dict. col.75

Briscoe, Henry Vincent Aird (1888-   ). Eng. chemist.
Chambers—Dict. col.75

Brisson, Mathurin Jacques (1723-1806). Fr. zoologist.
Hammerton p300

Brissot, Pierre (1478-1522). Fr. physician.
Gordon—Medieval p594-595
Major—History (I) p463

Britton, Edgar Clay (1891-   ). Amer. chemist.
Curr. Biog. '52 p69-70 (por.69)

Britton, Nathaniel Lord (1859-1934). Amer. botanist.
N.A.S.—Biog. (19) p147-160 (por.147)

Britton, Wilton Everett (1868-1939). Amer. entomologist.
Osborn—Fragments p219 (por.351)

Broadbent, Sir William Henry (1835-1907). Eng. physician.
Hammerton p301 (por.301)
Major—History (2) p898

Broadhurst, Harry (1904?-   ). Eng. aero. pioneer.
Curr. Biog. '43 p77-78 (por.78)

Broca, Paul (1824-1880). Fr. anthropologist, physician, surgeon.

*Book—Pop. Sci. (4) p1145-1146
Chambers—Dict. col. 75-76
Hammerton p301
Leonardo—Lives p66-69

Major—History (2) p888-889
  (por.848)
Van Wagenen—Beacon p399-340
Williams—Story p419 (por.421)

Brock, Reginald Walter (1874-1935). Can. geologist.

G.S.A.—Proc. '35 p157-167 (por.157)

Brock, William S. (1895-   ). Amer. aero. pioneer.

Heinmuller—Man's p325 (por.325)

Brocklesby, Richard (1772-1797). Eng. physician.

Hammerton p302

Brode, Wallace Reid (1900-   ). Amer. chemist.

Curr. Biog. '58 p60-61 (por.60)

Broderip, William John (1780-1859). Eng. naturalist.

Gunther—Early XI p119
Hammerton p302

Brodie, Sir Benjamin Collins (1783-1862). Eng. surgeon.

Hammerton p302 (por.302)
Leonardo—Lives p69-71

Bröger, Waldemar Christopher (or Brogger, Waldemar Christofer) (1851-1940). Norw. geologist, mineralogist.

A.A.A.S.—Proc. (79) p8-10
G.S.A.—Proc. '40 p167-169 (por.167)

Broglie.   See **De Broglie, Louis Victor Pierre Raymond, Prince**

Brokaw, Augustus Van Liew (1863-1907). Amer. surgeon.

Leonardo—Lives p71-72

Bromfield, William (1712-1792). Eng. surgeon.

Leonardo—Lives p72-73

Brongniart, Alexandre (1770-1847). Fr. geologist, mineralogist.

Chambers—Dict. col.76
Geike—Founders p213-219

Hammerton p302
Woodruff—Devel. p176-177,265-266

Bronk, Detlev Wulf (1897-   ). Amer. physiologist.

Curr. Biog. '49 p76-78 (por.77)

Bronowski, Jacob (1908-   ). Pol.-   mathematician.
Curr. Biog. '58 p61-63 (por.62)
Newman—What p382-384

Brönsted, Johannes Nicolaus (1879-1947). Dan. chemist.
Chambers—Dict. col.76

Brooke-Popham.   See **Popham, Sir Henry Robert Moore Brooke-**

Brookins, Walter Richard (1888-   ). Amer. aero. pioneer.
Heinmuller—Man's p279 (por.279)

Brooks, Henry Harlow (1871-1936). Amer. physician.
Rowntree—Amid p227-229 (por.211)

Brooks, Matilda Moldenhauser (n.d.) Amer. physiologist, biologist.
Curr. Biog. '41 p108-109 (por.109)

Brooks, Thomas Benton (1836-1900). Amer. geologist.
Merrill—First p440-441 (por.441)

Brooks, William Keith (1848-1908). Amer. zoologist.
Jordan—Leading p427-455 (por.427)
N.A.S.—Biog. (7) p23-79 (por.23,71)

Broomall, Anna E. (1847-1931). Amer. physician.
Mead—Medical p29,30-31
  (por.,append.)

Brossard, Edgar Bernard (1889-   ). Amer. agriculturist.
Curr. Biog. '54 p118-120 (por.119)

Brouncker (or Brounker), **William, 2d Viscount** (1620-1684). Irish
  mathematician.
Ball—Short p312-313   Smith—Hist. I p410-411
Chambers—Dict. col.76

Broussais, François Joseph Victor (1772-1838). Fr. physician, surgeon.
Castiglioni—Hist. p699-700   Major—History (2) p664-667 (por.666)
Lambert—Medical p153   Sigerist—Great p287-290 (por.289)

Broussonet, Pierre Marie August (1761-1807). Fr. botanist, naturalist,
  physician.
Hawks—Pioneers p270

Brouwer, Dirk (1902-   ). Dutch-Amer. astronomer.
Curr. Biog. '51 p62-64

Brown, (Alexander) Crum (1838-1922). Scot. chemist.
Chambers—Dict. col.77

Brown, Arthur Whitten (1886-1948). Scot. aero. pioneer.
*Fraser—Heroes p55-86   La Croix—They p20-40
Hammerton p306

Brown, Charles Randall (1899-   ). Amer. aero. pioneer.
Curr. Biog. '58 p65-66 (por.65)

Brown, Dame Edith Mary (1864-1956). Eng. physician.
Lovejoy—Women p226

Brown, Ernest William (1866-1938). Eng. astronomer, mathematician.
N.A.S.—Biog. (21) p243-260 (por.243)

Brown, George Harold (1908-   ). Amer. radio pioneer.
Radio's 100 p284-287 (por.140)

Brown, Harold (1927-   ). Amer. physicist.
Curr. Biog. 1961 (Sept.) (por.)

Brown, Harrison (1917-   ). Amer. geochemist.
Curr. Biog. '55 p71-72 (por.71)

Brown, John (1735-1788). Scot. physician.
Hammerton p307   Major—History (2) p592-594 (por.592)
Lambert—Medical p152-153   Oliver—Stalkers p138-139
Lambert—Minute p152-153   Sigerist—Great p200-202

Brown, Rachel Fuller (1898   ). Amer. biochemist.
Yost—Women Mod. p64-79
(por.,front).

Brown, Robert (1773-1858). Scot. botanist.
Bodenheimer—Hist. p377   Oliver—Makers p108-125 (por.108)
Chambers—Dict. col.77   Schwartz—Moments (2) p549-550
Gilmour—British p33-34 (por.33)   *Snyder—Biology p58-62 (por.61)
Hammerton p307   Van Wagenen—Beacon p219-221
Hawks—Pioneers p263-266 (por.264) Woodruff—Devel. p243,266
Magie—Source p251   Year—Pic p126 (por.126)

Brown, Thomas Clachar (1882-1934). Amer. geologist.
G.S.A.—Proc. '34 p203-205 (por.203)

Brown, Winifred (1900-   ). Eng. aero. pioneer.
Hammerton p308 (por.308)

Browne, Charles Albert (1870-1947). Amer. agric. chemist.
Chymie V.I p11-14 (por.14)

Browning, John Moses (1855-1926). Amer. inventor.
Hammerton p309

Brownowski, Jacob (1908-   ). Polish-Eng. mathematician.
Curr. Biog. '58 p61-63 (por.62)
Newman—What p382-384

Bruce, Archibald (1778-1818). Amer. mineralogist, geologist.
Merrill—First p38-40
Smith—Chem. p219

Bruce, David (1855-1931). Aust. bacteriologist, physician.
Bulloch—Hist. p355   Hammerton p311
Chambers—Dict. col.78   Major—History (2) p916
*DeKruif—Microbe p252-277

Bruce, Eric (1855-1935). Brit. aero. pioneer.
Burge—Ency. p627

Bruce, Everend Lester (1884-1949). Can. geologist.
G.S.A.—Proc.'49 p121-122 (por.121)

Brücke, Ernst Wilhelm von (1819-1892). Ger. physiologist, physician.
Major—History (2) p886
Woodruff—Devel. p266

Brudus, Dionysius (1478-1522). Port. physician.
Gordon—Medieval p761

Brues, Charles Thomas (1879-1955). Amer. entomologist.
Osborn—Fragments p226

Bruhl, Julius Wilhelm (1850-1911). Pol. chemist.
A.A.A.S.—Proc. (78) p11
Smith—Torch. p39 (por.39)

Brunck, Heinrich von (1847-1911). Ger. chemist.
Smith—Torch. p40 (por.40)

Brunel, Isambard Kingdom (1806-1859). Eng. engineer, inventor.
*Book—Pop. Sci. (4) p1411-1412
Chambers—Dict. col.78-79
Goddard—Eminent p216-226
(por.216)
Hammerton p312-313
100 Great p589-594
People p50 (por.71)

Brunel, Sir Marc Isambard (1769-1849). Fr. engineer, inventor.
*Book—Pop. Sci. (4) p1412-1414
(por.1413)
Chambers—Dict. col.78
Hammerton p313 (por.313)
*Watson—Engineers p61-69 (por.60)

Bruner, Donald L. (1893-   ). Amer. aero. pioneer.
Holland—Arch. p62-78 (por.54)

Bruner, Lawrence (1856-1937). Amer. entomologist.
Osborn—Fragments p219-220
(por.348)

Brunfels (or Brunfelsius), **Otto** (1464/1488-1534). Ger. botanist,
physician, naturalist.
Arber—Herbals p52,55,61,202,206
207 (por.52)
Gordon—Medieval p660 (por.115)
Major—History (1) p462
Miall—Early p17-20
Reed—Short p64-65
Sarton—Six p132

Brunner, Jean (or Johann) **Conrad von** (1653-1727). Swiss anatomist,
physician.
Major—History (1) p563
Woodruff—Devel. p266

Bruno, Giordano (1548?-1600). It. nat. philosopher.
*Book — Pop. Sci. (7) p2474-2476
(por.2475)
Gordon—Romance p451 (por.451)
Gumpert—Trail p108
Osborn—Greeks p121-127
Sedgwick—Short p254
Williams—Great p122-128
Year—Pic p77 (por.77)

Bruno of Longoburgo (or Jamerius) (c.1252). It. surgeon.
Leonardo—Lives p73-74
Major—History (1) p353

Bruns, Viktor von (1812-1883). Ger. surgeon.
Leonardo—Lives p74

Brunschwig, Hieronymus (or Jerome of Brunswick) (c1450-1512/1533). Ger. physician, surgeon.
Chambers—Dict. col.79
Leonardo—Lives p75
Major—History (1) p434

Brunton, Sir Thomas Lauder (1844-1916). Scot physician.
Hammerton p313 (por.313)
Major—History (2) p905

Brunton, William (1777-1851). Scot. engineer.
Hammerton p313

Brush, George Jarvis (1813-1912). Amer. mineralogist.
N.A.S.—Biog. (10) p107-111 (por.107)

Bryan, George Hartley (1864-1928). Eng. mathematician, aero. pioneer.
Burge—Ency. p627

Bryan, Kirk (1888-1950). Amer. geologist.
G.S.A.—Proc. '50 p91-93 (por.91)

Bryce, James (1838-1922). Irish naturalist.
Osborn—Impr. p109-116 (por.109)

Buch, (Christian) Leopold, Baron von (1774-1853). Ger. geologist, paleontologist, mineralogist.
Adams—Birth p227-236,381-386 (por.228)
*Book—Pop. Sci. (2) p716
Chambers—Dict. col.79
Fenton—Giants p65-69 (por.14)
Geikie—Founders p141-149
Osborn—Greeks p309-310

Buchan, Alexander (1829-1907). Scot. meteorologist.
Chambers—Dict. col.79-80
Hammerton p315

Buchan, William (1729-1805). Scot. physician.
Hammerton p315

Buchanan, Robert MacNeil (1861-1931). Scot. bacteriologist.
Bulloch—Hist. p255

Buchanan, Thomas Drysdale (1876-1940). Amer. physician.
Curr. Biog. '40 p118

Bucher, Walter Herman (1888-   ). Amer. geologist.
Curr. Biog. '57 p84-86 (por.84)

Buchner, Edouard (1850-1902). Ger. chemist.

Bulloch—Hist. p355-356
Chambers—Dict. col.80
Farber—Nobel p29-32 (por.118)

Hammerton p316
Smith—Torch. p42 (por.46)

Buchner, Hans (1850-1902). Ger. bacteriologist.

Bulloch—Hist. p355-356

Buck, Laurence Perry (1913-1957). Amer. geologist.

G.S.A.—Proc. '57 p175

Buckland, Francis Trevelyan (1826-1880). Eng. naturalist, surgeon.

Hammerton p317
Van Wagenen—Beacon p347-349

Buckland, William (1784-1856). Eng. geologist, mineralogist.

Gregory—British p26 (por.25)
Gunther—Early XI p197-199 (por.198)

Woodruff—Devel. p266 (por.186)

Buckley, Oliver Ellsworth (1887-   ). Amer. physicist.

Progress—Science '41 p81-82 (por.82)

Budd, George (1808-1882). Eng. physician.

Hammerton p317

Budd, William (1811-1880). Eng. bacteriologist, physician.

Bulloch—Hist. p356

Buehler, Henry Andrew (1876-1944). Amer. geologist.

G.S.A.—Proc. '44 p155-160 (por.155)

Buerger, Leo (1879-1943). Austrian-Amer. physician, surgeon.

Kagan—Modern p110 (por.110)
Leonardo—Lives (Supp.I) p474-475

Buffon, Georges Louis Leclerc, Comte de (or Leclerc, George Louis) (1707-1788). Fr. naturalist.

Bodenheimer—Hist. p303-304
*Book—Pop. Sci. (4) p1146-1147
Bulloch—Hist. p356
Chambers—Dict. col.80-81
Davison—Founders p4-7
Geikie—Founders p8-12
Grainger—Guide p147-148
Hammerton p317-318 (por.318)
Locy—Biology p419-421 (por.420)

Miall—Early p359-390
Murray—Science p142-144
Osborn—Greeks p188-201
Peattie—Gather p113-119
Peattie—Green p57-68,71-76 (por.70)
Van Wagenen—Beacon p150-152
Weeks—Discovery p255 (por.255)
Woodruff—Devel. p253,266 (por.256)

Bugher, John Clifford (1901-   ). Amer. physician.
Curr. Biog. '53 p96-97 (por.97)

Bull, William Tillinghast (1849-1909). Amer. surgeon.
Leonardo—Lives p76-77

Bullard, Sir Edward Crisp (1907-   ). Eng. geophysicist.
Curr. Biog. '54 p128-130 (por.129)

Buller, Francis (1844-1905). Can. surgeon.
Leonardo—Lives p77-78

Bumm, Ernst von (1858-1925). Ger. gynecologist.
Bulloch—Hist. p356

Bumstead, Henry Andrews (1870-1920). Amer. physicist.
N.A.S.—Biog. (13) p107-123 (por.107)

Bunau-Varillá, Philippe Jean (1859/1860-1940). Fr. engineer.
Curr. Biog. '40 p125

Bundesen, Herman Niels (1882-1960). Ger. physician.
Curr. Biog. '48 p79-81 (por. 80)
    '60 p62

Bunker, George Maverick (1908-   ), Amer. aero. pioneer, engineer.
Curr. Biog. '57 p86-87 (por.86)

Bunsen, Robert Wilhelm Eberard von (1811-1899). Ger. chemist.
*Book—Pop. Sci. (3) p869
Chambers—Dict. col.81
*Darrow—Masters p206-213 (por.161)
Findlay—Hundred p320
Hammerton p319-320
Lenard—Great p324-338 (por.325)
Partington p235-236,238 (por.235)
Roberts—Chem. p151-159
Smith—Torch. p43 (por.43)
Van Wagenen—Beacon p295-297
Weeks—Discovery p364-373
    (por.369,370)
Williams—Great p340-344 (por.345)
Williams—Story p283-284 (por.277)
Woodruff—Devel. p266 (por.110)

Bunts, Frank Emory (1861-1928). Amer. surgeon.
Leonardo—Lives p78

Burbank, Luther (1849-1926). Amer. biologist, naturalist, botanist.
*Bolton—Famous p237-246 (por.236)
*Book—Pop. Sci. (2) p590-592
    (por.592)
*Bridges—Master p48-59 (por.50)
Carmer—Caval. p211-213
    (por.210,212)

(Continued)

Burbank, Luther—*Continued*
Chambers—Dict. col.81-82
*Compton—Conquests p86-100
*Darrow—Builders p10-12
*Everett—When p128-134 (por.128)
*Hylander—Scien. p106-122 (por.112)
*Ivins—Fifty p49-56 (por.51)
*Law—Modern p22-36 (por.32)
*Nisenson—Illus. p27 (por.27)

People p52-53
Sewell—Brief p206-207
*Simmons—Great p46-50 (por.56)
*Snyder—Biology p169-174 (por.171)
*Tappan—Heroes p106-114
Tuska—Inventors p82
Webb—Famous p68-81 (por.69)

Burchard, John Ely (1898-   ). Amer. engineer.
Curr. Biog. '58 p68-70 (por.69)

Burdon-Sanderson, John Scott (1828-1905). Eng. physiologist.
Gunther—Early XI p177-179
(por.178)
Hammerton p321-322 (por.321)

Burgess, Albert Franklin (1873-1953). Amer. entomologist.
Osborn—Fragments p236 (por.376)

Burgess, Carter Lane (1916-   ). Amer. aero. pioneer.
Curr. Biog. '57 p87-89 (por.88)

Burgess, Edward (1848-1891). Amer. entomologist.
Osborn—Fragments p207

Burgess, George Kimball (1874-1932). Amer. physicist.
N.A.S.—Biog. (30) p57-72 (por. 57)

Bürgi, Jobst (or Byrgius, Joost, Jost, Justus) (1552-1632). Swiss
mathematician.
Hofman—History p110-111   Smith—Hist. I p433
Hooper—Makers p192,193

Burmeister, Hermann Carl Conrad (1807-1892). Ger. entomologist.
Essig—Hist. p562-563 (por.562)

Burnet, Sir Frank MacFarlane (1899-   ). Austral. physician.
Curr. Biog. '54 p134-135 (por.135)

Burney, Leroy E. (1906-   ). Amer. physician, surgeon.
Curr. Biog. '57 p89-91 (por.90)

Burnham, Sherburne Wesley (1838-1921). Amer. astronomer.
MacPherson—Astron. p84-91
Williams—Great p290,471-472
(por.471)

Burns, Allan (1781-1813). Scot. surgeon.
Leonardo—Lives p79

Burnside, William (1852-1927). Eng. mathematician.
Hammerton p329

Burrell, Herbert Leslie (1856-1910). Amer. surgeon.
Leonardo—Lives p79-80

Burroughs, John (1837-1921). Amer. naturalist.
*Darrow—Builders p155-158   Osborn—Impr. p184-198 (por.184)
*Everett—When p135-142 (por.135)   Tracy—Amer. Nat. p86-99
Fitzhugh—Concise p91-92   Webb—Famous p82-93 (por.83)
*Law—Modern p37-49   Welker—Birds p124-135,149-150
*Milne—Natur. p115-122 (por.114)

Burrows, Sir George (1801-1887). Eng. physician.
Hammerton p329

Burrows, Ronald Montague (1867-1920). Eng. archaeologist.
Hammerton p329

Burt, Cyril Lodowic (1883-   ). Eng. psychologist.
Hammerton p329

Burton, Alan Chadburn (1904-   ). Eng. physiologist.
Curr. Biog. '56 p90-92 (por.91)

Burton, Eli Franklin (1879-1948). Can. physicist.
Progress—Science '41 p82-83 (por.83)

Burwash, Lachlin Taylor (1874-1940). Can. sci. explorer.
Curr. Biog. '41 p123

Busbeck, Augier Ghislan de (or Busbecq, Augier Chislen de) (1522-1592).
Belg. botanist.
Hawks—Pioneers p78

Busching, Anton Friedrich (1724-1793) Ger. geographer.
Hammerton p330

Bush, Vannevar (1890-   ). Amer. elec. engineer, inventor.
Curr. Biog. '40 p128-130 (por.130)   Fitzhugh—Concise p768
   '47 p80-82 (por.80)   Progress—Science '40 p83-84 (por.84)
Fisher—Amer. p239-241 (por.238)   *Yost—Engineers p47-59

Bushnell, David (1742?-1824). Amer. inventor.
Hylander—Invent. p200

Bussy, Antoine Alexandre Brutus (1794-1882). Fr. chemist.
Chambers—Dict. col.82
Weeks—Discovery p306,307-308
(por.306)

Butenandt, Adolf Friedrich Johann (1903-   ). Ger. chemist.
Chambers—Dict. col.82
Farber—Nobel p166-168

Butler, Charles (1559-1647). Eng. naturalist.
Miall—Early p87-93

Butler, Frank Hedges (1856-1928). Brit. aero. pioneer.
Burge—Ency. p627-628
Hammerton p331

Butler, Howard Crosby (1872-1922). Amer. archaeologist, naturalist.
Osborn—Impr. p207-212 (por.207)

Butlerov, Aleksander Mikhailovich (or Butlerow) (1828-1886). Rus.
chemist.
Partington—Short 281,316

Butlin, Henry Trentham (1845-1912). Eng. surgeon.
Leonardo—Lives p80-84

Butterfield, Kenyon Leech (1868-1935). Amer. agriculturist.
*Ivins—Fifty p217-219 (por.216)

Butts, Alfred Mosher (1899-   ). Amer. inventor.
Curr. Biog. '54 p145-146 (por.145)

Butts, Charles (1863-1946). Amer. geologist, paleontologist.
G.S.A.—Proc. '47 p125-126 (por.125)

Buwalda, John Peter (1886-1954). Amer. geologist.
G.S.A.—Proc. '55 p107-111 (por.107)

Buxton, Bertram Henry (1852-1934). Eng. bacteriologist.
Bulloch—Hist. p356

Buxton, Leonard Halford Dudley (1889-   ). Eng. anthropologist.
Hammerton p332 (por.332)

Buxton, Patrick Alfred (1892-1955). Eng. biologist, entomologist.
R.S.L.—Biog. (2) p69-80 (por. 69)

Buzzard, Sir Edward Farquhar (b.1871). Eng. physician.
Hammerton p332

Bybee, Halbert Pleasant (1888-1957). Amer. geologist.
G.S.A.—Proc. '57 p89-93 (por.89)

Byrd, Richard Evelyn (1888-1957). Amer. sci. explorer, aero. pioneer.
Curr. Biog. '42 p120-122 (por.121),
    '56 p95-98 (por.96)
*Darrow—Builders p92-105 (por.100)
Fitzhugh—Concise p92-94,769-770
*Fraser—Famous p123-150
*Fraser—Heroes p396-407,477-487,
    559-562
Hammerton p333 (por.333)
Heinmuller—Man's p48-67,320
    (por.58,320)
Huff—Famous (2d) p97-110 (por.96)
La Croix—They p107-119
*Lockhart—My p51 (por.49)
*Logie—Careers p290-308
Maitland—Knights p288-291,309-311
Morris—Ency. p641
Sewell—Brief p229-230
*Shippen—Bridle p119-124
*Snyder—Biology p432-436 (por.433)

Byrgius, Justus.   See **Bürgi, Jobst**

Byroade, Henry Alfred (1913-   ). Amer. engineer.
Curr. Biog. '52 p79-81 (por.80)

C

Cabanis, Pierre Jean Georges (1757-1808). Fr. physician.
Hammerton p335

Cable, Frank T. (1863-1945). Amer. engineer.
Hammerton p335

Cabot, Arthur Tracy (1852-1912). Amer. surgeon.
Leonardo—Lives p84-85

Cabot, Richard Clarke (1868-1939). Amer. physician.
Kagan—Modern p24 (por.24)
Major—History (2) p1029

Cabral, Sacadura (1892-1924). Port. aero. pioneer.
Heinmuller—Man's p312 (por.312)

Cacciopoli, Joseph (1852-1947). It. surgeon.
Leonardo—Lives p85

Cadet de Gassicourt, Louis Claude (1731-1799). Fr. chemist.
Chambers—Dict. col.83

Cadman, Sir John (1877-1941). Eng. engineer.
Hammerton p336

Cadwalader, Thomas (1708-1779). Amer. physician.
Major—History (2) p765

Cady, Hamilton Perkins (1874-1943). Amer. chemist.
Weeks—Discovery p478 (por.478)

Caelius Aurelianus (or Aurelianus, Caelius) (fl 5th cent.) Roman physician.
Gordon—Medieval p47-50   Major—History (1) p204-206
Hammerton p145

Caesar, Lawson (1870-1952). Can. entomologist.
Osborn—Fragments p204-205
(por.364)

Cagniard de la Tour, Charles (or Cagniard-Latour, Charles) (1777-1859).
Fr. physicist, engineer, inventor.
Bulloch—Hist. p356
Chambers—Dict. col.83

Cahours, Auguste Thomas (1813-1891). Fr. chemist.
Chambers—Dict. col.83   Smith—Torch. p44 (por.44)
Partington—Short p270

Cailletet, Louis Paul (1832-1913). Fr. physicist.
Chambers—Dict. col.83   Magie—Source p192-193
Hammerton p338

Caird, Sir James (1816-1892). Scot. agriculturist.
Hammerton p339

Caius, John (or Key, Kaye, Kees, Keys) (1510-1573). Eng. physician.
Chambers—Dict. col.84   Miall—Early p79-84
Gordon—Medieval p737-738   Raven—English p138-153
Major—History (1) p448-450

Caius Tranquillus Suetonius.   See **Suetonius, Gaius Tranquillus**

Cajori, Florian (1859-1930). Swiss mathematician, physicist, astronomer.
Swiss—Prom. p305-308

Calcagnini, Celio (1479-1541). It. astronomer.
Dreyer—Hist. p292-295

Caldani, Leopoldo Marco (1725-1813). It. anatomist, physiologist, physician.
Castiglioni—Hist. p600 (por.600)
Major—History (2) p636

Calderone, Frank Anthony (1901). Amer. physician.
Curr. Biog. '52 p81-83 (por.82)

Caldwell, Charles (1772-1853). Amer. chemist.
Chymia v.4 p129-157 (por.132)

Caldwell, George C. (1834-1907). Amer. chemist.
Browne—Hist. p475 (por.45)

Caldwell, William Edgar (1880-1943). Amer. gynecologist.
Curr. Biog. '43 p94

Calhoun, Abner Wellborn (1846-1910). Amer. surgeon.
Leonardo—Lives p85-86

Calippus.   See **Callippus.**

Calkins, Gary Nathan (1869-1943). Amer. protozoologist.
*Snyder—Biology p413-416 (por.414)

Callendar, Hugh Longbourne (1863-1930). Eng. physicist.
Chambers—Dict. col.84
Hammerton p341

Callippus (or Calippus) (4th cent. B.C.). Gr. astronomer.
Abetti—History p34-35
Smith—Hist. I p95

Callow, John Michael (1867-1940). Amer. min. engineer, metallurgist.
Curr. Biog. '40 p138

Calmette, Albert Léon Charles (1863-1933). Fr. bacteriologist.
Bulloch—Hist. p356-357   Hammerton p341
Grainger—Guide p148   Major—History (2) (por.968)

Calvert, Frederick Grace (1819-1873). Eng. chemsit.
Hammerton p342

Calvert, Philip Powell (b.1871). Amer. entomologist, zoologist.
Osborn—Fragments p233-234
   (por.364)

Camac, Charles Nicoll Bancker (1868-1940). Amer. physician.
Curr. Biog. '40 p138

Camara-Pestana, Luiz da (1863-1899). Port. bacteriologist.
Bulloch—Hist. p357

Camerarius, Joachim, the Younger (1534-1598). Ger. botanist.
Arber—Herbals p76-78,233,234
   (por.76)
Sarton—Six p135-136

Camerarius, Rudolf Jacob (1665-1721). Ger. botanist, physician.
Bodenheimer—Hist. p284   Reed—Short p95-96
Chambers—Dict. col.84   *Snyder—Biology p165
Hawks—Pioneers p220

Cameron, Charles Sherwood (1908-   ). Amer. physician.
Curr. Biog. '54 p146-148 (por.147)

Cameron, Irving Howard (1854-1933). Can. surgeon.
Leonardo—Lives p86-87

Camm, Sydney (1893-   ). Eng. aero. pioneer.
Curr. Biog. '42 p130-131 (por.131)

Campanus, Johannes (fl c.1260). It. mathematician.
Smith—Hist. I p218

Campbell, Douglas Houghton (1859-1953). Amer. botanist.
N.A.S.—Biog. (29) p45-53 (por.45)

Campbell, Henry Donald (1862-1934). Amer. geologist.
G.S.A.—Proc. '34 p209-211 (por.209)

Campbell, Marius (1858-1940). Amer. geologist.
G.S.A.—Proc. '40 p171-177 (por.171)

Campbell, Robert Burns (1892-1955). Amer. geologist.
G.S.A.—Proc. '55 p113-114 (por.113)

Campbell, William Wallace (1862-1938). Amer. astronomer.
Armitage—Cent. p157-159 (por.144)   N.A.S.—Biog. '49 p35-57 (por.35)
MacPherson—Astron. p239-245
(por.239)

Campbell, Willis Cohoon (1880-1941). Amer. physician, surgeon.
Curr. Biog. '41 p130

Camper, Pieter (1722-1789). Dutch anatomist, physician.
Locy—Biology p143-144 (por.144)   Woodruff—Devel. p266
Major—History (2) p636

Canano, Giovanni Batista (1515-1579). It. physician.
Gordon—Medieval p621-622

Candau, Marcolino Gomes (1911-   ). Brazil. physician.
Curr. Biog. '54 p148-150 (por.149)

Candee, Robert Chapin (1892-   ). Amer. aero. pioneer.
Curr. Biog. '44 p81-83 (por.82)

Candèze, Ernest Charles Auguste (1827-1898). Belg. entomologist.
Essig—Hist. p563-564 (por.564)

Candolle, Alphonse Louis Pierre Pyrame de (1806-1893). Fr. botanist.
Reed—Short p129

Candolle, Augustin Pyrame de (1778-1841). Swiss botanist.
Chamber—Dict. col.85   Hawks—Pioneers p243-244
Hammerton p347-348

Canning, Sir Samuel (1823-1908). Eng. engineer.
Hammerton p340

Cannizzaro, Stanislao (1826-1910). It. chemist.
*Book—Pop. Sci. (5) p1767   Partington p256-258,271 (por.257)
Chambers—Dict. col.85   Smith—Torch. p45 (por.45)
Findlay—Hundred p320   Tilden—Famous p174-187 (por.174)
Holmyard—Markers p265-266   Woodruff—Devel. p266 (por.118)
(por.265)

Cannon, Annie Jump (1863-1941). Amer. astronomer.
Curr. Biog. '41 p132   Progress—Science '41 p86-87
Hammerton p349   Yost—Women Sci. p27-43.

Cannon, Walter Bradford (1871-1945). Amer. physiologist, physician.

Curr. Biog. '45 p89
Fabricant—Why p104-105
Fisher—Amer. p95-96 (por.94)
*Hathaway—Partners p67-71
Moulton—Auto. p613-614
Rosen—Four p134-139,287-289

Rowntree—Amid p216-221 (por.210)
Major—History (2) p1029
Progress—Science '40 p87-88 (por.88)
16 Amer. p33-36
*Snyder—Biology p373-374 (por.373)

Cantle, Sir James (1851-1926). Scot. surgeon.

Hammerton p349

Canton, Allen A. (1889-1940). Amer. inventor, elec. engineer.

Curr. Biog. '40 p140

Canton, John (1718-1772). Eng. physicist.

Chambers—Dict. col.85
Hammerton p349

Cantor, Georg Ferdinand Ludwig Cantor (1845-1918). Rus. mathematician.

Bell—Men p555-579 (por., front.)
Cajori—Hist. p397-401

Hammerton p350
Muir—Men p217-240
Smith—Hist. 1 p510

Cantor, Moritz Benedikt (1829-1920). Ger. mathematician.

Smith—Hist. 1 p544

Capps, Stephen Reid (1881-1949). Amer. geologist.

G.S.A.—Proc. '49 p127-135 (por.127)

Carbone, Tito (1863-1904). It. bacteriologist.

Bulloch—Hist. p357

Cardano, Girolamo (or Cardan, Geronimo, Jerome, Hieronimo) (1501-1576). It. mathematician, physician.

Ball—Short p221-225
*Book—Pop. Sci. (4) p1414-1415,
(7) p2477
Cajori—Hist. p134-135
Castiglioni—Hist. p452 (por.451)
Chambers—Dict. col.85-86
Gordon—Medieval p725-728
(por.179)
Gordon—Romance p177-178
(por.177)
Gumpert—Trial p3-28
Hammerton p352

Hooper—Makers p88-92
Major—History (1) p379-383
(por.381)
Muir—Men p26-46
Rosen—Four p53-54,237-239
Sarton—Six p31-36,187-189 (por.33)
Sedgwick—Short p239.
Smith—Hist. I p295-297 (por.296)
Smith—Portraits (v.2) II, unp. (por.)
Woodruff—Devel. p266-267
Year—Pic p84 (por.84)

Cardi.   See **Cordus, Valerius**

Cardon, Philip Vincent (1889-   ). Amer. agriculturist.
Curr. Biog. '54 p155-157 (por.155)

Caritat.   See **Condorcet, Marie Jean Antoine Nicolas de Caritat, Marquis de**

Carle, Antonio (1854-1927) It. bacteriologist, physician, surgeon.
Bulloch—Hist. p357   Leonardo—Lives p87-88
Castiglioni—Hist. p1013 (por.1012)

Carleton, Mark Alfred (1866-1925). Amer. botanist, agriculturist.
*Darrow—Builders p179-183   *Men—Scien. p31-33
*DeKruif—Hunger p3-30 (por.2)

Carlisle, Sir Anthony (1768-1840). Eng. anatomist, surgeon.
Leonardo—Lives p88-89

Carlson, Anton Julius (1875-1956). Swed. physiologist.
Curr. Biog. '48 p93-95 (por.94)   N.A.S.—(35) p1-15 (por.1)
    '56 p102   Progress—Science '40 p89-90 (por.89)
Major—History (2) p977-978

Carlson, Earl R. (1897-   ). Amer. physician.
Fabricant—Why p86-88
*Truax—Doctors p122-132

Carmalt, William Henry (1836-1930). Amer. surgeon.
Leonardo—Lives p89

Carnarvon, George Edward Stanhope, 5th Earl of (1866-1923). Eng. archaeologist.
Ceram—Gods p175-206
Hammerton p355-356

Carnegie, Andrew (1835-1919). Scot.-Amer. inventor.
Abbott—Great p350-352 (por.351)   *Law—Modern p50-62
*Darrow—Masters p180-185   *Nisenson—Illus. p30 (por.30)
Fitzhugh—Concise p102-103   *Tappan—Heroes p228-236
Hammerton p356 (por.356)

Carney, Frank (1868-1934). Amer. geologist.
G.S.A.—Proc. '34 p213-216 (por.213)

Carnot, Lazare Nicholas Marguerite (1753-1823). Fr. mathematician.

Arago—Biog. p1-116
Ball—Short p428

Cajori—Hist. p276
Smith—Hist. I p494

Carnot, (Nicolas Léonard) Sadi (1796-1832). Fr. physicist.

Ball—Short p433
*Book—Pop. Sci. (5) p1768-1769
  (por.1768)
Chambers—Dict. col.86
Hammerton p356
Hart—Physicists p127-129

Lenard—Great p231-235 (por.231)
Magie—Source p220-221
Van Wagenen—Beacon p261-262
Woodruff—Devel. p54-55,61,62,267
Year—Pic. p119

Caro, Heinrich (1834-1910). Ger. chemist.

Smith—Torch. p46 (por.46)

Carossa, Hans (1878-1956). Ger. physician.

Rosen—Four p206-209

Carothers, Wallace Hume (1896-1937). Amer. chemist.

Chambers—Dict. col.86-87
N.A.S.—Biog. (20) p293-303 (por.293)
Wilson—Amer. p387-389 (por.387)

Carpenter, Sir Henry Cort Harold (1875-1940). Eng. metallurgist.

Curr. Biog. '40 p144.

Carpenter, Lewis Van (1895-1940). Amer. engineer.

Curr. Biog. '40 p145

Carpue, Joseph Constantine (1764-1846). Eng. physician, surgeon.

Thorwald—Century p70-84 (por.80)

Carr, Emma P. (1880-   ). Amer. chemist.

Curr. Biog. '59 p55-57 (por.56)

Carrel, Alexis (1873-1944). Fr. physician, surgeon, biologist.

*Book—Pop. Sci. (5) p1769-1770
  (por. 1769)
Chambers—Dict. col.87
Curr. Biog. '40 p145-146 (por.146),
  '44 p85
*Darrow—Builders p222-225
Hammerton p358
*Law—Modern p63-76 (por.64)

Leonardo—Lives (supp 1) p475-476
Major—History (2) p1029-1030
Progress—Science '40 p90 (por.90)
Ratcliffe—Modern p194-195,202-210
Rowntree—Amid p367-369 (por.362)
*Snyder—Biology p416-419 (por.417,
  436)
Stevenson—Nobel p73-77 (por.150)

Carrier, Willis Haviland (1876-1950.) Amer. engineer, inventor.

Progress—Science '41 p87-88 (por.87)
*Yost—Science p178-190

Carrington, Richard Christopher (1826-1875). Eng. astronomer.
Armitage—Cent. p51-52
Chambers—Dict. col.87
Hammerton p359
Shapley—Astron. p274

Carroll, James (1854-1907). Eng. physician.
Chambers—Dict. col.87-88
Major—History (2) p914-915
*Masters—Conquest p153-154
(por.158)

Carroll, Lewis. See **Dodgson, Charles Lutwidge**

Carson, John Renshaw (1887-1940). Amer. mathematician, elec. engineer.
Curr. Biog. '40 p146-147 (por.147)

Carson, Rachel Louise (1907-   ). Amer. biologist.
Curr. Biog. '51 p100-102 (por.101)

Carter, Henry Vandyke (1831-1897). Eng. pathologist.
Bulloch—Hist. p357

Carter, Howard (1873-1939). Eng. archaeologist.
Ceram—Gods p173-206
Hammerton p359-360

Carter, Huntly (1862-1942). Brit. psychiatrist, pathologist.
Curr. Biog. '42 p141

Cartwright, Edmund (1743-1823). Eng. inventor.
*Book—Pop. Sci. (4) p1415-1416
(por.1415)
Chambers—Dict. col.88
*Darrow—Masters p50-53
*Darrow—Thinkers p95-97
*Eberle—Invent. p21-25 (por.20)
*Epstein—Real p155-157
Gunther—Early XI p173-174
(por.176)
Hammerton p360 (por.360)
*Hartman—Mach. p11-13
*Larsen—Prentice p66-68
Law—Civiliz. p92-96
*Parkman—Conq. p54-62

Carty, John Joseph (1861-1932). Amer. engineer.
*Darrow—Builders p260-265
N.A.S.—Biog. (18) p69-85 (por.69)

Carus Lucretius. See **Lucretius**

Carvajal, Gaspar de (1504-1584). Sp. sci. explorer, naturalist.
Von Hagen—Green p31-32

Carver, George Washington (c1864-1943). Amer. agric. chemist, botanist.

Borth—Pioneers p226-240 (por.238)
*Cooper—Twenty p141-158 (por.140)
Curr. Biog. '40 p148-150 (por.149),
 '43 p106.
Huff—Famous (2d) p111-119
 (por.113)

*Hughes—Negroes p69-76 (por.69)
 Morris—Ency. p642
*Simmons—Great p51-57 (por.51)
 Thomas—50 Amer. p348-357
*Yost—Science p147-162

Casál, Gaspar (1679-1759). Sp. physician.

Major—History (2) p630

Casamajor, Paul (1831-1887). Fr.-Amer. chemist.

Browne—Hist. p495

Case, Ermine Cowles (1871-1953). Amer. geologist, paleontologist.

G.S.A.—Proc. '54 p93-101 (por.93)

Casey, Thomas Lincoln (1831-1896). Amer. engineer.

N.A.S.—Biog. (4) p125-134

Casey, Thomas Lincoln (1857-1925). Amer. entomologist.

Essig—Hist. p565-567 (por.565)
Osborn—Fragments p175-176
 (por.359)

Caspersson, Törjborn O. (1910-   ). Swed. physician.

Robinson—100 p261-264 (por.261)

Cassegrain, N. (c.17th cent.). Fr. physician.

Chambers—Dict. col.88

Casserio, Giulio (1545-1616). It. anatomist, physician.

Major—History (1) p412

Cassin, John (1813-1869). Amer. ornithologist.

Welker—Bird p168-170

Cassini family (17th-19th cent.). It.-Fr. mathematicians, astronomers, etc.

Smith-Hist. I p368-370

Cassini, Alexandre Henri Gabriel de, Vicomte (1784-1832). Fr. botanist.

Chambers—Dict. col.89

Cassini, Giovanni Domenico (or Jean Dominique) (1625-1712). It.-Fr. astronomer.

*Book—Pop. Sci. (6) p1929
Chambers—Dict. col.88-89
Hammerton p362
Shapley—Astron. p72

Van Wagenen—Beacon p118-119
Vaucouleurs—Disc. p60-61
Woodruff—Devel. p267

Cassini, Jacques (1677-1756). Fr. astronomer.
Chambers—Dict. col.89

Cassini, Jacques Dominique de (Comte) (1748-1845). Fr. mathematician.
Chambers—Dict. col.89

Cassini de Thury, César François (1714-1784). Fr. astronomer, geographer.
Chambers—Dict. col.89

Cassiodorus, Flavius Magnus Aurelius (c.488/490-c566/575). Roman mathematician.
Ball—Short p133
Clagett—Greek p153-154,157,158

Casson, Stanley (1889-   ). Eng. archaeologist.
Hammerton p363 (por.363)

Castellani, Aldo (b.1875). It. physician.
Major—History (2) p973

Castillo Najera, Francisco (1886-1954). Mex. physician, surgeon, pathologist.
Curr. Biog. '46 p100-103 (por.101), '55 p110

Castle, William Ernest (b.1867). Amer. zoologist, biologist.
Chambers—Dict. col.90

Castner, Hamilton Young (1859-1899). Amer. chemist.
Chambers—Dict. col.90

Castro, Rodrigo de (1560-1675). Ger. physician.
Gordon—Medieval p762

Caswell, Alexis (1799-1877). Amer. astronomer, mathematician.
N.A.S.—Biog. (6) p363-372 (por.363)

Caswell, John (1655-1712). Eng. mathematician.
Smith—Hist. I p413

Cataldi, Pierre Antoine (or Pietro Antonio) (1548-1626). It. mathematician.
Chambers—Dict. col.90
Smith—Hist. I p303.

Catesby, Mark (1679-1749). Amer. naturalist, ornithologist, entomologist, botanist.
Bell—Early p50-51
Osborn—Fragments p11-12
Welker—Birds p10-14

Cathcart, Stanley Holman (1889-1953). Amer. geologist.
G.S.A.—Proc. '52 p97-98 (por.97)

Cathcart-Jones, Owen (1900-   ). Eng. aero. pioneer.
Hammerton p1447

Catlin, George (1796-1872). Amer. ethnologist, anthropologist.
Hammerton p367
Youmans—Pioneers p336-346
  (por.336)

Cato, Marcus Porcius, "The Censor" (234-149 B.C.). Rom. biologist.
Adams—Birth p48
Bodenheimer—Hist. p172
Gordon—Medicine p626-629

Cattell, James McKeen (1860-1944). Amer. psychologist.
Curr. Biog. '44 p88
N.A.S.—Biog. (25) p1-9 (por.1)

Caturani, Michele Gaetano (1873-1940). Amer. physician, gynecologist.
Curr. Biog. '40 p152 (por.152)

Cauchy, Augustin Louis, Baron (1789-1857). Fr. mathematician.
Ball—Short p469-471
Bell—Men p270-293 (por.,front.)
*Book—Pop. Sci. (7) p2480
Cajori—Hist. p368-369
Chambers—Dict. col.90
*Miller—Hist. p243-245
Smith—Hist. I p496-497 (por.497)
Smith—Portraits,v2, VIII, unp. (por.)
Woodruff—Devel. p30-31,267 (por.30)
Year—Pic. p117 (por.117)

Caudell, Andrew Nelson (1872-1936). Amer. entomologist.
Osborn—Fragments p238 (por.361)

Cauliaco.   See **Chauliac, Guy de**

Caus, Salomon de (1576-1626). Fr. engineer, physicist.
Hammerton p368

Cautley, Sir Proby Thomas (1802-1871). Eng. engineer.
Hammerton p368

Cavalieri, (Francesco) Bonaventura (1598-1647). It. mathematician.

Ball—Short p278-281
Cajori—Hist. p161-162
Hooker—Makers p240-241,249-252
Sedgwick—Short p278-280

Smith—Hist. I p362-363 (por.363)
Turnbull—Great p81
Year—Pic. p92 (por.92)

Cavendish, Henry (1731-1810). Eng. physicist, chemist.

Ball—Short p429-430
*Book—Pop. Sci. (5) p1770-1772
  (por.1771)
Burge—Ency. p628
Chalmers—Historic p262-263
Chambers—Dict. col.91
*Darrow—Masters p35-37 (por.32)
*Darrow—Thinkers p51-53
Gibson—Heroes p179-187
Gregory—British p44-45 (por.45)
Hammerton p369 (por.369)
Heinmuller—Man's p232 (por.232)
Holmyard—British p34-36 (por.35)
Holmyard—Chem. p83-87 (por.90)
Holmyard—Makers p177-186
  (por.178)
*Jaffe—Crucibles p73-92
Lenard—Great p145-149 (por.145)
Leonard—Crus. p241-260 (por.246)

Magie—Source p105-106
Major—History p613-614
Morgan—Men p31
Murray—Science p341-344
Partington—Short p99-104,150-151
  (por.100)
People p59-60
Ramsey—Essays p30-41
Roberts—Chem. p13-20
Robinson—Path. p239-264 (por.254)
Schwartz—Moments (1) p475-477
Smith—Torch. p47 (por.47)
Thomson—Great p31
Tilden—Famous p41-52 (por.41)
Van Wagenen—Beacon p166-167
Weeks—Discovery p84-87 (por.84)
Woodruff—Devel. p88,267
*Wright—Great p193-199
Year—Pic p103 (por.103)

Caventou, Joseph Bienamé (1795-1878). Fr. chemist.

Chambers—Dict. col.91

Caxton, William (1422-1491). Eng. inventor.

*Glenister—Stories p19-27
*Larsen—Prentice p7-8
Law—Civiliz. p120-122

Nisenson—Illus. p35
100 Great p532-537

Cayeux, Lucien (1864-1944). Fr. geologist.

G.S.A.—Proc. '47 p131-133 (por.131)

Cayley, Arthur (1821-1895). Eng. mathematician.

Ball—Short p475-476
Bell—Men p378-383,388-405
  (por.,front.)
Cajori—Hist. p342-343
Chambers—Dict. col.91-92
Hammerton p370
MacFarlane—Lectures p64-77
  (por.,front.)

*Miller—Hist. p257-259
Smith—Hist. I p465-467 (por.465)
Smith—Math. p128-129
Smith—Portraits v. 2. XI, unp.
  (por.)
Woodruff—Devel. p267 (por.30)

Cayley, Sir George (1773-1857). Eng. inventor, aero. pioneer.

Abbot—Great p225-226
*Bishop—Kite p81-86
Burge—Enyc. p628

*Cohen—Men p83-86,86,99-100
Heinmuller—Man's p237 (por.237)

Caylus, Anne Claude Philippe de Tubières de Pestels de Névis, Comte de (1692-1795). Fr. archaeologist.
Hammerton p370

Ceci, Antonio (1852-1920). It. surgeon.
Leonardo—Lives p90

Celli, Angelo (1857-1914). It. physician.
Castiglioni—Hist. p826-827,904
   (por.1096)
Major—History (2) p917

Cellini, Benvenuto (1500-1571). It. metallurgist.
Moulton—Auto. p47   Tuska—Invent. p114-115
*Science Miles. p42 (por.42)

CeLoria, Giovanni (1842-1920). It. astronomer.
MacPherson—Astron. p108-113
   (por.108)
MacPherson—Makers p216-217

Celsius, Anders (1701-1744). Swed. astronomer.
*Book—Pop. Sci. (4) p1416   Hart—Physicists p91
Chambers—Dict. col.92   Lindroth—Swedish p66-73
Hammerton p371-372   Year—Pic. p104 (por.104)

Celsus, (Aulus) Aurelius Cornelius (25 B.C.-50 A.D.) Rom. physician.
Atkinson—Magic p47-48   Hammerton p372
Castiglioni—Hist. p204-213   Lambert—Medical p46-47
Clagett—Greek p107-108   Lambert—Minute p46-47
Gordon—Medicine p664-671   Leonardo—Lives p90-92
   (por.665)   Major—History (1) p169-170

Cesalpino, Andrea (or Cesalpini, Cesalpinus) (1519-1603). It. botanist, physician.
Arber—Herbals p143,144,183,184   Leonardo—Lives p92-93
   (por.144)   Major—History (1) p492-494
Castiglioni—Hist. p436-440 (por.437)   (por.490)
Chambers—Dict. col.92   Miall—Early p36-39
Gordon—Medieval p622-625   Reed—Short p71-73
Hawks—Pioneers p184-187   Woodruff—Devel. p240,267
Lambert—Medical p122   Year—Pic. p81,82 (por.81)
Lambert—Minute p122

Cesnola, Luigi Palma di (1832-1904). Amer. archaeologist.
Hammerton p373

Ceulen, Ludolph van (or Keulen, Ludolf van) (1540-1610). Dutch mathematician.
Chambers—Dict. col.92
Smith—Hist. I p330-331

Ceva brothers (17th-18th cent.) It. mathematicians.
Smith—Hist. I p511-512

Ceva, Giovanni (1647?-1734). It. mathematician.
Chambers—Dict. col.92

Chabaneau, François (or Chavaneau) (1754-1842). Fr. chemist.
Chambers—Dict. col.93
Weeks—Discovery p244-246

Chabert, Philibert (1737-1814). Fr. bacteriologist.
Bulloch—Hist. p357

Chacon, Dionysio (Denis) Daca (or Daza) (c1510-c1596). Sp. physician, surgeon.
Gordon—Romance p535 (por.535)
Leonardo—Lives p146

Chadwick, Sir Edwin (1800-1890). Eng. physician.
Major—History (2) p879
Walker—Pioneers p71-86 (por.71)

Chadwick, George Halcott (1876-1953). Amer. geologist.
G.S.A.—Proc. '52 p101-105 (por.101)

Chadwick, Sir James (1891-   ). Eng. physicist.
Chambers—Dict. col.93
Curr. Biog. '45 p94-95 (por.94)
Heathcote—Nobel p331-338 (por.240)
Riedman—Men p112-115
Weber—College p568 (por.568)
Year—Pic. p211 (por.211)

Chaffee, Emory Leon (1885-   ). Amer. physicist.
Radio's 100 p218-219 (por.140)

Chain, Ernest Boris (1906-   ). Ger. pathologist, biochemist.
Calder—Science p90-91
Chambers—Dict. col.93
Grainger—Guide p148
*Larsen—Shaped p130-141 (por.97)
Stevenson—Nobel p230,233-237 (por.150)

Chalcidius (fl. 4th cent.) Rom. nat. philosopher.
Clagett—Greek p147-148

Chalmers, James (1782-1853). Scot. inventor.
Hammerton p374

Chamberlain, Francis L. (1905-   ). Amer. physician.
Curr. Biog. '59 p61-62 (por.61)

Chamberlain, Owen (1920-   ). Amer. physicist.
Curr. Biog. '60 p83-85 (por.84)

Chamberlain, Paul Mellen (1865-1940). Amer. engineer.
Curr. Biog. '40 p155-156

Chamberlain, William Isaac (1837-1920). Amer. agriculturist.
*Ivins—Fifty p309-314 (por.311)

Chamberland, Charles Édouard (1851-1908). Fr. bacteriologist.
Bulloch—Hist. p357
Chambers—Dict. col.93-94

Chamberlen family (16th, 17th cent.). Eng. physicians.
Atkinson—Magic p163-166
Major—History (1) p551

Chamberlen, Peter (1601-1683). Eng. physician.
Hammerton p376

Chamberlin, Clarence Duncan (1893-   ). Amer. aero. pioneer.
*Fraser—Heroes p461-474
Heinmuller—Man's p86-102,323
(por.99,323)
La Croix—They p100-106

Chamberlin, Rollin Thomas (1881-1948). Amer. geologist.
G.S.A.—Proc. '48 p135-140 (por.135)

Chamberlin, Thomas Chrowder (1843-1928). Amer. geologist.
*Book—Pop. Sci. (2) p717
Chambers—Dict. col.94
Fenton—Giants p302-317 (por.271)
Hammerton p376
Merrill—First p486-489 (por.450)
N.A.S.—Biog. (15) p307-393
(por.307,378)
Trattner—Arch. p332-350 (por.342)
Woodruff—Devel. p267 (por.206)

Chambers, Robert (1802-1871). Scot. geologist, biologist.
Osborn—Greeks p312-316
Progress—Science '40 p96
Woodruff—Devel. p203-204,256,267

Chamisso, Adelbert von (or Louis Charles Adélaide de Chamisso) (1781-1838). Fr.-Ger. naturalist, biologist, botanist.

Alden—Early p21-27
Bodenheimer—Hist. p360
Chambers—Dict. col.94

Dakin—Perennial p28-29
Essig—Hist. p620 (por.620)

Champier, Symphorien (1472-1539). Fr. physician.

Major—History (1) p422

Champneys, Sir Francis (1848-1930). Eng. physician.

Hammerton p378

Champollion-Figeac, Jean Francois (1790-1832). Fr. archaeologist.

Ceram—Gods p85-90,92-115

Champollion-Figeac, Jean Jacques (1778-1867). Fr. archaeologist.

Ceram—Gods p87-88

Chancourtois, Alexandre Émile Béguyer de (1819-1886). Fr. geologist.

Chambers—Dict. col.94-95
Weeks—Discovery p386-387,396
  (por.396)

Chandler, Charles Frederick (1836-1925). Amer. chemist.

Browne—Hist. p472-473 (por.29)
Killeffer—Eminent p11 (por.11)

N.A.S.—Biog. (14) p127-178 (por.127)

Chandler, Seth Carlo (1846-1913). Amer. astronomer.

Shapley—Astron, p377

Chandrasekhar, Subrahmanyan (1910-   ). Ind. astronomer.

Progress—Science '41 p88

Chantemesse, Andrè (1851-1919). Fr. bacteriologist, pathologist.

Bulloch—Hist. p358

Chanute, Octave (1832-1910). Fr.-Amer. aero. pioneer.

*Bishop—Kite p130-134
Burge—Ency. p628
*Cohen—Men p93-95

Hammerton p378
Heinmuller—Man's p255 (por.255)

Chapelle. See **La Chapelle, Marie Louise Dugès**

Chapin, Charles de Witt (1856-1941). Amer. public health worker.

Curr. Biog. '41 p146
16 Amer. p49-52

Chapin, S. F. (1839-1889). Amer. entomologist.
Essig—Hist. p567-568

Chapman, David Leonard (1869-1958). Eng. chemist.
R.S.L.—Biog. (4) p35-43 (por.35)

Chapman, Frank Michler (1864-1945). Amer. ornithologist, naturalist.
*Book—Pop Sci. (4) p1147-1148
  (por.1148)
Curr. Biog. '46 p108
*Milne—Natur. p135-142 (por.134)
N.A.S.—Biog. (25) p111-132 (por.111)
Peattie—Gather p293-296
Tracy—Amer. Nat. p190-198
Von Hagen—Green p345

Chapman, Sydney (1888-   ). Eng. physicist.
Curr. Biog. '57 p106-108 (por.107)

Chappe, Claude (1763-1805). Fr. engineer, inventor.
Appleyard—Pioneers p263-298
  (por.262,275)
*Epstein—Real p131

Chaptal, Jean Antoine Claude, Comte De Chanteloup (1756-1832). Fr. chemist.
Chambers—Dict. col.95
Hammerton p379
Partington—Short p177
Rosen—Four p60-63
Smith—Torch. p48 (por.48)
Weeks—Discovery p446 (por.446)

Charaka (Caraka) (c100 A.D.). Hindu surgeon.
Leonardo—Lives p93

Charcot, Jean Baptists Étienne Auguste (1867-1936). Fr. sci. explorer.
Hammerton p1447

Charcot, Jean Martin (1825-1893). Fr. neurologist, physician.
Castiglioni—Hist. p739-740 (por.740)
Chambers—Dict. col.95
Gordon—Romance p479 (por.479)
Hammerton p379
Major—History (2) p889-890
  (por.850)

Chard, Marie L. (1868-1938). Amer. physician.
Lovejoy—Women Phys. p53 (por.52)

Chardin.   See **Teilhard de Chardin, Pierre**

Chardonnet, Comte Hilaire Bernigaud de (1839-1924). Fr. chemist, physicist.
Law—Civiliz. p276-277

Charles, Jacques Alexandre César (1746-1823). Fr. physicist, aero. pioneer, inventor.

*Bishop—Kite p30-34
Burge—Ency. p628
Chambers—Dict. col.95-96
Hammerton p388
Heinmuller—Man's p233 (por.233)

*Larsen—Prentice p105,107-109
Law—Civiliz. p59-60,151-152
*Shippen—Bridle p49-56
Van Wagenen—Beacon p186-188

Charpentier, Jean de (1786-1855). Swiss mineralogist, geologist.

Woodruff—Devel. p268

Charrin, Albert (1856-1907). Fr. physiologist, pathologist.

Bulloch—Hist. p358

Chasles, Michel (1793-1880). Fr. mathematician.

Cajori—Hist. p292-294
Chambers—Dict. col.96

Hammerton p389
Smith—Hist. I p498

Chassaignac, Pierre-Marie-Édouard (1804-1879). Fr. surgeon.

Leonardo—Lives p94

Chasseboeuf.   See Volney, Constantin François de Chasseboeuf Comte de

Chassepot, Antoine Alphonse (1833-1905). Fr. inventor.

Hammerton p389

Chatelet, Emilie Marquise de. (or Gabrielle, Emilie Le Tonnelier de Breteuil) (1706-1749). Fr. mathematician, astronomer, physicist.

Coolidge—Six p23-25
Mozans—Woman p151-153,175-177,
   201-202

Chatelier, Henry Louis Le (1850-1936). Fr. chemist, metallurgist.

A.A.A.S.—Proc. (78) p31-32
Chambers—Dict. col.96

Partington—Short p341
Smith—Torch. p152 (por.152)

Chauliac, Guy de (or Cauliaco, Guido de). (c1300-c1370). Fr. physician, surgeon.

Castiglioni—Hist. p345-347
Gordon—Medieval p352-355 (por.51)
Hammerton p392
Leonardo—Lives p94-96

Major—Hist. (1) p310-312 (por.307)
Moulton—Auto. p38
Walsh—Catholic (2d) p93-115
   (por.93)
Year—Pic. (por.80)

Chauveau, Jean Baptiste Auguste (1827-1917). Fr. physiologist, pathologist.

Bulloch—Hist. p358

Chauvenet, William (1820-1870). Amer. mathematician.
N.A.S.—Biog. (1) p227-243

Chavaneau.   See **Chabaneau, François**

Chavez, Georges (1887-1910). Fr. aero. pioneer.
Heinmuller—Man's p282 (por.282)

Chebichev.   See **Tchebichev, Pafnutiy Lvovich**

Cheever, David W. (1831-1915). Amer. surgeon.
Kagan—Modern p91 (por.91)
Leonardo—Lives p97-99

Chekhov, Anton (1860-1904). Rus. physician.
Farmer—Doctor's p200

Chelius, Max Josef von (1794-1876). Ger. surgeon.
Leonardo—Lives p99-100

Chenevix, Richard (1774-1830). Irish chemist.
Hammerton p393

Cheney, George Monroe (1893-1952). Amer. geologist.
G.S.A.—Proc. '54 p103-106 (por.103)

Chennault, Claire Lee (1890-   ). Amer. aero. pioneer.
Heinmuller—Man's p354 (por.354)

Cherrie, George K. (1865-1948). Amer. naturalist.
Cutright—Great p42

Cherwell, Frederick Alexander Lindemann, 1st Baron (1886-1957). Eng.
physicist.
Chambers—Dict. supp., col.96-97   R.S.L.—Biog. (4) p45-69 (por.45)
Curr. Biog. '52 p100-102 (por.101)

Cheselden, William (1688-1752). Eng. anatomist, surgeon.
Chambers—Dict. col.97   Leonardo—Lives p100-101
Hammerton p393   Major—History (2) p632

Chesser, Elizabeth Sloan (1878-1940). Eng. physician.
Curr. Biog. '40 p166

Chevreul, Michel Eugène (1786-1889). Fr. chemist.
*Book—Pop. Sci. (5) p1772
Chambers—Dict. col.97
Hammerton p394 (por.394)
Partington—Short p221-223,237
  (por.222)

Smith—Torch. p49 (por.49)
Van Wagenen—Beacon p243-245
Weeks—Discovery p218,219 (por.218)

Cheyne, George (1671-1743). Scot. physician.
Farmer—Doctors' p11
Hammerton p395

Major—History (2) p629

Cheyne, John (1777-1836). Scot. physician.
Major—History (2) p681-682

Cheyne, William Watson (1852-1932). Eng. bacteriologist, surgeon.
Bulloch—Hist. p358
Hammerton p395

Chiarugi, Vincenzo (1759-1820). It. physician.
Castiglioni—Hist. p633-634 (por.634)

Chidlaw, Benjamin W. (1900-   ). Amer. aero. engineer.
Curr. Biog. '55 p116-118 (por.117)

Child, Charles Manning (1869-1954). Amer. biologist, zoologist.
N.A.S.—Biog. (30) p73-103 (por.73)

Childe, Henry Langdon (1781-1874). Eng. inventor.
Hammerton p395-396

Childe, Vere Gordon (1892-1957). Austral. archaeologist.
Hammerton p396 (por.396)
Schwartz—Moments (1) p109-110

Chisholm, George Brock (1896). Can. psychiatrist, public health worker.
Curr. Biog. '48 p104-105 (por.105)

Chittenden, Frank H. (1858-1928). Amer. entomologist.
Osborn—Fragments p190-191
  (por.358)

Chittenden, Russell Henry (1856-1943). Amer. physiologist, chemist.
Chambers—Dict. col.97
Killeffer—Eminent p19 (por.19)

N.A.S.—Biog. (24) p59-93 (por.59)

Chladni, Ernst Florens Friedrich (1756-1824/1827). Ger. physicist.
Chambers—Dict. col.98
Hammerton p397

Van Wagenen—Beacon p207-209

Chomel, August François (1788-1858). Fr. physician.
Major—History (2) p708

Chopart, François (1743-1795). Fr. surgeon.
Leonardo—Lives p101-103

Choulant, Johann Ludwig (1791-1861). Ger. physician.
Major—History (2) p709

Christensen, Leo Martin (1898-1955). Amer. chemist.
Borth—Pioneers p74-75,174-183
(por.182)

Christian, Henry Asbury (1876-1951). Amer. physician.
Major—History (2) p1030

Christiansen, Christian (1843-1917). Dan. physicist.
Chambers—Dict. col.98
Magie—Source p381

Christie, Samuel Hunter (1784-1865). Eng. mathematician.
Chambers—Dict. col.98

Christy, David (1802-c1867). Amer. geologist.
Merrill—First p255-256 (por.256)

Chrysippus (280-206 B.C.). Gr. nat. philosopher.
Gordon—Medicine p602 (por.602)

Chrysler, Walter Percy (1875-1940). Amer. engineer.
*White—Famous (3d) p17-27 (por.15)

Chu Hsi (or Chu Shï-kié, Chu Hi) (1130-1200). Chin. mathematician.
Smith—Hist. I p273

Chubb, Lewis Warrington (1882-1952). Amer. engineer.
Curr. Biog. '47 p108-110 (por.109).
'52 p106

Chuquet, Nicolas (c1445-c1500). Fr. mathematician.
Chambers—Dict. col.98
Smith—Hist. I p261

Church, Arthur Henry (1865-1937). Eng. botanist.
Gunther—Early XI p252-253
(por.252)

Church, Ellen (n.d.) Amer. aero. pioneer.
Knapp—New p73-85 (por.179)

Church, William (1859-1920). Amer. anthropologist.
Hammerton p401

Church, Sir William Selby (1837-1928). Eng. physician.
Hammerton p401

Ciamician, Giacomo Luigi (1857-1922). It. chemist.
Hammerton p402
Smith—Torch. p50 (por.50)

Cidenas (c343 B.C.). Babyl. astronomer.
Chambers—Dict. col.99

Cierva, Juan de la (or Cierva Codorniu) (1895-1936). Sp. aero. pioneer,
engineer, inventor.
Burge—Ency. p628
Daniel Gugg. p27-31 (por.26)
Daniel—Pioneer. p19-21 (por.18)
Hammerton p403
Heinmuller—Man's p313 (por.313)

Ciruelo, Pedro Sanchez (c1470-1560). Sp. mathematician.
Smith—Hist. I p344

Citois, François (1572-1652). Fr. physician.
Major—History (1) p478

Civiale, Jean (1792-1867). Fr. physician.
Castiglioni—Hist. p872 (por.872)
Leonardo—Lives p103-104
Thorwald—Century p35-38,40-46,51-
64 (por.80)

Clairaut, Alexis Claude (or Clairault) (1713-1765). Fr. mathematician.
Abetti—History p154-155
Ball—Short p373-374
Cajori—Hist. p244-245
Chambers—Dict. col.99
Hammerton p404
Smith—Hist. I p474-477
Van Wagenen—Beacon p156-158
Woodruff—Devel. p21,22,268

Claisen, Ludwig (1851-1930). Ger. chemist.
A.A.A.S.—Proc. (79) p10-11
Partington—Short p319

Clapeyron, Benoît-Paul-Émile (1799-1864). Fr. engineer.
A.A.A.S.—Proc. (77) p37-38

Clapp, Charles Horace (1883-1935). Amer. geologist.
G.S.A.—Proc. '35 p171-179 (por.171)

Clapp, Frederick Gardner (1879-1944). Amer. geologist.
G.S.A.—Proc. '44 p163-166 (por.163)

Clark, Alvan G. (1804-1887). Amer. astronomer, inventor.
Chambers—Dict. col.99   *Darrow—Thinkers p123-126 (por.124)
*Darrow—Masters p135-139 (por.289)   Wilson—Amer. p275,277 (por.277)

Clark, Sir Andrew (1826-1893). Scot. physician.
Hammerton p406 (por.406)

Clark, Bruce Lawrence (1880-1945). Amer. geologist.
G.S.A.—Proc. '46 p149-151 (por.149)

Clark, Eugenie (1922-   ). Amer. ichthyologist.
Curr. Biog. '53 p120-122 (por.121)

Clark, Henry James (1826-1873). Amer. biologist.
N.A.S.—Biog. (1) p317-326

Clark, Sir James (1788-1870). Scot. physician.
Hammerton p406

Clark, Josiah Latimer (1822-1898). Eng. engineer.
Chambers—Dict. col.99
Hammerton p406

Clark, Nancy Talbot (1825-1901). Amer. physician.
Lovejoy—Women p82-84
Mead—Medical p45,46

Clark, Robert Watson (1884-1948). Amer. geologist.
G.S.A.—Proc. '49 p139-140 (por.139)

Clark, Samuel Marmaduke Dinwiddie (1875-1925). Amer. surgeon.
Leonardo—Lives p104-105

Clark, Thomas (1801-1867). Scot. chemist.
Chambers—Dict. col.99-100
Hammerton p406

Clark, William Andrews (1839-1925). Amer. min. engineer, metallurgist.
*Wildman—Ist p67-77 (por.65)

Clark, William Bullock (1860-1917). Amer. geologist.
N.A.S. —Biog. (9) p1-12 (por.1)

Clark, William Mansfield (1884-   ). Amer. chemist.
Chambers—Dict. col.100

Clark, William Otterbein (1874-1952). Amer. geologist.
GS.A.—Proc. '54 p107-110 (por.107)

Clarke, Alexander Ross (1828-1914). Scot. geodesist.
Chambers—Dict. col.100

Clarke, Charles (1887-   ). Amer. physician.
Curr.Biog. '47 p120-122 (por.121)

Clarke, Edith (n.d.) Amer. elec. engineer.
Goff—Women p50-65

Clarke, Edward Daniel (1769-1822). Eng. mineralogist.
Weeks—Discovery p280 (por.280)

Clarke, Frank Wigglesworth (1847-1931). Amer. geologist, geochemist.
Browne—Hist. p478 (por.61)   Killeffer—Eminent p16 (por.16)
Chambers—Dict. col.100   N.A.S.—Biog. (15) p139-145 (por.139)

Clarke, John (1761-1815). Eng. physician.
Major—History (2) p702

Clarke, John Mason (1857-1925). Amer. paleontologist.
N.A.S.—Biog. (12) p183-222 (por.183)

Clarke, Warren Thompson (1863-1929). Amer. entomologist.
Essig—Hist p568-570 (por.569)

Clarke, William Branwhite (1798-1878). Eng. geologist.
Hammerton p407

Claude, Georges (1870-1960). Fr. chemist, physicist.
Chambers—Dict. col.100-101

Claudius Ptolemaeus.   See Ptolemy

Clausius, Rudolf (1822-1888). Ger. physicist.
*Book—Pop. Sci. (5) p1772-1773   Lenard—Great p296-298 (por.297)
Chalmers—Historic p263   Magie—Source p228
Chambers—Dict. col.101   Van Wagenen—Beacon p325-326
Crew—Physicists #8 (folder) (por.) Woodruff—Devel. p62,268
Hammerton p408

Clavius, Christopher (1537-1612). Ger. mathematician.
Smith—Hist. I p334-335 (por.334)
Walsh—Catholic (2d) p193-197
(por.193)

Clay, Charles (1801-1893). Eng. surgeon.
Hammerton p408

Clayton, John (1685?-1773). Eng.-Amer. botanist.
Chambers—Dict. col.101

Clayton, Richard (1811-1859). Eng.-Amer. aero. pioneer.
Heinmuller—Man's p239
Milbank—First p57-60

Cleaveland, Parker (1780-1858). Amer. geologist.
Merrill—First p45-46 (por.42)
Smith—Chem. p221

Clebsch, (Alfred) Rudolf Friedrich (1833-1872). Ger. mathematician.
Cajori—Hist. p313-314

Cleland, Herdman Fitzgerald (1869-1935). Amer. geologist.
G.S.A.—Proc. '35 p183-186 (por.183)

Clemensen, Erik Christian (1876?-1941). Dan.-Amer. chemist.
Curr. Biog. '41 p156

Clement, Martin Withington (1881-   ). Amer. engineer.
Curr. Biog. '46 p117-120 (por.118)

Clément-Desormes, Nicolas (?   -1841). Fr. chemist.
Chambers—Dict. col.101

Clemson, Thomas Green (1807-1888). Amer. min. engineer, mineralogist.
Smith—Chem. p219-220

Clendening, Logan (1884-1945). Amer. physician.
Curr. Biog. '45 p114
Major—History (2) p1030-1031
(por.993)

Cleomedes (fl.2d cent.). Gr. astron.
Smith—Hist. I p132

Clericus, Petrus.   See Petroncellus

Clerk, Sir Dugald (1854-1932). Scot. engineer.
Hammerton p411 (por.411)

Clerk-Maxwell.   See **Maxwell, James Clerk**

Clerke, Agnes Mary (1842-1907). Irish astronomer.
*Book—Pop. Sci. (6) p1929-1930   MacPherson—Astron. p114-118
Hammerton p411   (por.114)

Clermont-Ganneau, Charles Simon (1846-1923). Fr. archaeologist.
Hammerton p411

Cleve, Per Theodor (1840-1905). Swed. chemist.
Chambers—Dict. col.102   Weeks—Discovery p424-426,477
Smith—Torch. p51 (por.51)   (por.424,477)

Cleveland, Clement (1843-1934). Amer. surgeon.
Leonardo—Lives p105-106

Cleveland, Emeline Horton (1829-1878). Amer. physician, surgeon.
Lovejoy—Women p38-39
Mead—Medical p63

Clichtoveus, Jodocus (or Josse Van) (d.1543).
Smith—Hist. I p342

Clifford, William Kingdon (1845-1879). Eng. mathematician.
Cajori—Hist. p307   MacFarlane—Lectures p78-91
Chambers—Dict. col.102   (por.,front.)
                                Smith—Hist. I p467-468 (por.468)

Cline, Henry (1750-1827). Eng. surgeon.
Leonardo—Lives p106-107

Cline, John Wesley (1898-   ). Amer. physician, surgeon.
Curr. Biog. '51 p110-111 (por.110)

Clinton, George Perkins (1867-1937). Amer. botanist, agriculturist.
N.A.S.—Biog. (20) p183-188 (por.183)

Clodd, Edward (1840-1930). Eng. nat. philosopher.
Hammerton p414

Cloquet, Jules Germain (1790-1883). Fr. surgeon.
Leonardo—Lives p107-108

Cloud, Joseph (1770-1845). Amer. mineralogist.
Smith—Chem. p221

Clouston, Sir Thomas Smith (1840-1915). Brit. physician.
Hammerton p414-415

Clowes, William (1540-1604). Eng. surgeon.
Gordon—Medieval p681-683   Major—History (1) p454-455
Leonardo—Lives p108-109

Cluness, William Robert (1835-1918). Can. physician.
Jones—Memories p363-369 (por.363)

Clusius.   See **Lecluse, Charles de**

Clyde, George D. (1898-   ). Amer. engineer, agriculturist.
Curr. Biog. '58 p96-98 (por.97)

Coanda, Henri (1885-   ). Fr. aero. engineer, inventor.
Curr. Biog. '56 p116-118 (por.117)

Coatalen, Louis Helen (1879-   ). Fr. engineer.
Hammerton p415

Cobb, Collier (1862-1934). Amer. geologist, geographer.
*G.S.A—Proc. '35 p189-191 (por.189)

Cobb, Jerie (1931-   ). Amer. aero. pioneer.
*Curr. Biog. '61 (Feb.) (por.)

Cobb, Stanley (1887-   ). Amer. psychiatrist.
Fabricant—Why p127-128

Cober, Tobias (or Kober) (d.c.1625). Ger. physician.
Major—History (1) p551

Cobham, Sir Alan John (1894-   ). Eng. aero. pioneer.
Burge—Ency. p628-629   Heinmuller—Man's p318 (por.318)
Hammerton p417

Coblentz, William Weber (b.1873). Amer. physicist, astronomer.
Chambers—Dict. col.102
Curr. Biog. '54 p186-188 (por.187)

Cochrane, Alexander (1802-1865). Scot.-Amer. chem. engineer.
Haynes—Chem. (1) p57-73 (por.64)

Cochrane, Edward Lull (1892-   ). Amer. engineer.
Curr. Biog. '51 p117-119 (por.117)
N.A.S.—Biog. (35) p33-46 (por.33)

Cochrane, Jacqueline (1906-   ). Amer. aero. pioneer.
*Adams—Heroines p239-253 (por.248)   Curr. Biog. '40 p181-183 (por.182)
*Clymer—Modern p160-168 (por.82)   Heinmuller—Man's p352 (por.352)

Cochran-Patrick, Charles William Kennedy (1896-1933). Scot. aero.
pioneer.
Burge—Ency. p629

Cockburn, William (1669-1739). Scot. physician.
Major—History (1) p556

Cockcroft, Sir John Douglas (1897-   ). Eng. physicist, engineer.
Chambers—Dict. col.102,103   Larsen—Scrap. p146-147 (por.145)
(por.103)   Year—Pic. p212 (por.212)
Curr. Biog '48 p107-108 (por.108)

Cocker, Edward (1631-1675). Eng. mathematician.
Chambers—Dict. col.103
Smith—Hist. I p415-416

Cockerell, Theodore Dru Alison (1866-1948). Eng.-Amer. zoologist,
entomologist, biologist.
Essig—Hist. p570-573 (por.570)   Osborn—Fragments p176-177
Ewen—Rocky p95-116,185 (por.95)   (por.380)

Cockerill, William (1759-1832). Eng.-Fr. inventor.
Hammerton p418

Cocking, Robert (1777-1837). Eng. aero. pioneer.
*Bishop—Kite p70-71
Burge—Ency. p629

Coddington, Henry (c1800-1845). Eng. mathematician.
Chambers—Dict. col.104

Codivilla, Alessandro (1861-1912). It. physician, surgeon.
Castiglioni—Hist. p878 (por.877)   Leonardo—Lives p109
Kagan—Modern p93 (por.93)

Codos, Paul (1896-1940). Fr. aero. pioneer.
Heinmuller—Man's p193-203,347
(por.201,203,347)

Cody, Samuel Franklin (1861-1913). Amer.-Eng. aero. pioneer.
Burge—Ency. p629   Heinmuller—Man's p275 (por.275)
Hammerton p418

Coe, Urling C. (1881-   ). Amer. physician.
Fabricant—Why p148-149

Coffin, Frank Trenholm (1878-   ). Amer. aero. pioneer.
Heinmuller—Man's p286 (por.286)

Coffin, James Henry (1806-1873). Amer. meteorologist, mathematician, astronomer.
N.A.S.—Biog. (1) p257-264
Youmans—Pioneers p447-457
(por. 447)

Coffin, John Huntingtom (1815-1890). Amer. astronomer.
N.A.S.—Biog. (8) p1-7 (por.1)

Cogan, Thomas (1545?-1607). Eng. physician.
Gunther—Early XI p107-109

Coghill, George Ellett (1872-1941). Amer. anatomist, biologist.
N.A.S.—Biog. (22) p251-267 (por.251)
Progress—Science '41 p102-103

Cohen, Joshua I. (1801-1870). Amer. physician, otologist.
Kagan—Modern p128 (por.128)

Cohen, Julius Berend (1859-1935). Eng. chemist.
Chambers—Dict. col.104

Cohn, Edwin Joseph (1892-1953). Amer. biochemist, physician.
*Eberle—Modern p136,138-142   N.A.S.—Biog. (35) p47-72 (por.47)
Morris—Ency. p645   Robinson—100 p291-294 (por.291)

Cohn, Ferdinand (1828-1898). Ger. bacteriologist, botanist.
Bulloch—Hist. p358-359 (por.36)   Hammerton p419
Chambers—Dict. col.104   Locy—Biology p270-271 (por.271)
Grainger—Guide p149   Major—History (2) p892-893

Cohnheim, Julius (1839-1884). Ger. pathologist, physician.
Bulloch—Hist. p359
Castiglioni—Hist. p798-799 (por.798)
Hammerton p419
Kagan—Leaders p82-86
Kagan—Modern p150 (por.150)
Major—History (2) p901

Cohu, La Motte Turck (1895-   ). Amer. aero. pioneer.
Curr. Biog. '51 p123-124 (por.123)

Coindet, Jean François (1774-1834). Swiss physician.
Chambers—Dict. col.104
Weeks—Discovery p447-449 (por.447)

Coiter (or Coeiter, Coyter, Koiter), **Volcher** (1534-1600?). Dutch physician, anatomist.
Bodenheimer—Hist. p237
Major—History (1) p474-475

Colby, Charles DeWitt (1865-1941). Amer. physician.
Curr. Biog. '41 p159

Colden, Cadwallader (1688-1776). Amer. botanist.
Bell—Early p51

Cole, Fay-Cooper (1881-   ). Amer. anthropologist.
Progress—Science '40 p110 (por.110)

Cole, Francis Joseph (1872-1959). Eng. zoologist.
R.S.L.—Biog. (5) p37-44 (por.37)

Cole, Frank Nelson (1861-1926). Amer. mathematician.
Smith—Math. p140-141

Cole (or Coles) **William** (1626-1662). Eng. botanist, naturalist.
Arber—Herbals p252-255,262,263
Gunther—Early XI p51-52

Cole, William (1635-1716). Eng. physician.
Gunther—Early XI p288-290

Cole-Hamilton, John Beresford (1894-1945). Eng. aero. pioneer.
Curr. Biog. '45 p116-117

Coleman, Arthur (1852-1939). Can. geologist.
G.S.A.—Proc. '39 p167-171 (por.167)

Coles.   See **Cole, William** (1626-1662)

Coli, François (1890-1927). Fr. aero. pioneer.
Heinmuller—Man's p322 (por.322)
La Croix—They p55-81 (por.98)

Colin, Jean Jacques (1784-1865). Fr. chemist.
Chambers—Dict. col.105

Colles, Abraham (1773-1843). Irish surgeon.
Hammerton p422   Major—History (2) p680-681
Leonardo—Lives p109-111

Collie, Sir John (1860-1935). Scot. surgeon.
Hammerton p422

Collier, Arthur J. (1866-1939). Amer. geologist.
G.S.A.—Proc. '39 p181-183 (por.181)

Collin, V. (fl.1823). Fr. physician.
Major—History (2) p708

Collins, Edward Treacher (1862-1932). Eng. surgeon.
Hammerton p423

Collins, George Lewis (1874-1940). Amer. physician, public health worker.
Curr. Biog. '40 p184

Collins, John (1625-1683). Eng. mathematician.
Ball—Short p315-316

Collins, William Henry (1878-1937). Can. geologist.
G.S.A.—Proc. '37 p157-161 (por.157)

Collins, Sir William Job (b.1859). Eng. physician.
Hammerton p423-424

Collishaw, Raymond (1893-   ). Can. aero. pioneer.
Burge—Ency. p629

Collyer, Charles B. D. (1898-1928). Amer. aero. pioneer.
Heinmuller—Man's p126-136,330
   (por.133,330)

Collyer, John Lyon (1893-   ). Amer. engineer.
Curr. Biog. '47 p125-128 (por.126)

Colman, Norman Jay (1827-1911). Amer. agriculturist.
*Ivins—Fifty p359-363 (por.361)

Colombo, (Matteo) Realdo of Cremona (1516-1559?). It. anatomist, physician.
Castiglioni—Hist. p435-436   Major—History (1) p410,491-492
Gordon—Medieval p635-636   (por.493)

Colot family, (16th-18th cent.). Fr. physician, surgeon.
Leonardo—Lives (Supp.1) p476

Colt, Samuel (1814-1862). Amer. inventor.
*Burlingame—Mach. p105-115   *Larsen—Prentice p127-128
Hammerton p425   *Wildman—Famous (2d) p51-60
*Hylander—Invent. p206-207   (por.51)

Colton, Gardner Quincy (1814-1898). Amer. chemist.
Chambers—Dict. col.105

Columbus, Christopher (1446/1451-1506). It. sci. explorer.
Hawks—Pioneers p115-118 (por.108)   Tuska—Invent. p122
*Science—Miles. p25-28 (por.25)

Columbus, Matthaeus (or Mathew) **Realdus** (1500-1559). It. anatomist. physician, surgeon.
Lambert—Medical p121-122   Woodruff—Devel. p268
Lambert—Minute p121-122   Year—Pic p81
Leonardo—Lives (supp 1) p476-477

Columna, (or Colonna) **Fabius** (1567-1650). It. botanist.
Arber—Herbals p97-100,168,243
  (por.98)

Colwell, Ethel (n.d.) Can. aero. pioneer.
Knapp—New p117-128 (por.179)

Combe, Andrew (1797-1847). Scot. physiologist.
Hammerton p426

Combe, James S. (1796-1883). Scot. physician.
Major—History (2) p712

Commodus.   See **Verus, Lucius Aurelius**

Common, Andre Ainslie (1841-1903). Eng. astronomer.
Chambers—Dict. col.106

Compere, George (1858-1928). Amer. entomologist.

Essig—Hist. p574-575

Compton, Arthur Holly (1892-1962). Amer. physicist.

*Bolton—Famous p259-269
Chambers—Dict. col.106-107
  (por.107)
Curr. Biog. '40 p184-186 (por.185); '58
  p99-101 (por.100)
Fisher—Amer. p223-225 (por.222)
Hammerton p427
*Hartman—Mach. p9-11
Heathcote—Nobel p259-268 (por.240)
*Hylander—Scien. p160-163

Jaffe—Outposts p400-411 (por.378)
Morris—Ency. p645
Progress—Science '40 p111-112
  (por.112)
Riedman—Men p188-199 (por.200)
*Shippen—Design p196
Weber—College p447 (por.447)
Wilson—Amer. p394-395 (por.395)
Year—Pic p213 (por.213)

Compton, Karl Taylor (1887-1954). Amer. physicist.

*Bolton—Famous p259-269
Curr. Biog. '41 p161-163 (por.162,
  '54 p196

Fisher—Amer. p223-225 (por.222)
Fitzhugh—Concise p773-774

Comstock, Anna Botsford (1854-1930). Amer. entomologist.

Essig—Hist. p577 (por.577)
Osborn—Fragments p178 (por.350)

Smiths.—Misc. (84) p57-61
  (por.545.pl.4)

Comstock, Cyrus Vallou (1831-1910). Amer. engineer.

N.A.S.—Biog. (7) p195-201 (por.195)

Comstock, George Cary (1855-1934). Amer. astronomer.

N.A.S.—Biog. (20) p161-174
  (por.161).

Comstock, John Henry (1849-1931). Amer. entomologist.

Essig—Hist. p575-578 (por.576)
Hammerton p428
Osborn—Fragments p177-178
  (por.350)

Smiths.—Misc. (84) p57-61
  (por.545.pl.4)

Comte, (Isidore) Auguste Marie François Xavier (1798-1857). Fr. nat.
philosopher.

Chambers—Dict. col.107

Conant, James Bryant (1893-   ). Amer. chemist.

Chambers—Dict. col.107
Curr. Biog. '41 p163-165 (por.163),
  '51 p129-132 (por.130)
Fisher—Amer. p263-265 (por.262)

Fitzhugh—Concise p774-775
Progress—Science '41 p104-105
  (por.104)
*Snyder—Biology p320-321 (por.321)

Condamine, C. M. de La.   See **La Condamine, Charles Marie de**

Condit, Daniel Dale (1886-1955). Amer. geologist.
G.S.A.—Proc. '55 p115-118 (por.115)

Condon, Edward Uhler (1902-   ). Amer. physicist.
Curr. Biog. '46 p127-129 (por.128)   Progress—Science '40 p112-113
Newman—What p98-101   (por.113)

Condorcet, Marie Jean Antoine Nicolas de Caritat, Marquis de (1743-1794). Fr. mathematician.
Chambers—Dict. col.107-108   Smith—Hist. I p481-482
People p97

Congreve, Sir William, Bart (1772-1828). Eng. inventor.
Chambers—Dict. col.108   *Williams—Rocket p3-30 (por.114)
Hammerton p430-431

Coningham, Sir Arthur (1895-1948). Austral. aero. pioneer.
Curr.Biog. '44 p108-110 (por.109), '48
   p111

Conklin, Edwin Grant (1863-1952). Amer. biologist.
N.A.S.—Biog. ('31) p54-75 (por.54)

Conn, Herbert William (1859-1917). Amer. bacteriologist.
Bulloch—Hist. p359

Conn, Jerome W. (1907-   ). Amer. physician.
Rowntree—Amid p552-555
   (por.550)

Conneau, Jean (or Beaumont, André, pseud). Fr. aero. pioneer.
Heinmuller—Man's p288 (por.288)

Connell, Karl (1879?-1941). Amer. physician, surgeon, inventor.
Curr. Biog. '41 p168

Conner, Phineas Sanborn (1839-1909). Amer. surgeon.
Leonardo—Lives p111

Connolly, Joseph Peter (1890-1947). Amer. geologist.
G.S.A.—Proc. '47 p135-138 (por.135)

Connor, Harry P. (1890-   ). Amer. aero. pioneer.
Heinmuller—Man's p340 (por.340)

Conolly, John (1796-1866). Fr. physician.
Farmer—Doctors' p121

Conon of Samos (fl. 3d. cent.) Gr. mathematician.
Hammerton p431

Conrad, Frank (1874-1941). Amer. elec. engineer, inventor.
*Men—Scien. p13-15
Radio's 100 p180-183 (por.140)

Conrad, Timothy Abbott (1803-1877). Amer. geologist, paleontologist, naturalist.
Merrill—First p201-202 (por.188)
Youmans—Pioneers p385-393
(por.385)

Constantine the African (or Constantinus Africanus) (c1020-c1087). African physician, surgeon.
Gordon—Medieval p321-322   Major—History (1) p270
Leonardo—Lives p111-113   Sigerist—Great p90-93 (por.88)

Conte.   See also **Le Conte**

Conte, Nicolas Jacques (1755-1805). Fr. inventor.
Hammerton p436

Conybeare, William Daniel (1787-1857). Eng. geologist.
Hammerton p437
Woodruff—Devel. p268

Coode ,Sir John (1816-1892). Eng. engineer.
Hammerton p437

Cook, Albert John (1842-1916). Amer. entomologist.
Essig—Hist. p578-581 (por.579)
Osborn—Fragments p224-225
(por.348)

Cook, Charles Wilford (1882-1933). Amer. geologist.
G.S.A.—Proc. '33 p181-182 (por.181)

Cook, Frederick Albert (1865-1940). Amer. sci. explorer.
Curr. Biog. '40 p187 (por.187)
Hammerton p437

Cook, George Hammell (1818-1889). Amer. geologist.
Merrill—First p421-422 (por.422)
N.A.S.—Biog. (4) p135-143

Cook, James J. (1728-1779). Eng. sci. explorer, naturalist.
Alden—Early p7-9
Bodenheimer—Hist. p311
Hammerton p438-439 (por.438)
*Snyder—Biology p335

Cook, Melville (or Melvin) **Thurston** (1869-1952.). Amer. botanist, entomologist.
Osborn—Fragments p225 (por.364)

Cooke, Josiah Parsons (1827-1894). Amer. chemist, mineralogist.
Chambers—Dict. col.108
Killeffer—Eminent p9 (por.9)
N.A.S.—Biog. (4) p175-180
Smith—Chem. p301-306 (por.302)

Cooke, Matthew (1829-1887). Irish-Amer. entomologist.
Essig—Hist. p581-584 (por.582)

Cooke, Mordecai Cubitt (1825-1913). Eng. mycologist.
Hammerton p439

Cooke, Morris Llewellyn (1872-1960). Amer. engineer.
Curr. Biog. '50 p95-97, May'60
'60 p97

Cooke, Sir William Fothergill (1806-1879). Brit. elec. pioneer.
Hammerton p439

Coolidge, William David (1873-   ). Amer. phys. chemist.
Curr. Biog. '47 p132-135 (por.133)
Progress—Science '41 p105 (por.105)
Radio's 100 p169-171 (por.140)

Coon, Carleton Stevens (1904-   ). Amer. anthropologist, archaeologist.
Curr. Biog. '55 p136-138 (por.137)

Coons, Albert Hewett (1912-   ). Amer. physician.
Curr. Biog. '60 p97-98 (por.98)

Cooper, Sir Astley Paston (1768-1841). Eng. physician, surgeon.
Chambers—Dict. col.108-109.
Hale-White—Great p22-41
Hammerton p439-440 (por.440)
Leonardo—Lives p113-115
Major—History (2) p692-694
(por.693)

Cooper, Elias S. (1822-1862). Amer. surgeon.
Leonardo—Lives p115-117

Cooper, Ellwood (1829-1918). Amer. entomologist.
Essig—Hist. p585-587 (por.586)

Cooper, Hugh Lincoln (1865-1937). Amer. engineer.
*Lockhart—My p125 (por.124)

Cooper, James Graham (1856-1911). Amer. entomologist.
Essig—Hist. p588

Cooper, Peter (1791-1883). Amer. inventor.
*Book—Pop. Sci. (4) p1417-1418   Morris—Ency. p647
   (por.1417)   *Watson—Engineers p73-78 (por.72)
Goddard—Eminent p100-110
   (por.100)

Cooper, Thomas (1759-1839). Amer. chemist.
Bell—Early p52   Merrill—First p86-88 (por.87)
Jaffe—Men p78-103 (por.xxviii)   Smith—Chem. p128-146 (por.128)

Cope, Edward Drinker (1840-1897). Amer. paleontologist, naturalist.
*Book—Pop. Sci. (4) p1148-1150   N.A.S.—Biog. (13) p127-171 (por.127)
   (por.1149)   Osborn—Impr. p149-164 (por.149)
Hammerton p441   Van Wagenen—Beacon p383-385
*Hylander—Scien. p94-98 (por.98) Williams—Story p114-121,318-319
Jordan—Leading p313-340 (por.313)   (por.106)
Locy—Biology p105-339 (por.338) Woodruff—Devel. p268
Merrill—First p528-530 (por.514,528) Young—Biology p39-42

Copeland, Ralph (1837-1905). Brit. astronomer, sci. explorer.
MacPherson—Astron. p71-76 (por.71)

Copernicus, Nicholas (or Kopernik, Mikolaj) (1473-1543). Pol.
   astronomer.
Abetti—History p67-81 (por.5,146)   People p100
Ball—Great (por.33)   Sarton—Six p55-62 (por.56)
Ball—Short p213-214   Schwartz—Moments (1) p217-220
*Bolton—Famous p109 (por.1)   *Science—Miles p32-36 (por.32)
Book—Pop. Sci. (6) p1930-1931   Sedgwick—Short p194-203
Chambers—Dict. col.109 (por.110)   Sewell—Brief p44
*Cottler—Heroes p89-97   Shapley—Astron. p1
*Crowther—Scientists p13-47 (por.32) *Simmons—Great p12-13 (por.12)
Dreyer—Hist. p305-344   Smith—Hist. I p346-348 (por.347)
Fitzhugh—Concise p143-144   Smith—Portraits, vol. I, II, unp. (por.)
Gibson—Heroes p51-55   *Snyder—Biology p81-82
Ginzburg—Adven. p74-96 (por.80)   *Stevens—Science p13-15 (por.12)
Gumpert—Trail p105-108   Thomas—Scien. p23-32 (por.21)
Hammerton p441   Trattner—Arch. p11-45 (por.22)
Hart—Makers p69-78 (por.69)   Tuska—Invent. p122
Hooper—Makers p110-111   Van Wagenen—Beacon p58-61
Koestler—Sleep. p119-187   Vaucouleurs—Disc. p42-46
Lenard—Great p12-16 (por.13)   Williams—Great p111-122 (por.108)
Lodge—Pioneers p2-31 (por.12)   Wilson—Human p86-92
MacPherson—Makers p1-7   Woodruff—Devel. p142-145,268
   (por.,front)   (por.138)
Moulton—Auto. p58-59   Year—Pic. p74,75,77 (por.75)

Copland, James (1791-1870). Eng. physician.
Hammerton p441

Coppens, Willy (1892-   ). Belg. aero. pioneer.
Heinmuller—Man's p305 (por.305)

Coquillett, Daniel William (c1850/1856-1908/1911). Amer. entomologist.
Essig—Hist. p588-592 (por.589)
Osborn—Fragments p203-204
  (por.358)

Corbeil.   See **Aegidius, Pierre Gilles Corbeil de**

Cordier, Pierre Louis Antoine (1777-1862). Fr. min. engineer, geologist.
Woodruff—Devel. p268

Cordus, Euricius (1486-c1535). Ger. physician.
Gordon—Medieval p741
Hawks—Pioneers p140-143

Cordus, Valerius (or Cardi) (1515-1544). Ger. naturalist, botanist.
Arber—Herbals p74-76,157-159
Bodenheimer—Hist. p224
Gordon—Medieval p660
Hawks—Pioneers p141-143
Major—History (1) p471
Miall—Early p28
Reed—Short p65-66
Sarton—Six p135
Woodruff—Devel. p268-269

Cori, Carl Ferdinand (1896-   ). Amer. biochemist.
Chambers—Dict. col.109
Curr. Biog. '47 p135-137 (por.136)
Stevenson—Nobel p248-249,250-254
  (por.150)
Year—Pic p221 (por.221)

Cori, Gerty Theresa Radnitz (1896-1957). Czech. biochemist.
Curr. Biog. '47 p135-137 (por.136)
Lovejoy—Women p197 (por.198)
Stevenson—Nobel p249,250-254
  (por.150)
Year—Pic p221 (por.221)
Yost—Women Mod. p1-16
  (por.,front.)

Corliss, George H. (1817-1888). Amer. inventor, engineer.
Abbot—Great p163-165 (por.161)
Goddard—Eminent p110-121
  (por.110)
*Hodgins—Behemoth p260-264
*Hylander—Invent. p199-200

Cormontaingne, Louis de (c1697-1752). Fr. engineer.
Hammerton p443

Cornaro, Luigi (1467/1475-1566). Aust. hygienist.
Sarton—Six p202-204 (por.24)

Cornell, Ezra (1807-1874). Amer. inventor.
*Yost—Science p1-17

Cornet, George (1858-1915). Ger. bacteriologist, physician.
Bulloch—Hist. p359

Cornil, André Victor (1837-1908). Fr. bacteriologist.
Bulloch—Hist. p359

Corning, James Leonard (1855-1923). Amer. neurologist, physician, surgeon.
Robinson—Victory p295 (por.251)

Cornu, Marie Alfred (1841-1902). Fr. physicist.
Hammerton p444

Corradi, Giuseppe (1830-1907). It. surgeon.
Leonardo—Lives p117

Corrigan, Dominic John (1802-1880). Irish physician.
Major—History (2) p685-686
  (por.684)
Walsh—Makers p200-214

Corrigan, Douglas (1907-   ). Amer. aero. pioneer.
*Fraser—Famous p310-342 (por.222)   Heinmuller—Man's p353 (por.353)
*Fraser—Heroes p813-819 (por.814)

Cortesi, Giambattista (1554-1636). It. anatomist, surgeon.
Major—History (1) p477

Corvisart des Marets, Jean Nicholas (1755-1821). Fr. physician.
Castiglioni—Hist. p699 (por.699)   Lambert—Minute p213-214
Gordon—Romance p223 (por.223)   Major—History (2) p653-659
Lambert—Medical p213-214   (por.655)
                   Sigerist—Great p272-276 (por.273)

Cosmas, Saint (or Kosmas, Indicopleustes) (522-547). Egypt. astronomer.
Dreyer—Hist. p214-219
Major—History (1) p208,220
  (por.209)

Coste, Eugene (1859-1940). Can. geologist.
G.S.A.—Proc. '40 p185-188 (por.185)

Coster, Dirk (1889-   ). Dutch physicist, meteorologist.
Chambers—Dict. col.109
Weeks—Discovery p517,518 (por.518)

Coster, Lourens Janszoon (fl. 1440). Dutch inventor.
Wilson—Human p80-83

Costes, Dieudonné (1892-   ). Fr. aero. pioneer.
*Fraser—Heroes p535-539,577-582   Heinmuller—Man's p325,340
Hammerton p447   (por.325,340)

Cotes, Roger (1682-1716). Eng. mathematician.
Ball—Short p382-383   Smith—Hist. I p447-448
Cajori—Hist. p726   Woodruff—Devel. p269

Cotta, Bernhard von (1808-1879). Ger. geologist.
Hammerton p447
Woodruff—Devel. p177-178,269

Cottam, Clarence (1899-   ). Amer. biologist, naturalist.
*Milne—Natur. p174-175

Cotton, Sir Arthur Thomas (1803-1899). Eng. engineer.
Hammerton p448

Cottrell, Frederick Gardner (1877-1948). Amer. phys. chemist,
metallurgist.
Chambers—Dict. col.110   N.A.S.—Biog. (27) p1-7 (por.1)
Killeffer—Eminent p31 (por.31) *Yost—Science p207-223

Cotugno, Domenico (or Cotunnius) (1736-1822). It. physician, anatomist.
Castiglioni—Hist. p601 (por.599)
Major—History (2) p637

Couch, Jonathan (1789-1870). Eng. naturalist.
Hammerton p448

Coué, Emilé (1857-1926). Fr. physician.
Hammerton p448 (por.448)

Coues, Elliott (1842-1899). Amer. ornithologist.
*Book—Pop. Sci. (4) p1150-1152   N.A.S.—Biog. (6) p395-426
(por.1151)   (por.395)
Hammerton p448   Peattie—Gather. p267-272

Coulomb, Charles Augustin de (1736-1806). Fr. physicist, engineer.

Chalmers—Historic p263
Chambers—Dict. col. 110-111
Hart—Physicists p99-101
Lenard—Great p149-158 (por.158)
Magie—Source p97-98

Morgan—Men p30-31
Radio's 100 p22-24
Van Wagenen—Beacon p169-170
Woodruff—Devel. p52,55,269
Year—Pic. p105 (por.105)

Coulter, Calvin Brewster (1888-1940). Amer. pathologist, bacteriologist.

Curr. Biog. '40 p201

Coulter, John Merle (1851-1928). Amer. botanist.

N.A.S.—Biog. ('14) p99-108 (por.99)

Coulter, Thomas (1793-1843). Irish Botanist, naturalist.

Dakin—Perennial p34-35

Councilman, William Thomas (1854-1933). Amer. pathologist, physician.

Bulloch—Hist. p359
Cushing—Medical p285-298

Kagan—Modern p151 (por.151)
N.A.S.—Biog. (18) p157-167
   (por.157)

Couper, Archibald Scott (1831-1892). Scot. chemist.

Chambers—Dict. col.111
Findlay—Hundred p321

*Kendall—Young p105-115 (por.114)
Partington—Short p289-290

Coupet, Louis (1892-   ). Fr. aero. pioneer.

Heinmuller—Man's p308 (por.308)

Courmont, Jules (1865-1917). Fr. bacteriologist.

Bulloch—Hist. p360

Cournand, André F. (1895-   ). Fr.-Amer. physician.

Curr. Biog. '57 p117-119 (por.118)

Courtois, Bernard (1777-1838). Fr. chemist.

Chambers—Dict. col.111
Weeks—Discovery p442-446

Cousteau, Jacques-Yves (1911-   ). Fr. engineer, oceanographer.

Curr. Biog. '53 p127-129 (por.128)

Coutelle, Jean Marie Joseph (1748-1835). Fr. aero. pioneer.

Heinmuller—Man's p236 (por.236)

Cowdry, Edmund Vincent (1888-   ). Can. anatomist.

Curr. Biog. '48 p118-120 (por.119)
Progress—Science '41 p105-106

Cowell, Philip Herbert (1870-1949). Eng. astronomer.
Chambers—Dict. col.111

Cowper, William (1666-1709). Eng. surgeon, anatomist.
Hammerton p452
Major—History (2) p628-629

Cox, Alfred (1866-1954). Eng. physician.
Fabricant—Why p173-174

Cox, Harold Rea (1907-   ). Amer. bacteriologist.
Curr. Biog. '61 (Apr.) (por.)

Coxe, John Redman (1773-1864). Amer. chemist.
Smith—Chem. p223

Coxwell, Henry Tracey (1819-1900). Eng. aero. pioneer.
Burge—Ency. p629-630   Heinmuller—Man's p241 (por.241)
*Cohen—Men p40-41   *Shippen—Bridle p71-76
Hammerton p453

Coze, Léon (1817-1896). Fr. bacteriologist.
Bulloch—Hist. p360

Crafts, James Mason (1839-1917). Amer. physicist, chemist.
*Book—Pop. Sci. (5) p1773   Smith—Torch. p52 (por.52)
N.A.S.—Biog. (9) p159-169 (por.159)

Cragin, Edwin Bradford (1859-1918). Amer. surgeon.
Leonardo—Lives p117-118

Craig, Charles Franklin (1872-1950). Amer. physician.
Major—History (2) p1031

Craig, Cleo Frank (1893-   ). Amer. engineer.
Curr. Biog. '51 p141-142 (por.141)

Craig, Sir James (1861-1933). Irish physician.
Hammerton p454

Cramer, Gabriel (1704-1752), Swiss mathematician.
Ball—Short p371-372
Smith—Hist. 1 p.520

Crane, Evan Jay (1889-   ). Amer. chemist.
Browne—Hist. p495 (por.339)

Crane, Jocelyn (1909-   ). Amer. zoologist.
Yost—Women Mod. p108-123
(port.,front.)

Cranston, John A. (1625-1680). Amer. physician.
Weeks—Discovery p497,498 (por.498)

Crary, Donald (1917-1957). Amer. geologist.
G.S.A.—Proc. '57 p177

Crateas (c100-60 B.C.). Gr. physician.
Gordon—Medicine p637

Craw, Alexander (1850-1908). Scot.-Amer. entomologist.
Essig—Hist. p593-595 (por.593)

Crawford, Adair (1748-1795). Irish physician.
Chambers—Dict. col.112
Weeks—Discovery p302-303

Crawford, Frederick Coolidge (1891-   ). Amer. engineer.
Curr. Biog. '43 p151-153 (por.151)

Crawford, Morris Barker (1852-1940). Amer. physician.
Curr. Biog. '40 p203 (pop.203)

Crawford, Ralph Dixon (1873-1950). Amer. geologist.
G.S.A.—Proc. '50 p97-99 (por.97)

Credé, Carl Sigismund Franz (1819-1892). Fr. physician.
Atkinson—Magic p261-263

Credner, Carl Hermann (1843-1913). Ger. geologist.
Hammerton p457

Crell, D. Lorentz, von (1744-1816). Ger. chemist.
Weeks—Discovery p319 (por.319)

Cremona, Luigi (1830-1903). It. mathematician.
Cajori—Hist. p295-296
Hammerton p458
*Miller—Hist. p264-265

Cresson, Ezra Townsend (1838-1926). Amer. entomologist.
Essig—Hist. p595-597 (por.596)
Osborn—Fragments p186 (por.350)

Crichton-Browne, Sir James (1840-1938). Scot. physician, neurologist.
Hammerton p459 (por.459)

Crile, George Washington (1864-1942). Amer. physician, surgeon.
Castiglioni—Hist. p1002
Curr. Biog. '43 p154
Fabricant—Why p144-145
Hammerton p459
Leonardo—Lives p118-120
Major—History (2) p1031

Cripps, Richard Stafford (1889-1952). Eng. chemist.
R.S.L.—Biog. (1) p11-32 (por.11)

Cristofori, Bartolommeo (1655-1731). It. inventor.
*Pratt—Famous p77-79

Crocker, William (1876-1950). Amer. botanist.
Progress—Science '41 p106 (por.106)

Croll, James (1821-1890). Scot. geologist.
Hammerton p460

Croll, Oswald (1580-1609). Ger. physician.
Major—History (1) p552

Crommelin, Andrew Claude de la Cherois (1865-1939). Eng. astronomer.
Hammerton p461

Crompton, Rookes Evelyn Bell (1845-1940). Eng. elec. engineer.
Curr. Biog. '40 p207 (por.207)

Crompton, Samuel (1753-1827). Eng. inventor.
*Book—Pop. Sci. (4) p1419-1420 (por.1419)
Chambers—Dict. col.112
*Darrow—Masters p48-49 (por.160)
*Darrow—Thinkers p90-92
*Epstein—Real p152-154
Hammerton p461 (por. 461)
*Larsen—Prentice p64-66
Law—Civiliz. p88-90
Year—Pic p139 (por.139)

Cronin, Archibald Joseph (1896-   ). Scot. physician.
Fabricant—Why p108

Cronstedt, Axel Fredrik, Baron (1722-1765). Swed. chemist, metallurgist.
Chambers—Dict. col.112
Lindroth—Swedish p97-104
Weeks—Discovery p70-72,323 (por.323)

Crookes, Sir William (1832-1919). Eng. chemist, physicist.

*Book—Pop. Sci. (5) p1773-1774 (por.1774)
Chalmers—Historic p263-264
Chambers—Dict. col.112-113 (por.114)
*Darrow—Masters p330-331
Findlay—British p11-29 (por.11)
Findlay—Hundred p321
Hammerton p463-464 (por. 464)
Holmyard—British p59-61 (por.59)
Lenard—Great p344-350 (por.349)

Magie—Source p563-564
Partington—Short p353
Radio's 100 p68-70 (por.140)
Smith—Torch. p53 (por. 53,54)
Tilden—Famous p259-272 (por.**259**)
Van Wagenen—Beacon p360-361
Weeks—Discovery p374-377 (por.376)
Woodruff—Devel. p269
Year—Pic. p178,208 (por.178)

Crookshank, Edgar March (1858-1928). Eng. bacteriologist.

Bulloch—Hist. p360

Croone, William (1633-1684). Eng. physician.

Major—History (1) p558

Crosby, Dixi (1800-1873). Amer. surgeon.

Leonardo—Lives p120-121

Cross, Charles Frederick (1855-1935). Eng. chemist.

Chambers—Dict. col.113

Cross, Charles Whitman (1854-1949). Amer. geologist.

N.A.S.—Biog. (32) p100-104 (por.100)

Crosse, Andrew (1784-1855). Eng. elec. pioneer.

Hammerton p46

Crossfield, Alfred Scott (1921-   ). Amer. aero. pioneer, engineer, space pioneer.

Thomas—Men (2) p1-25 (por.106)

Crosson, Joseph Esler (1903-   ). Amer. aero. pioneer.

Potter—Flying p97-114 (por.114)

Crotch, George Robert (1842-1874). Amer. entomologist.

Essig—Hist. p598-600 (por.598)

Crum, Harry E. (1892-1955). Amer. geologist.

G.S.A.—Proc. '55 p121-122 (por.121)

Crum Brown.   See Brown, (Alexander) Crum

Crumbine, Samuel J. (1862-1954). Amer. physician.

Fabricant—Why p175-177

Crump, Norris Roy (1904-   ). Can. engineer.
Curr. Biog. '57 p121-123 (por.122)

Cruveilhier, Jean Baptiste (1791-1874). Fr. pathologist, anatomist.
Castiglioni—Hist. p690 (por.690)   Major—History (2) p673-675
Lambert—Medical p204   (por.674)

Cruz, Oswald (1872-1917). Brazil. physician, hygienist.
Major—History (2) p920,1003

Cruzen, Richard Harold (1897-   ). Amer. engineer, sci. explorer.
Curr. Biog. '47 p143-145 (por.144)

Ctesibius (or Ctesibios) (fl.2d cent. B.C.) Alex. physicist, inventor.
Matschoss—Great p13-15
Year—Pic. p39

Ctseias (fl.5th cent. B.C.). Gr. physician, surgeon.
Gordon—Medicine p495-496

Cubitt, Sir William, (1785-1861). Eng. engineer.
Hammerton p465

Cugnot, Nicolas Joseph (1725-1804). Fr. engineer.
Chambers—Dict. col.113   Law—Civiliz. p51-53
*Epstein—Real p64-65   Meyer—World p93
*Hodgins—Behemoth

Cullen, Glenn Ernest (1890-1940). Amer. biochemist.
Curr. Biog. '40 p213 (por. 213)

Cullen, William (1710-1790). Scot. physician.
Castiglioni—Hist. p585-586   Lambert—Minute p151-152
Chambers—Dict. col.114   Major—History (2) p589-591
Farmer—Doctors' p28   (por.590)
Holmyard—Makers p164-166   Oliver—Stalkers p138
   (por.164)   Sigerist—Great p199 (por. 200)
Lambert—Medical p151-152

Cullis, Winifred Clara (1875-1956). Eng. physiologist.
Curr. Biog. '43 p158-159 (por.158)

Culmann, Karl (1821-1881). Ger. mathematician, engineer.
Cajori—Hist. p296-297

Culpeper, Nicholas (1616-1654). Eng. botanist, physician.
Arber—Herbals p261,262,263   Major—History (1) p546
  (por.262)
Gordon—Medieval p605 (por.83)

Culver, Garry E. (1849-1938). Amer. geologist.
G.S.A.—Proc. '38 p143-145 (por. 143)

Culver, H. P. (1893-   ). Amer. aero. pioneer.
Heinmuller—Man's p304 (por.304)

Cuming, Hugh (1791-1865). Eng. naturalist.
Davison—Founders p35-37

Cummings, Bruce Frederick (or W. N. P. Barbellion, pseud.) (1889-1919). Eng. biologist, naturalist.
Hammerton p184

Cunningham, David Douglas (1843-1914). Eng. pathologist, bacteriologist, naturalist.
Bulloch—Hist. p360

Cunningham, James (d.1709). Scot. physician, botanist.
Reed—Short p92

Cunningham, William Francis (1885-1940). Amer. pathologist.
Curr. Biog. '41 p192

Curbull.   See **Aegidius, Pierre Gilles Corbeil de**

Curie, Irene.   See **Joliot-Curie, Irène**

Curie, Marja (or Marie) **Sklodowska** (1867-1934). Pol. phys. chemist, physicist.
*Bolton—Famous p211-221 (por.210)   *Darrow—Masters p238-252 (por.65)
*Book—Pop. Sci. (5) p1775 (por.1766)   *Darrow—Thinkers p288-290 (por.289)
*Bridges—Master p63-69 (por.66)   Farber—Nobel p46-49
Calder—Science p64-66   Findlay—Hundred p335
Castiglioni—Hist. p926 (por.1073)   Fitzhugh—Concise p152-153
Chambers—Dict. col. 114-115   Hammond—Stories p120-134
  (por.115)   (por.123)
*Compton—Conquests p136-149   Harrow—Chemists p155-176
  (por.122)   (por.155)
*Cottler—Heroes p156-165   Heathcote—Nobel p18-26 (por.240)
*Crowther—Scientists p181-221   *Jaffe—Crucibles p242-264
  (por.208)

(Continued)

Curie, Marja—*Continued*
*Kendall—Young p209-220
   (por.211,212,220)
*Larsen—Prentice p136-140
*Larsen—Scrap. p132-135 (por.144)
Law—Civiliz. p 290-294
Lovejoy—Women p161-163,172-173
   (por.162)
*McSpadden—How p231-244 (por.234)
Magie—Source p613
*Montgomery—Story p121-126
Moulton—Auto. p492-493
Mozans—Woman p221-222
*Nisenson—Illus. p47 (por.47)
*Nisenson—More p43 (por. 43)
100 Great p662-667
Partington—Short p364 (por.357)
People p103
*Pratt—Famous p130-131
Riedman—Men p17-45 (por. 41,56-57)

Schwartz—Moments (2) p888-890
*Science—Miles p276-279 (por. 276)
Sewell—Brief p218-219
*Shippen—Design p186-191
*Simmons—Great p58-62 (por.58)
Smith—Torch. p55 (por.55,56)
*Stevens—Science p142-147 (por.141)
Thomas—Scien. p265-280 (por.263)
Untermeyer—Makers p368-378
Van Wagenen—Beacon p426-430
Weber—College p70 (por.70)
Weeks—Discovery p485-507,531-534
   (por. 490,503)
*Williams—Ellis p208-224 (por.207)
Wilson—Amer. p333 (por.333)
Woodruff—Devel. p269
*Wright—Great p142-151
Year—Pic. p208 (por.208)

Curie, Pierre (1859-1906). Fr. physicist, chemist.
*Bolton—Famous p211-221 (por.210)
•Bridges—Master p62-69 (por.63)
Chambers—Dict. col.115
*Compton—Conquests p136-149
   (por.122)
Fitzhugh—Concise p152-153
Hammond—Stories p116-134
Heathcote—Nobel p18,22-26 (por.240)
*Kendall—Young p211-218 (por.211)
*Larsen—Prentice p136-140
Magie—Source p613

100 Great p662-667
Riedman—Men p17-45 (por.33,41)
Schwartz—Moments (2) p888-890
*Shippen—Design p186-191
*Simmons—Great p58-62 (por.58)
*Stevenson—Science p144-147
   (por.141)
Weber—College p60 (por.60)
Weeks—Discovery p484-507,531-534
   (por.484)
Wilson—Amer. p333 (por.333)
Year—Pic. p208 (por.208)

Curling, Thomas Blizard (1811-1888). Eng. surgeon.
Major—History (2) p882

Currie, James (1756-1805). Eng. physician.
Farmer—Dictors' p49

Curtis, Charles Gordon (1860-1953). Amer. inventor.
Hodgins—Behemoth p274-275

Curtis, Heber Doust (1872-1942). Amer. astronomer.
Curr. Biog. '42 p172
N.A.S.—Biog. (22) p275-284
   (por.275)

Curtis, William (1746-1799). Brit. botanist.
Gilmour—British p30

Curtiss, Charles Franklin (1863-1947). Amer. agriculturist.
Lockhart—My p41 (por.40)

Curtiss, Glenn Hammond (1878-1930). Amer. aero. pioneer.
Burge—Ency. p630
*Cohen—Men p142-146
*Fraser—Famous p46-71 (por.62)
Hammerton p468
Heinmuller—Man's p270 (por.270)
Maitland—Knights p84-111
  (por.66,87,102)
*Shippen—Bridle p108-112
*Wilman—Famous (2d) p77-92
  (por.77)

Curtius, Ernst (1814-1896) Ger. archaeologist.
Hammerton p468

Curtius, Theodor (1857-1928). Ger. chemist.
Chambers—Dict. col.116
Partington—Short p357-364
Smith—Torch. p57 (por.57)

Cusa, Nicholas of.   See **Nicholas of Cusa**

Cushier, Elizabeth (1837-1932). Amer. physician.
Mead—Medical p85-95

Cushing, Harvey William (1869-1939). Amer. physician, surgeon, neurologist.
Carmer—Caval. p217-219 (por.218)
Castiglioni—Hist. p1003-1004
  (por.1004)
Chambers—Dist. col.116
*Chandler—Medicine p109-113
  (por.108)
Gumpert—Trail p289-298
Hammerton p469
Kagan—Modern p208
Leonardo—Lives p121-124
Major—History (2) p958-959,1031-
  1032 (por.957)
*Montgomery—Story p176-178,
  193-195
Morris—Ency. p648
Moulton—Auto. p622-623
N.A.S.—Biog. (22) p49-54 (por.49)
Rosen—Four p277-278
Rowntree—Amid p71-74 (por.73)
Young—Scalpel p224-267 (por.232)

Cushman, Joseph Augustine (1881-1949). Amer. micropaleontologist, geologist.
G.S.A.—Proc. '51 p95-101 (por.95)

Cushny, Arthur Robertson (1866-1926). Scot. physician.
Castiglioni—Hist. p894 (por.894)

Cutbush, James S. (1788-1823). Amer. chemist.
Smith—Chem. p223-224

Cutler, Elliott Carr (1888-1947). Amer. surgeon.
Leonardo—Lives p124-125

Cutler, Manasseh (1742-1823). Amer. botanist.
Bell—Early p52-53

Cuvier, Georges Léopold Chrétien Frederic Dagobert, Baron (1769-1832).
Fr. naturalist, paleontologist, anatomist, zoologist.

Adams—Birth p263-268 (por.264)
Bodenheimer—Hist. p356
*Book—Pop. Sci. (4) p1152-1154
  (por.1153)
Chambers—Dict. col.116
*Darrow—Masters p88-92 (por.64)
Geikie—Founders p211-221
Gordon—Medicine p50 (por.50)
Hammerton p469 (por.469)
Locy—Biology p130-133,148-150,
  327-328 (por.152-153)
Moulton—Auto. p253

Osborn—Greeks p278-283
Peattie—Green p164-171
*Shippen—Micro. p97-106
*Snyder—Biology p83-89 (por.85)
Thomson—Great p53-59
Van Wagenen—Beacon p213-215
Williams—Story p91-98,111,300,
  321-322 (por. 92)
Woodruff—Devel. p200-202,269
  (por.176)
*World's Great p147-161 (por.152)
Year—Pic. p126 (por.126)

Cuyler, Robert Hamilton (1908-1944). Amer. geologist.
G.S.A.—Proc. '44 p171-173 (por.171)

Czerny, Vincenz (1842-1916). Czech. surgeon.
Leonardo—Lives p125-127

D

D'Abano, Pietro (or Petrus Aponensis) (1250-1316). It. physician,
astronomer.
Castiglioni—Hist. p330-332 (por.330)
Sigerist—Great p97-99 (por.97)

Daca-Chagon.   See **Chacon, Dionysio (Denis) Daca**

Da Costa, Jacob M. (1833-1900). W. Ind. physician.
Kagan—Modern p11 (por. 11)
Major—History (2) p897

Da Costa, John Chalmers (1863-1933). Amer. physician.
Rowntree—Amid p414-419 (por.407)

D'Acquapendente.   See **Fabricius ab Acquapendente, Hieronymus**

Dacus.   See **Harpestraeng, Henrik**

Daecke, Victor A. E. (1863-1918). Ger.-Amer. entomologist.
Osborn—Fragments p202-203

Dafoe, Allan Roy (1883-1943). Can. physician.

Curr. Biog. '43 p159

d'Agoty.   See **Agoty, Jacques Gautier d'**

Daguerre, Louis Jacques Mandé (1789-1851). Fr. inventor.

A.A.A.S.—Proc. (79) p11-12
*Book—Pop. Sci. (4) p1420-1421
Chambers—Dict. col.117
*Darrow—Masters p131-135 (por.160)
*Darrow—Thinkers p173-176 (por.174)
*Epstein—Real p125
Hammerton p471 (por.471)
*Larsen—Prentice p87-89
*Larsen—Scrap. p12-16 (por.24)
Law—Civiliz. p158-166
*McSpadden—How p145-159 (por.146)
Meyer—World p77-79
*Montgomery—Invent. p82-84
Smith—Torch. p58 (por.58)
Van Wagenen—Beacon p251-253
Williams—Great p350 (por.352)
Williams—Story p284-285 (por.281)
Year—Pic. p159,161 (por. 161)

Dahl, Anders (c18th cent.). Swed. botanist.

Chambers—Dict. col.117

Dahlberg, Erik Johanssen, Count (1625-1703). Swed. engineer.

Hammerton p471

Dahlgren, John Adolf (1809-1870). Amer. inventor.

Hammerton p471

Daimler, Gottlieb (1834-1900). Ger. inventor, engineer.

Chambers—Dict. col. 117
*Eberle—Invent. p87-92 (por.86)
*Epstein—Real p58,74-75
Hammerton p471-472 (por.472)
*Hodgins—Behemoth p313-316
*Larsen—Scrap p118-121 (por.112)
Law—Civiliz. p53-54
Matschoss—Great p292-298 (por.298)
*Pratt—Famous p37-40
Year—Pic. p186 (por.186)

Dake, Charles Laurence (1883-1934). Amer. geologist.

G.S.A.—Proc. '35 p195-198 (por.195)

Dakin, Henry Drysdale (1880-1952). Eng. chemist.

Chambers—Dict. col.117-118
Hammerton p472 (por.472)

d'Albe.   See **Fournier d'Albe, Edmund Edward**

Dalcroze, Émile Jaques (1865-1950). Swiss inventor.

Hammerton p472 (por.472)

Dale, Sir Henry Hallett (1875-   ). Eng. physiologist.

Chambers—Dict. col.118
Major—History (2) p963
Stevenson—Nobel p186,187-190 (por.150)
Year—Pic. p229 (por. 229)

Dale, Thomas Pelham (1821-1892). Eng. phys. chemist.
Chambers—Dict. col.118-119

D'Alechamps, Jacques (1513-1588). Fr. botanist, physician, surgeon.
Arber—Herbals p119,171-173   Leonardo—Lives p132
(por.117)
Hawks—Pioneers p164-165

D'Alembert.   See **Alembert, Jean Le Rond D'**

Dalen, Nils Gustav (1869-1937). Swed. engineer, inventor.
Chambers—Dict. col.119   *Men—Scien. p19-21
Hammerton p472   Weber—College p196 (por.196)
Heathcote—Nobel p102-107 (por.240)

Dall, William Healey (1845-1927). Amer. anthropologist, naturalist,
paleontologist, zoologist.
N.A.S.—Biog. (31) p92-106 (por.92)

Dallinger, William Henry (1842-1909). Eng. biologist.
Bulloch—Hist. p360
Hammerton p473

Dallmeyer, John Henry (1830-1883). Ger.-Eng. optician.
Hammerton p473

Da Lonigo.   See **Leoniceno, Nicolò**

Dalton, John (1766-1844). Eng. physicist, chemist, mathematician.
Ball—Short p431   N.A.S.—Biog. (3) p177-185
*Book—Pop. Sci. (5) p1775-1776   Partington—Short p167-174,178-179
(por. 1776)   (por. 168)
Chalmers—Historic p264   People p104-105
Chambers—Dict. col.119-120   Roberts—Chem. p63-71
*Darrow—Masters p111-113 (por.33) Schwartz—Moments (2) p768-770
Gibson—Heroes p214-225   Sedgwick—Short p361-363
Ginzburg—Advent. p200-218   *Shippen—Design p97-106
Hammerton p473 (por.473)   Smith—Torch. p59 (por.59)
Holmyard—British p37-39 (por.37)   *Stevens—Science p91-94 (por.90)
Holmyard—Chem. p111-125 (por.113) Thomas—Scien. p81-95 (por.79)
Holmyard—Great Chem. p75-84   Tilden—Famous p104-118 (por.104)
Holmyard—Makers p221-240   Trattner—Arch. p72-97 (por.86)
(por.221)   Van Wagenen—Beacon p211-213
*Jaffe—Crucibles p114—135   Williams—Story p168-169,182,
Lenard—Great p177-180,183-184   252-255,262 (por.254)
(por.177)   Woodruff—Devel. p84-86,269 (por.84)
Major—History (2) p810   *World's Great p129-144 (por.132)
Moulton—Auto. p231-232   Year—Pic. p123 (por.123)

Daly, Reginald Aldworth (1871-1957). Can.-Amer. geologist.
N.A.S.—Biog. (34) p31-53 (por.31)
Progress—Science '41 p108-109
  (por. 108)

Dam, (Carl Peter) Henrik (1895-   ). Dan. biochemist.
Chambers—Dict. col.120
Curr. Biog. '49 p135-136 (por. 136)

Stevenson—Nobel p216-217,218-220
  (por.150)

Damascenus, Janus.   See **Mesuë, Senior**

D'Amecourt, Gustave de Ponton (1825-1888). Fr. inventor, aero. pioneer.
Heinmuller—Man's p246

Dame Trot.   See **Trotula of Salerno**

Damian, Saint (fl. 303 A.D.). Arab. physician.
Major—History (1) p208,220
  (por.209)

Damon, Ralph Shepard (1897-   ). Amer. engineer, aero. pioneer.
Curr. Biog. '49 p136-138 (por.137)

Dampier, William (1652-1715). Eng. naturalist, sci. explorer.
Von Hagen—Green p97-98

Dana, Charles L. (1852-1935). Amer. neurologist.
Major—History (2) p1032

Dana, Edward Salisbury (1849-1935). Amer. mineralogist.
A.A.A.S.—Proc. (77) p51-52
G.S.A.—Proc. '35 p201-208 (por.201)

N.A.S.—Biog. (18) p349-358 (por.349)

Dana, James Dwight (1813-1895). Amer. geologist, mineralogist.
*Book—Pop. Sci. (2) p717-718
  (por.717)
*Darrow—Masters p331
Fenton—Giants p214-232 (por.175)
Hammerton p475
*Hylander—Scien. p77-84 (por.77)
Jaffe—Men p258-278 (por.xxviii)

Jordan—Leading p233-268 (por.233)
Merrill—First p262-264 (por.262,263)
N.A.S.—Biog. (9) p41-83 (por.41)
True—Smiths. p265-268 (por.266)
Van Wagenen—Beacon p298-300
Woodruff—Devel. p269 (por.186)
Young—Biology p38 (por.35)

Dana, James Freeman (1793-1827). Amer. chemist.
Smith—Chem. p221-222

Dana, Samuel Luther (1795-1868). Amer. chemist.
Smith—Chem. p222
Youmans—Pioneers p311-318
  (por.311)

Dandy, Walter Edward (1886-1946). Amer. pathologist, physician,
  surgeon.
Curr. Biog. '46 p139   Major—History (2) p1032
Leonardo—Lives p127-128

D'Anghiera.   See **Peter Martyr**

Daniell, John Frederick (1790-1845). Eng. physicist, chemist, inventor.
Chambers—Dict. col.120
Hammerton p476

D'Annunzio, Gabriele (1863-1938). It. aero. pioneer.
Heinmuller—Man's p291 (por.291)

Dansyz, Jean (1860-1928). Pol.-Fr. bacteriologist.
Bulloch—Hist. p360

Darboux, Jean Gaston (1842-1917). Fr. mathematician.
Cajori—Hist. p315
Chambers—Dict. col.120

Darby, Abraham (1676/1677-c1717). Eng. engineer.
Hart—Engineers p111-115

Darcet, Jean (1725-1801). Fr. chemist.
Smith—Torch. p61 (por.61)

Darcet, Jean Pierre Joseph (1777-1844). Fr. chemist.
Hammerton p478
Smith—Torch. p62 (por.62)

Daremberg, Charles Victor (1816-1872). Fr. physician.
Major—History (2) p883

D'Argelata, Pietro (d.1423). It. physician, surgeon.
Castiglioni—Hist. p370-371
Major—History (1) p355

d'Arlandes.   See **Arlandes, le Marquis d'**

d'Arsonval.   See **Arsonval, Jacques Arsène d'**

Dart, Raymond Arthur (1893-   ). Austral. anatomist.

Darton, Nelson Horatio (1865-1948). Amer. geologist.
G.S.A.—Proc. '48 p145-162 (por.145)

Darwin, Charles Robert (1809-1882). Eng. naturalist, biologist.
Bodenheimer—Hist. p396
*Bolton—Famous p121-160 (por.120)
*Book—Pop. Sci. (6) p2021-2022
    (por.2020)
Castiglioni p669-670 (por.670)
Chambers—Dict. col.120-121
    (por.122)
*Cottler—Heroes p328-338
*Crowther—Scientists. p137-180
    (por.129)
Cutright—Great p15-19 (por., front.)
*Darrow—Masters p162-171 (por.288)
Fitzhugh—Concise p155-157
Geikie—Founders p282-284
Gibson—Heroes p265-277 (por.266)
Gilmour—British p37
Ginzburg—Adven. p300-324 (por.288)
Gordon—Medicine p18 (por.18)
Gordon—Romance p43 (por.43)
Gregory—British p26-27 (por.24)
Hammerton p480-481 (por.480)
Hammond—Stories p136-165
    (por.146)
Holmyard—British p48-50 (por.48)
Lenard—Great p308-320 (por.317)
Locy—Biology p386-397,428-435
    (por.387,431)
Major—History (2) p810-813
    (por.811)
Makers—Modern p1-124
*Milne—Natur. p77-85 (por.76)
Moulton—Auto. p349-350
Murray—Science p154-212
*Nisenson—Illus. p48 (por.48)
Oliver—Stalkers p169-172 (por.170)
100 Great p610-618 (por.56)
Osborn—Greeks p327-345
Osborn—Impr. p33-70 (por.33)
Peattie—Green p285-296,304-325
    (por.front, 295)
People p107-108 (por.127)
Robinson—Path. p511-520 (por.518)
Schwartz—Moments (2) p659-662
Sci. Amer.—Lives p195-214 (por.197)
*Science—Miles. p173 (por.173)
Sewell—Brief p145-146
*Shippen—Micro. p119-131
*Snyder—Biology p113-123 (por.123)
*Sootin—Twelve p111-139
*Stevens—Science p113-119 (por.112)
Thomas—Scien. p133-147 (por.131)
Thomson—Great p88-93
Trattner—Arch. p211-240 (por.230)
Untermeyer—Makers p1-6
Van Wagenen—Beacon p286-287
Von Hagen—Green p167
Williams—Story p105-108,302-317
    (por.304)
*Williams—Ellis p130-153
Williams—Great p324 (por.324)
Wilson—Human p306-333 (por.324)
Woodruff—Devel. p269-270 (por.215)
*World's Great p331-353 (por.340)
Year—Pic. p128-129 (por.129)

Darwin, Erasmus (1731-1802). Eng. physiologist, physician.
*Book—Pop. Sci. (6) p2023 (por.2023)
Gordon—Medicine p17 (por.17)
Hamerton p481 (por.481)
Locy—Biology p421-422 (por.421)
Major—History (2) p636-637
Murray—Science p144-148
Osborn—Greeks p202-218
Williams—Story p290-291,296
    (por.290)
Woodruff—Devel. p253-254,270
    (por.256)

Darwin, Sir Francis (1848-1925). Eng. botanist.
Hammerton p481 (por.481)

Darwin, Sir George Howard (1845-1912). Eng. astronomer, mathematician.

Armitage—Cent. p43-44 (por.80)
*Book—Pop. Sci. (8) p2567-2568 (por.2568)
Cajori—Hist. p449-450
Chambers—Dict. col.121

Hammerton p481 (por.481)
MacPherson—Astron. p156-162 (por.156)
Shapley—Astron. p397 (por.403)
Woodruff—Devel. p252-254,256-258, 270

Darwin, Leonard (1850-1943). Eng. engineer.

Curr. Biog. '43 p160
Hammerton p481 (por.481)

Daubenton, Louis Jean Marie (1716-1799). Fr. anatomist.

Hammerton p482

Daubeny, Charles Giles Bridle (1795-1867). Eng. chemist, naturalist.

Gunther—Early XI p174-175 (por.176)

Daubrée, Gabriel Auguste (1814-1896). Fr. min. engineer, mineralogist, geologist.

Woodruff—Devel. p181,270

D'Aubuisson de Voisins, Jean François (1769-1819). Fr. geologist.

Fenton—Giants p63-65
Geikie—Founders p138-141

Dauglish, John (1824-1866). Scot. inventor.

Hammerton p482

Davaine, Casimir Joseph (1812-1882). Fr. pathologist, physician, biologist.

Bulloch—Hist. p361
Chambers—Dict. col.121-122

Da Varignana, Bartolomeo (d.1318). It physician.

Castiglioni—Hist. p340-341

Davenport, Charles Benedict (1866-1944). Amer. zoologist, biologist.

Curr. Biog. '44 p142
Hammerton p483

N.A.S.—Biog. '49 p75-91 (por.75)
*Snyder—Biology p149-152 (por.151)

Davenport, Eugene (1856-1941). Amer. agriculturist.

Curr. Biog. '41 p205
*Ivins—Fifty p325-328 (por.327)

Davenport, Thomas (1802-1851). Amer. inventor.

*Hodgins—Behemoth p217-221
*Hylander—Invent. p208-209

Davey, John (1846-1923). Eng.-Amer. agriculturist.
*Ivins—Fifty p199-209 (por.198)

David, Sir Tannatt William Edgeworth (1858-1934). Austral. geologist, sci. explorer.
*Bridges—Master p70-80 (por.70)   Hammerton p1448 (por.1448)
G.S.A.—Proc. '35 p215-237 (por.215)

David de Pomis.   See **Pomis, David de**

Davidson, Anstruther (1860-1932). Scot.-Amer. entomologist.
Essig—Hist. p600-601

Davidson, George (1825-1911). Eng. geographer, astronomer.
N.A.S.—Biog. (18) p189-204
  (por.189)

Davidson, J. Brownlee (1880-1957). Amer. agric. engineer.
*Yost—Engineers p77-90

Davidson, William (1593-c1669). Scot. chemist.
Chymie v.1 p149-151 (por.150)

Davidson, William Lee (1915-   ). Amer. physicist.
Curr. Biog. '52 p136-138 (por.137)

Da Vigo, Giovanni (1460-1525). It. physician, surgeon.
Castiglioni—Hist. p470-471
Leonardo—Lives p438-439

Da Vinci.   See **Vinci, Leonardo da**

Davis, Benjamin Oliver, Jr., (1912-   ). Amer. aero. pioneer.
Curr. Biog. '55 p150-151 (por.151)

Davis, Bergen (1869-1958). Amer. physicist.
N.A.S.—Biog. (34) p.65-78 (por.65)

Davis, Carroll Campbell (1888-   ). Amer. chemist.
Browne—Hist. p495-496 (por.411)

Davis, Charles Henry (1807-1877). Amer. sci. explorer.
N.A.S.—Biog. (4) p23-55

Davis, Edward W. (1888-   ). Amer. metallurgical engineer.
Curr. Biog. '55 p152-154 (por.153)

Davis, Harvey Nathaniel (1881-1952). Amer. engineer.
Curr. Biog. '47 p147-149 (por.147),
   '53 p148

Davis, Jess Harrison (1906-   ). Amer. engineer.
Curr. Biog. '56 p142-144 (por.143)

Davis, Sir Robert Henry (b.1870). Amer.-Can. inventor.
Pringle—Great p84-100

Davis, Tenney Lombard (1890-1949). Amer. chemist.
Chymia (3) p1-6 (por.2)

Davis, Watson (1896-   ). Amer. sci. writer.
Curr. Biog. '45 p139-140 (por.140)

Davis, William E. (1896-   ). Amer. physician.
Curr. Biog. '40 p229-230 (por.230)

Davis, William Elias Brownlee (1863-1902). Amer. surgeon, gynecologist.
Leonardo—Lives p129-130

Davis, William Morris (1850-1934). Amer. geologist, geomorphologist,
   meteorologist, geographer.
Chambers—Dict. col.122   Woodruff—Devel. p270 (por.206)
N.A.S.—Biog. (23) p263-280 (por.263)

Davis, William Virginius, Jr. (1902-   ). Amer. aero. pioneer.
*Fraser—Heroes p527-533

Davison, (Frederick) Trubee (1896-   ). Amer. sci. museum dir.
Curr. Biog. '45 p141-143 (por.142)

Davisson, Clinton Joseph (1881-   ). Amer. physicist.
Chambers—Dict. col.122-123   Weber—College p623 (por.623)
Heathcote—Nobel p353-362 (por.240)   Wilson—Amer. p398-399 (por.396)
Morris—Ency. p649   Year—Pic. p210,211 (por.211)
Progress—Science '41 p109-110
   (por. 109)

Davy, Sir Humphrey (1778-1829). Eng. chemist.
Abbot—Great p3-4 (por.5)   Chambers—Dict. col.123-124
*Book—Pop. Sci. (10) p3217-3218   (por.123)
   (por.3218)   Chymia v.5 p193-201
Chalmers—Historic p264-265   *Cottler—Heroes p146-155
                    (Continued)

Davy, Sir Humphrey—*Continued*
Crowther—Men p1-66 (por.8,64)
*Darrow—Masters p67-73 (por.321)
*Darrow—Thinkers p53-56 (por.54)
Defries—Pioneers p161-170
*Epstein—Real p54,123-124
Fülöp—Miller p52-71 (por.65)
Gibson—Heroes p226-247
Gregory—British p17,19 (por.19)
Hammerton p486 (por.486)
Hart—Makers p210-232 (por.210)
*Hodgins—Behemoth p116-117,
122-125
Holmyard—British p40-41 (por.40)
Holmyard—Great Chem. p90-97
Holmyard—Makers p260-262
(por.260)
*Kendall—Young p1-41 (por.3)
Lenard—Great p190-194 (por.194)
Magie—Source p161
Major—History (2) p809-810
Masters—Conquest p61-65

Moulton—Auto. p287
Partington—Short p180-191,211-212
(por.181)
People p109
Ramsay— Essays p42-56
Roberts—Chem. p72-83
Robinson—Victory p47-55 (por.51)
Schwartz—Moments (2) p781-782
Smith—Torch. p63 (por.63)
*Sootin—Twelve p67--85
*Stevens—Science p83-88 (por.82)
Taylor—Illus. p113,115,117
Tilden—Famous p78-103 (por.78)
Van Wagenen—Beacon p231-232
Weeks—Discovery p273-278,296,440
(por.273,296,440)
Williams—Story p225,241-242,
262-265,366 (por.3)
Woodruff—Devel. p270 (por.84)
*World's Great p189-204 (por.194)
Year—Pic. p123 (por.123)

Davy, John (1790-1868). Eng. physician.
Chambers—Dict. col.124-125

Dawkins, Sir William Boyd (1837-1929). Welsh geologist, archaeologist.
Gunther—Early XI p252
Hammerton p487 (por.487)

Dawson, Bertrand Edward, 1st Baron (d.1945). Eng. physician.
Hammerton p487

Dawson, Charles (1864-1916). Eng. paleontologist.
Hammerton p487

Dawson, Sir John William (1820-1899). Can. geologist. ornithologist.
*Book—Pop. Sci. (2) p718-719
(por.719)
Fenton—Giants p193-198 (por.190)
Hammerton p487

Merrill—First p491-492 (por.490)
Tracy—Amer. Nat. p180-189

Dawson of Penn, Bertrand Dawson, 1st Viscount (1886/-1945). Eng.
physician.
Curr. Biog. '45 p145

Day, Albert M. (1897-   ). Amer. biologist.
Curr. Biog. '48 p136-138 (por.137)

Day, David Talbot (1859-1925). Amer. geologist.
G.S.A.—Proc. '33 p185-187 (por.185)

d'Azyr.   See **Vicq d'Azur, Félix**

Deacon, Henry (1822-1877). Eng. chemist.
Chambers—Dict. col.125
Smith—Torch p65 (por.65)

Dean, George (1863-1914). Scot. bacteriologist.
Bulloch—Hist. p361

Dean, George Adam (1873-1956). Amer. entomologist.
Osborn—Fragments p235 (por.368)

Dean, H. Trendley (1893-   ). Amer. epidemiologist, dental surgeon.
Curr. Biog. '57 p137-138 (por.137)

Deane, James (1801-1858). Amer. geologist.
Merrill—First p562-563 (por.558)

Dearden, Harold (1882-   ). Eng. psychologist.
Hammerton p488

Deaver, John Blair (1855-1931). Amer. surgeon.
Kagan—Modern p97 (por.97)
Leonardo—Lives p130-132

De Ballore, Fernand de Montessus (1851-   ). Fr. seismologist.
Davison—Founders p160-176

de Bary.   See **Bary, Heinrich Anton de**

de Beaumont.   See **Beaumont, Jean Baptiste Armand Louis Léonce Élie**

de Beauvais.   See **Vincent of Beauvais**

De Bierne, André Louis (1874-   ). Fr. chemist.
Weeks—Discovery p493-499,507

De Bolya.   See **Bolyai, Farkas**

De Boodt, Anselm (1550-1632). Belg. mineralogist, naturalist.
Adams—Birth p161-163

De Bordeau, Theophile (1722-1776). Fr. physiologist.
Castiglioni—Hist. p586-588

De Brahm, William Gerard (1717-1799). Amer. hydrographer.
Bell—Early p53

Debray, Henri Jules (1827-1888). Fr. chemist.
Smith—Torch. p66 (por.66)
Weeks—Discovery p264 (por. 264)

De Breau.   See **Quatrefages de Bréau, Jean Louis Armand de**

De Broglie, Louis Victor Pierre Raymond, Prince (1892-   )
Chambers—Dict. col.125
Curr. Biog. '55 p67-69 (por.68)
Hammerton p302
Heathcote—Nobel p287-304
  (por.240)
Moulton—Auto. p547-548
Weber—College p491 (por.491)
Wilson—Amer. p396-397
Year—Pic. p210-211 (por.211)

De Broglie, Maurice, Duc (1875-   ). Fr. physicist.
Chambers—Dict. col.125

Debus, Heinrich (1824-1915). Ger. chemist.
Weeks—Discovery p366 (por.366)

Debye, Peter Joseph Wilhelm (1884-   ). Dutch-Amer. physicist.
Chambers—Dict. col.125-126
Farber—Nobel p147-151 (por.118)

De Candolle.   See **Candolle, Augustin Pyrame de**

de Carvajal.   See **Carvajal, Gasper de**

de Cauliaco.   See **Chauliac, Guy de**

de Chancourtois.   See **Chancourtois, Alexandre Émile Béguyer de**

De Chardin.   See **Teilhard de Chardin, Pierre**

De Chardonnet.   See **Chardonnet, Comte Hilaire Bernigaud de**

De Chauliac.   See **Chauliac, Guy de**

De Corbeil.   See **Aegidius, Pierre Gilles Corbeil de**

De Cormontaingne.   See **Cormontaingne, Louis de**

De Coulomb.   See **Coulomb, Charles Augustin de**

De Coursey, Elbert (1902-   ). Amer. pathologist, physician.
Curr. Biog. '54 p232-233 (por.232)

De Cusa.   See **Nicholas of Cusa**

de Dacia, Petrus. (c1300). Dan. astronomer, mathematician.
Copen.—Prom. p12-15

Dedekind, Julius Wilhelm Richard (1831-1916)
Bell—Men p516-525   Smith—Hist. 1 p509-510
Hammerton p490

De Dolomieu.   See **Dolomieu, Déodat Guy Silvain Tancrède Gratet de**

Dee, John (1527-1608). Eng. chemist, mathematician.
Smith—Hist. 1 p323-324 (por.322)
Smith—Torch. p67 (por.67)

De Elhuyar.   See **Elhuyar, Don Fausto d'**

Deere, John (1804-1886). Amer. inventor.
*Epstein—Real p169-170   Wilson—Amer. p138-139
*Ivins—Fifty p21-30 (por.22)   Year—Pic. p188 (por.189)

De Fagnano.   See **Fagnano, Guilio Carlo, Count de**

De Forest, Lee (1873-1961). Amer. inventor.
*Bachman—Great p291-292 (por.292)   Meyer—World p187-191 (por.189)
Chambers—Dict. col.126   *Montgomery—Invent. p67-71
Curr. Biog. '41 p213-215 (por.213)   *Montgomery—Story p197-199
  '61 (Oct.)   Morris—Ency. p650
*Darrow—Masters p331   *Patterson—Amer. p189-206
Hammerton p491   *Pratt—Famous p131-133
Hawks—Wireless p268,273-274   Radio's 100 p164-168 (por.140)
  (por.288)   *Towers—Beacon p231-245
*Hylander—Invent. p185-198   Wilson—Amer. p362-371 (por.362,
  (por.185)   368,371)
*Logie—Careers p14-36 (por.17)   Year—Pic. p179 (por.179)

De Fourcroy.   See **Fourcroy, Antoine François, Comte de**

De Geer, Carl (or Charles) (1720-1778). Swed. entomologist, biologist.
Essig—Hist. p601-602 (por.602)
Lindroth—Swedish p113-121

De Geer, Gerard Jakob de (1858-1943). Swed. geologist.
Curr. Biog. '43 p162   Lindroth—Swedish p219-225
G.S.A.—Proc. '43 p117-127
   (por.117)

De Golyer, Everette Lee (1886-1956). Amer. geologist.
G.S.A.—Proc. '57 p95-101 (por.95)
N.A.S.—Biog. (33) p65-71 (por.65)

De Gordon.   See **Gordon, Bernard de**

De Graaf.   See **Graaf, Regnier de**

De Gray.   See **Walsingham, Lord Gray, Thomas de**

De Gua de Malves.   See **Gua de Malves, Jean Paul de**

deHaen.   See **Haen, Anton de**

de Havilland.   See **Havilland, Sir Geoffrey de**

De Hevesy.   See **Hevesy, George von**

Deinostratus.   See **Dinostratus**

De Jean, Pierre François Marie Auguste (1780-1845). Fr. entomologist.
Essig—Hist. p603-604 (por.603)

Déjérine, Joseph Jules (1849-1917). Swiss neurologist.
Major—History (2) p965,1032

Dekkers, Frederick (1648-1720). Dutch physician.
Major—History (1) p561

DeKleine, William (1877-1957). Amer. physician.
Curr. Biog. '41 p217-218 (por.217)

DeKruif, Paul Henry (1890-   ). Amer. bacteriologist.
Curr. Biog. '42 p186-188 (por.186)

De la Bèche, Sir Henry Thomas (1796-1855). Eng. geologist.
Hammerton p492

De la Böe.   See **Sylvius, Franciscus**

de la Caille.   See **Lacaille, Nicolas Louis de**

De Lacaze-Duthiers.   See **Lacaze-Duthiers, (Félix) Henri de**

De la Cierva.   See **Cierva, Juan de la**

De la Condamine.   See **La Condamine, Charles Marie de**

De la Faye, Georges (1699-1781). Fr. surgeon.
Leonardo—Lives p164-165

Delafontaine, Marc (1837-1911). Swiss chemist.
Weeks—Discovery p420 (por.420)

Delagrange, Léon (1873-1910). Fr. aero. pioneer.
Burge—Ency. p630   Heinmuller—Man's p268 (por.268)
Hammerton p492

De la Hire.   See **La Hire, Philippe de**

De la Huerta.   See **Horto, Garcia ab**

De Lalande.   See **Lalande, Joseph Jérôme Lefrançais de**

De la Loubère.   See **La Loubère, Antoine de**

De Lamarck.   See **Lamarck, Jean Baptiste Pierre Antoine de Monet,
Chevalier de**

Delambre, Jean Baptiste Joseph (1749-1822). Fr. astronomer.
*Book—Pop. Sci. (8) p2568   Smith—Hist. 1 p492-494
Chambers—Dict. col.126

De La Mettrie.   See **La Mettrie, Julien Offrey de**

De Lana, Francesco (1631-1687). It. inventor, aero. pioneer.
Heinmuller—Man's p231- (por.231)

De Lange, Cornelia Catharina (1871-1950). Dutch physician.
Lovejoy—Women p185

Delany, Patrick Bernard (1845-1924). Amer. inventor.
Hammerton p493

De Laplace. See **Laplace, Pierre Simon, Marquis de**

De la Rive. See **La Rive, Auguste Arthur de**

de Laroche. See **Laroche, Raymonde, Baronne de**

De La Rue, Warren (1815-1889). Eng. astronomer, inventor.
Chambers—Dict. col.126-127
Hammerton p493

de La Sablière. See **La Sablière, Marguerite de**

De Laval. See **Laval, Carl Gustav Patrik de**

de La Vaulx. See **La Vaulx, Henri, Count de**

Delbrück, Max (1850-1919). Ger. inventor.
Smith—Torch. p72 (por.72)

Delcourt, Jules Dupuis (1802-1864). Fr. aero. pioneer.
Heinmuller—Man's p240 (por.240)

De Lee, Joseph Bolivar (1869-1942). Amer. physician, gynecologist.
Kagan—Modern p123 (por.123)

Delépine, Marcel (1871-   ). Fr. chemist.
Chambers—Dict. col.127

De Léscluse. See **Lécluse, Charles de**

De Lesseps. See **Lesseps, Ferdinand Marie, Vicomte de**

de L'Hopital. See **L'Hopital, Guillaume Francoise Antoine de**

d'Elhuyar. See **Elhuyar**

Delisle, Joseph Nicholas (1688-1768). Fr. astronomer, mathematician.
Chambers—Dict. col.127

Della Croce, Giovanni Andrea (fl.1573). It. surgeon.
Leonardo—Lives p132-133

Della Porta. See **Porta, Giovanni Gambattista Della**

Della Torre, Giacomo of Forli (or Jacopo da Forli) (d.1413/1414). It. physician.
Major—History (1) p354

Della Torre, Marc Antonio (c.1473-1506). It. anatomist, physician.
Major—History (1) p395-396

Dellinger, John Howard (1886-   ). Amer. physicist, engineer.
Radio's 100 p220-222 (por.140)

Delmedigo, Joseph Solomon (or Medigo, Joseph del) (1591-1655). Gr. physician.
Gordon—Medieval p763 (por.83)

De L'Obel.   See **L'Obel, Matthias de**

De Lobmayer.   See **Lobmayer, Geza de**

De Loureiro.   See **Loureiro, Juan de**

Delpech, Jacques Mathieu (1777-1832). Fr. surgeon.
Leonardo—Lives p133-135

Del Prete, Carol P. (1890-1928). It. aero. pioneer.
*Fraser—Heroes p549-550
Heinmuller—Man's p331- (por.331)

Del Rio, Andrés Manuel (1764-1849). Sp. mineralogist, paleontologist.
A.A.A.S.—Proc. (77) p39-40   Weeks—Discovery p147,197,225-233
Chambers—Dict. col.127   (por.147,197)

Deluc, Jean André (1727-1817). Swiss geologist.
Chambers—Dict. col.128
Hammerton p495

Demarcay, Eugene Anatole (1852-1903/1904). Fr. chemist.
A.A.A.S.—Proc. (81) p44-45   Smith—Torch. p75 (por.73)
Chambers—Dict. col.128   Weeks—Discovery p430-432
                                  (por.430)

De Margerie, Emmanuel Marie Pierre Martin Jacquin de (1862-1953). Fr. geologist.
R.S.L.—Biog. (1) p185-191 (por.185)

de Maricourt.   See **Peregrinus, Petrus**

de Maupertuis.   See **Maupertuis, Pierre Louis Moreau de**

de Mercado.   See **Mercado, Luiz de**

Demikhov, Vladimar Petrovitch (1916-   ). Rus. surgeon.
    Curr. Biog. '60 p111-112 (por.111)

Democedes (c 520 B.C.). Gr. physician.
    Gordon—Medicine p494-495

Democritus of Abdera (460-357/370 B.C.). Gr. nat. philosopher.
    *Book—Pop. Sci. (9) p2915-2916
      (por.2915)
    Cajori—Hist. p25
    Gordon—Medicine p474-479
    Hammerton p496 (por.496)
    Osborn—Greeks p57-59
    Sedgwick—Short p62-63
    Smith—Hist. 1 p80-81
    Turnbull—Great p22
    Van Wagenen—Beacon p9-11
    Wilson—Human p16-20

de Mofras.   See **Mofras, Duflot de**

Demoivre, Abraham (1667-1754). Fr.-Eng. mathematician.
    Ball—Short p383-384
    Cajori—Hist. p229-230
    Chambers—Dict. col.128
    Hooper—Makers p374-379
    Smith—Hist. 1 p450-451
    Woodruff—Devel. p21,285

de Mondeville.   See **Mondeville, Henri de**

de Montmort.   See **Montmort, Pierre-Rémond de**

Demorest, Max Harrison (1910-1942). Amer. geologist.
    G.S.A.—Proc. '42 p173-176 (por.173)

De Morgan, Augustus (1806-1871). Eng. mathematician.
    Ball—Short p474-475
    Cajori—Hist. p330-332
    Chambers—Dict. col.128-129
    Hammerton p496
    MacFarlane—Lectures p19-33
      (por.,front.)
    Smith—Hist. 1 p462

De Mott, Richard Hopper (1886-   ). Amer. engineer.
    Curr. Biog. '51 p157-159 (por.158)

Dempster, Arthur Jeffrey (1886-1950). Can. physicist.
    N.A.S.—Biog. (27) p319-329
      (por.319)
    Progress—Science '41 p113

De Munck, Victor C.B.A. (1920-1956). Dutch geologist.
G.S.A.—Proc. '57 p179

Dengel (Mother) Anna (1892-   ). Eng. physician.
Lovejoy—Women p229

Denis (or Denys), **Jean Baptiste** (1620-1704). Fr. physician, mathematician.
Major—History (1) p555

Denning, William Frederick (1848-1931). Eng. astronomer.
Chambers—Dict. col.129
MacPherson—Astron. p172-178
(por.172)

Dennis, Martin (1851-1916). Amer. chemist, inventor.
Chem. Ind. p17-18 (por.17)
Haynes—Chem. (1) p197-208
(por.200,201)

Dennis, Olive Wetzel (1885-1957). Amer. engineer.
Curr. Biog. '41 p220-221 (por.221)
Goff—Women p3-18

Denonvilliers, Charles Pierre (1808-1872). Fr. anatomist, surgeon.
Leonardo—Lives p135

Denys.   See **Denis, Jean Baptiste**

De Orta.   See **Horto, Garcia ab**

de Ortega.   See **Ortega, Juan de**

de Oviedo y Valdés.   See **Oviedo y Valdés, Gonzalo Fernandez de**

De Pinedo.   See **Pinedo, Francesco Marchese de**

de Pomis.   See **Pomis, David de**

de Pourtalès.   See **Pourtalès, Louis François de**

de Prony.   See **Prony, Gaspard Clair François Marie Riche, Baron de**

de Quervain.   See **Quervain, Fritz de**

de Réaumur.   See **Réaumur, René Antoine Ferchault de**

Derby, George Strong (1875-1931). Amer. physician.
Cushing—Medical p245-252

De Renzi, Salvatore (1800-1872). It. physician.
Castiglioni—Hist. p753 (por.753)

de Retines.   See **Robert de Ketene of Chester**

de Roberval.   See **Roberval, Gilles Personne de**

De Rossi, Michele Stefano (1834-1898). It. seismologist.
Davison—Founders p95-104

De Rozier.   See **Rozier, Jean François Pilâtre de**

de Saint-Come.   See **Saint-Come, Frère Jean de**

Desaguliers, John Theophilus (1683-1744). Eng. nat. philosopher.
Gunther—Early XI p296-297
  (por.297)

de St. Fond.   See **Faujas de Saint-Fond, Barthélemy de**

de Saint-Venant.   See **Barré de Saint-Venant, A.J.C.**

Desargues, Gérard (1593-1662). Fr. mathematician.
Ball-Short p257-258   Smith—Hist. 1 p383-384
Cajori—Hist. p166   Turnbull—Great p76-77
Chambers—Dict. col.129   Van Wagenen—Beacon p103-104
Sedgwick—Short p280-282   Woodruff—Devel. p270

De Sarzec.   See **Sarzec, Ernest de**

Desault, Pierre Joseph (1744-1795). Fr. anatomist, surgeon.
Leonardo—Lives p136-137

de Saussure.   See **Saussure.**

de Sauvages.   See **Sauvages, François Boissier de**

de Savitsch.   See **Savitsch, Eugene de**

Descartes, Renè (1596-1650). Fr. mathematician, nat. philosopher.

A.A.A.S.—Proc. (78) p10
Ball—Short p268-278
Bell—Men p35-55 (por.,front.)
Bodenheimer—Hist. p252
*Book—Pop. Sci. (9) p2916-2918
  (por.2910)
Cajori—Hist. p173-180
Castiglioni—Hist. p507-509 (por.507)
Chambers—Dict. col.129-130
  (por.130)
Fitzhugh—Concise p164-165
Gordon—Medieval p648-651
Gordon—Romance p116-117
  (por.117)
Hammerton—p499-500 (por.500)
Hart—Makers p125-137 (por.125)
Hart—Physicists p70-72
Hooper—Makers p206-221
Lambert—Medical p139-140
Lambert—Minute p139-140
Lenard—Great p52-53 (por.53)
Lodge—Pioneers p136-158 (por.148)
Magie—Source p50
Major—History (1) p480-484
  (por.480)
*Miller—Hist. p228-230
Moulton—Auto. p134
Muir—Men p47-76
Newman—Interp. p33-34
Osborn—Greeks p140-142
Robinson—Path. p123-151 (por.142)
Schwartz—Moments (1) p43-45
Sedgwick—Short p273-278
Sewell—Brief p56-57
Smith—Hist. 1 p371-377 (por.372)
Smith—Portraits v.L. VI unp (por.)
Suter—Gallery p76-84
Turnbull—Great p70-77
Van Wagenen—Beacon p104-105
Woodruff—Devel. p270 (por.8)
Year—Pic. p92 (por.86)

Desch, Cecil Henry (1874-1958). Eng. metallurgist.

R.S.L.—Biog. (5) p49-64 (por.49)

De Serres.   See **Serres, Olivier de**

De Seversky, Alexander Procofieff (1894-   ). Russ.-Amer. aero.
  pioneer.

Curr. Biog. '41 p222-223
  (por.222)
Heinmuller—Man's p348 (por.348)

Deshayes, Gérard Paul (1795-1875). Fr. geologist, naturalist.

Chambers—Dict. col.130
Woodruff—Devel. p208,270

De Sitter.   See **Sitter, Willem de**

Desmarest, Nicolas (1725-1815). Fr. geologist.

Fenton—Giants p34-38
Geikie—Founders p48-78
Woodruff—Devel. p270-271

Despars, Jacques (d.1457). Fr. physician.

Lambert—Medical p154

De Telkes.   See **Telkes, Maria de**

D'Etiolles.   See **Leroy D'Etiolles, Jean Jacques Joseph**

Detwiler, Samuel Randall (1890-1957). Amer. anatomist.
N.A.S.—Biog. (35) p85-99 (por.85)

Detwiller, Henry (1795-1887). Swiss physician.
Swiss—Prom. p119-122

de Ulloa.   See **Ulloa, Don Antonio de**

de Vauban.   See **Vauban, Sebastien le Prestre de**

Deventer, Hendrik van (1651-1739). Dutch obstetrician.
Major—History (1)

Devereaux, William Charles (1874?-1941). Amer. meteorologist.
Curr. Biog. '41 p223

Devèze, Jean (1753-1825). Fr. physician.
Major—History (2) p701

De Vighne, Harry Carlos (1876-1957). Amer. physician.
Fabricant—Why p160-163

de Vigni.   See **Vigni, Antoine François Saugrain De**

Deville, Charles Sainte-Claire (1814-1876). Fr. geologist.
Weeks—Discovery p353 (por.353)

Deville, Henri Étienne Sainte-Claire (1818-1881). Fr. chemist.
Chambers—Dict col.130-131   Partington—Short p339
Chymia (3) p205-221 (por.206)   Smith—Torch. p74 (por.74)
Hammerton p1177   Weeks—Discovery p353-355
                                           (por.353)

De Voe, Ralph Godwin (1883-   ). Amer. physician.
Curr. Biog. '44 p154-156 (por.155)

De Vries, Hugo (1848-1935). Dutch botanist, biologist.
Bodenheimer—Hist. p445   Schwartz—Moments (2) p698-700
Chambers—Dict. col.131   *Shippen—Men p169-173
Hammerton p503   *Snyder—Biology p138-140 (por.139)
Locy—Biology p408-410 (por.409)   Year—Pic. p225 (por.225)

De Vry, Herman A. (1877-1941). Amer. inventor.
Curr. Biog. '41 p223

Dewar, Sir James (1842-1923). Scot. chemist, physicist.
*Book—Pop. Sci. (10) p3218-3220
  (por.3219)
Chambers—Dict. col.132
*Darrow—Masters p332
Findlay—British p30-57 (por.30)
Findlay—Hundred p321
Gregory—British p20

Hammerton p503 (por.503)
Holmyard—British p66-68 (por.66)
Partington—Short p341
Smith—Torch. p76 (por.76)
Van Wagenen—Beacon p388-390
Woodruff—Devel. p271

Dewees, William Potts (1786-1841). Amer. physician, surgeon.
Leonardo—Lives p137-138
Major—History (2) p767

Dewey, Bradley (1887-   ). Amer. chemist.
Browne—Hist. p492 (por.169)

Dewey, John (1859-1952). Amer. psychologist.
N.A.S.—Biog. (30) p106-120
  (por.105)

Dewey, Richard (1845-1933). Amer. psychiatrist.
Rosen—Four p18-20,92-94

De Wolf, Frank Walbridge (1881-1957). Amer. geologist.
G.S.A.—Proc. '57 p105-107 (por.105)

Dexheimer, Wilbur App (1901-   ). Amer. engineer.
Curr. Biog. '55 p166-168 (por.167)

Dexter, Aaron (1750-1829). Amer. chemist.
Smith—Chem. p148

d'Hérelle, Felix-Hubert (1873-1949). Can. bacteriologist.
Bulloch—Hist. p372
Grainger—Guide p155

Dicaearchus of Messina (d.285 B.C.). Sicilian mathematician.
Smith—Hist. 1 p94

Dichter, Ernest (1907-   ). Austrian-Amer. psychologist.
Curr. Biog. '61 (Jan.) (por.)

Dickerson, Roy Ernest (1878-1944). Amer. geologist.
Curr. Biog. '44 p168
G.S.A.—Proc. '44 p174-177 (por.174)

Dickinson, Robert Latou (1861-1950). Amer. physician.
Curr. Biog. '50 p120-121, '51 p162

Dickinson, William Howship (1832-1913). Brit. physician.
Major—History (2) p896

Dickson, Alexander (1836-1887). Scot. botanist.
Oliver—Makers p300-301

Diderot, Denis (1713-1784). Fr. nat. philosopher.
Chambers—Dict. col.132   Osborn—Greeks p170-173
Murray—Science p135-140

Didorus Siculus (fl.44 B.C.). Gr. naturalist.
Adams—Birth p22-23

Diefendorf, Allen Ross (1871-1943). Amer. psychiatrist.
Curr. Biog. '43 p174

Dieffenbach, Johann Friedrich (1794-1847). Ger. surgeon.
Chambers—Dict. col.133   Thorwald—Century p65-68, 82-84
Leonardo—Lives p138-140

Diels, Otto (1876-1954). Ger. chemist.
Chambers—Dict. Supp.
Farber—Nobel p204,206-207
  (por.118)

Diesel, Rudolf (1858-1913). Ger. inventor, engineer.
*Bachman—Great p71   *Larsen—Shaped p199-202 (por.192)
*Book—Pop. Sci. (4) p1422-1423   Matschoss—Great p299-304
  (por.1423)   (por.299)
Chambers—Dict. col.133   *Montgomery—Invent. p209-212
Hammerton p507 (por.507)   *Science Miles. p257-262 (por.257)
*Larsen—Prentice p78-81   Year—Pic. p187 (por.187)
*Larsen—Scrap. p128-130 (por.129)

Dietrich, Amalie (1821-1891). Ger.-Austral. botanist.
Mozans—Woman p243-244

Dietz, David (1897-   ). Amer. sci. writer.
Curr. Biog. '40 p244-245 (por.244)

Dietz, Johann (1665-1738). Ger. physician, surgeon.
Rosen—Four p54-56,150-154

Dieulafoy, Auguste Marcel (1844-1920). Fr. archaeologist.
Hammerton p508

Dieulafoy, Georges (1839-1911). Fr. physician.
Major—History (2) p903

Dieulafoy, Jeanne Paule Henriette Rachel (née Magre) (1851-1916). Fr. archaeologist.
Mozans—Woman p318-321

Digby, Sir Kenelm (1603-1665). Eng. chemist.
Chymia v.2 p119-128 (por.126)   Major—History (1) p545
Gunther—Early XI p287

Digges, Leonard (d.1571?). Eng. mathematician.
Smith—Hist. 1 p321-322

Digges, Thomas (d.1595). Eng. mathematician.
Smith—Hist. 1 p321-322

Digman, Ralph Eriksen (1920-1953). Amer. geologist.
G.S.A.—Proc. '52 p173

Dimock, Susan (1847-1875). Amer. physician, surgeon.
Lovejoy—Women p86-87

Dines, William Henry (1865-1927). Eng. aero. pioneer.
Hammerton p509

Dinnendahl, Franz (1775-1826). Ger. engineer.
Matschoss—Great p119-127
  (por.117)

Dino del Garbo (d.1327). It. physician.
Major—History (1) p354

Dinostratus (or Deinostratus) (fl.c350 B.C.). Gr. mathematician.
Smith—Hist. 1 p92

D'Invilliers, Edward Vincent (1857-1928). Amer. geologist.
G.S.A.—Proc. '34 p221-222
  (por.221)

Diocles of Carystus (c. 3d cent. B.C.). Gr. physician.
Gordon—Medicine p546-548   Sigerist—Great p38-41
Major—History (1) p160   Smith—Hist. 1 p118

Diogenes Laërtius (fl. 3d cent.). Gr. physician.
Gordon—Medicine p464 (por.464)

Diogenes of Apollonia (fl. 5th cent.). Gr. nat. philosopher, physician.
Gordon—Medicine p462-465
Major—History (1) p114

Dionis, Pierre (1645-1718). Fr. surgeon.
Leonardo—Lives p140-141

Dionysius Periegetes (4th cent. or earlier?). Gr. geographer, naturalist.
Adams—Birth p25

Diophantus (c.3d-4th cent.). Gr. mathematician.
Ball—Short p103-110
Cajori—Hist. p60-62
Chambers—Dict. col.133
Clagett—Greek p117
Hammerton p510
Hooper—Makers p79-82
*Miller—Hist. p224-226
Sedgwick—Short p133-138
Smith—Hist. 1 p133-135
Turnbull—Great p49-53
Van Wagenen—Beacon p35-37
Woodruff—Devel. p12,271

Dioscorides, Pedanius (c50). Gr. physician.
Adams—Birth p23-25
Arber—Herbals p8-12
Bodenheimer—Hist. p177
Castiglioni—Hist. p215-216
Chambers—Dict. col.133
Gordon—Medicine p635-637
(por.636)
Hammerton p510
Hawks—Pioneers p77,78,79,80,81
Major—History (1) p175-176
(por.191)
Reed—Short p42-43
Van Wagenen—Beacon p29-30
Woodruff—Devel. p219,271

Dippel, Johann Konrad (1673-1734). Ger. chemist.
Hammerton p510

Dirac, Paul Adrien Maurice (1902-   ). Eng. physicist.
Chambers—Dict. col.134
Heathcote—Nobel p313,323-329
(por.240)
Weber—College p554 (por.554)
Year—Pic. p211 (por.211)

Dircks, Henry (1806-1873). Eng. engineer.
Hammerton p510

Dirichlet, Peter Gustav Lejeune (1805-1859). Ger. mathematician.
Ball—Short p454-455
Cajori—Hist. p438

Disney, Walter E. (1901-   ). Amer. inventor.
*Larsen—Scrap. p41,44-45,46
(por.49)

Distant, William Lucas (1845-1922). Eng. entomologist.
Osborn—Fragments p232-233

Ditmars, Raymond Lee (1876-1942). Amer. naturalist.
Curr. Biog. '40 p248-249 (por.249),   Progress—Science '40 p121-122
  '42 p202   (por.121)
*Milne—Natur. p172

Ditton, Humphry (1675-1715). Eng. mathematician.
Ball-Short p380
Chambers—Dict. col.134

Divers, Edward (1837-1912). Eng. chemist.
Partington—Short p353

Di Vigo, Giovanni (1460-1520). It. physician.
Major—History (1) p371-373

Dixon, Arthur Lee (1867-1955). Eng. mathematician.
R.S.L.—Biog. (1) p33-34 (por.33)

Dixon, Harold Baily (1852-1930). Eng. chemist.
A.A.A.S.—Proc. (81) p46-47   Findlay—Hundred p322
Chambers—Dict. col.134   Hammerton p510
Findlay—British p126-145 (por.126) Partington—Short p352

Dixon, Thomas F. (1881?-1949). Amer. space pioneer.
Thomas—Men (2) p26-43 (por.106)

Djuanda (1911-   ). Javanese engineer.
Curr. Biog. '58 p120-122 (por.121)

Dobbie, Sir James Johnston (1852-1924). Scot. chemist.
A.A.A.S.—Proc. (81) p47-49   Hammerton p511
Findlay—Hundred p322

Döbereiner, Johann Wolfgang (1780-1849). Ger. chemist.
A.A.A.S.—Proc. (77) p40-41   Smith—Torch p77 (por.77)
Chambers—Dict. col. 134-135   Weeks—Discovery p385-386
Partington—Short p343-344   (por.385)
  (por.343)

Dobson, Matthew (d.1784). Eng. physician.
Major—History (2) p634

Dodart, Denis (1634-1707). Fr. botanist, physician.
Major—History (1) p558

Dodge, Charles Richards (b.1847). Amer. entomologist.
Smiths.—Misc. (84) p41-43

Dodge, Raymond (1871-1942). Amer. psychologist.
Curr. Biog. '42 p203-204
N.A.S.—Biog. (29) p65-115 (por.65)

Dodgson, Charles Lutwidge (or Carroll, Lewis, pseud.) (1832-1898). Eng. mathematician.
Hammerton p359
Sci. Amer.—Lives p241-256
  (por.243)

Dodoëns, Rembert (or Dodonaeus) (1517-1585). Belg. botanist, physician.
Arber—Herbals p82,83,84,227,228,
  229,255 (por.81)
Hawks—Pioneers p166-169,171
Major—History (1) p472
Sarton—Six p141-143 (por.142)
Woodruff—Devel. p271

Doebner, Oskar Gustav (1850-1907). Ger. chemist, botanist, zoologist.
A.A.A.S.—Proc. (78) p32-33

Doherty, Robert Ernest (1885-   ). Amer. elec. engineer.
Curr. Biog. '49, p159-160 (por.160),
  '50 p121-122
*Yost.—Engineers p1-16

Doihara, Kenji (1883-1948). Japan. aero. pioneer.
Curr. Biog. '42 p205-207 (por.206)

Doisy, Edward Adelbert (1893-   ). Amer. biochemist.
Castiglioni—Hist. p943 (por.942)
Chambers—Dict. col.135
Curr. Biog. '49 p161-162 (por.161)
Stevenson—Nobel p217,220-222

d'Oisy, Pelletier (1892-   ). Fr. aero. pioneer.
Heinmuller—Man's p314 (por.314)

Dolbear, Amos Emerson (1837-1910). Amer. inventor.
Hawks—Wireless p129-138 (por.114)
Radio's 100 p74-76 (por.140)

Dold, Hermann (1882-   ). Ger. bacteriologist.
Bulloch—Hist. p361

Dolland, John (1706-1761). Eng. inventor.
*Book—Pop. Sci. (4) p1423-1424
  (por.1424)
Chambers—Dict. col.135
Hammerton p513-514
Woodruff—Devel. p162,271
Year—Pic. p104 (por.104)

Dodge, Charles Richards (1847- n.d.). Amer. entomologist.
Mead—Medical p42-43

Dolomieu, Déodat Guy Silvain Tancrède Gratet de (1750-1801). Fr.
geologist, seismologist.
*Book—Pop. Sci. (2) p719-720   Geikie—Founders p198
Davison—Founders p31-33   Hammerton p514

Domagk, Gerhard (1895-   ). Ger. biochemist.
Calder—Science p88-89   Grainger—Guide p149
Chambers—Dict. col.135-136   Major—History (2) p1006-1007
Curr. Biog. '58 p124-126 (por.125)   (por.1007)
*Eberle—Modern p51-57   Stevenson—Nobel p209-214
*Elwell—Sci. p71-72   (por.150)
                                  Year—Pic. p221,222 (pop.222)

Donaldson, Henry Herbert (1857-1938). Amer. biologist.
N.A.S.—Biog. (20) p229-237
(por.229)

Donaldson, Washington (1840-1875). Amer. aero. pioneer.
Milbank—First p136-139 (por.134)

Donati, Giovanni Battista (1826-1873). It. astronomer.
Chambers—Dict. col.136   MacPherson—Makers p164-165
Hammerton p515

Donati, Mario (1870-1946). It. surgeon.
Leonardo—Lives p141-142

Donders, Frans Cornelis (1818-1889). Dutch physiologist, physician,
ophthalmologist.
Castiglioni—Hist. p731 (por.731)   Woodruff—Devel. p271
Hammerton p515

Dondi, Giacomo (1298-1359). It. astronomer.
Major—History (1) p354

Donitz, Friedrich Karl Wilhelm (1838-1912). Ger. bacteriologist.
Bulloch—Hist. p361

Donnan, Frederick George (1870-1956). Irish phys. chemist.
Chambers—Dict. col.136
R.S.L.—Biog. (3) p23-35 (por.23)

Donné, Alfred (1801-1878). Fr. bacteriologist.
Bulloch—Hist. p362

Donnolo (Sabbatho Ben Abraham Ben Joel) (c913-982). It. physician.
Gordon—Medieval p256-260

Dooley, Thomas Anthony (1927-1961). Amer. physician.
Curr. Biog. '57 p148-150 (por.149),
'61 (Mr.)

Doolittle, James H. (1896-   ). Amer. aero. pioneer.
Curr. Biog. '42 p207-210 (por.209),
57 p150-152 (por.151)
Daniel—Pioneer p79-85 (por.78)
Heinmuller—Man's p344 (por.344)
Maitland—Knights p262-265
Montgomery—Invent. p246-248
Thomas—Men p.xiv-xv
Thomas—Men (2) p.xv-xvi
Thomas—Men (3) p1-30 (por.74)

Doppler, Christian Johann (1803-1853). Aust. mathematician, physicist.
Chambers—Dict. col.136
Hammerton p516
Van Wagenen—Beacon p276-279

D'Orbigny.   See **Orbigny, Alcide Dessalines d'**

Dorn, Friedrich Ernst (1848-1916). Ger. chemist.
Chambers—Dict. col.137
Weeks—Discovery p493-494

Dornberger, Walter (1895-   ). Ger. engineer.
Gartmann—Men p137-140 (por.160)
Thomas—Men (2) p44-63 (por.106)
Williams—Rocket p204-230
(por.114)

Dornier, Claude (1884-   ). Ger. aero. pioneer.
Heinmuller—Man's p336 (por.336)

Dörpfeld, Wilhelm (1853-1940). Ger. archaeologist.
Curr. Biog. '40 p255

Dorset, Marion (1872-1935). Amer. chemist, agriculturist.
*Darrow—Builders p193-197
*De Kruif—Hunger p69-97 (por.68)

Dorsey, John Syng (1783-1818). Amer. surgeon.
Leonardo—Lives p142-143
Major—History (2) p768-769

Douglas, Clifford Hugh (1879-1952). Scot. engineer.
Hammerton p518 (por.518)

Douglas, David (1798-1834). Scot. botanist.
Alden—Early p32-37 (por.33)
Dakin—Perennial p30-34

Douglas, Donald Wills (1892-   ). Amer. engineer, aero. pioneer.
Curr. Biog. '41 p231-233 (por.231),   Forbes—Fifty p93-99 (por.92)
  '50 p123-125 (por.124)   Heinmuller—Man's p298 (por.298)
Daniel—Pioneer p61-65 (por.60)

Douglas, James (1837-1918). Can. min. engineer, metallurgist.
John Fritz p85-87 (por.84)

Douglas, James Henderson, Jr. (1899-   ). Amer. aero. pioneer.
Curr. Biog. '57 p152-154 (por.153)

Douglas, Sir Sholto (1893-   ). Eng. aero. pioneer.
Curr. Biog. '43 p178-179 (por.179)

Douglas, Stewart Ranken (1871-1936). Eng. bacteriologist, physician.
Bulloch—Hist. p362

Douglas, Walter J. (1873?-1941). Amer. engineer.
Curr. Biog. '41 p233

Douglass, Andrew Ellicott (1867-1901). Amer. astronomer.
Chambers—Dict. col.137
Jaffe—Outposts p468-478

Douglass, William (1691-1752). Brit-Amer. physician.
Farmer—Doctors' p7

Dove, Heinrich Wilhelm (1803-1879). Ger. meteorologist.
Hammerton p519

Dover, Thomas (1660?-1742). Eng. physician.
Atkinson—Magic p100-101   Major—History (2) p628
Hammerton p519

Dow, Herbert Henry (1866-1930). Amer. chemist.
Haynes—Chem. (1) p259-278
  (por.264,265)

Dow, Willard Henry (1897-1949). Amer. chemist.
Curr. Biog. '44 p172-174 (por.173),
  '49 p168
Forbes—Fifty p101-106 (por.100)

Dowson, Joseph Emerson (1844-1940). Eng. inventor.
Hammerton p519-520

Drake, Daniel. (1785-1852). Amer. physician.
Atkinson—Magic p227-232
Castiglioni—Hist. p710 (por.710)
Flexner —Doctors p165-234
(por.165)
Major—History (2) p743-746
(por.745)
Rosen—Four p6-11,33-34,63-66

Drake, Edwin Laurentine (1819-1889).
Hartman—Mach. p100-102
Wilson—Amer. p169-170 (por.168)

Drake, (John Gibbs) St. Clair (1911-   ). Amer. anthropologist.
Curr. Biog. '46 p103-106 (por.105)

Drake, Noah Fields (1864-1945). Amer. geologist.
G.S.A.—Proc. '47 p141-147
(por.141)

Draper, Charles Stark (1901-   ). Amer. space pioneer.
Thomas—Men (3) p31-52 (por.74)

Draper, Henry (1837-1882). Amer. astronomer.
Chambers—Dict. col.137
N.A.S.—Biog. (3) p81-137
Williams—Great p356-359,368
(por.358)

Draper, John William (1811-1882). Eng.-Amer. chemist.
Browne—Hist. p471 (por.19)
Chambers—Dict. col.137
Findlay—Hundred p322
Hammerton p521
N.A.S.—Biog. (2) p349-382
Van Wagenen—Beacon p293-294
Williams—Great p351-352 (por.353)
Williams—Story p285 (por.285)
Wilson—Amer. p264-265 (por.264)

Drebbel, Cornelius van (1572-1634). Dutch inventor.
Hammerton p522

Dresser, John Alexander (1866-1954). Can. geologist.
G.S.A.—Proc. '57 p109-110 (por.109)

Drew, Charles Richard (1904-1950). Amer. physician, surgeon.
Curr. Biog. '44 p179-180 (por.179),
'50 p128
*Sterne—Blood p129-174
*Truax—Doctors p165-181

Dreyer, John Louis Emil (1852-1926). Dan. astronomer.
Hammerton p522

Dreyfus, Camille Edouard (b.1878). Swiss chemist.
Curr. Biog. '55 p174-175 (por.174)

Dreyse, Johann Nikolaus von (1787-1867). Ger. inventor.
Hammerton p522

Driesch, Hans Adolf Eduard (1867-1941). Ger. biologist.
Chambers—Dict. col.138
Hammerton p522

Drinker, Philip (1894-   ). Amer. inventor.
Montgomery—Story p84-86
Ratcliffe—Modern p49-53

Druce, George Claridge (1850-1932). Eng. botanist.
Gilmour—British p42-43

Drude, Paul Karl Ludwig (1863-1906). Ger. physicist.
Chambers—Dict. col.138
Hammerton p523

Drummond, Sir David (1852-1932). Brit. physician.
Hammerton p523

Drummond, Thomas (1790?-1835). Scot. naturalist.
Geiser—Natural. p55-78

Drury, Dru (1725-1803). Eng. naturalist.
Hammerton p523

Dryander, Johannes (or Eichmann, Johannes) (d.c.1560). Ger. anatomist,
    physician.
Major—History (1) p462

Dryden, Hugh Latimer (1898-   ). Amer. physicist.
Curr. Biog. '59 p99-100 (por.99)   Thomas—Men (2) p64-87 (por.106)
Daniel—Pioneer p131-135 (por.130)

Duane, William (1872-1935). Amer. physicist.
N.A.S.—Biog. (18) p23-34 (por.23)

Dubilier, William (1888-   ). Amer. engineer.
Radio's 100 p231-233 (por.140)

Dubis, Paul-Antoine (1795-1871). Fr. obstetrician, surgeon.
Leonardo—Lives p145

Dublin, Louis Israel (1882-   ). Lith.-Amer. public health worker.
Curr. Biog. '42 p221-223 (por.221)

Dubois, Eugène (1858-1941). Fr. anthropologist.
Curr. Biog. '41 p241
*Sootin—Twelve p195-212

Dubois, Jacques. See **Sylvius, Jacques Dubois**

DuBois-Reymond, Emil Heinrich (1818-1896). Ger. physiologist.
*Book—Pop. Sci. (10) 3220-3221   Major—History (2) p800,886
Chambers—Dict. col.61   Rosen—Four p247-252
Hammerton p525   Woodruff—Devel. p271
Locy—Biology p189-190 (por.189)

Dubos, René Jules (1901-   ). Fr.-Amer. bacteriologist.
Chambers—Dict. col.138   *Eberle—Modern p71-75
Curr. Biog. '52 p163-165 (por.164)

Dubridge, Lee Alvin (1901-   ). Amer. physicist.
Curr. Biog. '48 p161-163 (por.162)

Dubulier, William (1888-   ). Amer. engineer, inventor.
Curr. Biog. '57 p156-157 (por.157)

Du Chatelet. See **Chatelet, Emilie, Marquise de**

Duchenne, Guillaume Benjamin Amand (or Duchenne de Boulogne)
    (1806-1875). Fr. physician.
Chambers—Dict. col.138-139   Major—History (2) p880
Hammerton p525   Robinson—Path. p553-577
                                                             (por.562,571)

Duclaux, Pierre Émile (1840-1904). Fr. bacteriologist, chemist.
Bulloch—Hist. p362   Hammerton p1448-1449
Grainger—Guide p149

Ducrey, Augusto (b.1860). It. bacteriologist.
Bulloch—Hist. p362

Duddell, William Du Bois (1872-1917). Eng. engineer.
Chambers—Dict. col.139
Hammerton p526

Dudley, Benjamin Winslow (1785-1870). Amer. physician, surgeon.
Major—History (2) p741-743
    (por.742)

Dudley, Charles Benjamin (1842-1909). Amer. chemist.
Browne—Hist. p476-477 (por.45)

Dudley, Dud (1599-1684). Eng. inventor.
*Hartman—Mach. p31

Dudley, Paul (1675-1751). Amer. naturalist.
Bell—Early p54

Dudley, Sheldon Francis (1884-1956). Eng. epidemiologist.
R.S.L.—Biog. (2) p85-97 (por.85)

Du Fay, Charles François de Cisternay (1698-1739). Fr. chemist.
Chambers—Dict. col.139
Hart—Physicists p97
Magie—Source p398
Morgan—Men p24-27
Radio's 100 p17-19
*Shippen—Design p34-40
Taylor—Illus. p88

Duffy, James Joseph (1892?-1941). Amer. physician.
Curr. Biog. '42 p223

Dufour, Jean Marie Léon (1782-1865). Fr. entomologist.
Locy—Biology p100

Dufrénoy, Ours Pierre Armand Petit (1792-1857). Fr. geologist.
Chambers—Dict. col.139

Dugan, Raymond Smith (1878-1940). Amer. astronomer.
Curr. Biog. '40 p261-262 (por.262)

Duggar, Benjamin Minge (1872-1956). Amer. botanist, agriculturist, biologist.
Curr. Biog. '52 p166-169 (por.167)
N.A.S.—Biog. (32) p113-121
(por.113)
*Shippen—Men p208

Duggar, John Frederick (1868-1945). Amer. agriculturist.
*Ivins—Fifty p351-356 (por.353)

Duhamel-Dumonceau, Henri Louis (1700-1782). Fr. chemist, botanist, engineer, agriculturist.
Chambers—Dict. col.139-140
Reed—Short p105-106
Weeks—Discovery p270-271
(por.270)

Dujardin, Félix (1801-1860). Fr. zoologist.
Bulloch—Hist. p362
Locy—Biology p262-267 (por.265)
*Snyder—Biology p63-64

Duke-Elder, Sir William Stewart (1898-). Brit. ophthalmologist.
Hammerton p527

Dulong, Pierre Louis (1785-1838). Fr. chemist, physicist.
Chambers—Dict. col.140
Chymia (v.i.) p171-190 (por.172)
Hammerton p527
Magie—Source p178
Partington—Short p213-247
Smith—Torch. p78 (por.78)
Van Wagenen—Beacon p242-243

Dumas, Jean Baptiste André (1800-1884). Fr. chemist.
A.A.A.S.—Proc. (78) p23-24
Chambers—Dict. col.140
*Darrow—Masters p119-122 (por.33)
Findlay—Hundred p322-323
Hammerton p529 (por.529)
Partington—Short p226-227,269
  (por.227)
Roberts—Chem. p106-120
Smith—Torch. p79 (por.79)
Tilden—Famous p205-215 (por.205)
Van Wagenen—Beacon p269-271
Weeks—Discovery p377 (por.377)
Williams—Story p279-280,346,347
  (por.346)
Woodruff—Devel. p271

Dumée, Jeanne (fl.1680-1685). Fr. astronomer.
Mozans—Woman p171

Dumont, Allen Balcom (1901-). Amer. engineer.
Curr. Biog. '46 p162-164 (por.163)
Radio's 100 p276 (por.140)

Dumont, André Hubert (1809-1857). Belg. geologist.
Hammerton p530

Dunbar, Paul Brown (1882-). Amer. chemist.
Curr. Biog. '49 p180-182 (por.181)

Dunbar, William (1749-1810). Amer. astronomer, meteorologist,
  geographer, paleontologist.
Bell—Early p54

Dunbar, William Philipps (1863-1922). Amer. bacteriologist.
Bulloch—Hist. p362

Dunér, Nils Christopher (1839-1914). Swed. astronomer.
Chambers—Dict. col.140
MacPherson—Astron. p92-98
  (por.92)
MacPherson—Makers p176-177

Dunham, Edward Kellogg (1862-1922). Amer. bacteriologist.
Bulloch—Hist. p362

Dunlop, John Boyd (1840-1921). Scot. inventor.
Hammerton p532   *Larsen—Scrap. p114-116 (por.112)
*Larsen—Men p88-97 (por.80)   People p135

Dunn, Gano Sillick (1870-1953). Amer. elec. engineer.
N.A.S. Biog. (28) p31-39 (por.31)

Dunn, George W. (1814-1905). Amer. entomologist.
Essig—Hist. p605

Dunn, James H. (1853-1904). Amer. surgeon.
Leonardo—Lives p146-147

Dunn, Louis G. (1908-   ). Brit.-Amer. space pioneer.
Thomas—Men (3) p53-73 (por.74)

Dunne, John William (1875-1949). Irish aero. pioneer, inventor.
Burge—Ency. p630
Hammerton p532

Dunning, John Ray (1907-   ). Amer. physicist.
Chambers—Dict. col.141   Wilson—Amer. p415
Curr. Biog. '48 p165-167 (por.166)

Dunstan, Sir Wyndham Rowland (1861-1949). Eng. chemist.
Hammerton p533

Dupin, Pierre Charles (1784-1873). Fr. mathematician, engineer.
Cajori—Hist. p275-276

Du Pont, Francis Irénée (1873-1942). Fr. chemist.
Carmer—Caval. p273-276 (por.273)
Curr. Biog. '42 p225-226

Du Pont, Richard Chichester (1911-   ). Amer. aero. pioneer.
*Fraser—Heroes p681-685

Dupuytren, Baron Guillaume (1777-1835). Fr. anatomist, surgeon.
Castiglioni—Hist. p713-714 (por.715)   Major—Hist. (2) p648-650 (por.649)
Leonardo—Lives p148-149

Durafour, François (1890-   ). Swiss aero. pioneer.
Heinmuller—Man's p311 (por.311)

Durand, William Frederick (1859-1958). Amer. aero. pioneer, engineer.
Daniel Gugg. p51-57 (por.50)
Daniel—Pioneer p37-41 (por.36)

Durant, Charles Ferson (1805-1873). Amer. aero. pioneer.
Heinmuller—Man's p239 (por.239)
Milbank—First p49-55 (por.54)

Durante, Castor (d.1590). It. physician, botanist.
Arber—Herbals p102-103

Durante, Francesco (1845-1934). It. surgeon.
Leonardo—Lives p149-150

Dürer, Albrecht (1471-1528). Ger. mathematician.
Ball—Short p213   Smith—Hist. 1 p326-327
Hammerton p534 (por. 534)

Duret, Claude (d.1611). Fr. biologist, naturalist.
Osborn—Greeks p162

Durham, Herbert Edward (1866-1945). Eng. bacteriologist.
Bulloch—Hist. p362-363

Durocher, Marie Josefina (1809-1895). Fr.-Brazil. physician, obstetrician.
Lovejoy—Women p261-262

Duroziez, Paul Louis (1826-1897). Fr. physician.
Major—History (2) p891-892

Dury, Charles (1847-1931) Amer. entomologist.
Osborn—Fragments p212-213
  (por.351)

Duryea, Charles Edgar (1861/1862-1938). Amer. inventor.
Abbott—Great p216-219   Hodgins—Behemoth p316-318
*Epstein—Real p75-76

Dusch, Theodor von (1824-1890). Ger. bacteriologist.
Bulloch—Hist. p363

Du Simitière, Pierre E. (1736-1784). Amer. naturalist.
Bell—Early p54-55

Dusser de Barenne, Joannes Gregorius (1885-1940). Dutch-Amer.
  physiologist, neurologist.
Curr. Biog. '40 p267 (por.267)

Du Toit, Alexander Logie (1878-1948). S. Afr. geologist.
G.S.A.—Proc. '49 p141-145 (por.141)

Dutrochet, René Joachim Henri (1776-1847). Fr. physiologist, biologist.
Bodenheimer—Hist. p378   Schwartz—Moments (2) p553-554
Chambers—Dict. col.141

Dutton, Clarence Edward (1841-1912). Amer. geologist, seismologist.
*Book—Pop. Sci. (2) p720   Merrill—First p545 (por.546)
Davison—Founders p148-151   N.A.S.—Biog. (3) p132-141
                                            (por.132)

Duvalier, Francois (1907-   ). Haitian physician.
Curr. Biog. '58 p129-130 (por.129)

Du Vigneaud, Vincent (1901-   ). Amer. biochemist.
Chambers—Dict. Supp.   Progress—Science '41 p116
Curr. Biog. '56 p160-162 (por.161)

Dwinelle, Charles Hascall (b.1847). Amer. entomologist, agriculturist.
Essig—Hist. p605-608 (por.606)

Dyar, Harrison Gray (1866-1929). Amer. entomologist.
Essig—Hist. p608-610 (por.608)
Osborn—Fragments p199

Dye, Marie (1891-   ). Nutrition research worker.
Curr. Biog. '48 p169-170 (por.170)

Dye, William David (1887-1932). Brit. physicist.
Hammerton p536-537

Dyer, Edward (1651-1730). Brit. botanist.
Gunther—Early XI p112

Dyer, Rolla Eugene (1886-   ). Amer. surgeon, public health worker.
Ratcliffe—Modern p165-170

Dyke, Cornelius Gysbert (1900-1943). Amer. neurologist, physician.
Curr. Biog. '43 p189

Dyson, Sir Frank Watson (1868-1939). Eng. astronomer.
*Bridges—Master p81-94 (por.90)   Hammerton p537
Chambers—Dict. col.142

E

Eads, James Buchanan (1820-1887). Amer. inventor, engineer.

Book—Pop. Sci. (7) p2297-2298
Carmer—Caval. p280-283 (por. 283)
Goddard—Eminent p140-149
   (por.140)

Hammerton p537
N.A.S.—Biog. (3) p59-79
*Watson—Engineers p107-118
   (por.106)

Eagleson, James Beatty (1862-1928). Amer. surgeon.

Leonardo—Lives p150

Eaker, Ira Clarence (1896-   ). Amer. aero. pioneer.

Curr. Biog. '42 p226-227 (por.227)
Heinmuller—Man's p334 (por.334)

Earhart, Amelia (1898-1937). Amer. aero. pioneer.

*Adams—Heroines p157-176
   (por.168)
*Fraser—Famous p180-207
*Fraser—Heroes p545-547,629-637,
   701-711 (por. 702)
Hammerton p537 (por.537)

Heath—Amer. (4) p31 (por.31)
Heinmuller—Man's p115-125,330
   (por.122,330)
La Croix—They p185-194 (por.98)
Maitland—Knights p314-315
*Shippen—Bridle p140-146

East, Edward Murray (1879-1938). Amer. agriculturist, chemist, biologist.

N.A.S.—Biog. (23) p217-232
   (por.217)

Eastman, Charles Alexander (1858-1939). Amer. physician.

Faris—Men p57-68

Eastman, George (1854-1932). Amer. inventor.

Abbot—Great p361-366 (por.360)
*Darrow—Builders p280-288
   (por.286)
*Everett—When p45-52 (por.45)
*Forbes—Men p83-92 (por. 1)
Hammerton p538- (por. 538)
Law—Civiliz. p174-175

Meyer—World p80-82 (por.82)
*Montgomery—Invent. p86-89
*Wildman—Famous 1st p105-112
   (por.103)
Wilson—Amer. p266-272 (por.270)
*Wright—Great p236-238
Year—Pic. p164 (por.164)

Eastwood, Alice (1859-1953). Amer. botanist.

Dakin—Perennial p1-18 (por.,front.)

Eastwood, Arthur (1867-1936). Eng. bacteriologist.

Bulloch—Hist. p363

Eaton, Amos (1776-1842). Amer. chemist.

Bell—Early p55
Chymia (v.2) p4-10 (por.4)
Fenton—Giants p137-149 (por. 111)

Merrill—First p56 (por.56)
Youmans—Pioneers p111-118
   (por.111)

Eaton, Harry Nelson (1880-1944). Amer. geologist.
G.S.A.—Proc. '44 p181-184 (por.181)

Eaton, Walter Prichard (1878-   ). Amer. naturalist.
Tracy—Amer. Nat. p199-207

Eaves, Elsie (1898-   ). Amer. engineer.
*Fleischman—Careers p150
Goff—Women p77-81

Ebbinghaus, Hermann (1850-1909). Ger. psychologist.
Chambers—Dict. col. 143

Ebel, Isabel Caroline (1908-   ). Amer. aero. pioneer.
Knapp—New p169-179 (por.179)

Ebers, George (1837-1898). Ger. archaeologist.
Gordon—Medicine p211 (por.211)

Eberth, Carl Joseph (1835-1926). Ger. pathologist, anatomist, bacteriologist.
Bulloch—Hist. p363 (por.54)
Hammerton p538

Ebstein, Wilhelm (1836-1912). Pol. physician.
Kagan—Modern p210 (por.210)

Eccles, William Henry (1875-   ). Eng. physicist.
Radio's 100 p184 (por.140)

Echols, Oliver Patton (1892-   ). Amer. aero. pioneer.
Curr. Biog. '47 p187-189 (por.188)

Eckel, Edwin Clarence (1875-1941). Amer. geologist.
G.S.A.—Proc. '42 p179-182 (por.179)

Eckener, Hugo von (1868-1954). Ger. aero. pioneer.
Burge—Ency. p630
Daniel—Pioneer p51-55 (por.50)
*Fraser—Heroes p555-558,603-609
Hammerton p539
Heinmuller—Man's p274 (por.274)

Eckersley, Thomas Lydwell (1886-1959). Eng. physicist.
R.S.L.—Biog. (5) p69-73 (por.69)

Eckstein, Gustav (1890-   ). Amer. physiologist, ornithologist.
Curr. Biog. '42 p232-233 (por.232)
Peattie—Gather. p83-86

Eddington, Sir Arthur Stanley (1882-1944). Eng. astronomer.

Abetti—History p303-306
  (por 146 (30))
Armitage—Cent. p210-214 (por.176)
Chambers—Dict. col.143-144
  (por.143)
Curr. Biog. '41 p254-256 (por.255)
Hammerton p539 (por.539)

MacPherson—Makers p231-234
  (por.210)
People p136
Untermeyer—Makers p605-611
Williams—Great p429-430,453,465,
  499,531

Edgerton, Harold Eugene (1903-   ). Amer. elec. engineer.

Chambers—Dict. col.144

Edgerton, J. C. (1895-   ). Amer. aero. engineer.

Heinmuller—Man's p304 (por.304)

Edgeworth, Tannatt William.   See **David, Sir Tannatt William Edgeworth**

Edison, Thomas Alva (1847-1931). Amer. inventor.

Abbot—Great p136-144 (por.140)
*Bachman—Great p247-353
*Bolton—Famous p195-208 (por.194)
*Book—Pop. Sci. (7) p2299-2305
  (por.2296)
Carmer—Caval. p251-255
  (por.251,253,254)
Chambers—Dict. col.144-145
  (por.145)
*Cottler—Heroes p220-229
Crowther—Famous p299-401
  (por.304,336)
*Crowther—Inventors p87-122
  (por.128)
*Darrow—Builders p141-144
  (por.286)
*Darrow—Masters p265-280
  (por.321)
*Darrow—Thinkers p258-263
*Eberle—Invent. p103-110 (por.102)
*Epstein—Real p56
*Everett—When p15-22 (por.15)
*Forbes—Men p93-104 (por.1)
*Glenister—Stories p214-235 (por.214)
Hammerton p540-541 (por.540)
*Hartman—Mach. p181-192
*Hathaway—Partners p202-226
  (por.203)
Hawks—Wireless p140-148 (por.146)
*Hodgins—Behemoth p229-235
*Hylander—Invent. p158-173
  (por.184)
*Hyde—Modern p48-63
John Fritz p51-53 (por.50)
*Larsen—Men p22-46 (por.80)
*Larsen—Prentice p51-54
Law—Civiliz. p173-174,232-239

*Law—Modern p92-105 (por.96)
*Lockhart—My p143-163 (por.141)
*McSpadden—How p211-227
Matschoss—Great p314-332
  (por.315)
Meyer—World p183-184,248-251
  (por.184)
*Montgomery—Invent. p62-66
Morris—Ency. p654-655
*Morris—Heroes p301-308
N.A.S.—Biog. (15) p287-303
  (por.287)
*Nida—Makers p180-190
*Nisenson—Illus. p55 (por.55)
100 Great p654-661 (por.56)
*Parkman—Conq. p159-185
*Patterson—Amer. p122-135
People p136-138 (por.171)
*Perry—Four p205-260 (por.204)
*Pratt—Famous p84-91
Radio's 100 p79-84 (por.140)
*Science Miles. p217-223 (por.217)
Sewell—Brief p198-199
*Simmons—Great p40-45 (por.40)
*Tappan—Heroes p199-207 (por.205)
Thomas—50 Amer. p294-302
  (por.,front.)
Tuska—Invent. p83-84,97-99
Untermeyer—Makers p218-227
Van Wagenen—Beacon p400-403
Webb—Famous p163-175 (por.162)
*Wildman—Famous (1st) p115-127
  (por.,front.)
Wilson—Amer. p286-295
  (por.287,288)
*Wright—Great p209-226
Year—Pic. p174,182 (por.174,182)

Edmunds, Charles Wallis (1873-1941). Eng.-Amer. pharmacologist.
Progress—Science '41 p118

Edridge-Green, Frederick William (1863-1953). Eng. ophthalmologist.
Hammerton p541

Edrisi Mohammet.   See **Idrisi**

Edward, Thomas (1814-1886). Scot. naturalist.
Hammerton p546

Edwards, Henry (1830-1891). Eng.-Amer. entomologist.
Essig—Hist. p611-612 (por.611)
Osborn—Fragments p162 (por.347)

Edwards, Lena Frances (1900-   ). Amer. physician.
Knapp—Women p47-61 (por.47)

Edwards, Waldo B. (1905-   ). Amer. physician.
Curr. Biog. '43 p303 (por.302)

Edwards, William H. (1822-1909). Amer. naturalist.
Cutright—Great p22-23

Egen, P.N.C. (1793-1849). Ger. mathematician, physician, seismologist.
Davison—Founders p40-41

Eger, Ernest (1892-   ). Czech. engineer.
Curr. Biog. '42 p236-237 (por.236)

Eghbal, Manouchehr (1909-   ). Pers. physician.
Curr. Biog. '59 p106-107 (por.107)

Egloff, Gustav (1886-1955). Amer. chemist.
Curr. Biog. '40 p271-272 (por.272)

Ehrenberg, Christian Gottfried (1795-1876). Ger. naturalist, bacteriologist.
Bulloch—Hist. p363   Locy—Biology p106-107 (por.108)
Chambers—Dict. col.145-146

Ehrhorn, Edward MacFarlane (1862-1941). Amer. entomologist.
Essig—Hist. p613-614 (por.613)

Ehricke, Krafft A. (1917-   ). Ger. aero. pioneer., engineer.
Curr. Biog. '58 p130-132 (por.131)
Thomas—Men p1-22 (por.140, folio)

Ehrlich, Paul (1854-1915). Ger. bacteriologist.

Bodenheimer—Hist. p434
*Book—Pop.Sci. (6) p2023-2025
Bulloch—Hist. p363-364 (por.54)
Calder—Science p86-88
Castiglioni—Hist. p822-824 (por.823)
Chambers—Dict. col.145-146
*Chandler—Medicine p134 (por.132)
*De Kruif—Microbe p334-358
Gordon—Romance p337-338
   (por.337)
Grainger—Guide p150-151
Hammerton p548 (por. 548)
Kagan—Leaders p163-176 (por.162)
Kagan—Modern p156 (por.156)
Lambert—Medical p264-265

Lambert—Minute p264-265
Major—History (2) p933-935
   (por.933)
*Montgomery—Story p223-226
Oliver—Stalkers p205,213 (por.201)
Rosen—Four p108-110
Rowntree—Amid p430-435 (por.431)
*Science Miles p237-242 (por.237)
Sigerist—Great p384-388 (por.384)
Smith—Torch. p80 (por.80)
*Snyder—Biology p266-269 (por.268)
Stevenson—Nobel p46-56 (por.150)
*Traux—Doctors p108-121
Year—Pic. p131,221 (por.131)

Eichmann, Johannes.   See Dryander, Johannes

Eidmann, Frank Lewis (1887-1941). Amer. engineer.

Curr. Biog. '41 p257

Eielson, Carl Benjamin (1897-1929). Amer. aero. pioneer.

*Fraser—Heroes p541-543
Heinmuller—Man's p329 (por.329)

Maitland—Knights p292-296
Potter—Flying p33-72 (por.50)

Eiffel, Alexandre Gustave (1832-1923). Fr. engineer.

Hammerton p548
Year—Pic. p198 (por.198)

Eigenmann, Carl H. (1863-1927). Ger.-Amer. ichthyologist, zoologist.

N.A.S.—Biog. (18) p305-323
   (por.305)

Eijkman, Christiaan (1858-1930). Dutch physician, hygienist, bacteriologist.

Chambers—Dict. col.146
Grainger—Guide p151
Hammerton p548
Major—History (2) p1032-1033

*Men—Scien. p7-9
*Montgomery—Story p235-238
*Snyder—Biology p336-338
Stevenson—Nobel p134-135,136,137
   (por.150)

Einstein, Albert (1879-1955). Ger.-Swiss-Amer. math. physicist.

Armitage—Cent. p16-17 (por.48)
*Bolton—Famous p283-297 (por.282)
*Book—Pop. Sci. (9) p2920-2923
*Bridges—Master p95-103 (por.96)
Chambers—Dict. col.146-147
   (por.,front.), Supp.

*Cottler—Heroes p166-176
*Crowther—Scientists p223-269
   (por.209)
Curr. Biog. '55 p177-178, '41 p257-
   259 (por.287), '53 p178-181
   (por.179)

(Continued)

Einstein, Albert—*Continued*
* *Darrow—Masters p17-26 (por.32)
* Fitzhugh—Concise p191-193
* Ginzburg—Adven. p378-425 (por.384)
* Hammerton p549-550 (por.549)
* Hart—Makers p310-314 (por.310)
* Heathcote—Nobel p180-197 (por.240)
* Jaffe—Crucibles p376-378
* *Lewellen—Boy p233-254 (por.233)
* Ludovici—Nobel p151-164 (por.151)
* Makers—Modern p1-134
* *Men—Scien. p22-24
* Moulton—Auto. p520-521
* *Nisenson—Illus. p56 (por.56)
* People p138-139 (por.178)
* Pringle—Great p170-188 (por.176)
* R.S.L.—Biog. (1) p37-67 (por.37)

* Riedman—Men p86-105 (por.88)
* Robinson—100 p235-238 (por.235)
* Rowntree—Amid p523-528 (por.524)
* Schwartz—Moments (1) p92-93
* *Science Miles p292-294 (por.272)
* Sewell—Brief p220-221
* *Shippen—Design p117-125
* *Simmons—Great p63-64 (por.63)
* Thomas—Scien. p299-314 (por.297)
* Trattner—Arch. p375-403 (por.391)
* Untermeyer—Makers p533-541
* Van Wagenen—Beacon p432-433
* Weber—College p332 (por.332)
* Wilson—Human p367-389 (por.374)
* Woodruff—Devel. p41,71,271
* *Wright—Great p187-192
* Year—Pic. p205 (por.204,215)

Einthoven, Willem (1860-1927). Dutch physiologist.
* Castiglioni—Hist. p779 (por.778)
* Chambers—Dict. col. 147
* Hammerton p550 (por.550)
* Major—History (2) p1033
* *Montgomery—Story p53-55
* Rowntree—Amid p468-470 (por.466)
* Stevenson—Nobel p115-118 (por.150)

Eiseley, Loren Corey (1907-   ). Amer. anthropologist.
* Curr. Biog. June '60 (por.)

Eiselsberg, Anton von (1860-1939). Aust. physician, surgeon.
* Leonardo—Lives p150-151
* Major—History (2) p1033

Eisen, Gustavus Augustus (1847-1940). Swed.-Amer. entomologist, archaeologist, biologist.
* Curr. Biog. '40 p274
* Essig—Hist. p615-617 (por.615)

Eisendrath, Daniel N. (1867-1939). Amer. surgeon.
* Kagan—Modern p99 (por.99)

Eisenhower, Milton S. (1899-   ). Amer. agriculturist.
* Curr. Biog. '46 p173-175 (por.173)

Eisenstein, Ferdinand Gotthold Max (1823-1852). Ger. mathematician.
* Ball—Short p455-456
* Hammerton p550
* Smith—Hist. I p509

Ekeberg, Anders Gustaf (1767-1813). Swed. chemist, mineralogist.
* Chambers—Dict. col.147
* Weeks—Discovery p187-190 (por.188)

Elder, Albert Lawrence (1901-   ). Amer. chemist.
Curr. Biog. '60 p127-128 (por. 128)

Elder, John Munro (1858-1922). Can. surgeon.
Leonardo—Lives p151-152

Elder, Ruth (1904-   ). Amer. aero. pioneer.
Heinmuller—Man's p326 (por.326)
Maitland—Knights p314

Elhuyar, Don Fausto d' (1755-1833). Sp. chemist.
Chambers—Dict. col.147-148
Weeks—Discovery p122-124,143-145
   (por.124,145,151)

Elhuyar, Juan José de (d.1804). Sp. chemist.
Weeks—Discovery p122-124,143-148

Eliot, Martha May (1891-   ). Amer. physician, public health worker.
Curr. Biog. '48 p184-186 (por.185)

Elkin, Daniel Collier (1893-1958). Amer. surgeon.
Progress—Science '40 p130

Elkin, William Lewis (1855-1933). Amer. astronomer.
N.A.S.—Biog. (18) p175-186 (por.175)

Ellehammer, Jacob Christian H. (1871-1946). Dan. aero. pioneer.
Heinmuller—Man's p264 (por.264)

Ellerman, Ferdinand (1869-1940). Amer. astronomer.
Curr. Biog. '40 p275

Ellicott, Andrew (1754-1820). Amer. astronomer, meteorologist.
Bell—Early p55-56

Elliot, Daniel Giraud (1835-1915). Amer. naturalist.
*Book—Pop. Sci. (6) p2025-2026

Elliot, Walter (1888-1958). Scot. physiologist, agriculturist.
R.S.L.—Biog. (4) p73-79 (por.73)

Elliotson, John (1791-1868). Eng. physician, physiologist.
Hammerton p557   Robinson—Victory p70-74
Major—History (2) p710

Ellis, Carleton (1876-1941). Amer. chemist.
Curr. Biog. '41 p262

Ellis, Havelock (1859-1939). Eng. physician, psychologist.
Fabricant—Why p1-3
Rosen—Four p24-26,122-124

Ellis, Seth Hocket (1830-1904). Amer. agriculturist.
*Ivins—Fifty p211-215 (por.210)

Ellsworth, Lincoln (1880-1951). Amer. aero. pioneer, sci. explorer.
*Fraser—Heroes p297-334,735-742   Maitland—Knights p284-288
Heinmuller—Man's p318 (por.318)   *Shippen—Bridle p113-118

El Qasvini (or Sakarya Ben Muhemmed) (1203-1283). Pers. geographer.
biologist, botanist.
Bodenheimer—Hist. p216

Elsberg, Louis (1836-1885). Ger.-Amer. physician.
Kagan—Modern p130 (por.130)

Elsner, Henry L. (1857-1916). Amer. physician.
Kagan—Modern p16 (por.16)

Elsom, Katharine O'Shea (1903-   ). Amer. physician, nutritionist.
Knapp—Women p109-122 (por.109)

Elster, Julius (1854-1920). Ger. physicist.
Chambers—Dict. col.148
Weeks—Discovery p496-497

Elvehjem, Conrad Arnold (1901-   ). Amer. biochemist.
Curr. Biog. p188-190 (por.189)   Ratcliffe—Modern p106-107
Progress—Science '41 p124-125
(por.124)

Ely, Eugene (1886-1911). Amer. aero. pioneer.
Heinmuller—Man's p285 (por.285)

Emanuel, Victor (1898-   ). Amer. aero. pioneer.
Curr. Biog. '51 p182-184 (por.183)

Emerson, Gladys (1903-   ). Amer. biochemist
Yost—Women Mod. p140-155
(por.,front.)

Emerson, Robert (1903-1959). Amer. botanist.
N.A.S.—Biog. (35) p112-127
(por.112)

Emerson, Rollins Adams (1873-1947). Amer. agriculturist, geneticist.
N.A.S.—Biog. (25) p313-319
(por.313)

Emerson, Victor Lee (1863?-1941). Amer. inventor.
Curr. Biog. '41 p262

Emery, Alden H. (1901-   ). Amer. chemist.
Browne—Hist. p496 (por.183)

Émilie, Marquise du Châtelet (1706-1749). Fr. mathematician.
Smith—Hist. I p477-478 (por.478)

Emme, Eugene M. (1919-   ). Amer. space pioneer.
Thomas—Men (3) p.xvi

Emmerich, Rudolph (1852-1914). Ger. bacteriologist.
Bulloch—Hist. p364
Major—History (2) p1033

Emmet, Thomas Addis (1828-1919). Amer. surgeon, gynecologist.
Leonardo—Lives p152-154
Marr—Pioneer p63-101 (por.65,74)

Emmet, William Leroy (1858-1941). Amer. elec. engineer.
Curr. Biog. '41 p262
N.A.S.—Biog. (22) p233-248 (por.233)

Emmett, J. P. (1799-1842), Amer. chemist.
Smith—Chem. p224

Emmons, Ebenezer (1799-1863). Amer. geologist.
Fenton—Giants p152-154 (por.174)   Youmans—Pioneers p347-353
Merrill—First p109-111 (por.188)   (por.347)

Emmons, Samuel Franklin (1841-1911). Amer. geologist.
N.A.S.—Biog. (7) p307-330 (por.307)

Emmons, William Harvey (1876-1948). Amer. geologist.
G.S.A.—Proc. '49 p151-155 (por.151)

Empedocles of Agrigentum (490?-430? B.C.). Gr. nat. philosopher.

Gordon—Medicine p488-492
Major—History (1) p113-114,115
Osborn—Greeks p52-57

Sedgwick—Short p59-60
Van Wagenen—Beacon p8-9
Woodruff—Devel. p271

Encke, Johann Franz (1791-1865). Ger. astronomer.

*Book—Pop. Sci. (8) p2568-2569
Chambers—Dict. col.148

Hammerton p560
MacPherson—Makers p136-138

Endeley, Emmanuel M. Bela Lifaffe (1916-   ). Brit. physician.

Curr. Biog. '59 p108-109 (por.109)

Endemann, Samuel Theodore Hermann Carl (1842-1909). Ger.-Amer. chemist.

Browne—Hist. p496 (por.319)

Enders, John Franklin (1897-   ). Amer. bacteriologist.

Chambers—Dict. Supp.
Curr. Biog. '55 p182-183 (por.182)

Grainger—Guide p151

Endres, George (d.1932). Hung.-Amer. aero. pioneer.

*Fraser—Heroes p591-597
Heinmuller—Man's p343 (por.343)

Enene (c1500 B.C.). Egypt. engineer.

Matschoss—Great p5-7

Engelmann, George (1809-1884). Ger.-Amer. botanist, physician, meteorologist.

N.A.S.—Biog. (4) p1-21

Engelmann, Theodor Wilhelm (1843-1909). Ger. physiologist.

Chambers—Dict. col.148-149

Englebright, Harry Lane (1884-1943). Amer. min. engineer.

Curr. Biog. '43 p198

Engler, Adolf Heinrich Gustav Adolf (1844-1930). Ger. botanist.

Chambers—Dict. col.149

Engstrom, Elmer William (1901-   ). Amer. engineer.

Curr. Biog. '51 p186-188 (por.187)

Enock, Charles Reginald (b.1868). Eng. engineer.

Hammerton p561

Ent, Sir George (1604-1689). Eng. anatomist.

Major—History (1) p553-554

Eötvös, Roland, Baron von (1848-1919). Hung. physicist.

Chambers—Dict. col.149
Hammerton p561-562

Epicurus (341/342-270 B.C.). Gr. naturalist, nat. philosopher.

Gordon—Medicine p578-581
  (por.579)
Gordon—Romance p216-217
Hammerton p562 (por.562)

Osborn—Greek p90-91
Sedgwick—Short p85
Year—Pic. p33 (por.33)

Eppinger, Hans (1846-1916). Aust. anatomist.

Bulloch—Hist. p364

Erasistratus (300/310-250 B.C.). Gr. anatomist, physician.

Castiglioni—Hist. p185-186
Chambers—Dict. col.149-150
Gordon—Medicine p598-606
  (por.598)
Gordon—Romance p95-97
Hammerton p563

Lambert—Medical p31-36
Lambert—Minute p33-36
Leonardo—Lives p155
Major—History (1) p143-145
Sigerist—Great p46-50
Van Wagenen—Beacon p18-19

Eratosthenes (275-194 B.C.). Gr. geographer, astronomer.

Ball—Short p83-84
*Book—Pop. Sci. (8) p2569
Cajori—Hist. p38
Chambers—Dict. col. 150
Clagett—Greek p92-93,111
Dreyer—Hist. p174-176
Gordon—Medicine p607
Hammerton p563
Hooper—Makers p49-52

Schwartz—Moments (1) p150-151
*Science Miles p18-22 (por.18)
Sedgwick—Short p107-108
Smith—Hist. I p108-111
Van Wagenen—Beacon p23-24
Vaucouleurs—Disc. p26-28
Williams—Great p31-50,61,63
Woodruff—Devel. p136,137,272

Erb, Wilhelm Heinrich (1840-1921). Ger. physician, neurologist.

Major—History (2) p903

Erdheim, Jacob (1874-1937). Aust. pathologist.

Kagan—Modern p170 (por.170)

Erichsen, Sir John Eric (1818-1896). Eng. surgeon.

Hammerton p564
Leonardo—Lives p156-157

Ericsson, John (1803-1889). Swed.-Amer. inventor, engineer.

*Beard—Foreign p73-82 (por.80)
*Book—Pop. Sci. (7) p2305-2306

Chambers—Dict. col.150
*Darrow—Masters p332

(Continued)

Ericsson, John—*Continued*
    Goddard—Eminent 86-98 (por.86,90)
    Hammerton p564 (por.564)
    *Hodgins—Behemoth p200-207
    *Hylander—Invent. p86-95
    Iles—Leading p218-275 (por.218)
    Matschoss—Great p204-216 (por.216)
    *Morris—Heroes p296-300

    *Nida—Makers p65-73 (por.67)
    *Pratt—Famous p33-35,115-116
    Wilson—Amer. p204-205
    Year—Pic. p185 (por.185)
    Youmans—Pioneers p374-384
        (por.374)

Erigena, Johannes Scotus (or John the Scot; Eriugena). (815?-877?). Irish astronomer, nat. philosopher.
    Clagett—Greek p166-167
    Osborn—Greeks p112-113

Erlanger, E. Joseph (b.1874). Amer. physiologist, physician.
    Castiglioni—History p938,944,1127
        (por.945)
    Chambers—Dict. col.150-151

    Stevenson—Nobel p223,224-228
        (por.150)

Erlenmeyer, Emil, Sr. (1825-1909). Ger. chemist.
    Partington—Short p291,293-294,316
    Smith—Torch. p81 (por.81)

Ermengem, Émile-Pierre-Marie van (1851-1932). Belg. bacteriologist.
    Bulloch—Hist. p364

Ernst, Harold Clarence (1856-1922). Amer. bacteriologist.
    Bulloch—Hist. p364

Ervendberg, Louis Cachand (1809-1863). Ger.-Amer. naturalist.
    Geiser—Natural. p95-131

Erxleben.   See Leporin-Erxleben, Dorothea Christin

Escherich, Theodor (1857-1911). Ger. bacteriologist.
    Bulloch—Hist. p365

Eschscholtz, Johann Friedrich (1793-1831). Ger. naturalist, botanist, entomologist.
    Alden—Early p27-28
    Dakin—Perennial p28-29

    Essig —Hist p617-622 (por.618)

Esdaile, James (1808-1859). Scot. physician.
    Robinson—Victory p74-75

Esmarch, Erwin von (1855-1915). Ger. bacteriologist.
    Bulloch—Hist. p365

Esmarch, Johannes Friedrich August von (1823-1908)

Hammerton p566
Leonardo—Lives p157-158

Major—History (2) p888

Esnault-Pelterie, Robert (1881-   ). Fr. aero. pioneer.

Heinmuller—Man's p267 (por.267)
*Williams—Rocket p123-124,173-176

Espenschied, Lloyd (1889-   ). Amer. elec. engineer.

Radio's 100 p236-238 (por.140)

Espy, James Pollard (1785-1860). Amer. meteorologist.

Hammerton p567
Youmans—Pioneer p196-204
  (por.196)

Esson, William (1838-1916). Eng. chemist.

Findlay—Hundred p323

Este, Isabella d', Marchioness of Mantua (1474-1539). It. archaeologist.

Mozans—Woman p310-311

Estienne, Charles (1504-1564), Fr. anatomist.

Major—History (1) p402,404

Étard, Alexander Leon (1852-1910). Fr. chemist.

_ A.A.A.S.—Proc. (81) p49-50

Etiolles.   See Leroy D'Etiolles, Jean Jacques Joseph

Euclid (c330-275 B.C.). Gr. mathematician.

Ball—Short p52-62
*Book—Pop. Sci. (9) p2927-2928
  (por.2927)
Cajori—Hist. p29-34
Chambers—Dict. col.151
Clagett—Greek p55-56,58-59
Hammerton p570
Hart—Makers p34-38
Hofman—History p21-25
Hooper—Makers p45-49
Lenard—Great p2

*Miller—Hist. p216-219
Muir—Men p14-19
Sedgwick—Short p88-97
Smith—Hist. I p103-107
Smith—Portraits (v.2) unp. (por.)
Thomas—Scien. p4-6
Turnbull—Great p31-34
Van Wagenen—Beacon p19-21
Woodruff—Devel. p28,29,33,272
Year—Pic. p38 (por.38)

Eudemus of Rhodes (fl. 335 B.C.) Gr. mathematician.

Smith—Hist. I p94

Eudoxus of Cnidus (409?-356? B.C.). Gr. astronomer, mathematician.

Abetti—History p32-34
Ball—Short p44-46

Bell—Men p25-28
*Book—Pop. Sci. (8) p2570
(*Continued*)

Eudoxus of Cnidus—*Continued*
Cajori—Hist. p28
Clagett—Greek p57,86-89
Dreyer—Hist. p87-107
Sedgwick—Short p77-79
Smith—Hist. I p91-92
Turnbull—Great p24-29

Euler, Leonhard (1707-1783). Swiss physicist, mathematician.
Abetti—History p154-155
Ball—Short p393-400
Bell—Men p139 (por.,front.)
*Book—Pop. Sci. (9) p2928-2930
Cajori—Hist. p232-241
Chambers—Dict. col.151-152
Hammerton p571
Hooper—Makers p348-353
*Miller—Hist. p236-239
Muir—Men p138-156
Sedgwick—Short p326-328
Smith—Hist. I p520-524 (por.521)
Smith—Portraits (v.2) 1 unp. (por.)
Turnbull—Great p96-100
Van Wagenen—Beacon p154-156
Woodruff—Devel. p272
Year—Pic. 110 (por.110)

Euler-Chelpin, Hans Karl August Simon von (b.1873). Ger.-Swed. chemist.
Chambers—Dict. col.152
Farber—Nobel p112-113,115-117
   (por.118)
Hammerton p571

Euryphron of Cnidus (fl. 5th cent. B.C.). Gr. physician.
Gordon—Medicine p496

Eustachio, Bartolomeo (or Eustachius; Eustacchio; Eustacio; Eustachi)
   1520/1524-1574). It. anatomist, physician, surgeon.
Castiglioni—Hist. p427-428 (por.432)
Chambers—Dict. col.152
Gordon—Medieval p636
Leonardo—Lives p158-159
Locy—Biology p37-38
Major—History (1) p408-410
Van Wagenen—Beacon p71-72

Eutocius (c520). Gr. mathematician.
Clagett—Greek p168-169

Evans, Alice Catherine (1881-   ). Amer. bacteriologist.
Curr. Biog. '43 p198-200 (por.199)
*De Kruif—Men p146-175

Evans, Arthur Henry (1872-1950). Eng. surgeon.
Hammerton p572

Evans, Arthur John (1851-1941). Eng. archaeologist.
Ceram—Gods p56-57,60-67
Curr. Biog. '41 p264
Hammerton p573 (por.573)
People p143

Evans, Griffith (1835-1935). Eng. vet. surgeon.
Major—History (2) p898-899

Evans, Herbert McLean (1882-   ). Amer. anatomist, physiologist.
Curr. Biog. '59 p109-111 (por.110)   Jaffe—Outposts p180-183,256-258,
Jaffe—Men p437-482 (por.xxviii,441)   271 (por.251)
                                         *Snyder—Biology p343-345 (por.344)

Evans, Sir John (1823-1908). Eng. archaeologist.
Hammerton p573

Evans, Oliver (1755-1819). Amer. inventor.
*Burlingame—Mach. p19-33   *Hylander—Invent. p21-26
Goddard—Eminent p36-41 (por.35)   People p143
Hammerton p573   Wilson—Amer. p49,54-58 (por.54)

Evans, William Lloyd (1870-1954). Amer. chemist.
Browne—Hist. p490 (por.163)

Eve, Paul Fitzsimmons (1806-1877). Amer. physician, surgeon.
Leonardo—Lives (supp 1) p479-480

Evelyn, John (1620-1706). Eng. botanist.
Gunther—Early XI p61-64

Evershed, John (1864-1956). Eng. astronomer.
R.S.L.—Biog. (3) p41-48 (por.41)

Ewart, James Cossar (1851-1933). Scot. zoologist.
Chambers—Dict. col. 152

Ewing, Henry Elsworth (1893-   ). Amer. entomologist.
Osborn—Fragments p200 (por.370)

Ewing, James (1866-1943). Amer. pathologist.
Curr. Biog. '43 p200   N.A.S.—Biog. (26) p45-51 (por.45)
Major—History (2) p1033

Ewing, Sir James Alfred (1855-1935). Scot. physicist.
Hammerton p574

Ewing, William Maurice (1906-   ). Amer. oceanographer.
Curr. Biog. '53 p188-190 (por.189)

Ewins, Arthur James (1882-1957). Eng. chemist.
R.S.L.—Biog. (4) p81-90 (por.81)

Exner, Max Joseph (1871-1943). Aust.-Amer. epidemiologist.
Curr. Biog. '43 p200

Eyde, Samuel (1866-1940). Norw. chemist.
Curr. Biog. '40 p287

Eykman, Johan Frederick (1851-1915). Dutch chemist.
A.A.A.S.—Proc. (79) p14-15

Eyring, Henry (1901-   ). Mex.-Amer. chemist.
Curr. Biog. '61 (Oct.) (por.)

F

Faber, Johannes (or Malleus Haereticorum; Heigerlin) (1574-1629). Ger. botanist.
Chambers—Dict. col.153

Fabiola, Saint (d400). It. physician.
Mozans—Woman p272-274

Fabre, Henri (1883-   ). Fr. aero. pioneer.
Heinmuller—Man's p278 (por.278)

Fabre, Jean Henri (1823-1915). Fr. entomologist.
*Book—Pop. Sci. (6) p2026-2027 (por.2027)
Chambers—Dict. col. 153
Guinagh—Inspired p99-112
Hammerton p576 (por.576)
Hammond—Stories p69-95 (por.89)
*Milne—Natur. p107-112 (por.106)
Peattie—Green p326,332-346 (por.326)
Peattie—Lives p108-115 (por.108)
Thomson—Great p127-137
Tuska—Invent. p100-101
Van Wagenen—Beacon p331-333

Fabricius, Johann (1587-1615). Ger. astronomer.
*Book—Pop. Sci. (8) p2570-2571
Hammerton p576

Fabricius, Johann Christian (1743/1745-1808). Dan. entomologist.
Chambers—Dict. col.153-154
Copen.—Prom. p76-80
Esig—Hist. p622-625 (por.623)

Fabricius, Otto (1744-1822). Dan. naturalist, sci. explorer.
Copen.—Prom. p72-75

Fabricius ab Acquapendente, Hieronymus (or Fabrizio, Geronimo) (1537-1619). It. anatomist, surgeon.

Castiglioni—Hist. p427,473 (por.428)
Chambers—Dict. col. 153
Gordon—Medieval p637-638
Hammerton p576
Lambert—Medical p122-123
Lambert—Minute p122-123
Leonardo—Lives p159-161

Locy—Biology p41-42 (por.43)
Major—History (1) p411-412 (por.413)
Newman—Interp. p27-28
Sigerist—Great p139
Van Wagenen—Beacon p72-74
Woodruff—Devel. p272
Year—Pic. p81 (por.81)

Fabricius Hildanus (or Fabry, Wilhelm) (1560-1634). Ger. physician, surgeon.

Gordon—Medieval p684-685 (por.50)
Gordon—Romance p455 (por.455)
Lambert—Medical p116-118

Lambert—Minute p116-118
Leonardo—Lives p161-163
Major—History (1) p442-444 (por.443)

Fabry.   See **Fabricius Hildanus**

Faessler, Carl (1895-1957). Swiss mineralogist, geologist.

G.S.A—Proc '57 p113-114 (por.113)

Fagnano, Giulio Carlo, Count (or Fagnani) (1682/1690-1766). It. mathematician.

Ball—Short p372-373
Cajori—Hist. p225

Fahlberg, Constantin (1850-1910). Amer. chemist.

Chambers—Dict. col.154

Fahrenheit, Gabriel Daniel (1686-1736). Ger. physicist.

Chambers—Dict. col.154
Hammerton p577
Hart—Physicists p90-91

Magie—Source p131
Moulton—Auto. p206

Fairbairn, Sir William (1789-1874). Scot. engineer.

Hammerton p577

Fairbanks, Thaddeus (1796-1886). Amer. inventor.

Hammerton p577

Fairchild, David Grandison (1869-1954). Amer. botanist, agriculturist.

Curr. Biog. '53 p190-193 (por.191)   *Milne—Natur. p145-155 (por.144)
*Jewett—Plant p47-101

Fairchild, Herman LeRoy (1850-1943). Amer. geologist.

G.S.A.—Proc. '44 p185-216 (por.185)

Fairey, Charles Richard (1887-   ). Brit. aero. pioneer.
Burge—Ency. p630-631

Fairless, Benjamin F. (1890-   ). Amer. engineer.
Forbes—Fifty p109-116 (por.108)

Fajans, Kasimir (1887-   ). Pol.-Amer. phys. chemist.
Chambers—Dict. col.154-155
Weeks—Discovery p491,492 (por.492)

Falconer, Hugh (1808-1865). Scot. paleontologist.
Hammerton p578

Falconer, John (fl.1574). Eng. botanist.
Hawks—Pioneers p147,149

Falcucci, Nicholas of Florence (or Florentinus, Nicholas) (c1350-c1411). It. physician.
Major—Hist. (1) p354-355

Falk, Leslie A. (1915-   ). Amer. physician.
Farmer—Doctors' p235-237

Fall, Henry Clinton (1862-1939). Amer. entomologist.
Esig—Hist. p625-627 (por.626)
Osborn—Fragments p234 (por.378)

Fallén, Carl Friedrich (1764-1830). Swed. entomologist.
Essig—Hist. p693

Fallopius, Gabriel (or Fallopio, Gabriello) (1523-1562). It. anatomist.
*Book—Pop. Sci. (10) p3221-3222
Castiglioni—Hist. p425-427
Chambers—Dict. col.155-156
Gordon—Medieval p636-637
Hammerton p578-579
Leonardo—Lives p163-164
Locy—Biology p37-38 (por.37)
Major—History (1) p410-411
(por.411)
Van Wagenen—Beacon p62-63
Woodruff—Devel. p224,272
Year—Pic. p81 (por.81)

Fanning, John Thomas (1837-1911). Amer. engineer.
Hammerton p579

Faraday, Michael (1791-1867). Eng. chemist, physicist, inventor.
Abbot—Great p4-5 (por.8)
*Bolton—Famous p77-83 (por.76)
*Book—Pop. Sci. (10) p3222-3224
Chalmers—History p265-266
Chambers—Dict. col.156 (por.155)
Crew—Physicists #6 (por.)
(Continued)

Faraday, Michael—*Continued*
 Crowther—Men p67-126 (por.72,117)
 *Darrow—Masters p73-77 (por.321)
 *Darrow—Thinkers p38-41 (por.40)
 Defries—Pioneers p171-187
 Dibner—Ten p35-38 (por.36)
 *Epstein—Real p54-55
 Findlay—Hundred p323
 Fitzhugh—Concise p202-203
 Fülöp—Miller p67-71 (por.48)
 Gibson—Heroes p248-264
 Ginzburg—Advent. p229-252
  (por.240)
 Gregory—British p32-33 **(por.32)**
 Hammerton p579-580 (por.579)
 Hammond—Stories p96-114 (por.104)
 Hart—Makers p248-273 (por.248)
 Hart—Physicists p108-112
 *Hartman—Mach. p90-94
 Hawks—Wireless p53-59 (por.40)
 *Hodgins—Behemoth p118-135
 Holmyard—British p45-47 (por.45)
 *Kendall—Young p42-88 (por.3)
 Law—Civiliz. p199-204
 Lenard—Great p247-263 (por.262)
 *McSpadden—How p163-174
 Magie—Source p472-473
 Meyer—World p133-137 (por.134)
 Morgan—Men p39-62 (por.92)
 Moulton—Auto. p288-290

 *Nisenson—Illus. p61 (por.61)
 100 Great p595-603
 Partington—Short p192-194,212
  (por.193)
 People p144-145 (por.170)
 Radio's 100 p41-47 (por.140)
 Roberts—Chem. p99-105
 Schwartz—Moments (2) p856-858
 Sci. Amer.—Lives p127-140 (por.129)
 *Science Miles p145-150 (por.145)
 Sewell—Brief p146
 *Shippen—Design p70-81
 Smith—Torch. p82 (por.82)
 *Stevens—Science p97-102 (por.96)
 Taylor—Illus. p124-126,130
 Thomas—Scien. p117-129 (por.115)
 Tilden—Famous p152-169 (por.152)
 Tuska—Invent. p129-130
 Van Wagenen—Beacon p253-255
 *Williams—Ellis p109-128
 Williams—Story p208-209,234
  (por.211)
 Wilson—Human p249-274 (por.252)
 Woodruff—Devel. p57-58,272
  (por.52)
 *World's Great p241-273 (por.244)
 *Wright—Great p200-208
 Year—Pic. p121 (por.121)

Farlow, William Gilson (1844-1919). Amer. botanist.
 N.A.S. Biog. (11) (XXI-Memoirs)
  p1-18 (por.1)

Farman, Henry C. (1874-1934). Fr. aero. pioneer.
 Burge—Ency. p631   Heinmuller—Man's p265 (por.265)
 Hammerton p581

Farmer, Moses Gerrish (1820-1893). Amer. inventor.
 *Hylander—Invent. p209

Farnsworth, Arthur (1908?-1943). Amer. aero. pioneer.
 Curr. Biog. '43 p200

Farnsworth, Philo Taylor (1906-   ). Amer. inventor, engineer.
 *Bachman—Great p294-296 (por.294)   Radio's 100 p280-282 (por.140)
 *Montgomery—Invent. p97-100   Wilson—Amer. p400-401

Farny, George Wimbor (1882-1941). Rus. min. engineer.
 Curr. Biog. '41 p270

Farr, Wanda K. (1895-   ). Amer. biochemist.
Yost—Women Sci. p139-157

Farr, William (1807-1883). Eng. pub. health worker.
Walker—Pioneers p87-99 (por.87)

Farrar, John (1779-1853). Amer. mathematician.
Smith—Math. p96-97

Farrington, Oliver Cummings (1864-1933). Amer. geologist.
G.S.A.—Proc. '33 p193-205 (por.193)

Fauchard, Pierre (1678-1761). Fr. dental surgeon.
Moulton—Auto. p208

Faujas de Saint-Fond, Barthélemy de (1741-1819). Fr. geologist.
Geikie—Founders p198-199
Hammerton p582

Faust, Ernest Carroll (1890-   ). Amer. parasitologist.
Progress—Science '40 p163

Fawcett, Edward (1867-1942). Brit. anatomist.
Curr. Biog. '42 p264

Fay.   See **Du Fay, Charles François de Cisternay**

Faye, Hervé Auguste Étienne Albans (1814-1902). Fr. astronomer.
Armitage—Cent. p53-54   Chambers—Dict. col.156-157
*Book—Pop. Sci. (8) p2571   Hammerton p583

Fayrer, Sir Joseph (1824-1907). Eng. physician.
Hammerton p583

Fearn, Anne Walter (1868?-1939). Amer. physician.
Fabricant—Why p112-113

Featherstonhaugh, George W. (1780-1866). Amer. geologist.
Merrill—First p137-138,161-165
(por.138)

Fechner, Gustav Theodor (1801-1887). Ger. physicist, psychologist.
*Book—Pop. Sci. (6) p2028   Williams—Story p409,412 (por.413)
Hammerton p583

Fedden, Sir Roy Alfred Hubert (1885-   ). Eng. engineer, aero. pioneer.
Daniel—Pioneer p57-59 (por.56)

Fedeles, Fortunato (1550-1630). It. physician.
Gordon—Medieval p759

Fehleisen, Friedrich (1854-1924). Ger. surgeon.
Bulloch—Hist. p365

Fehling, Hermann von (1812-1885). Ger. chemist.
Chambers—Dict. col.157   Smith—Torch. p84 (por.84)
Hammerton p584

Felix, Arthur (1887-1956). Siles.-Pol. bacteriologist.
R.S.L.—Biog. (3) p53-75 (por.53)

Felix, Robert H. (1904-   ). Amer. psychiatrist.
Curr. Biog. '57 p182-183 (por.182)

Fellows, Sir Charles (1799-1860). Eng. archaeologist.
Hammerton p584

Fellows, Robert Ellsworth (1915-1949). Amer. geologist.
G.S.A.—Proc. '49 p159-162 (por.159)

Felt, Ephraim Porter (1868-1943). Amer. entomologist.
Essig—Hist. p627-629 (por.627)
Osborn—Fragments p231-232
  (por.352)

Felt, Harry Donald (1902-   ). Amer. aero. pioneer.
Curr. Biog. '59 p114-116 (por.115)

Feltz, Victor Timothée (1835-1893). Fr. bacteriologist.
Bulloch—Hist. p365

Fenger, Christian (1840-1902). Dan.-Amer. surgeon.
Leonardo—Lives p165-166
Major—History (2) p1033

Fenneman, Nevin Melancthon (1865-1945). Amer. geologist.
G.S.A.—Proc. '45 p215-225 (por.215)

Fenner, Clarence Norman (1870-1949). Amer. geologist.
G.S.A.—Proc. '51 p103-106 (por.103)

Ferber, Ferdinand (1862-1909). Fr. aero. pioneer.
Burge—Ency. p631
Heinmuller—Man's p261 (por.261)

Ferguson, Alexander Hugh (1853-1911). Can.-Amer. surgeon.
Leonardo—Lives p166

Ferguson, Archie Robert (1895-   ). Amer. aero. pioneer.
Potter—Flying p208-232 (por.210)

Ferguson, Harry George (1884-1960). Irish-Amer. inventor.
Curr. Biog. '56 p179-181 (por.179)
*Larsen—Shaped p161-175 (por.129)

Ferguson, James (1710-1776). Scot. astronomer.
Hammerton p587 (por.587)
MacPherson—Makers p84-87

Fergusson, James (1808-1886). Scot. archaeologist.
Hammerton p587

Fergusson, Sir William (1808-1877). Scot. physician, surgeon.
Hammerton p587   Major—History (2) p880-881
Leonardo—Lives (Supp.1) p480-481

Fermat, Pierre de (1601-1665). Fr. mathematician.
Ball—Short p293-301
Bell—Men p56-72 (por.,front.)
*Book—Pop. Sci. (11) p3813-3814
Cajori—Hist. p163-164,167-171
Chambers—Dict. col. 157-158
Hooper—Makers p222-223,286-288
Magie—Source p278
*Miller—Hist. p230-231
Sedgwick— Short p282-283
Smith—Hist. I p377-378 (por.377)
Smith—Portraits (2) III, unp. (por.)
Turnbull—Great p80-81
Van Wagenen—Beacon p109-110
Woodruff—Devel. p272 (por.8)
Year—Pic. p92-93 (por.93)

Fermi, Enrico (1901-1954). It. physicist.
A.A.A.S.—Proc. (82) p290-293
Chambers—Dict. Supp.,col.158
Curr. Biog. '45 p179-181 (por.179), '55 p202
Heathcote—Nobel p369-377 (por.240)
*Jaffe—Crucibles p379-396
Jaffe—Men p571-628 (por.xxviii)
N.A.S.—Biog. (30) p125-155 (por.125)
*Pratt—Famous p134-136
Progress—Science '40 p163
R.S.L.—Biog. (1) p69-75 (por.69)
Riedman—Men p150-171 (por.168, 169)
Robinson—100 p239-242 (por.239)
Weber—College p653 (por.653)
Weeks—Discovery p537-538
Wilson—Amer. p415-416 (por.414)
Year—Pic. p212 (por.212)

Fermor, Lewis Leigh (1880-1954). Eng. geologist.
R.S.L.—Biog. (2) p101-113 (por.101)

Fernald, Charles Henry (1838-1921). Amer. entomologist, zoologist.
Osborn—Fragments p178 (por.350)

Fernald, Henry Torsey (1866-1952). Amer. entomologist.
Osborn—Fragments p200 (por.353)

Fernald, M. E. (1839-1919). Amer. entomologist.
Osborn—Fragments p178

Fernald, Merritt Lyndon (1873-1950). Amer. botanist.
N.A.S.—Biog. (28) p45-64 (por.45)

Fernel, Jean François (or Joannes Fernelius) (1497-1558). Fr. physician.
Gordon—Medieval p596-597,757-758   Sarton—Six p191-196 (por.192)
Major—History (1) p419-423   Smith—Hist. I p308-309
 (por.421)

Ferrán y Clua, Jaime (1849-1929). Sp. bacteriologist.
Bulloch—Hist. p365

Ferranti, Sebastian Ziani de (1864-1930). Eng. inventor.
Hammerton p587

Ferrari, Ludovico (or Ferraro) (1522-1565). It. mathematician.
Ball—Short p225-226
Smith—Hist. I p300

Ferrarin, Arturo (1895-1941). It. aero. pioneer.
*Fraser—Heroes p549-550
Heinmuller—Man's p331 (por.331)

Ferrein, Antoine (1693-1769). Fr. physician.
Major—History (2) p632

Ferrel, William (1817-1891). Amer. meteorologist.
Hammerton p587-588
N.A.S.—Biog. (3) p265-299

Ferrero, Gina Lombroso (1872-1944). It. physician, psychologist.
Curr. Biog. '44 p205
Lovejoy—Women p203

Ferrier, Sir David (1843-1928). Scot. anatomist, neurologist.
Chambers—Dict. col.158
Hammerton p588

Ferris, Harry Burr (1865-1940). Amer. anatomist.
Curr. Biog. '40 p290

Fessenden, Reginald Aubrey (1866-1932). Can. physicist, inventor.
Hawks—Wireless p288-290 (por.288) Year—Pic. p179 (por.179)
Radio's 100 p137-141 (por.140)

Fewkes, Jesse Walter (1850-1930). Amer. enthnologist, geologist.
N.A.S.—Biog. (15) p261-267 (por.261)
True—Smiths. p123-125 (por.124)

Feynman, Richard Phillips (1918-   ). Amer. physicist.
Curr. Biog. '55 p205-207 (por.206)

Fibiger, Johannes Andreas Grib (1867-1928). Dan. pathologist, physician.
Castiglioni—Hist. p963,1126   Grainger—Guide p152
  (por.963)   Hammerton p589
Chambers—Dict. col.158-159   Stevenson—Nobel p120-124 (por.150)
Copen.—Prom. p190-193

Fibonacci, Leonardo (or Pisano, Leonardo) (1180?-1250?). It.
  mathematician.
Hooper—Makers p84   Smith—Hist. I p214-218 (por.214)
Sedgwick—Short p178-179

Ficino, Marsilio (1433-1499). It. nat. philosopher, hygienist.
Sarton—Six p201-202

Fick, Adolph Eugen (1829-1910). Ger. physiologist.
Chambers—Dict. col.159

Fiedler, Wilhelm (1832-1912). Ger. mathematician.
Cajori—Hist. p297

Field, Cyrus West (1819-1892). Amer. inventor.
Abbot—Great p91-92 (por.89)   Law—Civiliz. p213-215
*Book—Pop. Sci. (5) p1539-1540 *Morris—Heroes p153-158
*Darrow—Masters p332   *Tappan—Heroes p71-78
*Epstein—Real p134-135   Wilson—Amer. p172-177 (por.172)
*Hartman—Mach. p148-153

Field, George Hamilton (b.1850). Amer. entomologist.
Essig—Hist. p629-630 (por.629)

Field, Henry (1902-   ). Amer. anthropologist.
Curr. Biog. '55 p207-209 (por.208)

Field, Stephen Dudley (1846-1913). Amer. inventor.
*Hylander—Invent. p210

Filatov, Vladimir Petrovich (1875-1956). Rus. physician.
*Montgomery—Story p189-191

Filon, Lewis Napoleon George (1875-1937). Eng. mathematician.
Hammerton p591

Finch, Ruy Herbert (1890-1957). Amer. geologist.
G.S.A.—Proc. '57 p117-120 (por.117)

Finck, Thomas (1561-1646). Dan. mathematician.
Chambers—Dict. col.159

Findlay, Alexander (b.1874). Scot. chemist.
Chambers—Dict. col.159

Finke, Leonhard Ludwig (1747-1828?). Ger. physician.
Rosen—Four p239-241

Finkelstein, Heinrich (1865-1942). Ger. physician.
Kagan—Modern p54 (por.54)

Finkler, Rita V. (Sapiro) (1888-   ). Rus. physician.
Knapp—Women p165-184 (por.165)

Finlay, Carlos Juan (1833-1915). Cuban physician, biologist.
Castiglioni—Hist. p906 (por.906)   Major—History (2) p863-864,897
Grainger—Guide p152   (por.864)
                                                  *Shippen—Men p187-190

Finney, John Miller Turpin (1863-1942). Amer. physician, surgeon.
Leonardo—Lives p166-168   Rosen—Four p196-200
Major—History (2) p1034

Finsen, Niels Ryberg (1860-1904). Dan. physician.
Chambers—Dict. col.159   Hammerton p592
Copen.—Prom. p181-185   Major—History (2) p918-919
*DeKruif—Men p283-299 (por.285)   Stevenson—Nobel p15-19 (por.150)

Fioravanti, Leonardo (1518-1588). It. physician.
Major—History (1) p472

Fischer, Bernhard (1852-1915). Ger. surgeon.
Bulloch—Hist. p365

Fischer, Emil Hermann (1852-1919). Ger. chemist.
A.A.A.S.—Proc. (81) p50-55
*Book—Pop. Sci. (10) p3224-3226
  (por.3225)
Chambers—Dict. col.159-160
Farber—Nobel p7-11 (por.118)
Findlay—Hundred p324
Hammerton p592
Harrow—Chemists p207-239 (por.217)
Major—History (2) p921-922
Partington—Short p310-312,318
  (por.311)
Smith—Torch. p85 (por.85)
*Snyder—Biology p315
Van Wagenen—Beacon p406-408
Woodruff—Devel. p111-112,272-273
  (por.110)
Year—Pic. p124,221 (por.124)

Fischer, Hans (1881-1945). Ger. chemist.
Chambers—Dict. col.160
Curr. Biog. '45 p188
Farber—Nobel p118-123 (por.118)
Hammerton p592
*Snyder—Biology p319-320

Fischer, Isidor (1868-1943). Aust. gynecologist.
Kagan—Modern p209 (por.209)

Fischer, Otto Philip (1852-1932). Ger. chemist.
A.A.A.S.—Proc. (81) p55-56
Chambers—Dict. col.160
Findlay—Hundred p324

Fischer von Waldheim, Gotthelf (1771-1853). Ger.-Rus. entomologist.
Essig—Hist. p631-632 (por.631)

Fish, Marie Poland (1902-   ). Amer. ichthyologist.
Curr. Biog. '41 p280-281 (por.208)

Fishbein, Morris (1889-   ). Amer. physician.
Curr. Biog. '40 p297-299 (por.298)

Fisher, Clarence Stanley (1876-1941). Amer. archaeologist.
Curr. Biog. '41 p282

Fisher, Harry Linn (1885-   ). Amer. chemist.
Curr. Biog. '54 p276-278 (por.277)

Fisher, I. (1875-1934). Fr. aero. pioneer.
Heinmuller—Man's p293 (por.293)

Fisher, James T. (1864-1951). Amer. psychiatrist.
Fabricant—Why p109-111

Fisher, Lloyd Wellington (1897-1951). Amer. geologist.
G.S.A.—Proc. '51 p109-111

Fisk, James Brown (1910-   ). Amer. physicist.
Curr. Biog. '59 p120-122 (por.121)

Fiske, Bradley Allen (1854-1942). Amer. aero. pioneer, inventor.
Heinmuller—Man's p292 (por.292)

Fiske, James Porter (1866-1941). Amer. physician, surgeon.
Curr. Biog. '41 p283

Fiske, John (1842-1901). Amer. nat. philosopher.
Hubbard—Scientists (2) p135-151
    (por.135)

Fitch, Asa (1809-1879). Amer. entomologist.
Essig—Hist. p632-634 (por.632)
Smiths.—Misc. (84) p43-50
    (por.pl.1,p545)

Fitch, Aubrey Wray (1883-   ). Amer. aero. pioneer.
Curr. Biog. '45 (por.191)

Fitch, John (1743-1798). Amer. inventor.
Abbot—Great p181-182   *Hodgins—Behemoth p177-183
*Burlingame—Inv. p36-53   *Hylander—Invent. p11-20 (por.10)
Chambers—Dict. col.160-161   Law—Civiliz. p40-45
Goddard—Eminent p18-26   Wilson—Amer.p52-53
Hammerton p593-594

Fittig, Rudolf (1835-1910). Ger. chemist.
Chambers—Dict. col.161   Smith—Torch. p86 (por.86)
Hammerton p594   Weeks—Discovery p472 (por.472)
Partington—Short p316-317

Fitz, Reginald Heber (1843-1913). Amer. physician, pathologist.
Chambers—Dict. col.161   Rowntree—Amid p221-225 (por.222)
Kagan—Modern p151 (por.151)   Thorwald—Century p261-363
Major—History (2) p904 (por.851)

Fitzgerald, George Francis (1851-1901). Irish physicist.
Appleyard—Pioneers p235-237,244-   Hammerton p594
    250 (por.236)   Sci. Amer.—Lives p75-83 (por.77)
Chambers—Dict. col.161

Fitzgerald, Leslie Maurice (1898-   ). Amer. oral surgeon.
Curr. Biog. '54 p278-280 (por.279)

Fitzmaurice, James (1898-   ). Irish aero. pioneer.
Hammerton p595
Heinmuller—Man's p103-114,328
(por.111,238)

Fitzroy, Robert (1805-1865). Eng. meteorologist.
Hammerton p595

Fizeau, Armand Hyppolyte Louis (1819-1896). Fr. physicist.
Chambers—Dict. col.162
Hammerton p595
Magie—Source p340

Flack, Martin (1882-1931). Eng. aero. pioneer.
Burge—Ency. p631

Flaiani, Giuseppe (1741-1808). It. anatomist, physician, surgeon.
Castiglioni—Hist. p625 (por.625)

Flammarion, (Nicolas) Camille (1842-1925). Fr. astronomer.
*Book—Pop. Sci. (8) p2571-2572
Chambers—Dict. col.162-163
Hammerton p596
MacPherson—Astron. p119-128
(por.119)
MacPherson—Makers p194-197

Flamsteed, John (1646-1719). Eng. astronomer.
Abetti—History p141-142
Ball—Great p147-161 (por.155)
*Book—Pop. Sci. (8) p2572 (por.2572)
Chambers—Dict. col.163-164
(por.162)
Hammerton p596
MacPherson—Makers p73-75
100 Great p551-556
Shapley—Astron. p87
Vaucouleurs—Disc. p62-63
Williams—Great p174-175 (por.174)
Woodruff—Devel. p273

Flanders, Ralph Edward (1880-   ). Amer. engineer.
Curr. Biog. '48 p211-214 (por.213)
*Yost—Engineers p17-31

Fleck, Sir Alexander (1889-   ). Scot. chemist.
Curr. Biog. '56 p183-184 (por.183)
Weeks—Discovery p501 (por.501)

Fleming, Sir Alexander (1881-1955). Scot. bacteriologist, physician.
*Bolton—Famous p271-280 (por.270)
Calder—Science p82-86
Castiglioni—Hist. p1057-1058
(por.1057)
Chambers—Dict. Supp.,col.164
(por.163)
*Crowther—Doctors p177-207
(por.161)
Curr. Biog. '44 p208 (por.208), '55
p210-211
*Eberle—Modern p1-48
*Elwell—Sci. p73-75
(Continued)

Fleming, Sir Alexander—*Continued*
Grainger—Guide p152-153
*Larsen—Shaped p131-141 (por.97)
Ludovici—Nobel p165-177 (por.174)
Major—History (2) p1010-1011 (por.1011)
*Montgomery—Story p131-135
Pringle—Great p13-24 (por.64)
R.S.L.—Biog. (2) p117-124 (por.117)
Ratcliffe—Modern p42-43

Robinson—100 p280-283 (por.280)
Rowntree—Amid p438-446 (por.439)
*Science Miles. p298-304 (por.298)
*Shippen—Men p198-203 (por.198)
Stevenson—Nobel p229-230,231-237 (por.150)
*Truax—Doctors p154-164
Untermeyer—Makers p559-564
Year—Pic. p222 (por.222)

Fleming, John Adam (1877-1956). Amer. geophysicist.
Curr. Biog. '40 p302-303; '56 p184

Fleming, Sir John Ambrose (1849-1945). Eng. physicist.
A.A.A.S.—Proc. (77) p52-53
Chambers—Dict. col.164
Curr. Biog. '45 p194
Hammerton p598 (por.598)

Hawks—Wireless p261-268 (por.258)
Law—Civiliz. p220
Radio's 100 p90-94 (por.140)
Year—Pic. p179 (por.179)

Fleming, Sir Sandford (1827-1915). Scot.-Can. engineer.
Book—Pop. Sci. (5) p1541-1543 (por.1541)

Fleming, Williamina Paton (1857-1911). Scot.-Amer. astronomer.
Armitage—Cent. p174-175 (por.176)

Flemming, Walther (1843-1915). Ger. biologist.
Chambers—Dict. col.164-165

Fletcher, Alice Cunningham (1838-1923). Amer. ethnologist, anthropologist.
Mozans—Woman p322-323

Fletcher, Harvey (1884-   ). Amer. physicist.
Progress—Science '41 p156-157 (por.157)

Fletcher, James (1852-1908). Can. entomologist.
Osborn—Fragments p170-171 (por.347)

Fletcher, Sir Walter Morley (1873-1933). Eng. physician.
Hammerton p599

Flett, Sir John (1869?-1947). Scot. geologist.
G.S.A.—Proc. '49 p163-164 (por.163)

Flettner, Anton (1885-   ). Ger. engineer, inventor.
Chambers—Dict. col.165

Fleure, Herbert John (1877-   ). Brit. anthropologist.
Hammerton p599 (por.599)

Flexner, Simon (1863-1946). Amer. pathologist, physician.
*Book—Pop. Sci. (6) p2028-2030 (por.2029)
Bulloch—Hist. p365
Curr. Biog. '46 p192
Hammerton p599
Major—History (2) p979-980,1034 (por.981)
Rowntree—Amid p358-364 (por.362)
*Snyder—Biology p270 (por.269)
*Stirling—Polio p36-37 (por.37)

Flickinger, Don D. (1907-   ). Amer. physician, aero. pioneer, space pioneer.
Thomas—Men (3) p74-96 (por.74)

Flint, Austin (1812-1886). Amer. physician.
Castiglioni—Hist. p837 (por.837)
Major—History (2) p759-760

Florentinus, Nicholaus.   See **Falcucci, Nicholas of Florence**

Florey, Sir Howard Walter (1898-   ). Eng. pathologist.
Chambers—Dict. col.165
Curr. Biog. '44 p208-210 (por.209)
*Eberle—Modern p26-37,48
Grainger—Guide p153
*Larsen—Shaped p131-140 (por.97)
*Shippen—Men p204-207
Stevenson—Nobel p230,233-237 (por.150)

Florey, Lady Mary Ethel Reed (n.d.). Eng. physician.
Lovejoy—Women p251

Flourens, Marie Jean Pierre (1794-1867). Fr. physiologist.
Hammerton p600

Flower, Sir William Henry (1831-1899). Eng. zoologist.
Hammerton p600

Floyer, Sir John (1649-1734). Eng. physician.
Chambers—Dict. col.165
Gunther—Early XI p129-131 (por.129)
Hammerton p600
Major—History (1) p562

Fludd, Robert (1574-1637). Eng. physician.
Gunther—Early XI p202-203,239
Major—History (1) p545

Flügge, Carl (1847-1923). Ger. bacteriologist, hygienist.
Bulloch—Hist. p366

Foà, Pio (1848-1923). It. pathologist.
Castiglioni—Hist. p808 (por.807)

Fodor, Josef (1843-1901). Hung. bacteriologist.
Bulloch—Hist. p366

Foerste, August F. (1862-1930). Amer. geologist.
G.S.A.—Proc. '36 p143-150 (por.143)

Foës, Anutius (or Foëius, Anuce) (1528-1592). Fr. physician.
Major—History (1) p473

Fokker, Anthony Herman Gerard (1890-1939). Dutch engineer, aero. pioneer.
Hammerton p602 (por.602)
Heinmuller—Man's p285 (por.285)

Foligno.   See **Gentile da Foligno**

Folin, Otto (or Knut Olof) (1867-1934). Swed. chemist.
N.A.S.—Biog. (27) p47-70 (por.47)

Folsom, Justus W. (1871-1936). Amer. entomologist.
Osborn—Fragments p207 (por.365)

Fonck, René (1894-   ). Fr. aero. pioneer.
Arnold—Airmen p127-128   Heinmuller—Man's p321 (por.321)
Burge—Ency. p631-632

Fontana, Abbé Felice (1730?-1805). It. naturalist, physiologist.
Castiglioni—Hist. p580-581

Fontana, Franciscus (1580-1656). It. astronomer.
Chambers—Dict. col.165

Fontana, Nicola.   See **Tartaglia, Niccolò**

Fontenelle, Bernard le Bovier de (1657-1757). Fr. sci. writer.
Chambers—Dict. col. 166

Fonvielle, Wilfred de (1824-1914). Fr. aero. pioneer.
Hammerton p603

Foote, Harry Ward (1875-1942). Amer. chemist.
Curr. Biog. '42 p266

Foote, Paul Darwin (1888-   ). Amer. physicist.
Progress—Science '40 p168-169
(por.168)

Forbes, Edward (1815-1854). Brit. naturalist.
Chambers—Dict. col.166

Forbes, George (1849-1936). Eng. physicist.
Chambers—Dict. col.166

Forbes, James David (1809-1868). Scot. physicist.
Chambers—Dict. col.166-167
Van Wagenen—Beacon p287-289

Forbes, Sir John (1787-1861). Scot. physician.
Hammerton p603

Forbes, Stephen Alfred (1844-1930). Amer. entomologist.
N.A.S.—Biog. (15) p3-25 (por.3)
Osborn—Fragments p221
(por.337,354)

Forbush, Edward Howe (1858-1929). Amer. naturalist, ornithologist.
Tracy—Amer. Nat. p173-179

Forchhammer, Johan Georg (1794-1865). Dan. geologist.
Copen—Prom. p107-109

Forchheimer, Frederick (1853-1913). Amer. physician.
Kagan—Modern p16 (por.16)

Ford, Henry (1863-1947). Amer. inventor.
Abbot—Great p222-225 (por.221)
Borth—Pioneers p200-212
(por.76,206)
*Burlingame—Mach. p187-202
Curr. Biog. '44 p217-221 (por.217)
*Darrow—Builders p45-54
*Epstein—Real p76-77
Fitzhugh—Concise p216-217
*Forbes—Men p115-124 (por.1)
Hammerton p604 (por.604)
*Hartman—Mach. p213-217
*Hodgins—Behemoth p318-319
Huff—Famous (2d) p191-204
(por.190)
*Larsen—Men p144-166
*Larsen—Prentice p77-78
*Larsen—Scrap p124-127
Law—Civiliz. p55-58
*McSpadden—How p247-262
*Montgomery—Invent. p213-216
Morris—Ency. p660
*Nisenson—More p57 (por.57)
*Parkman—Conq. p310-324
People p147-148
Sewell—Brief p201-202
Thomas—50 Amer. p339-347
(por.,back)
Untermeyer—Makers p321-328
*Wildman—Famous (1st) p131-143
(por.129)

Ford, William E. (1878-1939). Amer. geologist, mineralogist.
G.S.A.—Proc. '39 p187-190 (por.187)

Ford, William Webber (1872-1941). Amer. bacteriologist.
Bulloch—Hist. p366   Progress—Science '41 p157
Curr. Biog. '41 p298

Fordos, Mathurin Joseph (1816-1878). Fr. bacteriologist.
Bulloch—Hist. p366

Foreest, Pieter van (or Forestus, Petrus) (1522-1597). Dutch physician.
Major—History (1) p473

Forel, August Henri (1848-1931). Swiss entomologist, psychologist, psychiatrist.
Chambers—Dict. col.167
Hammerton p605 (por.605)

Forel, François Alphonse (1841-1912). Swiss naturalist, seismologist. anatomist.
Davison—Founders p139

Forlanini, Carlo (1847-1918). It. physician, surgeon.
Castiglioni—Hist. p989 (por.988)
Leonardo—Lives p168-169

Forlanini, Enrico (1848-1930). It. aero. pioneer, engineer.
Heinmuller—Man's p249 (por.249)

Forman, Jonathan (1887-   ). Amer. physician.
Fabricant—Why p23-41

Forssman, Werner (1904-   ). Ger. physician.
Curr. Biog. '57 p190-192 (por.191)

Förster, Friedrich Wilhelm (b.1869). Ger. psychologist.
Hammerton p605

Forsyth, Alexander John (1769-1843). Scot. inventor.
*Pratt—Famous p106-111

Forsyth, Andrew Russell (1858-1942). Scot. mathematician.
Hammerton p605

Fortune, Robert (1813-1880). Scot. botanist.
Hammerton p606

Foshag, William Frederick (1894-1956). Amer. geologist.
G.S.A.—Proc. '56 p123-124 (por.123)

Foss, Joseph Jacob (1915-   ). Amer. aero. pioneer.
Curr. Biog. '55 p211-212 (por.211).

Foster, John Wells (1815-1873). Amer. geologist, paleontologist.
Merrill—First p280-284,302 (por.280)

Foster, Sir Michael (1836-1907). Eng. physiologist, physician.
Castiglioni—Hist. p784 (por.785)   Major—History (2) p899
Hammerton p606

Foster, William Chapman (1897-   ). Amer. engineer.
Curr. Biog '50 p152-154 (por.152)

Fothergill, John (1712-1780). Eng. physician.
Farmer—Doctors' p33
Hammerton p606-607
Major—History (2) p634

Foucault, Jean Bernard Léon (1819-1868). Fr. physicist.
Chambers—Dict. col.167   Shapley—Astron. p283
Hammerton p607   Van Wagenen—Beacon p309-310
Magie—Source p342-343   Williams—Great p355,558-559
      (por.356)

Foulois, Benjamin D. (1879-   ). Amer. aero. pioneer.
Heinmuller—Man's p270 (por.270)

Fouqúe, Ferdinand André (1828-1904). Fr. geologist, petrologist.
Woodruff—Devel. p273

Fourcroy, Antoine François, Comte de (1755-1809). Fr. chemist.
Chambers—Dict. col.167-168   Smith—Torch. p87 (por.87)
Hammerton p607   Weeks—Discovery p138 (por.138)
Partington—Short p177

Fourier, Jean Baptiste (1768-1830). Fr. mathematician.
Ball—Short p432-433   Hammerton p607
Bell—Men p183,191-204 (port.,front.)   Magie—Source p174
Cajori—Hist. p269-272   Woodruff—Devel. p26,54,273
Chambers—Dict. col.168   Year—Pic. p117 (por.117)

Fournier d'Albe, Edmund Edward (1863-1933). Eng. physicist, inventor.
Chambers—Dict. col.168
Hammerton p607

Fowler, Alfred (1868-1940). Eng. astro-physicist, astronomer.
Curr. Biog. '40 p310-311

Fowler, Carroll (b.1875). Amer. entomologist.
Essig—Hist. p634

Fowler, Sir John (1817-1898). Eng. engineer.
Hammerton p608

Fowler, Lydia Folger (1822-1879). Amer. physician.
Lovejoy—Women p8-21 (por.11)
Mead—Medical p41-42

Fowler-Billings, Katharine (1902-   ). Amer. geologist.
Curr. Biog. '40 p311

Fox, Sir Charles (1810-1874). Eng. engineer.
Hammerton p608

Fox, Robert Were (1789-1877). Eng. geologist.
Hammerton p609

Foye, Wilbur Garland (1886-1935). Amer. geologist.
G.S.A.—Proc. '35 p245-252 (por.249)

Fracastoro, Girolamo (or Fracastorius, Hieronymus) (1483-1553). It.
astronomer, physician.
Bulloch—Hist. p366
Castiglioni—Hist. p457-459
  (por.455,457)
Chambers—Dict. col.168-169
Dreyer—Hist. p296-301
Gordon—Medieval p703-708 (por.18)
Gordon—Romance p219,220-221
  (por.219)
Grainger—Guide p153-154
Hammerton p609 (por.609)
Major—History (1) p377-379 (por.376)
Moulton—Auto. p86-87
Oliver—Stalkers p69-73 (por.70)
Sarton—Six p211-212
Sigerist—Great p103-108 (por.104)
Year—Pic. p81 (por.81)

Fraenkel, Albert (1848-1916). Ger. physician.
Bulloch—Hist. p366
Kagan—Modern p152 (por.152)

Fraenkel, Carl (1861-1915). Ger. bacteriologist.
Bulloch—Hist. p366-367

Fraenkel, Eugen (1853-1925). Ger. pathologist, bacteriologist.
Bulloch—Hist. p367

Francis, Edward (1872-1957). Amer. bacteriologist.
   *De Kruif—Hunger p133-166 (por.132)

Francis, Thomas, Jr. (1900-   ). Amer. physician.
   *Stirling—Polio p90-95 (por.91)

Franck, James (1882-   ). Amer. physicist.
   Chambers—Dict. col.169
   Curr. Biog. '57 p192-194 (por.193)
   Heathcote—Nobel p229-248 (por.240)
   Progress—Science '41 p162-163
   Weber—College p399 (por.399)

Franco, Pierre (c1500-c1565). Fr. surgeon.
   Leonardo—Lives p170-171
   Major—History (1) p469

Frank, Albert Bernhard (1839-1900). Ger. botanist.
   Chambers—Dict. col.169

Frank, Johann Peter (1745-1821). Ger. physician, public health worker.
   Castiglioni—Hist. p644-645 (por.645)
   Major—History (2) p642-644
      (por.643)
   Sigerist—Great p243-257 (por.248)
   Walker—Pioneers p35-47 (por.35)

Frank, Lawrence Kelso (1890-   ). Amer. mental hygienist.
   Curr. Biog. '58 p146-147 (por.147)

Frank, Louis (1867?-1941). Amer. physician, surgeon.
   Curr. Biog. '41 p303

Frank, Mortimer (1874-1919). Amer. physician.
   Kagan—Modern p214 (por.214)

Frankland, Sir Edward (1825-1899). Eng. chemist.
   Chambers—Dict. col.170
   Findlay—Hundred p324
   Hammerton p614
   Partington—Short p273-274,294
      (por.275)
   Roberts—Chem. p193-200
   Smith—Torch. p88 (por.88)
   Tilden—Famous p216-227 (por.216)

Frankland, Percy Faraday (1858-1946). Eng. chemist, bacteriologist.
   Bulloch—Hist. p367

Franklin, Benjamin (1706-1790). Amer. inventor.
   Bell—Early p56-58
   *Bishop—Kite p20-24
   *Book—Pop. Sci. (11) p3815-3816
   *Burlingame—Inv. p16-33
   Carmer—Caval. p50-57 (por.57)
   Chambers—Dict. col.170 (por.169)
      (*Continued*)

Franklin, Benjamin—*Continued*

Crowther—Famous p17-134 (por.32)
*Darrow—Masters p332-333
Dibner—Ten p15-18 (por.16)
*Epstein—Real p49-50,107
Fitzhugh—Concise p222-224
Gibson—Heroes p134-163
*Goddard—Eminent p9-16 (por.8)
Hammerton p614-615 (por.614)
Hart—Makers p196-197 (por.196)
Hart—Physicists p98-99
*Hartman-Mach. p83-86
Hawks—Wireless p15-17 (por.10)
*Hodgins—Behemoth p90-95
Hylander—Invent. p1-10 (por.,front.)
*Hylander—Scien. p1-10
Jaffe—Men p23-51 (por.xxviii)
*Larsen—Prentice p36-39
*Lewellen—Boy p189-214 (por.189)
Magie—Source p400-401
Meyer—World p127-128 (por.128)
Milbank—First p4-8 (por.6)
Morgan—Men p28-29
Morris—Ency. p661

*Morris—Heroes p33-43
Moulton—Auto. p234-235
*Nida—Makers p42-49 (por.46)
Peattie—Lives p11-17 (por.11)
People p150 (por.7)
*Pratt—Famous p55-59,82-83
Radio's 100 p19-22 (por.140)
Schwartz—Moments (2) p846-847
Sci. Amer.—Lives p111-126 (por.113)
*Science Miles. p97 (por.97)
Sewell—Brief p86-87
*Shippen—Design p45-51
Smith—Math. p57-59
*Stevens—Science p51-56 (por.50)
Taylor—Illus. p91-93
Thomas—50 Amer. p1-11
Tuska—Invent. p78-79
Van Wagenen—Beacon p148-150
Wilson—Amer. p16-23 (por.16)
Woglom—Discov. p118-120
*World's Great p67-95 (por.78)
Year—Pic. p105 (por.105)
Youmans—Pioneers p1-23 (por.,front.)

Franklin, Charles Samuel (1879-   ). Eng. engineer.

Radio's 100 p196-198 (por.140)

Franklin, Edward Curtis (1862-1937). Amer. chemist.

Browne—Hist. p484 (por.117)
Killeffer—Eminent p21 (por.21)

Frapolli, Francesco (fl.1700's; d.1773). It. physician.

Major—History (2) p636

Frasch, Herman (1851?-1914). Ger.-Amer. chemist, inventor.

A.A.A.S.—Proc. (79) p15-17

Fraunhofer, Joseph von (1787-1826). Ger. physicist, optician, astronomer.

Armitage—Cent. p19-22 (por.48,XI)
*Book—Pop. Sci. (10) p3226
Chambers—Dict. col.170-171
Hammerton p616
Lenard—Great p196-204 (por.199)
MacPherson—Makers p159-162
  (por.106)

Shapley—Astron. p196
Van Wagenen—Beacon p247-248
Weeks—Discovery p364 (por.364)
Williams—Great p338-340 (por.348)
Woodruff—Devel. p273
Year—Pic. p119 (por.119)

Frazer, Sir James George (1854-1941). Scot. anthropologist.

Curr. Biog. '41 p309
Hammerton p616 (por.616)

Frazer, John Fries (1812-1872). Amer. chemist, physicist.

N.A.S.—Biog. (1) p245-256

Frear, Joseph Allen, Jr. (1903-   ). Amer. agriculturist.
Curr. Biog. '54 p289-291 (por.290)

Fred, Edwin Brown (1887-   ). Amer. bacteriologist.
Curr. Biog. '50 p156-157 (por.156)

Frederick II (1194-1250). Ger. biologist, ornithologist.
Bodenheimer—Hist. p210
Welker—Birds p3-4

Fredholm, Eric Ivar (1866-1927). Swed. mathematician.
Cajori—Hist. p393
Lindroth—Swedish p256-263

Freeman, Bruce Clark (1900-1940). Can. geologist.
G.S.A.—Proc. '40 p191-193 (por.191)

Freeman, John Ripley (1855-1932). Amer. engineer.
N.A.S.—Biog (17) p171-182 (por.171)

Freeman, Leonard (1860-1935). Amer. surgeon.
Leonardo—Lives p171

Freeman, Walter (1895-   ). Amer. neurologist.
Chambers—Dict. col.171

Freiberg, Albert Henry (1868-1940). Amer. surgeon.
Kagan—Modern p101 (por.101)

Freind, John (1675-1728). Eng. physician.
Gunther—Early XI p215 (por.212,216)
Major—History (2) p630

Frémont, John Charles (1813-1890). Amer. naturalist, sci. explorer.
Ewan—Rocky p21-33,211 (por.21)
*Nisenson—More p59 (por.59)

Frémy, Edmond (1814-1894). Fr. chemist.
Chambers—Dict. col.171   Weeks—Discovery p458-459 (por.459)
Hammerton p622

French, George Hazen (1841-1935). Amer. entomologist.
Osborn—Fragments p180-181
  (por.348)

French, Hollis (1868-1940). Amer. engineer.
Curr. Biog. '41 p311

Frénicle de Bessy, Bernard (c1602-1675). Fr. mathematician.
Smith—Hist. I p385

Frère Jean de Saint-Come.   See **Saint-Come, Frère Jean de**

Frerichs, Friedrich Theodor von (1819-1885). Ger. physician.
Major—History (2) p886

Fresenius, Karl Remigius (1818-1897). Ger. chemist.
Chambers—Dict. col.171-172   Smith—Torch. p89 (por.89)
Hammerton p622

Fresnel, Augustin Jean (1788-1827). Fr. physicist, engineer.
Arago—Biog. p171-279   Hart—Physicists p118-122
Ball—Short p436-437   Lenard—Great p196-213 (por.199)
*Book—Pop. Sci. (10) p3226-3228   Magie—Source p318
Chalmers—Historic p266   Van Wagenen—Beacon p250-251
Chambers—Dict. col.172   Williams—Story p200-204,225
Crew—Physicists #5 (folder) (por.)   (por.201)
Hammerton p622   Woodruff—Devel. p59,273
                                        Year—Pic. p120 (por.120)

Freud, Sigmund (1856-1939). Aust. neurologist, psychologist, psychoanalyst.
*Book—Pop. Sci. (6) p2031-2036   Jaffe—Outposts p219-225 (por.203)
Castiglioni—Hist. p1049-1051   Kagan—Modern p66 (por.66)
   (por.1050)   Major—History (2) p929-930 (por.929)
Chambers—Dict. col.172-173   Makers—Modern p1-132
   (por.174)   Moulton—Auto. p591-592
*Chandler—Medicine p103-106   People p151 (por.179)
   (por.102)   Rosen—Four p116-119,202-206
Fabricant—Why p42-43   *Science Miles. p245-249 (por.245)
Farmer—Doctors' p195   Sewell—Brief p219-220
Fitzhugh—Concise p228-229   Untermeyer—Makers p238-246
Gordon—Romance p508-513   Year—Pic. p224 (por.224)
Hammerton p622-623 (por.622)

Freundlich, Herbert (1880-1941). Ger. chemist.
Chambers—Dict. col.173
Curr. Biog. '41 p311

Frey, Joseph Miller (1818-1888). Amer. physician.
Jones—Memories p358-362 (por.358)

Freyer, Sir Peter Johnston (1852-1921). Brit. surgeon.
Hammerton p623

Friedberger, Ernst (1875-1932). Ger. bacteriologist.
Bulloch—Hist. p367

Friedel, Charles (1832-1899). Fr. mineralogist, chemist.
*Book—Pop. Sci. (10) p3228-3229   Partington—Short p318
Chambers—Dict. col.173   Smith—Torch. p90 (por.90)

Friedenwald, Aaron (1836-1902). Amer. physician.
Kagan—Modern p144 (por.144)

Friedenwald, Julius (1866-1941). Amer. physician.
Kagan—Modern p22 (por.22)

Friedheim, Carl (1858-1909). Swiss chemist.
Smith—Torch. p91 (por.91)

Friedlander, Alfred (1871-1939). Amer. physician.
Kagan—Modern p25 (por.25)

Friedländer, Carl (1847-1887). Aust. bacteriologist.
Bulloch—Hist. p367

Friedländer, Paul (1857-1923). Aust. chemist.
Smith—Torch. p92 (por.92)

Fries, Elias Magnus (1794-1878). Swed. botanist.
Chambers—Dict. col.173-174   Reed—Short p269
Lindroth—Swedish p178-185

Friese-Greene, William (1855-1921). Eng. inventor.
Chambers—Dict. col.174   *Larsen—Scrap p22-24 (por.32)
Hammerton p686   People p151-152
*Larsen—Men p47-68 (por.80)

Fripp, Sir Alfred Downing (1865-1930). Eng. surgeon.
Hammerton p623

Frisch, Johann Leonhard (1666-1743). Ger. naturalist.
Miall—Early p240-244

Frisch, Otto Robert (1904-   ). Dan.-Aust. physicist.
Chambers—Dict. col.175

Frisen (or Frisius).   See **Phryesen, Laurentius Frisen**

Frisius, Gemma (1508-1555). Dutch mathematician.
Smith—Hist. I p341-342

Fritz, John (1822-1913). Amer. engineer.
John Fritz p25-29 (por.24)

Froehlich, Jack E. (1921-   ). Amer. engineer.
Curr. Biog. '59 p134-135 (por.134)

Frolick, Per K. (1899-   ). Norw.-Amer.
Browne—Hist. p491 (por.169)

Fromm, Erich (1900-   ). Ger. psychoanalyst.
Newman—What p360-361

Frontinus, Sextus Julius (c40-103). Roman engineer, mathematician.
Sedgwick—Short p144
Smith—Hist. I p123-124

Frosch, Paul (1860-1928). Ger. bacteriologist.
Bulloch—Hist. p367

Frost, Edwin Brant (1866-1935). Amer. astronomer.
N.A.S.—Biog. (19) p25-39 (por.25)

Frothingham, Channing (1881-1959). Amer. physician.
Curr. Biog. '48 p232-234 (por.232) '59
  p135

Froude, William (1810-1879). Eng. engineer.
Chambers—Dict. col.175

Frye, Jack (1904-   ). Amer. aero. pioneer.
Curr. Biog. '45 p207-210 (por.208)

Fuchs, Carl (1838-1914). Ger.-Amer. entomologist.
Essig—Hist. p635-637 (por.636)

Fuchs, Emmanuel Lazarus (1833-1902). Ger. mathematician.
Smith—Hist. I p510

Fuchs, Klaus (1911-   ). Ger. physicist.
Robinson—100 p250-253 (por.250)

Fuchs, Leonhard (1501-1566). Ger. botanist.

Arber—Herbals p64,67,70,152,153,
212,215,217,219 (por.65)
Bodenheimer—Hist. p225
Castiglioni—Hist. p486
Chambers—Dict. col.175-176
Gordon—Medieval p659-660 (por.50)
Hammerton p626

Hawks—Pioneers p135-137
Major—History (1) p468
Miall—Early p24-28
Reed—Short p66-68
Sarton—Six p132 (por.133)
Year—Pic. p82 (por.82)

Fuchs, Sir Vivian E. (1908-   ). Eng. geologist.

Curr. Biog. '58 p152-153 (por.153)

Füchsel, George Christian (1722-1773). Ger. geologist.

Geikie—Founders p98-102
Woodruff—Devel. p206,273

Fuller, John Langworthy (1910-   ). Amer. biologist.

Curr. Biog. '59 p135-137 (por.136)

Fuller, Richard Buckminster (1895-1960). Amer. inventor, engineer.

Curr. Biog. p153-155 (por.153)

Fulton, John Farquhar (1837-1887). Can. physiologist.

Major—History (2) p979

Fulton, Robert (1765-1815). Amer. inventor, engineer.

Abbot—Great p185-187
*Bachman—Great p25-49 (por.32)
Bell—Early p58
*Book—Pop. Sci. (7) p2307-2308
Chambers—Dict. col.176
*Cottler—Heroes p190-200
*Darrow—Masters p103-106 (por.289)
*Darrow—Thinkers p69-75 (por.70)
*Eberle—Invent. p29-36 (por.28)
*Epstein—Real p85-86
Fitzhugh—Concise p232-234
Goddard—Eminent p43-48
Hammerton p627 (por.627)
*Hartman—Mach. p63-71
*Hathaway—Partners p151-162
*Hodgins—Behemoth p188-195
*Hylander—Invent. p45-58 (por.58)
Iles—Leading p40-74 (por.40)

*Larsen—Prentice p21-24
*Larsen—Shaped p176-181 (por.144)
Law—Civiliz. p46-50
Matschoss—Great p140-153 (por.141)
*Montgomery—Invent. p233-236
Morris—Ency. p662-663
*Morris—Heroes p96-100
*Nida—Makers p57-63,131 (por.59)
*Nisenson—Illus. p65 (por.65)
*Parkman—Conq. p222-241 (por.225)
*Patterson—Amer. p17-31
*Perry—Four p11-69 (por.10)
*Pratt—Famous p26-30
*Science Miles. p132-137 (por.132)
Sewell—Brief p112-113
Thomas—50 Amer. p97-104
   (por.,back)
Wilson—Amer. p61-71 (por.64)
Year—Pic. p146 (por.146)

Funk, Casimir (1884-   ). Pol.-Amer. biochemist.

Chambers—Dict. col.176
Curr. Biog. '45 p210-212 (por.211)

Rowntree—Amid p427-430 (por.423)
Year—Pic. p221 (por.221)

Funkhouser, William Delbert (1881-1948). Amer. entomologist.
Osborn—Fragments p199-200
  (por.367)

Furey, Warren William (1898-1958). Amer. physician.
Curr. Biog. '50 p160-161 (por.161)
  '59 p142

Furlong, Eustace L. (1874-1950). Amer. geologist.
G.S.A.—Proc. '51 p113-114 (por.113)

Furman, Nathaniel Howe (1892-   ). Amer. chemist.
Browne—Hist. p494 (por.227)
Curr. Biog. '51 p219-221 (por.220)

Furnas, Clifford Cook (1900-   ). Amer. engineer.
Curr. Biog. '56 p193-195 (por.194)

Fusch, Remacle (1500-1587). Flem. botanist.
Hawks—Pioneers p165-166

Futcher, Thomas Barnes (1871-1938). Can. physician.
Major—History (2) p1034

G

Gabb, William More (1839-1878). Amer. entomologist, geologist.
Essig—Hist. p638
N.A.S.—Biog. (6) p345-356 (por.345)

Gabriel, Siegmund (1851-1924). Ger. chemist.
A.A.A.S.—Proc. (79) p17-18

Gabritchewsky, Georgiy Norbertovich (1860-1907). Russ. bacteriologist.
Bulloch—Hist. p367

Gaddeson (or Gaddesden).   See **John of Gaddesden**

Gadolin, Johan (1760-1852). Finnish chemist.
A.A.A.S.—Proc. (81) p56-58   Weeks—Discovery p414-416
Chambers—Dict. col.177   (por.414,415)

Gadow, Hans Friedrich (1855-1928). Ger.-Eng. zoologist.
Hammerton p628

Gaffky, Georg Theodor August (1850-1918). Ger. bacteriologist.
Bulloch—Hist. p367-368
Chambers—Dict. col.177

Gagarin, Yuri (Alekseyevich) (1934-   ). Rus. space pioneer, astronaut.
Curr. Biog. '61 (Oct.) (por.)
Thomas—Men (3) p97-117 (por.74)

Gahn, Johan Gottlieb (1745-1818). Swed. chemist, mineralogist.
Chambers—Dict. col.177   Weeks—Discovery p73-77 (por.73)
Smith—Torch. p93 (por.93)

Gale, Henry Gordon (1874-1942). Amer. physicist.
Curr. Biog. '43 p223

Gale, Hoyt Stoddard (1876-1952). Amer. geologist.
G.S.A—Proc. '52 p107-111 (por.107)

Gale, Thomas (1507-1586/1587). Eng. surgeon.
Gordon—Medieval p680-681   Major—History (1) p454
Leonardo—Lives p171-172

Galen (or Claudius Galenes) (c130-200?). Gr. physician.
Adams—Birth p49
Atkinson—Magic p48-51,151-152
Bodenheimer—Hist. p178
*Book—Pop. Sci. (8) 2701-2702
Castiglioni—Hist. p217-226 (por.216)
Chambers—Dict. col.177-178
*Chandler—Medicine p9-11 (por.8)
Clagett—Greek p42-46
*Elwell—Sci. p25-26
Gordon—Medicine p697-723 (por.698)
Gordon—Romance p64-67,100-105 (por.33)
Hammerton p630 (por.630)
*Hathaway—Partners p10-15
Lambert—Medical p47-59 (por.52)
Lambert—Minute p47-59 (por.17)
Leonardo—Lives p173-174
Locy—Biology p23-26 (por.25)
Major—History (1) p188-202 (por.198)
*Masters—Conquest p19-21
Moulton—Auto. p28
Oliver—Stalkers p39-45 (por.41)
Partington—Short p15
Robinson—Path. p1-19 (por.14,15)
Schwartz—Moments (1) p181-183
Sedgwick—Short p146-147
*Shippen—Men p45-50
Sigerist—Great p68-77
*Snyder—Biology p177,179
Thomson—Great p13-16
Van Wagenen—Beacon p33-35
Wilson—Human p53-58
Woodruff—Devel. p236-239,273

Galilei, Galileo (1564-1642). It. astronomer.
Abetti—History p91-114 (por.146) (14)
Ball—Great p67-95 (por.73)
Ball—Short p247-251
Bodenheimer—Hist. p251
*Bolton—Famous p11-31 (por.10)
Book—Pop. Sci. (10) p3413-3415
Cajori—Hist. p171-172
Castiglioni—Hist. p509-510 (por.505)
Chambers—Dict. col.178-179 (por.178)
*Cottler—Heroes p98-107
Crew—Physicists #1 (folder) (por.)
*Crowther—Scientists p49-88 (por.33)
*Darrow—Masters p7-12 (por.161)
*Darrow—Thinkers p17-23 (por.22)
*Elwell—Sci. p35-36

(Continued)

Galilei, Galileo—*Continued*
*Epstein—Real p115-118
Fitzhugh—Concise p235-237
Gibson—Heroes p76-106
Ginzburg—Adven. p97-125 (por.97)
Gordon—Medieval p647-648
Gordon—Romance p118 (por.118)
Hammerton p631 (por.631)
Hart—Makers p103-124 (por.103)
Hart—Physicists p44-52
Hooper—Makers p194-201
Koestler—Sleep p353-378
Lenard—Great p24-39 (por.38)
*Lewellen—Boy p1-40 (por.1)
Lodge—Pioneers p80-135 (por.126)
MacPherson—Makers p31-48 (por.210)
*McSpadden—How p83-95 (por.90)
Magie—Source p1-2
Moulton—Auto. p63-64
Newman—Interp. p30-32
*Nisenson—Illus. p68 (por.68)
People p155-156 (por.173)
*Pratt—Famous p12-17
Schwartz—Moments (1) p240-242,332-333

*Science Miles p60 (por.60)
Sci. Amer. –Lives p3-20 (por.5)
Sedgwick—Short p217-226 (por.217)
Sewell—Brief p58-59
Shapley—Astron. p41
*Simmons—Great p14-16 (por.14)
Smith—Hist. I p363-366 (por.364)
Smith—Portraits (1), IV, unp. (por.)
*Stevens—Science p16-19 (por.12)
Suter—Gallery p85-102
Taylor—Illus. p53-67
Thomas-Scien. p35-38 (por.33)
Tuska—Invent. p124
Van Wagenen—Beacon p85-94
Vaucouleurs—Disc. p46-48
*Williams-Ellis p25-59
Williams—Great p155-165 (por.173)
Wilson—Human p157-188
Woodruff—Devel. p152-154,273-274 (por.43)
*World's Great p3-32 (por.4)
*Wright—Great p175-179
Year—Pic. p78,79,87 (por.78)

Gall, Franz Joseph (1758-1828). Ger. physiologist, anatomist, physician.
Castiglioni—Hist. p636
Chambers—Dict. col.179-180
Lambert—Minute p191-192
Major—History (2) p677-680 (por.679)

Gallatin, Albert (1761-1849). Swiss-Amer. enthnologist.
Morris—Ency. p603
Swiss—Prom. p88-97 (por.88)

Galle, Johann Gottfried (1812-1910). Ger. astronomer.
Hammerton p632

Galliher, Edgar Wayne (1907-1945). Amer. geologist.
G.S.A.—Proc. '45 p229-232 (por.229)

Galois, Évariste (1811-1832). Fr. mathematician.
Ball—Short p475
Bell—Men p362-377 (por.,front.)
Chambers—Dict. col.180
Miller—Hist. p251-253
Muir—Men p202-216
Murray—Science p338-339
Smith—Hist. I p498-499

Galton, Sir Francis (1822-1911). Eng. anthropologist, inventor, meteorologist, physicist, biologist.
*Book—Pop. Sci. (8) p2702-2703
Chambers—Dict. col.180
Hammerton p633 (por.633)
Locy—Biology p319-321 (**por.319**)
Moulton—Auto. p398
*Snyder—Biology p127-132 (por.128)
Thomson—Great p114-123
Van Wagenen—Beacon p320-321
Woodruff—Devel. p249,274

Galvani, Luigi (or Aloisio) (1737-1798). It. physicist, physiologist, physician, anatomist.

*Book—Pop. Sci. (11) p3665-3666 (por.3666)
Chambers—Dict. col.180-181
*Darrow—Masters p333
*Epstein—Real p50-51
Hammerton p633
Hart—physicists p101
*Hartman—Mach. p86-87
Hawks—Wireless p18-20 (por.20)
Hodgins—Behemoth p97-101
Law—Civiliz. p197
Lenard—Great p159-163 (por.158)

Magie—Source p420
Major—History (2) p637
Meyer—World p128-130 (por.129)
Morgan—Men p32-33
100 Great p564-568
Radio's 100 p24-26 (por.140)
*Science Miles p111 (por.111)
*Shippen—Design p52-57
Van Wagenen—Beacon p174-175
Walsh—Makers p113-131
Year—Pic. p106 (por.106)

Gamaliel VI (or Gamliel, R. Gamliel Bathrai) (400-425). Palest. physician.
Gordon—Medicine p787

Gamalieya (or Gamaleiia), **Nikolay Fyodorovich** (1859-1949). Russ. bacteriologist.
Bulloch—Hist. p368

Gambetta, Léon Michel (1838-1882). Fr. aero. pioneer.
*Shippen—Bridle p77-84

Gamliel.   See **Gamaliel VI**

Gamow, George (1904-   ). Russ.-Amer. physicist.
Curr. Biog. '51 p228-230 (por.229)

Gann, Thomas William Francis (1868-1938). Brit. archaeologist.
Hammerton p635

Ganong, William Francis (1864-1941). Can. botanist.
Progress—Science '41 p163

Ganswindt, Hermann (1856-1934). Ger. inventor, engineer.
Gartmann—Men p11-25 (por.16)

Gantt, L. Rosa H. (b.1875). Amer. physician.
Lovejoy—Women p352-355
Lovejoy—Women Phys. p205-209 (por.8)

Garand, John Cantius (1888-   ). Can. inventor.
Curr. Biog. '45 p221-224 (por.222)

Garcia da Orta.   See **Horto, Garcia ab**

Garcia, Manuel (1805-1906). Sp.-Fr. inventor
    Chambers—Dict. col.181   Wolom—Discov. p89-99
    *Montgomery—Story p45-47

Garden, Alexander (1730?-1791). Amer. naturalist, physician.
    Bell—Early p58-59

Gardiner, James Garfield (1883-   ). Can. agriculturist.
    Curr. Biog. '56 p200-202 (por.201)

Gardiner, John Stanley (1872-1946). Irish zoologist, biologist.
    Hammerton p635

Gardner, Ernest Arthur (1862-1939). Eng. archaeologist.
    Hammerton p636 (por.636)

Gardner, Lester Durand (1876-1956). Amer. aero. pioneer.
    Curr. Biog. '47 p225-227 (por.226)
    Daniel—Pioneer. p111-115 (por.110)

Gardner, Maude Elsa (1894-   ). Amer. aero. pioneer.
    Goff—Women p113-115

Gardner, Percy (1846-1937). Eng. archaeologist.
    Hammerton p636 (por.636)

Gariopontus (or Guarinpotus). (d1050). It. physician.
    Castiglioni—Hist. p302

Garman, Harrison (1858-1944). Amer. entomologist.
    Osborn—Fragments p188-189
      (por.360)

Garner, William Edward (1889-   ). Eng. chemist.
    Chambers Dict. col.181

Garnerin, André Jacques (1769-1823). Fr. aero. pioneer.
    *Bishop—Kite p58-63,68-69   Heinmuller—Man's p237 (por.237)
    Burge—Ency. p632   *Shippen—Bridle p43-48

Garré, Karl (1857-1928). Swiss bacteriologist, surgeon.
    Bulloch—Hist. p368

Garrett, Elizabeth.   See **Anderson, Elizabeth Garrett**

Garrison, Fielding Hudson (1870-1935). Amer. physician.
Castiglioni—Hist. p1112-1113   Major—History (2) p990-993 (por.992)
   (por.1112)
Kagan—Modern p208 (por.208)

Garrod, Sir Archibald Edward (1857-1936). Eng. physician.
Hammerton p638

Garros, Roland (1888-1918). Fr. aero. pioneer.
Hammerton p638
Heinmuller—Man's p288 (por.288)

Garstang, John (1876-1956). Eng. archaeologist.
Hammerton p638 (por.638)

Garstin, Sir William Edmund (1849-1925). Brit. engineer.
Hammerton p638

Gärtner, August (or Anton Hieronymus) (1848-1934). Ger. bacteriologist,
   hygienist, surgeon.
Bulloch—Hist. p368

Garvan, Francis Patrick (1875-1937). Amer. chemurgist.
Borth—Pioneers p142-184

Gascoigne, William (1612-1644). Eng. astronomer, inventor.
Woodruff—Devel. p274

Gaskell, W. H. (1847-1914). Brit. physician, physiologist.
Castiglioni—Hist. p784,946 (por.785)

Gaspard, Marie Humbert Bernard (1788-1871). Fr. physician.
Bulloch—Hist. p368

Gassendi (or Gassend), **Pierre** (1592-1655). Fr. mathematician.
Chambers—Dict. col.181

Gasser, Herbert Spencer (1888-   ). Amer. physiologist, physician.
Castiglioni—Hist. p944,1127 (por.945)   Curr. Biog. '45 p224-225 (por.224)
Chambers—Dict. col.181-182   Stevenson—Nobel p224-228 (por.150)

Gatling, Richard Jordan (1818-1903). Amer. inventor.
Hammerton p639 (por.639)
*Hylander—Invent. p207

Gatschet, Albert Samuel (1832-1907). Swiss ethnologist.
  Swiss—Prom. p211-213 (por.211)

Gattermann, Ludwig (1860-1920). Ger. chemist.
  Smith—Torch. p94 (por.94)

Gatty, Harold (1903-   ). Aust. aero. pioneer.
  *Fraser—Heroes p583-589
  Heinmuller—Man's p137-149,342
    (por.342)

Gaub, Jerome David (1705-1780). Dutch pathologist.
  Castiglioni—Hist. p608

Gauss, Karl Friedrich (1777-1855). Ger. astronomer.
  Abetti—History p171-172
  Ball—Short p447-454
  Bell—Men p218-269 (por.,front.)
  Cajori—Hist. p434-438
  Chambers—Dict. col.182-183
    (por.182)
  Dibner—Ten p31-34 (por.32)
  Hammerton p640
  Hooper—Makers p379-382
  Lenard—Great p240-247 (por.241)
  Magie—Source p519
  *Miller—Hist. p241-243
  Muir—Men p157-183
  Murray—Science p348-349
  Shapley—Astron. p183
  Smith—Hist. I p502-504 (por.503)
  Smith—Portraits (1) X, unp. (por.)
  Turnbull—Great p108-114
  Van Wagenen—Beacon p229-230
  Woodruff—Devel. p28-30,274 (por.30)
  Year—Pic. p116 (por.117)

Gautier, Armand (1837-1920). Fr. biochemist.
  Bulloch—Hist. p368
  Smith—Torch. p95 (por.95)

Gautier (or Gauthier), **Dagoty.**   See **Agoty, Jacques Gautier d'**

Gay, Frederick Parker (1874-1939). Amer. bacteriologist.
  Bulloch—Hist. p368
  N.A.S.—Biog. (28) p99-107 (por.99)

Gay-Lussac, Joseph Louis (1778-1850). Fr. chemist, physicist.
  A.A.A.S.—Proc. (78) p18-20
  *Book—Pop. Sci. (11) p3666-3667
    (por.3667)
  Chambers—Dict. col.183
  *Darrow—Masters p332
  Hammerton p643-644
  Lenard—Great p184-187 (por.186)
  Magie—Source p165-166
  Partington—Short p212,223-226
    (por.224)
  Roberts—Chem. p84-87
  Schwartz—Moments (2) p804-806
  Smith—Torch. p96 (por.96)
  Tilden—Famous p119-126 (por.119)
  Van Wagenen—Beacon p232-234
  Weeks—Discovery p333,336-341
    (por.333)
  Williams—Story p256-258,266-267
    (por.257)
  Woodruff—Devel. p274 (por.100)

Geber (or Jabir ibn-Hayyan) (c721-c.813?). Arab. chemist.

Cajori—Hist. p109-110
Chambers—Dict. col.183-184
Hammerton p643
Holmyard—Chem. p15-20,42-43
Holmyard—Great Chem. p9-17
Holmyard—Makers p49-63,79

Major—History (1) p234-236
Oliver—Stalkers p52-54
Partington—Short p28
Schwartz—Moments (1) p186-187
Smith—Torch. p98 (por.98)

Geddes, Sir Patrick (1854-1932). Scot. biologist.

Chambers—Dict. col.184
Defries—Pioneers p68-90

Hammerton p643

Geer.   See **De Geer**

Gegenbauer, Carl (1826-1903). Ger. anatomist.

*Book—Pop. Sci. (8) p2703-2704
Chambers—Dict. col.184
Hammerton p643

Locy—Biology p163-164 (por.164)
Woodruff—Devel. p274

Gehuchten, Arthur van (1861-1914). Fr. neurologist.

Great Names p69-71 (por.68)

Geiger, Hans (1882-   ). Ger. physicist.

Chambers—Dict. col.184-185
Year—Pic. p211 (por.211)

Geikie, (or Geike) **Sir Archibald** (1835-1924). Scot. geologist.

*Book—Pop. Sci. (5) p1659 (por.1660)
Chambers—Dict. col.185

Fenton—Giants p288-301
Hammerton p643-644 (por.644)

Geikie, James (1839-1915). Scot. geologist.

*Book—Pop. Sci. (5) p1660 (por.1660)
Chambers—Dict. col.185

Geinitz, Franz Eugen (b.1854). Ger. geologist, mineralogist, seismologist.

Davison—Founders p130-131

Geissler, Heinrich (1814-1879). Ger. inventor.

Hammerton p644

Geitel, Hans Friedrich (1855-1923). Ger. physicist.

Chambers—Dict. col.185-186
Weeks—Discovery p496-497

Gellibrand, Henry (1597-1636/1637). Eng. mathematician.

Smith—Hist. I p392

Geminus (fl c77 B.C.). Rhod. mathematician.
Smith—Hist. I p121

Geminus, Thomas (c1540-1560). Eng. physician.
Major—History (1) p470-471

Genet, Edmond Charles (1763-1834). Fr. aero. pioneer.
Heinmuller—Man's p238 (por.238)
Milbank—First p38-42

Genth, Frederick Augustus (1820-1893). Ger.-Amer. chemist, mineralogist.
Browne—Hist. p472 (por.29)   N.A.S.—Biog. (4) p201-221 (por.201)
Chambers—Dict. col.186   Smith—Chem. p261-263

Gentile da Foligno (d.1348). It. physician.
Major—History (1) p332

Gentry, Viola (1900-   ). Amer. aero. pioneer.
Heinmuller—Man's p328 (por.328)

Geoffroy, Étienne François "The Elder" (1672-1731). Fr. chemist.
Hammerton p645
Smith—Torch. p99 (por.99)

Geoffroy Saint-Hilaire, Étienne (1772-1844). Fr. naturalist.
Chambers—Dict. col.186   Osborn—Greeks p255-263
Hammerton p645   Williams—Story p300 (por.299)
Locy—Biology p423-426 (por.424)   Woodruff—Devel. p274

Geoffroy Saint-Hilaire, Isadore (1805-1861). Fr. zoologist.
Osborn—Greeks p294-296

George, Harold Lee (1893-   ). Amer. aero. pioneer.
Curr. Biog. '42 p292-293 (por.293)

Georgius Agricola.   See **Agricola, Georgius**

Geppert, August Julius (1856-1937). Ger. bacteriologist.
Bulloch—Hist. p369

Gerard, John (1545-1612). Eng. botanist.
Arber—Herbals p129,132,157   Hawks—Pioneers p177-180 (por.178)
  (por.130)   Major—History (1) p476
Chambers—Dict. col.186-187   Miall—Early p78-79
Gilmour—British p11-12 (por.11)   Raven—English p204-217
Hammerton p649   Reed—Short p70-71

Gerard, Ralph Waldo (1900-   ). Amer. physiologist.
Progress—Science '41 p178 (por.178)

Gerard of Cremona (1114?-1187). Sp. mathematician.
Ball—Short p166   Major—History (1) p271
Cajori—Hist. p119

Gerbert.   See **Sylvester II**

Gerbezius, Marcus (or Verbez). (d1718). Slov. physician.
Major—Hist. (1) p562

Gerdy, Pierre-Nicolas (1797-1856). Fr. surgeon.
Leonardo—Lives p174-175

Gergonne, Joseph Diaz (1771-1859). Fr. mathematician.
Cajori—Hist. p288-289
Smith—Hist. I p495-496

Gerhard, William Josiah (1873-1959). Amer. entomologist.
Osborn—Fragments p206 (por.360)

Gerhard, William Wood (1809-1872). Amer. physician.
Castiglioni—Hist. p709 (por.709)
Major—History (2) p759

Gerhardt, Charles Frédéric (1816-1856). Fr. chemist.
Chambers—Dict. col.187   Smith—Torch. p100 (por.100)
Findlay—Hundred p324-325   Woodruff—Devel. p274
Partington—Short p251-255,269-270
    (por.252)

Gericke, William Frederick (1884-   ). Amer. hydroponicist.
Ratcliffe—Modern p296-302

Germain, Sophie (1776-1831). Fr. mathematician.
Coolidge—Six p26-29
Mozans—Woman p154-157

Germer, Lester Halbert (1896-   ). Amer. physicist.
Wilson—Amer. p398-399 (por.396)

Gersdorff, (or Gerssdorff) **Hans von** (c.1480?-1540?). Ger. physician,
    surgeon.
Gordon—Medieval p683-684   Major—History (1) p434-436
Leonardo—Lives p175-176

Gershon, Ben-Shlomoh (fl. 13th cent.). Fr. biologist.
Bodenheimer—Hist. p217

Gerstacker, Carl Allan (1916-   ). Amer. chemist.
Curr. Biog. '61 (Oct.) (por.)

Gerster, Arpad Geza Charles (1848-1923). Amer. surgeon.
Leonardo—Lives p176-177

Gersuny, Robert (1844-1924). Aust. surgeon.
Leonardo—Lives p177-178

Gesell, Arnold Lucius (1880-1961). Amer. physician, psychologist,
    pediatrician.
Curr. Biog. '61 (Sept.)   Progress—Science '40 p185-186
Fabricant—Why p47-53   (por.185)

Gesner, Abraham (1797-1864). Can. geologist, physician, surgeon.
Merrill—First p180-181 (por.180)

Gesner, Konrad von (or Gessner, Conrad von). (1516-1565). Ger.-Swiss
    botanist, naturalist, zoologist.
Adams—Birth p176-183 (por.176)   Major—History (1) p438-440 (por.439)
Arber—Herbals p110-112, 113, 166,   Miall—Early p28-32,48-49
  168,233-234 (por.110)   Moulton—Auto. p89
Bodenheimer—Hist. p230   Sarton—Six p153-156,160 (por.24)
Castiglioni—Hist. p487   Sedgwick—Short p228
Chambers—Dict. col.187   *Snyder—Biology p15-17
Gordon—Medieval p660-661 (por.115)   Van Wagenen—Beacon p70-71
Hammerton p650   Woodruff—Devel. p223,274
Hawks—Pioneers p157-160   Year—Pic. p82 (por.82)
Locy—Biology p112-114 (por.114)

Getman, Frederick Hutton (1877-1941). Amer. chemist.
Curr. Biog. '42 p298

Gherardi, Bancroft (1873-1941). Amer. engineer.
N.A.S.—Biog. (30) p157-177 (por.157)

Ghini, Luca (1500-1556). It. botanist.
Hawks—Pioneers p145-146

Ghon, Anton (1866-1936). Aust. bacteriologist, path. anatomist.
Bulloch—Hist. p369

Giauque, William Francis (1895-   ). Can.-Amer. chemist.
Chambers—Dict. col.187
Curr. Biog. '50 p170-171 (por.170)
Farber—Nobel p199-203 (por.118)

Gibb, Alexander (1872-1958). Brit. engineer.
R.S.L.—Biog. (5) p75-85 (por.75)

Gibb, Claude Dixon (1898-1959). Austral. engineer.
R.S.L.—Biog. (5) p87-93 (por.87)

Gibbes, Lewis Reeve (1810-1894). Amer. chemist.
Weeks—Discovery p394-397 (por.394)

Gibbs, George (1861-1940). Amer. engineer.
Curr. Biog. '40 p334
Merrill—First p319 (por.319)

Gibbs, James E. (1829-1902). Amer. inventor.
Law—Civiliz. p111

Gibbs, Josiah Willard (1839-1903). Amer. chemist.
*Book—Pop. Sci. (11) p3668-3670 (por.3670)
Cajori—Hist. p476-477
Castiglioni—Hist. p792
Chambers—Dict. col.188
Crew—Physicists #10 (folder) (port.)
Crowther—Famous p227-297 (por.248)
Hammerton p653
Jaffe—Men p207-330 (por.xxviii)
Jordan—Leading p341-362 (por.341)
Killeffer—Eminent p13 (por.13)
Morris—Ency. p665-666
Moulton—Auto. p465-466
N.A.S.—Biog. (6) p373-391 (por.373)
Partington—Short p330-331,339 (por.330)
Smith—Chem. p343-349 (por.344)
Smith—Math. p146-148 (por.149)
Smith—Torch. p101 (por.101)
Van Wagenen—Beacon p381-383
Wilson—Amer. p298-305 (por.298,305)
Woodruff—Devel. p115-117,274-275 (por.75)
Year—Pic. p124 (por.124)

Gibbs, (Oliver) Wolcott (1822-1908). Amer. chemist.
Killeffer—Eminent p7 (por.7)
N.A.S.—Biog. (7) p1-18 (por.1)
Smith—Chem. p264-274 (por.264)
Smith—Torch. p102 (por.102)

Gibbs, William Francis (1886-   ). Amer. engineer.
Fisher—Amer. p209-211 (por.208)

Gibson, Arthur (1875-1959). Can. entomologist.
Osborn—Fragments p235 (por.361)

Gibson, Margaret Dunlop (1843-1920). Eng. archaeologist.
Mozans—Woman p327-333

Gibson, William (1788-1868). Amer. surgeon.
Leonardo—Lives p178-179

Giesel, Friedrich (or Fritz) **O.** (1852-1927). Ger. chemist.
Chambers—Dict. col.188

Gieson, Ira van (1866-1913). Amer. neurologist.
Bulloch—Hist. p369

Giffard, Henri (1825-1882). Fr. engineer, aero. pioneer.
*Bishop—Kite p50-55   Heinmuller—Man's p243 (por.243)
Burge—Ency. p632

Gifford, Sanford Robinson (1892-1944). Amer. ophthalmologist.
Curr. Biog. '44 p232-233

Gignoux, Maurice (1881-1955). Fr. geologist.
G.S.A.—Proc. '56 p127-130 (por.127)

Gilbert (c950-1003). Roman mathematician.
Smith—Hist. I p195-196

Gilbert, Grove Karl (1843-1918). Amer. geologist.
Chambers—Dict. col.188   Merrill—First p546-547 (por.546)
Fenton—Giants p269-287 (por.270)   Woodruff—Devel. p275 (por.196)

Gilbert, Sir Joseph Henry (1817-1901). Eng. chemist, agriculturist,
  botanist.
Chambers—Dict. col.188-189   *Ivins—Fifty p243-244 (por.242)
Gilmour—British p40-41   Oliver—Makers p233-242 (por.233)
Hammerton p655

Gilbert, William (1540/1544-1603). English physicist, physician.
*Book—Pop. Sci. (11) p3670-3671   Morgan—Men p19-22
Chambers—Dict. col.189   Moulton—Auto. p113-114
*Darrow—Masters p333-334   Radio's 100 p12-15 (por.140)
Dibner—Ten p7-10 (por.8)   Sarton—Six p94-98
Gregory—British p10   Schwartz—Moments (1) p324-325
Hammerton p655-656 (por.656)   *Science Miles. p52 (por.52)
Hart—Makers p95-97 (por.93)   Sedgwick—Short p228-229
Hart—Physicists p39-44   *Shippen—Design p19-24
Hawks—Wireless p6-7 (por.10)   Suter—Gallery p30-45
*Hodgins—Behemoth p69-72   Taylor—Illus. p81-82,84
Holmyard—British p11-14 (por.11)   Van Wagenen—Beacon p74-76
Magie—Source p387   Woodruff—Devel. p275
Major—History (1) p475-476   Year—Pic. p83
Meyer—World p126 (por.127)

Gilbertus Anglicus (or Dr. Desideralissimus) (c1170/1180-1230/1250). Eng. physician.
Atkinson—Magic p61-70   Major—History (1) p283-284
Gordon—Medieval p285-287

Gilbreth, Frank Bunker (1868-1924). Amer. engineer.
*Logie—Careers p312-326

Gilbreth, Lillian Evelyn (1878-   ). Amer. engineer.
*Clymer—Modern p1-11 (por.82)   Goff—Women p116-132
Curr. Biog. '40 p336-337 (por.337)   *Logie—Careers p312-326
'51 p233-235 (por.234)   *Watson—Engineers p139-142
*Fleischman—Careers p166   (por.138)
                                        Yost—Women Sci. p99-121

Giles, Barney McKinney (1892-   ). Amer. aero. pioneer.
Curr. Biog. '44 p233-235 (por.233)

Giles de Corbeil.   See **Aegidius, Pierre Gilles Corbeil de**

Gill, Charles (b.1805). Eng.-Amer. mathematician.
Smith—Math. p98-99

Gill, Sir David (1843-1914). Scot. astronomer.
Armitage—Cent. p77. (por.144)   MacPherson—Astron. p138-144
*Book—Pop. Sci. (10) p3415   (por.138)
Chambers—Dict. col.189   MacPherson—Makers p219-221
Hammerton p656-657   Shapley—Astron. p350

Gill, Theodore Nicholas (1837-1914). Amer. ichthyologist, zoologist, ecologist.
Book—Pop. Sci. (8) p2705
N.A.S.—Biog. (8) p313-322 (por.313)

Gillam, Harold (d.1943). Amer. aero. pioneer.
Potter—Flying p143-163 (por.147)

Gilles.   See **Gillius, Petrus**

Gilles de Corbeil.   See **Aegidius, Pierre Gilles Corbeil de**

Gillespie, Louis John (1886-1941). Amer. bacteriologist, agriculturist, biochemist.
Curr. Biog. '41 p321

Gillette, King Camp (1855-1932). Amer. inventor.
Hammerton p657

Gilliam, Tod David (1844-1923). Amer. surgeon.
Leonardo—Lives p179-181

Gillies, Sir Harold Delf (1882-1960). New Zeal. surgeon.
Hammerton p657

Gilliss, James Melville (1811-1865). Amer. astronomer.
N.A.S.—Biog. (1) p135-179

Gillius, Petrus (or Gilles). (1490-1554). Fr. naturalist.
Miall—Early p57-58

Gilmer, Thomas L. (1849-1931). Amer. oral surgeon.
Leonardo—Lives p181-182

Gilmore, Charles Whitney (1874-1945). Amer. geologist.
G.S.A.—Proc. '45 p235-239 (por.235)

Gilmore, John Washington (1872-1942). Amer. agronomist.
Curr. Biog. '42 p300

Gilmore, Melvin Randolph (1868-1940). Amer. ethnologist.
Curr Biog. '40 p338

Gimbernat, Don Antonio (1734-1816). Sp. surgeon.
Leonardo—Lives p182-183

Giordani, Francesco (1896-1961). Amer. chemist.
Curr. Biog. '57 p21-22,23,-24 (por.24)

Giordano, Davide (1864-1954). It. physician, surgeon.
Castiglioni—Hist. p1013 (por.1112)

Giovanni, Battista.   See Grassi, Giovanni Battista

Girard, Aimé (1830-1898). Fr. chemist.
Smith—Torch. p103 (por.103)

Girard, Albert (1595-1632). Dutch mathematician.
Ball—Short p234-235   Smith—Hist. I p423
Chambers—Dict. col.189-190

Giraud-Soulavie, Abbé (1752-1813). Fr. geologist.
Geikie—Founders p204-207

Girty, George Herbert (1869-1939). Amer. geologist.
G.S.A.—Proc. '39 p195-200 (por.195)

Gladstone, John Hall (1827-1902). Eng. chemist.
Chambers—Dict. col.190   Hammerton p660
Findlay—Hundred p325

Glaisher, James (1809-1903). Eng. aero. pioneer, astronomer, meteorologist.
Burge—Ency. p632   Hammerton p661
Chambers—Dict. col.190   *Shippen—Bridle p71-76
*Cohen—Men

Glanvill, Joseph (1636-1680). Eng. nat. philosopher.
Gunther—Early XI p148-149

Glaser, Donald Arthur (1926-   ). Amer. physicist.
Curr. Biog. '61 (Mr.) (por.)

Glasgow, Maud (1868-1955). Amer. physician.
Atkinson—Magic p267-269

Glauber, Johann Rudolph (1604-1668/1670). Ger. chemist, physician.
Chambers—Dict. col.190   Partington—Short p47-59 (por.57)
Hammerton p662   Smith—Torch. p104 (por.104)
Holmyard—Chem. p54-55   Weeks—Discovery p305 (por.305)

Glaucius of Taras (or Glaucias of Taros) (c.170 B.C.) Gr. physician.
Gordon—Medicine p610

Glazebrook, Sir Richard Tetley (1854-1935). Eng. physicist.
Hammerton p662 (por.662)

Gleason, Rachel Brooks (1820-1905). Amer. physician.
Mead—Medical p44-45

Gleichen, Wilhelm Friedrich (or Russworm). (1717-1783). Ger. bacteriologist.
Bulloch—Hist. p369

Glennan, Thomas Keith (1905-   ). Amer. engineer.
Curr. Biog. '50 p173-175 (por.174)

Glidden, Carlos (1834-1877). Amer. inventor.
*Larsen—Scrap. p65-69 (por.64).

Glisson, Francis (1597-1677). Eng. physician.
Castiglioni—Hist. p544-545
Major—History (1) p522

Glover, James W. (1868-1941). Amer. mathematician.
Progress—Science '41 p179

Glover, Townend (1813-1883). Eng.-Amer. entomologist.
Smiths.—Misc. (84). p35-41
(por.545,pl.1)

Glueck, Nelson (1900-   ). Amer. archaeologist.
Curr. Biog. '48 p243-245 (por.244)

Gmelin, Johann Friedrich (1748-1804). Ger. chemist.
Weeks—Discovery p332 (por.332)

Gmelin, Johann Georg (1709-1755). Ger. chemist.
Hammerton p664

Gmelin, Leopold (1788-1853). Ger. chemist.
Chambers—Dict. col.190-191
Partington—Short p214
Smith—Torch. p105 (por.105)
Weeks—Discovery p347-348 (por.348)

Godard, Eugène (1827-1890). Fr. aero. pioneer.
Heinmuller—Man's p246 (por.246)
Milbank—First p42-44

Goddard, Jonathan (c.1617-1675). Eng. physician, chemist.
Gunther—Early XI p52

Goddard, Robert Hutchings (1882-1945). Amer. physicist, inventor.
Curr. Biog. '45 p239
Gartmann—Men p35-47 (por.33)
*Science—Miles p305-312 (por.305,311)
Thomas—Men p23-46 (por.140,folio)
Williams—Rocket p70-110 (por.114)

Godfrey, Ambrose (1685-1756). Eng. chemist.
Weeks—Discovery p43,49-50 (por.43)

Goding, F. W. (1858-1933). Amer. entomologist.
Osborn—Fragments p233 (por.348)

Godlee, Sir Rickman John (1849-1925). Eng. physician, surgeon.
Chambers—Dict. col.191
Hammerton p665
Leonardo—Lives p183-184

Godman, Frederick DuCane (1834-1919). Eng. entomologist.
Osborn—Fragments p173

Goebel, Arthur (Art) (1893-   ). Amer. aero. pioneer.
*Fraser—Heroes p521-533
Heinmuller—Man's p324 (por.324)

Goebel, Karl Eberhardt von (1855-1932). Ger. naturalist.
Reed—Short p143-144

Goering.   See **Göring, Hermann Wilhelm**

Goessmann, Charles A. (1827-1910). Ger.-Amer. chemist.
Browne—Hist. p474 (por.35)

Goethals, George Washington (1858-1928). Dutch-Amer. engineer.
*Beard—Foreign p100-108 (por.104)
*Book—Pop. Sci. (7) p2415-2417
    (por.2416)
*Darrow—Builders p233-238
*Everett—When p77-83 (por.77)
*Forbes—Men p163-172 (por.1)
Hammerton p666
John Fritz p107-110 (por.106)
*Law—Modern p106-120 (por.113)
Morris—Ency. p666
*Tappan—Heroes p254-263
*Watson—Engineers p121-128
    (por.120)
Webb—Famous p201-222 (por.203)
*Wildman—Famous (2d) p111-120

Goethe, Johann Wolfgang von (1749-1832). Ger. biologist, naturalist.
Bodenheimer—Hist. p335
*Book—Pop. Sci. (11) p3817-3818
    (por.3817)
Hammerton p666-667 (por.666,667)
Murray—Science p153-154
Osborn—Greeks p267-277
Peattie—Green p269-278 (por.278)
Thomson—Great p59-66
Woodruff—Devel. p275
Year—Pic. p107 (por. 107)

Goldberger, Joseph (1874-1929). Amer. physician.
*Compton—Conquests p211-234
*Darrow—Builders p212-217 (por.195)
*De Kruif—Hunger p335-370 (por.334)
Ratcliffe—Modern p102-104
*Snyder—Biology p345-346 (por.346)
Tobey—Riders p270-272

Goldenweiser, Alexander A. (1880-1940). Amer. anthropologist.
Curr. Biog. '40 p339

Goldmark, Henry (1857-1941). Amer. engineer.
Curr. Biog. '41 p331

Goldmark, Peter Carl (1906-   ). Hung.-Amer. engineer, inventor.
Curr. Biog. '40 p339-340 (por.340)
    '50 p177-179 (por.178)

Goldsborough, John Byron (1864?-1943). Amer. engineer.
Curr. Biog. 43 p233

Goldschmiedt, Guido (1850-1915). Aust. chemist.
A.A.A.S.—Proc. (78) p21-22

Goldschmidt, Hans (1861-1923). Ger. chemist.
Chambers—Dict. p191
Smith—Torch. p106 (por.106)

Goldschmidt, Richard Benedikt (1878-   ). Ger.-Amer. biologist,
zoologist.
Chambers—Dict. col.191-192

Goldschmidt, Victor Moritz (1888-1947). Swiss geologist.
G.S.A.—Proc. '47 p149-152 (por.149)

Goldsmith, Alfred Norton (1887-   ). Amer. engineer.
Radio's 100 p224-226 (por.140)

Goldsmith, Lester Morris (1893-   ). Amer. engineer.
Curr. Biog. '40 p340-341

Goldsmith, Oliver (1728-1774). Irish physician.
Farmer—Doctors' p18

Goldstein, Eugen (1850-1930). Ger. physicist.
A.A.A.S.—Proc. (78) p29-30   Magie—Source p576
Chambers—Dict. col.192

Goldstein, Max Aaron (1870-1941). Amer. otologist, physician.
Kagan—Modern p133 (por.133)

Goldstine, Herman Heine (1913-   ). Amer. mathematician.
Curr. Biog. '52 p211-212

Goldthwait, James Walter (1880-1947). Amer. geologist.
G.S.A.—Proc. '48 p171-180 (por.171)

Goldwater, Sigismund (1873-1942). Amer. physician.
Kagan—Modern p207 (por.207)

Goler, George Washington (1864-1940). Amer. physician.
Curr. Biog. '40 p340

Golgi, Camillo (1843/1844-1926). It. physician, cytologist, pathologist.
Castiglioni—Hist. p722 (por.773)   Major—History (2) p906
Chambers—Dict. col.192   Stevenson—Nobel p32-33,34-36
Hammerton p669   (por.150)

Golitzin, Boris Borisovitch, Prince (1826-1916). Russ. physicist.
Hammerton p669

Golovina, Anastasia (d.1932). Bulg. physician.
Lovejoy—Women p210

Gomberg, Moses (1866-1947). Amer. chemist.
Browne—Hist. p486 (por.141)   Killeffer—Eminent p24 (por.24)
Chambers—Dict. col.192   Smith—Torch. p107 (por.107)

Gonzano.   See Oviedo y Valdés, Gonzalo Fernandez de

Gooch, Benjamin (fl. c1771-1792). Eng. surgeon.
Leonardo—Lives p184

Gooch, Sir Daniel (1816-1889). Eng. engineer.
Hammerton p671 (por.671)

Gooch, Frank Austin (1852-1929). Amer. chemist.
A.A.A.S.—Proc. (81) p58-59
N.A.S.—Biog. (15) p105-125
(por.105,119)

Goodale, George Lincoln (1839-1923). Amer. botanist.
N.A.S.—Biog. (11) p1-7 (por.1)

Goode, George Brown (1851-1896). Amer. ichthyologist, zoologist.
*Book—Pop. Sci. (8) p2705-2706   N.A.S.—Biog. (4) p145-174
(por.2706)   Oehser—Sons p92-106 (por.58)
Jordan—Leading p391-403 (por.391)

Goodfellow, George E. (1855-1910). Amer. surgeon.
Leonardo—Lives p184-186

Goodman, John D. (1794-1830). Amer. physician, surgeon.
Bell—Early p59

Goodricke, John (1764-1786). Eng. astronomer.
Chambers—Dict. col.193   Williams—Great p469-470
Shapley—Astron. p152

Goodsir, John (1814-1867). Scot. anatomist, pathologist.

Bulloch—Hist. p369

Goodyear, Charles (1800-1860). Amer. inventor.

A.A.A.S.—Proc. (78) p33-35
Abbot—Great p317-319 (por.319)
Carmer—Caval. p265-267 (por.266)
Chambers—Dict. col.193
*Darrow—Masters p334
*Darrow—Thinkers p190-194 (por.192)
Hammerton p671
*Hartman—Mach. p122-126
*Hylander—Invent. p96-108 (por.97)
Iles—Leading p176-217 (por.176)
*Larsen—Shaped p66-77 (por.48)
Law—Civiliz. p253-258

Meyer—World p253
*Montgomery—Invent. p165-169
Morris—Ency. p667
Morris—Heroes p171-176
*Nida—Makers p97-104 (por.100)
*Parkman—Conq. p110-131 (por.112)
Patterson—Amer. p62-72
*Tappan—Heroes p30-38
Tuska—Invent. p85
*Wildman—Famous (1st) p147-154
   (por.145)
Wilson—Amer. p124-129 (por.124)
*Wright—Great p234-236

Gordon, Bernard de (fl. 14th cent.). Fr. physician.

Gordon—Medieval p283-284 (por.114)
Major—History (1) p309-310

Gordon, Charles Henry (1857-1934). Amer. geologist.

G.S.A.—Proc. '34 p225-228 (por.225)

Gordon, Crawford, Jr. (1914-   ). Can. aero. pioneer.

Curr. Biog. '59 p170-172 (por.171)

Gordon, Neil E. (1886-1949). Amer. chemist.

Browne—Hist. p396-497 (por.411)

Gore, George (1826-1908). Eng. electrochemist.

Weeks—Discovery p458-459 (por.459)

Gore, John Ellard (1845-1910). Irish astronomer.

MacPherson—Astron. p145-155
   (por.145)
MacPherson—Makers p215-216

Gorgas, William Crawford (1854-1920). Amer. physician, surgeon, public health worker.

Atkinson—Magic p298-300
*Book—Pop. Sci. (7) p2417-2419
   (por.2417)
*Cottler—Heroes p307-318
*Darrow—Builders p206-210 (por.195)
Grainger—Guide p154
Hammerton p673
Lambert—Medical p293-300 (por.294)
Lambert—Minute p293-300 (por.289)
Law—Civiliz. p341

*Law—Modern p121-135 (por.128)
Major—History (2) p915
Rowntree—Amid p14-20 (por.18)
16 Amer. p53-56
*Snyder—Biology p225-230 (por.228)
*Tappan—Heroes p237-244
Tobey—Riders p182-185
Walker—Pioneers p227-238 (por.227)
*Yost—Science p100-116

Gorham, John (1783-1829). Amer. chemist.
Smith—Chem. p221

Göring, Hermann Wilhelm (1893-1946). Ger. aero. pioneer.
Curr. Biog. '41 p327-330 (por.327)
'46 p218

Gortner, Ross Aiken (1885-1942). Amer. biochemist.
N.A.S.—Biog. (23) p149-160 (por.149)

Goss, Albert S. (1882-   ). Amer. agriculturist.
Curr. Biog. '45 p241-243 (por.242)

Gossard, Harry A. (1868-1925). Amer. entomologist.
Osborn—Fragments p189 (por.372)

Gosse, Philip Henry (1810-1888). Eng. ornithologist, naturalist.
Peattie—Gather p205-209

Goudkoff, Paul Pavel (1880-1955). Rus.-Amer. geologist.
G.S.A.—Proc. '55 p127-130 (por.127)

Goudsmit, Samuel Abraham (1902-   ). Dutch-Amer. physicist.
Curr. Biog. '54 p304-306 (por.305)

Gould, Augustus Addison (1805-1866). Amer. naturalist.
N.A.S.—Biog. (5) p91-105 (por.91)

Gould, Benjamin Apthorp (1824-1896). Amer. astronomer.
Chambers—Dict. col.193   N.A.S.—Biog. (10) p155-170 (por.155)
Hammerton p676   Shapley—Astron. p324

Gould, Charles Newton (1868-1949). Amer. geologist.
G.S.A.—Proc. '49 p165-171 (por.165)

Gourmelen, Étienne (d.1593). Fr. physician.
Major—History (1) p477

Gower, Pauline (or Mary de Peauly) (1910-1947). Eng. aero. pioneer.
Curr Biog. '43 p241-242 (por.241)   Knapp—New p19-33 (por.179)
'47 p252

Gowers, Sir William Richard (1845-1915). Eng. neurologist.
Major—History (2) p906

Graaf, Regnier de (1641-1673). Dutch anatomist, physician, biologist.
Bodenheimer—Hist. p265
Chambers—Dict. col.193-194
Hammerton p678
Major—History (1) p534-536
Woodruff—Devel. p275

Grabau, Amadeus William (1870-1946). Amer. geologist, paleontologist.
G.S.A.—Proc. '46 p155-161 (por.155)

Grace, Eugene Gifford (1876-1960). Amer. engineer.
White—Famous (3d) p81-90 (por.79)

Grace, John Hilton (1873-1958). Eng. mathematician.
R.S.L.—Biog. (4) p93-96 (por.93)

Gracht, Willem A.J.M. van Waterschoot (1873-1943). Dutch geologist.
G.S.A.—Proc. '46 p231-233 (por.231)

Grade, Hans (b.1879). Ger. aero. pioneer, engineer.
Heinmuller—Man's p273 (por.273)

Graebe, Karl (1841-1927). Ger. chemist.
Chambers—Dict. col.194
Partington—Short p318
Smith—Torch. p108 (por.108,109,124)

Graefe, Albrecht (1828-1870). Ger. ophthalmologist.
Castiglioni—Hist. p730 (por.731)
Hammerton p679
Leonardo—Lives p186-187
Major—History (2) p892

Gräefe (or Gräfe), **Karl Ferdinand von** (1787-1840). Ger. surgeon.
Hammerton p679
Leonardo—Lives p187-188

Grafenburg.   See **Schenck von Grafenburg, Johann**

Gräffe, Carl Heinrich (1799-1873). Swiss mathematician.
Cajori—Hist. p364-365

Graham, Evarts Ambrose (1883-1957). Amer. physician, surgeon.
Curr. Biog. '52 p220-222 (por.221)
Fabricant—Why p114-115

Graham, Robert (1786-1845). Scot. botanist.
Oliver—Makers p291-293

Graham, Thomas (1805-1869). Scot. chemist.

Castiglioni—Hist. p688
Chambers—Dict. col.194
Findlay—Hundred p325-326
Hammerton p679-680
Partington—Short p245-247,270-271
    (por.246)

Ramsay—Essays p56-66
Roberts—Chem. p140-150
Smith—Torch. p110 (por.110)
Woodruff—Devel. p121-122,275

Graham, Wallace Harry (1910-   ). Amer. physician, surgeon.

Curr. Biog. '47 p254-257 (por.255)

Graham, William A. P. (1899-1934). Amer. geologist.

G.S.A.—Proc. '34 p233-235 (por.233)

Grahame-White, Claude (1879-   ). Eng. aero. pioneer.

Burge—Ency. p632
Hammerton p680

Heinmuller—Man's p282 (por.282)

Gram, Hans Christian Joachim (1853-1938). Dan. physician.

Bulloch—Hist. p369
Chambers—Dict. col.194-195

Grammateus, Henricus (or Scriptor, Schreiber, Schreyber, Heinrich)
    (b.1496). Ger. mathematician.

Smith—Hist. I p329-330

Gramme, Zénobe Théophile (1826-1901). Belg. inventor.

*Epstein—Real p55
Hammerton p680

Grange.   See **La Grange, Joseph Louis, Comte**

Granger, Walter (1872-1941). Amer. paleontologist, sci. explorer,
    geologist.

Curr. Biog. '41 p338-339
G.S.A.—Proc. '41 p159-166

Grant, Robert (1814-1892). Scot. astronomer.

Hammerton p681

Grapheus.   See **Grassus, Benvenutus**

Grasselli, Eugen Ramiro (1810-1882). It.-Amer. chemist.

Haynes—Chem. (1) p88-106 (por.89)

Grassi, Giovanni Battista (1854-1925). It. zoologist, entomologist.

*Book—Pop. Sci. (8) p2706-2707
Chambers—Dict. col.195

*De Kruif—Microbe p298-310
Major—History (2) p914

Grassman, Hermann Günther (1809-1877). Ger. mathematician.
Ball—Short p473-474
Cajori—Hist. p335-337

Grassus (or Grapheus), **Benvenutus** (fl. 12th cent.) Palest. ophthalmologist.
Leonardo—Lives p188-189
Major—History (1) p356

Gratiot, Charles (1786-1855). Swiss engineer.
Swiss—Prom. p79-81

Grau San Martin, Ramon (1887-   ). Cuban physician.
Curr. Biog. '44 p253-256 (por.254)

Graunt, John (1620-1674). Eng. inventor.
Major—History (1) p556
Moulton—Auto. p162

Graves, Alvin Cushman (1909-   ). Amer. physicist.
Curr. Biog. '52 p224-226 (por.225)

Graves, Robert James (1797-1853). Irish physician.
Atkinson—Magic p223
Hammerton p683
Lambert—Medical p217
Lambert—Minute p217
Major—History (2) p682-683 (por.682)
Walsh—Makers p168-185

Gravesande, Wilhelm Jacob Storm van s' (1688-1742). Dutch mathematician.
Smith—Hist. I p526

Gray, Asa (1810-1888). Amer. botanist.
*Book—Pop. Sci. (8) p2708-2709
*Darrow—Masters p334
Hammerton p683 (por.683)
*Hylander—Scien. p59-64 (por.53)
Jordan—Leading p211-231 (por.211)
Morris—Ency. p668
N.A.S.—Biog. (3) p161-175
Reed—Short p131-132
True—Smiths. p263-265 (por.263)
Van Wagenen—Beacon p289-291
Woodruff—Devel. p275
Young—Biology p45-46 (por.43)

Gray, Elisha (1835-1901). Amer. inventor.
*Darrow—Masters p334-335
Hammerton p683
*Hylander—Invent. p209-210

Gray, Etta (1880-   ). Amer. physician.
Lovejoy—Women Phys. p73-83 (por.7)

Gray, George Alphonso (1882-   ). Amer. aero. pioneer.
Heinmuller—Man's p295 (por.295)

Gray, Harold E. (1906-   ). Amer. aero. pioneer.
Heinmuller—Man's p355

Gray, Hawthorne (d.1927). Amer. aero. pioneer.
Fraser—Heroes p721-722

Gray, James Gordon (1876-1934). Scot. physicist.
Hammerton p1449

Gray, Stephen (d.1736). Eng. physicist.
Chambers—Dict. col.195
Hammerton p683-684
Hart—Physicists p96
Hodgins—Behemoth p78-91
Magie—Source p394
Taylor—Illus. p84,86,87
Van Wagenen—Beacon p145-146

Gray, Thomas de.   See **Walsingham, Lord Gray, Thomas de**

"Great Yü."   See **Yü**

Greathead, Henry (1757-1816). Eng. inventor.
Hammerton p684

Greathead, James Henry (1844-1896). Brit. engineer.
Hammerton p684

Greaves, John (1602-1652). Eng. (Barbados) mathematician, astronomer.
Gunther—Early XI p48-49 (por.48)
R.S.L.—Biog. (2) p129-136 (por.129)

Grebe, John J. (1900-   ). Ger.-Amer. phys. chemist.
Curr. Biog. '55 p240-241 (por.241)

Green, Arthur George (1864-1941). Eng. chemist.
Findlay—British p247-269 (por.247)

Green, Charles (1784-1870). Eng. aero. pioneer.
Burge—Ency. p632
*Cohen—Men p31-35
Hammerton p685
Heinmuller—Man's p238 (por.238)

Green, George (1793-1841). Eng. mathematician.
Chambers—Dict. col.195
Hammerton p685
Murray—Science p349-350

Green, Jacob (1790-1841). Amer. geologist.
Merrill—First p140-141 (por.140)

Green, Joseph Henry (1791-1863). Eng. surgeon.
Leonardo—Lives p189-190

Green, Lucille H. (d.1878). Amer. physician.
Lovejoy—Women p221-222

Greene, Catherine L. (1731-1794?). Amer. inventor.
Mozans—Woman p351-352

Greene, Cornelia A. (b.1831). Amer. physician.
Mead—Medical p47

Greene, Edward Lee (1843-1915). Amer. botanist, naturalist.
Ewan—Rocky p45-66 (por.45)

Greene, William Friese.   See **Friese-Greene, William**

Greener, William (1806-1869). Eng. inventor.
Hammerton p686

Greenewalt, Crawford Hallock (1902-   ). Amer. chem. engineer.
Curr. Biog. '49 p234-236 (por.235)

Greenhill, Sir Alfred (1847-1927). Eng. mathematician.
Hammerton p686

Greenhill, William Alexander (1814-1894). Eng. physician.
Major—History (2) p882-883

Greenwood, Allen (1866-1942). Amer. physician.
Curr. Biog. '42 p315

Gregg, John Robert (1867-1948). Irish inventor.
Hammerton p687

Gregor, William (1761-1817). Eng. chemist, mineralogist.
Chambers—Dict. col.195
Weeks—Discovery p318-320

Gregory, David (1661-1708). Scot. mathematician.
Ball—Short p379
Chambers—Dict. col.196
Gunther—Early XI p65
Smith—Hist. I p413

Gregory, Elisha Hall (1824-1906). Amer. surgeon.
Leonardo—Lives p190

Gregory, Herbert Ernest (1869-1952). Amer. geologist.
G.S.A.—Proc. '52 p115-121 (por.115)

Gregory, James (1638-1675). Scot. mathematician, inventor.
Ball—Short p313-314   Turnbull—Great p83-85
Chambers—Dict. col.196   Year—Pic. p93 (por.93)
Smith—Hist. I p409-410

Gregory, John Walter (1864-1932). Eng. geologist.
Hammerton p689 (por.689)

Gregory, Menas Sarkis (1872?-1941). Amer. psychiatrist.
Curr. Biog. '42 p315

Gregory, Sir Richard Arman (1864-1952). Eng. astronomer.
Hammerton p689

Gregory, William King (b.1876). Amer. paleontologist.
Progress—Science '41 p180

Gregory of Nyssa, Saint (c331-c396). Gr. nat. philosopher.
Osborn—Greeks p108

Grenfell, Bernard Pyne (1869-1926). Eng. archaeologist.
Hammerton p690

Grenfell, Sir Wilfred Thomason (1865-1940). Eng. physician, surgeon.
Curr. Biog. '40 p349 (por.349)   Peattie—Lives p169-176 (por.169)
Fabricant—Why p52-53   Progress—Science '40 p186-187
Hammerton p690 (por.690)   (por.187)
*Hyde—Modern p230-249   Rosen—Four p132-134
                                   Rowntree—Amid p520-522 (por.518)

Gresley, Sir Herbert Nigel (1876-1941). Brit. engineer.
Curr. Biog. '41 p345

Grew, Nehemiah (1641-1712). Eng. botanist.
Bodenheimer—Hist. p266   Major—History (1) p557
Chambers—Dict. col.196   Miall—Early p166-174
Gilmour—British p20-22   Oliver—Makers p44-64 (por.44)
Hammerton p691   Reed—Short p88-90
Hawks—Pioneers p199-203   *Snyder—Biology p164 (por.164)
Locy—Biology p56-57   Woodruff—Devel. p275

Grey of Fallodon, Sir Edward, Viscount (1862-1933). Eng. ornithologist.
Peattie—Gather. p309-311

Griess, Johann Peter (1829-1888). Ger. chemist.
Partington—Short p281,316
Smith—Torch. p111 (por.111)

Griffin, Bennett (1895-   ). Amer. aero. pioneer.
Heinmuller—Man's p172-182
(por.346)

Griffin, John D. (1906-   ). Can. psychiatrist.
Curr. Biog. '57 p220-221 (por.220)

Griffith, Francis Llewellyn (1862-1934). Brit. archaeologist.
Hammerton p693 (por.693)

Griffith, John Price Crozer (1856-1941). Amer. physician.
Curr. Biog. '41 p347
Progress—Science '41 p180

Griffith, William (1810-1845). Eng. botanist.
Oliver—Makers p178-191 (por.178)

Grignard, (François Auguste) Victor (1871-1935). Fr. chemist.
Chambers—Dict. col.196-197   Partington—Short p320
Farber—Nobel p50-52 (por.118)   Smith—Torch. p111 (por.111)

Grijns, Gerrit (1865-1944). Dutch biologist.
Bodenheimer—Hist. p448

Grimaldi, Francesco Antonio (1740-1784). It. seismologist.
Davison—Founders p26-27

Grimaldi, Francesco Maria (1618?-1663). It. physicist.
Chambers—Dict. col.197
Magie—Source p294

Grimaux, Louis (1835-1900). Fr. chemist.
Smith—Torch. p113 (por.113)

Grimshaw, Robert (1850-1941). Amer. engineer, inventor.
Curr. Biog. '41 p347

Griscom, John (1774-1852). Amer. chemist.
Smith—Chem. p224

Grisebach, August (1814-1879). Ger. naturalist, botanist.
Reed—Short p131

Grizodubova, Valentina Stepanova (1910?-   ). Rus. aero. pioneer.
Curr. Biog. '41 p347-348 (por.348)
Knapp—New p129-139 (por.179)

Grocco, Pietro (1856-1916). It. physician.
Castiglioni—Hist. p842 (por.842)

Gromov, Mikhail (1899-   ). Rus. aero. pioneer.
Heinmuller—Man's p352 (por.352)

Gronau, Wolfgang von (1893-   ). Ger. aero. pioneer.
*Fraser—Heroes p572-576,637-643
Heinmuller—Man's p337 (por.337)

Groombridge, Stephen (1755-1832). Eng. astronomer.
Hammerton p694 (por.694)

Gros, Edmund Louis (1869-1942). Amer. physician.
Curr. Biog. '42 p316

Grosbeck, John Arthur (1883-1914). Amer. entomologist.
Osborn—Fragments p206 (por.356)

Gross, Louis (1895-1937). Can. physician.
Kagan—Modern p47 (por.47)

Gross, Robert Ellsworth (1897-   ). Amer. aero. pioneer.
Curr. Biog. '56 p233-235 (por.233)

Gross, Samuel David (1805-1884). Amer. physician, surgeon.
Castiglioni—Hist. p850
Fabricant—Why p168-172
Leonardo—Lives (Supp I) p481-482
Major—History (2) p762-764
Rosen—Four p70-74,179-182,260-264

Gross, Samuel W. (1837-1889). Amer. surgeon.
Leonardo—Lives p191

Grosse, Aristid V. (1905-   ). Amer. chemist.
Chambers—Dict. col.197
Weeks—Discovery p497-498,516,538-539

Grosseteste, Robert, Bishop of London (or, nicknamed "Greathead") (c.1175-1253). Eng. naturalist.
Chambers—Dict. col.197-198
Gordon—Medieval p275-276

Grosvenor, Gilbert Hovey (b.1875). Amer. geographer.
Curr. Biog. '46 p228-230 (por.229)
Hammerton p695

Grosvenor, Graham Bethune (1884-1943). Amer. aero. pioneer.
Curr. Biog. '43 p255

Grosvenor, John (1742-1823). Eng. surgeon.
Gunther—Early XI p219

Grosvenor, Melville Bell (1901-   ). Amer. geographer.
Curr. Biog. '60 p171-173 (por.172)

Grote, Augustus Radcliffe (1841-1903). Eng.-Amer. entomologist.
Essig—Hist. p639-640 (por.639)

Grotefend, Georg Friedrich (1775-1853). Ger. philologist.
Ceram—Gods p223-231
Hammerton p695

Grotjahn, Alfred (1869-1932). Ger. physician.
Rosen—Four p291-292

Grove, Sir William Robert (1811-1896). Eng physicist, inventor.
Chambers—Dict. col.198
Hammerton p696

Groves, Leslie R. (1896-   ). Amer. engineer.
Curr. Biog. '45 p254-256 (por.255)

Gruber, Max (1853-1927). Aust. bacteriologist.
Bulloch—Hist. p369

Gruby, David (1810-1898). Hung. bacteriologist.
Bulloch—Hist. p370

Gruithuisen, Franz Paula von (1774-1852). Ger. surgeon, astronomer.
Bulloch—Hist. p370

Grumman, Leroy Randle (1895-   ). Amer. aero. pioneer.
Curr. Biog. '45 p256-259 (por.257)
Daniel—Pioneer p117-121 (por.116)

Grünbaum (later Leyton), **Albert Sidney Frankau** (1869-1921). Eng. bacteriologist.
Bulloch—Hist. p370

Grünpeck, Joseph (1470-1531). Ger. physician.
Major—History (1) p464

Gscheidlen, Richard (1842-1889). Ger. physiologist.
Bulloch—Hist. p369-370

Gua de Malves, Jean Paul de (c1712-1786). Fr. mathematician.
Smith—Hist. I p475

Guainierio, Antonio (d.1445). It. physician, surgeon.
Major—History (1) p355

Guedel, Arthur E. (1883-1956). Amer. anesthetist.
Robinson—Victory p285,308
(por.275)

Guenée, Achille (1809-1880). Fr. entomologist.
Essig—Hist. p640-642 (por.641)

Guenther, Konrad (b.1874). Ger. naturalist.
Von Hagen—Green p326

Guerick, Otto von (1602-1686). Ger. physicist, inventor.
A.A.A.S.—Proc. (81) p59-62
*Book—Pop. Sci. (11) p3671-3672
(por.3671)
Chambers—Dict. col.198
*Darrow—Masters p335
Dibner—Ten p11-14 (por.12)
Hammerton p697
Hart—Physicists p60-63
*Hartman—Mach. p51-53
Lenard—Great p54-62 (por.66)
Magie—Source p80
Matschoss—Great p71-83 (por.86)
Morgan—Men p23-24
Radio's 100 p15-16 (por.140)
*Shippen—Design p25-83
Taylor—Illus p60-61
Van Wagenen—Beacon p111-112
Year—Pic. p94 (por.94)

Guérin, Jules-René (1801-1886). Fr. surgeon.
Bulloch—Hist. p370

Guettard, Jean Étienne (1715-1786). Fr. geologist.

*Book—Pop. Sci. (5) p1661
Chambers—Dict. col.198-199
Fenton—Giants p27-34
Geike—Founders p12-46

Hammerton p697
Merrill—First p1-2
Woodruff—Devel. p275

Guggenheim, Daniel (1856-1930). Amer. aero. pioneer.

Forbes—Men p173-180 (por.1)
Morris—Ency. p669

Guggenheim, Harry Frank (1890-   ). Amer. aero. pioneer.

Curr. Biog. '56 p237-239 (por.237)
Heinmuller—Man's p322 (por.322)

Thomas—Men pxii

Guibert, Nicholas 1540/1547-1620). Fr. chemist, physician.

Chymia (v.2) p115-117

Guidi (or Guido).   See **Vidius, Guido**

Guillaume, Charles Édouard (1861-1938). Swiss physicist.

Chambers—Dict. col. 199
Hammerton p698

Heathcote—Nobel p173-179 (por.240)
Weber—College p315 (por.315)

Guillaume, Baron Dupuytren.   See **Dupuytren, Baron Guillaume**

Guillemeau, Jacques (1550-1613). Fr. surgeon.

Leonardo—Lives p192-194
Major—History (1) p476

Guinterius, Johannes (or Winter, Johannes). Ger. physician.

Major—History (1) p419

Guldberg, Cato Maximilian (1836-1902). Norw. mathematician, chemist.

Chambers—Dict. col.199-200
Findlay—Hundred p326

Partington—Short p325-326,339
   (por.326)
Woodruff—Devel. p114,275

Guldin, Paul (or Guldinus) (1577-1643). Swiss mathematician.

Ball—Short p252-253
Cajori—Hist. p159

Gull, Sir William Withey (1816-1890). Eng. physician.

Hale-White—Great p208-226
Major—History (2) p815-816
   (por.815)

Gullstrand, Allvar (1862-1930). Swed. ophthalmologist, physician.
Castiglioni—Hist. p1023 (por.1023)   Lindroth—Swedish p239-248
Chambers—Dict. col.200   Stevenson—Nobel p68-72 (por.150)
Hammerton p699

Gumpert, Martin (1897-   ). Ger. physician.
Curr. Biog. '51 p250-252 (por.251)

Gundersen, Gunnar (1897-   ). Amer. physician.
Curr. Biog. '59 p164-165 (por.164)

Gundlach, Johann Cristoph (or Johannes (Juan) Christopher) (1810-1896).
Ger.-Cuban entomologist.
Osborn—Fragments p31-32 (por.345)

Gunn, Moses (1822-1887). Amer. surgeon.
Leonardo—Lives p194-195

Gunning, John (d.1798). Eng. surgeon.
Leonardo—Lives p195

Gunter, Edmund (1581-1626). Eng. mathematician, astronomer.
Chambers—Dict. col.200   Hammerton p699
Gunther—Early XI p203   Smith—Hist. I p394-395

Günther, Carl Oscar (1854-1929). Ger. bacteriologist.
Bulloch—Hist. p370

Gunther, Robert Theodore (1869-1940). Eng. biologist.
Hammerton p699-700

Gurley, William Frank Eugene (1854-1943). Amer. paleontologist,
geologist.
G.S.A.—Proc. '43 p135-139 (por.135)

Gurlt, Ernst Julius (1825-1899). Ger. surgeon.
Leonardo—Lives p195-196
Major—History (2) p889

Gurney, Edmund (1847-1888). Eng. psychologist.
Hammerton p700

Gurney, Sir Goldsworthy (1793-1875). Eng. inventor.
Hammerton p700

Gutenberg, Johannes (or John, Johann) (1400?-1468). Ger inventor.
*Bachman—Great p187-205 (por.201)
*Book—Pop. Sci. (7) p2309-2310 (por.2309)
*Cottler—Heroes p179-189
*Darrow—Thinkers p107-113 (por.111)
*Eberle—Invent. p3-10
*Epstein—Real p104-105
Fitzhugh—Concise p261-263
*Glenister—Stories p13-19 (por.19)
Hammerton p701-702 (por.702)
*Hathaway—Partners p93-102 (por.95)
*Larsen—Prentice p3-7
Law—Civiliz. p116-119
*McSpadden—How p45-58 (por.50)
Matschoss—Great p39-48 (por.39)
Meyer—World p38-40
*Montgomery—Invent. p17-21
*Nida—Makers p1-9
*Nisenson—Illus. p75 (por.75)
*Pratt—Famous p8-12
Sewell—Brief p28
Wilson—Human p80-85 (por.84)

Guthrie, George James (1785-1856). Eng. surgeon.
Leonardo—Lives p196-198

Guthrie, George Wilkeston (1845-1915). Amer. surgeon.
Leonardo—Lives p198-199

Guthrie, Joseph Edward (1871-1935). Amer. entomologist.
Osborn—Fragments p222 (por.364)

Guthrie, Samuel (1782-1848). Amer. chemist, inventor.
Hammerton p702
Robinson—Path. p309-339
Robinson—Victory p175-190
Smith—Chem. p226-229

Guy, Henry Lewis (1887-1956). Welsh engineer.
R.S.L.—Biog. (4) p99-101 (por.99)

Guy, Raymond Frederick (1899-   ). Amer. engineer.
Curr. Biog. '50 p214-216 (por.215)

Guye, Phillippe-Auguste (1862-1922). Swiss chemist.
Smith—Torch. p114 (por.114)

Guynemer, Georges (1894-1917). Fr. aero. pioneer.
Arnold—Airmen p125-127
Burge—Ency. p632
Hammerton p702
Heinmuller—Man's (por.300)

Guyon, Jean Casimir Félix (1831-1920). Fr. physician, surgeon.
Castiglioni—Hist. p852 (por.852)
Leonardo—Lives (Supp 1) (p482-483)

Guyot, Arnold Henry (1807-1884). Swiss geologist, geographer.
Hammerton p702
N.A.S.—Biog. (2) p309-345
Swiss—Prom. p214-219 (por.214)
Van Wagenen—Beacon p284-286
Youmans—Pioneers p492-499 (por.492)

Guyot, Edmé Gilles (1706-1786). Fr. geographer, physician.
Woglom—Discov. p101-103

Guyton de Morveau, Louis Bernard, Baron (1737-1816). Fr. chemist, aero.
pioneer.
Hammerton p702   Weeks—Discovery p317 (por.317)
Heinmuller—Man's p234 (por.234)

Gwathmey, James Tayloe (1865-1944). Amer. anesthetist, physician.
Curr. Biog. '44 p262
Robinson—Victory p264 (por.274)

Gwinne, Matthew (1554-1627). Eng. physician.
Gunther—Early XI p238

Gyllenhal, Leonhard (1752-1840). Swed. entomologist.
Essig—Hist. p642-643 (por.642)

H

Haas, Arthur Erich (1884-1941). Bohem. physicist.
Curr. Biog. p358

Haber, Fritz (1868-1934). Ger. chemist.
Chambers—Dict. col.201   Partington—Short p341
Farber—Nobel 71-75 (por.118)   Smith—Torch. p115 (por.115)
Hammerton p703

Haber, Heinz (1913-   ). Ger. physicist.
Curr. Biog. '52 p237-238 (por.237)

Haddon, Alfred Cort (1855-1940). Eng. anthropologist, ethnologist.
Curr. Biog. '40 p356

Haden, Sir Francis Seymour (1818-1910). Eng. surgeon.
Hammerton p704 (por.704)

Hadfield, Sir Robert Abbott (1859-1940). Eng. metallurgist.
Chambers—Dict. col.201   Hammerton p704
Curr. Biog. '40 p357   John Fritz p119-121 (por.118)

Hadley, James (1821-1872). Amer. philologist.
N.A.S.—Biog. (5) p247-254 (por.247)

Hadley, John (1682-1744). Eng. astronomer, mathematician.
Chambers—Dict. col.201

Hadrian Junius (or Jonge, Adriaan de) (1511-1575). Dutch physician.
Major—History (1) p470

Haeckel, Ernest Heinrich (1834-1919). Ger. naturalist, biologist, nat. philosopher.
*Book—Pop Sci. (8) p2709-2710 (por.2700)
Chambers—Dict. col.201-202
*Darrow—Masters p335
Hammerton p704 (por.704)
Hubbard—Scientists (2) p1-24 (por.,front.)
Locy—Biology p439-441 (por.440)
Thomas—Scien. p233-244 (por.231)
Thomson—Great p158-161
Van Wagenen—Beacon p370-371
Woodruff—Devel. p275-276
Year—Pic. p129 (por.129)

Haen, Anton de (1704-1776). Dutch physician.
Major—History (2) p581-583 (por.582)
Sigerist—Great p210-218 (por.208)

Haenke.   See Hanke, Thaddeus

Haenlein, Paul (1835-1905). Ger. engineer, aero. pioneer.
Heinmuller—Man's p248 (por.248)

Haereticorum.   See Faber, Johannes

Haeser, Heinrich (1811-1884). Ger. physician.
Major—History (2) p881-882

Haffkine, Waldemar Mordecai Wolff (1860-1930). Rus. bacteriologist, physician.
Bulloch—Hist. p370-371
Hammerton p704
Kagan—Modern p157 (por.157)

Hafstad, Lawrence R. (1904-   ). Amer. physicist.
Curr. Biog. '56 p239-241 por.240)

Hagen, Hermann August (1817-1893). Ger.-Amer. entomologist.
Essig—Hist. p643-646 (por.644)
Osborn—Fragments p159-161 (por.338)
Smiths.—Misc. (184) p61-63 (por.545,pl.4)

Hagen, John P. (1908-   ). Can.-Amer. physicist.
Curr. Biog. '57 p225-227 (por.226)

Hagen, Victor Wolfgang von (1908-   ). Amer. naturalist, sci. explorer.
Curr. Biog. '42 p859-860 (por.859)

Haggard, William (1826-1901). Amer. surgeon.
Leonardo—Lives p199-200

Haggard, William David (1872-1940). Amer. gynecologist, physician, surgeon.
Curr. Biog. '40 p357

Hague, Arnold (1840-1917). Amer. geologist.
N.A.S.—Biog. (9) p21-36 (por.21)

Hahn, Otto (1879-   ). Ger. phys. chemist.
Chambers—Dict. col.202
Curr. Biog. '51 p252-253 (por.253)
Farber—Nobel p174-177 (por.118)
*Larsen—Scrap. p147-149
Progress—Science '40 p187
Weeks—Discovery p492,496-497,539-540
Year—Pic. p213 (por.213)

Hahneman, Samuel Christian Friedrich (1755-1843). Ger. physician.
Castiglioni—Hist. p591-592
Chambers—Dict. col.202-203
Farmer—Doctors' p118
Hammerton p705
Lambert—Medical p155-157
Lambert—Minute p155-157
Major—History (2) p695-698 (por.695)
Oliver—Stalkers p139-140
Year—Pic. p108 (por.108)

Hajek, Marcus (1861-1941). Hung. physician.
Kagan—Modern p131 (por.131)

Hakluyt, Richard (c1552-1616). Eng. geographer.
Hammerton p706

Halberstadt, Baird (1860-1934). Amer. geologist.
G.S.A.—Proc. '36 p159-161 (por.159)

Haldane, John Burdon Samderson (1892-   ). Brit. physiologist.
*Bridges—Master p104-116 (por.113)
Chambers—Dict. col.203
Curr. Biog. '40 p357-359 (por.358)
Hammerton p707 (por.707)
Year—Pic. p229 (por.229)

Haldane, John Scott (1860-1936). Scot. biologist.
Gunther—Early XI p145 (por.145)
Hammerton p707-708 (por.707)
Major—History (2) p961,1034-1035
*Wright—Great p125-132

Haldeman, George (1898-   ). Amer. aero. pioneer.
Heinmuller—Man's p326 (por.326)

Haldeman, Samuel S. (1812-1880). Amer. entomologist.

Essig—Hist. p646-647 (por.647)
N.A.S.—Biog. (2) p139-172
Osborn—Fragments p27 (por.338)
Osborn—Greek p310-311
Swiss—Prom. p229-233

Hale, Albert C. (1845-1921). Amer. chemist.

Browne—Hist. p497 (por.61)

Hale, George Ellery (1868-1938). Amer. astronomer.

Abetti—History p253-259
Armitage—Cent. p65-73 (por.80)
*Book—Pop. Sci. (10) p3416-3417 (por.3416)
Chambers—Dict. col.203-204
Hammerton p708
Jaffe—Outposts p421-449 (por.426)
MacPherson—Makers p179-182
N.A.S.—Biog. (21) p181-217 (por.181)
Williams—Great p419-421
Wilson—Amer. p352-361 (por.352)

Hale, William Jay (1876-1955). Amer. chemist, agriculturist.

Borth—Pioneers p47-85 (por.48)

Hale-White, Sir William (1857-1949). Eng. physician.

Hammerton p708

Hales, Stephen (1677-1761). Eng. physiologist, inventor, botanist, chemist.

Bodenheimer—Hist. p290
Chambers—Dict. col.204 (por.203)
Gilmour—British p22-27 (por.27)
Guinagh—Inspired p145-150
Hammerton p708
Hawks—Pioneers p228-230
Holmyard—Makers p161 (por.161)
Major—History (2) p609-613 (por.610)
Oliver—Makers p65-83 (por.65)
Partington—Short p90-93,150 (por.91)
Reed—Short p103-105
Schwartz—Moments (2) p600-601
Thomson—Great p34-38
Weeks—Discovery p111 (por.111)
Woglom—Discov. p11-29
Woodruff—Devel. p240-241,276 (por.236)

Halevi.   See **Abraham ibn David**

Halford, Sir Henry (1766-1844). Eng. physician.

Major—History (2) p705

Halim, Mustafa (Ahmed) ben (1921-   ). N. Afr. engineer.

Curr. Biog. '56 p241-243 (por.242)

Hall, Sir Alfred Daniel (1864-1942). Eng. agriculturist.

Hammerton p709

Hall, Arthur Lewis (1872-1955). Eng. geologist.

G.S.A.—Proc. '56 p137-138 (por.137)
R.S.L.—Biog. (2) p139-145 (por.139)

Hall, Asaph (1829-1907). Amer. astron.

Chambers—Dict. col. 204-205
Hammerton p709
MacPherson p25-31 (por.25)

N.A.S.—Biog. (6) p241-277 (por.241)
Shapley—Astron. p320
Smith—Math. p132-133

Hall, Charles Francis (1821-1871). Amer. sci. explorer.

*Book—Pop. Sci. (8) p2818-2821
Hammerton p709

Hall, Charles Martin (1863-1914). Amer. chemist, inventor.

*Bachman—Great p276-277 (por.276)
Chambers—Dict. col.205
Hammerton p709
*Kendall—Young p236-245 (por.241)
Law—Civiliz. p271-272
*Montgomery—Invent. p175-178

*Patterson—Amer. p148-160
*Science Miles. p263-269 (por.263)
Smith—Torch. p116 (por.116)
Weeks—Discovery p356-358 (por.356)
*Wright—Great p238-240

Hall, Edwin Herbert (1855-1938). Amer. physicist.

Magie—Source p541-542
N.A.S.—Biog. (21) p73-86 (por.73)

Hall, George M. (1891-1941). Amer. geologist.

G.S.A.—Proc. '41 p173-175 (por.173)

Hall, George Washington (1869-1941). Amer. neurologist.

Curr. Biog. '41 p361

Hall, Granville Stanley (1846-1924). Amer. psychologist.

N.A.S.—Biog. (12) p135-154 (por.135)

Hall, Henry Reginald Holland (1873-1930). Eng. archaeologist.

Hammerton p709 (por.709)

Hall, Sir James (1761-1832). Scot. geologist.

*Book—Pop. Sci. (5) p1661-1662
Geikie—Founders p184-191

Hammerton p709
Woodruff—Devel. p276 (por.206)

Hall, James (1811-1898). Amer. paleontologist, geologist.

*Book—Pop. Sci. (5) p1662
Fenton—Giants p150-164 (por.174)

Hammerton p709
Merrill—First p232-235 (por.232)

Hall, John (1575-1635). Eng. physician.

Hammerton p709

Hall, Marshall (1790-1857). Eng. physiologist, physician.

Chambers—Dict. col.205
Hale-White—Great p85-105
Hammerton p740

Major—History (2) p709
Woodruff—Devel. p276

Hall-Edwards, John Francis (1858-1926). Brit. physicist.
Hammerton p710

Halle, John (1529-1568). Eng. physician.
Major—History (1) p454

Haller, Albin (1849-1925). Fr. chemist.
A.A.A.S.—Proc. (77) p38-39
Smith—Torch. p116 (por.116)

Haller, Albrecht von (1708-1777). Swiss botanist, physician, physiologist, anatomist.
Bodenheimer—Hist. p307
Castiglioni—Hist. p609-612 (por.610)
Chambers—Dict. col.205-206
Cushing—Medical p266-284
Hammerton p710
Lambert—Medical p149-150
Lambert—Minute p149-150
Locy—Biology p181-182 (por.182)
Major—History (2) p573-577 (por.574)
Sigerist—Great p191-198,202,-204 (por.193)
Woodruff—Devel. p237-238,276 (por.236)

Halley, Edmund (1656-1742). Eng. mathematician, astronomer.
Abetti—History p142-143
Ball—Great p162-186 (por.167)
Ball—Short p379-380
*Book—Pop. Sci. (10) p3417-3418 (por.3417)
Chambers—Dict. col.206
Gregory—British p22 (por.12)
Gunther—Early XI p126-128 (por.126)
Hammerton p710
MacPherson—Makers p75-82
Moulton—Auto. p196-197
Schwartz—Moments (1) p305-306
*Science Miles. p91 (por.91)
Sedgwick—Short p302-303
Shapley—Astron. p94
Smith—Hist. I p405-406 (por.405)
Van Wagenen—Beacon p135-136
Vaucouleurs—Disc. p68-71
Williams—Great p202-217 (por.205)
Woodruff—Devel. p158,276 (por.138)
Year—Pic. p98,99 (por.99)

Hallier, Ernst (1831-1904). Ger. botanist.
Bulloch—Hist. p371

Halloran, Roy Dennis (1894-1943). Amer. psychiatrist.
Curr. Biog. '43 p272

Hallwachs, Wilhelm (1859-1922). Ger. physicist.
Magie—Source p578

Halpenny, Jasper (1869-1930). Can. surgeon.
Leonardo—Lives p200-201

Halphen, George-Henri (1844-1889). Fr. mathematician.
Cajori—Hist. p313

Halsted, George Bruce (1853-1922). Amer. mathematician.
Smith—Math. p139-140

Halsted, William Stewart (1852-1922). Amer. physician, surgeon.
Castiglioni—Hist. p852 (por.851)
Cushing—Medical p225-232
Kagan—Modern p95 (por.95)
Leonardo—Lives p201-203
Major—History (2) p855,858-859,913-914 (por.854)
*Montgomery—Story p163-167
N.A.S.—Biog. (17) p151-163 (por.151)
Robinson—Victory p252-253 (por.250)
Rowntree—Amid p63-66 (por.65)
Thorwald—Century p288-289,296-301
Young—Scalpel p199-217 (por.233)

Haly Abbas. See **Ali Abbas**

Haly, Jesu. See **Isa ben Ali**

Haly-Rodoam. See **Ali ibn-Rodhwan**

Hamel, Gustav (1889-1914). Eng. aero. pioneer.
Burge—Ency. p632

Hamilton, Alice (b.1869). Amer. physician.
Chandler—Medicine p117-122 (por.116)
Curr. Biog. '46 p234-236 (por.235)
Fabricant—Why p135-136
Rosen—Four p42-44,130-132,211-214
Yost—Women Sci. p44-61

Hamilton, Charles K. (1881-1914). Amer. aero. pioneer.
Heinmuller—Man's p281 (por.281)

Hamilton, Sir William (1730-1803). Eng. seismologist.
Davison—Founders p30-31

Hamilton, Sir William Rowan (1805-1865). Irish mathematician, astronomer.
Ball—Great p303-334 (por.313)
Ball—Short p472-473
Bell—Men p340-361 (por.,front.)
Cajori— Hist. p332-333
Chambers—Dict. col.206
Hammerton p714
MacFarlane—Lecture p34-49 (por., front.)
*Miller—Hist. p248-251
Sci. Amer.—Lives p61-74 (por.63)
Smith—Hist. I p461-462
Smith—Portraits (v.2), X, unp. (por.)
Turnbull—Great p115-118
Woodruff—Devel. p32,39-40,276

Hammar, Alfred Gottlieb (1880-1913). Swed. entomologist.
Osborn—Fragments p215

Hammer, Adam (1818-1878). Ger.-Amer. physician.
Major—History (2) p771

Hammon, William McDowell (1904-   ). Amer. microbiologist, physician.
Curr. Biog. '57 p233-235 (por.234)
*Sterling—Polio p53-54 (por.53)

Hammond, E. Cuyler (1912-   ). Amer. biologist.
Curr. Biog. '57 p235-237 (por.235)

Hammond, Graeme M. (1858-1944). Amer. neurologist.
Curr. Biog. '44 p266

Hammond, John Hays (1855-1936). Amer. min. engineer, inventor.
*Bernays—Outline p134
*Darrow—Builders p245-247
*Forbes—Men p181-190 (por.1)
Hammerton p714
Radio's 100 p229-231 (por.140)
*Wildman—Famous (2d) p123-132 (por.123)

Hamor, William Allen (1887-   ). Amer. chemist.
Browne—Hist. p497 (por.399)

Hampton, John (1799-1851). Eng. aero. pioneer.
Burge—Ency. p632

Hamusco, Juan Valverde di (c.1560). Sp. anatomist.
Major—History (1) p472

Hamy, Ernest Theodore (1842-1908). Fr. ethnologist.
Hammerton p715

Hance, James Harold (1880-1955). Amer. geologist.
G.S.A.—Proc. '57 p123-125 (por.123)

Hanckwitz, Ambrose Godfrey (or Godfrey, Ambrose) (1660-1741). Eng. chemist.
Weeks—Discovery p43-52 (por.48)

Hancock, Joy Bright (1898-   ). Amer. aero. pioneer.
Curr. Biog. '49 p241-243 (por.242)

Hanke, Thaddeus (or Haenke) (1761-1817). Bohem. botanist, naturalist.
Alden—Early p13

Hankin, Ernest Hanbury (1865-1939). Eng. bacteriologist, chemist.
Bulloch—Hist. p371

Hann, Julius (1839-1921). Aust. meteorologist.
Hammerton p717

Hannah, John Alfred (1902-   ). Amer. agriculturist.
Curr. Biog. '52 p241-243 (por.243)

Hannover, Adolph (1814-1894). Dan. physician, anatomist.
Copen.—Prom. p120-123

Hanriot, Maurice (1854-1933). Fr. chemist.
Smith—Torch. p118 (por.118)

Hansell, Clarence (1898-   ). Amer. engineer.
Radio's 100 p269-272 (por.140)

Hansen, Emil Christian (1842-1909). Dan. bacteriologist.
Bulloch—Hist. p371
Copen.—Prom. p161-164

Hansen, (Gerhard Henrik) Armauer (1841-1912). Norw. bacteriologist.
Bulloch—Hist. p371   Grainger—Guide p154-155
Chambers—Dict. col.207

Hansen, Niels Ebbesen (1866-1950). Dan.-Amer. bacteriologist, botanist.
*Beard—Foreign p123-131
*Jewett—Plant p1-25

Hansen, Peter Andreas (1795-1874). Dan. astronomer.
Hammerton p719

Hansen, William Webster (1909-1949). Amer. physicist.
N.A.S.—Biog. (27) p121-134 (por.121)

Hansom, Joseph Aloysius (1803-1882). Eng. inventor.
Hammerton p719

Hansteen, Christoph (1784-1873). Norw. astronomer.
Hammerton p719

Han Syin (pseud. of Elizabeth Comber) (1917-   ). Chin. physician.
Curr. Biog. '57 p237-238 (por.238)

Hantzsch, Arthur (1847-1935). Ger. chemist.
Chambers—Dict. col.207
Partington—Short p319

Harbison, John Stewart (1826-1912). Amer. entomologist.
Essig.—Hist. p647-649 (por.648)

Harcourt, Augustus George Vernon (1834-1919). Eng. chemist.
Findlay—Hundred p326

Harcourt, William Vernon (1789-1871). Eng. nat. philosopher.
Hammerton p720

Harden, Sir Arthur (1865-1940). Eng. chemist.
Chambers—Dict. col.207
Curr. Biog. '40 p363
Farber—Nobel p111-112,114-115 (por.118)
Findlay—British p270-284 (por.270)
Smith—Torch. p119 (por.119)

Hardy, Alister Clavering (1896-   ). Eng. biologist.
Chambers—Dict. col.207

Hardy, Sir William Bate (1864-1934). Eng. physiologist.
Hammerton p722

Hare, Robert (1781-1858). Amer. chemist.
Chambers—Dict. col.207-208
Kendall—Young p233-235 (por.240)
Killeffer—Eminent p4 (por.4)
Smith—Chem. p183-205 (por.front.)
Weeks—Discovery p247-248 (por.248)
Youmans—Pioneers p176-181 (por.176)

Harford, W. G. W. (1825-1911). Amer. entomologist.
Essig—Hist. p650-651 (por.650)

Hargrave, Lawrence (1850-1915). Austral. aero. pioneer.
*Bishop—Kite p113-117
Burge—Ency. p632-633
Heinmuller—Man's p252 (por.252)

Hargreaves, James (d.1778). Eng. inventor.
*Book—Pop. Sci. (9) p3045-3046
Chambers—Dict. col.208
*Darrow—Masters p41-44
*Epstein—Real p148-150
Hammerton p723
*Hartman—Mach. p5-7
*Larsen—Prentice p61-62
Law—Civiliz. p82-84
*Montgomery—Invent. p110-114
*Parkman—Conq. p38-48
*Pratt—Famous p79-81

Hargreaves, James (1834-1915). Eng. chemist.
Chambers—Dict. col.208

Harington, Charles Robert (1897-   ). Eng. chemist.
Chambers—Dict. col.208

Hariot.   See **Harriot, Thomas**

Harker, Alfred (1860-1938). Eng. geologist.
G.S.A.—Proc. '39 p207-208 (por.207)
Hammerton p723

Harkness, Harvey Wilson (1821-1901). Amer. physician.
Jones—Memories p370-374 (por.370)

Harkness, James (1864-1923). Amer. mathematician.
Smith—Math. p145

Harley, George (1829-1896). Eng. physician.
Major—History (2) p893

Harmer, Sir Sidney Frederic (1862-1950). Eng. zoologist.
Hammerton p723

Harmon, Clifford Burke (b.1868). Amer. aero. pioneer.
Heinmuller—Man's p275 (por.275)

Harmon, Millard Fillmore (1888-1945). Amer. aero. pioneer.
Curr. Biog. '42 p332-333 (por.333),
   '45 p271

Harnwell, Gaylord P. (1903-   ). Amer. physicist.
Curr. Biog. '56 p247-248 (por.247)

Harper, Robert Almer (1862-1946). Amer. botanist.
N.A.S.—Biog. (25) p229-237 (por.229)

Harpestraeng, Henrik (or Dacus, Henricus) (d.1244). Dan. med. writer.
Copen.—Prom. p9-11

Harrer, Heinrich (1912-   ). Aust. geographer.
Curr. Biog. '54 p321-323 (por.322)

Harriman, Edward Henry (1848-1909). Amer. inventor.
Abbot—Great p207-214 (por.209)

Harriot, Thomas (1560-1621). Eng. mathematician.

Ball—Short p237-238
Cajori—Hist. p156-157
Gunther—Early XI p110-111

Hammerton p725
Jaffe—Men p1-22
Smith—Hist. I p388-389

Harris, Sir Arthur Travers (1892-   ). Eng. aero. pioneer.

Curr. Biog. '42 p333-335 (por.334)

Harris, Gilbert Dennison (1864-1952). Amer. paleontologist.

G.S.A.—Proc. '52 p125-128 (por.125)

Harris, James Rendel (1852-1941). Brit. archaeologist.

Curr. Biog. '41 p366

Harris, Thaddeus William (1795-1856). Amer. entomologist.

Essig—Hist. p651-653 (por.652)
Smiths.—Misc. (84) p30-35
    (por.545,pl.1.)

Harris, Walter (1647-1732). Eng. physician.

Major—History (1) p561

Harrison, Archibald Cunningham (1864-1926). Amer. surgeon.

Leonardo—Lives p203-204

Harrison, Helen (n.d.). Can. aero. pioneer.

Knapp—New p86-99 (por.179)

Harrison, John (1693-1776). Eng. inventor.

Chambers—Dict. col.208-209

Harrison, Ross Granville (1870-1959). Amer. biologist.

Bodenheimer—Hist. p452
Chambers—Dict. col.209
Morris—Ency. p672
N.A.S.—Biog. (35) p132-154
    (por.132)

Progress—Science '41 p180-181
    (por.181)
Schwartz—Moments (2) p566-567

Harrison, William Henry (1892-   ). Amer. engineer.

Curr. Biog. '49 p255-256 (por.255)

Hart, Charles A. (1859-1918). Amer. entomologist.

Osborn—Fragments p237 (por.368)

Hart, Edward (1854-1931). Amer. chemist.

Browne—Hist. p497-498 (por.319)

Hart, Edwin Bret (1874-1953). Amer. agriculturist, biochemist.
*De Kruif—Hunger p284-297 (por.285)
N.A.S.—Biog. (28) p117-134 (por.117)

Harte, Richard Hickman (1855-1925). Amer. surgeon.
Leonardo—Lives p204-205

Harting, Pieter (1812-1885). Dutch naturalist.
Bulloch—Hist. p371

Hartley, Sir Charles Augustus (1825-1915). Brit. engineer.
Hammerton p727

Hartley, Edwin A. (1893-1926). Amer. entomologist.
Osborn—Fragments p218 (por.374)

Hartley, Frank (1856-1913). Amer. surgeon.
Leonardo—Lives p205-206

Hartley, Percival (1881-1957). Eng. biochemist, physiologist.
R.S.L.—Biog. (3) p81-97 (por.81)

Hartley, Walter Noel (1846-1913). Irish chemist.
Findlay—Hundred p326

Hartmann, Johannes Franz (1865-1936). Ger. astronomer.
Hammerton p727

Hartree, Douglas Rayner (1897-1958). Eng. math. physicist.
R.S.L.—Biog. (4) p103-113 (por.103)

Hartt, Charles Frederick (1840-1876). Amer. geologist.
Merrill—First p429-430 (por.430)

Hartweg, Karl Theodore (1812-1871). Ger. botanist, naturalist.
Alden—Early p47-48
Dakin—Perennial p36-38

Hartwell, John Augustus (1869-1940). Amer. physician.
Curr. Biog. '41 p369 (por.369)

Harun al Rashid (763/764-809). Arab. physician.
Major—History (1) p230,232
Smith—Hist. I p168

Harvey, Edmund Newton (1887-1959). Amer. physiologist, biologist.
Curr. Biog. '52 p247-248 (por.247)
Progress—Science '41 p181-182
(por.181)

Harvey, Gideon (1640-1700). Eng. physician.
Major—History (1) p560

Harvey, Hayward Augustus (1824-1893). Amer. inventor.
Hammerton p728

Harvey, Perry Williams (1869-1932). Amer. physician.
Cushing—Medical p253-265
(silhouette,265)

Harvey, Sir William (1578-1657). Eng. physician.
Atkinson—Magic p157-162
Bodenheimer—Hist. p243
*Book—Pop. Sci. (12) p3893-3895
(por.3895)
Castiglioni—Hist. p515-519 (por.516)
Chambers—Dict. col.209 (por.210)
*Chandler—Medicine p37-41 (por.36)
*Cottler—Heroes p251-259
*Crowther—Doctors p11-40 (por.64)
*Darrow—Masters p355
Fitzhugh—Concise p277-279
*Fox—Great p60-78 (por.60)
Ginzburg—Adven. p126-138 (por.128)
Gordon—Medieval p654-656 (por.51)
Gordon—Romance p38-39 (por.39)
Gregory—British p10-12
Gunther—Early XI p49-50 (por.50)
Hammerton p728-729 (por.728)
Holmyard—British p17-19 (por.17)
Lambert—Medical p123-138 (por.124)
Lambert—Minute p123-137 (por.128)
Locy—Biology p38-53, 180-181,198-
202 (por.44)
Major—History (1) p494-500
(por.495)
*Masters—Conquest p21-33 (por.24)
*Montgomery—Story p20-23
Moulton—Auto. p105
Newman—Interp. p28-30
*Nisenson—Illus. p78 (por.78)
Oliver—Makers p204-224 (por.204)
Oliver—Stalkers p89-93 (por.91)
100 Great p545-550 (por.56)
People p186-187
Schwartz—Moments (2) p575-578
Sci. Amer.—Lives p183-193 (por.185)
*Science Miles. p66 (por.66)
Sedgwick—Short p255-256
*Shippen—Micro. p55-59
Sigerist—Great p139-145 (por.144)
*Snyder—Biology p37-41 (por.39)
*Sterne—Blood p11-43
Thomson—Great p17-21
Tuska—Invent. p124-126
Van Wagenen—Beacon p99-101
*Williams-Ellis p61-84 (por.64)
Wilson—Human p119-128 (por.122)
Woodruff—Devel. p224-225,276
(por.224)
*World's Great p27-40 (por.12)
Year—Pic. p80,90 (por.90)
Young—Scalpel p57-74 (por.72)

Hasdai ibn-Shap-rut (or Hasdai ben Schaprut) (d.970/990?). Sp. physician.
Castiglioni—Hist. p275

Hasenöhrl, Friedrich (1874-1915). Aust. mathematician.
Lenard—Great p371-382 (por.371)

Haskins, Caryl Parker (1908-   ). Amer. physicist, biologist.
Curr. Biog. '58 p184-186 (por.185)

Haslett, Dame Caroline (1895-1957). Brit. engineer.
Curr. Biog. '50 p223-225 (por.224)
  '57 p244

Haslett, Elmer (1894-   ). Amer. aero. pioneer.
Arnold—Airmen p121-122

Hass, Hans (1919-   ). Aust. zoologist.
Curr. Biog. '55 p263-264 (por.263)

Hass, Henry Bohn (1902-   ). Amer. chemist.
Curr. Biog. '56 p254-256 (por.255)

Hasslacher, Jacob (1852-1921). Ger.-Amer. chemist.
Haynes—Chem. (1) p209-224
  (por.209)

Hassler, Ferdinand Rudolph (1770-1843). Amer. mathematician, engineer.
Smith—Math. p100-101
Swiss—Prom. p234-237 (por.234)

Hastings, Charles Sheldon (1848-1932). Amer. physicist.
N.A.S.—Biog. (20) p273-287 (por.273)

Hastings, John B. (1858-1942). Eng.-Amer. geologist.
G.S.A.—Proc. '42 p189-193 (por.189)

Hata, Sahachiro (1872-1938). Japan. bacteriologist.
Bulloch—Hist. p371

Hatch, Frederick Winslow (1821-1884). Amer. physician.
Jones—Memories p334-340 (por.334)

Hatchett, Charles (1765?-1847). Eng. chemist.
Chambers—Dict. col.209-210
Weeks—Discovery p183-185,206-224
  (por. 183,220)

Hauksbee, Francis (or Hawksbee). (d.c.1713). Eng. inventor, physicist.
Hammerton p731
Year—Pic. p104-105

Hauser, Gustav (b.1856). Ger. anatomist, bacteriologist.
Bulloch—Hist. p371

Hautefeuille, Paul Gabriel (1836-1902). Fr. chemist.
Smith—Torch. p120 (por.120)

Haüy, Abbé René Just (1743-1822). Fr. mineralogist.
Adams—Birth p205-207
Chambers—Dict. col.210-211
Hammerton p731
Van Wagenen—Beacon p179-181
Weeks—Discovery p331 (por.331)
Woodruff—Devel. p276

Havens, Beckwith (1890-   ). Amer. aero. pioneer.
Heinmuller—Man's p292 (por.292)

Havilland, Sir Geoffrey de (1882-   ). Eng. aero. pioneer.
Burge—Ency. p630
Daniel—Pioneer p145-147 (por.144)
Hammerton p732

Hawes, Harriet Boyd (b.1871). Amer. archaeologist.
Mozans—Woman p321-322

Hawker, Harry George (1888?-1919?). Austral. aero. pioneer.
Burge—Ency. p633
Hammerton p732 (por.732)
Heinmuller—Man p307 (por.307)

Hawkins, Alfred Cary (1887-1954). Amer. geologist.
G.S.A.—Proc. '54 p149

Hawkins, Caesar Henry (1798-1884). Eng. surgeon.
Leonardo—Lives p206-207

Hawks, Frank Monroe (1897-1937). Amer. aero. pioneer.
*Fraser—Famous p208-230 (por.222)
Heinmuller—Man's p333 (por.333)

Hawksbee.   See **Hauksbee, Francis**

Hawkshaw, Sir John (1811-1891). Eng. engineer.
Hammerton p733

Hawley, Alan Ramsay (1869-1938). Amer. aero. pioneer.
Heinmuller—Man's p264 (por.264)

Hawley, Paul Ramsey (1891-   ). Amer. physician.
Curr. Biog. '46 p248-250 (por.249)

Haworth, Leland John (1904-   ). Amer. physicist.
Curr. Biog. '50 p225-226 (por.226)

Haworth, Sir Walter Norman (1883-1950). Eng. chemist.
Chambers—Dict. col. 211
Farber—Nobel p152-155 (por.118)

Haxo, François Nicolas Benôit, Baron (1774-1838). Fr. engineer.
Hammerton p733

Hayden, Ferdinand Vandeveer (1829-1887). Amer. geologist.
Fenton—Giants p241-246 (por.255)   N.A.S.—Biog. (3) p395-408 (por.395)
Merrill—First p523-527 (por.500)

Hayden, Horace H. (1769-1844). Amer. pathologist, physiologist.
Atkinson—Magic p281
Merrill—First p85 (por.85)

Hayes, Samuel Perkins (1874-1958). Amer. psychologist.
Curr. Biog. '54 p325-327 (por.326)
    '58 p186

Hayford, John Fillmore (1868-1925). Amer. engineer.
N.A.S.—Biog. (16) p157-278 (por.157)

Haygarth, John (1740-1827). Eng. physician.
Major—History (2) p637

Haynes, Elwood G. (1857-1925). Amer. inventor.
Abbot—Great p219-222
Chambers—Dict. col.211

Hays, Isaac (1796-1879). Amer. physician.
Kagan—Modern p143 (por.143)

Hayward, Leland (1902-   ). Amer. aero. pioneer.
Curr. Biog. '49 p263-265 (por.263)

Hazeltine, (Louis) Alan (1886-   ). physicist, elec. engineer, inventor.
Curr. Biog. '48 p273-274 (por.273)
Radio's 100 p222-224 (por.140)

Head, Sir Henry (1861-1940). Eng. neurologist.
Curr. Biog. '40 p373
Rowntree—Amid p156-161 (por.159)

Headley, Rowland Patrick George John Allanson-Winn, 5th Baron (b.1855). Eng. engineer.
Hammerton p736

Heald, Henry Townley (1904-   ). Amer. engineer.
Curr. Biog. '52 p253-255 (por.254)

Heathcoat, John (1783-1861). Eng. inventor.
Hammerton p737

Heaton, Ross Leslie (1890-1950). Amer. geologist.
G.S.A.—Proc. '50 p101-102 (por.101)

Heaviside, Oliver (1850-1925). Eng. physicist.
A.A.A.S.—Proc. (78) p20-21
Appleyard—Pioneers p211-260
  (por.210)
Chambers—Dict. col.211-212
Hammerton p737
Hawks—Wireless p256 (por.258)
Radio's 100 p96-97 (por.140)

Heberden, William (1710-1801). Eng. physician.
Hammerton p737
Major—History (2) p598 (por.599)

Hebra, Ferdinand von (1816-1880). Aust. dermatologist.
Major—Hist. (2) p783-784
Robinson—Path. p611-621 (por.614)

Hecateus of Miletus (or Hecatus) (fl.c.500 B.C.). Gr. geographer.
Year—Pic. p33

Heck, Nicholas Hunter (1882-1953). Amer. seismologist, geologist.
G.S.A.—Proc. '54 p111-117 (por.111)

Hecker, Justus Friedrich Karl (1795-1850). Ger. physician.
Major—History (2) p711

Hedin, Sven Anders (1865-1952). Swed. geologist, sci. explorer,
  geographer.
*Book—Pop Sci. (8) p2820-2821
Curr. Biog. '40 p374-376 (por.375) '53
  p260
Lindroth—Swedish p249-255

Heer, Anna (d.1918). Swiss physician.
Lovejoy—Women p166-167

Hegenberger, Albert F. (1895-   ). Amer. aero. pioneer.
*Fraser—Heroes p492-502
Heinmuller—Man's p324 (por.324)
Maitland—Knights p318-327 (por.323)

Heidemann, Otto (1842-1916). Ger.-Amer. entomologist.
Essig—Hist. p653-654
Osborn—Fragments p203 (por.349)

Heidenhain, Rudolf Peter Heinrich (1834-1897). Ger. physiologist.
Major—History (2) p897-898

Heidingsfeld, M. L. (1871-1918). Amer. dermatologist.
Kagan—Modern p79 (por.79)

Heilbron, Sir Ian Morris (1886-1959). Scot. chemist.
Chambers—Dict. col.212

Heim, Albert (1849-1937). Swiss geologist, seismologist.
Davison—Founders p138-139
G.S.A.—Proc. '37 p169-171 (por.169)

Heim, Ludwig (b.1857). Ger. bacteriologist.
Bulloch—Hist. p372

Heim-Vogtlin, Marie (d.1916). Swiss physician.
Lovejoy—Women p165-167

Heinlein, Robert A. (1907-   ). Amer. engineer.
Curr. Biog. '55 p275-277 (por.276)

Heisenberg, Werner Karl (1901-   ). Ger. physicist.
Chambers—Dict. col.212
(por.105-106)
Curr. Biog. '57 p248-250 (por.249)
Heathcote—Nobel p306-312 (por.240)
Moulton—Auto. p554
Weber—College p521 (por.521)
Year—Pic. p211 (por.211)

Heiser, Victor George (b.1873). Amer. physician, public health worker.
Curr. Biog. '42 p360-362 (por.361)
Rosen—Four p223-226

Heising, Raymond Alphonsus (1888-   ). Amer. elec. engineer.
Radio's 100 p233-234 (por.140)

Heister, Lorenz H. (1683-1758). Ger. physician, surgeon.
Leonardo—Lives p207-208
Major—History (2) p630-631

Hektoen, Ludvig (1863-1951). Amer. pathologist.
Bulloch—Hist. p372
Curr. Biog. '47 p289-291 (por.290) '51
p267
N.A.S.—Biog. (28) p163-178 (por.163)

Heliodorus (fl.2d cent.). Gr. physician, surgeon.
Gordon—Medicine p683-684

Hell, Carl Magnus von (1849-1926). Ger. chemist.
A.A.A.S.—Proc. (77) p48

Heller, John Roderick, Jr. (1905-   ). Amer. physician.
Curr. Biog. '49 p267-268 (por.268)

Helmholtz, Hermann Ludwig Ferdinand von (1821-1894). Ger.
physiologist, anatomist, physicist.
Atkinson—Magic p223-224
*Book—Pop. Sci. (11) p3672-3673
Cajori—Hist. p474-475
Castiglioni—Hist. p688 (por.690)
Chambers—Dict. col.212-213
*Darrow—Masters p214-219 (por.161)
Ginzburg—Adven. p259-275
Gordon—Romance p224 (por.224)
Hammerton p740 (por.740)
Hart—Makers p281-282 (por.281)
Lenard—Great p292-295 (por.296)
Magie—Source p122
Major—History (2) p802-806 (por.803)
*Montgomery—Story p40-43
Moulton—Auto. p406-407
Murray—Science p66-74,95-101
Radio's 100 p54-55 (por.140)
Rosen—Four p253-254
Shapley—Astron. p311
Sigerist—Great p322-328 (por.328)
Van Wagenen—Beacon p316-318
Weeks—Discovery p373 (por.373)
Williams—Great p323,432 (por.323)
Williams—Story p227-228, 238,437
(por.237)
Woodruff—Devel. p276-277 (por.60)
Year—Pic. p122 (por.122)

Helmont, Jan Baptista van (1577?-1644?). Fr. chemist, physician.
Bodenheimer—Hist. p254
*Book—Pop. Sci. (11) p3673-3674
(por.3674)
Bulloch—Hist. p372
Castiglioni—Hist. p539-540
Chambers—Dict. col.213-214
Gordon—Medieval p611-614 (por.51)
Gordon—Romance p109,114-116
(por.109)
Hammerton p740
Holmyard—Chem. p51-54 (por.58)
Holmyard—Makers p119-124
(por.121)
Lambert—Medical p142-143
Lambert—Minute p142-143
Major—History (1) p500-503
(por.502)
Oliver—Stalkers p103-104
Partington—Short p44-54 (por.45)
Reed—Short p90-91
Schwartz—Moments (1) p199-200
Sigerist—Great p157-161 (por.160)
Smith—Torch. p246 (por.246)
Woodruff—Devel. p240,277

Helriegel, Hermann (1831-1895). Ger. biologist.
Chambers—Dict. col.214

Hempel, Walter Mathias (1851-1916). Ger. chemist.
A.A.A.S.—Proc. 18-19
Smith—Torch. p121 (por.121)

Hench, Philip Showalter (1896-   ). Amer. physician.
Chambers—Dict. (Supp.)
Curr. Biog. '50 p230-231 (por.231)
Morris—Ency. p674
Rowntree—Amid p538-543 (por.530)
Stevenson—Nobel p273,277-280
(por.150)

Henderson, Elmer Lee (1885-1953). Amer. surgeon.
Curr. Biog. '50 p223-233 (por.232)
'53 p263

Henderson, George Gerald (1862-1942). Scot. chemist.
Chambers—Dict. col.214

Henderson, George Hugh (1892-   ). Can. math. physicist.
Chambers—Dict. col.214-215

Henderson, Lawrence Joseph (1878-1942). Amer. biochemist.
  physiologist.
Curr. Biog. '42 p362   N.A.S.—Biog. (23) p31-50 (por.31)
Major—History (2) p978,1035

Henderson, Peter (1822-1890). Scot.-Amer. agriculturist.
*Ivins—Fifty p73-83 (por.75)

Henderson, Thomas (1798-1844). Scot. astronomer.
Chambers—Dict. col.215
MacPherson—Makers p146-151

Henderson, Yandell (1873-1944). Amer. physiologist.
Major—History (2) p1035

Henfrey, Arthur (1819-1859). Scot. botanist.
Oliver—Makers p192-203

Henke, Alfred (1903-1940). Ger. aero. pioneer.
Heinmuller—Man's p354 (por.354)

Henle, Friedrich Gustav Jakob (1809-1885). Ger. pathologist, anatomist.
Bulloch—Hist. p372   Kagan—Modern p9 (por.9)
Castiglioni—Hist. p677   Major—History (2) p797-799
Chambers—Dict. col.215   (por.799)
Grainger—Guide p155   Robinson—Path. p413-509
Kagan—Leaders p9-21 (por.10)   (por.439,455,479,502,503)
                                 Rosen—Four p245-247
                                 Sigerist—Great p350-353 (por.352)

Henniger, Arthur Rodolphe Marie (1850-1884). Ger. physician, chemist.
A.A.A.S.—Proc. (78) p26-27

Henoch, Eduard (1820-1910). Ger. physician.
Major—History (2) p886-887

Henri de Mondeville.   See Mondeville, Henri de

Henry, Joseph (1797/1799-1878). Amer. physicist, inventor.
Abbot—Great p5-7 (por.9)
*Book—Pop. Sci.. (11) p3674-3676
   (por.3675)
*Burlingame—Inv. p64-70,82-86
Chambers—Dict. col.215-216
Crowther—Famous p157-198
   (por.176,224)
*Darrow—Masters p140-147 (por.288)
*Darrow—Thinkers p36-37 (por.37)
Dibner—Ten p39-42 (por.40)
Hawks—Wireless p40-52 (por.40)
*Hylander—Scien. p44-52 (por.52)
Jaffe—Men p179-206 (por.xxviii)
Jordan—Leading p119-146 (por.119)
*Larsen—Prentice p55
Magie—Source p513-514
Meyer—World p145-147 (por.145)

Morris—Ency. p674-675
Moulton—Auto. p291-292
N.A.S.—Biog. (5) p1-35 (por.1)
Oehser—Sons p28-59 (por.26)
Radio's 100 p47-52 (por.140)
Sci. Amer.—Lives p141-153 (por.143)
*Science Miles p151-155 (por.151)
*Sootin—Twelve p87-109
True—Smiths. p274-280 (por.276)
Tuska—Invent. p129
Van Wagenen—Beacon p264-265
Wilson—Amer. p108-113 (por.113)
Woodruff—Devel. p277 (por.52)
Year—Pic. p176 (por.176)
Youmans—Pioneers p354-367
   (por.354)

Henry, William (1774/1775-1836). Eng. chemist.
Chambers—Dict. col.216
Hammerton p750

Weeks—Discovery p439 (por.439)

Henry, William Arnon (1850-1932). Amer. agriculturist.
*Ivins—Fifty p287-293 (por.289)

Henschel, August Wilhelm Eduard Theodor (1790-1856). Ger. physician.
Major—History (2) p708-709

Hensen, Victor (or Viktor). Ger. physiologist.
Chambers—Dict. col.216

Henshaw, Samuel (1852-1941). Amer. zoologist.
Progress—Science '41 p184-185

Henslow, John Stevens (1796-1861). Eng. botanist.
Hammerton p750
Oliver—Makers p151-163 (por.151)

Henson, William (1805-1888). Eng.-Amer. aero, pioneer, inventor.
*Bishop—Kite p87-92
Burge—Ency. p633

Heinmuller—Man's p241 (por.241)

Hepp, Edward (1851-1917). Ger. chemist.
A.A.A.S.—Proc. (79) p20-21

Heraclides of Tarentum (or Heracleides of Taras). (fl.1st, 2nd cent., B.C.). It. physician.

Castiglioni—Hist. p187
Gordon—Medicine p611-612

Sigerist—Great p52-55

Heraclides Ponticus (or Heracleides of Pontus). (fl. c.4th cent. B.C.). Gr. astronomer.

Abetti—History p35-36
Clagett—Greek p90

Dreyer—Hist. p123-135
Sedgwick—Short p85-86

Heraclitus (535/540-475 B.C.). Gr. nat. philosopher.

*Book—Pop. Sci. (11) p3819-3820
   (por.3819)
Gordon—Medicine p465-468
   (por.466)

Osborn—Greeks p51
Weeks—Discovery p1 (por.1)

Herder, Johann Gottfried von (1744-1803). Ger. nat. philosopher.

Osborn—Greeks p153-154

Herdman, Sir William Abbott (1858-1924). Scot. marine naturalist.

Hammerton p752

Hering, Ewald (1834-1918). Ger. physiologist, psychologist.

Chambers—Dict. col.216

Hermite, Charles (1822-1901). Fr. mathematician.

Ball—Short p478
Bell—Men p448-465 (por.,front.)
Cajori—Hist. p415-416

Chambers—Dict. col.216-217
*Miller—Hist. p260-262

Hernandez, Francisco (1514-1578). Sp. physician, naturalist.

Alden—Early p3-4

Herndon, Hugh, Jr. (1904-   ). Amer. aero. pioneer.

*Fraser—Heroes p623-628
Heinmuller—Man's p161-172,345
   (por.345)

Hero of Alexandria (c80 B.C.?). Gr. mathematician, inventor.

Ball—Short p88-91
*Book—Pop. Sci. (9) p3046-3047
Cajori—Hist. p43-44
Chambers—Dict. col.217
Clagett—Greek p29-31,76-80,117
Hammerton p752
*Hodges—Behemoth p30

Matschoss—Great p19-21
Meyer—World p24-27
Sedgwick—Short p123-125
Smith—Hist. I p125-126
Taylor—Illus. p36-38
Year—Pic. p39

Herod, William Rogers (1898-   ). Amer. engineer.

Curr. Biog. '51 p267-270 (por.268)

Heron-Allen, Edward (1861-1943). Eng. zoologist, biologist.

Hammerton p753

Herophilus (fl c.300 B.C.). Gr. anatomist, surgeon.

Castiglioni—Hist. p185
Chambers—Dict. col.217
Gordon—Medicine p594-598 (por.594)
Gordon—Romance p95-96
Lambert—Medical p31-36

Lambert—Minute p31-33
Leonardo—Lives p208-209
Major—History (1) p143,148
Sigerist—Great p43-46

Heroult, Paul Louis Toussaint (1863-1914). Fr. metallurgist, inventor.

Chambers—Dict. col.217-218
Law—Civiliz. p272-273

*Science Miles p263-269 (por.263)
Weeks—Discovery p357-358 (por.357)

Herreshoff, John Brown Francis (1850-1932). Amer. chem. engineer, metallurgist.

A.A.A.S.—Proc. (78) p6-7

Herrick, Francis Hobart (1858-1940). Amer. biologist.

Curr. Biog '40 p384 (por.384)

Herrick, Glenn W. (b.1870). Amer. entomologist.

Osborn—Fragments p202 (por.364)

Herrick, James B. (1861-1954). Amer. physician.

Fabricant—Why p89-84
Major—History (2) p713,949-950
(por.950)

Herschel, Caroline Lucretia (1750-1848). Ger.-Eng. astronomer.

Ball—Great p210-211,218 (por.207)
*Book—Pop. Sci. (10) p3422-3423
(por.3421)
*Darrow—Thinkers p121-123
Gibson—Heroes p188-202

Hammerton p754 (por.754)
Law—Civiliz. p179-182
Lodge—Pioneers p273-293 (por.287)
Mozans—Woman p182-190
Williams—Great p254-255 (por.253)

Herschel, Sir John Frederick William (1792-1871). Eng. astronomer.

Armitage—Cent. p8
Ball—Great p247-271 (por.253)
Ball—Short p441-442
*Book—Pop. Sci. (10) p3419-3420
(por.3419)
Chambers—Dict. col.218-219
Gregory—British p23-24 (por.24)
Hammerton p754 (por.754)
MacFarlane—Ten p131-141
(por.,front.)

Shapley—Astron. p238 (por.242)
Vaucouleurs—Disc. p107-110
Williams—Great p288-293,318-319
(por.317)
Williams—Story p63-65,326-327
(por.61)
Woodruff—Devel. p157,277
Year—Pic. p162 (por.162)

Herschel, Sir William (or Frederick William). (1738-1822). Ger.-Eng. **astronomer.**

Abetti—History p161-168
  (por.146 (25))
Armitage—Cent. p6-8
Ball—Great p200-218 (por.206)
*Bolton—Famous p59-75 (por.58)
*Book—Pop. Sci. (10) p3420-3422
  (por.3421)
Chambers—Dict. col.217-218
  (por.218)
*Darrow—Masters p58-63 (por.65)
*Darrow—Thinkers p121-123
Gibson—Heroes p188-213
Guinagh—Inspired p45-54
Hammerton p754
Hammond—Stories p49-68 (por.58)

Holmyard—British p42-44 (por.42)
Lodge—Pioneers p273-293 (por.285)
MacPherson—Makers p94-123
  (por.106)
People p189-190
Sedgwick—Short p333-334
Shapley—Astron. p140
Tuska—Invent. p93-94
Van Wagenen—Beacon p175-176
Vaucouleurs—Disc. p99-107
Williams—Great p251-265,272-273
  (por.253)
Woodruff—Devel. p159,277 (por.129)
*World's Great p99-125 (por.100)
Year—Pic. p111 (por.111)

Hersey, Henry Blanchard (1861-1948). Amer. aero. pioneer.

Heinmuller—Man's p262 (por.262)

Hershey, Oscar H. (1874-1939). Amer. geologist.

G.S.A.—Proc. '40 p195-197 (por.195)

Herskovits, Melville Jean (1895-   ). Amer. anthropologist.

Curr. Biog. '48 p282-284 (por.282)

Hertwig, Oscar (or Oskar) (1849-1922). Ger. embryologist.

Chambers—Dict. col.219
Hammerton p755

Locy—Biology p232 (por.231)

Herty, Charles Holmes, (1867-1938). Amer. chemist, agriculturist.

Borth—Pioneers p86-124
Browne—Hist. p482-483 (por.103)

Herty, Charles Holmes, Jr. (1896-1953). Amer. metallurgist, phys. chemist.

N.A.S.—Biog. (31) p114-119
  (por.114)

Hertz, Gustav (1887-1950). Ger. physicist.

Chambers—Dict. col.219
Heathcote—Nobel p229,230-248
  (por.240)

Weber—College p412 (por.412)

Hertz, Heinrich Rudolf (1857-1894). Ger. physicist, inventor.

Appleyard—Pioneers p109-140
  (por.108,112)
*Book—Pop. Sci. (11) p3676-3677
Chambers—Dict. col.219

Crew—Physicists #11 (folder) (por.)
*Darrow—Masters p297-299 (por.320)
Hammerton p755 (por.755)
*Hartman—Mach. p222-223
(Continued)

Hertz, Heinrich Rudolf—*Continued*
Hawks—Wireless p182-188 (por.178)
*Larsen—Prentice p149-150
Law—Civiliz. p220
Lenard—Great p358-371 (por.371)
Magie—Source p549-550
Meyer—World p192-197 (por.195)
*Montgomery—Invent. p147-150
Moulton—Auto. p455
*Pratt—Famous p67,68
Radio's 100 p113-117 (por.140)

Schwartz—Moments (2) p901-902
*Shippen—Design p172-178
*Sootin—Twelve p175-194
Tuska—Invent. p79-80
Van Wagenen—Beacon p416-418
Wilson—Human p346-357
Woodruff—Devel. p64-65, 277
   (por.60)
Year—Pic. p121,178 (por.121)

Hertzler, Arthur Emanuel (1870-1946). Amer. physician, surgeon.
Curr. Biog. '46 p255
Fabricant—Why p4-5

Rosen p200-201

Hertzsprung, Ejnar (1873-   ). Dan. astronomer.
Abetti—History p272-274

Herzog, Maurice (1919-   ). Fr. engineer.
Curr. Biog. '53 p263-265 (por.264)

Hess, Alfred H. (1875-1933). Amer. biochemist, physician.
Kagan—Modern p53 (por.53)

Hess, Dean Elmer (1917-   ). Amer. aero. pioneer.
Curr. Biog. '57 p252-253 (por.253)

Hess, Elmer (1889-1961). Amer. physician, urologist.
Curr. Biog. '56 p262-264 (por.263)
   '61 (Je.)

Hess, Germain Henri (1802-1850). Swiss chemist.
A.A.A.S.—Proc. (78) p33
   (81) p62

Chambers—Dict. col.220
Findlay—Hundred p326

Hess, Victor Francis (or Franz) (1883-   ). Aust.-Amer. physicist.
Chambers—Dict. col.220
Heathcote—Nobel p339-345 (por.240)

Progress—Science '41 p185 (por.185)
Weber—College p586 (por.586)

Hess, Walter Rudolf (1881-   ). Swiss physiologist.
Chambers—Dict. col.220
Stevenson—Nobel p260-264 (por.150)

Hesse, Curtis Julian (1905-1945). Amer. geologist.
G.S.A.—Proc. '45 p245-247 (por.245)

Hesse, Ludwig Otto (1811-1874). Ger. mathematician.
Cajori—Hist. p311-312

Hesse, Walther (1846-1911). Ger. bacteriologist.
Bulloch—Hist. p372-373

Hesselbach, Franz Kaspar (1759-1816). Ger. surgeon.
Leonardo—Lives p209-210

Heubner, Otto Johann Leonard (1843-1926). Ger. physician.
Rosen—Four p16-18,37-40,191-194

Heurne, Jan van (1543-1601). Dutch physician.
Major—History (1) p176

Hevelius, Johannes (1611-1687). Pol. astronomer.
Hammerton p756
Vaucouleurs—Disc. p57-58
Williams—Great p213-214 (por.214)
Year—Pic. p98

Hevesy, Georg von (1885-   ). Hung.-Swed. chemist.
Chambers—Dict. col.220-221
Curr. Biog. '59 p186-188 (por.187)
Farber—Nobel p170-173 (por.118)
Weeks—Discovery p517,518-519
   (por.517)
Year—Pic. p229 (por.229)

Hewett, Sir Frederick Stanley (1880-   ). Brit. surgeon.
Hammerton p756

Hewitson, William Chapman (1806-1878). Eng. naturalist.
Hammerton p756

Hewitt, C. Gordon (1885-1920). Eng.-Can. entomologist.
Osborn—Fragments p209-210
   (por.364)

Hewitt, John Theodore (1868-1954). Eng. chemist.
R.S.L.—Biog. (1) p79-96 (por.79)

Hewitt, Peter Cooper (1861-1921). Amer. inventor.
*Book—Pop. Sci. (9) p3047-3048
Hammerton p766

Hewson, William (1739-1774). Eng. physician.
Major—History (2) p637

Hey, William (1736-1819). Eng. surgeon.
Leonardo—Lives p211

Heyerdahl, Thor (1914-   ). Norw. ethnologist.
Curr. Biog. '47 p300-302 (por.301)

Heymans, Corneille (1890/1892-   ). Fr.-Belg. physiologist, biologist.
Chambers—Dict. col.221
Stevenson—Nobel p204-208 (por.150)

Heyrovsky, Jaroslav (1890-   ). Czech. phys. chemist.
Curr. Biog. '61 (July) (por.)
Weeks—Discovery p519, 520-521
(por.519)

Hiärne, Urban (or Hjarne) (1641-1724). Swed. chemist, physician, mineralogist.
Lindroth—Swedish p42-49
Weeks—Discovery p70-71 (por.70)

Hibbard, Henry D. (1856?-1942). Amer. engineer.
Curr. Biog. '42 p369

Hibbert, Harold (1877-1945). Eng. chemist.
N.A.S.—Biog. (32) p146-158
(por.146)

Hibbs, Russell A. (1869-1932). Amer. surgeon.
Leonardo—Lives p211-213

Hibler, Emmanuel von (1865-1911). Aust. bacteriologist.
Bulloch—Hist. p373

Hickling, Henry George Albert (1883-1954). Eng. geologist.
R.S.L.—Biog. (2) p149-155 (por.149)

Hickman, Henry Hill (1800-1829/1830). Eng. physician.
Fülöp—Miller p81-89   Robinson—Victory p56-65
Major—History (2) p713

Hicks, Beatrice A. (1919-   ). Amer. engineer.
Curr. Biog. '57 p255-257 (por.256)

Higgins, Daniel Franklin (1882-1930). Amer. geologist.
G.S.A.—Proc. '34 p237-242 (por.237)

Higgins, William (1768?-1825). Irish chemist.
Partington—Short p166-167,178

Higginson, William (1867?-1943). Amer. engineer.
Curr. Biog. '43 p297

Highmore, Nathaniel (1613-1685). Eng. anatomist, physician.
Gunther—Early XI p230-231   Major—History (1) p555
(por.230)
Hammerton p757

Highton, Henry (1816-1874). Eng. inventor.
Hawks—Wireless p86-90 (por.64)

Higinbotham, William A. (1910-   ). Amer. physicist.
Curr. Biog. '47 p304-305 (por.305)

Hilbert, David (1862-1943). Ger. mathematician.
Year—Pic. p202 (por.202)

Hildanus.   See **Fabricius Hildanus**

Hildebrand, Joel Henry (1881-   ). Amer. chemist.
Curr. Biog. '55 p280-282 (por.281)

Hildegard of Bingen, Saint (1098?-1179). Ger. physician, biologist,
zoologist.
Bodenheimer—Hist. p198   Major—History (1) p288-289
Gordon—Medieval p281-283   Mozans—Woman p169-170,233-235,
Gordon—Romance p301   277-280

Hildred, Sir William P. (1893-   ). Eng. aero. pioneer.
Curr. Biog. '56 p271-272 (por.271)

Hilgard,Eugene Woldemar (1833-1916). Ger.-Amer. agriculturist, chemist,
geologist.
*Ivins—Fifty p255-261 (por.254)   N.A.S.—Biog. (9) p95-142 (por.95)
Merrill—First p367-368,438,468-469
(por.295)

Hilgard, Julius Erasmus (1825-1890). Ger.-Amer. engineer.
N.A.S.—Biog. (3) p327-338

Hill, Archibald Vivian (1886-   ). Eng. biochemist, physiologist.
Castiglioni—Hist. p943, 1126   *Snyder—Biology p400-403 (por.408)
(por.942)   Stevenson—Nobel p102-103,104-105
Chambers—Dict. col.221   (por.150)

Hill, George William (1838-1914). Amer. astronomer, mathematician.
Cajori—Hist. p450
N.A.S.—Biog. (8) p275-302
(por.275)
Shapley—Astron. p362
Smith—Math. p129-131
Van Wagenen—Beacon p375-377
Woodruff—Devel. p277 (por.158)

Hill, Henry Barker (1849-1903). Amer. chemist.
A.A.A.S.—Proc. (77) p42-43
N.A.S.—Biog. (5) p255-264 (por.255)

Hill, James Peter (1873-1954). Scot. zoologist.
R.S.L.—Biog. (1) p101-115 (por.101)

Hill, John (1716-1775). Eng. botanist.
Hammerton p758
Hawks—Pioneers p255,256,257
Oliver—Makers p84-107 (por.84)

Hill, Justine Hamilton (1893-   ). Amer. bacteriologist.
Curr. Biog. '41 p384-385 (por.385)

Hill, Sir Leonard Erskine (1866-1952). Eng. physiologist.
Chambers—Dict. col.221-222
Hammerton p758

Hill, Robert Thomas (1858-1941). Amer. geologist.
Curr. Biog. '41 p385-386
G.S.A.—Proc. '43 p141-162 (por.141)
Progress—Science '41 p190

Hillary, William (1722-1763). Eng. physician.
Major—History (2) p635-636

Hilleboe, Herman Ertresvaag (1906-   ). Amer. physician.
Curr. Biog. '55 p284-286 (por.285)

Hillebrand, William F. (1853-1925). Amer. geochemist, mineralogist.
Browne—Hist. p479-480 (por.73)
Chambers—Dict. col.222
Killeffer—Eminent p17 (por.17)
N.A.S.—Biog. (12) p43-65 (por.43)
Weeks—Discovery p326,475
(por.326)

Hillig, Otto (1888-   ). Amer. aero. pioneer.
Heinmuller—Man's p342 (por.342)

Hillman, Edward Henry (1889-1934). Brit. aero. pioneer.
Burge—Ency. p633

Hilton, John (1804-1878). Eng. surgeon.
Hammerton p759

Hinds, Warren Elmer (1876-1935). Amer. entomologist.
Osborn—Fragments p236 (por.349)

Hine, James S. (1866-1929). Amer. entomologist.
Osborn—Fragments p213 (por.369)

Hingson, Robert Andrews (1913-   ). Amer. physician.
Curr. Biog. '43 p300-302 (por.301)

Hinkler, Herbert John Louis (1892-1933). Aust. aero. pioneer.
Burge—Ency. p633
Hammerton p760 (por.760)

Hinshelwood, Sir Cyril Norman (1897-   ). Eng. chemist.
Chambers—Dict. col.222
Curr. Biog. '57 p259-260 (por.259)

Hinton, Sir Christopher (1901-   ). Eng. engineer.
Curr. Biog. '57 p261-262 (por.261)

Hinton, Walter (1889-   ). Amer. aero. pioneer.
Heinmuller—Man's p306 (por.306)

Hipparchus (c.160-125 B.C.). Gr. astronomer.
Abetti—History p40-43
Ball—Short p86-88
*Book—Pop. Sci. (10) p3423-3424
Cajori—Hist. p43
Chambers—Dict. col.222
Clagett—Greek p71,94,96-98,177
Gordon—Medicine p607-608
Hammerton p760-761
Hooper—Makers p113-124
Lenard—Great p4-9
Sedgwick—Short p119-123
Smith—Hist. p119
Van Wagenen—Beacon p27-29
Vaucouleurs—Disc. p28-31
Williams—Great p64-80
Woodruff—Devel. p137-139,141-142,
    277-278
Year—Pic. p39

Hippias of Elias (fl.c.420 B.C.). Gr. mathematician.
Ball—Short p34-35
Sedgwick—Short p65
Smith—Hist. I p82

Hippocrates (460?-377? B.C.). Gr. physician.
Atkinson—Magic p36-43
Bodenheimer—Hist. p157
*Book—Pop. Sci. (12) p3895-3897
    (por.3897)
Castiglioni—Hist. p148-153 (por.150)
Chambers—Dict. col.222-223
*Chandler—Medicine p3-5 (por.2)
Clagett—Greek p36-40,46
*Elwell—Sci. p23-25
Fitzhugh—Concise p300-302
Gordon—Medicine p499-542
    (por.500)
Gordon—Romance p62,90-92
    (por.27)
Hammerton p761 (por.761)

(Continued)

Hippocrates—*Continued*
Hawks—Pioneers p52-54
Lambert—Medical p14-25 (por.16)
Lambert—Minute p14-25 (por.16)
Leonardo—Lives p213-215
*McSpadden—How p3-14
Major—History (1) p115-138
(por.136)
*Masters—Conquest p18-19
Moulton—Auto. p5
*Nisenson—Illus. p83 (por.83)
Oliver—Stalkers p22-32 (por.23)
Reed—Short p32

Schwartz—Moments (1) p18-20
*Science Miles. p9-11 (por.9)
Sedgwick—Short p63-64
*Shippen—Men p35-42
Sigerist—Great p29-37
*Simmons—Great p6-8 (por.6)
*Snyder—Biology p176-177 (por.176)
Tobey—Riders p42
Van Wagenen—Beacon p11-12
Wilson—Human p21-28
Woodruff—Devel. p218,278
Year—Pic. p29 (por.29)

Hippocrates of Chios (fl.5th cent. B.C.). Gr. mathematician.
Ball—Short p37-42
Cajori—Hist. p21-23

Sedgwick—Short p67-68
Turnbull—Great p18-20

Hirsch, August (1817-1894). Ger. pathologist.
Bulloch—Hist. p373
Kagan—Modern p209 (por.209)

Hirsch, Isaac Seth (1880-1942). Amer. radiologist.
Curr. Biog. '42 p377

Hirschberg, Julius (1843-1925). Ger. physician.
Kagan—Modern p147 (por.147)

Hirschfelder, Joseph Oakland (1911-   ). Amer. phys. chemist.
Curr. Biog. '50 p243-244 (por.244)

Hirst, Edmund Langley (1898-   ). Eng. chemist.
Chambers—Dict. col.223

Hirszfeld, Hanna (n.d.) Pol. physician, pediatrician.
Knapp—Women p137-150 (por.137)

His, Wilhelm (1831-1904). Swiss anatomist, biologist, embryologist,
physician.
Chambers—Dict. col.223
Locy—Biology p232 (por.233)

Major—History (2) p896
Rosen—Four p142-143

Hisinger, Wilhelm (or Hising) (1766-1852). Swed. geologist, mineralogist.
Weeks—Discovery p322-324,327
(por.327)

Hispanus.   See **John XXI, Pope**

Hiss, Philip Hanson, Jr. (1868-1913). Amer. bacteriologist.
Bulloch—Hist. p373

Hitchcock, Charles Baker (1906-   ). Amer. geographer, sci. explorer.
Curr. Biog. '54 p335-336 (por.335)

Hitchcock, Charles Henry (1836-1919). Amer. geologist.
*Book—Pop. Sci. (5) p1662
Merrill—First p402-403,604,635
  (por.404)

Hitchcock, Edward (1793-1864). Amer. geologist.
*Book—Pop. Sci. (5) p1663-1664
  (por.1663)
Merrill—First p152 (por.152)
N.A.S.—Biog. (1) p113-134
Woodruff—Devel. p278
Youmans—Pioneers p290-299
  (por.290)

Hittorf, Johann Wilhelm (1824-1914). Ger. physicist, chemist.
Chambers—Dict. col.223
Hammerton p763
Lenard—Great p344-355 (por.348)
Magie—Source p561
Partington—Short p340
Van Wagenen—Beacon p334-336

Hjelm, Peter Jacob (1746-1813). Swed. chemist.
Chambers—Dict. col.224
Weeks—Discovery p128-131

Hoagland, Dennis Robert (1884-1949). Amer. agriculturist, botanist,
  naturalist.
N.A.S.—Biog. (29) p123-135
  (por.123)

Hoard, William Dempster (1836-1918). Amer. agriculturist.
*Ivins—Fifty p105-113 (por.107)

Hobbs, Leonard (or "Luke") **Sinclair** (1896-   ). Amer. aero. pioneer,
  engineer.
Curr. Biog. '54 p336-338 (por.337)

Hobbs, William Herbert (1864-1953). Amer. geologist.
G.S.A.—Proc. '52 p131-134 (por.131)

Hobson, Ernest William (1856-1933). Eng. mathematician.
Hammerton p764

Hoche, Alfred E. (1865-1945). Ger. physician, psychiatrist.
Rosen—Four p26-28,279-281

Hochstetter, Ferninand von (1829-1884). Amer. geologist, seismologist.
Davison—Founders p131-132

Hodgen, John Thompson (1826-1882). Amer. surgeon.
Leonardo—Lives p215-216

Hodges, Nathaniel (1629-1688). Eng. physician.
Major—History (1) p547

Hodgkin, Dorothy Mary Crowfoot (1910-   ). Eng. chemist.
Calder—Science p92

Hodgkin, Thomas (1798-1866). Eng. physician, pathologist.
Castiglioni—Hist. p705 (por.705)   Major—History (2) p691-692
Chambers—Dict. col.224

Hodgkinson, Eaton (1789-1861). Eng. mathematician.
Hammerton p765

Hoe, Richard March (1812-1886). Amer. inventor.
Hammerton p765 (por.765)   *Montgomery—Invent. p22-25
*Hylander—Invent. p205   Morris—Ency. p676
Law—Civiliz. p126-127

Hoe, Robert (1784-1833.) Eng.-Amer. inventor.
Law—Civiliz. p126-127
*Montgomery—Invent. p22-25

Hoefer, Wolfgang (1614-1681). Ger. physician.
Major—History (1) p555

Hoene-Wronski.   See **Wronski, Józef Maria**

Hoernes, Rudolf (1850-1912). Aust. geologist, seismologist, paleontologist.
Davison—Founders p135-136

Höfer, Hans (b.1843). Aust. seismologist, geologist.
Davison—Founders p133-134

Hoff.   See **Van't Hoff, Jacobus Henricus**

Hoff, Karl Ernst Adolf von (1771-1837). Ger. geologist, seismologist.
Davison—Founders p39-40

Hoffman, Edward L. (1884-   ). Amer. aero. pioneer.
Holland—Arch. p113-126

Hoffman, Friedrich (1660-1741). Ger. physician.
Castiglioni—Hist. p584-585   Oliver—Stalkers p137
Major—History (2) p568-570
(por.569)

Hoffman, (Heinrich) Hermann (1819-1891). Ger. botanist.
Bulloch—Hist. p373

Hoffman, Joseph Gilbert (1909-   ). Amer. biophysicist.
Curr. Biog. '58 p193-195 (por.194)

Hofmann, August Wilhelm von (1818-1892). Ger. chemist.
*Book—Pop. Sci. (11) p3677-3678   Roberts—Chem. p160-175
(por.3677)   Smith—Torch. p122 (por.122,123,
Chambers—Dict. col.224-225   124)
Findlay—Hundred p327-328   Weeks—Discovery p374,375
Hammerton p766   (por.375)
Partington—Short p260-262,270   Woodruff—Devel. p109,278
(por.260)

Hofmann, Klaus Heinrich (1911-   ). Ger.-Amer. biochemist.
Curr. Biog. '61 (Apr.) (por.)

Hofmeister, Franz (1850-1922). Aust.-Ger. physiol. chemist.
A.A.A.S.—Proc. (78) p28-29

Hofmeister, Wilhelm Friedrich Benedict (1824-1877). Ger. biologist,
botanist.
Bodenheimer—Hist. p401   Thomson—Great p138-145
Chambers—Dict. col.225

Hogan, John Vincent Lawless (1890-   ). Amer. elec. engineer.
Radio's 100 p245-247 (por.140)

Hogben, Lancelot Thomas (1895-   ). Brit. physiologist, zoologist.
Chambers—Dict. col.225
Curr. Biog. '41 p396-398 (por.397)

Hogbom, Arvid Gustav (1857-1940). Swed. geologist.
G.S.A.—Proc. '40 p201-203 (por.201)

Hogg, Helen Sawyer (1905-   ). Can. astronomer.
Yost—Women Mod. p31-47
(por.,front.)

Hogyes, Andreas (1847-1906). Hung. pathologist, bacteriologist.
Bulloch—Hist. p373

Hohenheim, Theophrastus Bombastus von.   See **Paracelsus, Philippus Aureolus**

Hoiriis, Holger (1901-1942). Amer. aero. pioneer.
Heinmuller—Man's p342 (por.342)

Holaday, William Marion (1901-   ). Amer. engineer.
Curr. Biog. '58 p197-198 (por.198)

Holbrook, John Edwards (1794-1871). Amer. ichthyologist.
N.A.S.—Biog. (5) p47-66 (por.47)

Holden, Edward Singleton (1846-1914). Amer. astronomer.
N.A.S.—Biog. (8) p347-357 (por.347)

Holden, Perry Greeley (1865-1959). Amer. agriculturist.
*Ivins—Fifty p85-93 (por.84)

Holden, Roy Jay (1870-1945). Amer. geologist.
G.S.A.—Proc. '46 p167-171 (por.167)

Holland, Charles Thurstan (1863-1941). Eng. radiologist.
Curr. Biog. '41 p398

Holland, Clifford Milburn (1883-1924). Amer. engineer.
Carmer—Caval. p284-297 (por.285)
*Darrow—Builders p265-266

Holland, John Philip (1840-1914). Irish-Amer. inventor.
*Beard—Foreign p149-154   *Montgomery—Invent. p237-240
*Darrow—Masters p307-313 (por.289)   *Nida—Makers p133-134
*Darrow—Thinkers p325 (por.324)   *Pratt—Famous p116-121
*Hylander—Invent. p140-146

Holland, William Jacob (1848-1932). Moravian-Amer. entomologist, zoologist, paleontologist.
Osborn—Fragments p220 (por.353)

Hollander, Bernard (1864-1934). Aust.-Eng. physician.
Hammerton p771

Holley, Alexander Lyman (1832-1882). Amer. metallurgist, engineer.
Goddard—Eminent p122-131
(por.122)

Holman, Eugene (1895-   ). Amer. geologist.
Curr. Biog. '48 p291-294 (por.292)

Holmes, Arthur (1890-   ). Eng. geologist.
Chambers—Dict. col.225-226

Holmes, Harry Nicholls (1879-1958). Amer. chemist.
Browne—Hist. p490 (por.163)
Progress—Science '40 p195 (por.195)

Holmes, Oliver Wendell (1809-1894). Amer. physician.
Chambers—Dict. col.226
Fabricant—Why p140-141
Fitzhugh—Concise p303-305
Gordon—Romance p181-182
(por.181)
Kagan—Modern p182 (por.182)
Lambert—Medical p238-239
Lambert—Minute p238-239
Major—History (2) p756-759
(por.757)
Morris—Ency. p676
Moulton—Auto. p312-313
Oliver—Stalkers p167 (por.168)
Rosen—Four p12-16,36-37,74-76

Holmes, William Henry (1846-1933). Amer. anthropologist, archaeologist, geologist, ethnologist.
N.A.S.—Biog. (17) p223-237
(por.223)
True—Smiths. p138 (por.138)

Holtzhausen, Friedrich Wilhelm (1768-1827). Ger. engineer.
Matschoss—Great p116-119 (por.117)

Holywood, John of.   See **Sacrobosco, Johannes de**

Homans, John (1836-1903). Amer. surgeon.
Leonardo—Lives p216-218

Homberg, Wilhelm (or Willem) (1652-1715). Dutch-Eng. naturalist, chemist.
Weeks—Discovery p334-335

Home, David Milne (or Milne, David) (1805-1890). Scot. geologist, seismologist.
Davison—Founders p42-44

Home, Sir Evarard (1756-1832). Scot. physician.
Major—History (2) p703

Home, Francis (1719-1813). Scot. physician.
Major—History (2) p635

Honess, Arthur P. (1886-1942). Amer. geologist.
G.S.A.—Proc. '42 p195-198 (por.195)

Honess, Charles William (1885-1949). Amer. geologist.
G.S.A.—Proc. '51 p115 (por.115)

Hooke, Robert (1635-1703). Eng. chemist, physicist.
Ball—Short p315
Bulloch—Hist. p373-374
Chambers—Dict. col.226-227
Crowther—Founders p181-222
*Epstein—Real p130-131
Gregory—British p22
Gunther—Early XI p212-214
Hammerton p776 (por.776)
Hawks—Pioneers p196-197
Locy—Biology p55-56
Magie—Source p93
Major—History (1) p515
Miall—Early p135-145
Moulton—Auto. p169-170
Oliver—Stalkers p95
Partington—Short p78-81,148
Reed—Short p86
Schwartz—Moments (1) p387-388
Schwartz—Moments (2) p533-534
Sci. Amer.—Lives p31-44 (por.33)
Sedgwick—Short p268
*Snyder—Biology p48-53
Taylor—Illus. p68-70
Thomson—Great p28-29
Van Wagenen—Beacon p124-126
Woodruff—Devel. p226,278

Hooker, Sir Joseph (1817-1911). Eng. botanist.
*Book—Pop. Sci. (12) p3898
Chambers—Dict. col.227
Gregory—British p14 (por.14)
Hammerton p776
Oliver—Makers p302-323 (por.302)
Reed—Short p129-131
Van Wagenen—Beacon p306-307
Woodruff—Devel. p204,278

Hooker, Sir William Jackson (1785-1865). Eng. botanist.
Gilmour—British p34-40 (por.33)
Oliver—Makers p126-150 (por.126)

Hooton, Earnest Albert (1887-1954). Amer. anthropologist.
Curr. Biog. '40 p397-400 (por.398)
  '54 p32
Progress—Science '40 p195-196
  (por.196)

Hoover, Charles Franklin (1865-1927). Amer. physician.
Major—History (2) p1035

Hoover, Herbert Clark (1874-   ). Amer. min. engineer.
Curr. Biog. '43 p306-312 (por.307)
*Darrow—Builders p248-260 (por.132)
*Everett—When p116-122 (por.116)
Fitzhugh—Concise p310-311
Hammerton p776-777 (por.776)
Huff—Famous (2d) p265-274
  (por.264)
Morris—Ency. p677
*Nisenson—More p74 (por.74)
Sewell—Brief p227-228
*Wildman—Famous (2d) p161-169
  (por.161)

Hoover, Herbert Clark, Jr. (1903-   ). Amer. min. engineer.
Curr. Biog. '54 p342-344 (por.343)

Hope, James (1801-1841). Eng. physician.
Major—History (2) p713

Hope, John (1725-1786). Scot. botanist.
Oliver—Makers p287-290
Weeks—Discovery p114 (por.114)

Hope, Thomas Charles (1766-1844). Scot. chemist.
Chambers—Dict. col.228
Weeks—Discovery p298,303-304
   (por.298)

Hopkins, Andrew Delmar (1857-1948). Amer. biochemist, entomologist.
Osborn—Fragments p237 (por.359)

Hopkins, B. Smith (1873-1952). Amer. chemist.
Chambers—Dict. col.228   Weeks—Discovery p523-527
Progress—Science '41 p191-192   (por.523)

Hopkins, Cyril George (1866-1919). Amer. agric. chemist.
*Ivins—Fifty p269-273 (por.268)

Hopkins, Sir Frederick Gowland (1861-1947). Eng. biologist, botanist.
Chambers—Dict. col.228 (por.227)   Pringle—Great p71-83 (por.80)
Hammerton p777   *Snyder—Biology p337-339 (por.337)
Major—History (2) p1035 (por.940)   Stevenson—Nobel p135-136,138-142
People p196-197   (por.150)

Hopkins, Nevil Monroe (1873-1945). Amer. engineer.
Curr. Biog. '45 p293

Hopkins, Thomas Cramer (1861-1935). Amer. geologist.
G.S.A.—Proc. '35 p255-259
   (por.255)

Hopkins, William (1793-1866). Eng. geologist, seismologist,
   mathematician.
Davison—Founders p81-84

Hopkinson, John (1849-1898). Eng. engineer.
Hammerton p777-778

Hoppe-Seyler (Ernst) Felix Emmanuel (1825-1895). Ger. physiol. chemist.
Major—History (2) p891-892
Smith—Torch. p125 (por.125)

Horder, Thomas Jeeves Horder, 1st Baron (1871-1955). Eng. physician.
Curr. Biog. '44 p309-310 (por.309)   Hammerton p779
  '55 p291

Horgan, Stephen Henry (1854-1941). Amer. inventor.
Curr. Biog. '41 p408

Horn, George Henry (1840-1897). Amer. entomologist.
Essig—Hist. p654-658 (por.655)
Osborn—Fragments p163-164
  (por.338)

Hornaday, William Temple (1854-1937). Amer. zoologist, naturalist.
Hammerton p779
Tracy—Amer. Nat. p138-146

Horner, H. Mansfield (1903-   ). Amer. engineer, aero. pioneer.
Curr. Biog. '55 p291-293 (por.292)

Horner, Seward Ellis (1906-1954). Amer. geologist.
G.S.A.—Proc. '54 p119-121 (por.119)

Horner, William George (1786-1837). Eng. mathematician.
Smith—Hist. I p459

Horney, Karen Danielsen (1885-1952). Ger.-Amer. psychiatrist, physician, psychoanalyst.
Curr. Biog. '41 p409-410 (por.409)
  '53 p279

Hornsby, Thomas (1733-1810). Eng. astronomer.
Gunther—Early XI p195

Horrocks (or Horrox), **Jeremiah** (1617/1619-1641). Eng. astronomer.
Chambers—Dict. col.228-229   Shapley—Astron. p58
Gregory—British p21   Vaucouleurs—Disc. p56-57
Hammerton p780   Williams—Great p165-174

Horsfall, Frank Lappin, Jr. (1906-   ). Amer. physician.
Curr. Biog. '41 p410-411 (por.411)
  '61 (Jan.) (por.)

Horsford, Eben (1818-1893). Amer. chemist.
Smith—Torch. p126 (por.126)

Horsley, Sir Victor Alexander Haden (1857-1916). Eng. neurologist, surgeon.
Great Names p25-28 (por.24)　　Leonardo—Lives p218-220
Hammerton p780 (por.780)　　Major—History (2) p1035-1036

Horstmann, August Friedrich (1842-1929). Ger. chemist.
Partington—Short p339
Smith—Torch. p127 (por.127)

Horto, Garcia ab (or de Orta; de la Huerta; Orto; del Huete) (fl. 16th cent.). Port. physician.
Arber—Herbals p104,105　　Hawks—Pioneers p154-156
Gordon—Medieval p762-763

Horton, Frank (1878-1957). Eng. physicist.
R.S.L.—Biog. (4) p117-125 (por.117)

Hosack, David (1769-1835). Amer. physician.
Farmer—Doctors' p84　　Youmans—Pioneers p100-110
Major—History (2) p733-734　　(por.100)

Hoskins, Roy Graham (1880-　　). Amer. endrocrinologist.
Progress—Science '41 p192

Hotchkiss, Benjamin Berkeley (1826-1885). Amer. inventor.
Hammerton p781
*Hylander—Invent. p207-208

Hotchkiss, William Otis (1878-1954). Amer. geologist.
G.S.A.—Proc. '55 p133-136 (por.133)

Houghton, Douglas (1809-1845). Amer. geologist.
Merrill—First p207-208 (por.207)

Houssay, Bernardo Alberto (1887-　　). Argent. physiologist, physician.
Castiglioni—Hist. p949,965,1000　　Curr. Biog. '48 p295-297 (por.295)
1104 (por.948)　　Robinson—100 p299-302 (por.299)
Chambers—Dict. col.229　　Stevenson—Nobel p244-248 (por.150)

Houston, Alexander Cruickshank (1865-1933). Brit. bacteriologist.
Bulloch—Hist. p374
Hammerton p782

Houston, David Franklin (1866-1940). Amer. agriculturist.
  *Ivins—Fifty p387-391 (por.386)

Hovey, Otis Ellis (1864-1941). Amer. engineer.
  Curr. Biog. '41 p412

Howard, James Raley (1873-1954). Amer. agriculturist.
  *Ivins—Fifty p145-154 (por.147)

Howard, Leland Ossian (1857-1950). Amer. entomologist, biologist.
  Bodenheimer—Hist. p454
  *Book—Pop. Sci. (12) p3898-39CJ
    (por.3899)
  Essig—Hist. p658-664 (por.659)
  Jaffe—Outposts p285-313 (por.282)
  N.A.S.—Biog. (33) p87-102 (por. 87)
  Osborn—Fragments p164
    (por.346,352,380)
  *Snyder—Biology p253-259 (por.252)

Howard, Luke (1772-1864). Brit. meteorologist.
  Hammerton p783

Howe, Clarence Decatur (1886-1961). Can. engineer.
  Curr. Biog. '45 p295-297 (por.295)

Howe, Elias (1819-1867). Amer. inventor.
  Abbot—Great p250-258
  *Bachman—Great p121-141
  *Book—Pop. Sci. (9) p3048-3050
  *Burlingame—Mach. p156-161
  Chambers—Dict. col.229
  *Darrow—Masters p335
  *Darrow—Thinkers p149-158
    (por.150)
  Goddard—Eminent p78-84 (por.78)
  Hammerton p784
  *Hartman—Mach. p130-136
  *Hylander—Invent. p66-72
  Iles—Leading p338-368 (por.338)
  *Larsen—Scrap. p56-64 (por.64)
  *Larsen—Shaped p78-87 (por.49)
  Law—Civiliz. p106-109
  Meyer—World p67-75 (por.67)
  *Montgomery—Invent. p129-134
  Morris—Ency. p678
  *Morris—Heroes p159-165
  *Nida—Makers p81-84 (por.83)
  *Parkman—Conq. p87-103 (por.88)
  *Patterson—Amer. p73-84
  *Tappan—Heroes p47-53
  Tuska—Invent. p117-118
  Year—Pic. p157 (por.157)

Howe, Ernest (1875-1932). Amer. geologist.
  G.S.A.—Proc. '33 p211-223 (por.211)

Howe, Harrison Estell (1881-1942). Amer. chemist.
  Browne—Hist. p498 (por.371)
  Curr. Biog. '43 p315

Howe, Henry Marion (1848-1922). Amer. metallurgist.
  John Fritz p97-98 (por.96)
  N.A.S.—Biog. (11) (XXI Memoirs)
    p108 (por.1)

Howe, Marshall Avery (1867-1936). Amer. botanist.
N.A.S.—Biog. (19) p243-258
(por.243)

Howe, Samuel Gridley (1801-1876). Amer. surgeon.
*Faris—Men p75-85

Howe (or How), **William** (1620-1656). Eng. naturalist.
*Raven—English p298-305

Howell, Wallace Egbert (1914-   ). Amer. meteorologist.
Curr. Biog. '50 p262-264 (por.262)
*Shippen—Bridle p176-181

Howell, William Henry (1860-1945). Amer. physiologist.
Curr.Biog. '45 p297   N.A.S.—Biog. (26) p153-174
Major—History (2) p919   (por.153)
                                   Rowntree—Amid p99-101 (por.100)

Howland, John (1873-1926). Amer. physician.
Major—History (2) p1036

Hoxie, Charles A. (1867?-1941). Amer. inventor.
Curr. Biog. '41 p412

Hoxsey, Arch (1884-1910). Amer. aero. pioneer.
Heinmuller—Man's p284 (por.284)

Hoy, Filo (or Philo) Romaine (1816-1892). Amer. entomologist.
Osborn—Fragments p180

Hoyle, Fred (1915-   ). Eng. astronomer.
Curr. Biog. p191-193 (por.192)

Hoyt, Ross G. (1893-   ). Amer. aero. pioneer.
Heinmuller—Man's p334 (por.334)

Hrabanus.   See **Rabanus, Maurus**

Hrotsvitha.   See **Roswitha**

Hrdlicka, Ales (1869-1943). Bohem.-Amer. anthropologist.
Chambers—Dict. col.229
Curr. Biog. '41 p412-415 (por.413)
'43 p320
Jaffe—Outposts p52-80 (por.58)
N.A.S.—Biog. (23) p305-316
(por.305)
Progress—Science '41 p195-196
(por.195)

Hubaish ibn.   See **Alhazan**

Hubbard, Bernard Rosecrans (1888-   ). Can.-Amer. sci. explorer.
Curr. Biog. '43 p320-323 (por.321)
Progress—Science '40 p201-202
(por.201)

Hubbard, Harvey Guernsey (1850-1899). Amer. entomologist.
Osborn—Fragments p176-187
(por.350)

Hubbard, Joseph S. (1823-1863). Amer. astronomer.
N.A.S.—Biog. (1) p1-34

Hubbard, Oliver Payson (1809-1900). Amer. geologist.
Merrill—First p294-295 (por.295)

Hubble, Edwin Powell (1889-1953). Amer. astronomer.
Armitage—Cent. p237-238,240-241
(por.176)
Chambers—Dict. col.229
Jaffe—Men p483-531 (por.xxviii)
Jaffe—Outposts p493-516 (por.490)
Progress—Science '40 p202
Year—Pic. p218,219 (por.219)

Hubeny, Maximilian John (1880-1942). Amer. radiologist.
Curr. Biog. '42 p396

Huber, François (1750-1831). Swiss naturalist.
Chambers—Dict. col.230

Hübner, Jacob (1761-1826). Ger. entomologist.
Essig—Hist. p664-667 (por.664)

Huchard, Henri (1844-1910). Fr. physician.
Castiglioni—Hist. p840 (por.840)

Hudleston, Edmund Cuthbert (1908-   ). Austral. aero. pioneer.
Curr. Biog. '51 p285-286 (por.286)

Hudson, Clarence Walter (1867-1943). Amer. engineer.
Curr. Biog. '43 p323

Hudson, Claude Silbert (1881-1952). Amer. chemist.
N.A.S.—Biog. (32) p181-197
(por.181)

Hudson, George Henry (1855-1934). Amer. paleontologist, geologist.
G.S.A.—Proc. '34 p245-248
(por.245)

Hudson, Harold W. (1876?-1943). Amer. engineer.
Curr. Biog. '43 p323

Hudson, William Henry (1841-1922). Amer.-Eng. naturalist, ornithologist.
Cutright—Great p33-37
Hammerton p787 (por.786)
Peattie—Gather. p3-10
Von Hagen—Green p283-284

Huenefeld, Baron Guenther von (1892-1929). Ger. aero. pioneer.
Heinmuller—Man's p103-114,328
(por.111,328)

Hueppe, Ferdinand (1852-1938). Ger. surgeon, bacteriologist, hygienist.
Bulloch—Hist. p374

Huerta, de la (or Huete, del).   See **Horto, Garcia ab**

Hufeland, Christoph Wilhelm (1762-1836). Ger. physician.
Hammerton p786
Major—History (2) p703-704
Rosen—Four p31-33,162-163

Huggins, Sir William (1824-1910). Eng. astronomer.
Abetti—History p194-196
Armitage—Cent. p25-31 (por.48)
*Book—Pop. Sci. (10) p3424-3426
(por.3425)
Chambers—Dict. col.230
Hammerton p786 (por.786)
MacPherson—Astron. p8-17
(por.,front.)
MacPherson—Makers p167-170
Shapley—Astron. p290
Van Wagenen—Beacon p340-342
Williams—Great 344-349,357-358,467
(por.365)
Woodruff—Devel. p278 (por.158)

Hugh of Lucca (or Borgognoni, Ugo) (fl. 13th cent.). It. physician, surgeon.
Castiglioni—Hist. p335-336
Leonardo—Lives p220-222
Major—History (1) p293-294

Hughes, David Edward (1831-1900). Eng.-Amer. inventor.
*Book—Pop. Sci. (9) p3050-3051
Chambers—Dict. col.230
Hammerton p787 (por.787)
Hawks—Wireless p168-174 (por.162)
Radio's 100 p63-64 (por.140)

Hughes, Howard Robard (1905-   ). Amer. aero. pioneer.
Curr. Biog. '41 p421-422 (por.421)
*Fraser—Famous p287-309
Heinmuller—Man's p214-227,353
(por.224,353)

Huguenin, Julius Caesar (1840-1926). Swiss entomologist.
Essig—Hist. p667 (por.667)

Hui.   See Liu Hui

Hulett, George Augustus (1867-1955). Amer. phys. chemist.
N.A.S.—Biog. (34) p83-99 (por.83)

Hull, Albert Wallace (1880-   ). Amer. physicist.
Radio's 100 p199-201 (por.140)

Hull, Clark Leonard (1884-1952). Amer. psychologist.
N.A.S.—Biog. (33) p125-135
   (por.125)

Humason, Milton L. (1891-   ). Amer. astronomer.
Jaffe—Outposts p496-507 (por.507)

Humboldt, (Friedrich Heinrich) Alexander, Baron von (1769-1859). Ger.
   aturalist, geologist.

Adams—Birth p236-238
Alden—Early p18
*Book—Pop. Sci. (12) p3900-3901
Chambers—Dict. col.230-231
Cutright—Great p7-12 (por.40)
*Darrow—Masters p92-98 (por.64)
Davison—Founders p44-46
Fitzhugh—Concise p320-321
Hammerton p790 (por.790)
Hawks—Pioneers p269-270
Lenard—Great p187-188 (por.187)
Moulton—Auto. p332-333

People p198-199 (por.228)
Reed—Short p127
Shapley—Astron. p223
Thomas—Scien. p99-113 (por.97)
Van Wagenen—Beacon p215-217
Von Hagen—Green p145-146
Weeks—Discovery p148,151-154
   (por.148)
Williams—Story p175-177
   (por.,front.)
*World's Great p165-185 (por.168)
Year—Pic. p127 (por.127)

Hume, Edgar Erskine (1889-1952). Amer. physician.
Curr. Biog. '44 p315-319 (por.316)
   '52 p279

Hume, Edward H. (1876-1957). Amer. physician, surgeon.
Rosen—Four p215-218

Hummel, John James (1850-1902). Eng. chemist.
A.A.A.S.—Proc. (78) p12-13

Humphreys, Andrew Atkinson (1810-1883). Amer. engineer.
N.A.S.—Biog. (2) p201-215

Hunain ibn Ishaq (or Hunain ibn Al-Ibadi; Johannitius). Arab. physician.

Castiglioni—Hist. p266
Gordon—Medieval p145-146
Hammerton p792

Leonardo—Lives p222
Major—History (1) p233-234
*Shippen—Men p55

Hundt, Magnus (1449-1519). Ger. physician.

Major—History (1) p461

Hunefeld, Ehrenfried Gunther, Baron von (1892-1929). Ger. aero. pioneer.

Hammerton p792

Hung.   See Ko Hung

Hungerford, Herbert Barker (1885-   ). Amer. entomologist.

Osborn—Fragments p236 (por.371)

Hunsaker, Jerome Clarke (1886-   ). Amer. aero. pioneer, engineer.

Curr. Biog. '42 p400-402 (por.401)
Daniel Gugg. p33-41 (por.32)

Daniel—Pioneer p23-29 (por.22)
Holland—Arch. p7-25

Hunt, Arthur Surridge (1871-1934). Eng. archaeologist.

Hammerton p792

Hunt, Edward B. (1822-1863). Amer. engineer.

N.A.S.—Biog. (3) p29-41

Hunt, Harriot K. (1805-1875). Amer. physician.

Lovejoy—Women p78-80
Mead—Medical p20-21

Hunt, Reid (1870-1948). Amer. physiologist, physician.

Major—History (2) p1036
N.A.S.—Biog. (26) p25-37 (por.25)

Hunt, Robert Wollston (1838-1923). Amer. engineer, metallurgist.

John Fritz p75-77 (por.74)

Hunt, Thomas Sterry (1826-1892). Amer. chemist, mineralogist, geologist.

Browne—Hist. p472 (por.19)
Killeffer—Eminent p8 (por.8)
Merrill—First p446-448 (por.447)

N.A.S.—Biog. (15) p207-220
   (por.207)
Smith—Chem. p246-252 (por.252)

Hunt, Walter (1796-1859). Amer. inventor.

Abbot—Great p248-250
Meyer—World p66-67,253 (por.66)

Hunter, Croil (1893-   ). Amer. aero. pioneer.
Curr. Biog. '51 p291-293 (por.292)

Hunter, John (1728-1893). Scot. physiologist, anatomist, surgeon, pathologist.

Atkinson—Magic p187-193
*Book—Pop. Sci. (12) p3901-3902
  (por.2903)
Castiglioni—Hist. p596-598 (por.597)
Chambers—Dict. p231-232
Gordon—Romance p251,469
  (por.469)
Hammerton p793 (por.793)
*Hathaway—Partners p19-27
Lambert—Medical p168-175
  (por.174)
Lambert—Minute p168-175 (por.161)
Leonardo—Lives (supp.1) p483-485

Locy—Biology p144-146 (por.145)
Major—History (2) p602-606
  (por.602)
*Masters—Conquest p34-39
Newman—Interp. p113-159
Robinson—Path. p187-211
  (por.190,191)
Sigerist—Great p219-228 (por.224)
Van Wagenen—Beacon p161-162
Woodruff—Devel. p278-279
Year—Pic. p109 (por.109)
Young—Scalpel p79-107 (por.73)

Hunter, W. D. (1875-1925). Amer. entomologist.
Osborn—Fragments p189-190
  (por.376)

Hunter, Walter Samuel (1889-1954). Amer. psychologist.
N.A.S.—Biog. (31) p127-146
  (por.127)

Hunter, William (1718-1783). Scot. anatomist, physician.

Castiglioni—Hist, p596 (por.597)
Farmer—Doctors' p30
Lambert—Medical p168-175
Lambert—Minute p169-175

Leonardo—Lives (Supp.1) p485-486
Major—History (2) p601
Year—Pic. p109

Huntington, George Sumner (1861-1927). Amer. anatomist, physician, surgeon.
N.A.S.—Biog. (18) p245-276
  (por.245,260)

Huntington, Thomas W. (1849-1929). Amer. physician.
Jones—Memories p406-430
  (por.406,407)

Hurdon, Elizabeth (1868-1941). Eng.-Can. physician.
Lovejoy—Women p117-118

Hurley, Roy T. (1896-   ). Amer. aero. pioneer, engineer.
Curr. Biog. '55 p293-295 (por.294)

Hurst, Charles Chamberlain (1870-1947). Eng. biologist.
Hammerton p794

Hurston, Zora Neale (1901-   ). Amer. anthropologist.
Curr. Biog. '42 p402-404 (por.402)
Downs—Meet p58-59 (por.58)

Hurter, Julius (1842-1917). Swiss herpetologist.
Swiss—Prom. p242-243

Hutchins, Thomas (1730-1789). Amer. naturalist, sci. explorer, cartographer.
Bell—Early p59-60

Hutchinson, James (1752-1793). Amer. chemist.
Smith—Chem. p148

Hutchinson, James Alexander (1863-1929). Can. surgeon.
Leonardo—Lives p222-223

Hutchinson, Sir Jonathan (1828-1913). Eng. physician, surgeon.
Castiglioni—Hist. p851-852,865   Major—History (2) p893
Hammerton p795-796

Hutchison, Miller Reese (1876-1944). Amer. inventor.
Curr. Biog. '44 p323

Hutten, Ulrich von (1488-1523). Ger. physician.
Gordon—Medieval p622,710-712
    (por.242)

Hutton, Charles (1737-1823). Eng. mathematician.
Hammerton p796

Hutton, James (1726-1797). Scot. geologist.
Adams—Birth p239-245 (por.,front.)   Trattner—Arch. p46-71 (por.54)
*Book—Pop Sci. (5) p1664-1665   Van Wagenen—Beacon p160-161
Chambers—Dict. col.232   Williams—Story p19-23,97,125
Fenton—Giants p49-50 (por.15)   (por.18)
Geikie—Founders p150-184   Woodruff—Devel. p183-184,279
Hammerton p796   (por.176)
Holmyard—British p28-30 (por.28)   Year—Pic. p135 (por.135)

Huxham, John (1692-1768). Eng. physician.
Hammerton p796
Major—History (2) p633

Huxley, Julian Sorell (1887-   ). Eng. biologist.

Curr. Biog. '42 p406-408 (por.407)   Newman—What p254-255
Hammerton p796-797 (por.796)   Year—Pic. p229 (por.229)

Huxley, Thomas Henry (1825-1895). Eng. biologist.

*Book—Pop. Sci. (12) p3903-3904   Moulton—Auto. p385-386
Chambers—Dict. col.232-233   Osborn—Impr. p71-98 (por.71)
  (por.231)   People p200 (por. 229)
*Darrow—Masters p335-336   Thomas—Scien. p151-163 (por.149)
Fitzhugh—Concise p325-326   Thomson—Great p145-151
Gordon—Medicine p27 (por.27)   Van Wagenen—Beacon p345-347
Gordon—Romance p44 (por.44)   Williams—Story p117-118 (por.311)
Hammerton p797-798 (por.797)   Woodruff—Devel. p279 (por.248)
Hubbard—Scientists (2) p59-81   *World's Great p381-398
Locy—Biology p337-338,437-439   Year—Pic. p129 (por.129)
  (por.438)
Major—History (2) p813-815

Huygens, Christian (1629-1695). Dutch mathematician.

Ball—Short p301-305   Magie—Source p27
*Book—Pop. Sci. (10) p3426-3427   Meyer—World p53
Cajori—Hist. p182-183   Moulton—Auto. p153
Chambers—Dict. col.233-234   Schwartz—Moments (1) p373-374
*Cottler p108-116   *Science Miles p75-78 (por.75)
Crew—Physicists #2 (folder) (por.)   Sedgwick—Short p286-289 (por.286)
*Darrow—Masters p336   Shapley—Astron. p63
*Epstein—Real p57   Smith—Hist. p423-424 (por.424)
Hammerton p798 (por.798)   Trattner—Arch. p144-162 (por.150)
Hart—Makers p151-154 (por.151)   Van Wagenen—Beacon p120-122
Hart—Physicists p81-84   Vaucouleurs—Disc. p58-60
Lenard—Great p67-83 (por.82)   Williams—Great p193-197 (por.195)
*Lewellen—Boy p140-148 (por.141)   Woodruff—Devel. p279
MacPherson—Makers p48-54   Year—Pic. p93 (por.93)

Hyatt, Alpheus (1838-1902). Amer. naturalist, biologist, zoologist.

Hammerton p798   Osborn—Fragments p211
N.A.S.—Biog. (6) p311-321
  (por.311)

Hyatt, John Wesley (1837-1920). Amer. inventor.

Law—Civiliz. p268-270
*Wright—Great p231-234

Hyde, Henry Van Zile (1906-   ). Amer. physician.

Curr. Biog. '60 p195-197 (por.196)

Hyde, Jesse Early (1884-1936). Amer. paleontologist, geologist.

G.S.A.—Proc. '36 p163-172 (por.163)

Hyginus, Gaius Julius (fl.1st. cent. B.C.). Roman mathematician.

Smith—Hist. I p124-125

Hyman, Libbie Henrietta (1888-   ). Amer. zoologist.
Yost—Amer. Sci. p122-138

Hypatia of Alexandria (c370-415?). Gr. mathematician.
Ball—Short p111
Cajori—Hist. p50-51
Coolidge—Six p2021
Mozans—Woman p137-141,168,199-201
Smith—Hist. 1 p137

Hypsicles of Alexandria (fl. 2nd cent.). Gr. astronomer, mathematician.
Smith—Hist. 1 p119

Hyrtl, Joseph (1810-1894). Aust. physician, anatomist.
Atkinson—Magic p290
Major—History (2) p784-785

I

Ibn abt Usaybi'a (c1203-1629). Syr. physician.
Major—History (1) p264

Ibn al-Baytar (or al-Baitâr, al-Beiter). Arab. botanist, physician.
Castiglioni—Hist. p279-280
Major—History (1) p264

Ibn al Khatib (or Lisan al-din Abu Abdallah Muhammed ibn 'Abdallah al Salmani) (1313-1374/1375). Sp. physician.
Major—History (1) p265

Ibn al-Ibadi.   See **Hunain ibn Ishaq**

Ibn al Nafis (fl. 13th cent.) Arab. physician.
Major—History (1) p489-491

Ibn Ezra.   See **Abenezra**

Ibn Ishaq.   See **Abu Yakub ibn Ishaq**

Ibn Ishaq Johannitius.   See **Hunain ibn Ishaq**

Ibn Junis.   See **Ali Ben abi Said Abderrahman**

Ibn Korra.   See **Tabit ibn Korra**

Ibn Luka.   See **Kosta ibn Luka**

Ibn Masawayh.   See **Mesuë, Senior**

Ibn-Muham-mad.   See **Averroes**

Ibn Mûsâ.   See **Al-Khowarizmi, Mohammed ibn Mûsâ**

Ibn Qurra.   See **Tabit ibn Korra**

Ibn Rushd.   See **Averroes**

Ibn Sarabiun (Serabi).   See **Serapion, Senior**

Ibn-Shap-Rut.   See **Hasdai ibn-Shap-rut.**

Ibn Thabit.   See **Sinan ibn Thabit**

Ibn Yahya.   See **Isa ibn Yahya ibn Ibrahim**

Ibn Zuhr.   See **Avenzoar**

Ibnu'l Wäfid.   See **Aben-Guefit**

Idrisi (or Edrisi Mohammed) (1099-1154). Arab. geographer.
Hammerton p541, 801

Ilg, Francis Lillian (1902-   ). Amer. physician.
Curr, Biog, '56 p299,300-301
(por.299)

Illner, Karl (1886-   ). Aust. aero. pioneer.
Heinmuller—Man's p280 (por.280)

Ilyich, Ilya.   See **Metchnikoff, Élie**

Imhotep (c.2980 B.C.). Egypt. physician.
Hammerton p801

Imlay, Lorin Everett (1864-1941). Amer. engineer.
Curr. Biog. '41 p429

Immelmann, Max Franz (1890-1916). Ger. aero. pioneer.
Burge—Ency. p634
Heinmuller—Man's p298 (por.298)

Indicopleustes.   See **Cosmas, Saint**

Infeld, Leopold (1898-   ). Pol.-Can. physicist, mathematician.
Curr. Biog. '41 p429-431 (por.429)

Ingen-Hausz, Jan (or Ingenhousz) (1730-1799). Dutch physician, botanist, biologist.
Chambers—Dict. col.235   *Snyder—Biology p307-308 (por.307)
Reed—Short p107-108   Woodruff—Devel. p241,279
Schwartz—Moments (2) p612-614   Year—Pic. p107 (por.107)

Inglis, Elsie Maud (1864-1917). Brit. surgeon.
Hammerton p803
Lovejoy—Women p282-283,287-291

Ingold, Christopher Kelk (1893-   ). Eng. chemist.
Chambers—Dict. col.235

Ingrassia, Giovanni Filippo (or Ingrassias, Gian Filippo) (1510-1580). Sic. physician, anatomist.
Castiglioni—Hist. p428-429 (por.428)   Leonardo—Lives p224
Chambers—Dict. col.235   Major—History (1) p469-470
Gordon—Hist. p638

Innes, Robert Thornton Axton (1861-1933). Scot. astronomer.
Hammerton p803

Insull, Samuel (1858-1938). Eng.-Amer. elec. engineer.
*Forbes—Men p204-213

Invilliers.   See **D'Invilliers, Edward Vincent**

Ipatieff (or Ipatiev), **Vladimir Nikolaevich** (1867-1952). Rus.-Amer. chemist.
Chambers—Dict. col.236

Irons, Ernest Edward (1877-1959). Amer. physician.
Curr. Biog. '49 p293-295 (por.294)
    '59 p201

Irvine, Sir James Colquhoun (1877-1952). Scot. chemist.
Chambers—Dict. col.236

Irving, Frederick C. (1883-   ). Amer. physician.
Fabricant—Why p164-167

Isaac Judaeus (Israeli, Isaac,) (Abu Ya' quiti Ali-Israeli, or Isaac the Jew) (830/832-932?). Arab. physician.
Castiglioni—Hist. p273   Major—History (1) p247,262-263
Gordon—Medieval p166-170

Isa ben Ali (or Haly, Jesu) (c925 A.D.). Arab. physician.
Gordon—Medieval p146-147

Isa ibn Yahya ibn Ibrahim (c987). Arab. physician.
Gordon—Medieval p147-148

Iselin, Columbus O'Donnell (1904-   ). Amer. oceanographer.
Curr. Biog. '48 p305-306 (por.305)

Isidorus of Seville, Saint (or Isidore) (560/570-636). Span. mathematician, nat. philosopher.
Ball—Short p133-134   Smith—Hist. I p183-184
Clagett—Greek p157-159

Isla, Rodrigo Ruiz Diaz (1462-1542). Port. physician.
Major—History (1) p463

Isomura Kittoku (or Iwamura) (fl.c.1660). Jap. mathematician.
Smith—Hist. I p437-438

Israel, James (1848-1926). Ger. surgeon.
Bulloch—Hist. p374
Kagan—Modern p87 (por.87)

Israeli, Isaac.   See **Isaac Judaeus**

Ittner, Martin Hill (1870-1945). Amer. chemist.
Curr. Biog. '42 p409-411 (por.410)
    '45 p300

Iverson, Caroline (n.d.). Amer. aero. pioneer.
Knapp—New p100-116 (por.179)

Ives, Frederic Eugene (1856-1937). Amer. inventor.
Chambers—Dict. col.236   Meyer—World p242-244
Hammerton p809

Ives, Herbert Eugene (1882-1953). Amer. physicist.
N.A.S.—Biog. (29) p145-172
    (por.145)
Radio's 100 p210-212 (por.140)

Ives, James Edward (1865-1943). Amer. physicist.
Curr. Biog. '43 p340

Ivory, Sir James Edward (1765-1842). Scot. mathematician.
Ball—Short p439
Cajori—Hist. p273-274

Ivy, Andrew Conway (1893-   ). Amer. physiologist.
Progress—Science '40 p211-212
    (por.211)

Iwamura.   See Isomura Kittoku

J

Jabir, ibn-Hayyan.   See Geber

Jackson, Charles Thomas (1805-1880). Amer. physician, surgeon, chemist, geologist.
Fülop—Miller p124-125,131-135,214,   Robinson—Victory p108-118 (por.83)
    318-323 (por.177)   Thorwald—Century p147-148,158-
Gumpert—Trail p230-231,245-250   162,164-165 (por.80)
Merrill—First p120-121 (por.120)   Wilson—Amer. p107
*Morris—Heroes p189-191   Young—Scalpel p139,140,141,142,
                                              147,150-155 (por.154)

Jackson, Chevalier (1865-1958). Amer. physician, inventor.
Curr. Biog. '40 p426-427 (por.426)   Rowntree—Amid p410-414 (por.407)
*Montgomery—Story p56-60

Jackson, Daniel Dana (1870-1941). Amer. chem. engineer.
Curr. Biog. '41 p433

Jackson, Dunham (1888-1946). Amer. mathematician.
N.A.S.—Biog. (33) p142-171
    (por.142)

Jackson, James (1777-1867). Amer. physician.
Kagan—Modern p7 (por.7)   Rosen—Four p163-165
Major—History (2) p737-738

Jackson, James, Jr. (1810-1834). Amer. physician.
Farmer—Doctors' p103-104

Jackson, John (1887-1958). Scot. chemist.
R.S.L.—Biog. (5) p95-104 (por.95)

Jackson, Sir John (1851-1919). Eng. engineer.
Hammerton p810

Jackson, John Hughlings (1835-1911). Eng. neurologist.
Hale—White—Great p268-289
Major—History (2) p898

Jackson, Robert Tracy (1861-1948). Amer. geologist, paleontologist.
G.S.A.—Proc. '51 p117-119 (por.117)

Jackson, Samuel (1790-1872). Amer. physician.
Major—History (2) p769

Jacob, Sir Lionel (1853-1934). Eng. engineer.
Hammerton p810

Jacobi, Abraham (1830-1919). Ger.-Amer. physician.
*Book—Pop. Sci. (12) p4009-4010 (por.4010)
Castiglioni—Hist. p863 (por.863)
Hammerton p810 (por.810)
Kagan—Leaders p41-51
Kagan—Modern p52 (por.52)
Major—History (2) p1036-1037

Jacobi, Karl Gustav Jacob (1804-1851). Ger. mathematician.
A.A.A.S.—Proc. (79) p21
Ball—Short p462-464
Bell—Men p327-339 (por.,front.)
Cajori—Hist. p414-415
Chambers—Dict. col.237
Hammerton p810
Smith—Hist. I p506-507 (por.506)
Smith—Portraits (2), IX, unp. (por.)
Woodruff—Devel. p279 (por.36)

Jacobi, Mary Putnam (1842-1906). Amer. physician.
Farmer—Doctors' p166-167
Hammerton p810
Lovejoy—Women p73-75,158-160 (por.74)
Mead—Medical p37-40 (por.,append.)

Jacobi, Moritz Hermann von (1801-1874). Ger.-Rus. physicist, engineer, chemist.
A.A.A.S.—Proc. (79) p22-23

Jacobs, Aletta H. (1849-1929). Dutch physician.
Lovejoy—Women p183-184

Jacobs, Henry Barton (1858-1939). Amer. physician.
Kagan—Modern p208 (por.208)

Jacobsen, Carlyle (1902-   ). Amer. psychologist.
Chambers—Dict. col.237

Jacobson, Ludwig (1783-1843). Dan. surgeon.
Copen.—Prom. p97-99

Jacobson, Paul (1859-1923). Ger. chemist.
Smith—Torch. p128 (por.128)

Jacobson, Sigismund D. (1837-1894). Dan. surgeon.
Kagan—Modern p145 (por.145)

Jacobus (c.460). Gr. physician.
Major—History (1) p221

Jacopi, Giulo (1898-   ). Aust. archaeologist.
Curr. Biog. '59 p201-203 (por.202)

Jacquard, Joseph Marie (1752-1834). Fr. inventor.
*Book—Pop. Sci. (9) p3051-3053   Hammerton p811 (por.811)
   (por.3051)   Law—Civiliz. p96-98
Chambers—Dict. col.237

Jäger, Gustav (1832-1917). Ger. zoologist.
Hammerton p811

Jamerius.   See **Bruno of Longoburgo**

James, Charles (1880-1928). Eng.-Amer. chemist.
Chambers—Dict. col.237-238   Weeks—Discovery p433-434,522
Smith—Torch. p129 (por.129)   (por.522)

James, Edwin (1797-1861). Amer. botanist, naturalist.
Ewan—Rocky p13-20,237-238
   (por.13)

James, Robert (1705-1776). Eng. physician.
Hammerton p813

James, William (1842-1910). Amer. psychologist.
Chambers—Dict. col.238   Moulton—Auto. p416-417
Morris—Ency. p682

Jameson, Mrs. Anna Brownell Murphy (1794-1860). Irish archaeologist,
   iconographer.
Mozans—Woman p313-316

Jameson, Robert (1774-1854). Scot. mineralogist, geologist.
Fenton—Giants p62-63   Woodruff—Devel. p279
Geikie—Founders p192-193

Jamieson, Leland Shattuck (1904-1941). Amer. aero. pioneer.
Curr. Biog. '41 p433

Jamin, Jules Célestin (1818-1886). Fr. physicist.
Chambers—Dict. col.238

Janas, Sigmund (1899-   ). Amer. aero. pioneer.
Curr. Biog. '50 p275-277 (por.276)

Janet, Pierre Marie Félix (1859-1947). Fr. neurologist, psychologist.
Chambers—Dict. col.238-239   Major—History (2) p965,1037
Hammerton p814

Janeway, Theodore Caldwell (1872-1917). Amer. physician.
Hammerton p814

Janney, Eli Hamilton (1831-1912). Amer. inventor.
Abbot—Great p199-200

Jansen, Zacharias (c.1600). Dutch optician.
Chambers—Dict. col.239
*Darrow—Masters p336

Janssen, Charles L. (1886-1941). Belg.-Amer. physician, surgeon.
Curr. Biog. '41 p433

Janssen, Pierre Jules César (1824-1907). Fr. astronomer.
Armitage—Cent. p56-57   MacPherson—Makers p171-172
Chambers—Dict. col.240   Shapley—Astron. p308 (por.309)
Hammerton p814-815   Weeks—Discovery p474,475
MacPherson—Astron. p18-24   (por.474,475)
  (por.18)   Williams—Great p374 (por.375)

Janus Damascenes.   See **Mesuë, Senior**

Japp, Francis Robert (1848-1925). Scot. chemist.
Chambers—Dict. col.240

Jaques-Dalcroze.   See **Dalcroze, Émile Jaques**

Jastrow, Joseph (1863-1944). Amer. psychologist.
Curr. Biog. '44 p328

Jauregg.   See **Wagner-Jauregg, Julius von**

Jean Baseilhac.   See **Saint-Come, Frère Jean de**

Jeans, Sir James Hopwood (1877-1946). Eng. mathematician, physicist, astronomer.
Armitage—Cent. p245-246 (por.177)   Hammerton p815-816 (por.816)
Chambers—Dict. col.240-241   Schwartz—Moments (2) p966-967
Curr. Biog. '41 p433-435 (por.434),
  '46 p283

Jefferies, John (1744-1810). Amer. surgeon.
Burge—Ency. p634
Peattie—Gather. p151-155

Jefferson, Mark (1863-1949). Amer. geologist.
G.S.A.—Proc. '49 p175-176
  (por.175)

Jefferson, Thomas (1743-1826). Amer. inventor, mathematician, zoologist.
Bell—Early p60-62   Smith—Math. p59-63
*Epstein—Real p168,178   Young—Biology p32-34 (por.35)

Jeffery, George Barker (1891-1957). Eng. mathematician.
R.S.L.—Biog. (4) p129-136
  (por.129)

Jefford, Jack Theodore (1910-   ). Amer. aero. pioneer.
Potter—Flying p234-252 (por.242)

Jeffrey, John (1826-1853). Scot. botanist.
Dakin—Perennial p38

Jeffreys, Harold (1891-   ). Eng. geophysicist.
Chambers—Dict. col.241

Jeffries, John (1744-1819). Amer. aero. pioneer, physician, surgeon.
Milbank—First p10-16
*Shippen—Bridle p57-63

Jelliffe, Smith Ely (1866-1945). Amer. neurologist.
Curr. Biog. '45 p302

Jellinek, Elvin Morton (1890-   ). Amer. physiologist.
Curr. Biog. '47 p334-335 (por.335)

Jenkin, (Henry Charles) Fleeming (1833-1885). Eng. engineer.
Hammerton p818

Jenkins, Charles Francis (1867-1934). Amer. inventor.
*Hylander—Invent. p174-184   Radio's 100 p141-143 (por.140)
*Montgomery—Invent. p90-93   Year—Pic. p245 (por.245)

Jenks, Leon E. (1876-1940). Amer. chemist.
Curr. Biog. '40 p431

Jenner, Edward (1749-1823). Eng. physician.
A.A.A.S.—Proc. (77) p43
Atkinson—Magic p204-209
Bodenheimer—Hist. p340
*Book—Pop. Sci. (12) p3905-3906
  (por.3906) (13) p4511
Castiglioni—Hist. p642-644 (por.643)
Chambers—Dict. col.241 (por.239)
*Chandler—Medicine p45-49 (por.44)
*Cottler—Heroes p269-277
*Darrow—Masters p125-127 (por.64)
*Elwell—Sci. p66-68
Farmer—Doctors' p71-76
Fitzhugh—Concise p349-350
*Fox—Great p79-97 (por.79)
Hale-White—Great p1-21
Hammerton p818 (por.818)
Lambert—Medical p230-238
  (por.232)
Lambert—Minute p230-238 (por.256)
Law—Civiliz. p308-311
Major—History (2) p606,609
  (por.608)
*Masters—Conquest p39-46 (por.40)
*Montgomery—Story p206-210
Moulton—Auto. p278-279
Murray—Science p1-19
Newman—Interp. p146-148
Oliver—Stalkers p144-149 (por.145)
100 Great p582-588 (por.56)
Robinson—Path. p213-238 (por.230)
Schwartz—Moments (2) p717-718
*Science Miles p120-124 (por.120)
*Shippen—Men p105-114
Sigerist—Great p261 (por.264)
*Snyder—Biology p181-187
*Sterling—Polio p45-47 (por.46)
Thomson—Great p66-71
Tobey—Riders p63-65
*Truax—Doctors p46-54
Tuska—Invent. p99
Van Wagenen—Beacon p195-198
Walker—Pioneers p48-58 (por.48)
Walsh—Makers p87-111
Williams—Story p42-43 (por.41)
Woglom—Discov. p75-81

Jenner, Sir William (1815-1898). Eng. physician.
Chambers—Dict. col.241-242
Hammerton p818

Jennings, Allen Henson (1866-1918). Amer. entomologist.
Osborn—Fragments p204

Jennings, Frank Dormer (1880-1934). Amer. surgeon.
Leonardo—Lives p224-225

Jennings, Herbert Spencer (1868-1947). Amer. zoologist, naturalist, geneticist, biologist.
Progress—Science '41 p210-211
  (por.210)
Snyder—Biology p360-363 (por.361)

Jensen, Carl Oluf (1864-1934). Dan. bacteriologist.
Bulloch—Hist. p374

Jerger, Joseph A. (1881-1950). Eng. physician.
Fabricant—Why p80-82

Jerome, Chauncey (1793-1868). Amer. inventor.
*Burlingame—Mach. p123-128

Jerome of Brunswick.   See **Brunschwig, Hieronymus**

Jervis-Smith, Frederick (1848-1911). Eng. engineer.
Gunther—Early XI p234-235
(por.235)

Jewett, Frank Baldwin (1879-1949). Amer. elec. engineer, physicist.
Curr. Biog. '46 p283-285 (por.284)   N.A.S.—Biog. (27) p239-260
  '50 p277   (por.239)
Holland—Ind. p33-55 (por.33)   Progress—Science '40 p212-213
                                         (por.212)

Jewett, Frank Fanning (1844-1926). Amer. chemist.
Weeks—Discovery p354 (por.354)

Jex-Blake, Sophia (1840-1912). Eng. physician.
Lovejoy—Women p144-157 (por.146)
Mozans—Woman p305-307

Jobert de Lamballe, Antoine (1799-1867). Fr. surgeon.
Leonardo—Lives p225-226

Joblot, Louis (1645-1723). Fr. bacteriologist.
Bulloch—Hist. p374

Joest, Ernst (1873-1926). Ger. bacteriologist.
Bulloch—Hist. p374-375

Johanitius.   See **Hunain ibn Ishaq**

Johannes.   See **Actarius, Johannes**

Johannes Anglicus.   See **John of Gaddesden**

Johannes de Mirfeld.   See **John of Mirfeld**

Johannsen, Wilhelm Ludwig (1857-1927). Dutch botanist, geneticist.
Chambers—Dict. col.242
Copen.—Prom. p177-180

John XXI, Pope (or Petrus Hispanus) (d.1277). Port. physician.
Gordon—Medieval p276-281
Walsh—Catholic (2d) p61-90 (por.61)

John of Arderne (or John of Arden) (1307-1380/1390). Eng. surgeon.
Castiglioni—Hist. p347
Gordon—Medieval p376-380
Hammerton p108
Leonardo—Lives p21-23
Major—History (1) p314-316, 450-451
(por.451)

John of Gaddesden (or Johannes Anglicus) (c.1280-1361). Eng. physician.
Gordon—Medieval p373-376
Major—History (1) p325-326

John of Mirfeld (or Johannes de Mirfeld) (d.1407). Eng. physician.
Gordon—Medieval p380-383
Leonardo—Lives p226-227

John of Vigo.   See **Vigo, Giovanni**

Johne, (Heinrich) Albert (1839-1910). Ger. bacteriologist.
Bulloch—Hist. p375

Johnson, Amy.   See **Mollison, Amy Johnson**

Johnson, Arthur Newhall (1870-1940). Amer. engineer.
Curr. Biog. '41 p431

Johnson, Charles William (1863-1932). Amer. entomologist.
Osborn—Fragments p237 (por.356)

Johnson, Clifton Wood (1905-1954). Amer. geologist.
G.S.A.—Proc. '54 p151

Johnson, Douglas Wilson (1878-1944). Amer. geologist.
Curr. Biog. '44 p328
G.S.A.—Proc. '44 p223-233 (por.223)
N.A.S.—Biog. (24) p197-220 (por.197)

Johnson, John Monroe (1878-   ). Amer. engineer.
Curr. Biog. '45 p306-309 (por.307)

Johnson, Joseph B. (1893-   ). Amer. engineer.
Curr. Biog. '56 p312-314 (por.313)

Johnson, Loren Bascom Taber (1875-1941). Amer. psychiatrist.
Curr. Biog. '42 p423

Johnson, Samuel William (1830-1909). Amer. agric. chemist.
Browne—Hist. p471-472 (por.19)   Smith—Chem. p275-276
N.A.S.—Biog. (7) p203-215 (por.203)

Johnson, Thomas (1604/1605-1644). Eng. botanist.
Arber—Herbals p134,135,237,238,239   Major—History (1) p553
Gilmour—British p12-13   Raven—English p273-297
Hawks—Pioneers p182-183

Johnson, Treat Baldwin (1875-1947). Amer. chemist.
N.A.S.—Biog. (27) p83-95 (por.83)

Johnson, William Woolsey (1841-1927). Amer. mathematician.
Smith—Math. p137-138

Johnston, George Ben (1853-1916). Amer. surgeon.
Leonardo—Lives p227-229

Johnston, Herrick Lee (1898-   ). Amer. chemist.
Chambers—Dict. col.242

Johnston, John (1881-   ). Scot.-Amer. chemist.
Progress—Science '41 p211-212
    (por.211)

Johnston-Lavis, Henry James (1856-1914). Eng. physician, seismologist.
Davison—Founders p85-86

Johnstone, Ralph (1886-1910). Amer. aero. pioneer.
Heinmuller—Man's p283 (por.283)

Johnstrup, Johannes Frederik (1818-1894). Dan. geologist.
Copen—Prom. p131-133

Joliot, Jean Frédéric (or Joliot-Curie) (1900-1958). Fr. physicist.
Calder—Science p70-71   *Kendall—Young p220-223 (por.221)
Chambers—Dict. col.242   Progress—Science '40 p213
Curr. Biog. '46 p294-296 (por.295) Riedman—Men p136-149 (por.152)
    '58 p213   Weeks—Discovery p505,531-541
Farber—Nobel p145-146 (por.118)   (por.505)
                                   Year—Pic. p212 (por.212)

Joliot-Curie, Irène (1897-1956). Fr. physicist.

Calder—Science p70-71
Chambers—Dict. col.242-243
Curr. Biog. '40 p435-436 (por.435)
  '56 p314
Farber—Nobel p143-145 (por.118)

*Kendall—Young p220-223 (por.221)
Progress—Science '40 p213
Riedman—Men p130-136 (por.152)
Weeks—Discovery p503,505,531-541
  (por.503,505)
Year—Pic. p212 (por.212)

Joly, John (1857-1933). Irish geologist, physicist.

Chambers—Dict. col.243
G.S.A.—Proc. '34 p251-252

Hammerton p829

Jonas, August Frederick (1858-1934). Amer. surgeon.

Leonardo—Lives p229-230

Jones, Charles Sherman (or "Casey"). Amer. aero. pioneer.

Heinmuller—Man's p296 (por.296)
Maitland—Knights p270-272

Jones, Frank Morton (b.1869). Amer. entomologist.

Osborn—Fragments p234 (por.352)

Jones, Frederick Wood (1879-1954). Eng. anatomist, anthropologist.

R.S.L.—Biog. (1) p119-129 (por.119)

Jones, Sir Harold Spencer (1890-1960). Eng. astronomer.

Curr. Biog. '55 p308-310 (por.309)
  '61 (Jan.)

Jones, John (1729-1791). Amer. surgeon.

Leonardo—Lives p230-231

Jones, John Matheis (1912-   ). Amer. aero. pioneer.

*Fraser—Heroes p823-827

Jones, Lewis Ralph (1864-1945). Amer. agriculturist.

N.A.S.—Biog. (31) p156-167 (por.156)

Jones, Marcus Eugene (1852-1934). Amer. botanist, naturalist, geologist, min. engineer.

Ewan—Rocky p79-86, 240-241
  (por.79)

Jones, Sir Robert (1858-1933). Welsh surgeon.

Hammerton p830
Kagan—Modern p93 (por.93)

Leonardo—Lives p232-233

Jones, Walter (Jennings) (1865-1935). Amer. physiol. chemist.
  N.A.S.—Biog. (20) p79-133 (por.79)

Jones, William (1675-1749). Welsh mathematician.
  A.A.A.S.—Proc. (77) p44-45

Jones, William Richard (1839-1889). Amer. engineer.
  Goddard—Eminent p132-138
    (por.132)

Jordan, Camille (Marie Ennemond Camille) (1838-1922). Fr. mathematician.
  Chambers—Dict. col.243

Jordan, David Starr (1851-1931). Amer. zoologist, biologist.
  Hylander—Scien. p123-130

Jordan, Edwin Oakes (1866-1936). Amer. bacteriologist.
  Bulloch—Hist. p375
  N.A.S.—Biog. (20) p197-218 (por.197)

Jordan, Frank Craig (1865-1941). Amer. astronomer.
  Curr. Biog. '41 p448
  Progress—Science '41 p212

Jordan, Louise (1908-   ). Amer. paleontologist, geologist.
  Goff—Woman p161-167

Jordan, Sara Murray (1884-1959). Amer. physician.
  Curr. Biog. '54 p367-369 (por.368)
    '60 p208

Jordan, Whitman Howard (1851-1931). Amer. agriculturist.
  *Ivins—Fifty p295-302 (por.294)

Jordanus Nemorarius (c.1220). Ger. mathematician.
  Ball—Short p171-174
  Smith—Hist. I p226-227

Joshee, Anandibai (1865-1887). Ind. physician.
  Lovejoy—Women p223-224

Joubert, Jules (1834-1910). Fr. physicist.
  Bulloch—Hist. p375

Joubert, Laurent J. (1529-1583). Fr. physician.
  Major—History (1) p473

Joule, James Prescott (1818-1889). Eng. physicist.
*Book—Pop. Sci. (12) p4010-4011
Chalmers—Historic p266
*Chambers—Dict. col.244
Crew—Physicists #7 (folder) (por.)
Crowther—Men p127-197 (por.144)
Gregory—British p31-32 (por.31)
Hammerton p832
Hart—Makers p285-286 (por.285)
Hart—Physicists p129-131
Lenard—Great p286-292 (por.283)
Magie—Source p203
Moulton—Auto. p292-293
Murray—Science p86-92
People p207-208
Van Wagenen—Beacon p307-308
Williams—Story p213-214,217-218 (por.219)
Woodruff—Devel. p61,62,81,279
Year—Pic. p122 (por.122)

Joutel, Louis H. (1858-1916). Amer. entomologist.
Osborn—Fragments p205-206

Joyce, Thomas Athol (1878-1942). Eng. anthropologist, ethnologist.
Hammerton p832-833 (por.832)

Judaeus, Asaf.   See **Asaph Ha-Ropheh of Syria**

Judaeus, Isaac.   See **Isaac Judaeus**

Judd, Charles Hubbard (1873-1946). Brit.-Amer. psychologist.
Curr. Biog. '46 p299

Judd, John Wesley (1840-1916). Eng. geologist.
Hammerton p833

Judd, Walter Henry (1898-   ). Amer. physician, surgeon.
Curr. Biog. '49 p308-310 (por.309)

Juhanna Abu'l Faraj.   See **Bar-Hebraeus**

Julian, Percy Lavon (1899-   ). Amer. chemist.
Curr. Biog. '47 p338-340 (por.339)
Downs—Meet p56-57 (por.56)

Jullien, Pierre (1814-1876). Fr. aero. pioneer.
Heinmuller—Man's p243

Jung, Carl Gustav (1875-1961). Swiss psychologist.
Chambers—Dict. col.244-246
Curr. Biog. '43 p359-362 (por.360)
    '53 p299-302 (por.300)
Curr. Biog. 1961 (Sept.)
Hammerton p834 (por.834)
People p209
Year—Pic. p224 (por.224)

Jung, Joachim (1587-1657). Ger. botanist, physician, mathematician.
Hawks—Pioneers p191,193   Woodruff—Devel. p279
Reed—Short p81-83

Jungfleisch, Emile-Clement (1839-1916). Fr. chemist.
Smith—Torch. p130 (por.130)
Weeks—Discovery p401 (por.401)

Junkers, Hugo (1859-1935). Ger. aero. pioneer.
Burge—Ency. p634

Jussieu de (family) (17th, 18th cent.). Fr. botanists.
Hammerton p834
Hawks—Pioneers p241-243

Jussieu, Adrien de (1797-1853). Fr. botanist.
Hawks—Pioneers p243 (por.244)

Jussieu, Antoine de (1686-1758). Fr. botanist, physician.
Hawks—Pioneers p241-243 (por.246)

Jussieu, Antoine Laurent de (1748-1836). Fr. botanist.
Chambers—Dict. col.246
Miall—Early p352-358

Jussieu, Bernard de (1699?-1777). Fr. botanist.
Hawks—Pioneers p241-243 (por.244)   Reed—Short p101-102
Miall—Early p351-352,353-358   Van Wagenen—Beacon p140-141

Just, Ernest Everett (1883-1941). Amer. zoologist.
Progress—Science '41 p212

K

Kablick, Josephine (b.1787). Bohem. paleontologist.
Mozans—Woman p242-243

Kaempffert, Waldemar (1877-1956). Amer. sci. writer.
Curr. Biog. '43 p362-365 (por.363)

Kahlbaum, Georg Wilhelm August (1853-1905). Ger. phys. chemist.
Smith—Torch. p131 (por.131)

Kahlenberg, Louis Albert (1870-1941). Amer. chemist.
Progress—Science '41 p212

Kahn, Albert (1869-1942). Ger.-Amer. engineer.
Curr. Biog. '42 p429-431 (por.430)

Kalbfleisch, Martin (1804-1873). Dutch-Amer. chemist.
Haynes—Chem. (1) p42-56 (por.44)

Kalm, Peter (1715/1716-1779) Swed. botanist, entomologist,
ornithologist, sci. explorer.
Osborn—Fragments p12
Peattie—Gather p97-100

Kalmus, Herbert Thomas (1881-   ). Amer. metallurgist, physicist,
chemist.
Curr. Biog. '49 p311-313 (por.312)

Kamel Muhammed.   See **Al-Damiri**

Kamerlingh Onnes.   See **Onnes, Heike Kamerlingh**

Kammerer, Paul (1880-1926). Austrian biologist.

Kammermeister.   See **Camerarius, Joachim, the Younger**

Kanavel, Allen Buckner (1874-1938). Amer. surgeon.
Leonardo—Lives p233-234

Kane, Elisha Kent (1820-1857). Amer. sci. explorer.
*Book—Pop. Sci. (8) p2824-2825

Kane, Sir Robert John (1809-1890). Irish chemist.
Chambers—Dict. col.247

Kant, Immanuel (1724-1804). Ger. nat. philosopher.
Hammerton p837-838 (por.837)   Suter—Gallery p123-126
Osborn—Greeks p146-152   Williams—Great p244-247,265-269
Shapley—Astron. p117   (por.245)

Kanthack, Alfredo Antunes (1863-1898). Eng. bacteriologist, pathologist.
Bulloch—Hist. p375

Kantrowitz, Arthur (1913-   ). Amer. physicist, space pioneer.
Thomas—Men (3) p118-137 (por.74)

Kapitza, Peter Leonidovich (or Pëtr, Pyotr Katitsa) (1894-   ). Rus. physicist.
Chambers—Dict. col.248-249   *Larsen—Scrap. p147 (por.145)
Curr. Biog. '55 p317-318 (por.318)

Kaplan, Joseph (1902-   ). Hung.-Amer. physicist.
Chambers—Dict. col.249
  (por.247-248)
Curr. Biog. '56 p316-318 (por.317)

Kapp, Gisbert (1842-1922). Austrian-Ger. engineer.
Hammerton p838

Kappel, Frederick R. (1902-   ). Amer. engineer.
Curr. Biog. '57 p289-291 (por.290)

Kapteyn, Jacobus Cornelius (1851-1922). Dutch astronomer.
Armitage—Cent. p159-160 (por.144)   MacPherson—Makers p221-226
Chambers—Dict. col.249   (por.106)
Hammerton p838   Shapley—Astron. p350
MacPherson—Astron. p185-191
  (por.185)

Karelitz, George Boris (1895-1943). Rus.-Amer. engineer.
Curr. Biog. '43 p368

Kármán, Theodore von (1881-   ). Hung.-Amer. physicist, aerodynamicist.
Curr. Biog. '55 p623-624 (por.623)
Robinson—100 p273-276 (por.273)

Karpinsky, Alexander Petrovich (1847?-1935?). Rus. geologist.
G.S.A.—Proc. '36 p175-192 (por.175)

Karrer, Paul (1889-   ). Swiss chemist.
Chambers—Dict. col. 249
Farber—Nobel p156-159 (por.118)

Kasner, Edward (1878-1955). Amer. mathematician.
Curr. Biog. '43 p368-370 (por.369)   N.A.S.—Biog. (31) p180-197 (por.180)
  '55 p319   Progress—Science '40 p213-214
                                            (por.214)

Kast, Ludwig W. (1877-1941). Amer. physician.
Curr. Biog. '41 p456

Kater, Henry (1777-1835). Eng. physicist.
Chambers—Dict. col.249-250
Hammerton p839

Kaufmann.   See Mercator, Nicolaus

Kay, George Frederick (1873-1943). Amer. geologist.
    G.S.A.—Proc. '43 p169-172 (por.169)

Kay, John (fl.1733-1764). Eng. inventor.
    *Darrow—Masters p50
    *Epstein—Real p146-148
    Hammerton p840

    *Hartman—Mach. p3-5
    *Larsen—Prentice p60-61
    Law—Civiliz. p91-92

Kaye.   See Caius, John

Kayser, Heinrich (1853-1940). Ger. physicist.
    R.S.L.—Biog. (1) p135-140 (por.135)

Kearton, Cherry (1871-1940). Eng. naturalist.
    Hammerton p840-841
    Peattie—Gather p65-68

Keeble, Sir Frederick (1870-1952). Eng. biologist, physiologist, botanist.
    Hammerton p842

Keeler, James Edward (1857-1900). Amer. astronomer.
    *Book—Pop. Sci. (14) p4641-4643
        (por.4642)
    Chambers—Dict. col.250
    N.A.S.—Biog. (5) p231-241 (por. 231)

    Shapley—Astron. p394
    Williams—Great p383-386 (por.384)

Keen, William Williams (1837-1932). Amer. physician, surgeon.
    Hammerton p842
    Leonardo—Lives (Supp. 1) p486-487

    Major—History (2) p1037

Keenan, Walter Francis, Jr. (1884-1940). Amer. engineer.
    Curr. Biog. '40 p448 (por.448)

Kees.   See Caius, John

Keesom, Wilhelmus Hendrikus (1876-   ). Dutch physicist.
    Chambers—Dict. col.250

Keilin, David (n.d.). Eng. biologist.
    Chambers—Dict. col.250

Keith, Sir Arthur (1864/1866-1955). Scot. anthropologist.
    Chambers—Dict. col.251,supp.
    G.S.A.—Proc. '44 p241-244 (por.241)
    Hammerton p842 (por.842)

    N.A.S.—Biog. (29) p191-196 (por.191)
    R.S.L.—Biog. (1) p145-156 (por.145)

Kekulé von Stradonitz, Friedrich August (1829-1896). Ger. chemist.

*Book—Pop. Sci. (12) p4012
Chambers—Dict. col.251
Chymia (1) p157-158 (por.158)
Findlay—Hundred p328
Hammerton p843
Holmyard—Great Chem. p105-110
Holmyard—Makers p280-281

*Kendall—Young p116-125 (por.115)
Moulton—Autobiog. p287-288
Partington—Short p286-292,294-295 (por.286)
Roberts—Chem. p201-207
Smith—Torch. p132-133 (por.132)
Van Wagenen—Beacon p353-354
Woodruff—Devel. p105,106,279-280

Kellems, Vivien (1896-   ). Amer. engineer.

Goff—Women p215-227

Keller, Kaufman Thuma (1885-   ). Amer. engineer.

Curr. Biog. '47 p344-346 (por.345)

Kellicott, David S. (1842-1898). Amer. entomologist.

Osborn—Fragments p232 (por.350)

Kellogg, Arthur Remington (1892-   ). Amer. biologist.

Curr. Biog. '49 p317-319

Kellogg, John Harvey (1852-1943). Amer. inventor, physician, surgeon.

Curr. Biog. '44 p336

Kellogg, Vernon Lyman (1867-1937). Amer. zoologist.

*Bernays—Outline p349
Essig—Hist. p668-670 (por.668)

N.A.S.—Biog. (20) p245-252 (por.245)
Osborn—Fragments p182

Kelly, Everett Lowell (1905-   ). Amer. psychologist.

Curr. Biog. '55 p322-324 (por.323)

Kelly, Howard Atwood (1858-1943). Amer. physician, surgeon.

Curr. Biog. '43 p370
Hammerton p843
Kagan—Modern p122 (por.122)

Leonardo—Lives (Supp. 1) p487-489
Major—History (2) p855,859,918 (por.854)
Rowntree—Amid p66-68 (por.64)

Kelly, Mervin J. (1894-   ). Amer. physicist.

Curr. Biog. '56 p329-331 (por.329)

Kelly, Oakley G. (n.d.). Amer. aero. pioneer.

*Fraser—Heroes p119-148
Maitland—Knights p256-257 (por.250)

Kelly, William (1811-1888). Amer. inventor.
*Burlingame—Inv. p91-114   *Parkman—Conq. p298-309
*Hartman—Mach. p108-111

Kelser, Raymond Alexander (1892-1952). Amer. bacteriologist.
N.A.S.—Biog. (28) p199-217
(por.199)

Kelvin, William Thomson, Lord (1824-1907). Scot. mathematician, physicist.
*Bolton—Famous p179-193 (por.178)
*Book—Pop. Sci. (12) p4013-4014
(por.4015)
Cajori—Hist. p472-474
Chambers—Dict. col.251-253
(por.252)
Crowther—Men p199-256
(por.218,242,252)
*Darrow—Masters p157-161 (por.32)
Gibson—Heroes p278-307
Gregory—British p15-16 (por.15)
Hammerton p843-844 (por.843)
Hart—Makers p274-303 (por.274)
Hart—Physicists p131-135
Holmyard—British p51-53 (por.51)
John Fritz p33-35 (por.32)
*Larsen—Shaped p88-100 (por.80)
Lenard—Great p298-307 (por.297)
Lodge—Pioneers p372-378 (por.373)
MacFarlane—Ten p55-70
(por.,front.)
Magie—Source p236-237
Morgan—Men p78-82
Moulton—Auto. p467-468
100 Great p634-639
Radio's 100 p55-57 (por.140)
Ramsay—Essays p89-100
Shapley—Astron. p261
Thomas—Scien. p219-229 (por.217)
*Towers—Beacon p114-129 (por.114)
Van Wagenen—Beacon p337-338
Williams—Great p432,518-524
(por.521)
Williams—Story p218-223,227,235,236
(por.219)
Woodruff—Devel. p280 (por.60)
Year—Pic. p122 (por.122,156)

Kemp, James Furman (1859-1926). Amer. geologist.
N.A.S.—Biog. (16) p1-8 (por.1)

Kendall, Edward Calvin (1886-   ). Amer. chemist.
Chambers—Dict. col.253
Curr. Biog. '50 p292-294 (por.293)
*Darrow—Builders p228-230
Morris—Ency. p684
Robinson—100 p287-290 (por.287)
Rowntree—Amid p534-538 (por.531)
*Snyder—Biology p370-371 (por.373)
Stevenson—Nobel p272-273,274-280
(por.150)

Kennard, A. E. (d.1934). Eng. surgeon.
Hammerton p846 (por.846)

Kennaway, Ernest Laurence (1881-1958). Eng. physiol. chemist.
R.S.L.—Biog. (4) p139-150 (por.139)

Kennedy, Sir Alexander Blackie William (1847-1928). Eng. engineer.
Hammerton p846

Kennelly, Arthur Edwin (1861-1939). Amer. elec. engineer.
Chambers—Dict. col.253   Radio's 100 p129-131 (por.140)
N.A.S.—Biog. (22) p83-94 (por.83)

Kent, Arthur Atwater (1873-1949). Amer. inventor, elec. engineer.
White—Famous (3d) p145-154
(por.143)

Kenyatta, Jomo (1893?-   ). Afr. anthropologist.
Curr. Biog. '53 p311-314 (por.312)

Kepler, Johannes (1571-1630). Ger. mathematician, astronomer.
Abetti—History p115-124
(por.146-(15))
Ball—Great p96-115 (por.103)
Ball—Short p254-257
*Book—Pop. Sci. (14) p4643-4646
(por.4643)
Cajori—Hist. p159-160
Chambers—Dist. col.253-255
(por.254)
Dreyer—Hist. p372-412
Fitzhugh—Concise p373-375
Gibson—Heroes p67-75
Gregory—British p20,21
Gumpert—Trail p110-112
Hammerton p847 (por.847)
Hart—Makers p79-92 (por.79)
Hofman—History p119-120
Hooper—Makers p201-206
Koestler—Sleep. p225-282,378-422
Lenard—Great p39-47 (por.39)
Lodge—Pioneers p56-79 (por.76)
MacPherson—Makers p18-31
(por.,front.)
People p213-214
Schwartz—Moments (1) p265-266
Sedgwick—Short p210-217 (por.210)
Shapley—Astron. p29
*Simmons—Great p17-18 (por.17)
Smith—Hist. 1 p416
Smith—Portraits (2) 111, unp.(por.)
*Stevens—Science p23-28 (por.22)
Turnbull—Great p65-69
Van Wagenen—Beacon p94-99
Vaucouleurs—Disc. p51-53
Walsh—Catholic (2d) p202
Williams—Great p141-155 (por.156)
Wilson—Human p129-156 (por.148)
Woodruff—Devel. p147-150,280
(por.138)
Year—Pic. p74,76,87,92,95 (por.76)

Kerckring, Thomas (1640-1693). Ger. physician.
Major—History (1) p560

Kern, Vincenz von (1760-1829). Aust. surgeon.
Leonardo—Lives p234-235

Kerr, Forrest A. (1896-1938). Amer. geologist.
G.S.A.—Proc. '38 p147-149 (por.147)

Kerr, John (1824-1907). Scot. physicist.
Chambers—Dict. col.255

Kerr, John Graham (1869-1957). Brit. zoologist.
Hammerton p848
R.S.L.—Biog. (4) p155-164 (por.155)

Kerr, Wahington Caruthers (1827-1885). Amer. geologist.
Merrill—First p475-476 (por.476)

Kersey, John (1616-1695?). Eng. mathematician.
Gunther—Early XI p304 (por.304)

Kerst, Donald William (1911-   ). Amer. physicist.
Curr. Biog. '50 p300-301 (por.300)

Kesselring, Albert (1887-   ). Ger. aero. pioneer.
Curr. Biog. '42 p455-456 (por.455)

Kessler, Henry H. (1896-   ). Amer. physician.
Curr. Biog. '57 p296-297 (por.297)

Ketelaer, Vincent (fl.1669). Dutch physician.
Major—History (1) p563

Ketham, Johannes de (fl.1480). Ger. physician.
Major—History (1) p463-464

Kettering, Charles Franklin (1876-1958). Amer. engineer, inventor.
Curr. Biog. '40 p453-454 (por.453)   N.A.S.—Biog. (34) p106-116
  '51 p330-332 (por.330)   (por.106)
*Hylander—Invent. p202-203   *Shumway—Famous p223-232
*Montgomery—Invent. p217-222   (por.221)
    *Yost—Science p191-206

Keulen.   See Ceulen, Ludolph van

Key, Ben Witt (1883-1940). Amer. physician, surgeon.
Curr. Biog. '40 p454

Key, Charles Aston (1793-1849). Eng. surgeon.
Leonardo—Lives p235-236

Key (or Keyes), **John.   See Caius, John**

Keyes, Edward Lawrence (1843-1924). Amer. surgeon.
Leonardo—Lives p236-238

Keyes, Regina Flood (1870-194?). Amer. surgeon.
Lovejoy—Women Phys. p69-70

Keyhoe, Donald Edward (1897-   ). Amer. aero. pioneer.
Curr. Biog. '56 p338-339 (por.338)

Keys, David A. (1890-   ). Can. physicist.
    Curr. Biog. '58 p224-225 (por.224)

Kharasch, Morris Selig (1895-1957). Rus.-Amer. chemist.
    N.A.S.—Biog. p123-132 (por.123)

Khatib.   See **Ibn al Khatīb**

Khayyám, Omar.   See **Omar Khayyám**

Khunrath.   See **Kunrath, Heinrich**

Kidd, John (1775-1851). Eng. chemist, physician.
    Chambers—Dict. col.255
    Gunther—Early XI p220-221
       (por.221)

Kidder, George Wallace, Jr. (1902-   ). Amer. biologist, biochemist.
    Curr. Biog. '49 p322-324 (por. 323)

Kieldahl, Johan (1849-1900). Dan. chemist.
    Smith—Torch. p136 (por.136)

Kikuchi, Dairoku (1855-1917). Japan. mathematician, seismologist.
    Davison—Founders p203-204

Killian, James Rhyne, Jr. (1904-   ). Amer. engineer.
    Curr. Biog. '49 p324-325 (por.324)
       '59 p229-231 (por.230)

Kimball, James Henry (1862-1943). Amer. meteorologist, aero. pioneer.
    Curr. Biog. '44 p340
    Heinmuller—Man's p327 (por.327)

Kimball, Wilbur R. (1863-1940). Amer. inventor, engineer, aero. pioneer.
    Curr. Biog. '40 p457

Kimble, George Herbert Tinley (1908-   ). Eng. geographer, meteorologist.
    Curr. Biog. '52 p307-309 (por.308)

Kindelberger, James Howard (1895-   ). Amer. aero. pioneer, engineer.
    Curr. Biog. '51 p342-343 (por.342)

Kindle, Edward Martin (1869-1940). Amer. geologist, paleontologist.
    G.S.A.—Proc. '40 p209-216 (por.209)

King, Albert Freeman Africanus (1841-1914). Eng. physician.
Major—History (2) p903-904

King, Clarence (1842-1901). Amer. geologist.
Fenton—Giants p235-249 (por.254)   N.A.S.—Biog. (6) p25-54 (por.25)
Merrill—First p537-540 (por.538)

King, Franklin Hiram (1848-1911). Amer. agric. chemist, geologist,
physicist.
*Ivins—Fifty p263-267 (por.262)

King, Harold (1887-1956). Brit. chemist.
R.S.L.—Biog. (2) p157-166 (por.157)

King, Leonard William (1869-1919). Eng. archaeologist.
Hammerton p851

King, Louis Vessot (1886-1956). Can. inventor, math. physicist.
R.S.L.—Biog. (3) p101-107 (por.101)

King, Samuel Archer (1828-1914). Amer. aero. pioneer.
Heinmuller—Man's p245 (por.245)
Milbank—First p142-146 (por.150)

Kingsford-Smith, Sir Charles Edward (1899-1935). Austral. aero. pioneer.
*Fraser—Heroes p547-549,567-571,
697-700
Heinmuller—Man's p329 (por.329)

Kingzett, Charles Thomas (1852-1935). Eng. chemist.
A.A.A.S.—Proc. (81) p67-68

Kinnersley, Ebenezer (1711-1778). Amer. physicist.
Bell—Early p62

Kinsey, Alfred Charles (1894-   ). Amer. zoologist, biologist.
Curr. Biog. '54 p379-381 (por.380)
'56 p340

Kipping, Frederic Stanley (1863-1949). Eng. chemist.
Chambers—Dict. col.255

Kipping, Sir Norman Victor (1901-   ). Eng. elec. engineer.
Curr. Biog. '49 p329-330 (por.330)

Kirby, William (1759-1850). Eng. entomologist.
Essig—Hist. p670-672 (por.671)
Hammerton p854

Kirch, Maria (1670-1720). Ger. astronomer.
Mozans—Woman p173-174

Kircher, Athanasius (1601-1680). Ger. mathematician, inventor.
Bodenheimer—Hist. p273-274
Bulloch—Hist. p375
Chambers—Dict. col.255-256
Gordon—Medieval p565 (por.243)
Gordon—Romance p221,223-224
(por.221)
Major—History (1) p529-531
(por.530)
Oliver—Stalkers p94
Osborn—Greeks p163
Walsh—Catholic (2d) p207)

Kirchhoff, Gustav Robert (1824-1887). Ger. physicist.
Armitage—Cent. p22-24 (por.48)
Chambers—Dict. col.256
Hammerton p854 (por.854)
Lenard—Great p324-338 (por.324)
MacPherson—Makers p162-164
Magie—Source p354
Shapley—Astron. p279
Smith—Torch. p135 (por.135)
Van Wagenen—Beacon p336-337
Weeks—Discovery p367-373
(por.367,370)
Williams—Great p340-343 (por.341)
Woodruff—Devel. p65,280
Year—Pic. p120 (por.120)

Kirk, Charles Townsend (1876-1945). Amer. geologist.
G.S.A.—Proc. '45 p249-250 (por.249)

Kirk, Edwin (1884-1955). Amer. geologist.
G.S.A.—Proc. '56 p141-144 (por.141)

Kirk, Norman Thomas (1888-1960). Amer. physician, surgeon.
Curr. Biog. '44 p353-355 (por.353)
'60 p217

Kirkaldy, George Willis (1873-1910). Brit. entomologist.
Osborn—Fragments p233 (por.376)

Kirkes, William Senhouse (1823-1864). Eng. physician.
Major—History (2) p887-888

Kirkland, Archie Howard (1873-1931). Amer. entomologist.
Osborn—Fragments p199 (por.359)

Kirkman, Thomas Penyngton (1806-1895). Eng. mathematician.
Cajori—Hist. p323
MacFarlane—Lectures p122-133
(por., front.)

Kirkwood, Daniel (1814-1895). Amer. astronomer.
Hammerton p854
Shapley—Astron. p305

Kirsch, August (1817-1894). Pol. physician.
Major—History (2) p884

Kirtland, Jared Potter (1793-1877). Amer. geologist, zoologist, physician.
N.A.S.—Biog. (2) p127-138

Kirwan, Richard (1733-1812). Irish chemist.
Chambers—Dict. col.256
Hammerton p854
Partington—Short p178
Weeks—Discovery p299 (por.299)

Kisevalter, George (1883-1941). Rus.-Amer. aero. pioneer, engineer.
Curr. Biog. '41 p471

Kistiakowsky, George Blogden (1900-   ). Amer. chemist.
Curr. Biog. Nov. '60 p219-220
(por.219)

Kitaibel, Paul (1757-1817). Hung. chemist, botanist.
Chambers—Dict. col.256-257
Weeks—Discovery p159,172-181
(por.159)

Kitasato, Shibasaburo (or Kitazato) (1852-1931). Japan. bacteriologist.
Bulloch—Hist. p375
Chambers—Dict. col.257
Grainger—Guide p155-156
Hammerton p854
Major—History (2) p1037-1038

Kitson, Harry Dexter (1886-1959). Amer. psychologist.
Curr. Biog. '51 p348-350 (por.349)
'59 p231

Kitt, Theodore (1858-1941). Ger. pathologist.
Bulloch—Hist. p376

Kittoku.   See **Isomura Kittoku**

Kjeldahl, Johan Gustav Christoffer Thorsager (1849-1900). Dan. chemist.
A.A.A.S.—Proc. (77) p47-48
Chambers—Dict. col.257
Copen.—Prom. p169-172

Klaproth, Martin Heinrich (1743-1817). Ger. chemist.
Chambers—Dict. col.257
Hammerton p856
Lenard—Great p180-183 (por.177)
Partington—Short p178
Smith—Torch. p137 (por.137)
Weeks—Discovery p130-131, 169-181, 320 (por.131, 320)

Klaus, Karl Karlovich (or Claus) (1796-1864). Rus. chemist.
Chambers—Dict. col.257-258
Weeks—Discovery p260-265 (por.260)

Klebs, Edwin (Theodore Albrecht) (1834-1913). Ger.-Amer. pathologist, bacteriologist.
Bulloch—Hist. p376
Castiglioni—Hist. p1113 (por.815)
Hammerton p856
Law—Civiliz. p335
Major—History (2) p843-844 (por.843)

Klee, Waldemar G. (1853-1891). Dan.-Amer. entomologist.
Essig—Hist. p672-673

Klein, Christian Felix (1849-1925). Ger. mathematician.
A.A.A.S.—Proc. (77) p41-42

Klein, Emanuel (1844-1925). Yugoslav. bacteriologist.
Bulloch—Hist. p376

Klein, Felix (1849-1925). Ger. mathematician.
Cajori—Hist. p356

Kleist, E. G. von (c.1745). Pomer. inventor.
Walsh—Catholic (2d) p170-172

Kleitman, Nathaniel (1895-   ). Rus.-Amer. physician.
Curr. Biog. '57 p306-308 (por.307)

Klemin, Alexander (1888-   ). Eng. aero. pioneer.
Holland—Arch. p79-93

Klenck, Hermann (1813-1881). Ger. physicist.
Bulloch—Hist. p376-377

Kligler, Israel Jacob (1889-1944). Rus. bacteriologist.
Kagan—Modern p177 (por.177)

Klingenstierna, Samuel (1689-1785). Swed. mathematician.
Lindroth—Swedish p59-65

Klipstein, August (1848-1926). Ger.-Amer. chemist.
Haynes—Chem. (1) p165-181
(por.168)

Klipstein, Ernest C. (1851-1922). Amer. chemist.
Haynes—Chem. (1) p182-196
(por.184)

Klopsteg, Paul E. (1889-   ). Amer. engineer, physicist.
Curr. Biog. '59 p231-233 (por.232)

Kluckhohn, Clyde (Kay Maben) (1905-1960). Amer. anthropologist.
Curr. Biog. '51 p350-352 (por. 352)   Newman—What p316-318
Oct. '60

Klumpp, Theodore George (1903-   ). Amer. physician.
Curr. Biog. '58 p232-234 (por.233)

Kluyver, Albert Jan (1888-1956). Dutch biochemist.
R.S.L.—Biog. (3) p109-122 (por.109)

Knab, Frederick (1865-1918). Ger. entomologist.
Osborn—Fragments p204

Knapp, Ludwig Friedrich (1814-1904). Ger. chemist.
Smith—Torch. p138 (por.138)

Knapp, Seaman Asahel (1833-1911). Amer. agriculturist.
*Ivins—Fifty p221-228 (por.220)

Knapp, Vernon (1899-1954). Amer. geologist.
G.S.A.—Proc. '55 p187

Knaus, Warren (b.1858). Amer. entomologist.
Osborn—Fragments p174-175
(por.339)

Knight, James H. (or Jack) (1893-   ). Amer. aero. pioneer.
Heinmuller—Man's p311 (por.311)

Knight, Thomas Andrew (1759-1838). Eng. agriculturist.
Bodenheimer—Hist. p346   Gilmour—British p28
Chambers—Dict. col.258

Knopf, Sigard Adolphus (1857-1940). Amer. physician.
Curr. Biog. '40 p461 (por. 461)

Knorr, Ludwig (1859-1921). Ger. chemist.
Partington—Short p320

Knox, Robert (1791-1862). Scot. anatomist.
Hammerton p858

Knudsen, Vern Oliver (1893-   ). Amer. physicist.
Progress—Science '40 p214-215
(por.215)

Knutsford, Sir Henry Holland, Viscount (1788-1873). Eng. physician.
Hammerton p858-859 (por.858)

Köbel, Jakob (1470-1533). Ger. mathematician.
Smith—Hist. (1) p336-337

Koch, Robert (1843-1910). Ger. bacteriologist, physician.
*Book—Pop. Sci. (12) p3906
(por.3906)
Bulloch—Hist. p377 (por.72)
Castiglioni—Hist. p813-816 (por.815)
Chambers—Dict. col.258
*Cottler—Heroes p287-295
*Darrow—Masters p336
*De Kruif—Microbe p105-144
*Elwell—Sci. p59-63
Farmer—Doctors' p174-176
Fitzhugh—Concise p379-381
*Fox—Great p204-225 (por.204)
Grainger—Guide p156-158
Hammerton p859 (por.859)
Lambert—Medical p259-263 (por.262)
Lambert—Minute p259-263 (por.272)
Law—Civiliz. p331-334
Locy—Biology p300-302 (por.301)
Major—History (2) p836-842
(por.837)
*Montgomery—Story p113-117
*Nisenson—Illus. p95 (por.95)
Oliver—Stalkers p189-195 (por.190)
People p232
Progress—Science '41 p213-214
Robinson—Path. p713-746
(por.718,719,734,735)
Rowntree—Amid p44-46 (por.45)
Schwartz—Moments (2) p726-728
Science Miles p201-204 (por.201)
Sigerist—Great p366-372 (por.268)
*Snyder—Biology p194-199 (por.197)
Stevenson—Nobel p25-31 (por.150)
Thorwald—Century p279-289,
291-293 (por.368)
Van Wagenen—Beacon p390-392
Walker—Pioneers p178-192 (por.178)
Woodruff—Devel. p280
Year—Pic. p131 (por.131)

Kocher, (Emil) Theodor (1841-1917). Swiss physician, surgeon.
Castiglioni—Hist. p1013-1014
(por.1014)
Chambers—Dict. col.258-259
Hammerton p859
Leonardo—Lives (Supp.1) p489
Major—History (2) p970-971,1038
(por.970)
Stevenson—Nobel p57-61 (por.150)

Koebele, Albert (1852-1924). Ger. entomologist.
Essig—Hist. p673-680 (por.675)
Osborn—Fragments p191-192
(por.351)

Koehl, Hermann (1888-1938). Ger. aero. pioneer.
Heinmuller—Man's p103-104,328
(por.111,328)

Koelliker.   See **Kölliker, Rudolf Albert von**

Koenig, Friedrich.   See **König, Friedrich**

Koenig, (or Konig), **Karl Rudolph** (1832-1901). Ger. physicist.
Chambers—Dict. col.259

Koenigs, Wilhelm (1851-1906). Ger. chemist.
A.A.A.S.—Proc. (79) p23-24

Koffka, Kurt (1886-1941). Ger.-Amer. psychologist.
Chambers—Dict. col.259   Progress—Science '41 p214
Curr. Biog. '42 p469

Kofoid, Charles Atwood (1865-1947). Amer. zoologist, geologist.
N.A.S.—Biog. (26) p121-133 (por.121)

Köhl, Hermann (1881-1938). Ger. aero. pioneer.
Hammerton p859

Kohler, Elmer Peter (1865-1938). Amer. chemist.
N.A.S.—Biog. (27) p265-284 (por.265)

Köhler, Wolfgang (1887-   ). Ger.-Amer. psychologist.
Chambers—Dict. col.259

Kohlrausch, Friedrich Wilhelm Georg (1840-1910). Ger. physicist.
Chambers—Dict. col.260
Hammerton p859

Ko Hung (4th cent.). Chin. chemist.
Partington—Short p34

Kolbe, (Adolph Wilhelm) Hermann (1818-1884). Ger. chemist.
Chambers—Dict. col.260   Partington—Short p274-280,294
Findlay—Hundred p328   Smith—Torch. p139 (por.139)

Koldewey, Robert (1855-1925). Ger. archaeologist.
Ceram—Gods p279-296

Kolle, Wilhelm (1868-1935). Ger. bacteriologist.
Bulloch—Hist. p377

Koller, Carl (or Karl) (1857-1944). Aust. ophthalmologist, surgeon.
Kagan—Modern p146 (por.146)   Robinson—Victory p246-256
Major—History (2) p1038   (por.236)

Kölliker, Rudolph Albert von (or Koelliker, Albrecht) (1817-1905). Swiss anatomist, biologist, zoologist, histologist, physiologist.

*Book—Pop. Sci. (12) p3907
Chambers—Dict. col.260
Hammerton p859

Locy p171-172,224 (por.173)
Major—History (2) p883-884

Kolmer, John A. (1886-   ). Amer. pathologist, physician.

Progress—Science '40 p215-216 (por.215)

Kolreuter, Joseph Gottlieb (1733-1806). Ger. botanist.

*Snyder—Biology p165-169 (por.167)

Kolster, Frederick Augustus (1883-   ). Swiss engineer.

Radio's 100 p212-216 (por.140)

König, Friedrich (or Koenig) (1774-1833). Ger. inventor.

Hammerton p859
*Larsen—Prentice p8-11
*Larsen—Scrap. p52-55 (por.64)

*Larsen—Shaped p184-188 (por.145)
Meyer—World p46-48

Koplik, Henry (1858-1927). Amer. physician.

Chambers—Dict. col.261

Kopp, Hermann Franz Moritz (1817-1892). Ger. phys. chemist.

Chambers—Dict. col.261
Findlay—Hundred p329

Partington—Short p338-339
Smith—Torch. p140 (por.140)

Köppen, Wladimir P. (1846-1940). Rus. meteorologist.

Chambers—Dict. col.261

Korányi, Alexander (1866-1944). Hung. physician.

Major—History (2) p1038

Korn, Arthur (1870-1945). Ger. physicist.

Radio's 100 p155-156 (por.140)

Körner, Wilhelm (1839-1925). Ger.-It. chemist.

Partington—Short p292-293,317

Kosmas.   See Cosmas, Saint

Kossel, Albrecht (1853-1927). Ger. physiol. chemist.

Chambers—Dict. col.261
Hammerton p860

Stevenson—Nobel p62-67 (por.150)

Kossel, (Alexander August Richard) Hermann (1864-1925). Ger. botanist, hygienist.
Bulloch—Hist. p377-378

Kossel, Walter (1888-   ). Ger. physicist.
Chambers—Dict. col.261-262

Kosta ibn Luka (864-923). Arab. physician.
Gordon—Medicine p148

Kotinsky, Jacob (1873-1928). Rus.-Amer. entomologist.
Osborn—Fragments p235

Koto, Bunjiro (or Bundjiro) (1856-1935). Japan, geologist, seismologist.
Davison—Founders p204-205
G.S.A.—Proc. '35 p263-265 (por.263)

Kóu Shóu-King (1231-1316). Chin. astronomer, mathematician.
Smith—Hist. 1 p272

Kovalevski, Alexander Onufrievich (1840-1901). Rus. geologist, embryologist.
Hammerton p861   Van Wagenen—Beacon p385-386
Locy—Biology p224 (por.225)

Kovalevski, Sonya (or Kovalevskaya, Sofya Vasilievna) (1850-1891). Rus. mathematician.
Bell—Men p423-429 (por.,front.)   Hammerton p861
Cajori—Hist. p456   Mozans—Woman p161-166
Coolidge—Six p29-31

Kovarik, Alois Francis (1880-   ). Amer. physicist.
Chambers—Dict. col.262

Kowalewsky.   See **Kovalevski**

Kraepelin.   See **Krapelin, Emil**

Krafft, Johann Daniel (c.1677). Ger. chemist.
Weeks—Discovery p41-49

Krafft-Ebing, Richard von (1840-1902). Ger. physician.
Hammerton p861
Major—History (2) p1038-1039

Krafftheim, Johann Crato von (1519-1585). Ger. physician.
Major—History (1) p472

Krapelin, Emil (or Kraepelin) (1856-1926). Ger. psychiatrist.
Chambers—Dict. col.262
Major—History (2) 1038

Kraske, Paul (1851-1930). Ger. surgeon.
Leonardo—Lives p238

Kraus, Charles August (b.1875). Amer. chemist.
Browne—Hist. p489 (por.163)
Chambers—Dict. col.262

Kraus, Friedrich (1858-1936). Bohem. physician.
Major—History (2) p1039

Kraus, Paul S. (d.1956). Amer. geologist.
G.S.A.—Proc. '56 p183

Kraus, Rudolf (1868-1932). Aust. bacteriologist, immunologist.
Bulloch—Hist. p378

Krause, Allen Kramer (1881-1941). Amer. physician.
Curr. Biog. '41 p476   Progress—Science '41 p214 (por.214)
Major—History (2) p1039

Krause, Fedor (1857-1927). Ger. surgeon.
Leonardo—Lives p238-239

Krebs, Hans Adolf (1900-   ). Ger.-Brit. physiologist, biochemist.
Chambers—Dict. Supp.
Curr. Biog. '54 p384-385 (por.384)

Krekeler, Heinz Ludwig (1906-   ). Amer. chemist.
Curr. Biog. '51 p358-360 (por.359)

Kremer.   See **Mercator, Gerardus**

Kress, Wilhelm (1846-1913). Aust. engineer, aero. pioneer.
Heinmuller—Man's p257 (por.257)

Krick, Irving Parkhurst (1906-   ). Amer. meteorologist.
Curr. Biog. '50 p312-314 (por.313)

Krieger, Philip (1900-1940). Amer. geologist.
G.S.A.—Proc. '43 p177-180 (por.177)

Krimer, Wenzel (1795-1834). Morav. physician.
Rosen—Four p66-68

Kroeber, Alfred Louis (1876-1960). Amer. archaeologist.
Curr. Biog. '58 p236-238 (por.237)
'60 p226

Krogh, (Schack) August Steenberg (1874-1949). Dan. physiologist.
Chambers—Dict. col.262-263   Rowntree—Amid p171-174 (por.172)
Hammerton p862   Stevenson—Nobel p96-100 (por.150)
Major-History (2) p1039

Kronecker, (Karl) Hugo (1839-1914). Ger. physiologist.
Kagan—Modern p185 (por.185)
Major—History (2) p901-902

Kronecker, Leopold (1823-1891). Ger. mathematician.
Bell—Men p466-483 (por.,front.)   Miller—Hist. p262-263
Cajori—Hist. p362-363

Kronfeld, Robert (1904-   ). Aust. aero. pioneer.
Hammerton p862

Kruesi, John Heinrich (1843-1899). Swiss inventor, engineer.
Swiss—Prom. p244-250 (por.244)

Krupp, Alfred (1812-1887). Eng. engineer.
Goddard—Eminent p234-239
(por.234)
Matschoss—Great p216-244 (por.217)

Krupp (von Bohlen und Halbach) Alfred Felix Alwyn (1907-   ). Ger. engineer.
Curr. Biog. '55 p341-343 (por.341)

Kruse, Walther (1864-1943). Ger. bacteriologist, hygienist.
Bulloch—Hist. p378

Krutch, Joseph Wood (1893-   ). Amer. naturalist.
Curr. Biog. '59 p236-238 (por.237)

Kuhlmann, Frederick (1876-1941). Amer. psychiatrist.
Curr. Biog. '41 p477

Kuhn, Adam (1741-1817). Amer. physician.
Major—History (2) p730 (por.730)

Kuhn, Richard (1900-   ). Aust. chemist.
Chambers—Dict. col.263
Farber—Nobel p160-161

Kuhne, Wilhelm (or Willy) (1837-1900). Ger. physiologist.
Chambers—Dict. col.263-264
Major—Hist (2) p899-900

Kuiper, Gerard P. (1905-   ). Dutch-Amer. astronomer.
Curr. Biog. '59 p240-241 (por.241)
Progress—Science '40 p216 (por.216)

Kumm, (Herman) Henry William (1901-   ). Ger.-Amer. physician.
Curr. Biog. '55 p343-345 (por.344)

Kummel, Henry Barnard (1867-1945). Amer. geologist.
G.S.A.—Proc. '45 p253-256 (por.253)

Kummer, Ernst Eduard (1810-1893). Ger. mathematician.
Ball—Short p458-459
Bell—Men p510-516 (por., front.)
Cajori—Hist. p442-443
Smith Hist. 1 p507-508

Kunckel, Johann von Löwenstern (1630-1702/1703). Ger. chemist.
Holmyard—Chem. p74-77
Partington—Short p61-62 (por.61)
Smith—Torch. p141 (por.141)
Weeks—Discovery p29,34-35,41-50
   (por.29)

Kundt, August Eduard Eberhard (1839-1894). Ger. physicist.
Chambers—Dict. col.264
Hammerton p863
Magie—Source p382

Kunrath, Heinrich (or Khunrath, Conrad) (1560?-1605). Ger. physician, chemist.
Chymia (3) p243 (por., front.)

Küpper, Klaus (1930-1957). Aust. micropaleontologist.
G.S.A.—Proc. '57 p181

Kurchatov, Igor Vasilievich (1903-1960). Rus. physicist.
Curr. Biog. '57 p312-313 (por.313)
   Apr. '60 p226

Kusch, Polykarp (1911-   ). Amer. physicist.
Chambers—Dict. Supp.
Curr. Biog. '56 p348-350 (por.349)

Kussmaul, Adolf (1822-1902). Ger. physician.
Major—History (2) p887
Rosen—Four p11-12,84-87,185,186

Kuter, Laurence Sherman (1905-   ). Amer. aero. pioneer.
Curr. Biog. '48 p360-362 (por.361)

Kützing, Friedrich Traugott (1807-1893). Ger. bacteriologist.
Bulloch—Hist. p376

L

La Boë.   See **Sylvius, Franciscus**

Lacaille, Nicolas Louis de (1713-1762). Fr. astronomer.
Chambers—Dict. col.265   Vaucouleurs—Dict. p75-77
Hammerton p865

Lacaze-Duthiers, (Félix) Henri de (1821-1901). Fr. anatomist, biologist, naturalist.
Locy—Biology p158 (por.159)
Woodruff—Devel. p280

Lacépède, Bernard Germaine Étienne de la Ville, Comte de (1756-1825). Fr. naturalist.
Hammerton p865

La Chapelle, Marie Louise Dugès (1769-1822). Fr. physician.
Mozans—Woman p293-294

La Condamine, Charles Marie de (1701-1774). Fr. math. geographer.
Chambers—Dict. col.265
Von Hagen—Green p124-125

Lacroix, François Antoine Alfred (1863-1944). Fr. mineralogist, geologist.
G.S.A.—Proc. '48 p183-185 (por.183)
Woodruff—Devel. p280

Lacroix, Sylvestre François (1765-1843). Fr. mathematician.
Smith—Hist. 1 p492

Ladenburg, Albert (1842-1911). Ger. chemist.
Partington—Short p317-318
Smith—Torch. p142 (por.142)

Laënnec, René Théophile Hyacinthe (1781-1826). Fr. physician.
*Book—Pop. Sci. (12) p3907-3908
Castiglioni—Hist. p700-702 (por.703)
Chambers—Dict. col.265
*Elwell—Sci. p33-35
Farmer—Dictors' p95
*Fox—Great p98-120 (por.98)
Gordon—Romance p493 (por.493)
Hammerton p866
Kagan—Modern p8 (por.8)
Lambert—Medical p214-217 (por.220)
Lambert—Minute p214-217 (por.241)
Major—History (2) p660-664 (por.660)
*Montgomery—Story p30-32
Moulton—Auto. p299-300
Oliver—Stalkers p152-154 (por.153)
Robinson—Path. p341-359 (por.350)
Rowntree—Amid p42,44 (por.42)
*Science Miles p142-144 (por.142)
*Shippen—Men p101-103
Sigerist—Great p283-287 (por.288)
Truax—Doctors p38-45
Walsh—Makers p133-164

Lafar, Franz (b.1865). Aust. bacteriologist.
Bulloch—Hist. p378

La Farge, Oliver Hazard Perry (or Oliver II) (1901-   ). Amer. archaeologist, anthropologist.
Progress—Science '40 p216-217 (por. 216)

Lagrange, Joseph Louis, Comte (1736-1813). Fr. astronomer, mathematician.
Abetti—History p156-157
Ball—Short p401-412
Bell—Men p153-171 (por.,front.)
Cajori—Hist. p250-259
Chambers—Dict. col.265-266
Hammerton p867
Hooper—Makers p353-360
Lodge—Pioneers p254-272
MacPherson—Makers p87-88
Magie—Source p61
*Miller—Hist. p239-241
Sedgwick—Short p329-330
Shapley—Astron. p131
Smith—Hist. 1 p482-486
Smith—Portraits (1) IX, unp.(por.)
Turnbull—Great p103-107
Van Wagenen—Beacon p173-174
Vaucouleurs—Disc. p83-84
Williams—Great p269 (por.270)
Williams—Story p15 (por.14)
Woodruff—Devel. p23-25,280 (por.22)

Laguerre, Edmond (1834-1886). Fr. mathematician.
Woodruff—Devel. p280

Laguna, Andres A. (1499-1563). Sp. physician.
Gordon—Medieval p761 (por.178)

Lahey, Frank Howard (1880-1953). Amer. physician, surgeon.
Curr. Biog. '41 p485-486 (por.485)
'53 p337

La Hire (or La Hyre), **Philippe de** (1640-1718). Fr. mathematician. astronomer.
Cajori—Hist. p166-167
Smith—Hist. 1 p386

Lahm, Frank Purdy (b.1877). Amer. aero. pioneer.
Heinmuller—Man's p261 (por.261)

Laidlaw, Sir Patrick Playfair (1881-1940). Scot. physician.
Curr. Biog. '40 p476

Laird, Donald Anderson (1897-   ). Amer. psychologist.
Curr. Biog. '46 p318-320 (por.319)

Lake, Simon (1866-1945). Amer. engineer, inventor.
Curr. Biog. '45 p332   *Darrow—Thinkers p320-322 (por.321)
*Darrow—Masters p313-314 (por.289)   *Hylander—Invent. p201-202

Lalande, Joseph Jérôme Lefrançais de (1732-1807). Fr. astronomer.
Chambers—Dict. col.266   Vaucouleurs—Disc. p77
Hammerton p868   Woodruff—Devel. p281

La Loubère, Antoine de (1600-1664). Fr. mathematician.
Smith—Hist. 1 p385

Lamarck, Jean Baptiste Pierre Antoine de Monet, Chevalier de (1774-1829). Fr. naturalist, paleontologist.
Adams—Birth p268   Osborn—Greeks p226-255
Bodenheimer—Hist. p351   Peattie—Green p141-149,151-164,
*Book—Pop. Sci. (12) p3908-3909   171-185 (por.150,167)
Chambers—Dict. col.266-267   Schwartz—Moments (2) p647-649
*Darrow—Masters p82-88 (por.64)   *Shippen—Micro. p107-117
Ginzburg—Adven. p290-299   *Snyder—Biology p106-113 (por.107)
Gordon—Medicine p33 (por.33)   *Stevens—Science p75-80 (por.74)
Gumpert—Trail p161-194   Thomson—Great p45-53
Hammerton p868-869 (por.868)   Van Wagenen—Beacon p182-184
Locy—Biology p131-132,328-330,   Williams—Story p293-298 (por.294)
  375-386 (por.379)   Wilson—Human p234-248
Major—History (2) p638   Woodruff—Devel. p254-255,281
Moulton—Auto. p246-247   (por.256)
Murray—Science p148-153   Year—Pic. p128 (por.128)

Lamb, Arthur Becket (1880-1952). Amer. chemist.
Browne—Hist. p487 (por.145)
N.A.S.—Biog. (29) p201-229
  (por.201)

Lamb, George (1870-1911). Brit. bacteriologist.
Bulloch—Hist. p378

Lamb, Sir Horace (1849-1934). Eng. mathematician, physicist.
Hammerton p870

Lamb, Willis Eugene (1913-   ). Amer. physicist.
A.A.A.S.—Proc. (82) p294-297   Curr. Biog. '56 p357-358 (por.357)
Chambers—Dict. Supp.

Lambert, Johann Heinrich (1728-1777). Ger. mathematician, physicist,
    astronomer.
Ball—Short p400-401   Shapley—Astron. p126
Cajori—Hist. p245-247   Williams—Great p242-244
Chambers—Dict. col.267

Lambert, Sylvester Maxwell (1882-1947). Amer. physician.
Curr. Biog. '41 p486-487 (por.486)
    '47 p372

Lambert, William Vincent (1897-   ). Amer. geneticist.
Curr. Biog. '55 p345-347 (por.345)

Lambie, Jack (1909-   ). Amer. aero. pioneer.
Heinmuller—Man's p204-213,351
    (por.212,351)

Lamé, Gabriel (1795-1870). Fr. mathematician, engineer.
Cajori—Hist. p467-468
Chambers—Dict. col.267-268

La Mettrie, Julien Offrey de (1709-1751). Fr. biologist, physician.
Bodenheimer—Hist. p298

Lamme, Benjamin Garver (1864-1924). Amer. inventor, engineer.
*Hodgins—Behemoth p252-256

Lamont, Johann von (or John) (1805-1879). Scot.-Ger. astronomer,
    physicist.
Armitage—Cent. p50-51
Hammerton p871

La Mountain, John (1830-1878). Amer. aero. pioneer.
Milbank—First p62-64

Lamy, Claude Auguste (1820-1878). Fr. chemist.
Chambers—Dict. col.268
Weeks—Discovery p376-378 (por.378)

Lana, Francesco (1631-1687). It. aero. pioneer.
Burge—Ency. p634

Lanchester, Frederick William (1868-1946). Eng. engineer, aero. pioneer.
Burge—Ency. p634   Daniel—Pioneer p15-17 (por.14)
Daniel Gugg. p19-25 (por.18)   Hammerton p872

Lanciani, Rudolfo Amadeo (1846-1929). It. archaeologist.
Hammerton p872

Lancisi, Giovanni Maria (1654-1720). It. physician.
Castiglioni—Hist. p562-563 (por.563)
Major—History (1) p539-542
   (por.541)

Land, Edwin Herbert (1909-   ). Amer. inventor, physicist.
Chambers—Dict. col.268   *Montgomery—Invent. p188-190
Curr. Biog. '53 p339-341 (por.340)

Landen, John (1719-1790). Eng. mathematician.
Cajori—Hist. p247-248   Smith—Hist. 1 p457
Hammerton p873

Landes, Henry (1867-1936). Amer. mineralogist, geologist.
G.S.A.—Proc. '36 p207-210 (por.207)

Landis, Walter Savage (1881-   ). Amer. chemist.
Chambers—Dict. col.268

Landolt, Hans Heinrich (1831-1910). Swiss-Ger. chemist.
Findlay—Hundred p329   Smith—Torch. p143 (por.143)
Partington—Short p316

Landsteiner, Karl (1868-1943). Aust.-Amer. pathologist, biologist,
   physician.
Bulloch—Hist. p378-379   Major—History (2) p1039-1040
Castiglioni—Hist. p976-977 (por.977)   (por.986)
Chambers—Dict. col.268-269   *Montgomery—Story p185-187
Curr. Biog. '43 p424   Rowntree—Amid p374-376 (por.362)
*Eberle—Modern p90-91,110-115   *Snyder—Biology p281-282 (por.280)
Grainger—Guide p158   *Sterne—Blood p83-127
Kagan—Modern p166 (por.166)   Stevenson—Nobel p143-147 (por.150)
                                         *Sterling—Polio p35-36 (por.35)

Lane, Jonathan Homer (1819-1880). Amer. physicist.
N.A.S.—Biog. (3) p253-262

Lane, Levi Cooper (1828-1902). Amer. surgeon.
Leonardo—Lives p239-241

Lane, Sir (William) Arbuthnot (1856-1943). Eng. surgeon.
Chambers—Dict. col.269
Curr. Biog. '43 p424
Hammerton p874 (por.874)
Leonardo—Lives p241-242

Lane-Poole, Stanley (1854-1931). Eng. archaeologist.
Hammerton p874

Lanfranchi, Guido (or Lanfranc of Milan) (c.1250-1315). It. physician. ..
Castiglioni—Hist. p337 (por.337)
Gordon—Medieval p350-351
(por.146)
Leonardo—Lives p242-245
Major—Hist. (1) p316-318 (por.317)

Lange, Carl Georg (1834-1900). Dan. psychologist, physician.
Chambers—Dict. col.269
Copen.—Prom. p152-155

Lange, Johannes (1485-1565). Ger. physician.
Gordon—Medieval p614-615
Major—History (1) p432,465
(por.433)

Langen, Eugen (1833-1895). Ger. engineer.
Matschoss—Great p283-292 (por.281)

Langenbeck, Bernhard Rudolph Konrad (1810-1887). Ger. surgeon.
Leonardo—Lives p245-246

Langenbeck, Conrad Johann Martin (1776-1851). Ger. surgeon.
Leonardo—Lives p246-247

Langevin, Paul (1872-1946). Fr. physicist.
Chambers—Dict. col.269

Langley, John Newport (1852-1925). Eng. physiologist.
Chambers—Dict. col.269-270

Langley, Samuel Pierpont (1834-1906). Amer. physicist, astronomer.
Armitage—Cent. p81-84 (por.80)
*Bishop—Kite p153-160
*Book—Pop. Sci. (9) p3053-3054
Burge—Ency. p634-635
(*Continued*)

Langley, Samuel Pierpont—*Continued*
Chambers—Dict. col.270
*Cohen—Men p106-113
*Darrow—Builders p90-92
*Darrow—Masters p336-337
Hammerton p875
Heinmuller—Man's p254 (por.254)
*Hylander—Invent. p203-204
Jaffe—Men p331-355
Maitland—Knights p31-34 (por.38)
Moulton—Auto. p469-470
N.A.S.—Biog. (7) p245-258 (por.245)

Oehser—Sons p110-140 (por.75)
*Parkman—Conq. p325-330
Shapley—Astron. p345
*Shippen—Bridle p92-100
*Sootin—Twelve p213-230
*Tappan—Heroes p217-227
True—Smiths. p286-293 (por.288)
Van Wagenen—Beacon p367-368
Williams—Great p435-438 (por.436)
Wilson—Human p358-366
*Yost—Science p47-63

Langmuir, Arthur Comings (1872-1941). Amer. chemist.
Curr. Biog. '41 p492

Langmuir, Irving (1881-1957). Amer. chemist.
Browne—Hist. p485-486 (por.141)
Chambers—Dict. col.270-271
(por.271)
Curr. Biog. '40 p478-480 (por.479)
'50 p320-322 (por.322), '57 p317
Farber—Nobel p132-136 (por.118)
Hammerton p875-876
*Hylander—Scien. p131-138 (por.113)
Jaffe—Crucibles p313-348
*Kendall—Young p246-260 (por.256)

Killeffer—Eminent p32 (por.32)
Morris—Ency. p685-686
Partington—Short p366,380 (por.363)
Progress—Science '40 p217 (por.217)
R.S.L.—Biog. (4) p167-179 (por.167)
Radio's 100 p201-204 (por.140)
Robinson—100 p254-257 (por.254)
*Science Miles p295-297 (por.295)
Wilson—Amer. p372-279
(por.375,376)
Year—Pic. p250 (por.250)

Langsdorff, Georg Heinrich von (1774-1852). Ger. physician, naturalist.
Alden—Early p19-21

Lankester, Sir Edwin Ray (1847-1929). Eng. biologist, morphologist, embryologist.
*Book—Pop. Sci. (13) p4563-4564
(por.4564)
Bulloch—Hist. p379
Chambers—Dict. col.271

Gunther—Early XI p102-103
(por.102)
Hammerton p876
Thomson—Great p161-170

Lanston, Tolbert (1844-1913). Amer. inventor.
Chambers—Dict. col.271-272

La Pérouse, Jean François, Comte de Galaup, (1741-1788). Fr. sci. explorer, naturalist.
Alden—Early p9-12

La Peyronie, François De (1678-1747). Fr. surgeon.
Leonardo—Lives p247-249

Lapham, Increase Allen (1811-1875). Amer. naturalist, geologist.
Merrill—First p484-486 (por.485)

Laplace, Pierre Simon, Marquis de (1749-1827). Fr. mathematician, astronomer.

A.A.A.S.—Proc. (77) p41
Abetti—History p157-160
Armitage—Cent. p131-134
Ball—Great p219-232 (por.227)
Ball—Short p412-421
Bell—Men p172-182 (por., front.)
*Book—Pop.Sci. (14) p4646-4647
Cajori—Hist. p259-266
Chambers—Dict. col.272
*Darrow—Masters p63-66 (por.65)
Fitzhugh—Concise p393-394
Hammerton p877-878 (por.878)
Hooper—Makers p360-363
Lenard—Great p218-223 (por.219)
Lodge—Pioneers p254,272
MacPherson—Makers p88-93
Murray—Science p337-338
Schwartz—Moments (1) p309-310
Sci.Amer.—Lives p45-58 (por.47)
Sedgwick—Short p330-333
Shapley—Astron. p155
Smith—Hist. 1 p486-487 (por.486)
Smith—Portraits (2) VII, unp.(por.)
Van Wagenen—Beacon p198-199
Vaucouleurs—Disc. p84-85
Williams—Great p269-273 (por.268)
Wilson—Human p219-221
Woodruff—Devel. p281 (por.148)
Year—Pic. p111 (por.111)

La Porte, Arthur E. (1896-   ). Amer. aero. pioneer.

Heinmuller—Man's p355 (por.355)

Lapp, Ralph Eugene (1917-   ). Amer. physicist.

Curr. Biog. '55 p347-349 (por.347)

Lapparent, Albert Cochon de (1839-1908). Fr. geologist.

Hammerton p878

Lapworth, Arthur (1872-1941). Scot. chemist.

Findlay—British p353-367 (por.353)
Partington—Short p321

Lapworth, Charles (1842-1920). Scot. geologist.

Chambers—Dict. col.272-273

La Ramée.   See Ramus, Petrus

Larghi, Bernardino (1812-1877). It. surgeon.

Leonardo—Lives p249

Largus.   See Scribonius Largus

La Rive, Auguste Arthur de (1801-1873). Swiss physicist.

A.A.A.S.—Proc. (79) p13-14
Hammerton p493

Larmor, Sir Joseph (1857-1942). Irish mathematician.

Hammerton p878

Laroche, Raymonde, Baronne de (1886-1919). Fr. aero. pioneer.
Heinmuller—Man's p276 (por.276)

Larrey, Dominique Jean, Baron (1766-1842). Fr. surgeon.
Leonardo—Lives p249-251
Major—History (2) p645-647
   (por.646)

Lartet, Edouard (1801-1871). Fr. archaeologist.
Hammerton p879

La Sablière, Marguerite de (1636-1693). Fr. astronomer.
Mozans—Woman p171-173

Lasaulx, Arnold von (1839-1886). Ger. mineralogist, seismologist.
Davison—Founders p128-129

Lashley, Karl Spencer (1890-1958). Amer. psychologist.
Chambers—Dict. col.273   R.L.S.—Biog. (5) p107-114 (por.107)
N.A.S. (35) p163-195 (por.163)

Lasker, Mary Woodard (Mrs. Albert D.) (1900-   ). Amer. health
   worker.
Curr. Biog. '59 p245-247 (por.246)
R.S.L.—Biog. (5) p107-114 (por.107)

Lassaigne, Jean-Louis (1800-1859). Fr. chemist.
A.A.A.S.—Proc. (78) p30

Lassar, Oskar (1849-1907). Ger. physician, dermatologist.
Kagan—Modern p77 (por.77)
Major—History (2) p1040

Lassell, William (1799-1880). Eng. astronomer.
*Book—Pop. Sci. (14) p4648
Chambers—Dict. col.273

Lassone, Joseph Marie François (1717-1788). Fr. chemist, physician.
Chambers—Dict. col.273

Latham, Hubert (1883-1912). Fr. aero. pioneer.
Heinmuller—Man's p271 (por.271)

Latimer, Wendell Mitchell (1893-1955). Amer. chemist.
N.A.S.—Biog. (32) p221-229 (por.221)

Latrobe, Benjamin Henry (1764-1820). Eng.-Amer. engineer.
Morris—Ency. p686

Lattes, Cesare Mansueto Giulio (1924-   ). Brazil. physicist.
Curr. Biog. '49 p342-344 (por.343)

Lauchen.   See Rheticus, George Joachim

Laue, Max Theodor Felix von (1879-1960). Ger. physicist.
Chambers—Dict. col.273-274   Heathcote—Nobel p118-124 (por.240)
Hammerton p882   Weber—College p222 ((por.222)

Laufer, Berthold (1874-1934). Ger.-Amer. anthropologist, archaeologist.
N.A.S.—Biog. (18) p43-56 (por.43)

Laüger, Paul (1896-   ). Swiss chemist.
Curr. Biog. '45 p340-342 (por.341)

Laugier, Henri (1888-   ). Fr. physician, hygienist.
Curr. Biog. '48 p371-372 (por.371)

Laugier, Stanislas (1799-1872). Fr. surgeon.
Leonardo—Lives p251-252

Laurence, William Leonard (1888-   ). Lith. sci. writer.
Curr. Biog. '45 p342-344 (por.343)

Laurens, André du (1558-1609). Fr. physician.
Major—History (1) p477-478

Laurent, Auguste (1807-1853). Fr. chemist.
Chambers—Dict. col.274   Hammerton p883
Chymie (4) p85-114   Partington—Short p248-250,269
Findlay—Hundred p329-330   (por.249)
                                    Smith—Torch. p144 (por.144)

Laval, Carl Gustav Patrik de (1845-1913). Swed. engineer, inventor.
*Book—Pop. Sci. (4) p1421-1422   *Hodgins—Behemoth p269-273
  (por.1421)   *Ivins—Fifty p13-20 (por. 15)
Chambers—Dict. col.274

Lavater, Johann Kaspar (1741-1801). Swiss nat. philosopher.
Castiglioni—Hist. p636 (por.637)

La Vaulx, Henri, Count de (1870-1930). Fr. aero. pioneer.
Heinmuller—Man's p258 (por.258)

Laveran, Charles Louis Alphonse (1845-1922). Fr. bacteriologist, physician.

Castiglioni—Hist. p826 (por.827)
Chambers—Dict. col.275
Hammerton p884
Major—History (2) p860-862,907-908
*Men—Scien. p37-39

*Shippen—Men p178-182 (por.174)
*Snyder—Biology p207-209 (por.209)
Stevenson—Nobel p41-45 (por.150)
Walker—Pioneers p206-217 (por.206)

La Verrier.   See Leverrier, Urbain Jean Joseph

Lavoisier, Antoine Laurent (1743-1794). Fr. chemist.

*Book—Pop. Sci. (12) p4016-4017
  (por.4016)
Chalmers—Historic p266-267
Chambers—Dict. col.275-276
  (por.275)
*Cottler—Heroes p128-137
*Darrow—Masters p37-40 (por.160)
*Darrow—Thinkers p50-51
Fitzhugh—Concise p397-309
Ginzburg—Advent. p176-199
Hammerton p884 (por.884)
Hammond—Stories p14-22 (por.20)
Holmyard—Chem. p102-111 (por.91)
Holmyard—Great Chem. p65-74
Holmyard—Makers p197-213
  (por.198)
*Jaffe—Crucibles p93-113
Leonard—Crus. p263-300 (por.278)
Major—History (2) p616-618
Moulton—Auto. p228-229
Mozans—Woman p214-216
Partington—Short p122-142,152
  (por.123)

Roberts—Chem. p41-53
Schwartz—Moments (1) p485-488
*Science Miles p117 (por.117)
Sci.Amer.—Lives p97-107 (por.99)
Smith—Torch. p145,148-149 (por.145)
*Snyder—Biology p306
*Stevens—Science p61-64 (por.58)
Taylor—Illus. p100-103, 123
Thomas—Scien. p69-77 (por.67)
Thomson—Great p31-34
Tilden—Famous p63-77 (por.63)
Tobey—Riders p259-260
Trattner—Arch. p98-120 (por.102)
Van Wagenen—Beacon p181-182
Weeks—Discovery p100,102-103,272
  (por.100,101)
Williams—Story p31-33 (por.37)
Wilson—Human p222-233 (por.230)
Woglom—Discov. p41-43
Woodruff—Devel. p82-84,281 (por.84)
Year—Pic. p100,103 (por.100)

Lavoisier, Madame (1758-1836). Fr. chemist.

Chymia (4) p13-29

Law, Ruth Bancroft (1887-   ). Amer. aero. pioneer.

Adams—Heroines p49-65 (por.56)
Heinmuller—Man's p294 (por.294)

Maitland—Knights p161-162

Lawes, Sir John Bennet, Bart (1814-1900). Eng. agriculturist.

Chambers—Dict. col.276
Gilmour—British p40-41

Hammerton p885 (por.885)
*Ivins—Fifty p237-241 (por.240)

Lawrence, Charles Lanier (1882-   ). Amer. aero. pioneer.

Holland—Arch. p161-174

Lawrence, Ernest Orlando (1901-1958). Amer. physicist.
Chambers—Dict. col.276-277
(por. 277-278)
Curr. Biog. '40 p484-485 (por.485)
'52 p329-332 (por.330), '58 p239
Heathcote—Nobel p378-387 (por.240)
*Jaffe—Crucibles p349-373
Jaffe—Men p532-570 (por.xxviii)
Morris—Ency. p686
Moulton—Auto. p557-558
Progress—Science '40 p218-219
(por.218)
Riedman—Men p179-187
Weber—College p671 (por.671)

Lawrence, Sir William (1783-1867). Eng. surgeon.
Leonardo—Lives p252-253

Lawson, Andrew Cowper (1861-1952). Scot. geologist.
G.S.A.—Proc. '52 p141-144 (por.141)

Lawson, Isaac (d. 1747). Scot. physician.
Weeks—Discovery p62-63

Lawson, Ted. W. (1917-   ). Amer. aero. pioneer.
Curr. Biog. '43 p430-432 (por.431)

Layard, Sir Austen Henry (1817-1894). Fr.-Eng. archaeologist.
Ceram—Gods p240-265
Gordon—Medicine p183 (por.183)
Hammerton p887 (por.887)

Lazear, Jesse William (1866-1900). Amer. physician.
*Masters—Conquest p153-155
(por.158)
Snyder—Biology p224-225
Year—Pic. p133 (por.133)

Lea, Isaac (1792-1886). Amer. geologist, naturalist.
Merrill—First p158 (por.158)
Youmans—Pioneers p260-269
(por.260)

Lea, Matthew Carey (1823-1897). Amer. chemist.
N.A.S.—Biog. (5) p155-203 (por.155)
Smith—Chem. p277-301 (por.278)

Leake, Chauncey D. (1896-   ). Amer. physiologist, chemist.
Curr. Biog. Apr. '60 (por.)
Robinson—Victory p255,307-308
(por.274)

Leaming, Jacob Spicer (1815-1885). Amer. agriculturist.
*Ivins—Fifty p57-68 (por.58)

Leathes, John Beresford (1864-1956). Swiss physiologist.
R.S.L.—Biog. (4) p185-190 (por.185)

Leavey, Edmond Harrison (1894-   ). Amer. engineer.
Curr. Biog. '51 p367-369 (por.368)

Leavitt, Henrietta (1868-1921). Amer. astronomer.
Armitage—Cent. p180-181
Williams—Great p455,457-460
   (por. 458)

Le Baron, William (1814-1876). Amer. entomologist.
Osborn—Fragments p221 (por.354)

Lebaudy, Paul (1858-1918). Fr. aero. pioneer.
Heinmuller—Man's p259 (por.259)

Lebaudy, Pierre (1861-1924). Fr. aero. pioneer.
Heinmuller—Man's p259 (por.259)

Lebedev, Pëtr Nikolajevich (1866-1912). Rus. physicist.
Chambers—Dict. col.277

Le Bel, Joseph Achille (1847-1930). Fr. chemist.
Findlay—Hundred p330
Smith—Torch. p150 (por.150)

Leber, Ferdinand Joseph von (1727-1808). Aust. surgeon.
Atkinson—Magic p214-217

Leblanc, Nicolas (1742-1806). Fr. chemist, inventor, surgeon.
*Book—Pop. Sci. (9) p3055
Chambers—Dict. col.277-278
Hammerton p888
Smith—Torch. p151 (por.151)

Le Bon, Gustave (1841-1931). Fr. physician.
Hammerton p888

Le Bris, Jean-Marie (d.1872). Fr. aero. pioneer.
*Bishop—Kite p99-105
*Shippen—Bridle p85-91

Lebrix, Joseph (1895-1931). Fr. aero. pioneer.
*Fraser—Heroes p535-539
Heinmuller—Man's p325 (por.325)

Le Cat, Claude-Nicolas (1700-1768). Fr. surgeon.
Leonardo—Lives p253-254

Le Chatelier.   See Chatelier, Henry Louis Le

Leclanché, Georges (1839-1882). Fr. chemist.
Chambers—Dict. col.278

Le Clerc, Daniel (1652-1728). Swiss physician.
Castiglioni—Hist. p751 (por.751)

Lécluse, Charles de (or Lescluse; Clusius) (1524/1526-1609). Fr. botanist, physician.
Arber—Herbals p84-89,155,156,   Miall—Early p72-74
  229,230 (por.84)   Reed—Short p68-69
Chambers—Dict. col.278-279   Sarton—Six p143-144 (por.24)
Hawks—Pioneers p165,169-171
  175-176

Le Conte, John (1818-1891). Amer. physicist.
N.A.S.—Biog. (3) p369-389

Le Conte, John Lawrence (1825-1883). Amer. entomologist.
Essig—Hist. p680-685 (por.681)   Osborn—Fragments p163 (por.338)
N.A.S.—Biog. (2) p216-293

Le Conte, Joseph (1823-1901). Amer. geologist.
*Book—Pop. Sci. (5) p1665-1666   N.A.S.—Biog. (6) p147-211 (por.147)
Merrill—First p468 (por.478)

Lecoq' de Boisbaudran.   See Boisbaudran, Paul Emile Lecoq de

Lederberg, Joshua (1925-   ). Amer. geneticist.
Curr. Biog. '59 p251-252 (por.251)

Ledermüller, Martin Frobenius (1719-1769). Ger. naturalist.
Bulloch—Hist. p379

Ledingham, John Charles Grant (b.1875). Can. bacteriologist.
Bulloch—Hist. p379

Le Dran, Henri François (1685-1773). Fr. surgeon.
Leonardo—Lives p254-255

Lee, James (1715-1795). Eng. botanist.
Hawks—Pioneers p255

Lee, Tsung-Dao (1926-   ). Chin. physicist.
Curr. Biog. '58 p240-241 (por.240)

Lee, William (c. 1589-1610). Eng. inventor.
Hammerton p890
Year—Pic. p139 (por.139)

Leech, Paul Nicholas (1889-1941). Amer. chemist.
Curr. Biog. '41 p504

Leeds, Albert Ripley (1843-1902). Amer. chemist.
Browne—Hist. p498

Lees, George Martin (1898-1955). Irish geologist.
R.S.L.—Biog. (1) p163-172 (por.163)

Lees, James Henry (1875-1935). Eng.-Amer. geologist.
G.S.A.—Proc. '36 p215-216 (por.215)

Leeuwenhoek (or Leuwenhoek), **Anton van** (1632-1723). Dutch naturalist, microscopist.
Bodenheimer—Hist. p269
*Book—Pop. Sci. (13) p4565-4566
    (por.4565)
Bulloch—Hist. p379
Castiglioni—Hist. p528-530 (por.529)
Chambers—Dict. col.279
*Compton—Conquests p271-294
*Cottler—Heroes p260-268
*De Kruif—Microbe p3-24
*Elwell—Sci. p47-50
*Epstein—Real p119-120
Gordon—Medieval p644-645 (por.19)
Gordon—Romance p41,222 (por.41)
Grainger—Guide p158-159
Guinagh—Inspired p83-95
Hammerton p891 (por.891)
Lambert—Medical p199-200 (por.198)
Lambert—Minute p199-200 (por.193)
Law—Civiliz. p321-322
Locy—Biology p77-88 (por.79)
Major—History (1) p531-534
    (por.532)
Meyer—World p52-53
Miall—Early p200-223
*Milne—Natur. p11-18 (por.10)
Montgomery—Story p92-96
Moulton—Auto. p158
Oliver—Stalkers p97-102
Peattie—Green p52-55
People p425-426 (por.272)
Reed—Short p86-87
Schwartz—Moments (1) p411-413
*Science Miles p81 (por.81)
*Shippen—Micro. p78-83
*Simmons—Great p19-24 (por.19)
*Snyder—Biology p53-58 (por.56)
*Sterling—Polio p24-27 (por.24)
Taylor—Illus p70,72
Van Wagenen—Beacon p122-124
*Williams-Ellis p84-108 (por.85)
Woodruff—Devel. p227-228,281
    (por.236)
Year—Pic. p91 (por.91)

Lefèbvre, Eugène (1878-1909). Fr. aero pioneer.
Heinmuller—Man's p272 (por.272)

Lefroy, Harold Maxwell (1877-1925). Eng. entomologist.
Hammerton p891

Legagneaux, Georges (1882-1914). Fr. aero pioneer.
Heinmuller—Man's p274 (por.274)

Legendre, Adrien Marie (1752-1833). Fr. mathematician.
A.A.A.S.—Proc. (81) p68-70
Ball—Short p421-425
Cajori—Hist. p266-269
Chambers—Dict. col.279
Hammerton p891
Smith—Hist. p487-490 (por.488)
Van Wagenen—Beacon p200-201
Woodruff—Devel. p26,281

Legge, Alexander (1866-1933). Amer. agriculturist.
White—Famous (3d) p157 (por.155)

Lehmann, Johann Gottlob (d. 1767). Ger. mineralogist, geologist.
Adams—Birth p375-378
Geikie—Founders p96-98

Lehmann, Karl Bernhard (1858-1961). Ger. bacteriologist, hygienist.
Bulloch—Hist. p379

Leibniz (or Leibnits), **Gottfried Wilhelm, Baron von** (1646-1716). Ger. mathematician.
Ball—Short p353-365
Bell—Men p117-130 (por.,front.)
Cajori—Hist. p205-218
Castiglioni—Hist. p579
Chambers—Dict. col.279-280
Geikie—Founders p7-8
Hammerton p892 (por.892)
Hart—Makers p165-167 (por.166)
Hooper—Makers p325-342
Lambert—Medical p141
Lambert—Minute p141
Lenard—Great p111-118 (por.124)
Magie—Source p51
Major—History (2) p566
*Miller—Hist. p235-236
Osborn—Greeks p142-146
Sedgwick—Short p301-302
Smith—Hist. 1 p417-418 (por.419)
Smith—Portraits (1) VIII, unp.(por.)
Van Wagenen—Beacon p132-135
Weeks—Discovery p41-47 (por.44)
Woodruff—Devel. p281 (por.8)
Year—Pic. p96,110 (por.96)

Leicester, Thomas William Coke, Earl of (1754-1842). Eng. agriculturist.
Hammerton p893

Leidy, Joseph (1823-1891). Amer. naturalist, paleontologist, geologist.
*Book—Pop. Sci. (13) p4566-4568
Hammerton p893
*Hylander—Scien. p85-89 (por.88)
Major—History (2) p771
N.A.S.—Biog. (17) p335-370 (por.335)
Osborn—Impr. p131-148 (por.131)
Van Wagenen—Beacon p328-330
Woodruff—Devel. p281-282
Young—Biology p42-43 (por.41)

Leigh-Mallory, Sir Trafford Leigh (1892-   ). Eng. aero. pioneer.
Curr. Biog. '44 p401-403 (por.402)

Leishman, Sir William Boog (1865-1926). Scot. bacteriologist.
Bulloch—Hist. p380
Chambers—Dict. col.280
Hammerton p893
Major—History (2) p920
Walker—Pioneers p252-263 (por.252)

Leith, Charles Kenneth (1875-1956). Amer. geologist.
Chambers—Dict. col.280
G.S.A.—Proc. '56 p147-155 (por.147)
N.A.S.—Biog. (33) p180-195 (por.180)

Lelong, B. M. (1858-1901). Amer. entomologist.
Essig—Hist. p685-687 (por.686)

Lemaitre, Abbé Georges Edouard (1894-   ). Belg. mathematician, astrophysicist.
Chambers—Dict. col.281

LeMay, Curtis Emerson (1906-   ). Amer. aero. pioneer.
Curr. Biog. '54 p403-405 (por.404)

Lemery, Nicolas (1645-1715). Fr. chemist.
Holmyard—Chem. p70
Holmyard—Makers p124-132 (por.124)
Partington—Short p59-60,149 (por.60)
Smith—Torch. p153 (por.153)
Weeks—Discovery p24-28 (por.25)

Lemoine, Émile Michel Hyacinth (1840-1912). Fr. mathematician, engineer.
Cajori—Hist. p299-300

Lemonnier, Pierre Charles (1715-1799). Fr. astronomer.
Chambers—Dict. col.281

Lenard, Philipp E. A. von (1862-1947). Ger. physicist.
Chambers—Dict. col.281
Hammerton p894
Heathcote—Nobel p34-40 (por.240)
Weber—College p94 (por.94)

Leng, Charles W. (1859-1941). Amer. entomologist.
Osborn—Fragments p183-184 (por.351,357)

Lennard-Jones, Sir John Edward (1894-1954). Eng. chemist, physicist.
Chambers—Dict. col.281-282
R.S.L.—Biog. (1) p175-181 (por.175)

Lenoir, (Jean Joseph) Étienne (1822-1900). Fr. inventor.
Chambers—Dict. col.282
*Epstein—Real p58

Lenormant, François (1837-1883). Fr. archaeologist.
Hammerton p896

Lenox-Conyngham Gerald Ponsonby (1866-1956). Irish geophysicist.
R.S.L.—Biog. (3) p129-139 (por.129)

Lenz, Heinrich Friedrich Emil (1804-1865). Ger. physicist.
Chambers—Dict. col.282   Magie—Source p511
Hammerton p896

Leonard, Raymond Jackson (1887-1937). Amer. geologist.
G.S.A.—Proc. '38 p153-154 (por.153)

Leonardo da Vinci.   See **Vinci, Leonardo da**

Leonardo Fibonacci (1180?-1250?). It. mathematician.
Ball—Short p167-170   Hammerton p897
Cajori—Hist. p120-124

Leone, Carcano (1536-1606). It. surgeon.
Leonardo—Lives p255

Leonhard, Karl Casar von (1779-1862). Ger. mineralogist, geologist.
Woodruff—Devel. p176,282

Leoniceno, Nicolò (or Leonicenus Da Lonigo) (1428-1524). It. physician.
Castiglioni—Hist. p373-374   Major—History (1) p373-375
Gordon—Medieval p536-537,589-590   (por.374)
  (por.146)

Leonidas (or Leonides) **of Alexandria** (fl. 1st cent.). Rom. physician,
  surgeon.
Gordon—Medicine p694

Leopold, Aldo (1886-   ). Amer. naturalist.
*Milne—Natur. p174-175

Leporin-Erxleben, Dorothea Christin (1715-1762). Ger. physician.
Lovejoy—Women p189-190
Mozans—Woman 293

Lepsius, Karl Richard (1810-1884). Ger. archaeologist.
Ceram—Gods p115-116,121-123

Leroy, Paul Georges (1927-1955). Belg.-Amer. geologist.
G.S.A.—Proc. '55 p189

Leroy D'Etiolles (or Etolles) **Jean Jacques Joseph** (1798-1860). Fr. surgeon.
Leonardo—Lives p255-256

Léscluse. See **Lécluse, Charles de**

Lesley, J. Peter (1819-1903). Amer. geologist.
Merrill—First p498-499 (por.496)
N.A.S.—Biog. (8) p155-240 (por.155)

Leslie, Sir John (1766-1832). Scot. physicist, mathematician.
Chambers—Dict. col.282
Hammerton p900 (por.900)

L'Esperance, Elise Depew Strang (1879?-1959). Amer. physician, pathologist.
Curr. Biog. '50 p340-341 (por.341)
    '59 p256

Lesquerreux, Leo (1806-1889). Swiss-Amer. geologist, paleobotanist.
Merrill—First p383 (por.380)   Youmans—Pioneers p458-463
N.A.S.—Biog. (3) p187-212   (por.458)

Lesseps, Ferdinand Marie, Vicomte de (1805-1894). Fr. engineer.
Hammerton p900 (por.900)   Year—Pic. p197 (por.197)
100 Great p619-624

Lesueur, Charles Alexandre (1778-1846). Fr.-Amer. naturalist.
Youmans—Pioneers p128-139
    (por.128)

Letourneau, Robert Gilmore (1888-   ). Amer. inventor.
Curr. Biog. '58 p244-245 (por.245)

Lettsom, John Coakley (1744-1815). Virgin Isl. physician.
Farmer—Doctors' p40
Major—History (2) p638

Leuckhart, (Karl Georg Friedrich) Rudolph (1822/1823-1898). Ger. zoologist, biologist.
Bodenheimer—Hist. p409   Locy—Biology p135-136 (por.136)
Hammerton p901

Leupold, Jacob (1674-1727). Ger. engineer.
Matschoss—Great p113-116 (por.116)

Levaditi, Constantin (1874-1928). Rom.-Fr. bacteriologist, physician.
Bulloch—Hist. p380

Levanevsky, Sigismund (1902-1937). Rus. aero. pioneer.
Heinmuller—Man's p351 (por.351)

Levene, Phoebus Aaron Theodore (1869-1940). Amer. biochemist.
Chambers—Dict. col.282-283   Kagan—Modern p188 (por.188)
Curr. Biog. '40 p497 (por.497)   N.A.S.—Biog. (23) p75-86 (por.75)

Leverett, Frank (1859-1943). Amer. geologist.
G.S.A.—Proc. '43 p183-185 (por.183)
N.A.S.—Biog. (23) p203-208 (por.203)

Leverrier, Urbain Jean Joseph (1811-1872). Fr. astronomer.
Abetti—History p214-217   MacPherson—Makers p151-157
Armitage—Cent. p113-115 (por.144) Shapley—Astron. p249 (por.251)
Ball—Great p335-353   Van Wagenen—Beacon p294-295
Ball—Short p494   Williams—Great p313-316 (por.313)
*Book—Pop. Sci. (14) p4649   Woodruff—Devel. p282
Chambers—Dict. col.283   Year—Pic. p118 (por. 118)
Hammerton p902

Levine, Philip (1900-   ). Rus.-Amer. bacteriologist, serologist, physician.
Curr. Biog. '47 p388-390 (por.389)
*Eberle—Modern p111-117,119

Lewis, Agnes Smith (1843-1926). Scot. archaeologist.
Mozans—Woman p327-333

Lewis, Albert Buell (1867-1940). Amer. anthropologist.
Curr. Biog. '40 p498 (por.498)

Lewis, Clyde Augustine (1913-   ). Amer. aero. pioneer.
Curr. Biog. '50 p342-343 (por.342)

Lewis, Dean DeWitt (1874-1941). Welsh-Amer. physician, surgeon.
Curr. Biog. '41 p510-512 (por.511)   Major—History (2) p1040
Leonardo—Lives (Supp.) p489-491

Lewis, Francis Park (1855-1940). Can. oculist.
Curr. Biog. '40 p498

Lewis, George T. (1817-1900). Amer. chemist.
Haynes—Chem. (1) p107-123
(por.112)

Lewis, George William (1882-1948). Amer. aero. pioneer, engineer.
Daniel Gugg. p59-62 (por.58)　　　N.A.S. Biog. (25) p297-311 (por.297)
Daniel—Pioneer p43-49 (por.42)　　Progress—Science '41 p214-215
　　　　　　　　　　　　　　　　(por.215)

Lewis, Gilbert Newton (1875-1946). Amer. chemist.
Chambers—Dict. col.283　　　　　Partington—Short p361 (por.361)
Killeffer—Eminent p30 (por.30)　　Schwartz—Moments (1) p84-85
Morris—Ency. p687　　　　　　　Smith—Torch. p154 (por.154)
N.A.S.—Biog. (31) p210-224
(por.210)

Lewis, Isaac Newton (1858-1931). Amer. inventor.
Hammerton p903

Lewis, Margaret Reed (1881-　　). Amer. anatomist, physiologist.
Progress—Science '40 p221 (por.221)

Lewis, Thomas (1881-1945). Welsh pathologist.
Major—History (2) p1040

Lewis, Timothy Richards (1841-1886). Welsh bacteriologist, physician, surgeon, public health worker.
Bulloch—Hist. p380
Walker—Pioneers p166-177 (por.166)

Lewis, Warren Kendall (1882-　　). Amer. chemist.
Chambers—Dict. col.283

Lewis, William Cudmore McCullagh (1885-1956). Eng. phys. chemist.
R.S.L.—Biog. (4) p193-200 (por.193)

Ley, Willy (1906-　　). Ger.-Amer. zoologist, engineer.
Curr. Biog. '41 p512-513 (por.513)　Williams—Rocket p122-124,145-146,
　'53 p356-359 (por.357)　　　　　148-149, 156-157, 160-165
　　　　　　　　　　　　　　　167-169, 207-208

Leybourn, William (1626-c.1700). Eng. mathematician.
Smith—Hist. p414-415

Leyden, Ernst Vicktor von (1832-1910). Ger. physician.
Major—History (2) p896-897

Leydig, Franz (1821-1908). Ger. entomologist, histologist, zoologist.
Locy—Biology p102-103,175-176
(por.175)

Leyton.   See **Grünbaum, Albert Sidney Frankau**

L'Hopital, (or L'Hospital), **Guillaume Françoise Antoine de** (1661-1704).
Fr. mathematician.
Ball—Short p369-370
Smith—Hist. 1 p384 (por.384)

Lhuilier, Simon-Antoine (1750-1840). Swiss mathematician.
Smith—Hist. I p525 (por.525)

Lhwyd, Edward (1660-1709). Welsh botanist.
Gunther—Early XI p250-251

Li, Katherine Yueh-Yuin (1911-   ). Chin. physician, surgeon.
Knapp—Women p1-15 (por.1)

Libavius, Andreas (or L'bau) (1540?-1616). Ger. chemist, physician.
Chambers—Dict. col.283-284   Partington—Short p56
Holmyard—Chem. p51   Sarton—Six p114-115
Holmyard—Makers p117-119

Libby, Willard Frank (1908-   ). Amer. chemist.
Curr. Biog. '54 p406-407 (por.406)

Libman, Emanuel (1872-1946). Amer. pathologist.
Major—History (2) p1040 (por.956)
Rowntree—Amid p225-227 (por.211)

Lichtheim, Ludwig (1845-1928). Ger. physician.
Bulloch—Hist. p380
Kagan—Modern p63 (por.63)

Lichtwitz, Leopold (1876-1943). Siles. physician.
Kagan—Modern p25 (por.25)

Liddel, Urner (1905-   ). Amer. physicist.
Curr. Biog. '51 p371-372 (por.371)

Liddell, Duncan (1561-1613). Scot. mathematician, chemist, physician.
Chymia (1) p140-142 (por.141,142)

Lie, Marius Sophus (1842-1899). Norw. mathematician.

Ball—Short p477-478
Cajori—Hist. p354-356
Chambers—Dict. col.284
Hammerton p904
*Miller—Hist. p265-268
Murray—Science p339-341
Smith—Hist. I p527
Woodruff—Devel. p36,282

Lieber, Oscar M. (1830-1862). Amer. geologist.
Merrill—First p323-325 (por.324)

Lieberkühn, Johann Nathaniel (1711-1746). Ger. anatomist.
Major—History (2) p634

Liebermann, Carl (or Karl) (1842-1914). Ger. chemist.
Partington—Short p318
Smith—Torch. (por.124,155)

Liebig, Justus, Baron von (1803-1873). Ger. chemist.

Bodenheimer—Hist. p388
*Book—Pop. Sci. (12) p4017-4018
  (por.4017)
Bulloch—Hist. p380
Chambers—Dict. col.284-285
*Darrow—Masters p116-119 (por.33)
Findlay—Hundred p330-331
Hammerton p904 (por.904)
Holmyard—Great Chem. p98-104
Holmyard—Makers p275-277
  (por.277)
Major—History (2) p791-793
  (por.792)
Moulton—Auto. p286
Partington—Short p228-230,237-238
  (por.229)
Roberts—Chem. p126-139
Smith—Torch. p156-157 (por.156)
*Snyder—Biology p311
Tilden—Famous p188-204 (por.188)
Van Wagenen—Beacon p279-281
Weeks—Discovery p349,453-454
  (por.349)
Woodruff—Devel. p282 (por.100)
Year—Pic. p123,124,250 (por.124)

Liggett, Louis Kroh (1875-1946). Amer. pharmacist.
*Wildman—Famous (2D) p185-193
  (por.185)

Lilienthal, Otto (1848-1896). Ger. aero. pioneer.

*Bishop—Kite p118-124
Burge—Ency. p635
Cohen—Men p87-89
Hammerton p905
*Hartman—Mach. p235-237
Heinmuller—Man's p251 (por.251)
*Larsen—Prentice p112-114

Lillie, Frank Rattray (1870-1947). Can.-Amer. zoologist.
N.A.S.—Biog. (30) p179-236
  (por.179)
Progress—Science '41 p215 (por.215)

Lillie, Ralph Stayner (1875-1952). Can.-Amer. physiologist, zoologist.
Progress—Science '41 p215-216

Linacre, Thomas (c.1460-1524). Eng. physician.
Chambers—Dict. col.285
Gordon—Medieval p588-589
(por.243)
Gunther—Early XI p154 (por.154)
Hammerton p906 (por.906)
Major—History (1) p447-448
(por.447)

Lincecum, Gideon (1793-1874). Amer. naturalist.
Geiser—Natural. p199-214

Linck (or Link) **Johann Heinrich** (1675-1735). Ger. pharmacist.
Weeks—Discovery p51,71 (por.51)

Lind, James (1716-1794). Scot. physician.
Chambers—Dict. col.285
Gordon—Romance p387,388-389
(por.387)
Hammerton p907
Major—History (2) p596-597
(por.597)
Walker—Pioneers p23-34 (por.23)

Lind, Samuel Colville (1879-   ). Amer. chemist.
Browne—Hist. p489-490 (por.163)
Chambers—Dict. col.285

Lindbergh, Anne Spence Morrow (1907-   ). Amer. aero. pioneer.
*Adams—Heroines p215-236 (por.232)
Curr. Biog. '40 p505-508 (por.507)
*Fraser—Heroes p609-614,665-676

Lindbergh, Charles (1902-   ). Amer. aero. pioneer.
Burge—Ency. p635
Curr. Biog. '41 p513-518, '54 p410-413
(por.411)
*Darrow—Builders p105-115 (por.101)
Fitzhugh—Concise p410-411
*Fraser—Famous p151-179 (por.62)
*Fraser—Heroes p431-458,537-539,
609-614,665-676 (por.,front.)
Hammerton P907-908 (por.907)
Heinmuller—Man's p68-85,323
(por.82,323)
Huff—Famous (2d) p345-356
(por.344)
La Croix—They p82-99 (por.98)
Maitland—Knights p307-309
Ratcliffe—Modern p204-208
*Shippen—Bridle p125-132
*Snyder—Biology p436-439 (por.436)

Linde, Karl (or Carl) **von** (1842-1934). Ger. chemist, engineer.
Chambers—Dict. col.286
Matschoss—Great p343-352
(por.352)
Smith—Torch. p159 (por.159)

Lindemann, F. A.   See **Cherwell, Frederick Alexander Lindemann, 1st
Baron**

Linden, Johann Antonides van der (1609-1664). Dutch anatomist, botanist.
Major—History (1) p554-555

Lindenblad, Nils Erik (1895-   ). Swed. inventor.
Radio's 100 p263-266 (por.140)

Lindenthal, Gustav (1850-1935). Aust.-Amer. engineer.
Hammerton p908
*Wildman—Famous (2d) p197-206
  (por.197)

Lindgren, Waldemar (1860-1939). Swed.-Amer. geologist.
G.S.A.—Proc. '49 p177-189 (por.177)

Lindheimer, Ferdinand Jakob (1801-1879). Ger.-Amer. naturalist.
Geiser—Natural. p132

Lindley, John (1799-1865). Eng. botanist.
Hammerton p908 (por.908)
Oliver—Makers p164-177 (por.164)

Lindsay, James Bowman (1799-1862). Scot. elec. engineer.
Hammerton p908
Hawks—Wireless p76-85 (por.64)

Lindsley, Thayer (1882-   ). Amer. geologist.
Curr. Biog. '57 p325-327 (por.326)

Linell, Martin Larsson (1849-1897). Swed.-Amer. entomologist.
Osborn—Fragments p222-223

Link, Edwin A. (1904-   ). Amer. inventor, aero. pioneer.
*Montgomery—Invent. p249-252

Linnaeus, Carolus (or von Linné, Carl) (1707-1778). Swed. botanist.
Bodenheimer—Hist. p286
*Bolton—Famous p49-57 (por.48)
*Book—Pop. Sci. (13) p4568-4570
Chambers—Dict. col.286,287
  (por.286)
*Darrow—Masters p78-82 (por.64)
Essig—Hist. p687-690 (por.688)
Gilmour—British p30
Hammerton p908-909 (por.909)
Hawks—Pioneers p232-238
  (por.,front.)
Hubbard—Scientists (2) p25-57
  (por.25)
Lenard—Great p314-317 (por.316)
Lindroth—Swedish p81-91
Locy—Biology p118-130 (por.124)
Major—History (2) p635 (por.653)
Miall—Early p310-336
*Milne—Natur. p21-31 (por.20)
Moulton—Auto. p210
Murray—Science p142
Osborn—Greeks p185-188
(*Continued*)

Linnaeus, Carolus—*Continued*
Peattie—Green p78-114,116-124,126-129 (por.78,119)
Peattie—Lives p89-97 (por.89)
People p244-245
Reed—Short p99-101
Schwartz—Moments (2) p636-638
*Shippen—Micro. p85-96 (por.84)

*Snyder—Biology p18-27 (por.21,25)
*Stevens—Science p43-47 (por.42)
Thomson—Great p38-41
Van Wagenen—Beacon p152-154
Woodruff—Devel. p231-232,282 (por.256)
Year—Pic. p101,107 (por.107)

Linton, Ralph (1893-1953). Amer. anthropologist.
N.A.S.—Biog. (31) p236-247 (por.236)

Lipmann, Fritz Albert (1899-   ). Ger.-Amer. biochemist.
Chambers—Dict. Supp.
Curr. Biog. '54 p413-415 (por.413)

Lippershey, Hans (d.c.1619). Dutch optician, inventor.
Meyer—World p52
*Pratt—Famous p14-15
Williams—Great p156-157 (por.157)

Lippman, Gabriel (1845-1921). Fr. physicist.
Chambers—Dict. col.287-288
Hammerton p909
Heathcote—Nobel p65-69 (por.240)
Weber—College p131 (por.131)
Weeks—Discovery p486 (por.486)

Lisan al-dīn abū Abdallah.   See **Ibn al Khatib**

Lissajous, Jules Antoine (1822-1880). Fr. physicist.
Chambers—Dict. col.288

Lister, Joseph, 1st Baron Lister of Lyme Regis (1827-1912). Eng. surgeon.
Atkinson—Magic p283-288
*Book—Pop. Sci. (13) p4375-4378, 4570-4571 (por.4377)
Bulloch—Hist. p380-381 (por.130)
Castiglioni—Hist. p718-719 (por.719)
Chambers—Dict. col.288 (por.287)
*Chandler—Medicine p77-81 (por.76)
*Cottler—Heroes p296-306
Crowther—Doctors p82-112 (por.96)
*Elwell—Sci. p56-59
Farmer—Doctors' p149
Fitzhugh—Concise p411-412
Fox—Great p178-203 (por.178)
Grainger—Guide p159-160
Hale-White—Great p246-267
Hammerton p910-911 (por.910)
*Hathaway—Partners p43-51 (por.45)
Holmyard—British p56-58 (por.56)
Kagan—Modern p89 (por.89)
Lambert—Medical p276-288 (por.286)
Lambert—Minute p276-288 (por.288)
Law—Civiliz. p329-330
Leonardo—Lives (Supp.-) p491-493
Locy—Biology p302-303 (por.302)
Major—History (2) p821-827 (por.823)
*Masters—Conquest p104-109 (por.106)
Miall—Early p130-134
*Montgomery—Story p157-162
Moulton—Auto. p434
Murray—Science p255-304
100 Great p640-647
Oliver—Stalkers p186-187 (por.187)
Schwartz—Moments (2) p746-747

(Continued)

Lister, Joseph—*Continued*
*Science Miles p194 (por.194)
*Shippen—Men p145-155 (por.144)
Sigerist—Great p376-379 (por.376)
*Snyder—Biology p199-205
Thorwald—Century p244-247,260-280
    (por.241)
Tobey—Riders p138-162
*Truax—Doctors p89-107
Van Wagenen—Beacon p351-352

Walker—Pioneers p154-165 (por.154)
*Williams-Ellis p189-207 (por.206)
Williams—Story p327-329, 382-386
    (por.383)
Wilson—Human p295,303-304
    (por.,front.)
Year—Pic. p132 (por.132)
Young—Scalpel p165-193 (por.185)

Liston, Robert (1794-1847). Scot. surgeon.
Chambers—Dict. col.288-289
Hammerton p911
Leonardo—Lives p256-257

Major—History (2) p710-711
Robinson—Victory p141-149
Thorwald—Century p112-123

Litchfield, Paul Weeks (1875-1958). Amer. chem. engineer.
Curr. Biog. '50 p343-346 (por.344)

Lithotomos.   See Ammonius

Little, Arthur Dehon (1863-1935). Amer. chemical engineer, inventor.
Browne—Hist. p481-482 (por.103)
*Darrow—Builders p130-134

Holland—Ind. p149-169 (por.149)

Little, Clarence Cook (1888-   ). Amer. biologist, geneticist.
Curr. Biog. '44 p416-418 (por.417)
Progress—Science '41 p216-217
    (por.216)

Littré, Alexis (1658-1725?). Fr. physician, surgeon, anatomist.
Leonardo—Lives p258

Littré, (Maximilien Paul) Émile (1801-1881). Fr. physician.
Major—History (2) p879-880
Rosen—Four p259-260

Liu Hui (fl.c.263). Chin. mathematician.
Smith—Hist. I p142

Liverside, Archibald (1847-1927). Eng. chemist.
Hammerton p912

Livingston, (Milton) Stanley (1905-   ). Amer. physicist.
Curr. Biog. '55 p368-369 (por.368)

Li Yeh (1178-1265). Chin. mathematician.
Smith—Hist. p270

Lizars, John (1783-1860). Scot. surgeon.
Leonardo—Lives p258-259

Ljotchitch-Milochevitch, Draga (d.1927). Yugoslav. physician.
Lovejoy—Women p209

Ljungberg, Ernst Carl Robert (1897-   ). Swed. aero. pioneer.
Curr. Biog. '55 p369-370 (por.370)

Lloyd, Edwin Russell (1882-1955). Amer. geologist.
G.S.A.—Proc. '55 p139-140 (por.139)

Lloyd, Humphrey (1800-1881). Irish optician.
Chambers—Dict. col.289

Lloyd, Samuel (1860-1926). Amer. surgeon.
Leonardo—Lives p259-260

Lobatchevsky, Nikolas Ivanovitch (1793-1856). Rus. mathematician.
Bell—Men p294-306 (por.,front.)
Cajori—Hist. p303
Chambers—Dict. col.289
Muir—Men p184-201
Smith—Hist. I p529-530 (por.530)
Smith—Portraits (1) XI, unp. (por.)
Van Wagenen—Beacon p258-259
Woodruff—Devel p28,282
Year—Pic. p117 (por.117)

L'Obel, Matthias de (or Lobelius, Lobel) (1538-1616). Flem. botanist,
naturalist.
Arber—Herbals p89-91,176-179
(por.90)
Chambers—Dict. col.290
Hawks—Pioneers p168-170,174,181,
239 (por.168)
Major—History (1) p457
Miall—Early p32-35
Sarton—Six p145-147 (por.24)

Lobmayer, Geza De (1880-1940). Hung. surgeon.
Leonardo—Lives p260-261

Lobry, de Bruyn Cornelius Adriann (or de Bruyn, Cornelius Adriann
Lobry) (1857-1904). Dutch chemist.
Smith—Torch. p40 (por.41)

Locke, John (1632-1704). Eng. physician.
Gunther—Early XI p210-211
Lambert—Medical p140-141
(por.140)
Lambert—Minute p140-141 (por.129)
Major—History (1) p557-558

Lockhart-Mummery, John Percy (1875-1957). Eng. surgeon.
Hammerton p916

Lockhead, William (1864-1928). Can. entomologist.
Osborn—Fragments p205 (por.356)

Lockyer, Sir Joseph Norman (1836-1920). Eng. astronomer.

Abetti—History p205-206
Armitage—Cent. p54-55 (por.80)
*Book—Pop. Sci. (14) p4649-4650
Chambers—Dict. col.290
Hammerton p916 (por.916)
Law—Civiliz. p279-280
MacPherson—Astron. p62-70

MacPherson—Makers p172-173
Shapley—Astron. p353
Van Wagenen—Beacon p373-375
Weeks—Discovery p476
  (por.475,476)
Williams—Great p374-383 (por.380)
Woodruff—Devel. p88-282

Lodge, Sir Oliver Joseph (1851-1940). Eng. physicist.

A.A.A.S.—Proc. (79) p24-27
*Book—Pop.Sci. (12) p4018-4019
  (por.4019)
*Bridges—Master p129-138 (por.130)
Chambers—Dict. col.290-291
Curr. Biog. '40 p514 (por.514)

*Darrow—Masters p337
Gregory—British p34,36 (por.40)
Hammerton p916-917 (por.917)
Hawks—Wireless p240-246 (por.228)
Radio's 100 p102-106 (por.140)
Year—Pic. p178 (por.178)

Loeb, Jacques (1859-1924). Ger.-Amer. biologist, biophysiologist.

Bodenheimer—Hist. p436
*Book—Pop. Sci. (13) p4572-4574
  (por.4573)
Castiglioni—Hist. p768,769 (por.769)
Chambers—Dict. col.291
Hammerton p917

Kagan—Modern p187 (por.187)
N.A.S.—Biog. (13) p318-368
  (por.318)
Ratcliffe—Modern p198-200
*Snyder—Biology p353-360 (por.355)

Loeb, Leo (1869-1959). Ger.-Amer. pathologist.

N.A.S.—Biog. (35) p205-219
  (por.205)

Loeffler, (or Loffler) Friedrich August Johannes (1852-1915). Ger. bacteriologist.

Bulloch—Hist. p381
DeKruif—Hunger p102-118 (por.105)

Hammerton p917

Loening, Grover Cleveland (1888-   ). Amer. aero. pioneer.

Heinmuller—Man's p299 (por.299)

Loew, Hermann (1807-1879). Ger. entomologist.

Essig—Hist. p691-693 (por.691)

Loewe, Walter Siegfried (1884-   ). Ger. pharmacologist.

Curr. Biog. '47 p392-394 (por.393)

Loewi, Otto (b.1873). Ger. pharmacologist.

Chambers—Dict. col.291
Stevenson—Nobel p187,190-195
  (por.150)

Loewinson-Lessing, Franz Julievitch (1861-1939). Rus. geologist.

G.S.A.—Proc. '40 p277 (por.277)

Loewy, Raymond Fernand (1893-   ). Fr.-Amer. engineer.
Curr. Biog. '53 p368-370 (por.369)

Logan, James (1674-1751). Amer. astronomer, mathematician.
Bell—Early p62-63

Logan, Thomas M. (1808-1876). Amer. physician.
Jones—Memories p383-405 (por.383)

Logan, Sir William Edmond (1798-1875). Can. geologist.
Fenton—Giants p179-190 (por.191)   Woodruff—Devel. p282
Merrill—First p415-416 (por.416)

Logan, William Newton (1869-1941). Amer. geologist.
G.S.A.—Proc. '41 p177-182 (por.177)

Lombardi, Francia (1897-   ). It. aero. pioneer.
Heinmuller—Man's p347 (por.347)

Lombroso, Cesare (1836-1909). It. physician, psychiatrist.
Castiglioni—Hist. p739 (por.739)
Chambers—Dict. col.291-292

Lombroso-Ferrero.   See **Ferrero, Gina Lombroso**

Lomm, Josse (or Loom, Joost van; Lommius, Jodocus) (c.1560). Dutch
physician.
Major—History (1) p466

Lomonósov, Micháil Vasílievíc (or Vasilievich) (1711-1765). Rus.
chemist.
Smith—Torch. p160 (por.160)
Year—Pic. p102 (por.102)

Long, Crawford Williamson (1815-1878). Amer. physician, surgeon.
Atkinson—Magic p253-260
Castiglioni—Hist. p723 (por.723)
Chambers—Dict. col.292
Flexner—Doctors p297-310 (por.292)
Fülöp—Miller p98-105 (por.105)
Hammerton p918
Law—Civiliz. p312-314
Leonardo—Lives p261-262
Major—History (2) p752-753
  (por.753)
Moulton—Auto. p320-321
Robinson—Victory p83-91 (por.83)
*Snyder—Biology p288-291 (por.290)
*Shippen—Men p135-138
*Truax—Doctors p68-70,85,87
Williams—Story p373-374 (por.371)
Wilson—Amer. p105 (por.104)
Young—Scalpel p137-138,151
  (por.154)

Long, John Harper (1856-1918). Amer. chemist.
Browne—Hist. p478-479 (por.61)

Long, Perrin Hamilton (1899-   ). Amer. physician.
*Montgomery—Story p128-130

Longcope, Warfield Theobald (1877-1953). Amer. pathologist, physician.
N.A.S.—Biog. (33) p205-213 (por.205)

Longomontanus (or Severin, Christian) (1562-1647). Dan. astronomer.
Year—Pic. p77 (por.77)

Longshore, Hannah Myers (1819-1902). Amer. physician.
Lovejoy—Women p28-30

Longstretch, Miers Fisher (1819-1891). Amer. astronomer.
N.A.S.—Biog. (8) p137-140 (por.137)

Lonigo.   See **Leoniceno, Nicolò**

Lonsdale, William (1794-1871). Eng. geologist.
Chambers—Dict. col. 292
Hammerton p919

Loom.   See **Lomm, Josse**

Loomis, Elias (1811-1889). Amer. mathematician, astronomer, meteorologist.
N.A.S.—Biog. (3) p213-240

Loomis, Frederic (1877-1949). Amer. gynecologist, obstetrician.
Fabricant—Why p69-71

Loomis, Frederick Brewster (1873-1937). Amer. geologist, paleontologist.
G.S.A.—Proc. '37 p173-177 (por.173)

Loomis, Mahlon (1826-1886). Amer. inventor.
Radio's 100 p58-59 (por.140)

Lopez, Rita Lobato (b.1866). Brazil. physician.
Lovejoy—Women p262-263 (por.263)

Loraine, Robert (1876-1935). Eng. aero pioneer.
Burge—Ency. p635
Hammerton p920

Lord, Frederick Taylor (1875-1941). Amer. physician.
Curr. Biog. '42 p530

Lorentz, Hendrik Antoon (1853-1928). Dutch physicist.
*Book—Pop. Sci. (2) p4019-4020
Chalmers—Historic p267
Chambers—Dict. col.292-293
Hammerton p920
Heathcote—Nobel p9-17 (por. 240)
Smith—Torch. p161 (por.161)
Weber—College p31 (por.31)

Lorenz, Adolf (1855-1946). Aust. physician, surgeon.
Leonardo—Lives (Supp.1) p493-495
Major—History (2) p1040-1041
(por.927)

Lorenz, Konrad Zacharias (1903-   ). Aust. naturalist.
Curr. Biog. '55 p372-374 (por.373)

Lorenz, Ludvig Valentin (1829-1891). Dan. physicist.
Copen.—Amer. p148-151

Lorge, Irving Daniel (1905-1961). Amer. psychologist.
Curr. Biog. '59 p267-269 (por.268)
'61 (Apr.)

Lorquin, Pierre Joseph Michel (1797-1873). Fr. entomologist.
Essig—Hist. p694-697 (por.695)

Loschmidt, Joseph (1821-1895). Aust. physicist.
Chambers—Dict. col.293

Loughlin, Gerald Francis (1880-1946). Amer. geologist.
G.S.A.—Proc. '46 p173-179 (por.173)

Louis, (Pierre) Charles Alexander (1787-1872). Fr. physician.
Castiglioni—Hist. p702 (por.700)
Lambert—Medical p203
Lambert—Minute p203-204
Major—History (2) p671-673
(por.672)

Loureiro, Juan de (1715-1796). Port. naturalist.
Reed—Short p109-110

Louyet, Paulin (1818-1850). Belg. chemist.
Weeks—Discovery p457 (por.457)

Love, Edward G. (1850-1919). Amer. chemist.
Browne—Hist. p498-499 (por.117)

Love, Nancy (1914-   ). Amer. aero. pioneer.
Knapp—New p47-60 (por.179)

Lovejoy, Esther Pohl (1869-   ). Amer. physician.
Lovejoy—Women p192,309 (por.309)   Mead—Medical p75,76,77
Lovejoy—Women Phys. p34-35   (por.,append.)
   (por. 20,29,44)

Lovelace, W. Randolph II (1907-   ). Amer. space pioneer, physician.
Thomas—Men (2) p89-112 (por.106)

Lovell, (Alfred Charles) Bernard (1913-   ). Eng. physicist.
Calder—Science p80
Curr. Biog. '59 p269-271 (por.270)

Loven, Sven Ludwig (1809-1895). Swed. zoologist, biologist.
Lindroth—Swedish p176-192

Lovering, Joseph (1813-1892). Amer. astronomer, mathematician.
N.A.S.—Biog. (6) p327-339 (por.327)

Low, Albert Peter (1861-1942). Can. geologist.
G.S.A.—Proc. '43 p195-198 (por.195)

Low, Archibald Montgomery (1888-1956). Eng. engineer, inventor.
*Bridges—Master p139-150 (por.142)   *Larsen—Shaped p211-216 (por.193)
Hammerton p925

Lowdermilk, Walter Clay (1888-   ). Amer. agriculturist.
Curr. Biog. '49 p363-364 (por.363)
Progress—Science '41 p217-218
   (por.217)

Lowe, Peter (1550/1559-1610/1612). Scot. physician, surgeon.
Gordon—Romance p443 (por.443)   Major—History (1) p477
Leonardo—Lives p262-263

Lowe, Thaddeus Sobieski C. (1832-1913). Amer. aero. pioneer, inventor.
Carmer—Caval. p244-247 (por.244)   *Shippen—Bridle p64-70
Heinmuller—Man's p244 (por.244)   Smith—Torch. p162 (por.162)
Milbank—First p119-130 (por.126)   Wilson—Amer. p184-187 (por.186)

Lowell, Francis Cabot (1775-1817). Amer. inventor.
Wilson—Amer. p88-89

Lowell, Percival (1855-1916). Amer. astronomer.
Armitage—Cent. p89-90   MacPherson—Astron. p206-216
*Book—Pop. Sci. (14) p4650-4651   (por.206)
   (por.4651)   MacPherson—Makers p197-201
Chambers—Dict. col.293   Shapley—Astron. p388
Hammerton p926

Löwenstern.   See **Kunckel, Johann von Löwenstern**

Lower, Richard (1631-1691). Eng. physiologist, anatomist, physician.
Gunther—Early XI p209-210   Woodruff—Devel. p282-283
  (por.209)
Major—History (1) p517-519
  (por.517)

Löwig, Carl (1803-1890). Ger. chemist.
Chambers—Dict. col.293-294
Weeks—Discovery p449-450
  (por.449)

Lowry, Philip Rosemond (1896-1931). Amer. entomologist.
Osborn—Fragments p215 (por.374)

Lowry, Thomas Martin (1874-1936). Eng. chemist.
Findlay—British p402-418 (por.402)

Lozier, Clemence Sophia (1813-1888). Amer. physician.
Lovejoy—Women p63-67

Lubarsch, Otto (1860-1933). Ger. anatomist.
Bulloch—Hist. p381

Lubbock, Sir John, Lord Avebury (1834-1913). Eng. anthropologist,
  entomologist.
*Book—Pop. Sci. (13) p4574-4575
  (por.4575)
Van Wagenen—Beacon p364-365

Lubbock, Sir John William (1803-1865). Eng. mathematician, astronomer.
Hammerton p927

Luca di Borgo.   See **Pacioli, Luca**

Luckhardt, Arno Benedict (1885-   ). Amer. physiologist.
Robinson—Victory p305 (por.274)

Lucretius (or Carus Titus Lucretius) (99/95-55 B.C.). Rom. naturalist.
Adams—Birth p32-35   Moulton—Auto. p15
Castiglioni—Hist. p204   Osborn—Greeks p91-97
Clagett—Greek p101-104   Schwartz—Moments (1) p154-155
Gordon—Medicine p661-663   Sedgwick—Short p144-145
Hammerton p928 (por.928)

Ludwig, Carl Friedrich Wilhelm (1816-1895). Ger. physiologist.
Atkinson—Magic p291
Castiglioni—Hist. p778-779 (por.778)
Chambers—Dict. col.294
Hammerton p929-930
Locy—Biology p188-189 (por.188)
Major—History (2) p790-791
Rosen—Four p247-252
Woodruff—Devel. p283

Ludwig, Karl Drais von. See **Sauerbronn, Karl Drais, Baron von**

Ludwig, Wilhelm Friedrich von (1790-1865). Ger. surgeon.
Leonardo—Lives p263

Lufberry, Raoul Gervais Victor (1885-1918). Fr. aero. pioneer.
Arnold—Airmen p122-123
Maitland—Knights p196-203

Lugeon, Maurice (1870-1953). Fr.-Swiss geologist.
G.S.A.—Proc. '54 p123-132 (por.123)

Luka. See **Kosta ibn Luka**

Luke, Frank, Jr. (d.1918). Amer. aero. pioneer.
Arnold—Airmen p118-120
Maitland—Knights p207-212

Lull, Richard Swann (1867-1957). Amer. geologist, paleontologist.
G.S.A.—Proc. '57 p127-131
(por.127)

Lully, Raymond (or Lull, Raymon; Lului, Raimondo; Dr. Illuminatus) (c.1235-1315/1316). Majorca chemist, physician.
Major—History (1) p308-309
Partington—Short p39-40
Three Famous p9-75

Lumière, Antoine (1839-1911). Fr. inventor.
Law—Civiliz p176-177

Lumière, Louis Jean (1864-1948). Fr. chemist.
Chambers—Dict. col.294
*Larsen—Scrap. p31-34

Lummer, Otto R. (1860-1925). Ger. physicist.
Chambers—Dict. col.294

Lumsden, Leslie Leon (1875-1946). Amer. physician, public health worker.
Ratcliffe—Modern p171-178

Lunardi, Vincenzo (or Vincent) (1759-1806). It. aero. pioneer.
Burge—Ency. p635   Heinmuller—Man's p234 (por.234)
Hammerton p930

Lund, Peter Wilhelm (1801-1880). Dan. zoologist, botanist, paleontologist.
Cohen.—Prom. p110

Lundholm, Carl Olaf (1850-1934). Swed.-Scot. chemist.
Hammerton p930

Lunge, George (1839-1923). Swiss chemist.
Smith—Torch. p163 (por.163)

Lupton, Charles Thomas (1878-1935). Amer. geologist.
G.S.A.—Proc. '35 p273-280 (por.273)

Lusitanus (or Lusitanius), **Amatus Juan Roderigo** (1511-1568). Port.
 physician.
Gordon—Medieval p629-640,753-755
Major—History (1) p470

Lusk, Graham (1866-1932). Amer. physiologist.
N.A.S.—Biog. (21) p95-130 (por.95)

Lustgarten, Sigmund (1858-1911). Aust. bacteriologist, dermatologist.
Bulloch—Hist. p381

Lustig, Alessandro (1857-1937). It. bacteriologist, pathologist.
Bulloch—Hist. p381

Lutz, Frank Eugene (1879-1943). Amer. biologist, entomologist.
Curr. Biog. '44 p426

Lydekker, Richard (1849-1915). Brit. naturalist.
Hammerton p932

Lyell, Sir Charles (1797-1875). Scot. geologist.
Bodenheimer—Hist. p375
*Book—Pop. Sci. (5) p1666-1667
   (por.1667)
Chambers—Dict. col.295
*Darrow—Masters p337
Davison—Founders p41-42
Fenton—Giants p84-97 (por.30)
Geikie—Founders p281-282
Gunther—Early XI p97-99
Hammerton p932-933 (por.933)
Locy—Biology p332-334 (por.333)
Moulton—Auto. p341-343
Murray—Science p42-65
Osborn—Greeks p325-326
*Snyder—Biologist p88-93 (por.91)
*Stevens—Science p105-109 (por.104)
Van Wagenen—Beacon p263-264
Williams—Story p99-102 (por.141)
Woodruff—Devel. p185-186,283
   (por.169)
*World's Great p277-295 (por.282)
Year—Pic. p135 (por.135)

Lyman, Henry Herbert (1854-1914). Amer. entomologist.
Osborn—Fragments p208-209

Lyman, Joseph (1906-   ). Amer. aero. pioneer, engineer.
Radio's 100 p282-284 (por.140)

Lyman, Theodore (1833-1897). Amer. zoologist.
N.A.S.—Biog. (5) p141-151
(por.141)

Lyman, Theodore (1874-1954). Amer. physicist.
N.A.S.—Biog. (3) p237-256
(por.237)

Lynch, Daniel Francis (1902-   ). Amer. oral surgeon.
Curr. Biog. '55 p374-376 (por.375)

Lynch, John Joseph (1894-   ). Eng. seismologist.
Curr. Biog. '46 p358-360 (por.359)

Lyndon, Edward (1879-1940). Amer. elec. engineer.
Curr. Biog. '40 p529-530

Lyonet (or Lyonnet), **Pierre** (1707-1789). Dutch entomologist, naturalist.
Locy—Biology p89-95 (por.90)   Woodruff—Devel. p283
Miall—Early p291-293

Lyons, Harry (1900-   ). Amer. oral pathologist.
Curr. Biog. '57 p336-337 (por.337)

Lyot, Bernard Ferdinand (1897-   ). Fr. astronomer.
Abetti—History p249-250,262-266,
284-286

Lysenko, Trofim Denisovich (1898-   ). Rus. biologist.
Chambers—Dict. col.295-296   Robinson—100 p265-268 (por.265)
Curr. Biog. '52 p364-366   Year—Pic. p225 (por.255)

Lyte, Henry (1529-1607). Eng. botanist.
Arber—Herbals p125,126,127,128
Gilmour—British p10-11

M

Maanen, Adriann van (1884-1946). Dutch-Amer. astronomer.
Chambers—Dict. col.297

Maberry, Charles Frederic (1850-1927). Amer. chemist.
A.A.A.S.—Proc. (78) p5

McAdam, John Loudon (1756-1836). Scot. engineer.
Hammerton p935
*Ivins—Fifty p31-34 (por.32)

McAdie, Alexander George (1863-1943). Amer. meteorologist.
Curr. Biog. '43 p469

MacAlister, Sir Donald (1854-1934). Scot. physician.
Hammerton p935 (por.935)

MacAlister, Robert Alexander Stewart (1870-1950). Irish archaelogist.
Hammerton p935

MacBride, Ernest William (1866-1940). Irish zoologist.
Hammerton p1451

McBride, Katharine Elizabeth (1904-   ). Amer. psychologist.
Curr. Biog. '42 p541-542 (por.542)

McBurney, Charles (1845-1913). Amer. surgeon.
Kagan—Modern p92 (por.92)
Leonardo—Lives p302-304

McCallie, Samuel Washington (1856-1933). Amer. geologist.
G.S.A.—Proc. '33 p227-230 (por.227)

MacCallum, William George (1874-1944). Can. pathologist.
Curr. Biog. '44 p430   N.A.S.—Biog. (23) p339-353
Major—History (2) p1041   (por.339)

McCarthy, Kenneth Cecil (1902-   ). Can. physician.
Curr. Biog. '53 p385-386 (por.385)

MacCartney, William Napier (1862-1940). Amer. physician.
Curr. Biog. '40 p530
Fabricant—Why p150-157

McCash, Andrew James (1858-1908). Amer. surgeon.
Leonardo—Lives p304-305

McCaskey, Hiram Dwyer (1871-1936). Amer. geologist.
G.S.A.—Proc. '37 p183-189 (por.183)

Macías, Ramón (1856-1916). Mex. surgeon.
Leonardo—Lives p265-266

Macie, Lewis (or Louis).   See **Smithson, James**

McClean, Sir Francis (1876-1955). Eng. aero. pioneer.
Burge—Ency. p635

McClintock, Emory (1840-1916). Amer. mathematician.
Smith—Math. p133-134

Macloskie, George (1834-1920). Amer. entomologist.
Osborn—Fragments p227

McClung, Clarence Erwin (1870-1946). Amer. biologist, zoologist.
Bodenheimer—Hist. p449

McClure, Sir Robert John le Mesurier (1807-1873). Irish sci. explorer.
Hammerton p937

McColloch, J. W. (1889-1929). Amer. entomologist.
Osborn—Fragments p214

McCollum, Elmer Verner (1879-   ). Amer. physiol. chemist.
Chambers—Dict. col.297   Progress—Science '41 p218 (por.218)
Jaffe—Outposts p245-280 (por.250)

McConachie, G. W. Grant (1909-   ). Can. aero. pioneer.
Curr. Biog. '58 p258-260 (por.259)

McCone, John A. (1902-   ). Amer. engineer.
Curr. Biog. '59 p272-274 (por.273)

MacConkey, Alfred Theodore (1861-1931). Eng. bacteriologist.
Bulloch—Hist. 382

McConnell, Richard George (1857-1942). Can. geologist.
G.S.A.—Proc. '44 p265-267 (por.265)

McConnell, Wilbur Ross (1881-1920). Amer. entomologist.
Osborn—Fragments p215

McCook, Henry Christopher (1837-1911). Amer. entomologist.
Osborn—Fragments p205 (por.256)

McCord, Carey P. (1886-   ). Amer. physician.
Rosen—Four p231-233

MacCormac, Sir William (1836-1901). Eng. physician, surgeon.
Leonardo—Lives (Supp.1) p495-496

McCormick, Cyrus Hall (1809-1884). Amer. inventor.
Abbot—Great p303-306
Bachman—Great p142-160
*Burlingame—Mach. p83-99
Carmer—Caval. p228-231 (por.228)
*Darrow—Builders p2-6
*Darrow—Thinkers p160-170
*Eberle—Invent. p69-74 (por.68)
*Epstein—Real p175-177
*Forbes—Men p240-249 (por.1)
*Hartman—Mach. p198-203
*Hathaway—Partners p195-202
*Hylander—Invent. p59-65 (por.59)
Iles—Leading p276-314 (por.276)
*Ives—Fifty p41-46 (por.40)
*Larsen—Prentice p81-83
Law—Civiliz. p112-115
Meyer—World p244 (por.243)
*Montgomery—Invent. p125-128
*Morris—Heroes p166-170
*Nida—Makers p74-80
*Parkman—Conq. p8-26
*Patterson—Amer. p32-48
*Pratt—Famous p51-52
*Tappan—Heroes p20-29
*Tuska—Invent. p117
*Wildman—Famous (1st) p167-178
   (por.165)
Wilson—Amer. p139-143 (por.140)
Year—Pic. p188 (por.188)

McCormick, Edward James (1891-   ). Amer. surgeon.
Curr. Biog. '53 p390-392 (por.390)

McCourt, Walter Edward (1884-1943). Amer. geologist.
G.S.A.—Proc. '43 p201-204 (por.201)

McCoy, Alexander Watts (1889-1944). Amer. geologist.
G.S.A.—Proc. '44 p271-276
   (por.271)

McCoy, George Walter (1876-1952). Amer. chemist.
DeKruif—Men p176-203

McCoy, Herbert Newby (1870-1945). Amer. chemist.
Weeks—Discovery p429 (por.429)

McCrae, Thomas (1870-1935). Can. physician.
Major—History (2) p1041-1042

McCudden, James T. (d.1918). Brit. aero. pioneer.
Burge—Ency. p636

McCullagh, James (1809-1847). Irish mathematician, physicist.
Murray—Science p356

McCune, Charles Andrew (1879-1940). Amer. engineer.
Curr. Biog. '40 p536

McCune, Francis Kimber (1906-   ). Amer. engineer.
Curr. Biog. '61 (Mar.) (por.)

McCurdy, James A. D. (1886-   ). Amer. aero. pioneer.
Heinmuller—Man's p269 (por.269)

MacDonald, Donald Francis (1875-1942). Can. geologist.
G.S.A.—Proc. '49 p197-199 (por.197)

MacDonald, Greville (b.1856). Eng. physician.
Farmer—Doctors' p198

McDonnell, Edward Orrick (1891-   ). Amer. aero. pioneer.
Holland—Arch. p145-160

MacDougall, William (1871-1938). Eng. psychologist.
Hammerton p639-640 (por.639)

McDowell, Ephraim (1771-1830). Amer. physician, surgeon.
Atkinson—Magic p241-249
Castiglioni—Hist. p727-728 (por.727)
Flexner—Doctors p121-162 (por.121)
Kagan—Modern p86 (por.86)
Leonardo—Lives p305-306
Major—History (2) p738-741 (por.739)
*Shippen—Men p125-132 (por.125)
Thorwald—Century p13-14 (por.48)
Young—Scalpel p112-123

Macelwane, James Bernard (1883-1956). Amer. geologist.
G.S.A.—Proc. '56 p159-161 (por.159)
N.S.A.—Biog. (31) p254-275 (por.254)

Macewen, Sir William (1848-1924). Scot. surgeon.
Leonardo—Lives p264-265

McFadyean, John (1853-1941). Scot. bacteriologist, pathologist, surgeon.
Bulloch—Hist. p382

MacFadyen, Allan (1860-1907). Scot. bacteriologist.
Bulloch—Hist. p382

McFarland, Marvin W. (1919-   ). Amer. aero. pioneer, space pioneer.
Thomas—Men (2) p. xvi-xvii
Thomas—Men (3) p.xvi

MacFarlane, James Rieman (1858-1938). Amer. geologist.
G.S.A.—Proc. '39 p211-212 (por.211)

McGee, Anita Newcomb (b.1864). Amer. physician, surgeon.
Mead—Medical p66

McGhee, George Crews (1912-   ). Amer. geologist.
Curr. Biog. '50 p367-369 (por.368)

MacGillivray, Alex Dyar (1868-1924). Amer. entomologist.
Osborn—Fragments p207-208

McGlashan, Charles Fayette (b.1847). Amer. entomologist.
Essig—Hist. p704-705

McGrady, Edward (1906-   ). Amer. sci. explorer, biologist.
Curr. Biog. '57 p339-341 (por.340)

McGraw, Theodore A. (1839-1921). Amer. surgeon.
Leonardo—Lives p306-307

McGregor, Gordon Roy (1901-   ). Can. aero. pioneer.
Curr. Biog. '54 p431-433 (por.432)

McGuire, Hunter H. (1835-1900). Amer. surgeon.
Leonardo—Lives p307-308
Major—History (2) p771

Mach, Ernst (1838-1916). Aust. physicist.
Chambers—Dict. col.297-298   *Science Miles p198-200 (por.198)
Hammerton p940-941   Year—Pic p120 (por.120)

McHale, Kathryn (1890-   ). Amer. psychologist.
Curr. Biog. '47 p415-416 (por.416)

Macie, Lewis (or Louis).   See **Smithson, James**

McIndoo, Norman Eugene (1881-   ). Amer. entomologist.
Osborn—Fragments p198 (por.341)

McIntire, Ross T. (1889-1959). Amer. physician, surgeon.
Curr. Biog. '45 p266-268 (por.267)
Feb.'60 p250

MacIntosh, Charles (1766-1843). Scot. inventor.
Hammerton p941

McIver, Pearl (1893-   ). Amer. public health worker.
Curr. Biog. '49 p378-380 (por.379)

Mack, Pauline Beery (1891-   ). Amer. chemist.
Curr. Biog. '50 p373-374 (por.373)

Mackay, Angus (1840-1932). Can. agriculturist.
*DeKruif—Hunger p33-66 (por.32)

MacKay, Clarence Hungerford (1874-1938). Amer. engineer.
*Shumway—Famous (4th) p255-262
(por.253)

MacKay, Helen Marion MacPherson (1891-   ). Scot. physician.
Hammerton p942

McKeen, John E. (1903-   ). Amer. chem. engineer.
Curr. Biog. '61 (Je.) (por.)

McKenna, Charles F. (1861-1930). Amer. chemist.
Browne—Hist. p499 (por.49)

MacKenzie, Chalmers Jack (1888-   ). Can. engineer.
Curr. Biog. '52 p379-381 (por.379)

MacKenzie, Sir James (1853-1925). Scot. physician.
Chambers—Dict. col.298   Rowntree—Amid p462-465,468
Hammerton p943   (por.466)
Major—History (2) p946-949,1041
(por.947)

MacKenzie, Sir Morell (1837-1892). Eng. surgeon.
Hammerton p943 (por.943)

MacKenzie, Richard James (1821-1854). Scot. surgeon.
Leonardo—Lives p266-267

McKenzie, Robert Tait (1867-1938). Can. surgeon.
Hammerton p943

M'Lachlan, Robert (1837-1904). Eng. entomologist.
Essig—Hist. p707-708 (por.707)

McLaughlin, George Dunlap (1887-   ). Amer. chemist.
Holland—Ind. p310-321 (por.310)

MacLaurin, Colin (1698-1746). Scot. mathematician.
Ball—Short p384-388
Cajori—Hist. p228-229
Chambers—Dict. col.298-299
Hammerton p944
Smith—Hist. I p452-454 (por.453)
Turnbull—Great p101-103
Van Wagenen—Beacon p138-140
Woodruff—Devel. p283
Year—Pic. p110 (por.110)

MacLean, Donald (1839-1903). Can. surgeon.
Leonardo—Lives p267

MacLean, John (1771-1814). Amer. chemist.
Bell—Early p63
Smith—Chem. p147-148 (por.148)

McLean, William Hannah (b.1877). Brit. engineer.
Hammerton p944

McLennan, John Cunningham (1867-1935). Can. physicist.
Chambers—Dict. col.299

McLennan, John Ferguson (1827-1881). Scot. ethnologist.
Hammerton p944

MacLeod, John James Rickard (1876-1935). Scot. physiologist.
Chambers—Dict. col.299
Hammerton p944-945
Major—History (2) p1041
Stevenson—Nobel p110,112-114
    (por.150)

Maclure, William (1763-1840). Scot.-Amer. geologist.
Bell—Early p63-64
Fenton—Giants p128-131 (por.95)
Hammerton p945
Merrill—First p31-37,46-47 (por.32)

McMechan, Francis Hoeffer (1879-1939). Amer. anesthetist.
Robinson—Victory p266 (por.275)

MacMillan, Donald Baxter (b.1874). Amer. geologist, aero. pioneer,
    anthropologist, sci. explorer.
Curr. Biog. '48 p402-404 (por.402)
*Fraser—Heroes p337-362

McMillan, Edwin Mattison (1907-   ). Amer. phys. chemist.
Chambers—Dict. Supp.   Morris—Ency. p691-692
Curr. Biog. '52 p382-384 (por.383)

McMillan, Franklin R. (1882-   ). Amer. engineer.
Holland—Ind. p254-264 (por.254)

MacMurchy, Helen (1862-1953). Can. physician.
Lovejoy—Women p116-117

McMurtrie, William (1851-1913). Amer. chemist.
A.A.A.S.—Proc. (79) p27-28
Browne—Hist. p477-478 (por.49)

McMurtry, Louis (1850-1924). Amer. surgeon.
Leonardo—Lives p308-309

McNally, Margaret (n.d.). Amer. engineer.
Goff—Women p168-176

MacNeven (or McNevin), **William James** (1763-1841). Irish-Amer. chemist.
Chymia (2) p17-25 (por.20)
Smith—Chem. p224

MacNider, William deBerniere (1881-1951). Amer. physician.
N.A.S.—Biog. (32) p238-261
    (por.238)

MacPhail, Sir Andrew (1864-1938). Can. pathologist, physician.
Hammerton p946

MacPherson, Hector (1888-   ). Scot. astronomer.
Hammerton p946

McPherson, William (1864-1951). Amer. chemist.
Browne—Hist. p486 (por.141)

Macquer, Pierre Joseph (1718-1784). Fr. chemist.
Chambers—Dict. col.299

Macready, John A. (1887-   ). Amer. aero. pioneer.
*Fraser—Heroes p119-148   Maitland—Knights p256-258
Heinmuller—Man's p312 (por.312)   (por.250)

MacVicar, Donald George (d.1956). Amer. geologist.
G.S.A.—Proc. '56 p185

McWeeney, Edmond Joseph (1864-1925). Irish bacteriologist.
Bulloch—Hist. p382

Maddox, Ernest Edmund (1860-1933). Eng. surgeon.
Hammerton p947

Maddox, Richard Leach (1816-1902). Eng. inventor, physician, chemist.
Year—Pic. p162 (por.162)

Madison, James (1749-1812). Amer. nat. philosopher.
Bell—Early p64

Mädler, Johann Heinrich (1794-1874). Ger. astronomer.
Chambers—Dict. col.299-300
MacPherson—Makers p138-144

Madsen, Thorvald (1870-1957). Dan. bacteriologist.
Bulloch—Hist. p382

Maffucci, Angiolo (1847-1903). It. anatomist, bacteriologist.
Bulloch—Hist. p382

Magati, Cesare (1579-1647). It. surgeon.
Leonardo—Lives p267-269

Magee, James Carre (1883-   ). Irish-Amer. physician, surgeon.
Curr. Biog. '43 p486-488 (por.487)

Magendie, François (1783-1855). Fr. physiologist, physician.
*Book—Pop. Sci. (13) p4575-4576
Castiglioni—Hist. p680
Chambers—Dict. col.300
Hammerton p948
Major—History (2) p675-677
(por.676)
Woodruff—Devel. p283

Maggi, Bartolommeo (1516?-1552). It. physician, surgeon, anatomist.
Gordon—Medieval p679-680
Leonardo—Lives p269-270
Major—History (1) p471

Magill, Mary J. (1855-1891). Amer. physician.
Jones—Memories p436-437

Magnol, Pierre (1638-1715). Fr. botanist, physician.
Hawks—Pioneers p239 (por.240)

Magnus, Albertus.   See **Albertus Magnus, Saint, Count von Böllstadt**

Magnus, Heinrich Gustav (1802-1870). Ger. chemist, physicist.
A.A.A.S.—Proc. (81) p70-71   Weeks—Discovery p161 (por.161)
Hammerton p948

Magnuson, Paul B. (1884-   ). Amer. physician, surgeon.
Curr. Biog. '48 p406-408 (por.407)

Magoffin, Ralph Van Deman (1874-1942). Amer. archaeologist.
Curr. Biog. '42 p557

Mahan, Dennis Hart (1802-1871). Amer. engineer.
N.A.S.—Biog. (2) p29-37

Mailhouse, Max (1857-1941). Amer. physician, neurologist.
Curr. Biog. '41 p551

Maillet, Benoît de (1656-1738). Fr. evolutionist.
Osborn—Greeks p163-167

Maimonides (or Moses ben Maimon) (1135-1204/1209). Arab.-Sp. physician.
Atkinson—Magic p58-59   Gordon—Romance p107-108
Bodenheimer—Hist. p204   (por.107)
Castiglioni—Hist. p277-278 (por.279)   Major—History (1) p256-257
Gordon—Medieval p219-236
  (por.210)

Main, Charles Thomas (1856-1943). Amer. engineer.
Curr. Biog. '43 p488

Maitland, Edward Maitland (1880-1921). Brit. aero. pioneer.
Burge—Ency. p636

Maitland, Lester J. (1888-   ). Amer. aero. pioneer.
*Fraser—Heroes p492-502   Maitland—Knights p318-327
Heinmuller—Man's p324 (por.324)   (por.323)

Makemson, Maud Worcester (1891-   ).
Curr. Biog. '41 p552-554 (por.553)

Makins, Sir George Henry (1853-1933). Eng. surgeon.
Hammerton p951

Malfatti, Giovanni Francesco Giuseppe (1731-1807). It. mathematician.
Smith—Hist. I p515

Malgaigne, Joseph François (1806-1865). Fr. surgeon.
Leonardo—Lives p270-271
Major—History (2) p775

Malinowsky, Bronislaw Kasper (1884-1942). Pol. anthropologist.
Chambers—Dict. col.300   Hammerton p952
Curr. Biog. '41 p554-556 (por.555)
   '42 p561

Mall, Franklin Paine (1862-1917). Amer. anatomist, pathologist, physician.
Major—History (2) p919
N.A.S.—Biog. (16) p65-116 (por.65)

Mallet, John William (1832-1912). Irish-Amer. chemist.
Browne—Hist. p473 (por.29)   Smith—Chem. p276-277
Killeffer—Eminent p10 (por.10)

Mallet, Robert (1810-1881). Irish seismologist, engineer.
Davison—Founders p65-81

Mallinckrodt, Edward (1845-1928). Amer. chemist.
Haynes—Chem. (1) p143-164
   (por.144)

Mallory, Frank Burr (1862-1941). Amer. pathologist.
Curr. Biog. '41 p556-557   Progress—Science '41 p221
Kagan—Modern p159 (por.159)

Mallory, Lester Dewitt (1904-   ). Amer. agriculturist.
Curr. Biog. Sept. '60

Mallus Haereticorum.   See **Faber, Johannes**

Mally, Fred William (1868-1939). Amer. entomologist.
Osborn—Fragments p235

Malmgren, Finn (1895-1928). Swed. meteorologist.
Hammerton p952

Malone, George Wilson (1890-   ). Amer. engineer.
Curr. Biog. '50 p380-382 (por.381)

Malott, Clyde Arnestt (1887-1950). Amer. geologist.
G.S.A.—Proc. '50 p105-108 (por.105)

Malpighi, Marcello (1628-1694). It. physician, anatomist.

Bodenheimer—Hist. p258
Castiglioni—Hist. p522-524 (por.523)
Chambers—Dict. col.300-301
Gordon—Medieval p644-645 (por.210)
Hammerton p953
Hawks—Pioneers p198-199
Lambert—Medical p197-199
Lambert—Minute p197-199
Locy—Biology p58-67,202-205 (por.59,204)
Major—History (1) p508-511 (por.509)
Miall—Early p145-166
Oliver—Stalkers p95-96
Peattie—Green p43-45
Reed—Short p1628-1694
Robinson—Path. p 153-185 (por.174)
Schwartz—Moments (2) p594-595
*Shippen—Micro. p70-75
Sigerist—Great p147-149 (por.145)
*Snyder—Biology p41-45 (por.42)
*Sterne—Blood p44-79
Van Wagenen—Beacon p119-120
Woodruff—Devel. p229-230,283 (por.236)
Year—Pic. p90,91 (por.92)

Malus, (Étienne) Stephen Louis (1775-1812). Fr. physicist, engineer.

Arago—Biog. p117-170
Chambers—Dict. col.301
Hart—Physicists p117-118
Magie—Source p315

Mamun, al-, Caliph Abdallah (786-833). Arab. physician.

Gordon—Medieval p137-139
Major—History (1) p230-232
Smith—Hist. I p169

Manardus, Johannes Giovanni Monardi (1462-1536). It. physician.

Major—History (1) p461

Manchot, Wilhelm (b.1869). Ger. chemist.

Chambers—Dict. col.301

Mandelstamm, Max (1839-1912). Lith. physician.

Kagan—Modern p146 (por.146)

Manfredi, Eustachio (1674-1739). It. mathematician.

Smith—Hist. I p512

Manfredi, Gabriel (1681-1761). It. mathematician.

Smith—Hist. I p512

Mangiagalli, Luigi (1849-1928). It. surgeon.

Leonardo—Lives p271

Mann, Albert Russell (1880-1947). Amer. agriculturist.

*Ivins—Fifty p343-350 (por.345)

Mann, B. Pickmann (1848-1926). Amer. entomologist.

Osborn—Fragments p171 (por.362)

Mannerheim, Carl Gustav von (1804-1854). Swed. entomologist.
Essig.—Hist. p698-700 (por.698)

Mannock, Edward (d.1918). Brit. aero. pioneer.
Burge—Ency. p636

Mansfield, George Rogers (1875-1917). Amer. geologist.
G.S.A.—Proc. '48 p187-193
(por.187)

Mansfield, Wendell Clay (1874-1939). Amer. geologist.
G.S.A.—Proc. '39 p213-215 (por.213)

Manson, Sir Patrick (1844-1922). Scot. bacteriologist, physician, parasitologist.
Bodenheimer—Hist. p422
Castiglioni—Hist. p984 (por.827)
Chambers—Dict. col.301-302
Hale-White—Great p290-303
Hammerton p956 (por.956)
Major—History (2) p905-906
*Masters—Conquest p128-149
(por.,front.)
*Montgomery—Story p109-111
Walker—Pioneers p193-205

Mansur, al- (or Muwaffaq, Abu Mansur) (fl.10th cent.). Pers. chemist.
Holmyard—Chem. p27-28

Manzolini, Anna Morandi (1716-1774?). It. anatomist.
Lovejoy—Women p202
Mozans—Woman p236-237

Mapes, James Jay (1805-1866). Amer. agric. chemist.
Haynes—Chem. (1) p74-87 (por.77)

Maragliano, Edoardo (1849-1940). It. physician.
Castiglioni—Hist. p843 (por.988)
Major—History (2) p972

Marble, John Putnam (1897-1955). Amer. geologist.
G.S.A.—Proc. '55 p143-144 (por.143)

Marbut, Curtis Fletcher (1863-1935). Amer. agriculturist, geologist.
G.S.A.—Proc. '36 p221-224 (por.221)

Marcet, Alexander (1770-1822). Swiss physician, chemist.
Weeks—Discovery p164 (por.164)

Marcet, Jane (1785-1858). Swiss physician, chemist.
Smith—Torch. p164 (por.164)

Marchiafava, Ettore (1847-1935). It. pathologist.

Castiglioni—Hist. p808 (por.807)
Major—History (2) p908

Marconi, Marchese Guglielmo (1874-1937). It. inventor, elec. engineer.

Abbot—Great p129-133 (por.128)
*Bachman—Great p287-290 (por.288)
*Bolton—Famous p223-234 (por.222)
*Book—Pop. Sci. (12) p4211-4213
    (por.4212)
*Bridges—Master p151-161 (por.158)
Chambers—Dict. col.302
*Cottler—Heroes p230-238
*Crowther—Inventors p125-162
    (por.129)
*Darrow—Builders p134-141
*Darrow—Masters p294-305 (por.320)
*Darrow—Thinkers p343-347
    (por.343)
*Eberle—Invent. p121-126 (por.120)
*Epstein—Real p137-138
Fitzhugh—Concise p442-443
Hammerton p958-959 (por.958)
*Hartman—Mach. p223-230
*Hathaway—Partners p124-130
    (por.125)
Hawks—Wireless p220-255 (por.228)
Heathcote—Nobel p70-81 (por.240)
*Larsen—Men p98-120 (por.80)
*Larsen—Prentice p150-157
Law—Civiliz. p216-219
*Nida—Makers p192-200 (por.192)
*Nisenson—More p92 (por.92)
100 Great p668-673
*Parkman—Conq. p396-408
*Pratt—Famous p66-70
Radio's 100 p171-180 (por.140)
*Science Miles p286-291 (por.286)
Sewell—Brief p209-210
*Towers—Beacon p199-230 (por.202)
Tuska—Invent. p80-81
Untermeyer—Makers p478-483
Van Wagenen—Beacon p430-432
Weber—College p145 (por.145)
Year—Pic. p179,243 (por.179,243)

Marcou, Jules (1824-1898). Fr.-Amer. geologist.

Merrill—First p308-310 (por.309)

Marett, Robert Ranulph (1866-1943). Eng. anthropologist.

Curr. Biog. '43 p497
Hammerton p960 (por.960)

Marey, Étienne Jules (1830-1904). Fr. physiologist, aero. pioneer.

Heinmuller—Man's p248 (por.248)

Margerie.   See **de Margerie, Emmanuel Marie Pierre Martin Jacquin de**

Marggraf, Andreas Sigismund (1709-1782). Ger. chemist.

Chambers—Dict. col.302
Hammerton p961
Smith—Torch. p165 (por.165)
Weeks—Discovery p344,455 (por.58)

Mariano Barletta, Santo de (1490-1550). It. surgeon.

Gordon—Medieval p678-679

Maricourt.   See **Peregrinus, Petrus**

Marie, Pierre (1853-1940). Fr. neurologist.

Major—History (2) p1041 (por.964)

Mariette, Auguste Édouard (1821-1881). Fr. archaeologist.
Ceram—Gods p128-136

Marignac, Jean Charles Galissard de (1817-1894). Swiss chemist.
Chambers—Dict. col.303
Partington—Short p353
Smith—Torch p166 (por.166)
Weeks—Discovery p423-424
(por.421)

Marine, David (1880-   ). Amer. pathologist.
Rowntree—Amid p382-384

Marinus of Tyre (fl.2nd cent.). Gr. geographer, mathematician.
Gordon—Medicine p689-690
Smith—Hist. I p129-130

Mariotte, Edmé (1620?-1684). Fr. physicist.
Chambers—Dict. col.303
Hammerton p963
Lenard—Great p64-66
Magie—Source p88
Reed—Short p91

Marius (or Mayr), **Simon** (1570-1624). Ger. astronomer.
Chambers—Dict. col.303

Marjolin, Jean-Nicolas (1780-1850). Fr. surgeon.
Leonardo—Lives p271-272

Mark, Herman Francis (1895-   ). Aust.-Amer. chemist.
Curr. Biog. '61 (May) (por.)

Markham, Beryl (1920-   ). Eng. aero. pioneer.
Curr. Biog. '42 p570-572 (por.570)
*Fraser—Heroes p755-761,781-784
(por.756)

Marmorek, Alexander (1865-1923). Pol.-Fr. physician, bacteriologist.
Kagan—Modern p162 (por.162)

Marriott, Alice Lee (1910-   ). Amer. ethnologist.
Curr. Biog. '50 p382-383 (por.383)

Marriott, Frederick (b.1805). Eng.-Amer. aero. pioneer.
Milbank—First p90-93

Mar Samuel.   See **Samuel, Mar**

Marsh, George Perkins (1801-1882). Amer. anthropologist.
N.A.S.—Biog. (6) p71-80 (por.71)

Marsh, James (1794-1846). Eng. chemist.
Chambers—Dict. col.303-304

Marsh, Othniel Charles (1831-1899). Amer. paleontologist.
*Book—Pop. Sci. (13) p4576-4578
Chambers—Dict. col.304
*Hylander—Scien. p89-94 por.89)
Jaffe—Men p279-306 (por.xxviii)
Jordan—Leading p283-312 (por.283)
Locy—Biology p340 (por.339)
Merrill—First p458-459,528-530,592 (por.528)
N.A.S.—Biog. (20) p1-58 (por.1)
Van Wagenen—Beacon p354-356
Williams—Story p114-121 (por.112)
Woodruff—Devel. p283 (por.196)
Young—Biology p39-40 (por.41)

Marshall, Charles Herbert (1898-   ). Amer. physician.
Curr. Biog. '49 p406-407 (por.406)

Marshall, Clara (1848-1931). Amer. physician.
Mead—Medical p30

Marshall, W. W. (d.1918). Amer. entomologist.
Osborn—Fragments p215-216

Marshall, William Stanley (1866-1947). Amer. entomologist.
Osborn—Fragments p197-198
(por.339,352)

Marsilio Ficino.   See **Ficino, Marsilio**

Martin, Archer John Porter (1910-   ). Eng. biochemist.
Chambers—Dict. Supp.
Curr. Biog. '53 p417-419 (por.418)

Martin, Charles James (1866-1955). Eng. biochemist, bacteriologist, physiologist.
Bulloch—Hist. p382-383
R.S.L.—Biog. (2) p173-204 (por.173)

Martin, Collier Ford (1873-1941). Amer. physician.
Curr. Biog. '41 p562

Martin, Edward (1859-1938). Amer. surgeon.
Leonardo—Lives p272-274

Martin, Emmanuel.   See **De Margerie, Emmanuel Marie Pierre Martin Jacquin de**

Martin, Franklin Henry (1857-1935). Amer. gynecologist, physician, surgeon.
Fabricant—Why p116-126
Leonardo—Lives (Supp 1) p496-497

Martin, George Curtis (1875-1943). Amer. geologist, geographer.
G.S.A.—Proc. '44 p247-254 (por.247)

Martin, Glenn Luther (1886-1955). Amer. aero. pioneer.
Curr. Biog. '43 p500-505 (por.501)   Heinmuller—Man's p277 (por.277)
Daniel—Pioneer p67-71 (por.66)   Holland—Arch. p192-205
Forbes—50 p299-306 (por.298)   Maitland—Knight p112-115

Martin, Lawrence (1880-1955). Amer. geologist.
G.S.A.—Proc. '55 p147-149 (por.147)

Martin, Lillien Jane (b.1851). Amer. psychologist.
Curr. Biog. '42 p575-577 (por.576)

Martin, Sydney (1860-1924). Eng. phys. chemist, physician.
Bulloch—Hist. p383

Martin, Walter Bramblett (1888-   ). Amer. physician.
Curr. Biog. '54 p443-445 (por.443)

Martini, Friedrich (1832-1897). Aust. inventor.
Hammerton p967

Martino, Gaetano (1900-   ). It. physiologist.
Curr. Biog. '56 p418-420 (por. 419)

Martland, Harrison Stanford (1883-1954). Amer. physician, pathologist.
Curr. Biog. '40 p565-566
    '54 p477

Marvel, Carl S. (1894-   ). Amer. chemist.
Browne—Hist. p491-492 (por.169)

Marvin, Charles Frederick (1858-1943). Amer. meteorologist, inventor.
Curr. Biog. '43 p506

Marvin, Harry (1863-1940). Amer. inventor.
Curr. Biog. '40 p566

Marx, George (1838-1895). Ger. entomologist.
Essig —Hist. p700-702 (por.700)
Osborn—Fragments p214

Marzotto, Gaetano, Count (1894-   ). It. agriculturist.
Curr. Biog. '53 p421-422 (por.421)

Masawaih.   See **Mesuë**

Mascagni, Paolo (1752-1815). It. physician.
Castiglioni—Hist. p600-601
  (por.598)
Major—History (2) p639

Mascheroni, Lorenzo (1750-1800). It. mathematician, physicist.
Smith—Hist. I p516-517 (por.516)

Maschke, Heinrich (1853-1908). Ger.-Amer. mathematician.
Smith—Math. p144-145

Masham, Samuel Cunliffe-Lister, 1st Baron (1815-1906). Eng. inventor.
Hammerton p972

Maskell, William Miles (1840-1898). Eng. entomologist.
Essig—Hist. p702-704 (por.703)

Maskelyn, Nevil Story (or Storey, Mervin Herbert Nevil) (1823-1911). Eng. astronomer.
Abetti—History p148-149
Chambers—Dict. col.304
Gunther—Early XI p270-271
  (por.270)
Hammerton p972
Shapley—Astron. p133
Williams—Great p247-251
  (por.248)

Maslama al-Majriti of Madrid (d.1007). Span. astronomer, mathematician, chemist.
Holmyard—Chem. p23-26
Holmyard—Makers p77

Massa Nicolo (1499-1569). It. physician.
Gordon—Medieval p758
Major—History (1) p467

Massooa.   See **Mesuë, Senior**

Matas, Rudolph (1860-1950). Amer. physician, surgeon.
Robinson—Victory p253,296
  (por.275)

Mather, Cotton (1663-1728). Amer. nat. philosopher.
Bell—Early p64-65

Mather, Kirtley Fletcher (1888-   ). Amer. geologist.
Curr. Biog. '51 p414-416 (por.415)

Mather, William Williams (1804-1859). Amer. geologist, chemist,
  mineralogist, agriculturist.
Merrill—First p173-174 (por.188)   Youmans—Pioneers p402-409
Smith—Chem. p225-226   (por.402)

Mathews, Edward Bennett (1869-1944). Amer. geologist.
G.S.A.—Proc. '44 p259-262 (por.259)

Mathews, John Alexander (1872-1935). Amer. chemist, metallurgist.
Holland—Ind. p129-148 (por.129)

Matskevich, Vladimir Vladimirovich (1910-   ). Rus. agriculturist.
Curr. Biog. '55 p407-409 (por.408)

Matson, George Charlton (1873-1940). Amer. geologist.
G.S.A.—Proc. '40 p229-231 (por.229)

Mattern, James (1906-   ). Amer. aero. pioneer.
Heinmuller—Man's p172-182,346
  (por.182,346)

Matthes, François Emile (1874-1948). Dutch-Amer. geologist.
G.S.A.—Proc. '55 p153-166 (por.153)

Mattioli, Pietro Andrea (or Matthioli; Mattiolus, Pierandrea) (1501-1577).
  It. botanist.
Arber—Herbals p92-97 p221,223,224,   Major—History (1) p468-469
  225 (por.93)   Sarton—Six p137-139 (por.138)
Castiglioni—Hist. p485 (por.485)   Woodruff—Devel. p283
Gordon—Medieval p659   Year—Pic. p82 (por.82)
Hawks—Pioneers p79,80

Maucini, Joseph J. (1893-1955). Amer. geologist.
G.S.A.—Proc. p187

Maudslay, Henry (1771-1831). Eng. engineer.
Goddard—Eminent p198-204
(por.198)
Matschoss—Great p189-197
(por.188)

Maughan, Russell L. (1893-   ). Amer. aero. pioneer.
*Fraser—Heroes p213-244   Maitland—Knights p253-256
Heinmuller—Man's p315 (por.315)

Maunder, Edward Walter (1851-1928). Eng. astronomer.
MacPherson—Astron. p192-200
(por.192)

Maupertuis, Pierre Louis Moreau de (1698-1759). Fr. mathematician,
astronomer.
Chambers—Dict. col.304-305   Smith—Hist. I p473-474 (por.473)
Hammerton p975   Year—Pic. p111 (por.111)
Osborn—Greeks p167-170

Mauriceau, François (1637-1709). Fr. obstetrician, physician.
Castiglioni—Hist. p555-556 (por.556)   Major—History (1) p558
Gordon—Medieval p693-695

Maurolico (or Maurolycus), **Franciscus** (1494-1575). It. mathematician.
Cajori—Hist. p141-142   Smith—Hist. I p301-302 (por.301)
Sarton—Six p84-85

Maurus, Harbanus.   See **Rabanus, Maurus**

Maury, Carlotta Joaquina (1874-1938). Amer. geologist, paleontologist.
G.S.A.—Proc. '38 p157-161 (por.157)

Maury, Matthew Fontaine (1806-1873). Amer. hydrographer,
oceanographer.
Chambers—Dict. col.305   Van Wagenen—Beacon p281-282
Jaffe—Men p207-232 (por.xxviii)   Williams—Story p178-180 (por.179)
*Stevens—Science p131-137 (por.130)   Youmans—Pioneers p464-474
(por.464)

Mauser, Paul von (1838-1914). Ger. inventor.
Hammerton p976

Mawson, Sir Douglas (1882-1958). Austral. geologist, sci. explorer.
*Book—Pop. Sci. (9) p3176-3177   R.S.L.—Biog. (5) p119-124 (por.119)
(por.3177)
Hammerton p976

Maxim, Sir Hiram Stevens (1840-1916). Amer.-Eng. aero. pioneer, inventor.

*Bishop—Kite p140-145
*Book—Pop. Sci. (12) p4213-4215
  (por.4213)
Burge—Ency. p636
*Cohen—Men p104-106
Hammerton p977
Heinmuller—Man's p253 (por.253)
*Larsen—Prentice p128-129
Tuska—Invent. p107,116-117

Maxim, Hudson (1853-1927). Amer. inventor.

*Book—Pop. Sci. (12) p4215-4216
  (por.4215)
Hammerton p977
*Wildman—Famous (1st) p181-192
  (por.179)

Maxwell, James Clerk (or Clerk-Maxwell) (1831-1879). Scot. physicist.

Appleyard—Pioneers p3-30
  (por.3,14,15)
*Book—Pop. Sci. (13) p4335-4336
  (por.4336)
Cajori—Hist. p474
Chalmers—Historic p267-268
Chambers—Dict. col.305,306,307
  (por.306)
Crew—Physicists #9 (folder) (port.)
Crowther—Men p259-326
  (por.,front.,282)
*Darrow—Masters p337
Dibner—Ten p43-46 (por.44)
Gibson—Heroes p308-321
Ginzburg—Adven. p252-257
Gregory—British p34-35 (por.35)
Hammerton p978 (por.978)
Hawks—Wireless p175-183 (por.178)
Holmyard—British p54-55 (por.54)
Law—Civiliz. p176,220
Lenard—Great p339-343 (por.348)
MacFarlane—Ten p7-21 (por.,front.)
Magie—Source p257-258
Meyer—World p194-197 (por.195)
Morgan—Men p82-84
Moulton—Auto. p450-451
Radio's 100 p65-68 (por.140)
Sci. Amer.—Lives p155-180 (por.157)
Shapley—Astron. p274
*Shippen—Design p165-171
Van Wagenen—Beacon p357-358
Williams—Great p321 (por.322)
Williams—Story p227,230,242-244
  (por.201)
Woodruff—Devel. p62-67,283-284
  (por.60)
Year—Pic. p122 (por.122)

May, Charles Henry (1861-1943). Amer. ophthalmologist.

Curr. Biog. '44 p458

Maybach, Wilhelm (1846-1929). Ger. engineer.

Matschoss—Great p294-298 (por.298)

Mayer.   See also **Mayor**

Mayer, Alfred Marshall (1836-1897). Amer. physicist.

*Book—Pop. Sci. (13) p4336-4338
N.A.S.—Biog. (8) p243-266
  (por.243)

Mayer, Johann Tobias (1723-1762). Ger. astronomer, mathematician.

Abetti—History p149
Hammerton p979

Mayer, Julius Robert von (1814-1878). Ger. physicist, physician.

Bodenheimer—Hist. p394
Chalmers—Historic p268
Chambers—Dict. col.307
Gumpert—Trail p197-225
Hammerton p979
Lenard—Great p271-286 (por.282)

Magie—Source p196-197
Sigerist—Great p323
Van Wagenen—Beacon p301-303
Williams—Story p435-436 (por.219)
Woodruff—Devel. p61,284

Mayerne, Sir Theodore Turquet (1573-1655). Swiss physician.

Major—History (1) p552

Maynard, Harold Bright (1902-   ). Amer. engineer.

*Yost—Engineers p91-106

Mayo family (19th, 20th cent.). Amer. physicians. See also names of individuals.

Castiglioni—Hist. p1007 (por.1008)
Cooper—Twenty p237-254 (por.236)
Cushing—Medical p299-302
Huff—Famous (2nd) p369-379
   (por.371,378)

Major—History (2) p997-998
   (por.997)
*Men—Scien. p34-36

Mayo, Charles Horace (1865-1939). Amer. physician, surgeon.

Chambers—Dict. col.307
Clapesattle—Doctors p159-712
   (por.274,403,626)
Hammerton p979
Kagan—Modern p88 (por.88)

Leonardo—Lives (Supp.1) p497-499
*Lockhart—My p229 (por.228)
Rowntree—Amid p271-278 (por.273)

Mayo, Charles William (1898-   ). Amer. physician, surgeon.

Curr. Biog. '41 p566-568 (por.567)
   '54 p448-450 (por.449)

Rowntree—Amid p278-381 (por.279)

Mayo, William James (1861-1939). Amer. physician, surgeon.

Chambers—Dict. col.307
Clapesattle—Doctors p159-712
   (por.274,403,274)
Kagan—Modern p88 (por.88)

Leonardo—Lives (Supp.1) p501-502
Rowntree—Amid p263-271 (por.265)

Mayo, William Worrall (1819-1911). Eng.-Amer. physician, surgeon.

Clapesattle—Doctors p9-473 (por.82)
Kagan—Modern p88 (por.88)

Leonardo—Lives (Supp.I) p501-502
Rowntree—Amid p257-262 (por.259)

Mayo-Robson, Arthur William (1853-1933). Eng. surgeon.

Leonardo—Lives p274-276

Mayo-Smith, Richmond (1854-1901). Amer. econ. statistician.

N.A.S.—Biog. (10) p73-76 (por.73)

Mayor, Alfred Goldsborough (1868-1922). Amer. marine biologist.
N.A.S.—Biog. (11) (XXI-Memoirs)
  p1-10 (por.1)

Mayow (or Mayouwe, Mayo), **John** (1640-1679). Eng. chemist, physiologist.
Chambers—Dict. col.307-308
Hammerton p979
Holmyard—Chem. p66-70 (por.59)
Holmyard—Makers p154-158
  (por.155)
Major—History (1) p519-521
  (por.520)
Partington—Short p80-84,148
  (por.80)
Smith—Torch. p167 (por.167)
Thomson—Great p29
Weeks—Discovery p90-92 (por.92)
Woodruff—Devel. p284

Mazzotti, Count Franco (1904-   ). It. aero. pioneer.
Heinmuller—Man's p347 (por.347)

Mc.   Names beginning with **Mc** prefix are listed as if spelled **Mac**

Mead, Kate Campbell (1867-1941). Amer. physician.
Curr. Biog. '41 p568
Lovejoy—Women Phys. p19-20
  (por.7)

Mead, Margaret (1901-   ). Amer. anthropologist.
Clymer—Modern p120-128 (por.82)
Curr. Biog. '40 p569-570
  '51 p421-423 (por.422)
Progress—Science '41 p226 (por.226)
Yost—Women Sci. p214-232

Mead, Richard (1673-1754). Eng. physician.
Hammerton p980
Major—History (2) p629-630
Tobey—Riders p56

Mead, Warren Judson (1883-1960). Amer. geologist.
Chambers—Dict. col.308
N.A.S.—Biog (35) p252-268
  (por.252)

Mease, James (1771-1846). Amer. physician.
Bell—Early p65-66

Méchain, Pierre François André (1744-1804). Fr. astronomer.
Chambers—Dict. col.308
Smith—Hist. I p491

Mechnikov.   See **Metchnikoff, Élie**

Meckel, Johann Friedrich (1781-1833). Ger. anatomist, embryologist.
Locy—Biology p162-163   Woodruff—Devel. p284
Osborn—Greeks p306-307

Medawar, Peter Brian (1915-   ). Brit. zoologist.
Curr. Biog. '61 (Apr.) (por.)

Medigo.   See **Delmedigo, Joseph Solomon**

Meek, Fielding Bradford (1817-1876). Amer. paleontologist, geologist.
Merrill—First p527-528 (por.380,526)
N.A.S.—Biog. (4) p75-80

Mees, Charles Edward Kenneth (1882-   ). Eng.-Amer. chemist.
*Darrow—Builders p288-290 (por.286)   Progress—Science '41 p236-237
Holland—Ind. p224-239 (por.224)   (por.237)

Megenberg, Kunrat von (1309-1374). Ger. physician.
Gordon—Medieval p393

Meggers, William Frederick (1888-   ). Amer. physicist.
Weeks—Discovery p520 (por.520)

Mehaffey, Joseph Cowles (1889-   ). Amer. engineer.
Curr. Biog. '48 p439-440 (por.440)

Meigen, Johann Wilhelm (1763-1845). Ger. entomologist.
Essig—Hist. p693

Meigs, Montgomery C. (1816-1892). Amer. engineer.
N.A.S.—Biog. (3) p311-326

Meiling, Richard Lewis (1908-   ). Amer. physician.
Curr. Biog. '50 p390-392 (por.391)

Meinzer, Oscar Edward (1876-1948). Amer. geologist.
G.S.A.—Proc. '48 p197-202 (por.197)

Meissner, Georg (1829-1905). Ger. physiologist, bacteriologist.
Bulloch—Hist. p383

Meitner, Lise (1878-   ). Aust. physicist.
Chambers—Dict. col.309   *Shippen—Design p126-128
Curr. Biog. '45 p393-395 (por.394)   Weeks—Discovery p492,497,539
Jaffe—Crucibles p374-376   Year—Pic. p213 (por.213)
*Larsen—Scrap. p148-149,152   Yost—Women Mod. p17-30
    (por.145)   (por.,front.)
Riedman—Men p119-121, 123

Meldola, Raphael (1849-1915). Eng. dentist.

A.A.A.S.—Proc. p46-47   Hammerton p982
Findlay—British p96-125 (por.96)

Mellanby, Sir Edward (1884-1955). Eng. physiologist, biologist, physician.

R.S.L.—Biog. (1) p193-218 (por.193)

Melloni, Macedonio (1798-1854). It. physicist.

Chambers—Dict. col.309

Melsens, Louis Henri Frédéric (1814-1886). Belg. chemist.

Findlay—Hundred p331

Melsheimer family (18th., 19th. cent.) Ger., Amer. entomologists.

Osborn—Fragments p13-24

Meltzer, Samuel J. (1851-1924). Rus.-Amer. physiologist, physician.

Kagan—Modern p187 (por.187)   N.A.S.—Biog. (11) (XXI-Memoirs)
Major—History (2) p1042   p1014 (por.1)
                                 Rowntree—Amid p364-367 (por.363)

Melvill, Thomas (1726-1753). Scot. physicist.

Chambers—Dict. col.309

Melville, Herman (1819-1891). Amer. naturalist.

Von Hagen—Green p201-202

Menaechmus (373-325 B.C.). Gr. mathematician.

Ball—Short p46-47   Turnbull—Great p20
Chambers—Dict. col.309-310

Mendel, Gregor Johann (or Johann Gregor) (1822-1884). Aust. botanist, biologist.

Bodenheimer—Hist. p416   Schwartz—Moments (2) p681-683
*Book—Pop. Sci. (13) p4578-4580 *Science Miles p182-187 (por.182)
  (por.4579)   Sewell—Brief p177-178
Castiglioni—Hist. p770 (por.770) *Shippen—Micro. p159-166
Chambers—Dict. col.310   *Snyder—Biology p133-138 (por.133)
*Cottler—Heroes p339-347   Stevens—Science p123-127 (por.122)
*Darrow—Masters p337-338   Thomas—Scien. p187-197 (por.185)
Ginzburg—Adven. p358-377   Thomson—Great p108-114
Gordon—Romance p49-50   Van Wagenen—Beacon p324-325
Guinagh—Inspired p57-66   Wilson—Human p334-345
Lenard—Great p321-324 (por.324) Woglom—Discov. p177-193
Hammerton p983-984 (por.983)   Woodruff—Devel. p249-250,284
Locy—Biology p315-319 (por.316)   (por.248)
Major—History (2) p887   Year—Pic. p133 (por.133)
Moulton—Auto. p578-579

Mendel, Lafayette Benedict (1872-1935). Amer. phys. chemist, physiologist, biochemist.

Castiglioni—Hist. p791 (por.792)
Chambers—Dict. col.310

Kagan—Modern p190 (por.190)
N.A.S.—Biog. (18) p123-137 (por.123)

Mendeleeff (or Mendelev, Mendeleev), **Dmitri Ivanovitch** (1834-1907). Rus. chemist.

*Book—Pop. Sci. (13) p4338-4339
Chalmers—Historic p268-269
Chambers—Dict. col.310-311 (por.311-312)
Chymia (I) p67-74
*Darrow—Masters p122-124 (por.33)
Findlay—Hundred p331
Hammerton p984 (por.984)
*Harrow—Chemists p19-40 (por.19)
Holmyard—Great Chem. p122-128
Holmyard—Makers p268-273
*Jaffe—Crucibles p199-218

*Kendall—Young p186-200 (por.187)
Moulton—Auto. p286
Partington—Short p346-349,354 (por.347)
Roberts—Chem. p208-219
Schwartz—Moments (2) p819-821
Smith—Torch. p168 (por.168)
Tilden—Famous p241-258 (por.241)
Van Wagenen—Beacon p368-370
Weeks—Discovery p390-396 (por.390,393)
Woodruff—Devel. p284 (por.100)
Year—Pic. p123,124 (por.124)

Mendenhall, Charles Elwood (1872-1935). Amer. physicist.

N.A.S.—Biog. (18) p1-20 (por.1)

Mendenhall, Thomas Corwin (1841-1924). Amer. meteorologist, geophysicist.

N.A.S.—Biog. (16) p331-346 (por.331)

Menecrates (or Menocrates), **Tiberius Claudius of Zeophleta** (c.30 A.D.). Roman physician.

Gordon—Medicine p550-551
Major—History (1) p219

Menelaus (fl.c.100). Gr. mathematician.

Smith—Hist. I p126-127

Ménétriés, Edouard (1802-1861). Fr.-Rus. entomologist.

Essig—Hist. p706-707 (por.706)

Menninger, Karl Augustus (1893-   ). Amer. psychiatrist.

Curr. Biog. '49 p442-444 (por.443)

Menninger, William Claire (1899-   ). Amer. psychiatrist.

Curr. Biog. '45 p400-402 (por.400)

Menocrates.   See **Menecrates, Tiberius Claudius of Zeophleta**

Menzel, Donald Howard (1901-   ). Amer. astronomer.
Curr. Biog. '56 p430-432 (por.431)

Menzies, Archibald (1754-1842). Scot. naturalist, botanist, physician,
surgeon.
Alden—Early p15-18 (por.14)
Dakin—Perennial p25-27

Mercado, Luiz de (1520-1606). Sp. physician.
Major—History (1) p473

Mercalli, Giuseppe (1850-1914). It. geologist, seismologist.
Davison—Founders p104-113

Mercator, Gerardus (or Gerhard Kremer) (1512-1594). Flem.
mathematician, geographer.
Chambers—Dict. col.312-313
Hammerton p985

Mercator, Nicolaus (or Kaufman) (c.1620-1687). Ger. mathematician.
astronomer, engineer.
Chambers—Dict. col.313
Smith—Hist. I p434

Mercer, John (1791-1866). Eng. chemist.
Chambers—Dict. col.313
Hammerton p985

Merck, George Wilhelm (1894-   ). Amer. chemist.
Curr. Biog. '46 p387-390 (por.388)

Mercuriale, Girolamo (or Mercuralis, Hieronymus, Jerome) (1530-1606).
It. physician, surgeon.
Gordon—Medieval p755 (por.147)   Major—History (1) p474
Leonardo—Lives p276-277

Mercurio, Scipione (1538-1616). It. obstetrician.
Major—History (1) p475

Meredith, Edwin Thomas (1876-1928). Amer. agriculturist.
*Ivins—Fifty p393-399 (por.392)

Mergenthaler, Ottmar (1854-1899). Ger.-Amer. inventor.
*Bachman—Great p205-207   *Book—Pop. Sci. (12) p4216-4217
*Beard—Foreign p167-174   Chambers—Dict. col.313
(Continued)

Mergenthaler, Ottmar—*Continued*
Hammerton p987
*Hylander—Invent. p205-206
Iles—Leading p393-432 (por.393)
*Larsen—Shaped p195-199 (por.177)
Law—Civiliz. p123-125
Meyer—World p42-43 (por.40)

*Montgomery—Invent. p33-36
Morris—Ency. p694
*Nida—Makers p147-150
*Patterson—Amer. p161-173
*Pratt—Famous p73-75

Merian, Maria Sibylla (1647-1717). Swiss naturalist.
Mozans—Woman p240-242

Merian, Peter (1795-1883). Swiss naturalist, physicist, chemist, geologist, seismologist.
Davison—Founders p38

Merica, Paul Dyer (1889-1957). Amer. metallurgist.
N.A.S.—Biog. (33) p226-234
  (por.226)
Progress—Science '41 p242-243

Mermoz, Jean (1901-1936). Fr. aero. pioneer.
Heinmuller—Man's p399 (por.339)
La Croix—They p144-159

Merrett (or Merret), **Christopher** (1614-1695). Eng. naturalist.
Gunther—Early XI p287-288
Raven—English p305-338

Merriam, Clinton Hart (1855-1942). Amer. naturalist, zoologist.
Curr. Biog. '42 p585
N.A.S.—Biog. '47 p1-26 (por.1)

Merriam, John Campbell (1869-1945). Amer. paleontologist, geologist.
Curr. Biog. '45 p402
G.S.A.—Proc. '46 p183-187 (por.183)

Hammerton p987
N.A.S.—Biog. (26) p209-217
  (por.209)

Merrill, Elmer Drew (1876-1956). Amer. botanist, agriculturist.
N.A.S.—Biog. (32) p273-301
  (por.273)

Merrill, George Perkins (1854-1929). Amer. geologist.
N.A.S.—Biog. (17) p33-41 (por.33)

Merrill, Grayson (1912-   ). Amer. space pioneer, engineer.
Thomas—Men p.xv-xvi
Thomas—Men (2) p.xvii

Thomas—Men (3) p.xvi-xvii

Merrill, Henry T. (or Dick) (1897-   ). Amer. aero. pioneer.
Heinmuller—Man's p204-213,351
  (por.210,212,351)

Merriman, Mansfield (1848-1925). Amer. mathematician, engineer.
Smith—Math. p136-137

Mersenne, Marin (1588-1648). Fr. mathematician, nat. philosopher.
Ball—Short p306-307
Chambers—Dict. col.313-314
*Lewellen—Boy p107-136 (por.107)
Magie—Source p115
Smith—Hist. I p380-381 (por.379)
Van Wagenen—Beacon p101-103

Mertens, Karl Heinrich (1796-1832). Ger. physician, surgeon, naturalist, botanist.
Alden—Early p38
Dakin—Perennial p27-28

Méry, Jean (1645-1722). Fr. surgeon.
Major—History (1) p561

Mesmer, Franz (or Friedrich) (1734-1815). Aust. physician.
Castiglioni—Hist. p587-590 (por.588)
Chambers—Dict. col.314
Fülöp—Miller p28-35 (por.48)
Gordon—Romance p120,499
  (por.499)
Hammerton p987
Lambert—Medical p187-189
Lambert—Minute p187-189
Major—History (2) p623-627
  (por.624)
Robinson—Victory p67-69

Messerschmitt, Wilhelm (1898-   ). Ger. inventor, aero. pioneer.
Curr. Biog. '40 p575-576 (por.575)

Mesuë, Junior (Masawaih al-Marindi) (c.1015). Arab. physician.
Gordon—Medieval p180-181
Major—History (1) p263

Mesuë, Senior (or Massooa, Massoua, Yuhanna ibn Masawaih, Damascenus, Janus) (777-857). Arab. physician.
Gordon—Medieval p143-144
Major—History (1) p232-233

Metchnikoff, Élie (or Mechnikov, Ilya, Ilyich) (1845-1916). Rus. zoologist, bacteriologist, biologist.
Bodenheimer—Hist. p439
*Book—Pop. Sci. (14) p4925-4927
  (por.4927)
Bulloch—Hist. p383 (por.148)
Castiglioni—Hist. p777,1126
  (por.821)
Chambers—Dict. col.308
*Cottler—Heroes p319-327
DeKruif—Microbe p207-233
Gordon—Medicine p40 (por.40)
(Continued)

Metchnikoff, Élie—*Continued*
Gordon—Romance p217 (por.217)
Grainger—Guide p161-162
Hammerton p988 (por.988)
Kagan—Modern p154 (por.154)
Lambert—Medical p263-264
Lambert—Minute p263-264
Major—History (2) p906-907
*Montgomery—Story p118-120

Robinson—Path. p747-770 (por.758)
*Snyder—Biology p273-278 (por.276)
*Sootin—Twelve p157-173
Stevenson—Nobel p46-51 (por.150)
Van Wagenen—Beacon p396-397
Woglom—Discov. p145-159
(por.,front.)

Metford, William Ellis (1824-1879). Eng. inventor.
Hammerton p988

Metlinger, Bartolomaeus (15th cent.). Ger. physician.
Gordon—Medieval p394-395

Metrodorus (c.4th cent., B.C.). Gr. nat. philosopher.
Gordon—Medicine p599 (por.599)

Mettauer, John Peter (1787-1875). Amer. surgeon.
Leonardo—Lives p277-278

Mettrie. See **La Mettrie, Julien Offrey de**

Metzelthin, Pearl Violette (1894-1947). Amer. health worker.
Curr. Biog. '42 p587-588 (por.587)
'48 p446

Meusnier, Jean Baptiste Marie (1745-1793). Fr. aero. pioneer.
Chambers—Dict. col.314
Heinmuller—Man's p235 (por.235)

Meyer, Adolf (1866-1950). Swiss psychiatrist.
Jaffe—Outposts p233-239 (por.202)
Major—History (2) p1042

Meyer, Editha Paula (Chartkoff) (1903-   ). Amer. engineer.
Goff—Women p19-44

Meyer, Frank (1875-1918). Dutch-Amer. botanist.
*Jewett—Plant p102-139

Meyer, (Julius) Lothar (1830-1895). Ger. chemist.
Chambers—Dict. col.314-315
Findlay—Hundred p331
Hammerton p989
Partington—Short p346,349,354
(por.346)

Smith—Torch. p169 (por.169)
Weeks—Discovery p389-391
(por.389)

Meyer, Karl Friedrich (1884-   ). Swiss-Amer. pathologist, bacteriologist.
  Curr. Biog. '52 p416-419 (por.417)

Meyer, Victor (1848-1897). Ger. chemist.
  *Book—Pop. Sci. (13) p4340-4342
  Chambers—Dict. col.315
  Hammerton p989
  Harrow—Chemist p177-195 (por.177)
  Partington—Short p312-315,318 (por.314)
  Roberts—Chem. p232-243
  Smith—Torch. p170 (por.170)

Meyer, Wilhelm (1824-1895). Dan. physician.
  Copen—Prom. p138-142

Meyer, Willy (1854-1932). Ger.-Amer. surgeon.
  Kagan—Modern p96 (por.96)
  Leonardo—Lives p278-279

Meyerhof, Otto Fritz (1884-1951). Ger. physiologist, biochemist.
  Chambers—Dict. col.315-316
  Hammerton p989
  N.A.S.—Biog. (34) p153-163 (por.153)
  Stevenson—Nobel p103,106-108 (por.150)

Michael Scot.   See **Scot, Michael**

Michaelis, Leonor (1875-1949). Ger.-Amer. biochemist.
  N.A.S.—Biog. (31) p282-292 (por.282)

Michaux, André (1746-1802). Fr. botanist.
  Bell—Early p66
  Peattie—Green p201-215

Michaux, François André (1770-1855). Fr. botanist, naturalist.
  Bell—Early p68

Michell, John (1724-1793). Eng. physicist, astronomer, seismologist.
  Chambers—Dict. col.316
  Davison—Founders p12-24
  Hammerton p992

Michel-Levy, Augustus (1847-1911). Fr. geologist.
  Van Wagenen—Beacon p392-394
  Woodruff—Devel. p181,182,284

Michelson, Albert Abraham (1852-1931). Ger.-Amer. physicist.

A.A.A.S.—Proc. (81) p72-75
*Book—Pop. Sci. (13) p4342-4344
  (por.4343)
Chalmers—Historic p269
Chambers—Dict. col.316-317
  (por.315)
*Darrow—Builders p164-167
*Darrow—Masters p338
Hammerton p992-993
Heathcote—Nobel p52-64 (por.240)
*Hylander—Scien. p156-160 (por.141)
Jaffe—Men p356-382 (por.xxviii)

*Law—Modern p136-149 (por.145)
Magie—Source p369
Morris—Ency. p695
N.A.S.—Biog. (19) p121-141
  (por.121,141)
Smith—Torch. p172 (por.172)
*Stevens—Science p151-156 (por.150)
Weber—College p117 (por.117)
Wilson—Amer. p209-219,308
  (por.309,312)
Year—Pic. p203 (por.203)

Midgley, Thomas, Jr. (1889-1944). Amer. chemist, inventor.

Browne—Hist. p491 (por.169)
Chambers—Dict. col.317
Curr. Biog. '44 p469

N.A.S.—Biog. '47 p361-376 (por.361)
*Wright—Great p240-242

Miers, Sir Henry Alexander (1858-1942). Brit. mineralogist.

Hammerton p993

Migula, Walter (b.1863). Ger. botanist, bacteriologist.

Bulloch—Hist. p383

Mikulicz-Radecki, Johann von (1850-1905). Pol. physician, surgeon.

Leonardo—Lives p279-280
Major—History (2) p912

Thorwald—Century p330,339-345
  (por.368)

Miles, (Maxine Frances) Mary (Forbes-Robertson) (1900/1901). Eng. aero. pioneer.

Curr. Biog. '42 p596-597 (por.597)
Knapp—New p61-72 (por.179)

Mill, Hugh Robert (1861-1950). Scot. meteorologist.

Hammerton p994

Miller, Arthur McQuiston (1861-1929). Amer. geologist.

G.S.A.—Proc. '35 p283-284 (por.283)

Miller, Benjamin LeRoy (1874-1944). Amer. geologist.

G.S.A.—Proc. '44 p277-279 (por.277)

Miller, Charles Jefferson (1874-1936). Amer. surgeon.

Leonardo—Lives p280-282

Miller, Dayton Clarence (1866-1941). Amer. physicist.

Curr. Biog. '41 p581
N.A.S.—Biog. (23) p61-66
  (por.61)

Progress—Science p249

Miller, George Abram (1863-1951). Amer. mathematician.
N.A.S.—Biog. (30) p257-312
(por.257)

Miller, Harriet (or Olive Thorne Miller) (1831-1918). Amer. naturalist, ornithologist.
Tracy—Amer. Nat. p116-129

Miller, Hugh (1802-1856). Scot. geologist.
*Book—Pop. Sci. (5) p1667-1668   Guinagh—Inspired p69-79
(por.1667)
Fenton—Giants p199-213 (por.191)

Miller, Joseph Leggett (1867-1937). Amer. physician.
Major—History (2) p1042

Miller, Leo Edward (1887-   ). Amer. naturalist, sci. explorer.
Cutright—Great p40-41

Miller, Olive Thorne.   See **Miller, Harriet**

Miller, Oskar von (1855-1934). Ger. elec. engineer.
Matschoss—Great p352-367
(por.353)

Miller, Philip (1691-1771). Eng. botanist.
Hammerton p995

Miller, William H. (1896-   ). Amer. aero. pioneer, engineer.
Holland—Ind. p322-338 (por.322)

Miller, William Hallowes (1801-1880). Welsh mineralogist, crystallographer.
A.A.A.S.—Proc. (79) p29-30

Miller, William Nash (1866-1940). Can. chemist.
Curr. Biog. '40 p582 (por.582)

Miller, Willoughby Dayton (1853-1907). Amer. bacteriologist, dentist.
Bulloch—Hist. p383-384

Millikan, Robert Andrews (1868-1953). Amer. physicist.
*Book—Pop. Sci. (13) p4343-4345   *Bridges—Master p162-168 (por.164)
(por.4345)   Chambers—Dict. col.317 (por.318)
(Continued)

Millikan, Robert Andrews—*Continued*
  Curr. Biog. '40 p584-585 (por.585)
    '52 p425-428 (por.426), '54 p462
  *Darrow—Builders p158-164
  Fisher—Amer. p69-72 (por.68)
  Hammerton p996
  Heathcote—Nobel p206-217 (por.240)
  Huff—Famous (2d) p381-391
    (por.383)

*Hylander—Scien. p139-145 (por.140)
Jaffe—Outposts p324-368 (por.330)
*Law—Modern p150-161 (por.152)
Morris—Ency. p695-696
N.A.S.—Biog. (33) p241-269
  (por.241)
Weber—College p365 (por.365)

Milne, David.   See Home, David Milne

Milne, Edward Arthur (1896-1950). Eng. astronomer, astrophysicist.
  Chambers—Dict. col.318

Milne, John (1850-1913). Eng. seismologist, min. engineer.
  Davison—Founders p177-184
  Hammerton p996

Milne-Edwards, Henri (1800-1885). Fr. zoologist, anatomist, physiologist.
  Chambers—Dict. col.318-319   Woodruff—Devel. p284
  Locy—Biology p157-158 (por.157)

Milner, Samuel Roslington (1875-1958). Eng. physicist.
  R.S.L.—Biog. (5) p129-146
    (por.129)

Minchin, Edward Alfred (1866-1915). Brit. biologist.
  Gunther—Early XI p55-56

Miner, Neil Alden (1898-1947). Amer. geologist.
  G.S.A.—Proc. '49 p201-207 (por.201)

Minkowski (or Minkowsky), **Hermann** (1864-1909). Rus.-Ger.
  mathematician.
  Chambers—Dict. col.319
  Woodruff—Devel. p285 (por.36)

Minkowski (or Minkowsky), **Oscar** (1858-1931). Rus. physician.
  Kagan—Modern p18 (por.18)
  Major—History (2) p917-918

Minot, Charles Sedgwick (1852-1914). Amer. biologist, embryologist,
  anatomist.
  Castiglioni—Hist. p775   N.A.S.—Biog. (9) p263-275 (por.263)
  Kagan—Modern p182 (por.182)   Osborn—Fragments p206-207

Minot, George Richards (1885-1950). Amer. physician.

Castiglioni—Hist. p998 (por.998)
Chambers—Dict. col.319
DeKruif—Men p88-116 (por.108)
Hammerton p1451
Major—History (2) p1042
(por.1002)

*Montgomery—Story p79-82
Rowntree—Amid p395-398 (por.390)
Stevenson—Nobel p172-173;175-177
(por.150)
*Truax—Doctors p133-153

Miquel, Pierre (1850-1922). Fr. bacteriologist.

Bulloch—Hist. p384

Mirfeld (or Mirfield).   See **John of Mirfeld**

Mitchell, Elisha (1793-1857). Amer. geologist, botanist.

Merrill—First p114-116 (por.114)
Youmans—Pioneers p279-289
(por.279)

Mitchell, Henry (1830-1902). Amer. hydrographer.

N.A.S.—Biog. (20) p141-147
(por.141)

Mitchell, John (d.1768). Amer. physician, botanist.

Bell—Early p66-67
Farmer—Doctors' p16

Mitchell, John Kearsley (1798-1858). Amer. physician.

Castiglioni—Hist. p708

Mitchell, Maria (1818-1889). Amer. astronomer.

*Book—Pop. Sci. (15) p4999-5000
(por.5000)
Carmer—Caval. p207-209 (por.207)
Heath—Amer. (4) p11 (por.11)

Law—Civiliz. p183-184
Mozans—Woman p190-192
*Tappan—Heroes p54-60

Mitchell, Sir Peter Chalmers (1864-1945). Scot. zoologist.

Hammerton p999 (por.999)

Mitchell, Samuel Latham (1764-1831). Amer. naturalist.

Bell—Early p67
Fenton—Giants p132 (por.110)
Major—History (2) p766-767

Merrill—First p17-21 (por.18)
Smith—Chem. p148-150 (por.150)
Youmans—Pioneers p71-80 (por.71)

Mitchell, Silas Weir (1829-1914). Amer. physician, neurologist.

*Book—Pop. Sci. (14) p4927-4928
Castiglioni—Hist. p888 (por.888)
Hammerton p999
Kagan—Leaders p27-40
Kagan—Modern p62 (por.62)

Major—History (2) p895-896
N.A.S.—Biog. (32) p334-340
(por.334)
Rowntree—Amid p405-410 (por.406)

Mitchell, William ("Billy") Lendrum (1879-1936). Amer. aero. pioneer.
Heinmuller—Man's p319 (por.319)   Morris—Ency. p696
Maitland—Knights p275-279

Mitscher, Marc Andrew (1887-   ). Amer. aero. pioneer.
Curr. Biog. '44 p476-480 (por.478)

Mitscherlich, Eilhardt (1794-1863). Ger. chemist.
Chambers—Dict. col.319-320   Smith—Torch. p173 (por.173)
Partington—Short p202,213 (por.203)

Mittag-Leffler, Magnus Gösta (1846-1927). Swed. mathematician.
Hammerton p1000

Mittelholzer, Walter (1894-1935). Swiss aero. pioneer.
Heinmuller—Man's p327 (por.327)

Mivart, St. George Jackson (1827-1900). Eng. nat. philosopher.
Hammerton p1000

Mixter, Samuel Jason (1855-1926). Amer. surgeon.
Leonardo—Lives p282-283

Möbius, Augustus Ferdinand (1790-1868). Ger. mathematician, astronomer.
Cajori—Hist. p289

Moch, Jules Salvador (1893-   ). Fr. engineer.
Curr. Biog. '50 p400-402 (por.401)

Modjeski (or Modrzejewski), **Ralph** (1861-1940). Pol.-Amer. engineer.
Curr. Biog. '40 p589-590
N.A.S—Biog. (23) p243-261
  (por.243)

Moebius, Paul Julius (1853-1907). Ger. physician.
Major—History (2) p1043

Moën, Lars (1901-   ). Belg. engineer.
Curr. Biog. '41 p590-592 (por.591)

Mofras, Duflot de (1810-1884). Fr. naturalist, botanist.
Alden—Early p48-49

Mohammed ibn Mûsâ.   See Al-Khowarizmi, Mohammed ibn Mûsâ

Mohl, Hugo von (1805-1872). Ger. botanist.
*Book—Pop. Sci. (14) p4929-4930
Chambers—Dict. col.320
Hammerton p1000
Locy—Biology p268-270 (por.269)
*Snyder—Biology p74-75 (por.76)
Williams—Story p338-339,343-344
   (por.344)

Mohler, John Robbins (1875-1952). Amer. agriculturist, bacteriologist, pathologist.
*DeKruif—Hunger p101-129 (por.100)
Ratcliffe—Modern p235-247

Mohr, Georg (1640-1697). Dan. mathematician.
Copen.—Prom. p44-47

Mohr, Karl Friedrich (1806-1879). Ger. chemist.
Chymia (3) p191-203
Hammerton p1000-1001
Smith—Torch. p174 (por.174)

Mohs, Friedrich (1773-1839). Ger. mineralogist.
Chambers—Dict. col.320

Moir, Sir Ernest William (1862-1933). Brit. engineer.
Hammerton p1001

Moir, James Reid (1879-1944). Eng. archaeologist.
Hammerton p1001

Moisant, John B. (1868-1910). Amer. aero. pioneer.
Heinmuller—Man's p284 (por.284)
Maitland—Knights p141-144

Moisant, Mathilde (1886-1910). Amer. aero. pioneer.
*Adams—Heroines p3-26 (por.24)
Heinmuller—Man's p290 (por.290)

Moissan (Ferdinand Frederic), Henri (1852-1907). Fr. chemist.
A.A.A.S.—Proc. (81) p75-78
*Book—Pop. Sci. (13) p4345-4347
Chambers—Dict. col.320
*Darrow—Masters p338
Farber—Nobel p25-28 (por.118)
Findlay—Hundred p331-332
Hammerton p1001
*Harrow—Chemists p135-154
   (por.135)
Partington—Short p350-351,354
Smith—Torch. p175 (por.175)
Van Wagenen—Beacon p405-406
Weeks—Discovery p188,458-464
   (por.188,460,464)
Woodruff—Devel. p285

Moisseiff, Leon Solomon (1872-1943). Amer. engineer.
Curr. Biog. '43 p534

Molengraaff, Gustaaf Adolf Frederik (1860-1942). Dutch geologist.
G.S.A.—Proc. '43 p205-206 (por.205)

Molinetti, Antonio (d.1673/1675). It. anatomist, surgeon.
Major—History (1) p553

Moller, Frederick (d.1944). Eng.-Amer. aero. pioneer.
Potter—Flying p122-137 (por.146)

Mollison, Amy Johnson (1903/1904-1941). Eng. aero. pioneer.
Burge—Ency. p636
Curr. Biog. '41 p439
*Fraser—Heroes p563-567,655-659
Hammerton p1002 (por.1002)
Heinmuller—Man's p183-192,346
  (por.189,346)
*Shippen—Bridle p133-139

Mollison, James Allan (1905-   ). Scot. aero. pioneer.
Burge—Ency. p636
*Fraser—Heroes p643-648,781-786
Hammerton p1002 (por.1002)
Heinmuller—Man's p183-192,346
  (por.189,346)

Molloy, Daniel Murrah (1892-1944). Amer. sanitarian.
Curr. Biog. '44 p480

Monardes, Nicolás (1493-1578). Sp. botanist, physician.
Arber—Herbals p105-109 (por.107)
Major—History (2) p715-716
  (por.715)

Mond, Ludwig (1839-1909). Ger.-Eng. chemist.
Chambers—Dict. col.321
Hammerton p1003 (por.1003)
Smith—Torch. p176 (por.176)

Mondeville, Henri de (1260-1320). Fr. physician, surgeon.
Castiglioni—Hist. p338,341
Gordon—Medieval p352
Lambert—Medical p78-79
Lambert—Minute p78-79
Leonardo—Lives p283-284
Major—History (1) p319-322
  (por.320)

Mondino de' Luzzi (or Mundinus; Remondino; De Luicci) (1270/1275-1326). It. surgeon, anatomist, physician.
Castiglioni—Hist. p341-345
Gordon—Medieval p331-333,422-426
  (por.51)
Lambert—Medical p99-100
Lambert—Minute p99-100
Leonardo—Lives p284-285
Major—History (1) p300-302
  (por.301)

Monge, Gaspard, Comte de Péluse (1746-1818). Fr. mathematician, physician.
Ball—Short p426-428
Bell—Men p183-191,204 (por.,front.)
Cajori—Hist. p274-275
Chambers—Dict. col.321
Hammerton p1004
Smith—Hist. I p490-491 (por.490)
Van Wagenen—Beacon p188-190
Woodruff—Devel. p285 (por.22)

Moniz, (Antonio) Egas (1874-1955). Port. neurologist, surgeon.
Chambers—Dict. col.321-322
Stevenson—Nobel p264-271 (por.150)

Monro family (17th-19th cent.). Scot. anatomists.
Castiglioni—Hist. p594 (por.594)

Monro, Alexander I (1697-1767). Scot. anatomist.
Castiglioni—Hist. p594 (por.594)
Leonardo—Lives p285-286

Montagnana, Bartolommeo (d.1460). It. physician.
Major—History (1) p355

Montalembert, Marc René, Marquis de (1714-1800). Fr. engineer.
Hammerton p1006

Montalto, Eliahu (or Philotheus, Elijah) (1550-1616). It. physician.
Gordon—Medieval p762

Montessori, Maria (1870-1952). It. physician.
Curr. Biog. '40 p591-592 (por.591)   Lovejoy—Women p203
   '52 p434

Montgolfier brothers (18th, 19th cent.). Fr. aero. pioneers.
*Bishop—Kite p14-19   Law—Civiliz. p59-66
Burge—Ency. p636-637   Meyer—World p233
*Cohen—Men p13-17,19-20 People p287-288
*Epstein—Real p88   *Shippen—Bridle p28-34
Hammerton p1008 (por.1008) Year—Pic. p153 (por.153)
*Larsen—Prentice p104-105,106-107

Montgolfier, Jacques Étienne (1745-1799). Fr. inventor, aero. pioneer.
Chambers—Dict. col.322   100 Great p569-574
Heinmuller—Man's p232 (por.232) Tuska—Invent. p112-113

Montgolfier, Joseph Michael (1740-1810). Fr. inventor.
Chambers—Dict. col.322   100 Great p569-574
Heinmuller—Man's p232 (por.232) Tuska—Invent. p112-113

Montgomery, Deane (1909-   ). Amer. mathematician.
Curr. Biog. '57 p372-374 (por.373)

Montgomery, Helen Marie (1911-   ). Amer. aero. pioneer.
Knapp—New p140-156 (por.179)

Montgomery, John Joseph (1858-1911). Amer. aero. pioneer.
*Cohen—Men p90-93   Maitland—Knights p34-35
Heinmuller—Man's p250 (por.250)

Montgomery, Joseph Fauntleroy (1812-1883). Amer. physician.
Jones—Memories p344-348

Montmort, Pierre-Rémond de (1678-1719). Fr. mathematician.
Smith—Hist. I p471

Montucla, Jean Étienne (1725-1799). Fr. mathematician.
Smith—Hist. I p540 (por.540)

Moon, William (1818-1894). Eng. inventor.
Hammerton p1009

Moore, Carl R. (1892-   ). Amer. zoologist.
Progress—Science '41 p259

Moore, Eliakim Hastings (1862-1932). Amer. mathematician.
N.A.S.—Biog. (17) p83-99 (por.83)
Smith—Math. p141-144 (por.143)

Moore, Gideon E. (1842-1895). Amer. chemist.
Browne—Hist. p312 (por.319)

Moore, Hugh Kelsea (1872-1939). Amer. chem. engineer.
Holland—Ind. p170-185 (por.170)

Moore, James Edward (1852-1918). Amer. surgeon.
Leonardo—Lives p286-287
N.A.S.—Biog. (29) p235-243
  (por.235)

Moore, Merrill (1903-1957). Amer. psychiatrist.
Fabricant—Why p13-18

Moore, Sir Norman (1847-1922). Eng. physician.
Kagan—Modern p12 (por.12)
Major—History (2) p908

Moore, Samuel Preston (1813-1889). Amer. surgeon.
Leonardo—Lives p287-288

Moore-Brabazon, John Cuthbert (1884-   ). Eng. aero. pioneer.
Burge—Ency. p636

Morax, Victor (1866-1935). Swiss bacteriologist.
Bulloch—Hist. p384

Moreau, Von (1905-1939). Ger. aero. pioneer.
Heinmuller—Man's p354 (por.354)

Moreell, Ben (1892-   ). Amer. engineer.
Curr. Biog. '46 p409-412 (por.410)

Morehouse, Daniel Walter (1876-1941). Amer. astronomer.
Curr. Biog. '41 p595

Morestead, Thomas (1375?-1450). Eng. surgeon.
Leonardo—Lives p289

Morgagni, Giovanni Battista (1682-1771). It. anatomist, physician, pathologist.
Castiglioni—Hist. p601-608 (por.602)
Chambers—Dict. col.322
Gordon—Romance p71 (por.71)
Hammerton p1011
Lambert—Medical p200-201 (por.202)
Lambert—Minute p200-201 (por.208)
Major—History (2) p585-588 (por.586)
Oliver—Stalkers p141-142
Sigerist—Great p229-236 (por.232)
Walsh—Makers p27-51
Year—Pic. p108 (por.108)

Morgan, Agnes Fay (1884-   ). Amer. chemist.
Progress—Science '41 p260 (por.260)

Morgan, Arthur Ernest (1878-   ). Amer. engineer.
Curr. Biog. '56 p449-451 (por.450)
*Yost—Engineers p32-46

Morgan, Augustus de.   See **De Morgan, Augustus**

Morgan, Conway Lloyd (1852-1936). Eng. psychologist, zoologist.
Hammerton p1011

Morgan, George Dillon (1894-1950). Amer. geologist.
G.S.A.—Proc. '51 p121-123 (por.121)

Morgan, Gilbert Thomas (1870-1940). Eng. chemist.
Findlay—British p316-352 (por.316)
Partington—Short p321

Morgan, Harcourt Alexander (b.1867). Amer. entomologist.
Ratcliffe—Modern p226-233 (por.224)

Morgan, John (1735-1789). Amer. physician.

Castiglioni—Hist. p599 (por.661) Major—History (2) p718-721
Flexner—Doctors p2-53 (por.3)   (por.719)

Morgan, Lewis Henry (1818-1881). Amer. anthropologist, ethnologist.

*Book—Pop. Sci. (14) p4930 N.A.S.—Biog. (6) p219-237 (por.219)
Hammerton p1012

Morgan, Thomas Alfred (1887-). Amer. engineer.

Curr. Biog. '50 p409-411 (por.409)

Morgan, Thomas E. (1906-). Amer. physician.

Curr. Biog. '59 p308-310 (por.309)

Morgan, Thomas Hunt (1866-1945). Amer. zoologist, biologist.

Bodenheimer—Hist. p455   Moulton—Auto. p586
Chambers—Dict. col.322   N.A.S.—Biog. (33) p283-299
Curr. Biog. '46 p418   (por.283)
Fisher—Amer. p57-59 (por.56) Osborn—Fragments p227 (por.375)
*Hylander—Scien. p176-178 *Shippen—Micro. p178-182
Jaffe—Men p383-436 (por. xxviii) Snyder—Biology p153-156 (por.155)
Jaffe—Outposts p40-46 (por.10) Stevenson—Nobel p165-170
Ludovici—Nobel p178-184 (por.175) (por.150)
Morris—Ency. p697-698   Year—Pic. p225 (por.225)

Morgenroth, Julius (1871-1924). Ger. bacteriologist.

Bulloch—Hist. p384

Morin, Arthur Jules (1795-1880). Fr. mathematician.

Chalmers—Historic p269

Morison, Robert (1620-1683). Scot. botanist.

Gilmour—British p14-16   Oliver—Makers p16-28 (por.8)
Hammerton p1012   Reed—Short p83-84
Hawks—Pioneers p206-207 (por.206)

Morley, Edward Williams (1838-1923). Amer. chemist, physicist.

Browne—Hist. p477 (por.49) N.A.S.—Biog. (11) (XXI Memoirs)
Chambers—Dict. col.323   p1-6 (por.1)
Killeffer—Eminent p12 (por.12) Smith—Torch. p177 (por.177)
Magie—Source p369   Year—Pic. p203 (por.203)

Moro, Abbé Anton Lazzaro (1687-1740). It. geologist.

Adams—Birth p365-372
Fenton—Giants p25-26

Morris, John Gottlieb (1803-1895). Amer. entomologist.

Osborn—Fragments p167-168
(por.347)

Morris, Lewis Coleman (1872-1923). Amer. surgeon.
Leonardo—Lives p289-291

Morris, Robert Tuttle (1857-1945). Amer. physician, surgeon.
Fabricant—Why p95-98

Morrison, Herbert Knowles (1854-1885). Amer. entomologist.
Essig —Hist. p709-710 (por.709)

Morse, Albert Pitts (1863-1935). Amer. entomologist.
Essig—Hist. p710-712 (por.711)

Morse, Edward Sylvester (1838-1925). Amer. zoologist, naturalist, entomologist.
N.A.S.—Biog. (17) p3-19 (por.3)
Osborn—Fragments p150-151
  (por.357)

Morse, Harmon Northrup (1848-1920). Amer. chemist.
Chambers—Dict. col.323-324
N.A.S.—Biog. (11) (XXXI Memoirs)
  p1-11 (por.1)

Morse, Harold Marston (1892-   ). Amer. mathematician.
Curr. Biog. '57 p380-382 (por.381)

Morse, John Lovett (1865-1940). Amer. physician.
Curr. Biog. '40 p598

Morse, Philip McCord (1903-   ). Amer. physicist.
Curr. Biog. '48 p461-463 (por.462)

Morse, Samuel Finley Breese (1791-1872). Amer. inventor.
Abbot—Great p80-85 (por.80)
*Bachman—Great p208-226
*Book—Pop. Sci. (12) p4217-4220
  (por.4219)
Carmer—Caval. p233-235
  (por.232,235)
Chambers—Dict. col.323-324
*Cottler—Heroes p201-210
*Darrow—Masters p148-157 (por.32)
*Darrow—Thinkers p135-146
  (por.136)
*Eberle—Invent. p59-65 (por.58)
*Epstein—Real p132-134
Fitzhugh—Concise p486-488
Hammerton p1014-1015 (por.1015)
*Hartman—Mach. p138-147
*Hathaway—Partners p102-113
  (por.103)
Hawks—Wireless p67-75 (por.72)
*Hylander—Invent. p73-85 (por.96)
Iles—Leading p119-175 (por.119)
*Larsen—Prentice p44-48
*Larsen—Shaped p39-54 (por.32)
Law—Civiliz. p207-212
Meyer—World p147-158 (por.146)
*Montgomery—Invent. p47-52
Morris—Ency. p698-699
*Morris—Heroes p145-152
(Continued)

Morse, Samuel Finley Breese—*Continued*
  *Nida—Makers p160-169
  *Parkman—Conq. p350-378 (por.352)
  *Patterson—Amer. p49-61
  *Perry—Four p133-201 (por.132)
  *Pratt—Famous p59-63
  Radio's 100 p35-41 (por.140)
  Sewell—Brief p127-128

  *Towers—Beacon p55-104
  Tuska—Invent. p103-104
  Wilson—Amer. p116-123
    (por.117,122)
  Year—Pic. p166-168 (por.166)
  Youmans—Pioneers p234-249
    (por.234)

Mortillet, Louis Laurent Gabriel (1821-1898). Fr. anthropologist.
  Hammerton p1015

Morton, Henry (1836-1902). Amer. engineer.
  N.A.S.—Biog. (8) p143-151 (por.143)

Morton, Henry Holdich (1861-1940). Amer. physician.
  Curr. Biog. '40 p598

Morton, John Chalmers (1821-1888). Brit. agriculturist.
  Hammerton p1015

Morton, John Jamieson, Jr. (1886-   ). Amer. surgeon.
  Curr. Biog. '55 p430-432 (por.431)

Morton, Julius Sterling (1832-1902). Amer. agriculturist.
  *Ivins—Fifty p373-377 (por.372)

Morton, Richard (1637-1698). Eng. physician.
  Major—History (1) p558

Morton, Rosalie Slaughter (b.1876). Amer. physician, surgeon.
  Fabricant—Why p9-12
  Mead—Medical p67

  Rosen—Four p124-127

Morton, Samuel George (1799-1851). Amer. geologist, physician, naturalist.
  Merrill—First p117 (por.117)

Morton, William Thomas Green (1819-1868). Amer. dentist.
  Carmer—Caval. p201-203 (por.201)
  *Darrow—Masters p127-130 (por.64)
  *Elwell—Sci. p122-124
  Flexner—Doctors p311-332 (por.311)
  *Fox—Great p145-177 (por.145)
  Fülöp-Miller p111-162,170-303
    (por.128)
  Gumpert—Trail p229-251

  Hammerton p1015
  Jaffe—Men p154-178 (por.xxviii)
  Lambert—Medical p273-274
    (por.274)
  Lambert—Minute p273-275 (por.273)
  Law—Civiliz. p315-317
  Major—History (2) p753-756
  *Montgomery—Story p148-152
  (Continued)

Morton, William Thomas Green—*Continued*
Morris—Ency. p699
*Morris—Heroes p187-189
Moulton—Auto. p320
Robinson—Victory p119-133 (por.83)
*Science Miles p177 (por.177)
*Shippen—Men p137-143
*Snyder—Biology p292-294
*Tappan—Heroes p39-46

Thorwald—Century p102-105,107-110, 145-164 (por.80)
*Truax—Doctors p74-88
Williams—Story p369-370 (por.367)
Wilson—Amer. p106-107 (por.107)
Young—Scalpel p139,140-147,150-155 (por.154)

Morveau, Louis Bernard Guyton de (1737-1816). Fr. chemist.
Hammerton p1015

Mosander, Carl Gustav (1797-1858). Swed. chemist.
Chambers—Dict. col.324
Weeks—Discovery p416-423 (por.416)

Moschcowitz, Alexis Victor (1865-1933). Hung.-Amer. physician.
Kagan—Modern p119 (por.119)

Moscicki, Ignace (or Ignacy) (1867-1946). Pol. chemist, inventor.
Curr. Biog. '46 p421

Moseley, Corliss Champion (1894-   ). Amer. aero. pioneer.
Heinmuller—Man's p309 (por.309)

Moseley, Henry Gwyn-Jeffreys (1887-1915). Eng. physicist.
Chambers—Dict. col.324
Gunther—Early XI p235-236 (por.235)
Hammerton p1016
Jaffe—Crucibles p289-311

*Kendall—Young p203-209 (por.187)
Partington—Short p360-361,380 (por.361)
Smith—Torch. p178 (por.178)
Weeks—Discovery p513-517 (por.514)

Moseley, Henry Nottidge (1844-1891). Eng. zoologist, naturalist.
Gunther—Early XI p100-102 (por.101)

Moses ben Maimon.   See **Maimonides**

Mosher, Eliza M. (1846-1928). Amer. physician.
Lovejoy—Women phys. p50-52 (por.7)
Mead—Medical p49 (por.,append.)

Mosso, Angelo (1846-1910). It. physiologist.
Major—History (2) p973-974 (por.973)

Motschulsky, Victor Ivanovich (1810-1871). Rus. entomologist.
Essig—Hist. p712-715 (por.713)

Mott, Valentine (1785-1865). Amer. pathologist, surgeon.
Leonardo—Lives p291-292
Major—History (2) p734-735
(por.735)

Moufet, Thomas (1553-1604). Scot.-Eng. naturalist.
Miall—Early p84-87
Raven—English p172-191

Mouillard, Louis Pierre (1834-1897). Fr. aero. pioneer.
Heinmuller—Man's p244 (por.244)

Moulton, Forest Ray (1872-1952). Amer. astronomer.
Chambers—Dict. col.324-325   Williams—Great p386-387,396,398
Curr. Biog. '46 p421-423 (por.422)
'53 p437

Mountain.   See **La Mountain, John**

Moureu, Charles (1863-1929). Fr. chemist.
Smith—Torch. p179 (por.179)

Mouromtseff, Ilia Emmanuel (1881-1954). Rus.-Amer. physicist,
elec. engineer.
Radio's 100 p208-212 (por.140)

Moya, (Alonzo) Manuel A. de (1906-   ). Dom. Rep. agriculturist.
Curr. Biog. '57 p384-386 (por.385)

Moyle, Don (1902-   ). Amer. aero. pioneer.
Heinmuller—Man's p344 (por.344)

Moyle, John (c.1640-1713). Eng. surgeon.
Leonardo—Lives p292-293

Moyle, Walter (1672-1721). Eng. naturalist.
Gunther—Early XI p93-94

Moynihan, Berkeley George Andrew, 1st Baron Moynihan of Leeds (1865-
1936). Eng. surgeon.
Hammerton p1017   Major—History (2) p1043
Leonardo—Lives p293-295

Mudd, Henry Hodgen (1844-1899). Amer. surgeon.
Leonardo—Lives p295-297

Mudge, Benjamin Franklin (1817-1879). Amer. geologist.
Merrill—First p423-425 (por.423)

Muhlenberg, Gotthilf Henry Ernst (1753-1815). Amer. botanist.
Bell—Early p67-68
Youmans—Pioneers p58-70 (por.58)

Muir, Frederick A. G. (d.1931). Eng. entomologist.
Osborn—Fragments p185-186
(por.367)

Muir, John (1838-1914). Scot.-Amer. naturalist.
*Beard—Foreign p184-193
*Milne—Natur. p125-132 (por.124)
Osborn—Impr. p184,198-205
(por.198)
Peattie—Gather. p29-35
Peattie—Lives p63-73 (por.63)
*Tappan—Heroes p179-188
Tracy—Amer. Nat. p100-115
Welker—Birds p151-152

Muir, Robert (1864-1959). Scot. pathologist.
R.S.L.—Biog. (5) p149-171 (por.149)

Mulder, Gerardus Johannes (1802-1880). Dutch chemist.
Chambers—Dict. col.325

Müller, Franz Joseph, Baron von Reichenstein (1740-1825). Aust. chemist,
mineralogist.
Chambers—Dict. col.325
Weeks—Discovery p157-159,170-172

Müller, Friedrich von (1858-1941). Ger. physician.
Major—History (2) p923,1043
(por.924)
Rowntree—Amid p167-170 (por.159)

Muller, Hermann Joseph (1890-   ). Amer. biologist, geneticist.
Chambers—Dict. col.325-326
Curr. Biog. '47 p458-460 (por.459)
Ludovici—Nobel p185-188 (por.175)
Progress—Science '40 p249

Müller, Johann (or Regiomontanus) (1436-1476). Ger. astronomer.
Ball—Short p201-205
Cajori—Hist. p131-132
(Continued)

Müller, Johann—*Continued*
Chambers—Dict. col.379
Dreyer—Hist. p289-292
Hammerton p1135
Sedgwick—Short p193-194
Smith—Hist. I p259-260

Stevenson—Nobel p238-243 (por.150)
Van Wagenen—Beacon p53-55
Walsh—Catholic (2d) p119-145
(por.119)

Müller, Johann Friedrich Theodor (or Fritz) (1821-1897). Ger. zoologist, biologist.
Chambers—Dict. col.325

Van Wagenen—Beacon p315-316

Müller, Johannes Peter (1801-1858). Ger. physiologist, biologist.
Bodenheimer—Hist. p364
*Book—Pop. Sci. (14) p4930-4931
Castiglioni—Hist. p684-685 (por.685)
Chambers—Dict. col.326
Gordon—Romance p122 (por.122)
Hammerton p1019
Lambert—Medical p204-205
Locy—Biology p163,184-188
(por.187)
Major—History (2) p788-790 (por.789)

Rosen—Four p20-21
Schwartz—Moments (2) p618-619
Sigerist—Great p307-311 (por.305)
*Snyder—Biology p64-65
Thomson—Great p86-88
Van Wagenen—Beacon p273-275
Walsh—Makers p215-250
Woodruff—Devel. p285
Year—Pic. p125 (por.125)

Müller, Karl Ottfried (1797-1840). Ger. archaeologist.
Hammerton p1019

Müller, Otto Frederick (1730-1784). Dan. biologist, naturalist.
Bulloch—Hist. p384-385
Chambers—Dict. col.326

Copen—Prom. p60-64

Müller, Paul (1899/1900-   ). Swiss chemist.
Chambers—Dict. col.326-327
Grainger—Guide p162

Stevenson—Nobel p255-259 (por.150)

Mulsant, Etienne (1797-1880). Fr. entomologist.
Essig—Hist. p715-717 (por.716)

Mundinus.   See **Mondino de'Luzzi**

Munro, John Cummings (1856-1910). Amer. surgeon.
Leonardo—Lives p297-298

Munroe, Charles Edward (1849-1938). Amer. chemist.
A.A.A.S.—Proc. (77) p43-44
Browne—Hist. p477 (por.49)

Munster, Sebastian (1489-1552). Ger. geographer.
Hammerton p1020

Münsterberg, Hugo (1863-1916). Ger. psychologist.
Hammerton p1020 (por.1020)

Munthe, Axel Martin Fredrik (1857-1949). Swed. physician.
Hammerton p1020

Muralt, Johannes (1645-1733). Swiss physician.
Major—History (1) p563

Murat, Queen Carolina. See **Bonaparte, Maria Annunciata, later Carolina**

Murchison, Sir Roderick Impey (1792-1871). Scot. geologist.
Chambers—Dict. col.327
Fenton—Giants p108-110 (por.94)
Geikie—Founders p247-256
Hammerton p1021 (por.1021)
Williams—Story p138-139 (por.137)
Woodruff—Devel. p285 (por.186)

Murdock, George John (1858-1942). Amer. inventor.
Curr. Biog. '42 p618

Murdock, George Peter (1897-   ). Amer. anthropologist.
Curr. Biog. '57 p390-392 (por.391)

Murdock, William (1754-1839). Scot. inventor, engineer.
*Book—Pop. Sci. (12) p4220-4222
Goddard—Eminent p174-180
  (por.174)
Hammerton p1021
*Hartman—Mach. p72-73
Larsen—Shaped p181-184 (por.145)
*Parkman—Conq. p139-157
Smith—Torch. p180 (por.180)

Murphree, Eger Vaughan (1898-   ). Amer. engineer.
Curr. Biog. '56 p455-457 (por.456)

Murphy, Gardner (1895-   ). Amer. psychologist.
Curr. Biog. May'60 (por.)
Progress—Science '41 p260-261
  (por.260)

Murphy, James Bumgardner (1884-1950). Amer. physiologist, physician.
N.A.S.—Biog. (34) p183-192 (por.183)

Murphy, John Benjamin (1857-1916). Amer. physician, surgeon.
Leonardo—Lives p298-299
Major—History (2) p1043
Rowntree—Amid p209,212-216
  (por.211)
Thorwald—Century p364-369
Webb—Famous p336-353 (por.337)

Murphy, Robert Cushman (1887-   ). Amer. naturalist.
Cutright—Great p41
*Milne—Natur. p172-173
Peattie—Gather. p135-139
Von Hagen—Green p356-357

Murphy, Walter J. (1899-   ). Amer. chemist.
Browne—Hist. 499 (por.371)

Murphy, William Parry (1892-   ). Amer. physician.
Chambers—Dict. col.327-328
Stevenson—Nobel p173,177-179
  (por.150)

Murray, Dwight Harrison (1888-   ). Amer. physician.
Curr. Biog. '57 p392-394 (por.393)

Murray, George Redmayne (1865-1939). Eng. pathologist.
Major—History (2) p919-920

Murray, Harold Watson (1906-1948). Amer. geologist.
G.S.A.—Proc. '49 p209-210 (por.209)

Murray, Sir John (1841-1914). Brit. biologist, geographer, oceanographer, marine zoologist.
Chambers—Dict. col.328
Hammerton p1022

Murray, Thomas Edward (1891-   ). Amer. engineer.
Cur. Biog. '50 p417-418 (por.417)

Murray, William Spencer (1873-1942). Amer. engineer.
Curr. Biog. '42 p618

Murri, Augusto (1841-1932). It. physician.
Castiglioni—Hist. p842 (por.842)

Murtfeldt, Mary E. (1848-1913). Amer. entomologist.
Osborn—Fragments p165-166
  (por.343)

Musa, Antonius (fl.25). Rom. physician.
Gordon—Medicine p634
Major—History (1) p167

Musgrave, William (1657-1721). Eng. anatomist, physician.
Gunther—Early XI p139 (por.138)

Musick, Edwin C. (1894-1938). Amer. aero. pioneer.
*Fraser—Famous p263-266   Heinmuller—Man's p350 (por.350)
*Fraser—Heroes p729-734

Muspratt, James (1793-1886). Irish chemist.
Chambers—Dict. col.328
Hammerton p1022

Musschenbroek, Pieter van (1692-1761). Dutch physicist, mathematician.
Chambers—Dict. col.328   Radio's 100 p16-17
Hart—Physicists p97-98   Year—Pic. p105 (por.105)

Mussey, Reuben D. (1780-1866). Amer. surgeon.
Leonardo—Lives p299-302

Mussolini, Bruno (1918-1941). It. aero. pioneer.
Curr. Biog. '41 p603

Muti, Ettore (1902-1943). It. aero. pioneer.
Curr. Biog. '43 p548

Mutis, José Celestino (1732-1808). Sp. botanist, naturalist, physician.
Weeks—Discovery p245 (por.245)

Mütter, Thomas D. (1811-1859). Amer. physician.
Major—History (2) p770

Muybridge, Eadweard (or Muggeridge, Edward James) (1830-1904). Eng.
inventor.
*Book—Pop. Sci. (12) p4222   Year—Pic. p163 (por.163)
*Larsen—Scrap. p19-20 (por.25)

Mydorge, Claude (1585-1647). Fr. mathematician.
Smith—Hist. I p378-279

Myers, Frederic William Henry (1843-1901). Eng. psychologist.
*Book—Pop. Sci. (13) p4484-4485
(por.4485)

Myers, Walter (1872-1901). Eng. bacteriologist.
Bulloch—Hist. p385

N

Nadar, A. (or Tournachon, Felix) (1820-1910). Fr. aero. pioneer.
Heinmuller—Man's p245 (por.245)

Naegeli.   See **Nägeli, Karl Wilhelm von**

Nafis.   See **Ibn al Nafis**

Nägeli, Karl Wilhelm von (or Naegeli, Carl von) (1817-1891). Swiss botanist, physicist.

Bodenheimer—Hist. p403
Bulloch—Hist. p385
Chambers—Dict. col.329

Hammerton p1025
Locy—Biology p269 (por.268)
Reed—Short p144-145

Nagyrapolt.   See **Szent-Györgyi, Albert von Nagyrapolt**

Nancride, Charles Beylard Guerard de (1847-1921). Amer. surgeon.

Leonardo—Lives p309-310

Nansen, Fridtjof (1861-1930). Norw. sci. explorer, zoologist.

*Book—Pop. Sci. (9) p3178-3179
Hammerton p1025 (por.1025)

Napier, John, Laird of Merchiston (1550-1617). Scot. mathematician.

A.A.A.S.—Proc. (78) p4-5
Ball—Short p235-236
Cajori—Hist. p149-150
Chambers—Dict. col.329
Chymia (1) p142-145 (por.144)
Hammerton p1026
Holmyard—British p15-16 (por.15)
Hooper—Makers p169-190

People p296-297
Smith—Hist. I p389-391 (por.389)
Smith—Portraits (1) V, unp. (por.)
Turnbull—Great p59-65
Van Wagenen—Beacon p83-85
Woodruff—Devel. p285 (por.8)
Year—Pic. p83,84 (por.84)

Nasini, Raffaello (1854-1931). It. chemist.

Weeks—Discovery p340,477 (por.340)

Nasir-Eddin.   See **Nassr-ed-Din**

Nasmyth, James (1808-1890). Scot. engineer.

Chambers—Dict. col.329-330
Goddard—Eminent p228-233 (por.228)

Hammerton p1029
Matschoss—Great p197-204 (por.189)

Nason, Henry Bradford (1831-1895). Amer. chemist.

Browne—Hist. p474-475 (por.35)

Nasse, Christian Friedrich (1778-1851). Ger. physician.

Major—History (2) p707

Nassr-ed-Din (or Nasir-Eddin) (1201?-1274). Arab. astronomer, mathematician.

Cajori—Hist. p108

Naudin, Charles Victor (1815-1899). Fr. botanist.
Osborn—Greeks p296-300

Naumann, Karl Friedrich (1797-1873). Ger. mineralogist.
Woodruff—Devel. p177,285

Naunyn, Bernard (1839-1925). Ger. physician.
Major—Hist. (2) p902-903
Rosen—Four p94-97,186-191

Neal, Herbert Vincent (1869-1940). Amer. biologist.
Curr. Biog. '40 p612 (por.612)

Nebel, Rudolf (1897-   ). Ger. aero. pioneer.
Gartmann—Men p84-90
*Williams—Rocket p152-157

Neckam, Alexander (or Nequam) (1157-1217). Eng. nat. philosopher.
Chambers—Dict. col.330
Raven—English p4-8

Needham, Claude Ervin (1894-1951). Amer. geologist.
G.S.A.—Proc. '51 p125-126 (por.125)

Needham, James G. (1868-1957). Amer. entomologist.
Osborn—Fragments p234 (por.373)

Needham, John Turberville (1713-1781). Eng. bacteriologist.
Bulloch—Hist. p385
Oliver—Stalkers p123-126

Needham, Joseph (1900-   ). Eng. biochemist.
Hammerton p1030

Neelsen, Friedrich (Carl Adolf) (1854-1894). Ger. bacteriologist, path. anatomist.
Bulloch—Hist. p385

Nef, John Ulric (1862-1915). Swiss-Amer. chemist.
N.A.S.—Biog. (34) p204-220 (por.204)

Negri, Adelchi (1876-1912). It. bacteriologist.
Bulloch—Hist. p385

Negrin, Juan (1892-1956). Sp. physiologist.
Curr. Biog. '45 p427-429 (por.427)
'57 p398

Neilson, James Beaumont (1792-1865). Scot. inventor.
Hammerton p1031

Neisser, Albert (1855-1916). Ger. bacteriologist, dermatologist.
Bulloch—Hist. p385
Grainger—Guide p162

Neisser, Max (1869-1938). Ger. bacteriologist, hygienist.
Bulloch—Hist. p385-386

Nélaton, Auguste (1807-1873). Fr. physician, surgeon.
Castiglioni—Hist. p715 (por.715)   Major—History (2) p880
Leonardo—Lives p310-311

Nelson, Erik Henning (1888-   ). Swed.-Amer. aero. pioneer.
Holland—Arch. p45-61

Nemorarius.   See **Jordanus Nemorarius**

Nencki, Marcel (1847-1901). Pol. bacteriological chemist.
Bulloch—Hist. p386

Nequam.   See **Neckam, Alexander**

Nernst, Walther Hermann (1864-1941). Ger. phys. chemist, physicist.
Chambers—Dict. col.330-331   Partington—Short p337-338,340-341
Curr. Biog. '42 p631   (por.337)
Farber—Nobel p77-81 (por.118)   Progress—Science '41 p268
Hammerton p1032   Smith—Torch. p181 (por.181)
                                      Woodruff—Devel. p121,285 (por.118)

Nervi, Pier Luigi (1891-   ). It. engineer.
Curr. Biog. '58 p300-301 (por.300)

Nesmeianov, Aleksandr N. (1899-   ). Rus. chemist.
Curr. Biog. '58 p301-303 (por.302)

Nestorius (or Nestor) (d.c.451). Syr. nat. philosopher.
Atkinson—Magic p53-54   *Shippen—Men p51-54
Hammerton p1033

Netherwood, Douglas Blakeshaw (1885-1943). Amer. aero. pioneer.
Curr. Biog. '43 p551

Netter, Arnold (1855-1936). Fr. bacteriologist.
Bulloch—Hist. p386

Neuburger, Max (1868-1955). Aust. neurologist.
Castiglioni—Hist. p1106-1107
(por.1107)

Neufeld, Fred (b.1869). Pol. bacteriologist.
Bulloch—Hist. p386

Neuman, Leo Handel (1868-1941). Amer. physician.
Curr. Biog. '41 p610

Neumann, Franz Ernst (1798-1895). Ger. chemist.
Hammerton p1033

Neumann, Gaspard (or Caspar) (1683-1737). Ger. chemist.
Weeks—Discovery p31-32,60,306

Neumann, Heinrich (1864-1939). Aust. physician.
Curr. Biog. '40 p612
Kagan—Modern p135 (por.135)

Newberry, John Strong (1822-1892). Amer. geologist.
Hammerton p1034
Merrill—First p363-365 (por.360)
N.A.S.—Biog. (6) p1-15 (por.1)
Woodruff—Devel. p285-286

Newbigin, Marion (d.1934). Scot. geologist.
Hammerton p1034

Newcomb, Simon (1835-1909). Can.-Amer. astronomer.
Armitage—Cent. p40 (por.80, XIX)
*Book—Pop. Sci. (15) p5000-5002
(por.5001)
Cajori—Hist. p451
Chambers—Dict. col.331
Hammerton p1035
*Hylander—Scien. p99-105 (por.99)
Jordan—Leading p363-389 (por.363)
MacPherson—Astron. p40-50 (por.40)
N.A.S.—Biog. (10) p1-18 (por.1)
Shapley—Astron. p326
Smith—Math. p131-132
Van Wagenen—Beacon p371-373
Williams—Great p79,413,559-560
(por.,front.)
Woodruff—Devel. p286 (por.158)

Newcomen, Thomas (1663-1729). Eng. inventor, engineer.
*Book—Pop. Sci. (12) p4223-4224
Chambers—Dict. col.332
*Epstein—Real p44
Goddard—Eminent p155-159
Hammerton p1035
Hart—Engineers p73-78
*Hartman—Mach. p57-59
*Hodgins—Behemoth p37-38

Newcomer, Francis Kosier (1889-   ). Amer. engineer.
Curr. Biog. '50 p423-425 (por.423)

Newell, Homer Edward, Jr. (1915-   ). Amer. physicist, mathematician.
Curr. Biog. '54 p485-487 (por.486)

Newland, David H. (1872-1943). Amer. geologist.
  G.S.A.—Proc. '43 p209-212 (por.209)

Newlands, John Alexander Reina (1838-1898). Eng. chemist.
  Chambers—Dict. col.332
  *Kendall—Young p182-186 (por.186)
  Partington—Short p344,345,354
  Weeks—Discovery p387-389 (por.387)

Newman, Sir George (1870-1948). Brit. bacteriologist.
  Hammerton p1035

Newport, George (1803-1854). Eng. anatomist.
  Locy—Biology p100-102

Newsholme, Sir Arthur (1857-1943). Brit. physician.
  Hammerton p1035

Newsom, Carroll Vincent (1904-   ). Amer. mathematician.
  Curr. Biog. '57 p401-403 (por.402)

Newton, Alfred (1829-1907). Eng. zoologist, ornithologist.
  Hammerton p1035
  People p302

Newton, Sir Charles Thomas (1816-1894). Brit. archaeologist.
  Hammerton p1035-1036

Newton, Hubert Anson (1830-1896). Amer. astronomer, mathematician.
  N.A.S.—Biog. (4) p99-120
  Smith—Math. p135-136

Newton, Sir Isaac (1642-1727). Eng. mathematician.
  Abetti—History p133-140
    (por.146#21)
  Ball—Great p116-146 (por.126)
  Ball—Short p319-352
  Bell—Men p90-116 (por.,front.)
  *Bolton—Famous p33-47 (por.32)
  *Book—Pop. Sci. (13) p4485-4487
    (por.4487)
  Cajori—Hist. p191-205
  Chambers—Dict. col.332-333
    (por.331)
  Chymia (2) p27-36
  *Cottler—Heroes p117-127
  Crew—Physicists #3 (por.)
  *Crowther—Founders p223-287
    (por.224)
  *Crowther—Scientists p89-136
    (por.128)
  *Darrow—Masters p13-17 (por.32)
  *Darrow—Thinkers p120-121
  Gibson—Heroes p107-133
  Ginzburg—Adven. p139-175
    (por.145)
  Gregory—British p22-23 (por.8)
  Hammerton p1036-1037 (por.1036)
  Hart—Makers p128-172 (por.138)
  Hart—Physicists p73-81
  Holmyard—British p23-27 (por.23)
  Holmyard—Makers p217-221
    (por.218)
  Hooper—Makers p274-324
  Lenard—Great p83-111 (por.83)

(Continued)

Newton, Sir Isaac—*Continued*
*Lewellen—Boy p41-70,137-164
(por.41)
Lodge—Pioneers p159-229
(por.,front.)
MacPherson—Makers p55-71
(por.210)
*McSpadden—How p99-111 (por.106)
Magie—Source p30-31
Meyer—World p35-37
*Miller—Hist. p231-235
Moulton—Auto. p171-173
Muir—Men p105-137
*Nisenson—Illus. p116 (por.116)
Oliver—Stalkers p132 (por.133)
100 Great p557-563
People p302
Schwartz—Moments (1) p55-57,278-
280,393-394
*Science Miles p87 (por.87)
Sci. Amer.—Lives p21-30 (por.23)
Sedgwick—Short p290-300

Sewell—Brief p72-73
Shapley—Astron. p74
*Shippen—Design p137-147
*Simmons—Great p25-26 (por.25)
Smith—Hist. I p398-404 (por.399)
Smith—Portraits (1), VII, unp. (por.)
Smith—Torch. p182 (por.182)
*Stevens—Science p32-39 (por.30)
Taylor—Illus. p74-78
Thomas—Scien. p51-65 (por.49)
Turnbull—Great p86-94
Van Wagenen—Beacon p126-130
Vaucouleurs—Disc. p54-56
Williams—Great p180-190 (por.188)
Wilson—Human p189-207 (por.194)
Woodruff—Devel. p18-25,47-50,153-
158,286 (por.,front.)
*World's Great p45-62 (por.46)
*Wright—Great p180-186
Year—Pic. p95 (por.95)

Newton, John (1823-1895). Amer. engineer.
N.A.S.—Biog. (4) p233-240

Nicaise, Jules Edouard (1838-1896). Fr. physician.
Major—History (2) p900

Nicander (c.135 B.C.). Gr. physician.
Gordon—Medicine p613

Nicholas of Cusa (or Nicolaus Cusanus) (1401-1464). Ger. physicist.
Dreyer—Hist. p282-288   Major—History (1) p356
Hart—Physicists p30-32

Nicholls, Francis (or Frank) (1699-1778). Eng. anatomist, physician.
Gunther—Early XI p95

Nichols, Edward Leamington (1854-1937). Amer. physicist.
N.A.S.—Biog. (21) p343-354
(por.343)

Nichols, Ernest Fox (1869-1924). Amer. physicist.
N.A.S.—Biog. (12) p99-127 (por.99)

Nichols, Henry Lambard (1823-1915). Amer. physician.
Jones—Memories p375-381 (por.375)

Nichols, Ruth Rowland (1901-   ). Amer. aero. pioneer.
Adams—Heroines p87-113 (por.104)
Heinmuller—Man's p338 (por.338)

Nichols, William Henry (1852-1930). Amer. chemist.
A.A.A.S.—Proc. (81) p78-80   *Darrow—Builders p295-299 (por.287)
Browne—Hist. p483 (por.117)   Forbes—Men p260-267 (por.1)

Nichols, William Thomas (1901-   ). Amer. engineer.
Curr. Biog. '53 p457-458 (por.458)

Nicholson, Henry Alleyne (1844-1899). Scot. paleontologist.
Hammerton p1038

Nicholson, John William (1881-1955). Eng. mathematician.
R.S.L.—Biog. (2) p209-213 (por.209)

Nicholson, Seth Barnes (1891-   ). Amer. astronomer.
Chambers—Dict. col.333-334

Nicholson, William (1753-1815). Eng. engineer, physicist.
Chambers—Dict. col.334
Magie—Source p431-432

Nickles, Samuel (1833-1908). Swiss physician, surgeon.
Swiss—Prom. p123-124

Nicol, William (1768-1851). Scot. physicist.
Chambers—Dict. col.334

Nicolaier, Arthur (b.1862). Ger. bacteriologist, physician.
Bulloch—Hist. p386

Nicole, François (1683-1758). Fr. mathematician.
Smith—Hist. I p472-473

Nicolet, Jean (1598-1642). Fr. geologist, sci. explorer.
Merrill—First p153-154

Nicolet, Marcel (1912-   ). Belg. astrophysicist.
Curr. Biog. '58 p308-310 (por.309)

Nicolle, Charles Jules Henri (1866-1936). Fr. bacteriologist.
Bulloch—Hist. p386   Hammerton p1039
Chambers—Dict. col.334   Major—History (2) p1043-1044
Grainger—Guide p163   (por.938)
                                       Stevenson—Nobel p130-133 (por.150)

Nicolò of Bresci.   See **Tartaglia, Niccolò**

Nicols, Thomas (fl.1659). Eng. geologist.
Adams—Birth p163-164

Nicomachus (fl.c.100). Gr. mathematician.
Cajori—Hist. p58-59   Sedgwick—Short p125-126
Clagett—Greek p116   Smith—Hist. I p127-129

Nicomedes (fl.c.150 B.C.). Gr. mathematician.
Smith—Hist. I p118

Nielsen, Arthur Charles (1897-   ). Amer. engineer.
Curr. Biog. '51 p459-461 (por.459)

Niepce, Joseph Nicéphore (1765-1833). Fr. inventor, physicist.
*Bock—Pop. Sci. (12) p4224-4225   Law—Civiliz. p155-157
*Epstein—Real p124-125   Meyer—World p77-78
Hammerton p1039   Year—Pic. p159,160 (por.160)
*Larsen—Scrap. p11-12 (por.25)

Nier, Alfred Otto Carl (1911-   ). Amer. physicist.
Jaffe—Crucibles p311-382

Nieuport, Édouard (1875-1911). Fr. aero. pioneer.
Heinmuller—Man's p277 (por.277)

Nieuwland, Julius Arthur (1878-1936). Amer. botanist, chemist.
Chambers—Dict. col.334-335

Nilson, Lars Fredrik (1840-1899). Swed. physicist, chemist.
Chambers—Dict. col.335   Smith—Torch. p183 (por.183)
Findlay—Hundred p332   Weeks—Discovery p403-407
                                (por.403)

Nilsson, Sven (1787-1883). Swed. zoologist.
Lindroth—Swedish p172-177

Nilsson-Ehle, Herman (1873-1949). Swed. botanist, geneticist.
Lindroth—Swedish p264-270

Nipkow, Paul Gottlieb (1860-1940). Ger. inventor.
Curr. Biog. '40 p618   Radio's 100 p128-129 (por.140)
*Larsen—Prentice p157-159

Nitze, Max (1848-1906). Ger. inventor, surgeon.
Chambers—Dict. col.335
Leonardo—Lives p312-313

Nixon, Alexander Butler (1820-1889). Amer. physician.
Jones—Memories p449-453 (por.449)

Nobel, Alfred Bernhard (1833-1896). Swed. chemist, engineer, inventor.
*Book—Pop. Sci. (12) p4225-4228   People p306-307
Chambers—Dict. col.335   *Pratt—Famous p7-8
*Darrow—Masters p220-227 (por.321)   Sewell—Brief p207
Hammerton p1041-1042 (por.1042)   Smith—Torch. p184 (por.184)
*Larsen—Shaped p111-129 (por.96)   Van Wagenen—Beacon p362-364
Moulton—Auto. p288   Year—Pic. p141 (por.141)

Nobile, Umberto (1885-   ). It. engineer, sci. explorer, aero. pioneer.
Hammerton p1042

Nobili, Leopoldo (1784-1835). It. physicist, inventor.
Chambers—Dict. col.335-336

Noble, Alfred (1844-1914). Amer. engineer.
John Fritz p63-65 (por.62)

Noble, Sir Andrew (1832-1915). Eng. physicist.
Hammerton p1042

Noble, Gladwyn Kingsley (1894-1940). Amer. biologist.
Curr. Biog. '41 p614 (por.614)

Nocard, Edmond Isidore Étienne (1850-1903). Fr. biologist.
Bulloch—Hist. p386
Chambers—Dict. p336

Noddack, Ida Eva (1896-   ). Ger. chemist.
Chambers—Dict. col.336
Weeks—Discovery p519-520,527

Noddack, Walter Karl Friedrich (1893-   ). Ger. chemist.
Chambers—Dict. col.336
Weeks—Discovery p519-520,527

Noé, Adolf Carl (1873-1939). Aust. geologist.
G.S.A.—Proc. '39 p219-225 (por.219)

Noelting, (Domingo) Emilio (1851-1922). Dan.-Ger. chemist.
A.A.A.S.—Proc. (79) p30-31

Nöggerath, Johann Jakob (1788-1877). Ger. mineralogist, seismologist.
Davison—Founders p121-123

Noguchi, Hideyo (1876-1928). Japan. bacteriologist.

Bulloch—Hist. p386-387
Chambers—Dict. col.336
*Darrow—Builders p210-212
Grainger—Guide p163
Major—History (2) p1044
*Masters—Conquest p162-163
    (por.164)

Osborn—Fragments p234-235
    (por.352)
*Shippen—Men p196-197
*Snyder—Biology p230-234 (por.232)
Tobey—Riders p186-189
*Williams-Ellis p239-244 (por.239)

Nollet, Jean Antoine, Abbé (1700-1770). Fr. physicist.

Chambers—Dict. col.337
Magie—Source p403

Walsh—Catholic (2d) p165-169
    (por.149)

Nonius.   See **Nunes, Pedro**

Nordau, Max Simon (1849-1923). Ger.-Hung. physician, psychologist.

*Book—Pop. Sci. (14) p4931-4932
Kagan—Modern p65 (por.65)

Norden, Carl Lukas (1880-   ). Dutch inventor, engineer.

Curr. Biog. '45 p432-434 (por.433)

Nordenskiöld, (or Nordenskjold) **Baron Nils Adolf Erik** (1832-1901). Swed. sci. explorer.

Hammerton p1043 (por.1043)
Lindroth—Swedish p204-213

Nordhoff, Heinz (1899-   ). Ger. engineer.

Curr. Biog. '56 p467-469 (por.468)

Nordmann, Charles (1881-1940). Fr. astronomer.

Curr. Biog. '40 p618

Norris, Henry Hutchinson (1873-1940). Amer. engineer.

Curr. Biog. '40 p620

Norris, James Flack (1871-1940). Amer. chemist.

Browne—Hist. p484-485 (por.133)
Curr. Biog. '40 p620 (por.620)
    (por.322)

Norstad, Lauris (1907-   ). Amer. aero. pioneer.

Curr. Biog. '59 p326-328

North, Elisha (1771-1843). Amer. physician.

Major—History (2) p767-768

Northrop, John Howard (1891-   ). Amer. biochemist.
Chambers—Dict. col.337-338
Curr. Biog. '47 p472-474 (por.473)
Farber—Nobel p184,185-186
(por.118)

Northrop, John Knudsen (1895-   ). Amer. aero. pioneer, engineer.
Curr. Biog. '49 p458-460 (por.459)

Northrup, Edwin Fitch (1866-1940). Amer. engineer.
Curr. Biog. '40 p620

Norton, John P. (1822-1852). Amer. agric. chemist.
Smith—Chem. p231

Norton, Thomas Herbert (1851-1941). Amer. chemist.
Curr. Biog. '42 p635
Progress—Science '41 p268-269
Weeks—Discovery p326 (por.326)

Norton, William A. (1810-1883). Amer. astronomer.
N.A.S.—Biog. (2) p189-199

Norton, William Harmon (1856-1944). Amer. geologist.
G.S.A.—Proc. '46 p199-206 (por.199)

Norway, Nevil Shute.   See **Shute, Nevil**

Nothnagel, Carl Wilhelm Heimann (1841-1905). Ger. physician.
Major—History (2) p904

Notman, James Geoffrey (1901-   ). Can. engineer.
Curr. Biog. '58 p312-313 (por.313)

Nott, Josiah Clark (1804-1873). Amer. physician, ethnologist.
Major—History p769

Novaro, Giacomo Filippo (1843-1934). It. surgeon.
Leonardo—Lives p313

Novy, Frederick George (1864-1957). Amer. bacteriologist.
N.A.S.—Biog. (33) p326-340 (por.326)

Noyes, Arthur Amos (1866-1936). Amer. chemist.
*Book—Pop. Sci. (13) p4347
Browne—Hist. p479 (por.73)
Killeffer—Eminent p23 (por.23)
N.A.S.—Biog. (31) p322-330
(por.322)

Noyes, Blance Wilcox (1900-   ). Amer. aero. pioneer.
 Adams—Heroines p137-153 (por.144)

Noyes, William Albert (1857-1941). Amer. chemist.
 Browne—Hist. p483 (por.117)   N.A.S.—Biog. (27) p179-195
 Curr. Biog. '41 p616   (por.179)
 Killeffer—Eminent p20 (por.20)   Progress—Science '41 p269

Noyes, William Albert, Jr. (1898-   ). Amer. chemist.
 Browne—Hist. p492 (por.183)
 Curr. Biog. '47 p478-480 (por.479)

Nuck, Anton (1650-1692). Dutch anatomist, surgeon.
 Major—History (1) p562

Nuckols, William Preston (1905-   ). Amer. aero. pioneer.
 Curr. Biog. '52 (p450-451)

Nunenmacher, Frederick William (b.1870). Amer. entomologist.
 Essig—Hist. p717-719 (por.717)

Nunes, Pedro (or Nonius, Nunez) (1492/1502-1577/1598). Port.
  mathematician.
 Cajori—Hist. p142
 Smith—Hist. I p348-349

Nungesser, Charles (1892-1927). Fr. aero. pioneer.
 Arnold—Airmen p128   Heinmuller—Man's p322 (por.322)
 Hammerton p1047   La Croix — They p55-81 (por.98)

Nuttall, George Henry Faulkner (1862-1937). Amer. biologist,
  entomologist.
 Osborn—Fragments p231 (por.341)

Nuttall, Thomas (1786-1859). Eng. botanist, ornithologist, naturalist.
 Alden—Early p42-46 (por.44)   Mozans—Woman p323-324
 Bell—Early p68   Peattie—Gather. p169-173
 *Book—Pop. Sci. (14) p4932-4934   Youmans—Pioneers p205-214
   (por.4933)   (por.205)
 Dakin—Perennial p35-36   Young—Biology p34 (por.35)

Nuysement, Jacques de (fl.1621). Fr. chemist.
 Chymia (2) p113-114

Nylander, Olof O. (1864?-1943). Swed. geologist, mineralogist.
 Curr. Biog. '43 p563

Nyrop, Donald William (1912-   ). Amer. aero. pioneer.
Curr. Biog. '52 p451-453 (por.452)

O

Oates, Lawrence Edward Grace (1880-1912). Brit. sci. explorer.
Hammerton p1048 (por.1048)

Oatman, Ira E. (1819-1888). Amer. physician.
Jones—Memories p349-352 (por.349)

Obel.   See **L'Obel, Matthias de**

Obermeier, Otto Hugo Franz (1843-1873). Ger. bacteriologist.
Bulloch—Hist. p387

Oberth, Hermann Julius (1894-   ). Rom. physicist.
Curr. Biog. '57 p416-418 (por.417)   *Williams—Rocket p111-143
Gartmann—Men p48-73 (por.64)

Obruchev, Vladimir Afanasevich (1863-1956). Rus. geologist.
G.S.A.—Proc. '57 p135-136 (por.135)

Ochsner, Albert John (1858-1925). Amer. surgeon.
Leonardo—Lives p314-316   Swiss—Prom. p125-126 (por.125)
Major—History (2) p1044

Ocker, William C. (1876-1942). Amer. aero. pioneer.
Curr. Biog. '42 p636

Odling, William (1829-1921). Eng. chemist.
Gunther—Early XI p292

O'Donnell, Emmett, Jr. (1906-   ). Amer. aero. pioneer.
Curr. Biog. '48 p479-481 (por.480)

O'Dwyer, Joseph (1841-1898). Amer. physician.
Major—History (2) p904
Walsh—Makers p323-356

Oenopides of Chios (fl.5th cent., B.C.). Gr. astronomer.
Smith—Hist. I p79-80

Öersted, Anders Sandoë (1816-1872). Dan. naturalist.
Copen.—Prom. p128-130

Oersted, Hans Christian (1777-1851). Dan. chemist, physicist.
A.A.A.S.—Proc. (79) p32-33
Abbott—Great p1-2 (por.4)
Appleyard—Pioneers p143-176
  (por.142,174)
*Book—Pop. Sci. (13) p4347-4348
Chalmers—Historic p269-270
Chambers—Dict. col.339
Copen.—Prom. p89-93
*Darrow—Masters p338-339
*Epstein—Real p53-54
Hammerton p1049
Hart—Makers p198-199 (por.199)
Hart—Physicists p105-106
*Hartman—Mach. p88-89
Hawks—Wireless p24-27 (por.26)
*Hodgins—Behemoth p104-109,125
Lenard—Great p213-218 (por.218)
Magie—Source p436-437
Meyer—World p131-133 (por.132)
Radio's 100 p31-34 (por.140)
Tuska—Invent. p127-128
Van Wagenen—Beacon p217-219
Weeks—Discovery p345-346 (por.345)
Williams—Story p207 (por.201)
Year—Pic. p121 (por.121)

Ogden, Francis Barber (1783-1857). Amer. inventor, engineer.
*Pratt—Famous p33-35

Ogle, John William (1824-1905). Eng. mathematician, physician.
Gunther—Early XI p234 (por.234)

Ogston, Alexander (1844-1929). Scot. bacteriologist.
Bulloch—Hist. p387 (por.164)

O'Harra, Cleophas C. (1866-1935). Amer. geologist.
G.S.A.—Proc. '35 p289-292 (por.289)

Ohm, George Simon (1787-1854). Ger. physicist.
Appleyard—Pioneers p179-208
  (por.178,181)
Chambers—Dict. col.339
Dibner—Ten p27-30 (por.28)
Hammerton p1050 (por.1050)
Hart—Makers p233-247 (por.233)
Hart—Physicists p103-105
Hodgins—Behemoth p113-115
Lenard—Great p236-240 (por.240)
Magie—Source p465
Radio's 100 p34-35 (por.140)
Tuska—Invent. p128
Van Wagenen—Beacon p248-250
Year—Pic. p121 (por.121)

Oisy.   See d'Oisy, Pelletier

Oken, (or Ockenfuss), **Lorenzo** (1779-1851). Ger. biologist, naturalist.
Locy—Biology p160-161,241-242
Murray—Science p140-141
Osborn—Greeks p180-185

Olbers, Heinrich Wilhelm Matthäus (1758-1840). Ger. astronomer, physician.
Chambers—Dict. col.340
McPherson—Makers p127-131
Shapley—Astron. p177
Williams—Great p281-288 (por.285)
Williams—Story p45-47 (por.55)

Oldham, Thomas (1816-1878). Irish geologist.
Davison—Founders p84-85

Olebar, Augustus Henry (1897-   ). Eng. aero. pioneer.
Hammerton p1054

Oliphant, Marcus Laurence Elwin (1901-   ). Austral. physicist.
Curr. Biog. '51 p468-469 (por.468)

Oliver, James (1823-1908). Scot. inventor.
*Epstein—Real p170-171

Oliver, James Edward (1829-1895). Amer. mathematician.
N.A.S.—Biog. (4) p57-73

Olivier, Guillaume Antoine (1756-1814). Fr. naturalist, entomologist.
Essig—Hist. p719-721 (por.720)

Olmsted, Denison (1791-1859). Amer. geologist, chemist.
Merrill—First p95-96 (por.94)   Youmans—Pioneers p250-259
Smith—Chem. p223   (por.250)

Olson, Harry Ferdinand (1902-   ). Amer. engineer.
Curr. Biog. '55 p465-466 (por.465)   Tuska—Invent. p92
Radio's 100 p277-278 (por.140)

Olszevski, Karol Stanislov (1846-1915). Pol. chemist.
Chambers—Dict. col.340

Omar Khayyám (c.1045-1123). Pers. astronomer, mathematician.
Cajori—Hist. p107-108   Smith—Hist. I p286
Hammerton p1051-1052

O'Meara, Barry Edward (1786-1836). Irish surgeon.
Hammerton p1052

Omeliansky, Vasil Leo (b.1867). Rus. bacteriologist.
Bulloch—Hist. p387

Omlie, Phoebe Fairgrave (1902-   ). Amer. aero. pioneer.
*Adams—Heroines p69-84 (por.72)
Knapp—New p157-168 (por.179)

Omori, Fusakichi (1868-1923). Japan. seismologist.
Davison—Founders p210-230

O'Neal, Edward Asbury (1875-   ). Amer. agriculturist.
Curr. Biog. '46 p436-438 (por.437)

Onnes, Heike Kamerlingh (1853-1926). Dutch physicist.
Chambers—Dict. col.340
Hammerton p1052
Heathcote—Nobel p108-117
   (por.240)
Smith—Torch. p184 (por.184)
Weber—College p210 (por.210)

Onsager, Lars (1903-   ). Norw. chemist.
A.A.A.S.—Proc. (82) p298-300
Curr. Biog. '58 p321-322 (por.321)

Opel, Fritz (1899-   ). Ger. rocket pioneer, aero. pioneer.
Gartmann—Men p82-84
Heinmuller—Man's p336 (por.336)
*Williams—Rocket p147-148

Oppenheimer, J. Robert (1904-   ). Amer. physicist.
Chambers Dict. col.341
Curr. Biog. '45 p438-440 (por.439)
*Pratt—Famous p135-136
Pringle—Great p189-206 (por.177)
Progress—Science '41 p269
Riedman—Men p200-217 (por.201)
Robinson—100 p247-249 (por.247)
Schwartz—Moments (2) p978-979
Year—Pic. p213 (por.213)

Orbigny, Alcide Dessalines d' (1802-1857). Fr. paleontologist, naturalist.
Hammerton p1053
Von Hagen—Green p182-183

Ordóñez, Ezequiel (1867?-1950). Mex. geologist.
G.S.A.—Proc. '50 p111-112 (por.111)

Oreibasios.   See **Oribasius of Pergamus**

Oresme (or Oresmus), **Nicole** (1323/1330-1382). Fr. mathematician.
Ball—Short p178-180
Cajori—Hist. p127
Smith—Hist. I p239-240

Orfila, Matthieu Joseph Bonaventure (or Matheo, José Bonaventura)
   (1787-1853). Fr.-Sp. chemist.
Hammerton p1053
Major—History (2) p708
Weeks—Discovery p139 (por.139)

Oriani, Barnaba (1752-1832). It. astronomer.
Abetti—Hist. p174-175

Oribasius of Pergamos (c325-c400). Gr. physician.
Gordon—Medicine p723-724
Gordon—Medieval p45-47
Lambert—Medical p60-61
Lambert—Minute p62-63
Leonardo—Lives p316-318
Major—History (1) p210-211

Orlebar, Augustus H. (1897?-1943). Eng. aero. pioneer.
Curr. Biog. '43 p566

Ormerod, Eleanor Anne (1828-1901). Eng. entomologist.
Hammerton p1055 (por.1055)
Mozans—Woman p246-253

Orr, Hiram Winnett (1877-1956). Amer. physician, surgeon.
Curr. Biog.'41 p638-639 (por.639)

Orr, Sir John Boyd (1880-1941). Scot. biologist.
Chambers—Dict. col.341
Curr. Biog. '46 p440-443 (por.442)

Orr, Louis McDonald (1899-1961). Amer. physician.
Curr. Biog. '60 p303-304 (por.303)
  '61 (July)

Orsted.   See Oersted, Hans Christian

Orta, (or Orto) **G. ab**   See **Horto, Garcia ab**

Ortega, Juan de (fl.1512-1567). Sp. mathematician.
Smith—Hist. I p344-345

Ortelius, Abraham (1527-1598). Dutch geographer.
Hammerton p1056

Orth, Johannes (1847-1923). Ger. pathologist, bacteriologist.
Bulloch—Hist. p387
Major—History (2) p908-909

Orto, (or Orta, de)   See **Horto, Garcia ab**

Orton, Edward Francis Baxter (1829-1899). Amer. geologist.
Merrill—First p453-454 (por.452)

Orville, Howard Thomas (1901-1960). Amer. meteorologist, aerologist.
Curr. Biog. '56 p473-475 (por.474)
  '60 p304

Osborn, Fairfield (1887-   ). Amer. naturalist.
Curr. Biog. '49 p463-465 (por.464)

Osborn, Henry Fairfield (1857-1935). Amer. geologist, paleontologist, biologist.

G.S.A.—Proc. '44 p287-292 (por.287)
Hammerton p1056 (por.1056)
*Hylander—Scien. p146-155 (por.,front.)
Moulton—Auto. p564
N.A.S.—Biog. (19) p53-88 **(por.53)**

Osborn, Herbert (1856-1954). Amer. entomologist.

Essig—Hist. p721-724 (por.722)

Osborne, Oliver Thomas (1862-1940). Amer. physician.

Curr. Biog. '40 p626

Osborne, Thomas Burr (1859-1929). Amer. biochemist.

N.A.S.—Biog. (14) p261-284 (por.261)

O'Shaughnessy, Laurence (1900-1940). Eng. surgeon.

Leonardo—Lives p318-319

Osler, Sir William (1849-1919). Can. physician.

A.A.A.S.—Proc. (77) p45
*Book—Pop. Sci. (14) p4934
Castiglioni—Hist. p834-835 (por.835)
Chambers—Dict. col.341-342
*Chandler—Medicine p85-92 (por.84)
Farmer—Doctors' p215
Hammerton p1056 (por.1056)
Kagan—Leaders p96-125
Kagan—Modern p14 (por.14)
Lambert—Medical p319-331 (por.328)
Lambert—Minute p319-331 (por.304)
Major—History (2) p854,856-859, 909-911 (por.854)
*Montgomery—Story p219-220,221
Moulton—Auto. p605-606
Newman—Interp. p227-247
Rowntree—Amid p61-62 (por.59)
*Science Miles p232 (por.232)
Sigerist—Great p397-401 (por.400)
16 Amer. p9-12

Osten Sacken, Carl Robert (1828-1906). Rus. entomologist.

Essig —Hist. p724-727 (por.725)

Ostwald, Wilhelm (1853-1932). Ger. chemist.

*Book—Pop. Sci. (13) p4348-4349 (por. 4349)
Chambers—Dict. col.342
Chymia (2) p57-64
Farber—Nobel p37-41 (por.118)
Findlay—Hundred p332
Hammerton p1057 (por.1057)
Partington—Short p336,340 (por.303)
Smith—Torch. p186 (por.186)
Woodruff—Devel. p63,118,119,286

Otto, John Conrad (1774-1844). Amer. physician.

Major—History (2) p768

Otto, Nikolaus August (1832-1891). Ger. engineer, inventor.

Chambers—Dict. col.342
Matschoss—Great p280-292 (por.281)
Year—Pic. p184 (por.184)

Oughtred, William (1574/1575-1660). Eng. inventor, mathematician.
Ball—Short p238-239
Cajori—Hist. p157-158
Chambers—Dict. col.342-343
Smith—Hist. I p392-394

Overholser, Winfred (1892-   ). Amer. psychiatrist.
Curr. Biog. '53 p466-468 (por.467)

Oviedo y Valdés, Gonzalo Fernandez de (1478-1557). Sp. biologist, naturalist, sci. explorer.
Bodenheimer—Hist. p223
Miall—Early p60-64
Von Hagen—Green p16-17

Ovington, Earle (1879-1936). Amer. aero. pioneer.
Heinmuller—Man's p289 (por.289)

Owen, David Dale (1807-1860). Scot. geologist.
Fenton—Giants p166-178 (por.175)
Merrill—First p196-199 (por.196)
Youmans—Pioneers p500-508 (por.500)

Owen, Sir Richard (1804-1892). Eng. anatomist, paleontologist, zoologist, physiologist, physician.
*Book—Pop. Sci. (14) p4934-4936 (por.4935)
Chambers—Dict. col.343-344
Hammerton p1059 (por.1059)
Locy—Biology p158-160,334 (por.161,335)
Major—History (2) p810
Merrill—First p357,358,396,556 (por.456)
Murray—Science p320-323
Osborn—Greeks p316-320
Williams—Story p363 (por.155)
Woodruff—Devel. p286

Owens, Robert Bowie (1870-1940). Amer. chemist, elec. engineer, physicist.
Chambers—Dict. col.344
Curr. Biog. '40 p626
Weeks—Discovery p502,503 (por.502)

P

Pacchioni, Antonio (1665-1726). It. anatomist, physician.
Castiglioni—Hist. p526-527 (por.528)
Major—History (2) p628

Pacciolo.   See **Pacioli, Luca**

Pacheco e Chaves, Joao (1916-   ). Brazil. agriculturist, engineer.
Curr. Biog. '54 p497-499 (por.498)

Pacini, Filippo (1812-1883). It. anatomist, physiologist.
Bulloch—Hist. p387
Van Wagenen—Beacon p297-298

Pacinotti, Antonio (1841-1912). It. physicist, inventor.
Year—Pic. p176 (por.176)

Pacioli, Luca (or Paccioli; Sepulchri, Far Luca di Borgo Sancti) (1450?-1520?). It. mathematician.
Ball—Short p208-212   Sedgwick—Short p232-234
Sarton—Six p28,29 (por.24)

Pack, Herbert J. (1892-1930). Amer. entomologist.
Osborn—Fragments p218-219

Packard, Alpheus Spring (1839-1905). Amer. entomologist, zoologist.
Essig—Hist. p727-729 (por.728)   Osborn—Fragments p147-148
N.A.S.—Biog. (9) p181-207 (por.181)   (por.346)

Packard, Winthrop (1862-1943). Amer. naturalist.
Curr. Biog. '43 p568

Paddon, Harry Locke (1880-1939). Brit. physician.
Curr. Biog. '40 p626

Page, Frederick Handley (1885-   ). Eng. aero pioneer.
Burge—Ency. p637
Hammerton p1062

Pagel, Julius Leopold (1851-1912). Pomer. physician.
Kagan—Modern p210 (por.210)
Major—History (2) p912

Pagenstecher, Hermann (1844-1932). Ger. physician.
Hammerton p1062

Paget, Sir James (1814-1899). Eng. physician, surgeon, pathologist.
Castiglioni—Hist. p851 (por.851)   Leonardo—Lives (supp.1) p502-503
Hale-White—Great p159-176   Major—History (2) p816-818
Hammerton p1062   (por.817)
      Rosen—Four p79-84

Paixhans, Henri Joseph (1783-1854). Fr. inventor.
*Pratt—Famous p110-113

Palache, Charles (1869-1954). Amer. geologist, mineralogist.
G.S.A.—Proc. '57 p137-139 (por.137)
N.A.S.—Biog. (30) p313-328
      (por.313)

Palfyn, Jean (1650-1730). Belg. anatomist, surgeon.
Major—History (1) p562

Palissy, Bernard (c1510-1589). Fr. nat. philosopher.
Chambers—Dict. col.345
Hammerton p1064
Sarton—Six p164-171
Smith—Torch. p187 (por.187)
Weeks—Discovery p65-66 (por.65)
Woodruff—Devel. p286

Pallas, Peter Simon (1741-1811). Ger. geologist, naturalist, zoologist.
Adams—Birth p378-381
Geikie—Founders p80-84
Weeks—Discovery p136-137
(por.137)

Palletta, Giovan-Battista (1747-1832). It. pathologist, surgeon.
Leonardo—Lives p319

Palmer, Albert deForest (1869-1940). Amer. physicist.
Curr. Biog. '40 p628

Palmer, Robert Hastings (1882-1948). Amer. geologist.
G.S.A.—Proc. '49 p211-212 (por.211)

Palmieri, Luigi (1807-1896). It. physicist, inventor, mathematician, seismologist.
Davison—Founders p87-91

Paltauf, Richard (1858-1924). Aust. bacteriologist, pathologist.
Bulloch—Hist. p387-388

Pancoast, Joseph (1805-1882). Amer. surgeon.
Leonardo—Lives p319-321

Pancoast, William Henry (1835-1897). Amer. surgeon.
Leonardo—Lives p321-322

Paneth, Frederick Adolphus (1887-   ). Aust.-Brit. chemist.
Chambers—Dict. col.345

Pangborn, Clyde E. (1894-   ). Amer. aero. pioneer.
*Fraser—Heroes p623-628
Heinmuller—Man's p161-172,345
(por.345)

Panhard, René (1841-1908). Fr. engineer, inventor.
Chambers—Dict. col.345-346

Panum, Peter Ludwig (1820-1885). Dan. pathologist, physiologist, bacteriologist, physician.

Bulloch—Hist. p388
Copen.—Prom. p134-137

Grainger—Guide p163-164

Papin, Denis (1647?-1712?). Fr. physicist, inventor.

*Book—Pop. Sci. (12) p4228-4229
Chambers—Dict. col.346
*Epstein—Real p43-44,57,82
Hammerton p1066

*Hartman—Mach. p53-55
Hart—Engineers p71-73
*Larsen—Prentice p12-16
Lenard—Great p11 (por.125)

Pappus, Alexandrinus (c.3rd., 4th. cent.). Gr. mathematician.

Ball—Short p99-101
Cajori—Hist. p49-50
Chambers—Dict. col.346
Clagett—Greek p53-54,55,117-118

Hammerton p1066
Sedgwick—Short p132-133,137-138
Smith—Hist. I p136-137
Turnbull—Great p44-49

Paracelsus, Philippus Aureolus (or Theophrastus Bombastus von Hohenheim) (1493?-1541). Swiss physician, chemist.

Arber—Herbals p248-250 (por.249)
Atkinson—Magic p120-125
Bodenheimer—Hist. p236
Castiglioni—Hist. p444-451 (por.444)
Chambers—Dict. col.346-347
 (por.347)
*Darrow—Masters p339
*Elwell—Sci. p26-27
Gordon—Medieval p597-602,605-611
 (por.19)
Gordon—Romance p112-114
Hammerton p1066 (por.1066)
Holmyard—Chem. p46-51 (por.49)
Holmyard—Great Chem. p33-39
Holmyard—Makers p106-115
 (por.107)
Jaffe—Crucibles p18-33
Lambert—Medical p91-98 (por.92)
Lambert—Minute p91-98 (por.96)
Leonard—Crus. p91-130 (por.118)

Leonardo—Lives (Supp.1) p503-504
Major—History (1) p383-393
 (por.385-388)
Moulton—Auto. p52-53
Oliver—Stalkers p63-69 (por.64)
Partington—Short p41-44 (por.43)
People p310,327 (por.364)
Robinson—Path. p49-67 (por.62,63)
Rosen—Four p147-150
Sarton—Six p108-114,178-187
 (por.24)
*Science Miles p37-41 (por.37)
*Shippen—Men p74-77
Sigerist—Great p109-121
 (por.112,120)
Smith—Torch. p188-189 (por.188)
*Snyder—Biology p179-180
Three Famous p137-186 (por.136)
Wilson—Human p93-104
Year—Pic. p80 (por.80)

Paré, Ambroise (1510/1517-1590). Fr. physician, surgeon.

Atkinson—Magic p141-149
*Book—Pop. Sci. (14) p4936-4937
Castiglioni—Hist. p474-479 (por.478)
Chambers—Dict. col.348
*Chandler—Medicine p31-34 (por.30)
*Elwell—Sci. p28-29
*Fox—Great p31-59 (por.31)
Gordon—Medieval p665-668,671-677,
 697 (por.211)
Gordon—Romance p403-406
 (por.403)
Hammerton p1067

Lambert—Medical p110-116
 (por.112)
Lambert—Minute p110-116 (por.113)
Law—Civiliz. p304-307
Leonardo—Lives p322-324
Major—History (1) p425-431
 (por.427)
*Masters—Conquest p121-122
Moulton—Auto. p91
Oliver—Stalkers p79-84 (por.80)
Robinson—Path. p99-122
 (por.118-119)

(*Continued*)

Paré, Ambroise—*Continued*
Sarton—Six p199-201 (por.24)
*Shippen—Men p77-79
Sigerist—Great p130-137 (por.137)
Tobey—Riders p134,136

*Truax—Doctors p3-16
Tuska—Invent. p85-86
Young—Scalpel p32-51 (por.56)

Parham, Frederick W. (1856-1927). Amer. surgeon.
Leonardo—Lives p324-325

Park, Henry (1744-1831). Eng. surgeon.
Leonardo—Lives p325

Park, Mungo (1771-1805/1806). Scot. physician, surgeon, sci. explorer.
*Book—Pop. Sci. (9) p3181-3183
(por.3183)

Park, Roswell (1852-1914). Amer. surgeon.
Leonardo—Lives p326-327

Park, William Hallock (1863-1939). Amer. bacteriologist, physician.
Grainger—Guide p164
Kagan—Modern p161 (por.161)
*Snyder—Biology p265-266 (por.265)

Parker, George Howard (1864-1955). Amer. zoologist.
Progress—Science '41 p276-277
(por.277)

Parker, Henry Webster (b.1822). Amer. entomologist.
Osborn—Fragments p157-158

Parkes, Alexander (1813-1890). Eng. chemist, inventor.
Chambers—Dict. col.348

Parkes, Charles Theodore (1842-1891). Amer. surgeon.
Leonardo—Lives p327-328

Parkes, Edmund Alexander (1819-1876). Eng. physician.
Hammerton p1067
Walker—Pioneers p126-136 (por.126)

Parkinson, James (1755-1824). Eng. physician, surgeon, paleontologist.
Chambers—Dict. col.348
Major—History (2) p701

Parkinson, James H. (1859-1926). Irish-Amer. physician.
Jones—Memories p443-448 (por.443)

Parkinson, John (1567-1650). Eng. botanist.
Arber—Herbals p135,136,137,174   Hawks—Pioneers p188-190
  (por.136)   Raven—English p248-273
Chambers—Dict. col.348-349
Gilmour—British p12

Parks, William Arthur (1868-1936). Can. paleontologist.
G.S.A.—Proc. '36 p229-231 (por.229)

Parmelee, Ruth A. (n.d.). Amer. physician.
Lovejoy—Women p341-343 (por.344)
Lovejoy—Women Phys. p143-145
  p173-184

Parmenides of Elea (5th cent., B.C.). Gr. nat. philosopher.
Gordon—Medicine p469-470   Sedgwick—Short p59
Hammerton p1068   Smith—Hist. I p81

Parmentier, Antoine Augustin (1737-1813). Fr. chemist.
Smith—Torch. p190 (por.190)

Parr, Albert Eide (1900-   ). Norw.-Amer. zoologist, oceanographer.
Curr. Biog. '42 p640-642 (por.641)

Parr, Samuel W. (1857-1931). Amer. chemist.
Browne—Hist. p485 (por.141)

Parran, Thomas (c.1655). Amer. physician, surgeon.
Fisher—Amer. p257-260 (por.256)

Parran, Thomas, Jr. (1892-   ). Amer. physician, surgeon.
Curr. Biog. '40 p629-631 (por.630)   Ratcliffe—Modern p180-183 (por.180)
Progress—Science '40 p268-269
  (por.269)

Parrish, Rebecca (1869-1952). Amer. physician.
Lovejoy—Women p242

Parrish, Wayne W. (1907-   ). Amer. aero. pioneer.
Curr. Biog. '58 p327-329 (por.328)

Parrott, Percival John (1874-1953). Eng.-Amer. entomologist.
Osborn—Fragments p201-202

Parry, Angenette (1858?-1939). Amer. physician.
Lovejoy—Women Phys. p314
  (por.7,28)

Parry, Caleb Hilliard (1755-1822). Eng. physician.
Major—History (2) p600

Parry, Charles Christopher (1823-1890). Amer. physician, botanist, naturalist.
Ewan—Rocky p34-44,278-279
(por.34)

Parseval, August von (1861-1942). Ger. inventor, aero. pioneer.
Curr. Biog. '42 p642
Heinmuller—Man's p263 (por.263)

Parsons, Arthur Leonard (1873-1957). Amer. geologist, mineralogist.
G.S.A.—Proc. '57 p145 (por.145)

Parsons, Sir Charles Algernon (1854-1931). Eng. engineer, inventor.
Abbot—Great p169-171
*Book—Pop. Sci. (15) p5019-5021
(por.5020)
*Bridges—Master p169-180 (por.173)
Chambers—Dict. col.349
*Epstein—Real p47
Hammerton p1069
*Larsen—Men p69-87 (por.80)
Matschoss—Great p304-314 (por.314)

Parsons, Charles Lathrop (1867-1954). Amer. chemist.
Browne—Hist. p499-500 (por.175)
Chambers—Dict. col.349

Parsons, Elsie Worthington (1857?-1941). Amer. anthropologist.
Curr. Biog. p642
Progress—Science '41 p277

Parsons, John Herbert (1868-1957). Eng. ophthalmologist.
R.S.L.—Biog. (4) p205-213 (por.205)

Parsons, William, Earl of Rosse (1800-1867). Irish astronomer.
Ball—Great p272-288 (por.273)
*Book—Pop. Sci. (15) p5169-5170
Shapley—Astron. p255
Vaucouleurs—Disc. p119-120
Williams—Great p347-348 (por.348)

Partridge, Earle Everard (1900-   ). Amer. aero. pioneer.
Curr. Biog. '55 p472-474 (por.473)

Parvin, Theophilus (1829-1899). Amer. surgeon.
Leonardo—Lives p328-329

Pascal, Blaise (1623-1662). Fr. mathematician.
Ball—Short p281-288   Bell—Men p73-89 (por.,front.)
(Continued)

Pascal, Blaise—*Continued*
  *Book—Pop. Sci. (14) p4745-4746
  Cajori—Hist. p164-165
  Chambers—Dict. col.349-350
  Hammerton p1069-1070 (por.1069)
  Hart—Makers p180
  Hart—Physicists p56-59
  Hooper—Makers p223-232
  Law—Civiliz. p132-134
  Lenard—Great p49-50 (por.53)
  *Lewellen—Boy p94-103 (por.93)
  Magie—Source p73
  Moulton—Auto. p145

  Muir—Men p77-104
  People p327-328
  Schwartz—Moments (1) p351-352
  Sedgwick—Short p283-286
  Smith—Hist. I p381-383 (por.381)
  Smith—Portraits (2), V, unp. (por.)
  *Sootin—Twelve p9-28
  Suter—Gallery p102-115
  Turnbull—Great p77-80
  Van Wagenen—Beacon p114-116
  Year—Pic. p92 (por.92)

Pasteur, Louis (1822-1895). Fr. chemist, biologist.

  Atkinson—Magic p224-225
  Bodenheimer—Hist. p426
  *Bolton—Famous p163-176 (por.162)
  *Book—Pop. Sci. (14) p4937-4940
  Bulloch—Hist. p388-389 (por.164)
  Castiglioni—Hist. p810-813 (por.811)
  Chambers—Dict. col.350-352
    (por.350)
  *Chandler—Medicine p69-74 (por.68)
  *Cottler—Heroes p278-286
  *Crowther—Doctors p41-81 (por.65)
  *Darrow—Masters p186-197 (por.288)
  *DeKruif—Microbe p57-104,145-183
  *Elwell—Sci. p51-55
  Findlay—Hundred p332
  Fitzhugh—Concise p513-515
  Ginzburg—Adven. p325-357
    (por.336)
  Gordon—Romance p225-226
    (por.225)
  Grainger—Guide p164-168
  Hammerton p1070-1071 (por.1071)
  Hammond—Stories p167-193
    (por.178)
  *Hathaway—Partners p30-43
    (por.31)
  Holmyard—Great Chem. p111-116
  *Hyde—Modern p100-121
  Kagan—Modern p149 (por.149)
  Kendall—Young p126-145 (por.148)
  Lambert—Medical p240-259
    (por.250)
  Lambert—Minute p240-259 (por.257)
  Law—Civiliz. p322-328
  Locy—Biology p288-289,294-300
    (por.295)
  *McSpadden—How p177-192 (por.178)
  Major—History (2) p829-836
    (por.831)
  *Masters—Conquest p82-100 (por.84)
  *Montgomery—Story p103-105

  Moulton—Auto. p428-429
  Murray—Science p213-254
  Newman—Interp. p193-225
  *Nisenson—Illus. p121 (por.121)
  Oliver—Stalkers p175-191 (por.176)
  100 Great p625-633
  Osborn—Impr. p117-130 (por.117)
  Partington—Short p300-302,315-316
    (por.301)
  People p328-329
  Roberts—Chem. p176-184
  Robinson—Path. p677-712
    (por.702,703)
  Rowntree—Amid p44 (por.43)
  Schwartz—Moments (2) p737-739
  *Science Miles. p188 (por.188)
  Sewell—Brief p178-179
  *Shippen—Men p115-124 (por.115)
  Sigerist—Great p360-365 (por.360)
  *Simmons—Great p28-32 (por.28)
  Smith—Torch. p191 (por.191,192)
  *Snyder—Biology p187-194
    (por.188,191)
  *Sterling—Polio p27-29,48-50 (por.29)
  Thomas—Scien. p201-215 (por.199)
  Thomson—Great p123-127
  Thorwald—Century p256-258
    (por.368)
  Tobey—Riders p80-103 (por.80)
  Trattner—Arch. p272-301 (por.294)
  Untermeyer—Makers p102-112
  Van Wagenen—Beacon p327-328
  Walker—Pioneers p137-153 (por.137)
  Walsh—Makers p291-321
  *Williams-Ellis p155-188 (por.166)
  Williams—Story p375-380,387,390
    (por.391)
  Wilson—Human p275-305 (por.280)
  Woodruff—Devel. p110,286 (por.110)
  Year—Pic. p130 (por.130)

Patin, Guy (1601-1672). Fr. physician.
Castiglioni—Hist. p519 (por.508)
Major—History (1) p458-460
  (por.459)

Paton, Stewart (1865-1942). Amer. psychiatrist.
Curr. Biog. '42 p647

Patrick, Mason Mathews (1863-1942). Amer. aero. pioneer.
Curr. Biog. '42 p648

Patterson, Austin McDowell (1876-1956). Amer. chemist.
Browne—Hist. p500 (por.339)

Patterson, Harry Norton (1853-1919). Amer. botanist, naturalist.
Ewan—Rocky p73-78,279 (por.73)

Patterson, John H. (1844-1922). Amer. inventor.
*Forbes—Men p268-277 (por.1)

Patterson, Robert (1743-1824). Amer. mathematician.
Bell—Early p68-69
Smith—Math. p96

Patton, Leroy Thompson (1880-1957). Amer. geologist.
G.S.A.—Proc. '57 p149-151 (por.149)

Patton, William Hampton (1853-1918). Amer. entomologist.
Osborn—Fragments p221-222

Pauchet, Victor (1869-1936). Fr. surgeon.
Leonardo—Lives p329-330

Paul, Robert W. (1869-1943). Brit. engineer, inventor.
*Larsen—Scrap. p27-29 (por.33)

Paul of Aegina (or Paulus Aegineta) (7th cent.). Gr. physician, surgeon.
Gordon—Medieval p60-65
Hammerton p1074
Lambert—Medical p65
Lambert—Minute p65-68
Leonardo—Lives p330-332
Major—History (1) p215-217

Paulhan, Louis (1883/1886-   ). Fr. aero. pioneer.
Hammerton p1074
Heinmuller—Man's p279 (por.279)

Pauli, Wolfgang Ernst (1900-1958). Aust.-Swiss physicist.
Chambers—Dict. col.352
Curr. Biog. '46 p468-470 (por.469)
Heathcotte—Nobel p411-421
    (por.240)
R.S.L.—Biog. (5) p175-187 (por.175)
Weber—College p721 (por.721)

Pauling, Linus Carl (1901-   ). Amer. chemist, biochemist.
Browne—Hist. p493 (por.227)
Chambers—Dict. Supp. col.351
Curr. Biog. '49 p473-475 (por,474)
Morris—Ency. p703
Year—Pic. p250 (por.250)

Pausanias (2d cent.). Gr. geographer.
Hammerton p1074-1075

Pavlov, Ivan Petrovich (1849-1936). Rus. physiologist.
A.A.A.S.—Proc. (77) p49
Bodenheimer—Hist. p450
Castiglioni—Hist. p781-782 (por.781)
Chambers—Dict. col.352-353
    (por.351)
*Crowther—Doctors p113-144 (por.96)
Hammerton p1075 (por.1075)
Major—History (2) p975-977
    (por.976)
Robinson—Path. p771-787 (por.778)
Rowntree—Amid p174-178
    (por.158,603)
Sci. Amer.—Lives p215-225 (por.216)
*Snyder—Biology p394-400 (por.398)
Stevenson—Nobel p20-24 (por.150)
Year—Pic. p229 (por.229)

Payne, Joseph Frank (1840-1910). Austral. physician.
Major—History (2) p903

Payne-Gaposchkin, Cecilia Helena (1900-   ). Eng.-Amer. astronomer.
Curr. Biog. '57 p421-423 (por.422)

Payr, Erwin (1871-1946). Aust. surgeon.
Major—History (2) p1044

Peabody, Francis Weld (1881-1927). Amer. physician.
Kagan—Modern p33 (por.33)

Peacock, George (1791-1858). Eng. mathematician.
Ball—Short p441
Cajori—Hist. p273
MacFarlane—Lectures p7-18
    (por.,front.)
Smith—Hist. I p459-460

Peacock, Martin Alfred (1898-1950). Scot. geologist.
G.S.A.—Proc. '51 p127-131 (por.127)

Peale, Charles Willson (1741-1827). Amer. naturalist.
Bell—Early p69

Peale, Mundy Ingalls (1906-   ). Amer. aero. pioneer.
Curr. Biog. '56 p485-487 (por.486)

Peale, Titian Ramsey (1799/1800-1885). Amer. entomologist, naturalist.
Osborn—Fragments p25

Péan, Jules Émile (1830-1898). Fr. physician-surgeon.
Thorwald—Century p311-312,317-326
(por.368)

Pearl, Raymond (1879-1940). Amer. biologist.
Curr. Biog. '41 p658
Hammerton p1075
Major—History (2) p1044-1045
N.A.S.—Biog. (22) p295-310
(por.295)
Progress—Science '40 p269-270
(por.270)

Pearse, Dorothy Norman Spicer (1908-   ). Eng. aero. pioneer, engineer.
Goff—Women p133-158

Pearson, Chester Charles (1906-   ). Amer. aero. pioneer, engineer.
Curr. Biog. '50 p442-444 (por.443)

Pearson, Jay Frederick Wesley (1901-   ). Amer. marine zoologist.
Curr. Biog. '53 p477-479 (por.478)

Pearson, Karl (1857-1936). Brit. mathematician, geneticist.
Hammerton p1076

Pearson, Thomas Gilbert (1873-1943). Amer. ornithologist.
Curr. Biog. '43 p574

Pearsons, Daniel Kimball (1820-1912). Amer. physician.
*Faris—Men p99-109

Peary, Robert Edwin (1856-1920). Amer. sci. explorer, engineer.
*Book—Pop. Sci. (11) p3885-3887
(por.3886)
*Darrow—Builders p70-76
Fitzhugh—Concise p517-519
Hammerton p1076
*Law—Modern p162-175 (por.168)
Morris—Ency. p703
*Science Miles. p250 (por.250)
Sewell—Brief p200-201
*Tappan—Heroes p245-253
Tuska—Invent. p102-103
Webb—Famous p354-372 (por.355)

Peaslee, Edmund Randolph (1814-1878). Amer. physician, surgeon, gynecologist.
Marr—Pioneer p103-120 (por.104)

Peattie, Donald Culross (1898-   ). Amer. botanist.
Curr. Biog. '40 p639-640 (por.639)
*Milne—Natur. p173
Moulton—Auto. p639

Pechmann, Hans von (1850-1902). Ger. chemist.
A.A.A.S.—Proc. (78) p14-15
Partington—Short p316

Peck, James Lincoln Holt (1912-   ). Amer. aero. pioneer.
Curr. Biog. '42 p653-655 (por.654)

Peck, William Dandridge (1763-1822). Amer. entomologist.
Essig. Hist. p729-732 (por.730,731)

Peckham, John (c.1240-1292). Eng. nat. philosopher.
Smith—Hist. I p224

Pecquet, Jean (1622-1674). Fr. anatomist, physician.
Chambers—Dict. col.353
Major—History (1) p557

Pedanius.   See **Dioscorides, Pedanius**

Pegge, Sir Christopher (1765-1822). Eng. anatomist.
Gunther—Early XI p118-119

Pegoud, Adolphe (1889-1915). Fr. aero. pioneer.
Heinmuller—Man's p297 (por.297)

Peirce, Benjamin (1809-1880). Amer. mathematician, astronomer.
*Book—Pop. Sci. (15) p5002-5003   Smith—Math. p119-120 (por.121)
Cajori—Hist. p338-340

Peirce, Benjamin Osgood (1854-1914). Amer. mathematician, physicist.
N.A.S.—Biog. (8) p437-464 (por.437)
Smith—Math. p124

Peirce, Charles Sanders (1839-1914). Amer. mathematician, psychologist.
*Book—Pop. Sci. (14) p4747-4748)
Morris—Ency. p703-704

Péligot, Eugène Melchior (1811-1890). Fr. chemist.
Chambers—Dict. col.353-354   Weeks—Discovery p132-133,136
Smith—Torch. p193 (por.193)   (por.136)

Pell, John (1610-1685). Eng. mathematician.
Ball—Short p316
Smith—Hist. I p411-412

Pelletier, Bertrand (1761-1797). Fr. chemist.
Weeks—Discovery p243 (por.242)

Pelletier, Pierre Joseph (1788-1842). Fr. chemist.
Chambers—Dict. col.354
Smith—Torch. p194 (por.194)

Pélouze, Théophile Jules (1807-1867). Fr. chemist.
Smith—Torch. p195 (por.195)

Peltier, Jean Charles Athanase (1785-1845). Fr. physicist.
Chambers—Dict. col.354

Pena, Pierre (16th cent.). Fr. botanist.
Hawks—Pioneers p167,168,169

Penard, Eugène (b.1855). Swiss naturalist, protozoologist.
Ewan—Rocky p89-94,282 (por.89)

Pénaud, Alphonse (1850-1880). Fr. aero. pioneer, inventor.
*Bishop—Kite p106-112
Heinmuller—Man's p247 (por.247)

Pender, Sir John (1816-1896). Scot. engineer.
Hammerton p1079

Pendlebury, Charles (1854-1941). Eng. mathematician.
Hammerton p1079

Pendray, George Edward (1901-   ). Amer. rocket pioneer.
*Williams—Rocket p174-183,188-189

Penfield, Samuel Lewis (1856-1906). Amer. mineralogist.
N.A.S.—Biog. (6) p119-140 (por.119)

Penfield, Wilder Graves (1891-   ). Amer. neurosurgeon.
Curr. Biog. '55 p477-480 (por.478)

Pengelly, William (1812-1894). Eng. geologist.
Hammerton p1079

Pennant, Thomas (1726-1798). Brit. naturalist, zoologist.
Gunther—Early XI p131-132
(por.133)
Hammerton p1080

Penney, Sir William George (1909-   ). Brit. atomic physicist.
Chambers—Dict. Supp.
Curr. Biog. '53 p482-485 (por.483)

Pennington, Mary Engle (1872-1952). Amer. biol. chemist, engineer.
Goff—Women p183-214
Yost—Women Sci. p80-98

Penny, Thomas (c.1530-1589). Eng. botanist.
Chambers—Dict. col.354
Raven—English p153-171

Penrose, Charles B. (1862-1925). Amer. gynecologist, surgeon.
Leonardo—Lives p332-333

Pepper, William, Jr. (1843-1898). Amer. physician.
Castiglioni—Hist. p836 (por.836)

Percival, James Gates (1795-1856). Amer. geologist.
Merrill—First p168-170,320 (por.295)

Percy, Pierre François (1754-1825). Fr. physician, surgeon.
Major—History (2) p647

Peregrinus, Petrus (or Peter the Pilgrim, Peter de Maricourt) (c.13th cent.).
Fr. inventor.
Chambers—Dict. col.354
*Shippen—Design p16-18

Pergande, Theodore (1840-1916). Ger.-Amer. entomologist.
Essig—Hist. p733-734 (por.733)
Osborn—Fragments p180 (por.348)

Periegetes.   See **Dionysius Periegetes**

Perkin, Arthur George (1861-1937). Amer. chemist.
Findlay—British p219-246 (por.219)

Perkin, Sir William Henry (Senior) (1838-1907). Eng. chemist.
*Book—Pop. Sci. (9) p3038 (por.3039)
Chambers—Dict. col.355
*Darrow—Masters p228-237 (por.321)
*Darrow—Thinkers p271-275
  (por.272)
Findlay—Hundred p333
Hammerton p1083
Harrow—Chemists p1-18 (por.1)
Holmyard—British p62-65 (por.62)
*Kendall—Young p89-91 (por.96,97)
Law—Civiliz. p263-267
Moulton—Auto. p28
Partington—Short p317
Roberts—Chem. p220-231
Smith—Torch. p196 (por.196)
Van Wagenen—Beacon p277-280
Woodruff—Devel. p287

Perkin, William Henry, Jr. (1860-1929). Eng. chemist.
Chambers—Dict. col.355
Findlay—British p176-218 (por.176)
Findlay—Hundred p333
Partington—Short p320
Smith—Torch. p197 (por.197)

Perkins, Edward Henry (1886-1936). Amer. geologist.
G.S.A.—Proc. '36 p237-238 (por.237)

Perkins, George Henry (1844-1933). Amer. geologist.
G.S.A.—Proc. '33 p235-237 (por.235)

Perkins, Richard Marlin (1905-   ). Amer. herpetologist, ichthyologist.
Curr. Biog. '51 p481-482 (por.482)

Perkins, Robert Cyril Layton (1866-1955). Eng. entomologist, zoologist.
R.S.L.—Biog. (2) p215-229 (por.215)

Perla, David (1900-   ). Amer. pathologist, physician.
Curr. Biog. '40 p646-647 (por.647)

Perlman, Alfred E. (1902-   ). Amer. engineer.
Curr. Biog. '55 p481 (por.483)

Perrault, Claude (1613-1688). Fr. physician, anatomist, naturalist.
Miall—Early p229,231-232

Perret, Frank Alvord (1862-1943). Amer. volcanologist.
Curr. Biog. '43 p574-575

Perrey, Alexis (1807-1882). Fr. mathematician, seismologist, meteorologist, astronomer.
Davison—Founders p47-64

Perrin, Francis Henri (1901-   ). Fr. atomic physicist.
Curr. Biog. '51 p483-484 (por.483)

Perrin, Jean Baptiste (1870-1942). Fr. physicist, chemist.
Chambers—Dict. col.355
Heathcote—Nobel p249-258
  (por.240)
Magie—Source p580
Smith—Torch. p198 (por.198)
Weber—College p431 (por.431)

Perrot, Georges (1832-1914). Fr. archaeologist.
Hammerton p1083

Perry, John (1850-1920). Irish inventor, mathematician, engineer.
Hammerton p1083

Perry, John (1840-1921). Amer. physician, surgeon.
Farmer—Doctors' p162
Merrill—First p604-605 (por.251)

Perry, Joseph Hartshorn (1858-1934). Amer. geologist.
G.S.A.—Proc. '35 p297-300 (por.297)

Persoon, Christiann Hendrik (1761/1770-1836). Dutch physician, botanist.
Reed—Short p268

Pertik, Otto (1852-1913). Hung. path. anatomist.
Bulloch—Hist. p389

Perty (Joseph Anton) Maximilian (1804-1884). Ger. naturalist.
Bulloch—Hist. p389

Pervukhin, Mikhail G. (1904-   ). Rus. engineer.
Curr. Biog. '56 p487-488 (por.488)

Petavel, Sir Joseph Ernest (1873-1936). Eng. physicist.
*Bridges—Master p181-195
Hammerton p1085

Peter, Luther Crouse (1869-1942). Amer. ophthalmologist.
Curr. Biog. '43 p578

Peter de Maricourt.   See **Peregrinus, Petrus**

Peter Martyr (or D'Anghiera, Pietro Martire de) (1457-1526). It. sci. explorer, naturalist.
Von Hagen—Green p3

Peter of Abano.   See **Abano, Pietro d'**

Peter of Spain.   See **John XXI, Pope**

Peter the Pilgrim.   See **Peregrinus, Petrus**

Peters, George Armstrong (1859-1907). Can. surgeon.
Leonardo—Lives p333-334

Peters, John Punnett (1887-1955). Amer. archaeologist.
N.A.S.—Biog. (31) p347-362
(por.347)

Peters, LeRoy Samuel (1882-1941). Amer. physician.
Curr. Biog. '42 p660

Petersen, C. G. Johannes (1860-1928). Dan. marine biologist.
Copen.—Prom. p186-189

Peterson, Reuben (1862-1942). Amer. gynecologist.
Curr. Biog. '43 p578

Peterson, Roger Tory (1908-   ). Amer. ornithologist.
Curr. Biog. '59 p354-356 (por.355)

Petiscus.   See **Pitiscus, Bartholomäus**

Petit, Alexis Thérèse (1791-1820). Fr. physicist.
Chambers—Dict. col.355-356
Magie—Source p178

Petit, Jean Louis (1674-1750). Fr. surgeon.
Chambers—Dict. col.356   Major—History (2) p630
Leonardo—Lives p334-335

Petrén, Karl (1868-1927). Swed. physician.
Major—History (2) p1045

Petri, Richard Julius (1852-1921). Ger. bacteriologist.
Bulloch—Hist. p389

Petrie, William Matthew Flinders (1853-1942). Eng. archaeologist.
Ceram—Gods p137-140,149-153   Hammerton p1088 (por.1088)
Curr. Biog. '42 p662

Petroncellus (or Petrus Clericus) (c.1030). It. physician.
Castiglioni—Hist. p302-303

Petrunkevitch, Alexander (b.1875). Rus.-Amer. archaeologist, zoologist.
Kinkead—Spider p3-73

Petrus Clericus.   See **Petroncellus**

Petrus de Dacia (c.1300). Dan. mathematician.
Copen.—Prom. p12-15

Petrus Gillius.   See **Gillius, Petrus**

Petrus Hispanus.   See **John XXI, Pope**

Petruschky, Johannes (Theodor Wilhelm) (b.1863). Ger. bacteriologist.
Bulloch—Hist. p389

Pettenkofer, Max Joseph von (1818-1901). Ger. bacteriologist, hygienist, physician.
Castiglioni—Hist. p749
Grainger—Guide p168-169
Gumpert—Trail p253-286
Major—History (2) p884-886
Sigerist—Great p390-393 (por.392)
Smith—Torch. p199 (por.199)
Walker—Pioneers p115-125 (por.115)

Petterson, Sven Otto (1848-1941). Swed. chemist.
Chambers—Dict. col.356
Weeks—Discovery p321 (por.321)

Pettit, Edison (1890-   ). Amer. astronomer.
Chambers—Dict. col.356

Petty, Sir William (1623-1687). Eng. anatomist, physician.
Gunther—Early XI p184-186
Major—History (1) p556-557
Moulton—Auto. p162

Peurbach.   See **Purbach, Georg**

Peyer, Johann Konrad (or Jean Conrad) (1653-1712). Swiss physician, anatomist.
Major—History (1) p563
Woodruff—Devel. p287

Pfaff, Johann Friederich (1765-1825). Ger. mathematician.
Ball—Short p425

Pfeffer, Wilhelm (1845-1920). Ger. botanist.
Chambers—Dict. col.357

Pfeiffer, August (1848-1919). Ger. bacteriologist, hygienist.
Bulloch—Hist. p389

Pfeiffer, Richard Friedrich Johann (1858-1945). Ger. bacteriologist.
Bulloch—Hist. p389-390 (por.202)
Chambers—Dict. col.357
R.S.L.—Biog. (2) p237-244 (por.237)

Pflüger, Eduard Friedrich Wilhelm (1829-1910). Ger. physiologist.
Chambers—Dict. col.357
Hammerton p1088
Major—History (2) p894

Pfolspeundt, Heinrich von (1450/1460-1533). Ger. physician, surgeon.
Gordon—Medieval p395-398   Major—History (1) p432-433
Leonardo—Lives p335-337

Phalen, William Clifton (1877-1949). Amer. geologist.
G.S.A.—Proc. '49 p213-215 (por.213)

Phelan, Gregory J. (1822-1902). Amer. physician.
Jones—Memories p341-343 (por.341)

Philinus of Cos (fl.c.250 B.C.). Gr. physician.
Gordon—Medicine p609-610

Philips, Robert William (1857-1939). Scot. physician.
Rowntree—Amid p46 (por.51)

Phillips, Alexander Hamilton (1866-1937). Amer. mineralogist.
G.S.A.—Proc. '36 p241-246 (por.241)

Phillips, Everett Franklin (1878-1951). Amer. entomologist, apiculturist.
Osborn—Fragments p201

Phillips, Everett Franklin Le Prince (d.1890?). Fr. inventor.
*Burlingame—Inv. p145-147

Phillips, Horatio F. (1845-1912). Eng. engineer, aero, pioneer, inventor.
Burge—Ency. p637
Heinmuller—Man's p253

Phillips, John (1800-1874). Eng. geologist.
Chambers—Dict. col.357-358   Hammerton p1091
Gunther—Early XI p317-318   Woodruff—Devel. p287
   (por.318)

Phillips, Theodore Evelyn Reece (1868-1942). Eng. astronomer.
Curr. Biog. '42 p662
Hammerton p1092

Phillips, Wendell (1921-   ). Amer. archaeologist, sci. explorer.
Curr. Biog. '58 p333-334 (por.333)

Philo of Byzantium (20 B.C.-A.D. c.50). Alex. nat philosopher.
Chambers—Dict. col.358
Taylor—Illus. p35-36

Philolaus (fl.c.425 B.C.). Gr. mathematician.
Smith—Hist. I p81-82

Philoponus, Joannes (6th cent.). Gr. nat. philosopher.
Clagett—Greek p142,169-176

Philumenos (c.250). Gr. gynecologist, obstetrician, surgeon.
Leonardo—Lives p337

Phryesen, Laurentius Frisen (or Frisius) (c.1490). Dutch physician.
Major—History (1) p461-462

Physick, Philip Syng (1768-1837). Amer. physician, surgeon.
Castiglioni—Hist. p721 (por.721)   Major—History (2) p731-732
Leonardo—Lives p338

Piaget, Jean (1896-   ). Swiss psychologist, zoologist.
Curr. Biog. '58 p334-336 (por.335)

Piazzi, Giuseppe (1746-1826). It. astronomer.
Abetti—History p169-170   Shapley—Astron. p180
*Book—Pop. Sci. (15) p5003-5004   Williams—Great p277-281
Chambers—Dict. col.358   Woodruff—Devel. p287
Hammerton p1092

Picard, Charles Émile (1856-1941). Fr. mathematician.
Chambers—Dict. col.358
Curr. Biog. '42 p662

Picard, Jean (1620-1682). Fr. astronomer.
Chambers—Dict. col.358-359

Piccard, Auguste (1884-1962). Swiss physicist.
Chambers—Dict. col.359   Hammerton p1093
Curr. Biog. '47 p515-517 (por.516)   Heinmuller—Man's p341 (por.341)
*Cohen—Men p62-65   Pringle—Great p101-122 (por.81)
*Fraser—Heroes p649-655

Piccard, Jean Felix (1884-   ). Swiss aero. pioneer, chemist, engineer.
Curr. Biog. '47 p515-517 (por.517)   Pringle—Great p101-122 (por.81)
*Fraser—Heroes p691-697

Piccio, Pierre Ruggerio (1880-   ). It. aero. pioneer.
Heinmuller—Man's p300 (por.300)

Pick, Lewis Andrew (1890-1956). Amer. engineer.
Curr. Biog. '46 p480-482 (por.481)
'57 p425

Pickard, Greenleaf Whittier (1877-1956). Amer. elec. engineer, inventor.
Radio's 100 p187-189 (por.140)

Pickering, Charles (1805-1878). Amer. naturalist.
Alden—Early p50-51

Pickering, Edward Charles (1846-1919). Amer. astronomer.
Abetti—History p226-227
Armitage—Cent. p149-151 (por.144)
*Book—Pop. Sci. (15) p5004-5006
   (por.5005)
Chambers—Dict. col.359
Hammerton p1093
MacPherson—Astron. p163-171
   (por.163)
MacPherson—Makers p177-179
N.A.S.—Biog. (15) p169-178
   (por.169)
Shapley—Astron. p367
Williams—Great p365-370,469-470
   (por.365)
Wilson—Amer. p275-276 (por.276)
Woodruff—Devel. p287 (por.158)

Pickering, William H. (1910-   ). New Zeal.-Amer. physicist.
Curr. Biog. '58 p336-337 (por.337)
Thomas—Men (2) p113-133
   (por.106)

Pickering, William Henry (1858-1938). Amer. astronomer.
*Book—Pop. Sci. (15) p5006
   (por.5006)
Chambers—Dict. col.359-360
MacPherson—Astron. p225-233
   (por.225)
MacPherson—Makers p201-205
Williams—Great p320,390-392
   (por.390)

Pictet, Raoul Pierre (1842/1846-1929). Swiss physicist.
Chambers—Dict. col.360
Magie—Source p194

Piel, Gerard (1915-   ). Amer. sci. writer.
Curr. Biog. '59 p361-362 (por.361)

Pierce, George Washington (1872-1956). Amer. physicist.
N.A.S.—Biog. (33) p351-370 (por.351)
Radio's 100 p161-164 (por.140)

Pierce, (John) Robinson (1910-   ). Amer. engineer.
Curr. Biog. '61 (Feb.) (por.)

Pietro di Abano.   See **Abano, Pietro d'**

Pietro Curialti de Tossignano (c.1250). It. physician.
Gordon—Medieval p702-703

Pilatre de Rozier.   See **Rozier, Jean François Pîlatre de**

Pilcher, Lewis Stephen (1845-1934). Amer. physician, surgeon.
Leonardo—Lives (Supp.1) p504-506

Pilcher, Percy Sinclair (1866-1899). Eng. aero. pioneer, engineer.
*Bishop—Kite p125-129   Heinmuller—Man's p254 (por.254)
Burge—Ency. p637-638

Pinchot, Gifford (1865-1946). Amer. agriculturist.
*Ivins—Fifty p187-197 (por.186)

Pincus, Gregory (1903-   ). Amer. biologist, zoologist, physiologist.
Ratcliffe—Modern p196-198

Pinedo, Francesco Marchese de (1890-1933). It. aero. pioneer.
Hammerton p1095
Heinmuller—Man's p34-47,319
   (por.45,319)

Pinel, Philippe (1745/1755-1826). Fr. physician.
Bulloch—Hist. p390   Major—History (2) p651-653
Castiglioni—Hist. p634-635 (por.634)   (por.654)
Gordon—Romance p200 (por.200)   Sigerist—Great p276-282 (por.272)
                                  *Truax—Doctors p55-67

Pinsker, Leon (1821-1891). Pol. physician.
Kagan—Modern p204 (por.204)

Pintner, Rudolf (1884-1942). Eng.-Amer. psychologist.
Curr. Biog. '43 p599

Piorry, Pierre Adolphe (1794-1879). Fr. physician.
Major—History (2) p711

Piper, Charles Vancouver (1867-1926). Amer. entomologist.
Osborn—Fragments p201

Piper, William Thomas (1881-   ). Amer. aero. pioneer, engineer.
Curr. Biog. '46 p484-486 (por.485)

Pirogoff, Nicolai Ivanovich (1810-1881). Rus. physician, surgeon.
Kagan—Modern p87 (por.87)   Robinson—Victory p167-171
Leonardo—Lives p338-340   (por.170)

Pirquet, Clemens Freiherr von (1874-1929). Aust. physician,
   pathologist.
Bulloch—Hist. p390   *Montgomery—Story p62-64
Major—History (2) p1045 (por.944) Rowntree—Amid p165-167 (por.159)

Pirsson, Louis Valentine (1860-1919). Amer. petrographer, geologist.
N.A.S.—Biog. (34) p228-243 (por.228)

Pisano. See **Fibonacci, Leonardo**

Pitard, Jean (1228-1305). Fr. physician.
Gordon—Medieval p437,439
 (por.115)
Leonardo—Lives p341

Pitcairn, Harold Frederick (1897-   ). Amer. aero. pioneer.
Heinmuller—Man's p326 (por.326)

Pitiscus (or Petiscus), **Bartholomaüs** (1561-1613). Ger. mathematician.
Smith—Hist. I p331

Pitkin, Walter Boughton (1878-1953). Amer. psychologist.
Curr. Biog. '41 p671-672 (por.671)
 '53 p496

Pitman, Sir Isaac (1813-1897). Eng. inventor.
Hammerton p1096

Pitt-Rivers, Augustus Henry Lane Fox (1827-1900). Eng. archaeologist.
Hammerton p1097-1098
People p334-335

Pitzer, Kenneth Sanborn (1914-   ). Amer. chemist.
Curr. Biog. '50 p451-452 (por.451)

Planck, Max Karl Ernest Ludwig (1858-1947). Ger. physicist.
Chambers—Dict. col.360-361
 (por.362)
Hammerton p1099 (por.1099)
Heathcote—Nobel p151-166
 (por.240)
Moulton—Auto. p536-538
Schwartz—Moments (2) p956-957
Untermeyer—Makers p270-274
Weber—College p285 (por.285)
Woodruff—Devel. p42,68-70,287

Planté, (Raymond Louis) Gaston (1834-1889). Fr. physicist.
Chambers—Dict. col. 361
Hammerton p1099

Plantin, Christophe (1514/1520-1589). Fr. botanist.
Arber—Herbals p79-82,229,232,233,
 266
Hawks—Pioneers p172-175 (por.172)
Sarton—Six p139-140 (por.140)

Plaskett, John Stanley (1865-1941). Can. astronomer.
Curr. Biog. '41 p676
Progress—Science '41 p298-299
(por.298)

Plateau, Joseph Antoine Ferdinand (1801-1883). Belg. physicist.
Chambers—Dict. col.361   *Men—Scien. p1-3
Hammerton p1099

Plato (427?-347 B.C.). Gr. astronomer, mathematician.
Abetti—History p31-32
Ball—Short p42-44
Bodenheimer—Hist. p162-163
*Book—Pop. Sci. (14) p4749-4752
  (por.4751)
Cajori—Hist. p25-27
Clagett—Greek p32
Dreyer—Hist. p53-86
Fitzhugh—Concise p537-539
Gordon—Medicine p561-567
  (por.562)
Hammerton p1099-1100 (por.1099)
Hofman—History p19-20
Lambert—Medical p26-29
Lambert—Minute p26-27
*Nisenson—Illus. p126 (por.126)
*Nisenson—More p113 (por.113)
Sedgwick—Short p69-75
Sewell—Brief p7-8
Smith—Hist. I p87-90 (por.87)
Van Wagenen—Beacon p12-14
Woodruff—Devel. p287

Platter (or Platerus), **Felix** (1536-1614). Ger. anatomist.
Gordon—Medieval p638-639,697,754
  (por.114)
Major—History (1) p437-438
  (por.439)

Plattner, Karl Friedrich (1800-1858). Ger. metallurgist, mineralogist.
Hammerton p1101
Weeks—Discovery p371 (por.371)

Plaut, Hugo Carl (1858-1928). Ger. physician, agriculturist, bacteriologist.
Bulloch—Hist. p390

Playfair, John (1748-1819). Scot. mathematician, geologist.
Chambers—Dict. col.361   Woodruff—Devel. p287
Fenton—Giants p59-60

Playfair, Lyon Playfair, 1st Baron (1818-1898). Brit. chemist.
Hammerton p1101 (por.1101)
Smith—Torch. p200 (por.200)

Plenciz (or Plenkiz), **Marcus Antonius von** (1705-1786). Aust.
  bacteriologist, physician.
Bulloch—Hist. p390
Oliver—Stalkers p130-131

Plesman, Albert (1889-   ). Dutch aero. pioneer.
Curr. Biog. '53 p496-498 (por.497)

Pliny, the Elder (or Gaius Plinius Caecilius Secundus) (23-79). Rom. botanist, nat. philosopher.

Adams—Birth p36-47
Arber—Herbals p12
Bodenheimer—Hist. p174
Castiglioni—Hist. p213-214
Clagett—Greek p110-111
Fenton—Giants p12-14
Fitzhugh—Concise p539-541
Gordon—Medicine p671-675 (por.672)
Hawks—Pioneers p71-76 (por.56)
Lambert—Medical p45-46
Lambert—Minute p45-46
Locy—Biology p15-17 (por.16)
Moulton—Auto. p17-18
Osborn—Greeks p98
Reed—Short p41-43
Schwartz—Moments (1) p169-170
Sedgwick—Short p146
*Shippen—Micro. p29-32
*Snyder—Biology p13-14
Weeks—Discovery p3,22 (por.3)
Woodruff—Devel. p287

Plücker, Julius (1801-1868). Ger. mathematician, physicist.

A.A.A.S.—Proc. (79) p33-35
Cajori—Hist. p309-311
Chalmers—Historic p270
Chambers—Dict. col.361-362
Hammerton p1102
Smith—Hist. I. p505-506

Plummer, Frederick Byron (1886-1947). Amer. geologist, paleontologist.
G.S.A.—Proc. '47 p155-161 (por.155)

Plummer, Henry S. (1875-1936). Amer. physician.
Rowntree—Amid p286-288,384-388 (por.287)

Poey, Felipe (1799-1891). Cuban geologist, entomologist, naturalist.
Osborn—Fragments p30-31

Poggendorff, Johann C. (1796-1877). Ger. physicist.
Chambers—Dict. col.362

Poincaré, Jules Henri (1854-1912). Fr. mathematician.

Bell—Men p526-554 (por.,front.)
*Book—Pop. Sci. (15) p4972-4973
Cajori—Hist. p388-390
Chambers—Dict. col.362-363
Hammerton p1104 (por.1104)
*Miller—Hist. p268-274
Moulton—Auto. p509-510
Schwartz—Moments (1) p72-73
Smith—Hist. I p499
Smith—Portraits (2) XIII, unp. (por.)
Weeks—Discovery p486 (por.486)
Woodruff—Devel. p287 (por.36)
Year—Pic. p117 (por.117)

Poinsot, Louis (1777-1859). Fr. mathematician.
Hammerton p1104
Magie—Source p65

Poisson, Siméon Denis (1781-1840). Fr. mathematician.
Ball—Short p433-436
Cajori—Hist. p465-467
Chambers—Dict. col.363
Hammerton p1104
Woodruff—Devel. p287-288 (por.22)

Polando, John Lewis (1901-   ). Amer. aero. pioneer.
*Fraser—Heroes p597-602
Heinmuller—Man's p150-160,343
    (por.159,343)

Polanyi, Michael (1891-   ). Hung. phys. chemist.
Chambers—Dict. col.363-364

Politzer, Adam (1835-1920). Hung. physician.
Castiglioni—Hist. p868 (por.868)
Kagan—Modern p129 (por.129)

Pollender, Franz Aloys Antoine (1800-1879). Ger. bacteriologist.
Bulloch—Hist. p390-391

Pólya, Eugene (or Jeno) (1876-1944). Hung. surgeon.
Leonardo—Lives p341-343

Polybus (fl.c764-743 B.C.). Gr. physiologist.
Gordon—Medicine p546

Pomis, David de (c.1555). It. physician.
Gordon—Medieval p763

Poncelet, Jean Victor (1788-1867). Fr. mathematician, engineer.
Ball—Short p428-429
Bell—Men p206-217 (por.,front.)
Cajori—Hist. p287-288
Chambers—Dict. col.364
Hammerton p1107
Smith—Hist. I p496
Woodruff—Devel. p288

Pontin, M.M. af (1781-1858). Swed. physician.
Weeks—Discovery p297,299 (por.299)

Poole, Reginald Stuart (1832-1895). Eng. archaeologist.
Hammerton p1108 (por.1108)

Pope, William Jackson (1870-1939). Eng. chemist.
Findlay—British p285-315 (por.285)
Hammerton p1109
Partington—Short p321
Smith—Torch. p201 (por.201)

Popenoe, Paul Bowman (1888-   ). Amer. biologist.
Curr. Biog. '46 p487-488 (por.488).

Popenoe, Wilson (1892-   ). Amer. biologist, agriculturist.
*Jewett—Plant p140-173

Popham, Sir Henry Robert Brooke- (1878-1953). Brit. aero. pioneer.
Burge—Ency. p627

Popov, Aleksandr Stepanovich (1859-1905). Rus. physicist.
Chambers—Dict. col.364   Radio's 100 p127-128 (por.140)
Hawks—Wireless p202-204 (por.200)

Porro, Edoardo (1842-1902). It. physician, surgeon.
Leonardo—Lives p343
Thorwald—Century p200-202,210-
    219

Porta, Giovanni Giambattista Della (1538?-1615). It. physicist.
Arber—Herbals p251,255-257   Sarton—Six p85-88 (por.24)
Gordon—Medieval p700   Sedgwick—Short p229
Law—Civiliz. p145-146   Year—Pic. p84 (por.84)

Porta, Luigi (1800-1875). It. surgeon.
Leonardo—Lives p343-344

Porter, Charles Burnham (1840-1909). Amer. surgeon.
Leonardo—Lives p344-345

Porter, Charles Talbot (1826-1910). Amer. engineer.
John Fritz p57-59 (por.56)

Porter, Richard William (1913-   ). Amer. elec. engineer.
Curr. Biog. '58 p338-339 (por.338)

Porter, Rufus (1792-1884). Amer. aero. pioneer, inventor.
Milbank—First p73-78

Porter, Thomas Conrad (1822-1901). Amer. botanist, naturalist.
Ewan—Rocky p67-72,284-285
    (por.67)

Porter, William Nichols (1886-   ). Amer. chemist.
Curr. Biog. '45 p476-478 (por.477)

Post, Augustus (1873-1952). Amer. aero. pioneer.
Heinmuller—Man's p278 (por.278)

Post, Wiley (1899-1935). Amer. aero. pioneer.
  *Fraser—Famous p231-262 (por.222)   Heinmuller—Man's p137-149,342
  *Fraser—Heroes p583-589,671-676   (por.148,342)

Post, Wright (1766-1828). Amer. surgeon.
  Leonardo—Lives p345-347

Potain, Pierre Carl (1825-1901). Fr. physician.
  Major—History (2) p890-891

Pott, J. H. (1692-1777). Ger. chemist.
  Weeks—Discovery p22,32,74-75

Pott, Percival (1714-1788). Eng. surgeon.
  Gordon—Romance p456 (por.456)   Leonardo—Lives p347-349
  Hammerton p1110-1111   Major—History (2) p635

Potter, Ellen Culver (1871-1958). Amer. physician, pub. health worker.
  Lovejoy—Women p380-381

Potter, Nathaniel (1770-1843). Amer. physician.
  Major—History (2) p767

Potter, William Everett (1905-   ). Amer. engineer.
  Curr. Biog. '57 p435-436 (por.435)

Pouchet, Claude Servais Matthias (1790-1868). Fr. physicist.
  Chambers—Dict. col.364
  Hammerton p1111

Pouchet, Félix Archimède (1800-1872). Fr. naturalist, physician.
  Bulloch—Hist. p391 (por.220)
  Locy—Biology p286-288

Poulsen, Valdemar (1869-1942). Dan. inventor, elec. engineer.
  Curr. Biog. '42 p671   Meyer—World p212-214
  Hammerton p1111   Radio's 100 p153-155 (por.140)

Poulton, Sir Edward Bagnall (1856-1943). Eng. zoologist, entomologist.
  Curr. Biog. '44 p549

Pound, Roscoe (b.1870). Amer. botanist.
  Curr. Biog. '47 p523-525 (por.524)

Poupart, François (1661-1709). Fr. naturalist, physician.
  Major—History (2) p628

Pourtalès, Louis François de (1823/1824-1880). Swiss-Amer. zoologist, naturalist.
N.A.S.—Biog. (5) p79-87 (por.79)

Powdermaker, Hortense (1900-   ). Amer. anthropologist.
Curr. Biog. '61 (Feb.) (por.)

Powell, Cecil Frank (1903-   ). Eng. physicist.
Chambers—Dict. Supp.   Weber—College p801 (por.801)
Heathcote—Nobel p452-461 (por.240)

Powell, G. Harold (1872-1922). Amer. agriculturist.
*Ivins—Fifty p167-178 (por.166)

Powell, John Wesley (1834-1902). Amer. geologist, ethnologist.
*Book—Pop. Sci. (10) p3299-3300   N.A.S.—Biog. (8) p11-83 (por.11)
Fenton—Giants p250-268 (por.254)   Oehser—Sons p81-84 (por.58)
Merrill—First p548 (por.544)   True—Smiths. p103-113,123 (por.104)
Morris—Ency. p706   Woodruff—Devel. p288 (por.196)

Power, Sir D'Arcy (1885-1941). Eng. physician, surgeon.
Curr. Biog. '41 p684-685   Leonardo—Lives (Supp.1) p506-507
Kagan—Modern p98 (por.98)

Power, Henry (1623-1668). Eng. physician, nat. philosopher.
Bulloch—Hist. p391

Power, Thomas Sarsfield (1905-   ). Amer. aero. pioneer.
Curr. Biog. '58 p339-341 (por.340)

Powers, Charles Andrews (1858-1922). Amer. surgeon.
Leonardo—Lives p349-350

Powers, Sidney (1890-1932). Amer. geologist.
G.S.A.—Proc. '33 p243-250 (por.243)

Poynting, John Henry (1852-1914). Eng. physicist.
A.A.A.S.—Proc. (81) p80-81   Hammerton p1112
Chambers—Dict. col.364-365

Pozzi, Samuel Jean (1846-1918). Fr. surgeon.
Leonardo—Lives p350-351

Prain, Sir David (1857-1944). Brit. botanist.
Hammerton p1112

Prandtl, Ludwig (1875-1953). Ger. engineer, physicist, aero. pioneer.
Burge—Ency. p638
Daniel Gugg. p11-17 (por.10)
Daniel—Pioneer p9-13 (por.8)
R.S.L.—Biog. p193-199 (por.193)

Pratt, Joseph Hyde (1870-1942). Amer. geologist.
G.S.A.—Proc. '42 p201-204 (por.201)

Pravaz, Charles Gabriel (1791-1853). Fr. physician.
Fülop—Miller p354-355 (por.72)
*Montgomery—Story p154-155

Praxagoras of Cos (fl.4th cent., B.C.). Gr. physician, surgeon.
Gordon—Medicine p548-549
Leonardo—Lives p351

Preece, Sir William Henry (1834-1913). Welsh elec. engineer.
Hammerton p1112 (por.1112)
Hawks—Wireless p159-167 (por.162)
Radio's 100 p71-73 (por.140)

Pregl, Fritz (1869-1930). Aust. chemist.
Chambers—Dict. col.365
Farber—Nobel p90-93 (por.118)
Smith—Torch. p202 (por.202)

Prescott, Albert B. (1832-1905). Amer. physician, surgeon, chemist.
Browne—Hist. p474 (por.35)

Prescott, Samuel Cate (b.1872). Amer. bacteriologist, chemist.
Holland—Women p31-40 (por.31)

Preston, Ann (1813-1872). Amer. physician.
Lovejoy—Women p31-40 (por.31)
Mead—Medical p26-29 (por.,append.)

Prestwich, Sir Joseph (1812-1896). Eng. geologist.
Gunther—Early XI p319-320
Hammerton p1113

Prévost, Pierre (1751-1839). Swiss physicist, physician.
Chambers—Dict. col.365

Prewitt, Theodore F. (1832-1904). Amer. surgeon.
Leonardo—Lives p351-352

Price, Charles C. (1913-   ). Amer. chemist.
Curr. Biog. '57 p438-440 (por.439)

Price, Joseph (1853-1911). Amer. physician, surgeon, gynecologist.
Leonardo—Lives (Supp.) p507-508

Prichard, Hesketh (1876-1922). Brit. naturalist.
Cutright—Great p37-38

Prichard, James Cowles (1786-1848). Eng. ethnologist.
Hammerton p1113

Priestley, Joseph (1733-1804). Eng. chemist.
Bell—Early p69-70
Bodenheimer—Hist. p322
*Book—Pop. Sci. (13) p4349-4350
  (por.4350)
Chalmers—Historic p270-271
Chambers—Dict. col.365-366
  (por.366)
Chymia (1) p123-137
*Darrow—Masters p30-33 (por.160)
*Darrow—Thinkers p47-50 (por.48)
*Fülop—Miller p40-50 (por.48)
Gibson—Heroes p164-178
Gilmour—British p26
Gregory—British p46 (por.44)
Guinagh—Inspired p13-25
Hammerton p1113-1114 (por.1114)
Hammond—Stories p8-22
Holmyard—British p33-34 (por.33)
Holmyard—Chem. p87-90 (por.84)
Holmyard—Great Chem. p58-64
Holmyard—Makers p169-177
  (por.170)
*Jaffe—Crucibles p51-72
Killeffer—Eminent p1 (por.1)
Lenard—Great p144-145 (por.145)
Leonard—Crus. p201-237 (por.214)
Major—History (2) p614-615,637
  (por.615)
Moulton—Auto. p222-223
Partington—Short p110-121,151
  (por.111)
Reed—Short p106-107
Roberts—Chem. p21-31
Schwartz—Moments (1) p445-447
Sci. Amer.—Lives p87-96 (por.89)
*Science Miles. p100 (por.100)
Smith—Chem. p109-127 (por.111)
Smith—Torch. p203-204 (por.203)
*Snyder—Biology p305-306
*Stevens—Science p59-61 (por.58)
Thomson—Great p30-31
Tilden—Famous p32-40 (por.32)
Van Wagenen—Beacon p167-169
Weeks—Discovery p92-99 (por.93)
Williams—Story p31,34-35,40
  (por.30)
Wilson—Amer. p32-35 (por.32)
Wilson—Human p213-216 (por.214)
Woodruff—Devel. p288
Year—Pic. p103 (por.103)

Priestley, Joseph Hubert (1883-   ). Eng. botanist.
Hammerton p1114 (por.1114)

Prigosen, Rosa Elizabeth (n.d.). Amer. bacteriologist, pediatrician.
Fleischner—Careers p456

Prince, David (1816-1889). Amer. surgeon.
Leonardo—Lives p353-354

Prince, Morton, (1854-1929). Amer. neuropsychiatrist.
Kagan—Modern p202 (por.202)

Pringle, Sir John (1707-1782). Brit. physician.
Hammerton p1114 (por.1114)
Major—History (2) p594-595
Walker—Pioneers p13-22 (por.13)

Pringsheim, Ernst (1859-1917). Ger. physicist.
Chambers—Dict. col.367

Pringsheim, Nathaniel (1823-1894). Ger. botanist, biologist.
Chambers—Dict. col.367

Priscianus, Theodorus (c.400). Rom. physician.
Major—History (1) p220-221

Pritchard, Charles (1808-1893). Eng. astronomer.
Armitage—Cent. p145   Hammerton p1115
Gunther—Early XI p143 (por.142)

Pritchard, George Eric Campbell (?-1943). Eng. physician.
Hammerton p1115

Pritchard, Stuart (1882-1940). Amer. physician.
Curr. Biog. '40 p663 (por.663)

Proclus (410/412-485). Gr. mathematician.
Ball—Short p112
Smith—Hist. I p137-138

Proctor, Richard Anthony (1837-1888). Eng. astronomer.
*Book—Pop. Sci. (15) p5007-5008   MacPherson—Makers p212-215
Hammerton p1115

Prony, Gaspard Clair François Marie Riche, Baron de (1775-1839). Fr.
mathematician, engineer.
Van Wagenen—Beacon p205-207

Proskauer, Bernhard (1851-1915). Ger. chemist, bacteriologist, hygienist.
Bulloch—Hist. p391

Protospatharius, Theophilus (603/610-641/649). Alex. physician.
Gordon—Medieval p59-60
Major—History (1) p221-222

Proust, Joseph Louis (1754-1826). Fr. chemist.
Chambers—Dict. col.367   Smith—Torch. p205 (por.205)
*Darrow—Masters p339   Tilden—Famous p127-130 (por.127)
Hammerton p1116   Van Wagenen—Beacon p204-205
Partington—Short p153-154
  (por.154)

Prout, John (1810-1894). Brit. agriculturist.
Hammerton p1117

Prout, William (1785-1850). Eng. chemist, physician.

Chambers—Dict. col.367-368
Hammerton p1117

Partington—Short p210-211,213
Smith—Torch. p206 (por.206)

Prouty, William Frederick (1779-1949). Amer. geologist.

G.S.A.—Proc. '50 p115-116 (por.115)

Provancher, L'Abbé Leon (1820-1892). Can. entomologist.

Essig—Hist. p734-735 (por.734)

Prowazek, Stanislaus Joseph Matthias von (1875-1915). Bohem. zoologist.

Major—History (2) p1045

Prudden, George Henry (1893-   ). Amer. aero. pioneer.

Heinmuller—Man's p316 (por.316)

Prudden, Theophil Mitchell (1849-1924). Amer. pathologist.

N.A.S.—Biog. (12) p73-93 (por.73)

Psellus (or Psellos), **Michael Constantine** (11th cent.). Byzan. nat. philosopher.

Major—History (1) p353
Smith—Hist. I p197-198

Ptolemy I (or Ptolemy Soter) (367?-283 B.C.). Egypt. physician.

Gordon—Medicine p590-592
    (por.591)

Ptolemy (or Ptolomaeus, Claudius) (c.90-168). Gr.-Egypt. astronomer, mathematician, geographer.

Abetti—History p43-45
Ball—Great p7-29 (por.9)
Ball—Short p96-99
*Book—Pop. Sci. (15) p5008-5009
Cajori—Hist. p46-48
Chambers—Dict. col.368
Clagett—Greek p79-82,93-96
Dreyer—Hist. p191-206
Ginzburg—Adven. p65-73
Gordon—Medicine p608
Hammerton p1117-1118
Hart—Makers p46-50

Hooper—Makers p145-149
Schwartz—Moments (1) p172-174
Sedgwick—Short p126-132
Smith—Hist. I p130-131
Taylor—Illus. p29
Turnbull—Great p43-44
Van Wagenen—Beacon p30-33
Vaucouleurs—Disc. p31-36
Wilson—Human p59-62
Woodruff—Devel. p140-142,288
Year—Pic. p39,74

Puccinotti, Francesco (1794-1872). It. physician.

Castiglioni—Hist. p753-754 (por.754)

Pugh, Evan (1828-1864). Amer. chemist.

Smith—Chem. p231-235

Pugh, Herbert Lamont (1895-   ). Amer. physician, surgeon.
Curr. Biog. '51 p495-497 (por.496)

Pullman, George Mortimer (1831-1897). Amer. inventor.
Hammerton p1119
Law—Civiliz. p38-39
*Montgomery—Invent. p200-204
*Wildman—Famous (2d) p247-258
(por.247)
Wilson—Amer. p222-227

Pumpelly, Raphael (1837-1923). Amer. geologist, sci. explorer.
Merrill—First p419-420 (por.420)
N.A.S.—Biog. (16) p23-61 (por.23)

Punnett, Reginald Crundell (b.1875). Eng. biologist, geneticist.
Hammerton p1119

Pupin, Michael Idvorsky (1885-1935). Yugoslav.-Amer. inventor, physicist.
*Beard—Foreign p202-207 (por.204)
*Book—Pop. Sci. (13) p4350-4353
(por.4351)
Hammerton p1119
Huff—Famous (2d) p419-428
(por.421)
N.A.S.—Biog. (19) p307-318 (por.307)
Radio's 100 p123-124 (por.140)

Purbach (or Peuerbach), **Georg** (1423-1461). Aust. astronomer, mathematician.
Dreyer—Hist. p288-289
Van Wagenen—Beacon p52-53

Purcell, Edward Mills (1912-   ). Amer. physicist.
Chambers—Dict. Supp.
Curr. Biog. '54 p519-521 (por.520)

Purdie, Thomas (1843-1916). Eng. chemist.
Findlay—Hundred p333-334

Purkinje, Jan Evangelista (or Purkyne, Jan Evangel) (1787-1869). Czech. physiologist.
Chambers—Dict. col.368
Locy—Biology p267-268 (por.267)
Major—History (2) p708
Robinson—Path. p361-380
(por.366,367)
*Snyder—Biology p70-74 (por.71,74)

Purmann, Mattheus Gottfried (1649-1711). Ger. surgeon.
Leonardo—Lives p354-355
Major—History (1) p561

Pusey, William Allen (1865-1940). Amer. physician, dermatologist.
*Bernays—Outline p216
Curr. Biog. '40 p665

Putnam, Amelia.   See Earhart, Amelia

Putnam, Frederic Ward (1839-1915). Amer. anthropologist.
   N.A.S.—Biog. '36 p125-138 (por.125)

Putnam, J. Duncan (1855-1881). Amer. entomologist.
   Osborn—Fragments p158-159
      (por.348)

Putnam, James Jackson (1846-1918). Amer. neurologist, psychoanalyst.
   Kagan—Modern p64 (por.64)

Putnam, Tracy Jackson (1894-   ). Amer. neurologist.
   Chambers—Dict. col.369

Putt, Donald Lancaster (1905-   ). Amer. aero. pioneer, space pioneer.
   Curr. Biog. '60 p324-325 (por.324)
   Thomas—Men (3) p.xv

Putti, Vittorio (1880-1940). It. surgeon.
   Leonardo—Lives p355-357

Pyrrhon (365?-275? B.C.). Gr. nat. philosopher.
   Gordon—Medicine p610-611

Pythagoras (569/582-500/506 B.C.). Gr. mathematician.
   Atkinson—Magic p43-44
   Cajori—Hist. p17-19,55-57
   Chambers—Dict. col.369-370
   Clagett—Greek p35,56-57
   Dreyer—Hist. p35-52
   Ginzburg—Adven. p3-23
   Gordon—Medicine p480-486
      (por.481)
   Hammerton p1120-1121
   Hart—Physicists p5-7
   Lambert—Minute p9-10
   Lenard—Great p1-2
   Major—History (1) p111-113
      (por.135)
   Muir—Men p5-14
   Sedgwick—Short p49-54
   Smith—Hist. I p69-77
   Turnbull—Great p6-15
   Van Wagenen—Beacon p5-7
   Wilson—Human p7-12
   Woodruff—Devel. p10,133,288
   Year—Pic. p27 (por.27)

Pytheas (4th cent.) Gr. astronomer, geographer.
   Hammerton p1121

Q

Quain, Sir Richard (1816-1898). Irish physician.
   Hammerton p1121 (por.1121)

Quaintance, Altus Lacy (1870-1958). Amer. entomologist.
Osborn—Fragments p223 (por.358)

Quarles, Donald Aubrey (1894-   ). Amer. engineer, aero. pioneer.
Curr. Biog. '55 p495-497 (por.495)

Quatrefages de Breau, Jean Louis Armand de (1810-1892). Fr.
anthropologist, ethnologist, naturalist.
Hammerton p1121
Major—History (2) p881

Queeny, John F. (1859-1933). Amer. chemist.
Haynes—Chem. (1) p225-242
(por.225)

Quenstedt, Friedrich August (1809-1889). Ger. mineralogist,
paleontologist, geologist.
Woodruff—Devel. p288

Quervain, Fritz de (1868-1940). Swiss surgeon.
Leonardo—Lives p357-358

Quesada, Elwood Richard (1904-   ). Amer. aero. pioneer.
Curr. Biog. '50 p473-475 (por.474)
'60 p327-329 (por.328)

Quetelet, Lambert Adolphe Jacques (1796-1874). Belg. astronomer.
Cajori—Hist. p380   People p342-343
Chambers—Dict. col.371-372   Smith—Hist. I p526
Hammerton p1121

Queuille, Henri (1884-   ). Fr. physician.
Curr. Biog. '48 p505-506 (por.506)

Quick, Hazel Irene (n.d.). Amer. engineer.
Goff—Women p88-91

Quick, (John) Herbert (1861-1925). Amer. agriculturist.
*Ivins—Fifty p229-235 (por.231)

Quiggle, Dorothy (1903-   ). Amer. chem. engineer.
Goff—Women p82-87

Quimby, Edith Hinckley (1891-   ). Amer. biophysicist.
Curr. Biog. '49 p492-493 (por.492)
Yost—Women Mod. p94-107
(por.,front.)

Quimby, Harriet (1884-1912). Amer. aero. pioneer.
*Adams—Heroines p3-26 (por.24)   Maitland—Knights p160-161
Heinmuller—Man's p290 (por.290)

Quincke, Heinrich Irenäeus (1842-1922). Ger. physician.
Major—History (2) p904

Quirke, Terence Thomas (1886-1947). Eng. geologist.
G.S.A.—Proc. '47 p167-170 (por.167)

R

Rabanus, Maurus (or Maurus, Hrabanus; Rhabanus, Maurus) (c776-856).
Ger. mathematician.
Smith—Hist. I p188

Rabelais, François (1494?-1553). Fr. physician.
Castiglioni—Hist. p497-498 (por.500)   Lambert—Medical p98
Gordon—Medieval p590-592   Lambert—Minute p98
(por.,front.)   Major—History (1) p466
Hammerton p1122-1123 (por.1123)

Rabi, Isidor Isaac (1898-   ). Amer. physicist.
Chambers—Dict. col.373   Progress—Science '40 p328-329
Curr. Biog. '48 p509-510 (por.509)   Weber—College p704 (por.704)
Heathcote—Nobel p398-410 (por.240)   Year—Pic. p212 (por.212)
Morris—Ency. p707

Rabinoff, Sophie (1888-   ). Rus.-Amer. physician.
Knapp—Women p123-136 (por.123)

Rabinowitsch, Lydia (1871-1935). Lith. bacteriologist.
Bulloch—Hist. p391

Raborn, William Francis, Jr. (1905-   ). Amer. aero. pioneer.
Curr. Biog. '58 p346-348 (por.347)
Thomas—Men (3) p138-161 (por.74)

Radcliffe, John (1650-1714). Eng. physician.
Gunther—Early XI p82-85 (por.84)   Major—History (1) p562-563
Hammerton p1124

Radford, Arthur William (1896-   ). Amer. aero. pioneer.
Curr Biog. '49 p493-495 (por.494)

Radoshkowsky, Octavius John (or Bourmeister-Radoshkowsky) (1820-1895). Pol. entomologist.
Essig—Hist. p735-737 (por.736)

Rafinesque, Constantine Samuel (or Rafinesque-Schmaltz) (1783-1840). Fr.-Amer. naturalist.
Bell—Early p70-71
Jaffe—Men p104-129 (por.xxviii)
Osborn—Fragments p25-26 (por.342)
Peattie—Green p261-268 (por.245)
Rosen—Four p165-166
Youmans—Pioneers p182-195
   (por.182)
Young—Biology p28-30 (por.29)

Rahn, Johann Heinrich (d.1676). Swiss mathematician.
Chambers—Dict. col.373

Rakestraw, Norris Watson (1895-   ). Amer. chemist.
Browne—Hist. p500 (por.411)

Raman, Sir Chandrasekhara Venkata (1888-   ). Ind. physicist.
Chambers—Dict. col.373
Curr. Biog. '48 p510-512 (por.511)
Hammerton p1127
Heathcote—Nobel p297-304 (por.240)
Weber—College p507 (por.507)

Ramanujan, Srinivasa (or Aiyengar, Srinivasa Ramanuja) (1887-1920). Ind. mathematician.
Sci. Amer.—Lives p257-269 (por.259)

Ramazzini, Bernardino (1633-1714). It. physician.
Castiglioni—Hist. p564-566 (por.563)
Major—History (1) p542-543

Ramée.   See Ramus, Petrus

Ramey, Howard K. (1896?-1943). Amer. aero. pioneer.
Curr. Biog. '43 p608

Rammelsberg, Karl Friedrich (1813-1899). Ger. chemist, mineralogist, crystallographer.
Smith—Torch. p207 (por.207)
Weeks—Discovery p199 (por.199)

Ramo, Simon (1913-   ). Amer. engineer.
Curr. Biog. '58 p348-350 (por.348)
Thomas—Men (2) p134-154
   (por.106)

Ramon, Gaston (1886-   ). Fr. bacteriologist.
Grainger—Guide p169

Ramon y Cayal, Santiago (1852-1934). Sp. histologist, physician.

A.A.A.S.—Proc. (81) p81-84
Castiglioni—Hist. p772-773 (por.773)
Chambers—Dict. col. 373-374
Hammerton p1127

Locy—Biology p176-177 (por.176)
Major—History (2) p1045-1046
Rosen—Four p21-24,101-104,269-274
Stevenson—Nobel p33-34,36-37
    (por.150)

Ramsay, Andrew Crombie (1814-1891). Scot. geologist.

Fenton—Giants p110
Hammerton p1127-1128

Ramsay, Sir William (1852-1916). Scot. chemist.

A.A.A.S.—Proc. (81) p84-88
*Book—Pop. Sci. (13) p4353
    (por.4334)
Chambers—Dict. col.374
*Darrow—Masters p339
Farber—Nobel p17-20 (por.118)
Findlay—British p146-175 (por.146)
Findlay—Hundred p334
Hammerton p1128 (por.1128)
Harrow—Chemists p41-58 (por.41)

Holmyard—British p69-72 (por.69)
Holmyard—Great Chem. p129-135
Law—Civiliz. p280-281
Partington—Short p351-352,354
    (por.351)
Smith—Torch. p208 (por.208,209)
Tilden—Famous p273-287 (por.273)
Van Wagenen—Beacon p408-411
Weeks—Discovery p471-481
    (por.471,479)
Woodruff—Devel. p288

Ramsay, Sir William Mitchell (1851-1939). Scot. archaeologist.

Hammerton p1128

Ramsden, Jesse (1735-1800). Eng. mathematician.

Chambers—Dict. col.274-275

Ramsey, DeWitt Clinton (1888-   ). Amer. aero. pioneer.

Curr. Biog. '53 p505-507 (por.506)
    '61 (Dec.) p41

Ramus, Petrus (or Ramée, Pierre de la; La Ramee, Pierre) (1515-1572).
    Fr. mathematician.

Ball—Short p227
Sarton—Six p39-42 (por.40)

Smith—Hist. I p309-310

Ramusio, Giani Battista (1485-1557). It. geographer.

Hammerton p1128

Randall, John Turton (1905-   ). Eng. physicist.

Chambers—Dict. col.375

Randers, Gunnar (1914-   ). Norw. physicist.

Curr. Biog. '57 p446-448 (por.447)

Ranger, Richard Howland (1889-   ). Amer. radio engineer.
Radio's 100 p239-240 (por.140)

Rankine, Alexander Oliver (1881-1956). Eng. physicist.
R.S.L.—Biog. (2) p249-254 (por.249)

Rankine, William John Macquorn (1820-1872). Scot. engineer, physicist.
Cajori—Hist. p476   MacFarlane—Ten p22-37 (por.,front.)
Hammerton p1129   Murray—Science p356-358

Ranney, Waitstill R. (1792-1854). Amer. physician.
Farmer—Doctors' p111

Ransohoff, Joeph (1853-1921). Amer. surgeon.
Kagan—Modern p96 (por.96)
Leonardo—Lives p358-359

Ransom, Frederick Parlett Fisher (1850-1937). Eng. physician.
Bulloch—Hist. p391

Ransome, Frederick Leslie (1868-1935). Eng.-Amer. geologist.
G.S.A.—Proc. '36 p249-252 (por.249)
N.A.S.—Biog. (22) p155-163
  (por.155)

Ranson, Stephen Walter (1880-1942). Amer. neurologist.
Curr. Biog. '42 p686
N.A.S.—Biog. (23) p365-382
  (por.365)

Raoult, François Marie (1830-1901). Fr. chemist, physicist.
Chambers—Dict. col.375-376   Partington—Short p331-334,340
Findlay—Hundred p334   (por.332)
Hammerton p1129   Smith—Torch. p210 (por.210)
                                     Woodruff—Devel. p119-289

Raschig, Friedrich August (or Fritz) (1863-1928). Ger. chemist.
Chambers—Dict. col.376
Partington—Short p354-355

Rasmussen, Knud Johan Victor (1879-1933). Dan. sci. explorer.
Hammerton p1130

Rasori, Giovanni (1766-1837). It. physician.
Castiglioni—Hist. p592-593 (por.582)

Raspail, François Vincent (1794-1878). Fr. chemist.
Hammerton p1130

Raspe, Rudolph Erich (1737-1794). Ger. mineralogist, geologist.
Adams—Birth p187-188
Weeks—Discovery p124

Rassam, Hormuzd (1826-1910). Turk. archaeologist.
Ceram—Gods p273-274
Hammerton p1131

Rassweiler, Clifford Fred (1899-   ). Amer. chem. engineer.
Curr. Biog. '58 p352-353 (por.353)

Rathke, Martin Heinrich (1793-1860). Ger. anatomist, biologist.
Chambers—Dict. col.376   Major—History (2) p710
Locy—Biology p163   Woodruff—Devel. p289

Rattone, Georgio (1857-1930). It. pathologist.
Bulloch—Hist. p391

Raver, Paul Jerome (1894-   ). Amer. engineer.
Curr. Biog. '41 p698-699 (por.698)

Rawlinson, Sir Henry Creswicke (1810-1895). Eng. philologist.
Ceram—Gods p232-239

Ray (or Wray), **John** (1627/1628-1705). Eng. naturalist, botanist.
Adams—Birth p258   Locy—Biology p115-118,128
Bodenheimer—Hist. p281-282   (por.116)
Chambers—Dict. col.376 (por.375)   Miall—Early p99-130
Crowther—Founders p94-130   Oliver—Makers p28-43 (por.28)
  (por.128)   Reed—Short p84-86
Gilmour—British p16-20 (por.19)   Woodruff—Devel. p230,231,289
Hammerton p1132
Hawks—Pioneers p204-206,208-212
  (por.204)

Rayer, Pierre-François-Olive (1793-1867). Fr. physician, pathologist.
Bulloch—Hist. p391

Rayleigh, John William Strutt, Lord (1842-1919). Eng. mathematician, physicist.
*Book—Pop. Sci. (15) p5063-5064   Gregory—British p46 (por.32)
  (por.5062)   Hammerton p1132 (por.1132)
Chambers—Dict. col.377   Heathcote—Nobel p27-33 (por.240)
                    (*Continued*)

Rayleigh, John William Strutt, Lord—*Continued*
Law—Civiliz. p280-281
People p346
Smith—Torch. p211 (por.211,212)
Van Wagenen—Beacon p386-388

Weber—College p81 (por.81)
Weeks—Discovery p469-471 (por.470)
Woodruff—Devel. p289 (por.66)

Raynaud, Maurice (1834-1881). Fr. physician.
Major—History (2) p898

Razi. See **Rhazes**

Read, Albert Cushing (1887-   ). Amer. aero. pioneer.
*Fraser—Famous p91-105
Heinmuller—Man's p306 (por.306)

Read, Alexander (1586-1641). Scot. surgeon.
Leonardo—Lives p359-361

Read, Clare Sewell (1826-1905). Eng. agriculturist.
Hammerton p1132

Read, John (1884-   ). Eng. chemist.
Newman—What p152-153

Read, Nathan (1759-1849). Amer. engineer, inventor.
*Book—Pop. Sci. (15) p5021-5022
(por.5021)
Goddard—Eminent p29-34 (por.28)

Réaumur, René Antoine Ferchault de (1683-1757). Fr. naturalist,
physicist, entomologist.
Bodenheimer—Hist. p300
*Book—Pop. Sci. (15) p5064
Castiglioni—Hist. p612
Chambers—Dict. col.377
Hammerton p1133 (por.1133)
Law—Civiliz. p275-276

Locy—Biology p96 (por.98)
Major—History (2) p618-620
Miall—Early p244-278
Peattie—Green p67-73 (por.71)
Smith—Torch. p213 (por.213)
Woodruff—Devel. p289

Récamier, Joseph Claude Anthelme (1774-1856). Fr. physician,
gynecologist.
Major—History (2) p707

Recklinghausen, Friedrich Daniel von (1833-1910). Ger. anatomist.
Bulloch—Hist. p391-392
Major—History (2) p897

Reclus, Jean Jacques Élisée (1830-1905). Fr. geographer.
Hammerton p1133

Recorde (or Record), **Robert** (1510-1558). Eng. mathematician.
Ball—Short p214-215
Chambers—Dict. col.377-378
Gunther—Early XI p156
Sedgwick—Short p236-237
Smith—Hist. I p317-321

Redfield, Robert (1897-1958). Amer. anthropologist.
Curr. Biog. '53 p511-512 (por.511)
　'59 p379

Redi, Francesco (1626?-1697/1698). It. naturalist, physician.
Bodenheimer—Hist. p263
Bulloch—Hist. p392 (por.236)
Castiglioni—Hist. p543-544 (por.543)
Chambers—Dict. col.378
Grainger—Guide p169
Locy—Biology p279-281 (por.280)
Miall—Early p225-228
Oliver—Stalkers p113-116
Schwartz—Moments (1) p405-407
Sigerist—Great p170
*Snyder—Biology p413
Thomson—Great p23-24
Woodruff—Devel. p250,289

Redman, Lawrence V. (1880-1946). Amer. chemist.
Browne—Hist. p486-487 (por.145)

Redmayne, Sir Richard Augustine Studdert (1865-1955). Brit. engineer.
Hammerton p1133-1134

Redway, Jacques Wardlaw (1849-1942). Amer. geographer, meteorologist.
Curr. Biog. '43 p615

Redwood, Sir Boverton (1846-1919). Brit. chemist.
Hammerton p1134

Reed, Sir Edward James (1830-1906). Eng. naval engineer.
Hammerton p1134

Reed, Herbert Calhoun (1873-1940). Amer. chemist.
Curr. Biog. '40 p675

Reed, James, Sr. (1881-1941). Amer. engineer.
Curr. Biog. '41 p699

Reed, Philip D. (1899-   ). Amer. engineer.
Curr. Biog. '49 p506-507 (por.507)

Reed, Ralph Daniel (1889-1940). Amer. geologist.
G.S.A.—Proc. '40 p233-236 (por.233)

Reed, Walter (1851-1902). Amer. bacteriologist, surgeon, physician.

Atkinson—Magic p295-296
*Bolton—Famous p249-257 (por.248)
*Book—Pop. Sci. (14) p4940-4941
Carmer—Caval. p214-216 (por.214)
Chambers—Dict. col.378
*Chandler—Medicine p95-99 (por.94)
*Darrow—Builders p200-206 (por.195)
DeKruif—Microbe p311-333
Farmer—Doctors' p203
Grainger—Guide p169-170
Hammerton p1134
Law—Civiliz. p339-340
Major—History (2) p913 (por.863)
*Masters—Conquest p154-160 (por.158)
Morris—Ency. p707-708
Rowntree—Amid p8-14 (por.11)
*Shippen—Men p190-195
*Simmons—Great p36-39 (por.36)
*Snyder—Biology p218-224 (por.219)
Walker—Pioneers p218-226 (por.218)
*Williams-Ellis p229-234

Rees, Mina S. (1902-). Amer. mathematician.

Curr. Biog. '57 p453-455 (por.454)

Reese, Charles L. (1862-1940). Amer. chemist.

Browne—Hist. p487 (por.145)
Holland—Ind. p297-309 (por.297)

Reeside, John Bernard, Jr. (1889-1958). Amer. geologist.

N.A.S.—Biog. (35) p272-284 (por.272)

Reeve, Robert Campbell (1902-). Amer. aero. pioneer.

Potter—Flying p164-185 (por.178)

Reeve, Sidney Armor (1866-1941). Amer. engineer.

Curr. Biog. '41 p699

Reeves, George I. (b.1879). Amer. entomologist.

Osborn—Fragments p222

Regener, Erich (1881-). Ger. physicist.

Chambers—Dict. col.378-379

Regiomontanus. See **Müller, Johann**

Regnault, Henri Victor (1810-1878). Fr. chemist, physicist.

Chambers—Dict. col.379
Hammerton p1135
Weeks—Discovery p391 (por.391)

Rehn, Ludwig-Mettler (1849-1930). Ger. physician, surgeon.

Thorwald—Century p380-390

Reich, Ferdinand (1799-1882). Ger. chemist, physicist.

A.A.A.S.—Proc. (77) p38
Chambers—Dict. col.379-380
Weeks—Discovery p378-380 (por.378)

Reiche, Louis Jerome (1799-1890). Dutch-Fr. entomologist.
Essig—Hist. p738 (por.738)

Reichelderfer, Francis Wilton (1895-   ). Amer. meteorologist.
Curr. Biog. '49 p508-510 (por.508)
Progress—Science '41 p352-353
  (por.352)

Reichenbach, G. F. (1771-1826). Ger. engineer.
Matschoss—Great p127-140 (por.140)

Reichenbach, Karl, Baron von (1788-1869). Ger. naturalist.
Chambers—Dict. col.380
Hammerton p1135

Reichenstein.   See **Müller, Franz Joseph, Baron von Reichenstein**

Reichert, Karl Bogislaus (1811-1884). Ger. embryologist.
Major—History (2) p800

Reichstein, Tadeus (or Tadeusz) (1897-   ). Pol.-Swiss chemist.
Chambers—Dict. Supp.   Stevenson—Nobel p273-274,280-283
Curr. Biog. '51 p513-514 (por.514)   (por.150)

Reid, Harry F. (1859-1944). Amer. geologist.
G.S.A.—Proc. '44 p293-295 (por.293)
N.A.S.—Biog. (26) p1-4 (por.1)

Reid, James L. (1844-1910). Amer. agriculturist.
*DeKruif—Hunger p180-188 (por.181)
*Ivins—Fifty p69-72 (por.70)

Reid, Mont Rogers (1889-1943). Amer. physician, surgeon.
Curr. Biog. '43 p615

Reinach, Salomon (1858-1932). Fr. archaeologist.
Hammerton p1136

Reinecke, Leopold (1884-1935). Dutch geologist.
G.S.A.—Proc. '36 p259-267 (por.259)

Reinhold, Arnold William (1843-1921). Eng. physicist.
Chambers—Dict. col.380

Reinmuth, Otto (1900-   ). Amer. chemist.
Browne—Hist. p500-501 (por.411)

Reisner, George Andrew (1867-1942). Amer. archaeologist.
Curr. Biog. '42 p691

Reith, Sir John Charles Walsham (1889-   ). Brit. engineer.
Hammerton p1136

Remigus (or Remi; Remigius) **of Auxerre** (d.c.908). Fr. physician.
Smith—Hist. I p188

Remington, Philo (1816-1889). Amer. inventor.
Hammerton p1137
Wilson—Amer. p253-255 (por.253)

Remsen, Ira (1846-1927). Amer. chemist.
*Book—Pop. Sci. (15) p5064-5065
    (por.5065)
Browne—Hist. p478 (por.61)
Chymia (2) p14-15
Hammerton p1137
Harrow—Chemists p197-215
    (por.197)
*Hylander—Scien. p164-166
Killeffer—Eminent p15 (por.15)
N.A.S.—Biog. (14) p207-257
    (por.207)
Smith—Torch. p214 (por.214)
Weeks—Discovery p473 (por.473)

Renard, Charles (1847-1905). Fr. aero. pioneer.
Heinmuller—Man's p251 (por.251)

Renaudot, Théophraste (1584/1586-1653). Fr. physician.
Castiglioni—Hist. p574-575 (por.575)

Renault, Louis (1877-1944). Fr. engineer, inventor.
Hammerton p1138

Renaux, Eugène (b.1877). Fr. aero. pioneer.
Heinmuller—Man's p287 (por.287)

Rendle, Alfred Barton (1865-1937). Eng. botanist.
Hammerton p1138

Rennie, John (1761-1821). Scot. engineer.
Hammerton p1138 (por.1138)
*Watson—Engineers p47-57 (por.46)

Rentzel, Delos Wilson (1909-   ). Amer. aero. pioneer.
Curr. Biog. '48 p518-520 (por.519)

Renucci, Simon François (fl.1834-1847). Fr. physician.
Woglom—Discov. p121-131

Repsold, Johann Georg (1770-1830). Ger. engineer.
Chambers—Dict. col.380

Resser, Charles Elmer (1889-1943). Amer. geologist.
G.S.A.—Proc. '43 p217-221 (por.217)

Retines, de   See **Robert de Ketene**

Revelle, Roger (1909-   ). Amer. oceanographer, geologist.
Curr. Biog. '57 p455-457 (por.455)

Reverchon, Julien (1837-1905). Fr.-Amer. naturalist.
Geiser—Natural. p215-224

Reverdin, Frederic (1849-1931). Swiss chemist.
A.A.A.S.—Proc. (77) p45-46

Rey, Jean J. (1635-1682). Fr. physician.
Holmyard—Chem. p61-62
Partington—Short p84

Reybold, Eugene (1884-   ). Amer. engineer.
Curr. Biog. '45 p494-497 (por.495)

Reyes, Teodoro Flores (1873-1955). Mex. geologist.
G.S.A.—Proc. '55 p123-125 (por.123)

Reynard, Alphonse François (1842-1903). Belg. biologist.
Hammerton p1140

Reynolds, James A. (1887-1940). Amer. elec. engineer.
Curr. Biog. '40 p680 (por.680)

Reynolds, Osborne (1842-1912). Irish physicist, engineer, inventor.
Chalmers—Historic p271
Chambers—Dict. col.380

Rezzi.   See **Rhazes**

R. Gamliel Bathrai.   See **Gamaliel VI**

Rhabanus.   See **Rabanus, Maurus**

Rhabdas, Nicholas (fl.c.1341). Gr. mathematician.
Smith—Hist. I p235

Rhaeticus (or Rhäticus).   See **Rheticus, George Joachim**

Rhazes (or Razi; Al-Razi; Abú-Bakr Muhammad ibn Zakariyýa) (850/860-923/932). Pers. physician.

Castiglioni—Hist. p267-270
*Chandler—Medicine p15-16
Gordon—Medieval p152-156
(por.178)
Hammerton p70
Holmyard—Chem. p20-22
Holmyard—Great Chem. p19-21
Holmyard—Makers p63-67
Lambert—Medical p68-69
Lambert—Minute p68-69
Major—History (1) p236-241
Oliver—Stalkers p50-51
Partington—Short p28
Robinson—Path. p31-48 (por.38)
*Shippen—Men p55-56
Sigerist—Great p80-83

Rheticus, George Joachim (or Rhaeticus; G. J. von Lauchen) (1514-1576). Ger. astronomer, mathematician.

Ball—Short p226
Chambers—Dict. col.381
Hammerton p1141
Hooper—Makers p166-167
Koestler—Sleep. p153-190
Smith—Hist. I p333-334
Woodruff—Devel. p289

Rhijn, Pieter Johannes van (1886-   ). Dutch astronomer, astrophysicist.

Chambers—Dict. col.381
MacPherson—Makers p238-240
(por.210)

Rhine, Joseph Banks (1895-   ). Amer. psychologist.

Chambers—Dict. col.381
Curr. Biog. '49 p516-518 (por.517)

Rhoads, Cornelius Packard (1898-1959). Amer. physician, pathologist.

Curr. Biog. '53 p523-524
'59 p385

Rhodes, James Ford (1848-1927). Amer. physician.

Cushing—Medical p233-244

Ribbert, Hugo (1855-1920). Ger. anatomist.

Bulloch—Hist. p392

Ribot, Théodule Armand (1839-1916). Fr. psychologist.

Hammerton p1142

Riccati, Giordano, Count (1585-1639). It. mathematician.

Smith—Hist. I p513-514

Riccati, Jacopo Francesco, Count (1676-1754). It. mathematician, physicist.

Ball—Short p372
Smith—Hist. I p512-513 (por.513)

Ricci, Corrado (1858-1934). It. archaeologist.
Hammerton p1142

Ricci, Matteo (1552-1610). It. mathematician.
Smith—Hist. I p303-304

Ricciolo, Giovanni Battista (1598-1671). It. astronomer.
Walsh—Catholic (2d) p199-201

Ricco, Annibale (1844-1919). It. astronomer.
Abetti—History p206-208

Richard of Wallingford (d.1336). Eng. inventor.
Hammerton p1144

Richards, Alfred Newton (b.1876). Amer. pharmacologist.
Curr. Biog. '50 p488-490 (por.489)

Richards, Dickinson Woodruff (1895-   ). Amer. physician.
Curr. Biog. '57 p457-459 (por.457)

Richards, Ellen Henriette Swallow (1842-1911). Amer. chemist, sanitary
engineer.
Law—Civiliz. p286-289
Mozans—Woman p217-220
16 Amer. p57-60
Yost—Women Sci. p1-26

Richards, Theodore William (1868-1928). Amer. chemist.
*Book—Pop. Sci. (15) p5065-5066 (por.5066)
Browne—Hist. p482 (por.103)
Chambers—Dict. col.381-382
*Darrow—Builders p168-171 (por.287)
*Darrow—Masters p340
Farber—Nobel p61-64 (por.118)
Hammerton p1144
Harrow—Chemists p59-78 (por.59)
*Hylander—Scien. p166-169
Killeffer—Eminent p27 (por.27)
*Law—Modern p191-203 (por.193)
Partington—Short p355 (por.344)
Smith—Torch. p215 (por.215)
Weeks—Discovery p498 (por.498)

Richardson, Archibald Read (1881-1954). Eng. mathematician.
R.S.L.—Biog. (1) p223-236 (por.223)

Richardson, Sir Benjamin Ward (1828-1896). Eng. physician.
Hammerton p1144
Robinson—Victory p237-245

Richardson, Charles Henry (1862-1935). Amer. geologist.
G.S.A.—Proc. '35 p301-302 (por.301)

Richardson, George Burr (1872-1949). Amer. geologist.
G.S.A.—Proc. '51 p135-138 (por.135)

Richardson, Sir John (1787-1865). Scot. sci. explorer, surgeon, naturalist.
Hammerton p1144

Richardson, Maurice Howe (1851-1912). Amer. surgeon.
Kagan—Modern p94 (por.94)
Leonardo—Lives p361-362

Richardson, Sir Owen Willans (b.1879). Eng. physicist.
Chambers—Dict. col.382
Hammerton p1144
Heathcote—Nobel p278-286 (por.240)
R.S.L.—Biog. (5) p207-210 (por.207)
Weber—College p476 (por.476)

Richardson, William D. (1876-1936). Amer. chemist.
Browne—Hist. p501 (por.371)

Richarz, Stephen (1874-1934). Ger. geologist.
G.S.A.—Proc. '34 p253-256 (por.253)

Richet, Charles Robert (1850-1935). Fr. physiologist.
A.A.A.S.—Proc. (78) p27-28
Bulloch—Hist. p392
Chambers—Dict. col.382
Grainger—Guide p170
Hammerton p1146
Major—History (2) p1046 (por.943)
Stevenson—Nobel p73-83 (por.150)

Richman, Harry (1895-   ). Amer. aero. pioneer.
*Fraser—Heroes p750
Heinmuller—Man's p350 (por.350)

Richter, August Gottlieb (1742-1812). Ger. surgeon.
Leonardo—Lives p362-363

Richter, Hieronymus Theodor (1824-1898). Ger. chemist.
Chambers—Dict. col.382
Weeks—Discovery p380-382
(por.380)

Richter, Jeremias Benjamin (1762-1807). Ger. chemist.
Chambers—Dict. col.383
Partington—Short p161-163,178
(por.161)
Smith—Torch. p216 (por.216)

Richthofen, Manfred Freiherr von Rittmeister (1892-1918). Ger. aero.
pioneer.
Arnold—Airmen p128-129
Burge—Ency. p638
Hammerton p1147
Heinmuller—Man's p299 (por.299)

Richtmyer, Floyd Karker (1881-1939). Amer. physicist.
N.A.S.—Biog. (22) p71-76 (por.71)

Rickenbacker, Edward Vernon (1890-   ). Amer. aero. pioneer.
Arnold—Airmen p117-118
Curr. Biog. '52 p497-499 (por.497)
*Fraser—Famous p72-90
Heinmuller—Man's p303 (por.303)
Maitland—Knights p212-215
*Shippen—Bridle p154-162

Ricketts, Howard Taylor (1871-1910). Amer. pathologist.
Major—History (2) p936,1046
(por.937)
16 Amer. p25-28

Ricketts, Louise Davidson (1887-1940). Amer. min. engineer.
Curr. Biog. '40 p684
(por.937)

Rickey, James Walter (1871-1943). Amer. engineer.
Curr. Biog. '43 p622

Rickover, Hyman George (1900-   ). Rus.-Amer. engineer.
Curr. Biog. '53 p525-526 (por.525)

Ricksecker, Lucius Edgar (1841-1913). Amer. entomologist.
Essig—Hist. p738-741 (por.740)

Ricord, Philip (1799/1800-1889). Amer. physician.
Castiglioni—Hist. p735-736 (por.736)

Rideal, Eric Keightley (1890-   ). Eng. chemist.
Chambers—Dict. col.383

Ridenour, Nina (1904-   ). Amer. psychologist.
Curr. Biog. '51 p520-523 (por.521)

Ridgeway, Sir William (1853-1926). Irish archaeologist.
Hammerton p1147

Ridgway, Robert (1850-1929). Amer. ornithologist.
N.A.S.—Biog. (15) p57-68 (por.57)

Ridley, Henry Nicholas (1855-1956). Eng. botanist, geologist, agriculturist.
R.S.L.—Biog. (3) p141-149 (por.141)

Riedel, Klaus (1910-1944). Ger. rocket engineer.
Gartmann—Men p84-90
*Williams—Rocket p160-165,167-168,
    207-208

Riemann, Georg Friedrich Bernhard (1826-1866). Ger. mathematician.
Ball—Short p464-465
Bell—Men p484-509 (por.,front.)
Cajori—Hist. p421-423
Chambers—Dict. col.383-384
Hammerton p1148
Smith—Hist. 1 p508
Woodruff—Devel. p289 (por.36)
Year—Pic. p117 (por.117)

Ries, Heinrich (1871-1951). Amer. geologist.
G.S.A.—Proc. '51 p141-142 (por.141)

Riese, Adam (c.1489-1559). Ger. mathematician.
Smith—Hist. I p337-338 (por.337)

Riesman, David (1867-1940). Amer. physician.
Curr. Biog. '40 p684 (por.684)
Kagan—Modern p23 (por.23)

Rigby, Sir Hugh (1870-1944). Irish surgeon.
Hammerton p1148

Riggs, Austen Fox (1876-1940). Amer. neuropsychiatrist.
Curr. Biog. '40 p684

Righi, Augusto (1850-1920). It. physicist.
Hammerton p1148
Hawks—Wireless p189-191 (por.200)
Radio's 100 p94-95 (por.140)

Riiser-Larsen, Hjalmar (1890-   ). Norw. sci. explorer, aero. pioneer.
Curr. Biog. '51 p523-525 (por.523)

Riley, Charles Frederick Curtis (1872-1934). Eng.-Amer. entomologist.
Osborn—Fragments p228

Riley, Charles Valentine (1843-1895). Eng.-Amer. entomologist.
Essig—Hist. p741-745 (por.743)
Osborn—Fragments p151-157
    (por.347)
Smiths.—Misc. (84) p53-57
    (por.545,pl.2)

Ring, Barbara Taylor (1879-1941). Amer. psychiatrist.
Curr. Biog. '41 p713

Riolan, Jean (1577/1578-1657). Fr. anatomist, physician.
Castiglioni—Hist. p519 (por.508)

Ripley, Joseph (1854-1940). Amer. engineer.
Curr. Biog. '40 p685

Ritchey, George Willis (1864-1945). Amer. astronomer.
Hammerton p1149

Ritchey, Harold W. (1912-   ). Amer. space pioneer, phys. chemist.
Thomas—Men (3) p162-181 (por.74)

Ritchie, James (1864-1923). Brit. bacteriologist, pathologist.
Bulloch—Hist. p392

Ritt, Joseph Fels (1893-1951). Amer. mathematician.
N.A.S.—Biog. (29) p253-258
   (por.253)

Rittenhouse, David (1732-1796). Amer. astronomer.
Bell—Early p71-72   Youmans—Pioneer p47-57 (por.47)
Smith—Math. p55-57

Ritter, Johann (1776-1810). Ger. physicist.
Chambers—Dict. col.384

Ritzman, Ernest George (1875-1955). Swiss agriculturist.
Ratcliffe—Modern p280-290

Rivers, James John (1824-1913). Eng.-Amer. entomologist.
Essig—Hist. p746-747 (por.746)

Rivers, Thomas Milton (1888-   ). Amer. bacteriologist, physiologist,
   physician.
Curr. Biog. '60 p336-338 (por.337)
Progress—Science '41 p353 (por.353)

Rivers, William Halse Rivers (1864-1922). Eng. anthropologist.
Hammerton p1150

Rivière, Lazare (1589-1655). Fr. physician.
Major—History (1) p553

Rixford, Emmet (1867-1938). Amer. surgeon.
Leonardo—Lives p363-365

Rizzoli, Francesco (1809-1880). It. surgeon.
Leonardo—Lives p365-366

Roark, Louis (1890-1950). Amer. geologist.
G.S.A.—Proc. '51 p145-148 (por.145)

Robb, Hunter (1863-1940). Amer. gynecologist, physician.
Curr. Biog. '40 p685

Robbins, Frederick C. (1916-   ). Amer. bacteriologist.
Curr. Biog. '55 p183 (por.183)

Robbins, Will S. (b.1854). Amer. agriculturist.
*Ivins—Fifty p115-125 (por.114)

Robbins, William Jacob (1890-   ). Amer. botanist.
Curr. Biog. '56 p515-517 (por.516)

Robert brothers (c.1783). Fr. aero. pioneers.
Burge—Ency. p638

Robert, A. J. (1758-1820). Fr. aero. pioneer, inventor.
Heinmuller—Man's p233 (por.233)

Robert, Louis (1794-1835). Swiss-Fr. inventor.
Meyer—World p247-248

Robert de Ketene (or de Retines) **of Chester** (fl.c.1143). Eng. chemist.
Chambers—Dict. col.384
Holmyard—Makers p86-88

Roberts, Isaac Phillips (1833-1928). Amer. agriculturist.
*Ivins—Fifty p303-308 (por.305)

Roberts, Walter Orr (1915-   ). Amer. astronomer.
Curr. Biog. '60 p340-341 (por.341)

Roberts, William (1830-1899). Eng. physician.
Bulloch—Hist. p392

Roberts-Austin, Sir William Chandler (1843-1902). Eng. metallurgist.
Chambers—Dict. col.383

Robertson, Charles (1857-1935). Amer. entomologist.
Osborn—Fragments p184 (por.355)

Robertson, Sir Robert (1869-1949). Eng. chemist.
*Bridges—Master p196-207 (por.198)

Robertson, Robert Blackwood (1913-   ). Scot. physician.
Curr. Biog. '57 p471-472 (por.471)

Roberval, Gilles Personne de (or Personnier de) (1602-1675). Fr.
mathematician.
Ball—Short p307   Hammerton p1153
Cajori—Hist. p162-163   Smith—Hist. I p385
Chambers—Dict. col.384-385

Robeson, Eslanda (Cardoza) Goode (1896-   ). Amer. anthropologist.
Curr. Biog. '45 p505-507 (por.505)

Robin, Charles Philippe (1821-1885). Fr. biologist.
Bulloch—Hist. p392-393

Robinet, J. B. René (1735-1820). Fr. evolutionist.
Murray—Science p140
Osborn—Greeks p177-180

Robins, Benjamin (1707-1751). Eng. mathematician, engineer.
Cajori—Hist. p219-220
Hammerton p1154

Robinson, Benjamin Lincoln (1864-1935). Amer. botanist.
N.A.S.—Biog. (17) p305-314

Robinson, Harold Roper (1889-1955). Eng. physicist.
R.S.L.—Biog. (3) p161-171 (por.161)

Robinson, Houlton D. (1863?-1945). Amer. engineer.
Curr. Biog. '45 p507

Robinson, Hugh Armstrong (1881-   ). Amer. aero. pioneer.
Heinmuller—Man's p276 (por.276)

Robinson, James (1884-   ). Eng. physicist.
Hammerton p1154

Robinson, John Thomas Romney (1792-1882). Irish astronomer.
Chambers—Dict. col.385

Robinson, Sir Robert (1886-   ). Brit. chemist.
Chambers—Dict. col.385
Farber—Nobel p190-193 (por.118)

Robinson, Victor (1886-1947). Rus. physician.
Major—History (2) p1046

Robiquet, Pierre Jean (1780-1840). Fr. chemist.
Chambers—Dict. col.385

Robison, John (1739-1805). Scot. chemist, mathematician.
Hammerton p1155
Year—Pic. p110

Robison, Robert (1883-   ). Eng. biochemist.
Chambers—Dict. col.385

Robitzek, Edward Heinrich (1912-   ). Amer. physician.
Curr. Biog. '53 p535-537

Rockwell, Mabel MacFerran (1902-   ). Amer. elec. engineer.
Goff—Women p94-112

Rockwood, Charles Greene (1843-1913). Amer. seismologist.
Davison—Founders p144-146

Rodahl, Kaare (1917-   ). Norw. physiologist, physician.
Curr. Biog. '56 p524-525 (por.525)

Roddy, H. Justin (1856-1943). Amer. geologist.
G.S.A.—Proc. '43 p225-227 (por.225)

Rodgers, Calbraith P. (1879-1912). Amer. aero. pioneer.
Heinmuller—Man's p291 (por.291)

Rodgers, John (1812-1882). Amer. sci. explorer.
N.A.S.—Biog. (6) p81-92 (por.81)

Rodgers, John (1888-1926). Amer. aero. pioneer.
*Fraser—Famous p106-122
*Fraser—Heroes p365-391

Rodman, William Louis (1858-1916). Amer. surgeon.
Leonardo—Lives p366-367

Roe, Sir Alliott Verdon (1877-1958). Eng. aero. pioneer.
Burge—Ency. p638
Hammerton p1157

Roebling, Charles Gustavus (1849-1918). Amer. engineer.
Schuyler—Roeblings p310 (por.310)

Roebling, Ferdinand William, Jr. (1878-1926). Amer. engineer.
Schuyler—Roeblings p389-393
(por.390)

Roebling, John Augustus (1806-1869). Ger.-Amer. engineer.
*Darrow—Builders p239-242
Hammerton p1157
Morris—Ency. p709

Schuler—Roeblings p3-151
(por.,front.)
Watson—Engineers p93-103 (por.92)
Year—Pic. p194 (por.194)

Roebling, Washington Augustus (1837-1926). Amer. engineer.
*Darrow—Builders p242-244
Schuyler—Roeblings p155-285
(por.155,190)

Roemer, Ferdinand (1818-1891). Ger. geologist, naturalist.
Geiser—Natural. p148-171

Roemer, Olaus (or Römer, Ole) (1644-1710). Dan. astronomer.
Chambers—Dict. col.386
Copen.—Prom. p48-52
Hammerton p1159
Lenard—Great p66 (por.67)
Lodge—Pioneers p232-246
Magie—Source p335

Shapley—Astron. p70
Van Wagenen—Beacon p131-132
Vaucouleurs—Disc. p61-62
Williams—Great p200-202
Woodruff—Devel. p289
Year—Pic. p97 (por.97)

Roemer, Paul Heinrich (1876-1916). Ger. bacteriologist.
Bulloch—Hist. p393

Roentgen (or Röntgen), **Wilhelm Konrad** (1845-1923). Ger. physicist.
*Book—Pop. Sci. (15) p5067
Calder—Science p61-63
Castiglioni—Hist. p1065-1066
(por.1066)
Chalmers—Historic p271
Chambers—Dict. col.386
*Darrow—Masters p240-241
(por.320)
*Darrow—Thinkers p286-287
(por.286)
*Elwell—Sci. p98-101
Fitzhugh—Concise p580-581
Hammerton p1160-1161 (por.1161)
Heathcote—Nobel p2-8 (por.240)
*Larsen—Prentice p140-141
*Larsen—Scrap. p135-138 (por.144)

*McSpadden—How p195-207
(por.202)
Magie—Source p600
Major—History (2) p865-866,908
(por.866)
*Men—Scien. p25-27
Meyer—World p260-261
*Montgomery—Invent. p152-156
*Montgomery—Story p171-174
Moulton—Auto. p484-485
*Nisenson—Illus. p133 (por.133)
People p352-353
Schwartz—Moments (2) p867-869
*Science Miles. p205-210 (por.205)
*Shippen—Design p180-184
*Shippen—Men p156-162 (por.156)

(*Continued*)

Roentgen (or Röntgen), Wilhelm Konrad —*Continued*
Smith—Torch. p217 (por.217)
*Stevens—Science p141-142
Tuska—Invent. p92-93
Van Wagenen—Beacon p399-400
Weber—College p1 (por.1)
Wilson—Amer. p330-331
Woglom—Discov. p160-174
Year—Pic. p206 (por.206)

Roger, Georges Henri (1860-1946). Fr. pathologist, physiologist.
Major—History (2) p1046-1047

Roger of Palermo (or Ruggiero Frugardi) (fl.1108/1170). It. physician, surgeon.
Gordon—Medieval p442-446
Lambert—Medical p77-78
Lambert—Minute p77-78
Leonardo—Lives p367-368
Major—History (1) p278-280

Rogers brothers (19th cent.). Amer. chemists.
Smith—Chem. p235-239

Rogers, Arthur William (1872-1946). Eng. geologist.
G.S.A.—Proc. '46 p209-213 (por.209)

Rogers, Fairman (1833-1900). Amer. engineer.
N.A.S.—Biog. (6) p93-107 (por.93)

Rogers, Henry Darwin (1808-1866) Amer. geologist.
Merrill—First p167-168 (por.166)

Rogers, James Blythe (1802-1852). Amer. chemist.
Youmans—Pioneers p368-373 (por.368)

Rogers, John (1881-1926). Amer. aero. pioneer.
Heinmuller—Man's p317 (por.317)

Rogers, Mark Homer (1877-1941). Amer. physician, surgeon.
Curr. Biog. '41 p732

Rogers, Robert Empie (1813-1884). Amer. chemist.
N.A.S.—Biog. (5) p291-308 (por.291)
Smith—Chem. p235-239

Rogers, Vesta Marie (1909-   ). Austral.-Amer. physician.
Knapp—Women p17-31 (por.17)

Rogers, William Augustus (1832-1898). Amer. astronomer, physicist, mathematician.
N.A.S.—Biog. (6) (pt.11) p109-112 (por.109);(Pt.I in v.4, p185-199)

Rogers, William Barton (1804-1882). Amer. geologist.

G.S.A.—Proc. '35 p305-310
Merrill—First p185-187 (por.166)
N.A.S.—Biog. (3) p1-13

Smith—Math. p96
Youmans—Pioneers p410-418
(por.410)

Roget, Peter Mark (1779-1869). Eng.-Swiss physician.

Hammerton p1158
*Larsen—Scrap. p19 (por.18)

Rokitansky, Karl von, Baron (1804-1878). Aust. pathologist, physician, anatomist.

Castiglioni—Hist. p694-695
Major—History (2) p781-782

Oliver—Stalkers p155 (por.157)
Sigerist—Great p292-297 (por.296)

Roland of Parma (or Roland Caplutti) (fl.1250). It. surgeon.

Leonardo—Lives p368-369

Rolfs, Peter Henry (1865-1944). Amer. entomologist.

Osborn—Fragments p223-224

Rolleston, George (1829-1881). Eng. physician.

Gunther—Early XI p282-283
(por.282)

Rolleston, Sir Humphrey Davy (1862-1944). Eng. physician.

Hammerton p1159
Kagan—Modern p17 (por.17)

Major—History (2) p1047

Rollier, Auguste Henri (1874-1954). Swiss physician.

*Bridges—Master p208-213
DeKruif—Men p300-316

*Hathaway—Partners p51-59

Rolls, Charles Stewart (1877-1910). Eng. engineer, aero. pioneer.

Burge—Ency. p638
Hammerton p1159

Heinmuller—Man's p280 (por.280)

Roman, Nancy G. (1925-   ). Amer. astronomer.

Curr. Biog. '60 p345-347 (por.346)

Romanes, George John (1848-1894). Can. biologist, physiologist.

Hammerton p1159 (por.1159)

Romanoff, Alexis Lawrence (1892-   ). Rus.-Amer. zoologist.

Curr. Biog. '53 p542-544 (por.543)
Kinkead—Spider p77-153

Romanowsky, Dimitri Leonidowitsch (1861-1921). Rus. physician.
Bulloch—Hist. p393

Romberg, Moritz Heinrich (1795-1873). Ger. pathologist, neurologist.
Major—History (2) p711

Römer.   See **Roemer, Ferdinand**

Rominger, Carl Ludwig (1820-1907). Ger.-Amer. geologist.
Merrill—First p444-445 (por.444)

Ronald, Sir Francis (1788-1873). Eng. inventor.
Appleyard—Pioneers p301-331
  (por.300)
Hammerton p1160

Rondelet, Guillaume (1507-1566). Fr. naturalist, physician.
Chambers—Dict. col.386   Miall—Early p45
Hawks—Pioneers p163-164   Woodruff—Devel. p289-290
Major—History (1) p469

Ronne, Finn (1899-   ). Norw.-Amer. sci. explorer, engineer.
Curr. Biog. '48 p537-538 (por.538)

Röntgen.   See **Roentgen, Wilhelm Konrad**

Rood, Ogden Nicholas (1831-1902). Amer. physicist.
N.A.S.—Biog. (6) p447-469 (por.447)

Roosevelt, Kermit (1889-1943). Amer. sci. explorer.
Curr. Biog. '43 p628

Roosevelt, Nicholas J. (1767-1854). Amer. inventor.
*Burlingame—Inv. p56-57

Roosevelt, Quentin (1897-1918). Amer. aero. pioneer.
Heinmuller—Man's p304

Roosevelt, Theodore (1858-1919). Amer. naturalist.
Osborn—Impr. p165-182 (por.165)
Tracy—Amer. Nat. p147-154

Root, Amos Ives (or.A.I.). Amer. agriculturist.
*Ivins—Fifty p127-136 (por.126)

Roozeboom, Hendrik Willem Bakhuis (1854-1907). Dutch phys. chemist.

Chambers—Dict. col.387
Findlay—Hundred p334

Partington—Short p339-340
Woodruff—Devel. p290 (por.118)

Rosa, Edward Bennett (1861-1921). Amer. physicist.

N.A.S.—Biog. (16) p355-363
(por.355)

Rosanoff, Aaron Joshua (1878-1943). Amer. psychiatrist.

Curr. Biog. '43 p631

Roscoe, Sir Henry Enfield (1833-1915). Eng. chemist.

Chambers—Dict. col.387
Findlay—Hundred p334-335
Hammerton p1163

Partington—Short p352
Smith—Torch. p218 (por.218)
Weeks—Discovery p198-202,370
(por.201,370)

Rose, Bruce (1890-1956). Can. geologist.

G.S.A.—Proc. '56 p165 (por.165)

Rose, Heinrich (1795-1864). Ger. chemist.

Smith—Torch. p219 (por.219)
Weeks—Discovery p184,189
(por.189)

Rose, Valentin, the Younger (1762-1807). Ger. chemist.

Weeks—Discovery p130,133
(por.133)

Rose, William Cumming (1887-   ). Amer. biochemist.

Curr. Biog. '53 p545-547 (por.546)
Progress—Science '41 p353-354
(por.354)

Rosen, Carl George (1891-   ). Amer. engineer, inventor.

*Yost—Engineers p140-154

Rosenbach, Anton Julius Friedrich (1842-1923). Ger. bacteriologist, surgeon.

Bulloch—Hist. p393

Rosenbach, Ottomar (1851-1907). Ger. physician.

Kagan—Modern p15 (por.15)

Rosenbusch, Karl Harry Ferdinand (1836-1914). Ger. geologist.

Woodruff—Devel. p290 (por.196)

Rosengarten, George D. (1869-1936). Amer. chemist.
Browne—Hist. p485 (por.133)
Haynes—Chem. (1) p26-41
(por.26,27)

Rosenheim, Sigmund Otto (1871-1955). Ger. chemist.
R.S.L.—Biog. (2) p257-263 (por.257)

Rosenhof, August Johann Roesel von (1705-1759). Ger. entomologist, naturalist.
Locy—Biology p95 (por.97)
Miall—Early p293-303

Rosenstein, Nils Rosen (1706-1773). Swed. physician.
Lindroth—Swedish p74-80

Rosett, Joshua (1875-1940). Amer. neuro-anatomist.
Curr. Biog. '40 p697 (por.697)

Ross, Sir James Clark (1800-1862). Eng. sci. explorer.
*Book —Pop Sci. (14) p4820-4821
(por.4821)

Ross, Sir John (1777-1856). Scot. sci. explorer.
*Book—Pop. Sci. (14) p4821-4822
Hammerton p1164

Ross, Sir Ronald (1857-1932). Brit. bacteriologist, physician.
*Book—Pop. Sci. (14) p4941-4942
*Bridges—Master p214-227 (por.225)
Castiglioni—Hist p827-828
Chambers—Dict. col.387
*Crowther—Doctor p145-176 (por.160)
*DeKruif—Microbe p278-298
Fabricant—Why p99-100
Hale-White—Great p304-320
Hammerton p1164
Major—History (2) p916-917
Rosen—Four p110-112,274-277
*Snyder—Biology p209-217 (por.215)
Stevenson—Nobel p10-14 (por.150)

Rossby, Carl-Gustaf Arvid (1898-1957). Swed.-Amer. meteorologist.
N.A.S.—Biog. (34) p249-262 (por.249)

Rosse. See **Parsons, William, Earl of Rosse**

Rossi, Bruno (1905-   ). It.-Amer. physicist.
Chambers—Dict. col.387-388

Rossi, Maurice (1901-   ). Fr. aero. pioneer.
Heinmuller—Man's p193-203,347
(por.201,203,347)

Rösslin, Eucharius (c.1493). Ger. physician.
Major—History (1) p436-437

Rostand, Jean (1894-   ). Fr. biologist.
Curr. Biog. '54 p545-547 (por.546)

Roswitha (or Hrotsvitha; Hrotswitha). Ger. mathematician.
Smith—Hist. I p189

Rotch, Thomas Morgan (1849-1914). Amer. physician.
Major—History (2) p909

Roth, Justus Ludwig Adolf (1818-1892). Ger. mineralogist, geologist.
Woodruff—Devel. p178,290

Rothschild, Marcus A. (1887-1936). Amer. physician.
Kagan—Modern p36 (por.36)

Rouelle, Guillaume François (1703-1770). Fr. chemist.
Chambers—Dict. col.388   Smith—Torch. p220 (por.220)
Holmyard—Makers p189-196   Weeks—Discovery p37 (por.37)
  (por.191)

Rouphos.   See **Rufus of Ephesus**

Rous, Francis Peyton (b.1879). Amer. pathologist, physician.
Rowntree—Amid p376-377
  (por.363)

Rousset, François (1535-1590?). Fr. surgeon.
Leonardo—Lives p369
Major—History (1) p466

Routh, Edward John (1831-1907). Brit. mathematician.
Hammerton p1168-1169

Routley, T. Clarence (1889-   ). Can. physician.
Curr. Biog. '56 p532-533 (por.532)

Roux, Philibert Joseph (1780-1854). Fr. surgeon.
Leonardo—Lives p369-371

Roux, Pierre Paul Émile (1853-1933). Fr. bacteriologist, physician.
Bulloch—Hist. p393 (por.248)   Castiglioni—Hist. p813 (por.812)
(*Continued*)

Roux, Pierre Paul Émile—*Continued*
Chambers—Dict. col.388
*DeKruif—Microbe p184-206
Grainger—Guide p170
Hammerton p1169

Major—History (2) p967 (por.968)
Masters—Conquest p228-229
(por.228)
*Snyder—Biology p261,263

Roux, Wilhelm (1850-1924). Ger. zoologist, anatomist.
Bodenheimer—Hist. p435
Chambers—Dict. col.388-389
Hammerton p1169

Rovsing, Niels Thorkild (1862-1927). Dan. surgeon.
Leonardo—Lives p371-372

Rowe, Basil Lee (1896-   ). Amer. aero. pioneer.
Heinmuller—Man's p314 (por.314)

Rowland, Henry Augustus (1848-1901). Amer. physicist.
*Book—Pop. Sci. (5) p5068
(por.5068)
Chambers—Dict. col.389
Crew—Physicists #12 (por.,folder)
Hammerton p1169
Jordan—Leading p405-426 (por.405)
Magie—Source p365

Morris—Ency. p711
N.A.S.—Biog. (5) p115-134
(por.115)
Van Wagenen—Beacon p403-404
Wilson—Amer. p277 (por.277)
Woodruff—Devel. p296 (por.66)

Rowland, Sydney Domville (1872-1917). Eng. bacteriologist.
Bulloch—Hist. p393-394

Rowledge, Arthur John (1876-1957). Eng. engineer.
R.S.L.—Biog. (4) p215-223
(por.215)

Rowntree, Cecil (1880?-1943). Brit. physician, surgeon.
Curr. Biog. '43 p637

Rowntree, Leonard George (1883-   ). Can. physician.
Rowntree—Amid (see index)
(por.,front., 4,134)

Royce, Sir Frederick Henry (1863-1933). Eng. aero. pioneer, engineer.
Burge—Ency. p638
Hammerton p1169

Royce, Josiah (1855-1916). Amer. psychologist.
N.A.S.—Biog. (33) p381-391 (por.381)

Royer, Clemence Augustine (1830-1902). Fr. naturalist.
Mozans—Woman p245-246

Rozier, Jean François Pilâtre de (1756-1785). Fr. aero. pioneer.
*Bishop—Kite p25-34
Burge—Ency. p637
Heinmuller—Man's p233   (por.233)
*Shippen—Bridle p35-42
Smith—Torch. p221 (por.221)

Rubens, Heinrich (1865-1922). Ger. physicist.
Chambers—Dict. col.389

Rubín de la Borbolla, Daniel Fernando (1907-   ). Mex. anthropologist.
Curr. Biog. '60 p349-350 (por.350)

Rubner, Max (1854-1932). Ger. physiologist, hygienist.
*Snyder—Biology p327-329 (por.329)

Rücker, Sir Arthur William (1848-1915). Eng. physicist.
Chambers—Dict. col.389-390
Hammerton p1171

Rudbeck, Olof (or Olaus) (1630-1702). Swed. anatomist, botanist, physician.
Chambers—Dict. col.390
Lindroth—Swedish p33-41
Major—Hist. (1) p557

Rudnick, Dorothea (1907-   ). Amer. embryologist.
Yost—Women Mod. p156-170
  (por.,front.)

Rudolf, Christoff (c.1500). Ger. mathematician.
Chambers—Dict. col.390
Smith—Hist. 1 p328-329

Ruedemann, Rudolf (1864-1956). Amer. paleontologist, geologist.
G.S.A.—Proc. '57 p153-157 (por.153)

Rueff, Jacob (c.1500). Swiss physician, surgeon.
Leonardo—Lives (Supp.1)   p508
Major—History (1) p468

Ruel, Johannes Jean de la (or Ruellius) (1479-1537). Fr. physician, botanist.
Arber—Herbals p116
Major—History (1) p465

Ruff, Otto (1871-1939). Ger. chemist.
Partington—Short p355

Ruffer, Marc Armand (1859-1916/1917). Eng. bacteriologist, physician.
Bulloch—Hist. p394
Major—History (2) p1047-1048

Rufus of Ephesus (or Rouphos, Ruphos) (fl.c.100). Gr. physician, anatomist.

Castiglioni—Hist. p215
Gordon—Medicine p690-692

Leonardo—Lives p372-373
Major—History (1) p182-185

Ruhmkorff, Heinrich Daniel (1803-1877). Ger. inventor, physicist.

Chambers—Dict. col.390
Hammerton p1171

Radio's 100 p52-53

Rumford, Sir Benjamin Thompson, Count (or Thompson, Benjamin, Count Rumford) (1753-1814). Amer.-Brit. physicist.

A.A.A.S.—Proc. (82) p253-289
Ball—Short p430
*Book—Pop. Sci. (15) p5069-5070
  (por.5069)
Chalmers—Historic p273-274
Chambers—Dict. col.390-391
  (por.391)
*Darrow—Masters p340
Gregory—British p31 (por.30)
Guinagh—Inspired p29-41
Hammerton p1172
Hammond—Stories p23-48
Hart—Physicists p124-127
*Hylander—Scien. p11-21
Jaffe—Men p52-77 (por.xxviii)

Jordan—Leading p9-50 (por., front.)
Killeffer—Eminent p2 (por.2)
Lenard—Great p170-175 (por.176)
*Lewellen—Boy p165-188 (por.165)
Magie—Source p146
Major—History (2) p639 (por.619)
Moulton—Auto. p240
*Shippen—Design p155-164
Smith—Torch. p222 (por.222)
Stevens—Science p67-71 (por.66)
Trattner—Arch. p121-143 (por.134)
Van Wagenen—Beacon p202-204
Williams—Story p26-27 (por.25)
Wilson—Amer. p24-31 (por.24)
Woodruff—Devel. p290
Year—Pic. p104 (por.104)

Rumpf, Georg Eberhard (c.1628-1702). Ger. naturalist.

Reed—Short p92-93

Rumpler, Edmund (1872-1940). Ger. engineer, aero. pioneer.

Curr. Biog. '40 p699-700

Rumsey, James (1743-1792). Amer. inventor, engineer.

Chambers—Dict. col.391
Hylander—Invent. p199

Rumsey, William Earl (1865-1928). Amer. entomologist.

Osborn—Fragments p200

Runge, Carl David Tolmé (1856-1927). Ger. mathematician, physicist.

Chambers—Dict. col.392
Hammerton p1172

Runge, Friedlieb Ferdinand (1795-1867). Ger. chemist.

Chambers—Dict. col.392

Runkle, John Daniel (1822-1902). Amer. mathematician, astronomer.

Smith—Math. p132

Ruphos.   See **Rufus of Ephesus**

Rusby, Henry Hurd (1855-1940). Amer. botanist, sci. explorer.
Curr. Biog. '41 p742-743 (por.743)

Ruschenberger, William W. S. (1807-1895). Amer. physician.
Major—History (2) p769-770

Rusconi, Mauro (1776-1849). It. anatomist, embryologist.
Castiglioni—Hist. p678

Rush, Benjamin (1745-1813). Amer. physician.
Atkinson—Magic p195-201
Bell—Early p72-74
Carmer—Caval. p191-194 (por.192)
Castiglioni—Hist. p622 (por.622)
Chymia (4) p37-77 (por.,front.)
Fabricant—Why p106-107
Flexner—Doctors p57-117 (por.57)
Hammerton p1172
Major—History (2) p724-730 (por.725)
Rosen—Four p56-59,154-162

Rushmore, David Barker (1873-1940). Amer. elec. engineer.
Curr. Biog. '40 p700

Rusk, Howard Archibald (1899/1901-   ). Amer. physician.
Curr. Biog. '46 p527-529 (por.527)
Rowntree—Amid p529,530-534 (por.530)

Rusk, Jeremiah McLain (1830-1893). Amer. agriculturist.
*Ivins—Fifty p365-371 (por.364)

Russell, Bertrand Arthur William, 3rd Earl Russell (b.1872). Eng. mathematician.
Chambers—Dict. col.392
Curr. Biog. '51 p542-545 (por.544)
Hammerton p1173 (por.1173)
Newman—What p3-5
Untermeyer—Makers p450-457
Year—Pic. p202 (por.202)

Russell, Sir Edward John (b.1872). Eng. agriculturist.
Hammerton p1174

Russell, Elizabeth Shull (1913-   ). Amer. zoologist, geneticist.
Yost—Women Mod. p48-63 (por.,front.)

Russell, Harry Luman (1866-1954). Amer. bacteriologist.
Grainger—Guide p170-171

Russell, Henry Norris (1877-1957). Amer. astronomer.

Armitage—Cent. p204-208 (por.176)
Chambers—Dict. col.392-393
MacPherson—Makers p182-184

N.A.S.—Biog. (32) p354-362
(por.354)
R.S.L.—Biog. (3) p173-185 (por.173)

Russell, John Scott (1808-1882). Scot. engineer.

Hammerton p1174

Russom, Vaughn Walter (1891-1955). Amer. geologist.

G.S.A.—Proc. '55 p191

Russworm.   See **Gleichen, Wilhelm Friedrich**

Rutenberg, Pinhas (or Pinchas) (1879-1942). Rus. engineer.

Curr. Biog. '42 p727

Rutherford, Daniel (1749-1819). Scot. physician, chemist.

A.A.A.S.—Proc. (77) p50-51
Chambers—Dict. col.393

Oliver—Makers p290-291
Weeks—Discovery p87-89,106-118
(por.87)

Rutherford, Ernest, 1st Baron Rutherford of Nelson (1871-1937). New
Zeal. physicist.

*Book—Pop. Sci. (15) p5070-5071
(por.5071)
*Bridges—Master p228-236 (por.230)
Calder—Science p66-70,72
Chambers—Dict. col.393-394
(por.394)
*Darrow—Masters p340
Farber—Nobel p33-36 (por.118)
Gregory—British p39 (por.40)
Hammerton p1174 (por.1174)
Holmyard—British p76-77 (por.76)
*Larsen—Men p167-182
*Larsen—Scrap. p141-147 (por. 145)
Ludovici—Nobel p189-215 (por.212)

Moulton—Auto. p506-507
N.A.S.—Biog. (3) p415-441
Partington—Short p360-361 (por.359)
People p358,375
Radio's 100 p156-161 (por.140)
Riedman—Men p65-85 (por.72,73)
Schwartz—Moments (2) p934-935
*Science Miles. p280-285 (por.280)
*Shippen—Design p111-114
Smith—Torch. p223 (por.223)
Weeks—Discovery p495-496
(por.495)
Woodruff—Devel. p290 (por.66)
Year—Pic. p207,212 (por.212)

Rutherford, John (1695-1779). Scot. physician.

Weeks—Discovery p106-107

Rutherford, Lewis Morris (1816-1892). Amer. astronomer.

Woodruff—Devel. p68,90,290

Rutten, Louis Martin Robert (1884-1946). Dutch geologist.

G.S.A.—Proc. '46 p217-223 (por.217)

Rutty, John (1698-1775). Eng. physician.

Major—History (2) p633

Ruysch, Fredrik (1638-1731). Dutch anatomist, biologist.
Major—History (1) p559-560

Ruzicka, Leopold W. G. (1887-   ). Swiss chemist.
Chambers—Dict. col.394-395
Farber—Nobel p162-165 (por.118)

Ryan, Harris Joseph (1866-1934). Amer. elec. engineer.
N.A.S.—Biog. (19) p285-301
  (por.285)

Ryan, Tubal Lee, Jr. (1898-   ). Amer. aero. pioneer.
Curr. Biog. '43 p655-657 (por.655)

Rydberg, Johannes Robert (1854-1919). Swed. physicist.
Chambers—Dict. col.396
Lindroth—Swedish p214-218

Ryff, Walter Hermann (c.1545). Ger. physician.
Major—History (1) p465-466

S

Sabatier, Paul (1854-1941). Fr. chemist.
Chambers—Dict. col.397   Partington—Short p321
Curr. Biog. '41 p745   Smith—Torch. p224 (por.224)
Farber—Nobel p52-56 (por.118)

Sabatier, Raphael-Bienvenu (1732-1811). Fr. surgeon.
Leonardo—Lives p373-374

Sabin, Albert Bruce (1906-   ). Pol. pathologist, bacteriologist.
Curr. Biog. '45 p527-529 (por.528)
Progress—Science '41 p355-356
  (por.356)

Sabin, Florence Rena (1871-1953). Amer. physician, anatomist.
Curr. Biog. '45 p527-529 (por.528)   N.A.S.—Biog. (34) p271-305 (por.271)
  '53 p551   16 Amer. p41-44
Lovejoy—Women p109,126 (por.126)   Yost—Women p62-79

Sabine, Sir Edward (1788-1883). Eng. astronomer, physicist.
Chambers—Dict. col.397
Hammerton p1176

Sablière. See **La Sablière, Marguerite de**
Bulloch—Hist. p394

Sachs, Bernard (1858-1944). Amer. neurologist.
Curr. Biog. '44 p575

Sachs, Hans (b.1877). Ger. bacteriologist.
Bulloch—Hist. p394

Sachs, Julius von (1832-1897). Ger. botanist.
Chambers—Dict. col.397-398
*Snyder—Biology p311-312 (por.312)

Sacrobosco, Johannes de (or John of Holywood or of Halifax). Eng.
mathematician.
Ball—Short p174
Smith—Hist. I p221-222

Sadi-Carnot. See **Carnot, (Nicolas Léonard) Sadi**

Sadler, James (1751-1828). Eng. aero. pioneer.
Burge—Ency. p638-639
Gunther—Early XI p311-313
(por.312)

Sadler, William Windham (1796-1824). Eng. aero. pioneer.
Burge—Ency. p639

Safford, James Merrill (1822-1907). Amer. geologist.
Merrill—First p437-438 (por.112)

Sage, Balthasar-Georges (1740-1824). Fr. chemist.
Weeks—Discovery p71 (por.71)

Saha, Meghnad (1893-1956). Ind. astrophysicist.
R.S.L.—Biog. (5) p217-230 (por.217)

Sahli, Hermann (1856-1923). Swiss physician.
Kagan—Modern p17 (por.17)
Major—History (2) p971

Saint-Come, Frère Jean de (or Jean Baseilhac) (1703-1781). Fr. surgeon.
Leonardo—Lives p135-136

Saint Exupéry, Antoine de (1900-1944). Fr. aero. pioneer.
Curr. Biog. '45 p529

St. Fond.   See **Faujas de Saint-Fond, Barthélemy de**

St. Hilaire.   See **Geoffroy Saint-Hilaire**

St. Hildegard.   See **Hildegard of Bingen, Saint**

St. John, Charles Edward (1857-1935). Amer. astronomer.
N.A.S.—Biog. (18) p285-297
  (por.285)

St. Sebastian.   See **Sebastian, St.**

Saint Venant.   See **Barré de St.-Venant, A.J.C.**

Sainte-Claire-Deville.   See **Deville, Charles Sainte-Claire**

Sakel, Manfred Joshua (1906-1958). Aust. physician, psychiatrist.
Curr. Biog. '41 p747-748 (por.747)
Ratcliffe—Modern p128-131

Saladino Di Ascoli (fl.c.1450). It. physician.
Castiglioni—Hist. p372

Salaman, Redcliffe Nathan (1874-1955). Eng. physician, pathologist.
R.S.L.—Biog. (1) p239-243 (por.239)

Saleeby, Caleb Williams (b.1878). Eng. physician.
Hammerton p1179-1180

Saliceto (or Saliceti).   See **William of Saliceto**

Salisbury, Rollin D. (1858-1922). Amer. geologist.
*Book—Pop. Sci. (10) p3300-3301

Salk, Jonas Edward (1914-   ). Amer. physician, virologist.
Chambers—Dict. Supp.   Rowntree—Amid p544-549
Curr. Biog. '54 p551-553   *Stirling—Polio p70,78-97 por.79,92)

Salmon, Daniel Elmer (1850-1914). Amer. vet. pathologist.
Bulloch—Hist. p394

Salmon, George (1879-1904). Irish mathematician.
Smith—Hist. I p462

Salmon, Thomas W. (1876-1927). Amer. psychiatrist.
Farmer——Doctors' p218
Tobey—Riders p299-301

Salomonsen, Carl Julius (1847-1924). Dan. bacteriologist.
Bulloch—Hist. p394-395

Salter, Alfred (1873-1945). Brit. physician.
Curr. Biog. '45 p530

Salter, Andrew (1914-   ). Amer. psychologist.
Curr. Biog. '44 p579-581 (por.580)

Salvin, Osbert (1835-1898). Eng. entomologist.
Osborn—Fragments p173

Samson, Charles Rumney (1883-1931). Eng. aero. pioneer.
Burge—Ency. p639

Samuel, Mar (or Yarchanai, Samuel, or Marsamuel ben Abba ha Cohen)
(160/165-257) Babyl. physician, astronomer.
Gordon—Medicine p758-787

Sanctorius, Sanctorius (or Santorio, Santorio) (1561-1636). It. physician.
Castiglioni—Hist. p536-537
Chambers—Dict. col.398
*Elwell—Sci. p36-38
Gordon—Medieval p645-646
Major—History (1) p484-488
(por.485)
*Shippen—Men p97-99
Sigerist—Great p151-156 (por.152)
Year—Pic. p82 (por.82)

Sander, Bruno (1884-   ). Aust. geologist.
G.S.A.—Proc. '57 p71-72 (por.71)

Sanders, James Glossberger (1880-   ). Amer. entomologist.
Osborn—Fragments p200-201
(por.366)

Sanderson, (Ezra) Dwight (1878-1944). Amer. entomologist.
Osborn—Fragments p225-226

Sanderson, Ivan T. (1911-   ). Scot. naturalist.
Von Hagen—Green p378

Sanderson, John Scott Burdon (1828-1905). Eng. pathologist, physiologist.
Bulloch—Hist. p395

Sandifort, Edward (1740-1819). Dutch physician.
Major—Hist (2) p637-638

Sands, Henry Berton (1830-1888). Amer. surgeon.
Leonardo—Lives p377-378

Sanford, Oliver Nason (b.1847). Amer. entomologist.
Essig—Hist. p747-748 (por.748)

Sänger, Eugen (1905-   ). Bohem. engineer, rocket pioneer.
Gartmann—Men p99-113 (por.112)

San Martin.   See **Grau San Martin, Ramon**

Santo, Mariano (or Marianus Sanctus de Berletta) (c.1490-c1555). It.
surgeon.
Leonardo—Lives p378

Santorini, Giovanni Domenico (1681-1737). It. physician, anatomist.
Major—History p631

Santorio.   See **Sanctorius, Sanctorius**

Santos-Dumont, Alberto (1873-1932). Brazil. aero. pioneer, inventor.
Burge—Ency. p639   Hammerton p1185
*Cohen—Men p48-52,75,137-139   Heinmuller—Man's p259 (por.259)

Sappey, Marie Philibert (1810-1896). Fr. physician.
Major—History (2) p881-882

Sarapion.   See **Serapion of Alexandria**

Sarconi, Michele (1731-1797). It. physician, seismologist.
Davison—Founders p29-30

Sargent, Charles Sprague (1841-1927).
N.A.S.—Biog. (12) p247-258
(por.247)

Sarnoff, David (1891-   ). Rus. engineer.
*White—Famous (3d) p261-270
(por.259)
Year—Pic. p243 (por.243)

Sarton, George Alfred Léon (1884-1956). Belg. chemist.
Curr. Biog. '42 p734-735 (por.734)   Schwartz—Moments (1) p103-104
Major—History (2) p995

Sarzec, Ernest de (1836-1901). Fr. archaeologist.
Ceram—Gods p301-302

Satyrus (2d cent.). Gr. physician.
Gordon—Medicine p497

Sauerbronn, Karl Drais, Baron von (or Ludwig, Karl Friedrich Christian
Drais) (1785-1851). Ger. inventor.
*Larsen—Prentice p70-73

Saunders, William (1822-1900). Scot.-Amer. agriculturist.
*Ivins—Fifty p155-165 (por.157)

Saunders, William (1836-1914). Can. entomologist.
Osborn—Fragments p164-165
(por.350)

Saunderson, Nicholas (1682-1739). Eng. mathematician.
Smith—Hist. 1 p454 (por.455)

Saussure, Henri Louis Frederic de (1829-1905). Swiss entomologist.
Essig—Hist. p748-750 (por.749)

Saussure, Horace Bénédict de (1740-1799). Swiss physicist, geologist.
A.A.A.S.—Proc. (77) p36-37   Geikie—Founders p84-93
Adams—Birth p387-393   Hammerton p1187
Chambers—Dict. col.398   Woodruff—Devel. 290

Saussure, Nicholas Théodore de (1767-1845). Swiss botanist, chemist,
naturalist, biologist.
Bodenheimer—Hist. p345   Woodruff—Devel. p290-291
*Snyder—Biology p308-309

Sauvages, François Boissier de (1706-1767). Fr. physician.
Oliver—Stalkers p137-138

Sauveur, Albert (1863-1939). Belg.-Amer. metallurgist, metallographer.
N.A.S.—Biog. (22) p121-125
(por.121)

Sauveur, Joseph (1653-1716). Fr. mathematician.
Magie—Source p119

Savage, John Lucian (b.1879). Amer. engineer.
Curr. Biog. '43 p665-667 (por.665)

Savage, Thomas Edmund (1866-1947). Amer. geologist.
G.S.A.—Proc. '47 p173-174 (por.173)

Savart, Felix (1791-1841). Fr. physicist, physician.
Chambers—Dict. col.398-399
Magie—Source p441

Savery, Thomas (1650?-1715). Eng. engineer, inventor.
Hammerton—p1188   *Hartman—Mach. p55-56
Hart—Engineers p66-70

Savile, Sir Henry (1549-1622). Eng. mathematician.
Gunther—Early XI p45-46 (por.46)

Savitsch, Eugene de (1903-   ). Rus. physician, surgeon.
Fabricant—Why p137-139

Savonarola, Giovanni Michele (d.1440). It. physician.
Major—History (1) p355

Sawin, Martha A. (1815-1859). Amer. physician.
Mead—Medical p45

Sax, Adolphe Antoine Joseph (1814-1894). Belg. inventor.
*Larsen—Shaped p188-191 (por.176)

Saxton, Joseph (1799-1873). Amer. inventor.
N.A.S.—Biog. (1) p287-316

Saxtorph, Matthias (1740-1800). Dan. physician.
Copen.—Prom. p68-71

Say, Thomas (1787-1834). Amer. entomologist.
Bell—Early p74-75   Peattie—Green p253-255,258-259,
Essig—Hist. p750-756 (por.752)   260 (por.245)
Jaffe—Men p130-153 (por.xxviii)   Youmans—Pioneers p215-222
Osborn—Fragments p24-25 (por.337)   (por.215)

Sayers, J. (1913-   ). Brit. physicist.
Chambers—Dict. col.399

Sayles, Robert Wilcox (1878-1942). Amer. geologist.
Curr. Biog. '42 p737
G.S.A.—Proc. '43 p229-231 (por.228)

Sayre, Lewis Albert (1820-1900). Amer. surgeon.
Leonardo—Lives p378-380

Scaliger, Joseph Justus (1540-1609). Fr. chronologist.
Chambers—Dict. col.399
Hammerton p1190 (por.1190)

Scaliger, Julius Caesar (1484-1558). It.-Fr. physician.
Hammerton p1190
Weeks—Discovery p236-237 (por.236)

Scarlett, Francis Rowland (1875-1934). Eng. aero. pioneer.
Burge—Ency. p639

Scarpa, Antonio (1752?-1832). It. anatomist, physician.
Castiglioni—Hist. p601
Hammerton p1190
Leonardo—Lives p380-383
Major—History (2) p638-639

Schaefer, Vincent Joseph (1906-   ). Amer. chemist, meteorologist.
Curr. Biog. '47 p553-555 (por.553)

Schamberg, Jay Frank (1870-1934). Amer. dermatologist.
Kagan—Modern p79 (por.79)

Scharlieb, Dame Mary Dacomb (1845-1930). Eng. surgeon.
Hammerton p1191 (por.1191)

Schattenfroh, Artur (1869-1923). Aust. bacteriologist, hygienist.
Bulloch—Hist. p395

Schaudinn, Fritz Richard (1871-1906). Ger. zoologist.
Chambers—Dict. col. 399-400
*DeKruif—Men p207-228 (por.220)
Locy—Biology p303-304 (por.304)
Major—History (2) p930-931 (por.931)

Schaus, William (1859-1942). Amer. entomologist.
Osborn—Fragments p234 (por.359)

Scheele, Karl Wilhelm (1742-1786). Swed. chemist.
Chalmers—Historic p271-272
Chambers—Dict. col.400
*Darrows—Masters p33-35
Hammerton p1191
Holmyard—Chem. p90
Holmyard—Makers p186-189
Lenard—Great p140-144 (por.144)
Lindroth—Swedish p141-150
Major—History (2) p615-616
Partington—Short p104-109,151 (por.106)
Roberts—Chem. p32-40
(*Continued*)

Scheele, Karl Wilhelm—*Continued*
Robinson—Path. p265-281
(por.270,271)
Schwartz—Moments (1) p461-463
Smith—Torch. p225 (por.225)
Sootin—Twelve p29-46

Tilden—Famous p53-62 (por.53)
Van Wagenen—Beacon p177-178
Weeks—Discovery p99,102
(por.99,123)
Year—Pic. p103

Scheele, Leonard Andrew (1907-   ). Amer. physician, surgeon.
Curr. Biog. '48 p557-560 (por.558)

Scheffer, Henric Theophil (1710-1759). Swed. chemist, mineralogist.
Weeks—Discovery p243

Scheiner, Christopher (1575/1579-1650). Ger. inventor, astronomer.
Gordon—Medieval p698
Walsh—Catholic (20) p197-198,206

Scheiner, Julius (1858-1913). Ger. astronomer, astrophysicist.
MacPherson—Astron. p234-239
(por.234)

Schelling, Friedrich Wilhelm Joseph von (1775-1854). Ger. nat.
philosopher.
Major—History (2) p698-700
Osborn—Greeks p154-156

Schenck von Grafenburg, Johann (1530/1531-1598). Ger. physician.
Gordon—Medieval p758
Major—History (1) p474

Schereschewsky, Joseph Williams (1873-1940). Amer. physician.
Curr. Biog. '40 p719

Scheubel, Johann (1494-1570). Ger. mathematician.
Smith—Hist. I p329

Schiaparelli, Giovanni Virginio (1835-1910). It. astronomer.
Abetti—History p223-226
(por. 146 (27))
Armitage—Cent. p89,92-94,101-103,
129 (por.80)
*Book—Pop. Sci. (15) p5170-5172
Chambers—Dict. col.400
Hammerton p1191

MacPherson—Astron. p51-61
(por.51)
MacPherson—Makers p189-194
(por.106)
Shapley—Astron. p380 (por.382)
Williams—Great p331 (por.331)

Schichau, Ferdinand (1814-1896). Ger. engineer.
Hammerton p1191

Schick, Béla (b.1877). Hung.-Amer. bacteriologist, pediatrician.
Bulloch—Hist. p395   Law—Civiliz. p336-337
Curr. Biog. '44 p599-600 (por.600)

Schiff, Moriz (1823-1896). Ger. physiologist, biologist.
Kagan—Modern p184 (por.184)

Schilder, Paul Ferdinand (1886-1940). Aust.-Amer. psychiatrist.
Curr. Biog. '41 p756
Kagan—Modern p72 (por.72)

Schildhauer, Clarence (1896-   ). Amer. aero. pioneer.
Heinmuller—Man's p336 (por.336)

Schilt, C. Frank (1895-   ). Amer. aero. pioneer.
Maitland—Knights p272-275

Schimmelbusch, Curt (1860-1895). Ger. pathologist, surgeon.
Bulloch—Hist. p395

Schimper, Andreas Franz Wilhelm (1856-1901). Ger. botanist.
Bodenheimer—Hist. p443
Chambers—Dict. col.400-401

Schindler, John Albert (1903-1957). Amer. physician.
Curr. Biog. '56 p551-553 (por.552)

Schiödte, Jörgen Christian (1815-1884). Dan. zoologist.
Copen.—Prom. p124-127

Schlatter, Carl (1864-1934). Swiss surgeon.
Leonardo—Lives p383-384

Schlee, Edward F. (1890-   ). Amer. aero. pioneer.
Heinmuller—Man's p325 (por.325)

Schleiden, Johann (1804-1881). Ger. botanist.
Bodenheimer—Hist. p381
Castiglioni—Hist. p675
Locy—Biology p242-244 247-248
  (por.246)
Major—History (2) p796,880
Reed—Short p136
Robinson—Path. p396-411 (por.406)
*Shippen—Micro. p145-148
*Snyder—Biology p64-67 (por.65)
Thomson—Great p80-81
Williams—Story p331-332,343-345
  (por.330)
Woodruff—Devel. p291

Schlesinger, Frank (1871-1943). Amer. astronomer.
Curr. Biog. '43 p671
N.A.S.—Biog. '47 p105-124
(por. 105)

Schliemann, Heinrich (1822-1890). Ger. archaeologist.
Ceram—Gods p29-55   Hammerton p1193 (por.1193)
Guinagh—Inspired p115-129   People p376

Schlink, Frederick John (1891-   ). Amer. physicist, engineer.
Curr. Biog. '41 p756-758 (por.757)

Schmelkes, Franz Carl (1899-1942). Czech. chemist.
Curr. Biog. '43 p671

Schmidt, Bernhard (1879-1935). Ger. astronomer.
Chambers—Dict. col.401

Schmidt, Johann Friedrich Julius (1825-1884). Ger. astronomer.
Chambers—Dict. col.402   Hammerton p1193
Davison—Founders p129-130   MacPherson—Makers p185-187

Schmidt, Johannes (1877-1933). Dan. biologist.
Chambers—Dict. col.401-402

Schmiedeberg, Johann Ernst (1838-1921). Rus. pharmacologist.
Major—History (2) p900

Schmucker, Johann Leberecht (1712-1786). Ger. surgeon.
Leonardo—Lives p385

Schneider, Charles Prosper Eugène (1868-1942). Fr. engineer.
John Fritz p122-127 (por.124)

Schneider, Conrad Victor (1610-1680). Ger. physician.
Major—History (1) p555

Schneirla, Theodore Christian (1902-   ). Amer. psychologist.
..Curr. Biog. '55 p534-535 (por.535)

Schomburgk, Moritz Richard (1811-1891). Ger. botanist, naturalist.
Cutright—Great p20-22

Schönbein, Christian Friedrich (1799-1868). Ger. chemist.
A.A.A.S.—Proc. (77) p50   Hammerton p1193
Chambers—Dict. col.402   Smith—Torch. p228 (por.228)

Schöner, Johann (1477-1547). Ger. astronomer, geographer.
Smith—Hist. I p335

Schönfeld, Eduard (1828-1891). Ger. astronomer.
Hammerton p1194
MacPherson—Makers p187-189

Schönlein, Johann Lukas (1793-1864). Ger. physician, pathologist.
Bulloch—Hist. p395-396   Sigerist—Great p311-315 (por.312)
Major—History (2) p793-796
(por.794)

Schoolcraft, Henry Rowe (1793-1864). Amer. ethnologist, geologist,
naturalist.
Merrill—First p62-69 (por.63)
Youmans—Pioneers p300-310
(por.300)

Schooten, Van, family (16th, 17th cent. math.) Dutch mathematicians.
Smith—Hist. 1 p425

Schöpf, Johann David (1752-1800). Ger.-Amer. geologist, physician,
surgeon.
Merrill—First p4-6 (por.4)

Schorlemmer, Carl Wilhelm (1834-1892). Ger.-Eng. chemist.
Partington—Short p316
Smith—Torch. p229 (por.229)

Schott, Charles Anthony (1826-1901). Ger.-Amer. engineer, geodesist.
N.A.S.—Biog. (8) p87-115 (por.87)

Schottelius, Max (1849-1919). Ger. pathologist, bacteriologist, hygienist.
Bulloch—Hist. p396

Schotten, Carl Ludwig (1853-1910). Ger. chemist.
Smith—Torch. p231 (por.231)

Schottmüller, Hugo (1867-1936). Ger. physician, bacteriologist.
Bulloch—Hist. p396

Schouw, Joakim Frederik (1789-1852). Dan. botanist.
Copen.—Prom. p100-103

Schrader, Frank Charles (1860-1944). Amer. geologist.
G.S.A.—Proc. '45 p259-268 (por.259)

Schreyber.   See Grammateus, Henricus

Schriever, Bernard A. (1910-   ). Ger.-Amer. engineer, aero. pioneer.
Curr. Biog. '57 p497-498 (por.497)   Thomas—Men (3) p.xiv
Thomas—Men p47-65 (por.140,folio)

Schröder, Heinrich Georg Friedrich (1810-1885). Ger. bacteriologist.
Bulloch—Hist. p396

Schrödinger, Erwin (1887-   ). Aust. physicist.
Chambers—Dict. col. 402-403   Weber—College p541 (por.541)
Heathcote—Nobel p313-323 (por.240)   Year—Pic. p211 (por.211)
Moulton—Auto. p551

Schroeder, Rudolph William (1886-   ). Amer. aero. pioneer.
Curr. Biog. '41 p761-762 (por.761)
Heinmuller—Man's p310 (por.310)

Schroeter, Joseph (1835-1894). Ger. physician.
Bulloch—Hist. p396

Schröter, Johann Hieronymus (1745-1816). Ger. astronomer.
MacPherson—Makers p124-127

Schuchert, Charles (1858-1942). Amer. paleontologist, geologist.
Curr. Biog. '43 p676   N.A.S.—Biog. (27) p363-375
G.S.A.—Proc. '42 p217 (por.217)   (por.363)

Schuh, Franz (1804-1865). Aust. surgeon.
Leonardo—Lives p386-387

Schultes, Johann (1595-1645). It. physician.
Major—Hist. (1) p553

Schultz, Alfred Reginald (1876-1943). Amer. geologist.
G.S.A.—Proc. '44 p299-303
(por.299)

Schultz, Gustav Theodor August Otto (1851-1928). Ger. chemist.
A.A.A.S.—Proc. (79) p35-37

Schultze, Max Joseph Sigismund (1825-1874). Ger. anatomist, biologist.
*Locy—Biology p172,272-274,285-286   *Snyder—Biology p76-77 (por.77)
(por.273)   Van Wagenen—Beacon p342-343
*Shippen—Micro. p149-157   Woodruff—Devel. p244,291

Schulze, Franz (1815-1873). Ger. agric. chemist, bacteriologist.
Bulloch—Hist. p396

Schumacher, Heinrich Christian (1780-1850). Dan. astronomer.
Copen.—Prom. p94-96

Schuster, Sir Arthur (1851-1934). Brit. physicist.
A.A.A.S.—Proc. (79) p37-39
Hammerton p1196

Schutz, (Johann) Wilhelm (1839-1920). Ger. vet. pathologist.
Bulloch—Hist. p396

Schützenberger, Paul (1827/1829-1897). Fr. chemist.
Chambers—Dict. col.403   Weeks—Discovery p457 (por.433)
Smith—Torch. p231 (por.231)

Schwabe, Heinrich Samuel (1789-1875). Ger. astronomer.
Armitage—Cent. p50   MacPherson—Makers p134-136
Chambers—Dict. col.403   Shapley—Astron. p221
Hammerton p1196   Williams—Great p415-418

Schwann, Theodor (1810-1882). Ger. naturalist, physiologist, biologist.
Bodenheimer—Hist. p384   *Shippen—Micro. p141-148
Bulloch—Hist. p396-397   *Snyder—Biology p67-69 (por.65)
Chambers—Dict. col.404   Thomson—Great p80-81
Hammerton p1196   Trattner—Arch. p189-210 (por.199)
Locy—Biology p171,244-246,249-250,   Walsh—Makers p251-268
  285-287 (por.245)   Williams—Story p331-338,343-345,
Major—History (2) p796-797   376,404 (por.377)
Moulton—Auto. p326-327   Woodruff—Devel. p291 (por.248)
Robinson—Path. p389-396 (por.407)   Year—Pic. p125,126,127 (por.125)
Schwartz—Moments (2) p558-560

Schwarz, David (1845-1897). Hung. aero. pioneer.
Heinmuller—Man's p256 (por.256)

Schwarz, Eugene Amandus (1844-1928). Ger.-Amer. entomologist.
Essig—Hist. p756-758 (por.756)
Osborn—Fragments p192-195
  (por. 346)

Schwarz, Hermann Amandus (1843/1845-1921). Ger. mathematician.
Cajori—Hist. p431

Schwarzschild, Karl (1873-1916). Ger. astronomer.
Armitage—Cent. p152 (por.144)

Schweigger, Johann Salomo Christoph (1779-1857). Ger. physicist.
Chambers—Dict. col. 404

Schweinitz, Lewis David von (1780-1834). Amer. botanist, mycologist.
Youmans—Pioneers p167-175
(por.167)

Schweitzer, Albert (1875-   ). Fr. physician.
Curr. Biog. '48 p564-567 (por.565)   Rosen—Four p44-50,119-122
Fabricant—Why p59-62   Rowntree—Amid p516-520
Hammerton p1197   (por.518,519)
Untermeyer—Makers p500-505

Schwidetzky, Oscar (Otto Rudolf) (b.1874). Pol. inventor.
Curr. Biog. '43 p676-677 (por.676)

Scot, Michael (1175?-1224?). Scot. physician.
Major—History (1) p322-323

Scott, Arthur Carroll (1865-1940). Amer. physician.
Curr. Biog. '40 p721

Scott, Charles William Anderson (1903-   ). Eng. aero. engineer.
Hammerton p1198

Scott, Charlotte Angas (1858-1931). Amer. mathematician.
Mozans—Woman p166

Scott, Dukinfield Henry (1854-1934). Eng. botanist.
Hammerton p1198

Scott, Gayle (1894-1948). Amer. geologist.
G.S.A.—Proc. '48 p207-209 (por.207)

Scott, George Herbert (1888-1930). Eng. aero. pioneer.
Burge—Ency. p639
Heinmuller—Man's p309 (por.309)

Scott, Irving Day (1877-1955). Amer. geologist.
G.S.A.—Proc. '57 p163-164 (por.163)

Scott, Kate Frances (1890-   ). Amer. physician.
Curr. Biog. '48 p571-573 (por.572)

Scott, Patrick (fl.1628/1623). Scot. chemist.
Chymia (1) p149

Scott, Robert Falcon (1868-1912). Eng. sci. explorer.
*Book—Pop. Sci. (14) p4823-4827   Hammerton p1198-1199
  (por.4824)   *Nisenson—More p127 (por.127)

Scott, William Berryman (1858-1947). Amer. geologist, paleontologist.
G.S.A.—Proc. '48 p211-220 (por.211)
N.A.S.—Biog. '49 p175-191 (por.175)

Scouler, John (1804-1871). Scot. physician, naturalist.
Alden—Early p37-38

Scribonius Largus (fl.1st cent.). Rom. physician.
Gordon—Medicine p634-635
Major—History (1) p167-168

Scriptor.   See **Grammateus, Henricus**

Scrope, George Julius Poulett (or Thomson) (1797-1876). Eng.
Williams—Story p124 (por. 141)
Woodruff—Devel. p291

Scudder, Ida Scudder (1870-1960). Amer. physician.
Knapp—Women p63-78 (por.63)
Lovejoy—Women p227-228
  (por.228)

Scudder, Samuel Hubbard (1837-1911). Amer. entomologist, naturalist.
Essig—Hist. p758-762 (por.759)   Osborn—Fragments p161-162
N.A.S.—Biog. (10) p81-86 (por.81)

Scultetus, Johannes (or Schulte) (1595-1645). Ger. surgeon.
Leonard—Lives p387-388

Seaborg, Glenn Theodore (1912-   ). Amer. phys. chemist.
Chambers—Dict. col.404 (por.403)   Morris—Ency. p713
Curr. Biog. '48 p573-575 (por.574)
  '61 (Dec.) (por.)

Seabury, David (1885-1960). Amer. psychologist.
Curr. Biog. '41 p765-767 (por.766)
  '60 p367

Seagrave, Gordon Stifler (1897?-   ). Amer. physician, surgeon.
Curr. Biog. '43 p681-683 (por.682)   Rosen—Four p218-222
Fabricant—Why p83-85

Seaman, Arthur Edmund (1858-1937). Amer. geologist.
G.S.A.—Proc. '37 p191-194 (por.191)

Searle, George Frederick Charles (1864-1954). Eng. physicist.
R.S.L.—Biog. (1) p247-250
(por.247)

Sears, Paul Bigelow (1891-   ). Amer. botanist.
Curr. Biog. '60 p367-369 (por.368)

Sears, Robert Richardson (1908-   ). Amer. psychologist.
Curr. Biog. '52 p522-523 (por.523)

Seashore, Carl Emil (1866-1949). Amer. psychologist.
N.A.S.—Biog. (29) p265-303
(por.265)

Sebastian, St. (3d cent.). Rom. physician.
Major—History (1) p341 (por.340)

Sebokht, Severus (fl.c.650). Pers. mathematician.
Smith—Hist. 1 p166-167

Sebrell, William Henry, Jr. (1901-   ). Amer. physician, surgeon.
Curr. Biog. '51 p557-559 (por.557)
Progress—Science '41 p358

Secchi, Angelo (1818-1878). It. astronomer.
Abetti—History p188-194
Armitage—Cent. p171-172 (por.144)
*Book—Pop. Sci. (15) p5172-5174
Chambers—Dict. col.405
Hammerton p1201
MacPherson—Makers p165-167
Shapley—Astron. p299
Walsh—Catholic (2d) p208-214
(por.209)

Sederholm, Jakob Johannes (1863-1934). Fin. geologist.
G.S.A.—Proc. '34 p259-263 (por.259)

Sedgwick, Adam (1785-1873). Eng. geologist.
*Book—Pop. Sci. (10) p3301-3302
(por.3301)
Chambers—Dict. col.405
Fenton—Giants p98-108 (por.94)
Geikie—Founders p256-267
Hammerton p1201-1202

Sedgwick, William Thompson (1855-1921). Amer. bacteriologist, pub.
health worker.
Grainger—Guide p171
Moulton—Auto. p446-447
16 Amer. p45-48
Tobey—Riders p221-250
Year—Pic. p135 (por.135)

Sédillot, Charles-Emmanuel (1804-1883). Fr. surgeon.
Bulloch—Hist. p397

Seebach, Albert Ludwig von (1839-1880). Ger. geologist, seismologist.
Davison—Founders p126-128

Seebeck, Thomas Johann (1770-1831). Ger. physicist.
Chambers—Dict. col.405
Magie—Source p461

Seeliger, Hugo (1849-1924). Ger. astronomer.
Armitage—Cent. p219
*Book—Pop. Sci. (15) p5174-5175
Chambers—Dict. col.405
Hammerton p1202
MacPherson—Astron. p179-184
(por.179)
MacPherson—Makers p217-219

Sefström, Nils Gabriel (1787-1845). Swed. physician, chemist, mineralogist.
Chambers—Dict. col.405-406
Weeks—Discovery p194-198,409
(por.194,409)

Ségelas (or Ségalas) **Pierre-Salamon** (1792-1875). Fr. surgeon.
Leonardo—Lives p388

Segré, Emilio Gino (1905-   ). It.-Amer. physicist.
Curr. Biog. '60 p369-371 (por.369)

Seifert, Florence Barbara (1897-   ). Amer. chemist.
Curr. Biog. '42 p750-752 (por.751)

Seifert, Richard (1861-1919). Ger. chemist.
Smith—Torch. p232 (por.232)

Seitz, Frederick (1911-   ). Amer. physicist.
Curr. Biog. '56 p563-564 (por.563)

Seki, Kowa (or Taka Kazu) (1642?-1708). Japan. mathematician.
Smith—Hist. I p439-440

Sekiya, Seikei (1855-1896). Japan. seismologist.
Davison—Founders p208-210

Selden, George Baldwin (1846-1922). Amer. inventor.
*Men—Scien. p16-18
Wilson—Amer. p320-327 (por.321)

Selfridge, Thomas E. (1882-1908). Amer. aero. pioneer.
Heinmuller—Man's p269 (por.269)

Selmi, Francesco (1817-1881). It. chemist.
Bulloch—Hist. p397

Selwyn, Alfred Richard Cecil (1824-1902). Can. geologist.
Merrill—First p445-446 (por.446)

Selye, Hans (or Hugo Bruno) (1907-   ). Aust. endocrinologist.
Curr. Biog. '53 p564-566 (por.565)
Robinson—10 p295-298 (por.295)

Selys-Lonechamps, Michel Edmond de (1813-1900). Fr. entomologist.
Essig—Hist. p762-764 (por.763)

Semenov, Nikolai N. (1896?-   ). Rus. phys. chemist.
Curr. Biog. '57 p498-500 (por.499)

Semmelweis, Ignatz Philipp (1818-1865). Hung. physician, obstetrician.
Atkinson—Magic p271-278
Castiglioni—Hist. p725-726 (por.725)
*DeKruif—Men p35-58 (por.44)
*Elwell—Sci. p55-56
*Fox—Great p121-144 (por.121)
Grainger—Guide p171-172
Hammerton p1201
Kagan—Modern p121 (por.121)
Lambert—Medical p239-240
Lambert—Minute p239-240
Leonardo—Lives p389-390
Major—History (2) p785-787
Robinson—Path. p623-647
 (por.638,646)
Sigerist—Great p354-359 (por.353)
Thorwald—Century p223,226-244
 (por.240)

Semon, Sir Felix (1849-1921). Brit. physician.
Hammerton p1204

Semon, Waldo Lonsbury (1898-   ). Amer. chemist.
Curr. Biog. '40 p723-724 (por.723)

Senac, Jean Baptiste (1693-1770). Fr. physician.
Major—History (2) p632-633

Senator, Herman (1834-1911). Pol. physician.
Major—History (2) p898

Senderens, Jean Baptiste (1856-1937). Fr. chemist.
Chambers—Dict. col.406

Senebier, Jean (1742-1809). Swiss naturalist.
Chambers—Dict. col.406
Reed—Short p108-109

Seneca, Lucius Annaeus (4 B.C.?-AD 65). Sp. naturalist.
Adams—Birth p47-48   Hammerton p1204 (por.1204)
Clagett—Greek p108-109 (por.108)

Senefelder, Alois (1771-1834). Ger. inventor.
Hammerton p1204 (por.1204)

Senemut (c.1500 B.C.). Egypt. engineer.
Matschoss—Great p7-8

Senn, Milton John Edward (1902-   ). Amer. physician, psychiatrist.
Curr. Biog. '50 p527-528

Senn, Nicholas (1844-1908). Swiss-Amer. surgeon.
Leonardo—Lives p390-391   Swiss—Prom. p127-131 (por.127)
Major—History (2) p1048 (por.953)

Sennert, Daniel (1572-1637). Ger. physician.
Major—History (1) p551

Sensenich, Roscoe Lloyd (1882-   ). Amer. physician.
Curr. Biog. '49 p558-559

Serapion, Senior (or Yuhanna ibn Sarabiun) (9th cent.). Arab. physician.
Castiglioni—Hist. p267   Major—History (1) p264
Gordon—Medieval p150-151

Serapion of Alexandria (c.220 B.C.). Alex. physician.
Gordon—Medicine p610

Sergievsky, Boris (1888-   ). Amer. aero. pioneer.
Heinmuller—Man's p338 (por.338)

Serres, Olivier de (1539-1619). Fr. agriculturist, naturalist, biologist.
Bodenheimer—Hist. p238
Miall—Early p93-98

Serret, Joseph Alfred (1819-1885). Fr. mathematician.
Cajori—Hist. p314

Sertürner, Friedrich Wilhelm Adam (1783-1841). Ger. chemist.

Chambers—Dict. col.406   *Montgomery—Story p142-146
Fülöp—Miller p72-79 (por.72)

Servetus, Michael (1511-1553). Sp. physician.

Castiglioni—Hist. p434-435 (por.433)   Lambert—Minute p121
Chambers—Dict. col.406   Major—History (1) p491 (por.489)
Gordon—Medieval p632-635   Oliver—Stalkers p77-79 (por.78)
Gordan—Romance p111-112   Robinson—Path. p69-81 (por.74)
Gumpert—Trail p67-98   Sarton—Six p189-191
Lambert—Medical p121   Year—Pic. p80

Serviss, Frederick LeVerne (1895-1954). Amer. geologist.

G.S.A.—Proc. '55 p193

Setchell, William Albert (1864-1943). Amer. botanist.

N.A.S.—Biog. (23) p127-135
(por. 127)

Seth, Simeon (or Symeon) (c.1075). Byzantine physician.

Major—History (1) p353

Seton, Ernest Thompson (1860-1946). Scot. naturalist.

Curr. Biog. '43 p685-688 (por.686)   Tracy—Amer. Nat. p233-243
'46 p544

Severinus, Marcus Aurelius (or Severino, Marco Aurelio) (1580-1656). It. anatomist, surgeon.

Locy—Biology p142-143 (por.142)   Woodruff—Devel. p234,291
Major—History (1) p552

Severinus. See also **Sörensen.**

Seward, Sara C. (d.1891). Amer. physician.

Lovejoy—Women p221

Seybert, Adam (1773-1825). Amer. chemist.

Smith—Chem. p150-151

S'Gravesande. See **Gravesande, Wilhelm Jacob Storm van s'**

Shackleton, Sir Ernest Henry (1874-1922). Irish sci. explorer.

*Book—Pop. Sci. (14) p4828-4830
(por. 4828)
Hammerton p1207 (por.1207)

Shaler, Millard K. (1880-1942). Amer. geologist.
G.S.A.—Proc. '44 p305-307 (por.305)

Shaler, Nathaniel Southgate (1841-1906). Amer. geologist.
Merrill—First p478 (por.478)

Shanks, W. (c.1870). Eng. mathematician.
Chambers—Dict. col.406-407

Shapiro, Harry Lionel (1902-   ). Amer. anthropologist.
Curr. Biog. '52 p530-533 (por.531)

Shapley, Harlow (1885-   ). Amer. astrophysicist, astronomer.
Armitage—Cent. p223-228 (por.176)
Chambers—Dict. col. 407 (por.407)
Curr. Biog. '41 p776-778 (por.777)
'52 p533-535 (por.534)
Fisher—Amer. p201-202 (por.200)
MacPherson—Makers p234-238 (por.210)
Progress—Science '40 p375 (por.375)
Williams—Great p366,462-464, 490, 503-505
Year—Pic. p218 (por.218)

Sharp, Harry Clay (1871-1940). Amer. physician.
Curr. Biog. '40 p729 (por.729)

Sharp, Samuel (1700?-1780). Eng. oculist, surgeon.
Leonardo—Lives p391

Sharpey, William (1802-1880). Scot. physician.
Major—History (2) p880

Sharpey-Schafer, Edward (1850-1935). Eng. physiologist.
Major—History (2) p962,1048

Shattock, Samuel George (1852-1924). Eng. pathologist.
Bulloch—Hist. p397

Shattuck, Frederick Cheever (1847-1929). Amer. physician.
Kagan—Modern p13 (por.13)

Shattuck, George Burbank (1869-1934). Amer. geologist.
G.S.A.—Proc. '34 p271-274 (por.271)

Shattuck, Lemuel (1793-1859). Amer. pub. health worker.
Walker—Pioneers p59-70 (por.59)

Shaw, Anna Howard (1847-1919). Eng.-Amer. physician.
Hyde—Modern p122-141   Webb—Famous p444-448 (por.440)
Lovejoy—Women p301

Shaw, Eugene Wesley (1881-1935). Amer. geologist.
G.S.A.—Proc. '35 p311-315 (por.311)

Shaw, Henry Larned Keith (1873-1941). Amer. pediatrician.
Curr. Biog. '41 p780

Shaw, Louis Agassiz (1886-1940). Amer. pub. health worker, physician.
Curr. Biog. '40 p729

Shaw, Ralph Robert (1907-   ). Amer. inventor.
Curr. Biog. '56 p570-572 (por.571)

Shaw, Sir William Napier (1854-1945). Eng. meteorologist.
Chambers—Dict. col.407-408

Shea, Andrew B. (1903-   ). Amer. aero. pioneer.
Curr. Biog. '57 p500-502 (por.501)

Shear, Theodore Leslie (1880-1945). Amer. archaeologist.
Curr. Biog. '45 p544

Shedd, Solon (1860-1941). Amer. geologist.
G.S.A.—Proc. '41 p187-190 (por.187)

Shelly, Mary Josephine (1902-   ). Amer. aero. pioneer.
Curr. Biog. '51 p568-570 (por.569)

Shepard, Alan Bartlett, Jr. (1923-   ). Amer. astronaut, aero. pioneer.
Curr. Biog. '61 (Dec.) (por.)
Thomas—Men (3) p182-207 (por.74)

Shepard, Charles Upham (1804-1886). Amer. geologist, mineralogist, chemist.
Merrill—First p181-182 (por.181)
Youmans—Pioneers p419-427
  (por.419)

Shepard, Edward Martin (1854-1934). Amer. geologist.
G.S.A.—Proc. '34 p277-279 (por.277)

Shepherd, Francis John (1851-1929). Can. surgeon.
Leonardo—Lives p392-393

Sherard, William (1658/1659-1728). Eng. botanist, ornithologist.
Gunther—Early XI p243-244

Sheriff, Hilla (1903-   ). Amer. physician.
Lovejoy—Women Phys. p189-197
(por.185)

Sherman, Harry Mitchell (1854-1921). Amer. surgeon.
Leonardo—Lives p393-394

Sherman, Henry Clapp (1875-1955). Amer. biochemist.
Chambers—Dict. col.408   Curr. Biog. '55 p549
Curr. Biog. '49 p565-566 (por.565)   Progress—Science '40 p376

Sherrill, Richard E. (1899-1952). Amer. geologist.
G.S.A.—Proc. '52 p149-151 (por.149)

Sherrington, Sir Charles Scott (1861-1952). Eng. physiologist.
Chambers—Dict. col.408   Ludovici—Nobel p216-226 (por.213)
Great Names p41-43 (por.40)   *Snyder—Biology p404-408 (por.404)
Hammerton p1216   Stevenson—Nobel p154-155,156-159
                              (por.150)

Shesta, John (1901-   ). Rus.-Amer. inventor.
*Williams—Rocket p186-191, 197-202

Shields, James P. (1890-1953). Amer. engineer.
Curr. Biog. '53 p569

Shiga, Kiyoshi (1870-1957). Japan. bacteriologist.
Bulloch—Hist. p397

Shimek, Bohumil (b.1861). Amer. geologist, botanist, paleobotanist.
G.S.A.—Proc. '38 p169-170 (por.169)

Shine, Francis Wayles (1874-1941). Amer. ophthalmologist.
Curr. Biog. '41 p785

Shipley, Sir Arthur Everett (1861-1927). Brit. geologist.
Hammerton p1216

Shippen, William, Jr. (1736-1808). Amer. physician, surgeon.
Leonardo—Lives p394-396
Major—History (2) p721-723
(por.722)

Shiras, George (1859-1942). Amer. naturalist.
Curr. Biog. '42 p761

Shlomoh.   See Gershon Ben-Shlomoh

Shockley, William (1890-1953). Amer. physicist.
Curr. Biog. '51 p569-571 (por.570)
    '53 p569

Sholes, Christopher Latham (1819-1890). Amer. inventor.
*Darrow—Thinkers p227-236
*Hylander—Invent. p109-116
    (por.116)
Iles—Leading p315-337 (por.315)
*Larsen—Scrap. p64-71 (por.64)
*Larsen—Shaped p101-110 (por.81)
Law—Civiliz. p128-131
Meyer—World p59-63 (por.59)
*Montgomery—Invent. p26-31
*Nida—Makers p152-159 (por.153)
*Patterson—Amer. p85-95

Shóu-King.   See Kóu Shóu-King

Shoulders, Harrison H. (1886-   ). Amer. physician.
Curr. Biog. '46 p554-556 (por.555)

Shreeve, Herbert Edward (1873-1942). Amer. inventor, engineer.
Curr. Biog. '42 p764-765

Shreve, Earl Owen (1881-   ). Amer. elec. engineer.
Curr. Biog. '47 p572-575 (por.573)

Shriner, Ralph L. (1899-   ). Amer. chemist.
Browne—Hist. p501 (por.399)

Shuler, Ellis William (1881-1954). Amer. geologist.
G.S.A.—Proc. '54 p133-136 (por.133)

Shull, George Harrison (1874-1954). Amer. agriculturist, botanist.
*DeKruif—Hunger p197-232 (por.196)

Shute, Nevil (or Norway, Nevil Shute) (1899-   ). Eng. aero. pioneer, engineer.
Curr. Biog. '42 p767-769 (por.768)
    '60 p380

Sibald, Sir Robert (1641-1722). Scot. physician.
Hammerton p1218

Sibthorp, John (1758-1796). Eng. botanist.
Gunther—Early XI p150-151

Siculus.   See **Didorus Siculus**

Sidgwick, Nevil Vincent (1873-1952). Eng. chemist.
Chambers—Dict. col.408-409

Siebert, Katharine Burr (1897-   ). Amer. physicist.
Yost—Women Sci. p177-195

Siebold, Charlotte (1761-1859). Ger. physician.
Lovejoy—Women p190-191

Siebold, Karl Kasper von (1736-1807). Ger. anatomist, obstetrician, surgeon.
Leonardo—Lives p396-397

Siebold, Karl Theodor Ernst von (1804-1885). Ger. zoologist.
Locy—Biology p131-135 (por.135)

Siegbahn, Karl Manne Georg (1886-   ). Swed. physicist.
Chambers—Dict. col.409   Lindroth—Swedish p280-291
Heathcote—Nobel p218-228 (por.240)   Weber—College p380 (por.380)

Siemens family (9th cent.). Ger.-Eng. engineers, inventors.
Hammerton p1220 (por.1220)

Siemens, (Ernest) Werner von (1816-1892). Ger. engineer, inventor.
*Book—Pop. Sci. (15) p5022-5023   Matschoss—Great p261-280
Hammerton p1220 (por.1220)   (por.280)

Siemens, Frederick S. (1823/1826-1904). Ger. engineer, inventor.
Hart—Engineers p129-132

Siemens, (Karl) Wilhelm (or William) (1823-1883). Ger.-Eng. engineer, inventor.
*Book—Pop. Sci. (15) p5023-5025   Goddard—Eminent p270-280
Chambers—Dict. col.409   (por.273)

Sigerist, Henry Ernest (1891-1957). Fr. medical writer.
Curr. Biog. '40 p732-733 (por.733)   Rosen—Four p139-142,292-294
Major—History (2) p993-994
(por.993)

Signoret, Victor Antoine (1816-1889). Fr. entomologist.
Essig—Hist. p764-765 (por.764)
Osborn—Fragments p230 (por.355)

Sikorsky, Igor Ivan (1889-   ). Rus.-Amer. aero. engineer.
Curr. Biog. '56 p576-578 (por.577)
'40 p734-736 (por.735)
Daniel—Pioneer p137-143 (por.136)..

Heinmuller—Man's p1-33,296
(por.22,296)
*Larsen—Shaped p142-160 (por.128)
*Shippen—Bridle p163-169

Silberrad, Oswald John (1878-1960). Eng. chemist.
Hammerton p1221

Sillcox, Lewis Katcham (1886-   ). Amer. engineer.
Curr. Biog. '54 p570-572 (por.571)

Silliman, Benjamin, Sr. (1779-1864). Amer. geologist, chemist, physicist.
*Book—Pop. Sci. (10) p3302-3303
(por.3303)
Fenton—Giants p133-136 (por.110)
Hammerton p1221
*Hylander—Scien. p22-28 (por.28)
Jordan—Leading p89-117 (por.89)
Killeffer—Eminent p3 (por.3)
Major—History (2) p768
Merrill—First p23-24 (por.24)

N.A.S.—Biog. (1) p99-112
Smith—Chem. p179-183,207-208
(por.206)
Van Wagenen—Beacon p235-237
Weeks—Discovery p303-304
(por.304)
Woodruff—Devel. p193,291
Youmans—Pioneers p140-151
(por.140)

Silliman, Benjamin, Jr. (1816-1885). Amer. agric. chemist, mineralogist.
N.A.S.—Biog. (7) p115-133
(por.115)

Silvertop, Henry.   See **Witham, Henry of Lurtington**

Simitière.   See **Du Simitière, Pierre E.**

Simmons, Gustavus Lincoln (1832-1910). Amer. physician.
Jones—Memories p323-333 (por.322)

Simon, Sir Frances (or Franz Eugen) (1893-1956). Eng. physicist.
R.S.L.—Biog. (4) p225-250 (por.225)

Simon, Gustav (1824-1876). Ger. surgeon.
Leonardo—Lives p397-398
Major—History (2) p888

Thorwald—Century p180-188,190-199

Simon, Sir John (1816-1904). Eng. physician, pub. health worker, surgeon.
Hale-White—Great p189-207
Leonardo—Lives p398-399

Walker—Pioneers p100-114 (por.100)

Simonds, Frederic William (1853-1941). Amer. geologist.
Curr. Biog. '41 p797
G.S.A. —Proc. '41 p193-197
(por.193)

Simons, David G. (1922-   ). Amer. physician.
Curr. Biog. '57 p506-508 (por.507)

Simonsen, John Lionel (1884-1957). Brit. chemist.
R.S.L.—Biog. (5) p237-246 (por.237)

Simplicius (6th cent.). Gr. nat. philosopher.
Clagett—Greek p176-177

Simpson, Sir George Clarke (b.1878). Eng. meteorologist.
*Bridges—Master p237-244 (por.238)
Chambers—Dict. col.410

Simpson, Howard Edwin (1874-1938). Amer. geologist.
G.S.A.—Proc. '38 p174-180 (por.174)

Simpson, Sir James Young (1811-1870). Scot. physician.
Chambers—Dict. col.410
*Elwell—Sci. p125-126
Farmer—Doctors' p126
Fülöp—Miller p328-345 (por.328)
Hale-White—Great p143-158
Hammerton p1222 (por.1222)
Kagan—Modern p120 (por.120)
Lambert—Minute p274-275
Leonardo—Lives p399-400
Major—History (2) p818-821
*Masters—Conquest p67-81 (por.70)
100 Great p604-609
Murray—Science p20-38
Robinson—Path. p521-551 (por.530)
Robinson—Victory p191-208
  (por.171)
*Snyder—Biology p294-297
Thorwald—Century p122-135,138-139,
  260,263-275 (por.80)

Simpson, Maxwell (1815-1902). Irish chemist.
Chymia (4) p159-170 (por.160)
Findlay—Hundred p335

Simpson, Thomas (1710-1761). Eng. mathematician.
Ball—Short p388-390
Chambers—Dict. col.410
Hammerton p1223
Smith—Hist. 1 p457

Sims, James Marion (1813-1883). Amer. physician, surgeon, gynecologist.
Castiglioni—Hist. p728 (por.727)
Fabricant—Why p44-46
*Faris—Men p34-45
Farmer—Doctors' p159
Hammerton p1223
Kagan—Modern p121 (por.121)
Leonardo—Lives (Supp.1) p508-510
Major—History (2) p761
Marr—Pioneer p1-62 (por.2,9)
Rosen—Four p34-36,76-79,171-178

Sims, Winfield Scott (1844-1918). Amer. inventor.
Hammerton p1223

Simson, Sir Henry John Forbes (1872-1932). Brit. obstetrician.
Hammerton p1223

Sinan ibn Thabit (860-943). Arab. physician.
Gordon—Medieval p151

Sinclair, William John (1877-1935). Amer. geologist.
G.S.A.—Proc. '38 p185-186 (por.185)

Singer, Isaac Merritt (1811-1875). Amer. inventor.
Hammerton p1224 (por.1224)   *Wildman—Famous (1st) p247-256
Law—Civiliz. p109-110   (por.245)
Meyer—World p71-75 (por.71)   Wilson—Amer. p134-135 (por.134)

Singer, (Siegfried) Fred (1924-   ). Aust.-Amer. physicist.
Curr. Biog. '55 p555-556
   (por.555)

Singstad, Ole (1882-   ). Norw.-Amer. engineer.
*Yost—Engineers p107-121

Sinnott, Edmund Ware (1888-   ). Amer. botanist.
Curr. Biog. '48 p583-585 (por.585)

Sinnott, John Alexander (1884-1956). Can.-Irish physician.
R.S.L.—Biog. (2) p269-281
   (por.269)

Siple, Paul Allman (1908-   ). Amer. biologist, sci. explorer.
Curr. Biog. '57 p512-514 (por.513)

Sisler, James Donaldson (1896-1935). Amer. geologist.
G.S.A.—Proc. '35 p319-321 (por.319)

Sitter, Willem de (1872-1934). Dutch astronomer.
Chambers—Dict. col.410-411
MacPherson—Makers p226-229

Skidmore, Louis (1897-   ). Amer. engineer.
Curr. Biog. '51 p589-592

Skinner, Charles Edward (1865-1950). Amer. elec. engineer.
Holland—Ind. p265-281 (por.265)

Skinner, Henry (1861-1926). Amer. entomologist.
Osborn—Fragments p186 (por.360)

Skoda, Joseph (1805-1881). Czech. physician.
Castiglioni—Hist. p711   Oliver—Stalkers p155 (por.156)
Chambers—Dict. col.411   Sigerist—Great p297-300 (por.297)
Major—History (2) p782-783

Skraup, Zdenko Hans (1850-1910). Czech. chemist.
A.A.A.S.—Proc. (78) p13-14
Smith—Torch. p233 (por.233)

Slaby, Adolph Karl Heinrich (1849-1913). Ger. physicist.
Radio's 100 p87-89 (por.140)

Slater, John Elliot (1891-   ). Amer. engineer.
Curr. Biog. '51 p593-595 (por.594)

Slater, Samuel (1768-1835). Eng.-Amer. inventor.
Hartman—Mach. p36-38

Slaughter, Frank Gill (1908-   ). Amer. physician.
Curr. Biog. '42 p772 (por.772)

Slemon, Charles Roy (1904-   ). Can. aero. pioneer.
Curr. Biog. '56 p582-583 (por.582)

Slingerland, Mark Vernon (1864-1909). Amer. entomologist.
Osborn—Fragments p203 (por.346)

Slipher, Vesto Melvin (1875-   ). Amer. astronomer.
Chambers—Dict. col.411
MacPherson—Makers p229-231

Sloane, Sir Hans (1660-1753). Brit. botanist, physician.
Hammond p1225 (por.1225)   Reed—Short p91-92
Hawks—Pioneers p213-219 (por.214)   Weeks—Discovery p185,209
Major—History (2) p628   (por.185,209)

Slocum, Harvey (1887-1961). Amer. engineer.
Curr. Biog. '57 p520-521 (por.520)

Sloggett, Sir Arthur Thomas (1857-1929). Brit. surgeon.
Hammerton p1225

Slosson, Anne Trumbull (1838-1926). Amer. entomologist.
Osborn—Fragments p208 (por.356)

Sly, Maud (1879-1954). Amer. pathologist.
*Compton—Conquests p255-268   Jaffe—Outposts p130-160 (por.138)
Curr. Biog. '40 p743-745 (por.744)
    '54 p579

Small, Lyndon Frederick (1897-1957)
N.A.S.—Biog. (33) p397-407 (por.397)

Small, William (1734-1775). Amer. nat. philosopher.
Bell—Early p75

Smeaton, John (1724-1792). Eng. engineer.
*Glenister—Stories p-100-119   *Watson—Engineers p3-10 (por.2)
  (por.100)
Hammerton p1226

Smellie, William (1740-1795). Scot. obstetrician.
Hammerton p1226
Major—History (2) p630

Smidovich.   See **Veresaev, Vikenti**

Smith, Alexander (1865-1922). Amer. chemist.
Browne—Hist. p481 (por.87)
N.A.S.—Biog. (1) (XXI—Memoirs)
  p1-4 (por.1)

Smith, Art (1895-1926). Amer. aero. pioneer.
Maitland—Knights p135-139

Smith, Austin Edward (1912-   ). Can. physician.
Curr. Biog. '50 p533-535 (por.534)

Smith, Clara Eliza (1865?-1943). Amer. mathematician.
Curr. Biog. '43 p706

Smith, Cyril Stanley (1903-   ). Eng. phys. metallurgist.
Curr. Biog. '48 p585-587 (por.586)

Smith, Cyrus Rowlett (1899-   ). Amer. aero. pioneer.
Curr. Biog. '45 p554-556 (por.555)

Smith, David Tillerson (1898-   ). Amer. physician.
Curr. Biog. '50 p535-536 (por.536)

Smith, Edgar Fahs (1854-1928). Amer. chemist.
Browne—Hist. p476 (por.45)   Killeffer—Eminent p18 (por.18)
Chyma (1) p.ix-xiv (por.,front.)   N.A.S.—Biog. (17) p103-139
  (5) p11-20   (por.103)

Smith, Edwin (1822-1906). Amer. archaeologist.
Gordon—Medicine p205 (por.205)

Smith, Edwin Frink (1854-1927). Amer. agriculturist, bacteriologist.
N.A.S.—Biog. (21) p1-46 (por.1)

Smith, Elinor (1908-   ). Amer. aero. pioneer.
*Adams—Heroines p179-193 (por.184)
Heinmuller—Man's p337 (por.337)

Smith, Erwin Frank (1854-1927). Amer. pathologist.
Bulloch—Hist. p397
Grainger—Guide p172-173

Smith, Eugene Allen (1841-1927). Amer. geologist.
Merrill—First p476-477 (por.324)

Smith, Sir Francis Pettit (1808-1874). Eng. inventor.
Chambers—Dict. col.411-412

Smith, George (1840-1876). Eng. archaeologist.
Ceram—Gods p274-278

Smith, George Otis (1871-1944). Amer. geologist.
G.S.A.—Proc. '44 p309-325 (por.309)

Smith, Sir Grafton Elliot (1871-1937). Austral. anatomist, anthropologist.
Hammerton p1227

Smith, Henry John Stephen (1826-1883). Eng. mathematician.
Ball—Short p456-458
Cajori—Hist. p441-442
Chambers—Dict. col.412
McFarlane—Lectures p92-106 (por.,front.)
Smith—Hist. I p467

Smith, Herbert Huntington (1851-1919). Amer. entomologist.
Osborn—Fragments p230 (por.359)

Smith, Sir James Edward (1759-1828). Eng. botanist.
Gilmour—British p31 (por.29)
Hammerton p1227
Hawks—Pioneers p258-260

Smith, James Hopkins, Jr. (1909-   ). Amer. aero. pioneer.
Curr. Biog. '58 p390-392 (por.391)

Smith, John Bernard (1858-1912). Amer. entomologist.
Osborn—Fragments p166-167
(por.348)

Smith, John Lawrence (1818-1883). Amer. chemist.
Browne—Hist. p471 (por.19)   Smith—Chem. p252-261 (por.258)
Killeffer—Eminent p6 (por.6)   Weeks—Discovery p221,422 (por.422)
N.A.S.—Biog. (2) p217-237

Smith, Jonas Waldo (1861-1933). Amer. engineer.
John Fritz p101-103 (por.100)

Smith, Lowell H. (1892-   ). Amer. aero. pioneer.
Heinmuller—Man's p315 (por.315)

Smith, Nathan (1762-1829). Amer. physician, surgeon.
Leonardo—Lives p400-402   Rosen- -Four p166-168,244-245
Major—History (2) p765-766

Smith, Nathan Ryno (1797-1877). Amer. surgeon.
Leonardo—Lives p402-403

Smith, Philip Sidney (1877-1949). Amer. geologist.
G.S.A.—Proc. '49 p217-222 (por.217)

Smith, Ralph Ingram (1822-1927). Amer. entomologist.
Osborn—Fragments p217-218

Smith, Robert (1689-1768). Eng. mathematician.
Hammerton p1227

Smith, Sir Ross MacPherson (1892-1922). Austral. aero. pioneer.
Hammerton p1227-1228
Heinmuller—Man's p308 (por.308)

Smith, Roy Burnett (1875-1940). Amer. chemist.
Curr. Biog. '41 p799

Smith, Sidney Irving (1843-1926). Amer. zoologist.
N.A.S.—Biog. (14) p5-10 (por.5)

Smith, Stephen (1823-1922). Amer. physician.
*Yost—Science p30-46

Smith, Theobald (1859-1934). Amer. pathologist, bacteriologist.

Bulloch—Hist. p397-398 (por.262)
Castiglioni—Hist. p986 (por.985)
*DeKruif—Microbe p236-251
Grainger—Guide p173
Hammerton p1228
Morris—Ency. p715-716
N.A.S.—Biog. (17) p261-288 (por.261)
Schwartz—Moments (2) p758-759
16 Amer. p21-24
*Snyder—Biology p239-243 (por.241)

Smith, Warren Dupré (1880-1950). Amer. geologist.

G.S.A.—Proc. '50 p119-122 (por.119)

Smith, William (1769-1839). Eng. geologist, paleontologist.

Adams—Birth p268-276 (por.268)
Chambers—Dict. col.412
Fenton—Giants p70-83 (por.30)
Geike—Founders p224-238
Hammerton p1228
Locy—Biology p330-331
Murray—Science p328
*Science Miles. p138-141 (por.138)
Williams—Story p89-91 (por.139)
Woodruff—Devel. p207-209,291
(por.176)

Smith, William Wright (1875-1956). Scot. botanist.

R.S.L.—Biog. (3) p193-198 (por.193)

Smith, Willoughby (1828-1891). Eng. engineer.

Hawks—Wireless p164-1 (por.146)

Smithson, James (or Macie, Lewis, Louis) (1765-1829). Brit. chemist,
mineralogist.

Gunther—Early XI p278-279
Hammerton p1228
Oehser—Sons p1-13 (por.10)
True—Smiths. p213-225 (por.216,324)

Smyth, Charles Henry, Jr. (1866-1937). Amer. geologist.

G.S.A.—Proc. '37 p195-199 (por.195)

Smyth, Charles Piazzi (1819-1900). Brit. astronomer.

Hammerton p1229

Smyth, Henry Dewolf (1898-   ). Amer. physicist.

Curr. Biog. '48 p591-593 (por.592)

Smyth, Henry Lloyd (1862-1944). Can. geologist.

G.S.A.—Proc. '47 p177-189 (por.177)

Snell, Foster Dee (1898-   ). Amer. chemist.

Curr. Biog. '43 p718-719 (por.719)

Snell, Sir John (1869-1938). Eng. elec. engineer.

*Bridges—Master p245-258 (por.246)

Snell, (or Snellius) **Rudolph** (1546-1613). Dutch mathematician.
Smith—Hist. I p422-423

Snell, (or Snellius) **Willebrod van Roijen** (1591-1626). Dutch mathematician.
Ball—Short p254   Lenard—Great p51-52 (por.52)
Chambers—Dict. col.412-413

Snider, Jacob (1820-1866). Dutch-Amer. inventor.
Hammerton p1230

Snider, Luther Crocker (1882-1947). Amer. geologist.
G.S.A.—Proc. '47 p191-192 (por.191)

Snook, Homer Clyde (1878-1942). Amer. inventor, electrophysicist.
Curr. Biog. '42 p776

Snow, Sir Charles Percy (1905-   ). Eng. physicist.
Curr. Biog. '54 p584-585 (por.584)
'61 (Dec.) (por.)

Snow, Francis Huntington (1840-1908). Amer. entomologist, naturalist.
Osborn—Fragments p224 (por.347)

Snow, John (1813-1858). Eng. physician, surgeon.
Bulloch—Hist. p398   Robinson—Victory p219-228
Moulton—Auto. p302-303   (por.219)
                                         Thorwald—Century p136-138
                                           (por.240)

Snyder, Howard McCrum (1881-   ). Amer. physician.
Curr. Biog. '55 p562-564 (por.563)

Sobrero, Ascanio (1812-1888). It. chemist, inventor.
Chambers—Dict. col.413
*Pratt—Famous p6-7

Socrates (468/470-399 B.C.). Gr. nat. philosopher.
Fitzhugh—Concise p638-640   Sewell—Brief p5-6
Hammerton p1230-1231 (por.1231)   Smith—Hist. I p79
100 Great p20-25

Soddy, Frederick (1877-1956). Eng. chemist.
*Book—Pop. Sci. (15) p5071-5072   R.S.L.—Biog. (3) p203-213 (por.203)
  (por.5071)   Riedman—Men p110-112
Chambers—Dict. col.413;Supp.   Schwartz—Moments (2) p934-935
Farber—Nobel p82-85 (por.118)   Weeks—Discovery p502 (por.502)
Hammerton p1232 (por.1232)   Year—Pic. p211 (por.211)
Moulton—Auto. p496-497

Soderberg, Carl Richard (1895-   ). Swed. engineer.
Curr. Biog. '58 p395-396 (por.396)

Soemmering, Samuel Thomas von (1755-1830). Ger. naturalist, anatomist.
Hawks—Wireless p63-64 (por.64)
Major—History (2) p701-702

Solberg, Thorvald Arthur (1894-   ). Amer. engineer, aero. pioneer.
Curr. Biog. '48 p593-595 (por.594)
Heinmuller—Man's p348 (por.348)

Solinus, Caius Julius (fl.250). Latin naturalist.
Adams—Birth p50

Solis-Cohen, Jacob Da Silva (1838-1927). Amer. physician.
Kagan—Leaders p61-71 (por.61)
Kagan—Modern p130 (por.130)

Sollas, William Johnson (1849-1936). Eng. geologist.
G.S.A.—Proc. '37 p203-207 (por.203)
Hammerton p1232 (por.1232)

Solon (c.639-559 B.C.). Gr. astronomer, mathematician.
Smith—Hist. I p66

Solvay, Ernest (1838-1922). Belg. chemist.
Chambers—Dict. col.414
Smith—Torch. p234 (por.234)

Somerset, Edward (1601-1667). Eng. engineer, inventor.
Hart—Engineers p62-64

Somerville, Mary Fairfax (1780-1872). Scot. mathematician, physicist.
Coolidge—Six p25-26   Mozans—Woman p157-161,211-212
Hammerton p1234

Somerville, Sir William (1860-1932). Brit. agriculturist.
Hammerton p1234

Sommerfeld, Arnold Johannes Wilhelm (1868-1951). Ger. physicist.
Chambers—Dict. col.414
Curr. Biog. '50 p537-538 (por.537)
   '51 p598

Sömmering.   See **Soemmering, Samuel Thomas von**

Sonnenschein, Robert (1879-1939). Amer. physician.
Kagan—Modern p141 (por.141)

Sopwith, Thomas Octave Murdoch (1888-   ). Eng. aero. pioneer, inventor.
Burge—Ency. p640   Heinmuller—Man's p281 (por.281)
Hammerton p1235 (por.1235)

Soranus of Ephesus (2d cent.). Gr. physician, surgeon, gynecologist.
Castiglioni—Hist. p202-203   Leonardo—Lives p403-405
Gordon—Medicine p653-660   Major—History (1) p185-188
   (por.654)   Sigerist—Great p63-67

Sorby, Henry Clifton (1826-1908). Eng. chemist, geologist.
Chambers—Dict. col.414   Woodruff—Devel. p291-292
Hammerton p1235

Sorensen, Frank England (1903-   ). Amer. space pioneer.
Thomas—Men p.xvi   Thomas—Men (3) p.xvi-xviii
Thomas—Men (2) p.xviii

Sörensen, Peder (or Severinus, Petrus) (1540/1542-1602). Dan. physician.
Copen.—Prom. p16-19

Sörensen, (or Severinus) **Sören Peter Lauritz** (1868-1939). Dan. biochemist.
Chambers—Dict. col.414-415

Soter.   See **Ptolemy I**

Souchon, Edmond (1841-1929). Amer. surgeon.
Leonardo—Lives p405-406

South, Lillian H. (or Tye, Mrs. H. H.) (b.1878). Amer. bacteriologist.
Lovejoy—Women Phys. p355

Southworth, George Clark (1890-   ). Amer. engineer.
Radio's 100 p247-250 (por.140)

Southworth, James (1913-   ). Amer. physician.
Curr. Biog. '43 p303-304 (por.304)

Spaatz, Carl (1891-   ). Amer. aero. pioneer.
Heinmuller—Man's p335 (por.335)

Spahlinger, Henry (1882-   ). Swiss bacteriologist.
Chambers—Dict. col.415
Hammerton p1237

Spalding, Lyman (1775-1821). Amer. physician.
G.S.A.—Proc. '50 p125-127 (por.125)

Spallanzani, (Abbe') Lazzaro (1729-1799). It. biologist, naturalist.
Bodenheimer—Hist. p315
Bulloch—Hist. p398 (por.280)
Castiglioni—Hist. p612-613 (por.611)
Chambers—Dict. col.415
*DeKruif—Microbe p25-56
Geikie—Founders p199
Gordon—Romance p222,224-226
  (por.222)
Grainger—Guide p173-174
Locy—Biology p282-284 (por.283)
Major—History (2) p620-622 (por.621)
Oliver—Stalkers p126-129 (por.124)
Schwartz—Moments (1) p417-418
Thomson—Great p23-24
Van Wagenen—Beacon p164-165
Woodruff—Devel. p292

Sparrow, Stanwood Willston (1888-1952). Amer. engineer.
*Yost—Engineers p155-167

Spath, Leonard Frank (1882-1957). Brit. geologist.
R.S.L.—Biog. (3) p217-222 (por.217)

Spearman, Charles E. (1863-1945). Brit. psychologist.
Curr. Biog. '45 p569

Speight, Robert (1867-1949). New Zeal. geologist.
Major—History (2) p768

Spelterini, Eduard (1852-1931). Swiss aero. pioneer.
Heinmuller—Man's p272 (por.272)

Spemann, Hans (1869-1941). Ger. zoologist.
Chambers—Dict. col. 415-416
*Snyder—Biology p364-366 (por.365)
Stevenson—Nobel p180-185 (por.150)

Spencer, Sir Baldwin (1860-1929). Austral. ethnologist.
Hammerton p1238

Spencer, Charles Albert (1813-1881). Amer. optician.
Three—Amer. p15-33 (por.,front., 20)

Spencer, Herbert (1820-1903). Eng. biologist, nat. philospher.
Lambert—Medical p157-159 (por.158)
Lambert—Minute p157-159 (por.144)
Osborn—Greeks p311-312
Shapley—Astron. p285
Thomson—Great p100-108

Spencer, Herbert R. (1849-1900). Amer. optician.
Three—Amer. p53-74 (por.54)

Spencer, Percival H. (1897-   ). Amer. inventor.
Tuska—Invent. p87-88

Spencer, Roscoe Roy (1888-   ). Amer. physician, surgeon.
*DeKruif—Men p119-145

Spencer, Sir Walter Baldwin (1860-1919). Eng. biologist, ethnographer.
Gunther—Early XI p152

Spencer, William Kingdon (1878-1955). Eng. paleontologist.
R.S.L.—Biog. (2) p291-297 (por.291)

Spens, Thomas (1769-1842). Scot. physician.
Major—History (2) p705

Sperry, Elmer Ambrose (1860-1930). Amer. inventor, elec. engineer.
Chambers—Dict. col.416
*Darrow—Builders p117-123
*Darrow—Thinkers p359-361
Hammerton p1240
Holland—Ind. p56 (por.56)
*Montgomery—Invent. p245-248
N.A.S.—Biog. (28) p223-247 (por.223)
*Yost—Science p134-146

Sperry, Lawrence (1892-1923). Amer. aero. pioneer, inventor.
Heinmuller—Man's p297 (por.297)
Maitland—Knights p279-282

Sperti, George Speri (1900-   ). Amer. elec. engineer.
Curr. Biog. '40 p751 (por.751)

Speter, Max (1883-1942). Rom. inventor.
Weeks—Discovery p50 (por.50)

Speusippus (fl.347-339 B.C.). Gr. mathematician, nat. philosopher.
Hammond p1240
Smith—Hist. I p90

Spieghel, (or Spigelius) **Adriaan van den** (1578-1625). Belg. botanist, anatomist, surgeon.
Major—History (1) p552

Spiller, William Gibson (1863-1940). Amer. neurologist.
Curr. Biog. '40 p751 (por.751)

Spilsbury, Sir Bernard Henry (1877/1878-1947). Eng. physician, pathologist.
Hammerton p1240-1241

Spitzer, Lyman, Jr. (1914-   ). Amer. astrophysicist.
Curr. Biog. '60 p395-397 (por.398)

Spivak, Charles David (1861-1927). Rus. physician.
Kagan—Modern p20 (por.20)

Spock, Benjamin McLane (1903-   ). Amer. pediatrician.
Curr. Biog. '56 p599-601 (por.599)

Spoon, Charles (1609-1684). Fr. physician.
Major—History (1) p554

Spottiswoode, William (1825-1883). Eng. mathematician, physicist.
Chambers—Dict. col.416

Sprague, Embert Hiram (1875-1940). Amer. engineer.
Curr. Biog. '40 p753 (por.753)

Sprague, Frank Julian (1857-1934). Amer. elec. engineer.
Hammerton p1242
*Hodgins—Behemoth p239-245

Sprengel, Christian Konrad (1750-1816). Ger. botanist, biologist.
Bodenheimer—Hist. p337
Chambers—Dict. col.416

Sprengel, Hermann Johann Philipp (1834-1906). Ger.-Brit. chemist.
Chambers—Dict. col.417
Hammerton p1242

Sprengel, Kurt (1766-1833). Ger. botanist.
Major—History (2) p704-705

Springs, Elliott White (1896-   ). Amer. aero. pioneer.
Heinmuller—Man's p302 (por.302)

Spruce, Richard (1817-1893). Eng. naturalist, botanist.
Cutright—Great p31-33
Von Hagen—Green p245-246

Spurr, Josiah Edward (1870-1951?). Amer. geologist.
Chambers—Dict. col.417

Squibb, Edward Robinson (1819-1900). Amer. pharmacist.
Carmer—Caval. p277-269 (por.278)

Squier, George Owen (1865-1934). Amer. elec. engineer, inventor.
N.A.S.—Biog. (20) p151-157 (por.151)   *Towers—Beacon p257-265
Radio's 100 p131-132 (por.140)

Squier, J. Bentley (1873-1948). Amer. physician, surgeon.
Leonardo—Lives (Supp.1) p511

Sridhara (c.991). Ind. mathematician.
Smith—Hist. I p274-275,280

Stadler, Lewis John (1896-1954). Amer. agriculturist.
N.A.S.—Biog. (30) p329-347 (por.329)

Stahl, Georg Ernst (1660-1734). Ger. chemist, physician.
Castiglioni—Hist. p583-584 (por.582)
Chalmers—Historic p272
Chambers—Dict. col.417
Gordon—Romance p119-120
Hammerton p1244 (por.1244)
Holmyard—Chem. p58-61
Holmyard—Great Chem. p51-57
Holmyard—Makers p143-150
  (por.147)
Lambert—Medical p148-149
Lambert—Minute p148-149
Major—History (2) p566-568
  (por.567)
Oliver—Stalkers p136-137
Partington—Short p85-88 (por.86)
Roberts—Chem. p3-8
Schwartz—Moments (1) p207-208
Sigerist—Great p183-184 (por.184)
Smith—Torch. p235 (por.235)
Weeks—Discovery p82,269-270,295
  (por.82)

Stainbrook, Merrill Addison (1897-1956). Amer. geologist.
G.S.A.—Proc. '56 p167-169 (por.167)

Stakman, Elvin Charles (1885-   ). Amer. agriculturist, botanist.
Curr. Biog. '49 p580-582 (por.582)
Robinson—100 p269-272 (por.269)

Stål, Carl (1833-1878). Swed. entomologist.
Essig—Hist. p765-767 (por.766)

Stalnaker, John Marshall (1903-   ). Amer. psychologist.
Curr. Biog. '58 p407-408 (por.407)

Stamm, Martin (1847-1918). Swiss physician, surgeon.
Swiss—Prom. p132-133

Stanhope, Charles, 3rd Earl (1753-1816). Eng. inventor.
Chambers—Dict. col. 418
Hammerton p1245-1246

Stanley, Freelan O. (1849-1940). Amer. inventor.
Curr. Biog. '40 p754

Stanley, Wendell Meredith (1904-   ). Amer. biochemist.
Chambers—Dict. col.418
Curr. Biog. '47 p604-607 (por.605)
*Eberle—Modern p121-126
Farber—Nobel p185,186-189
   (por.118)
Morris—Ency. p716
Progress—Science '40 p386-387
*Snyder—Biology p235-236 (por.235)

Stanley, William (1858-1916). Amer. elec. engineer, inventor.
Chambers—Dict. col.418

Stanton, Timothy William (1860-1953). Amer. paleontologist, geologist.
G.S.A.—Proc. '54 p137-141 (por.137)

Stapp, John Paul (1910-   ). Amer. aero. pioneer, physician.
Curr. Biog. '59 p426-427 (por.426)
Thomas—Men p66-89 (por.140,folio)

Stark, Johannes (1874-1951). Ger. physicist.
Chambers—Dict. col.419
Hammerton p247
Heathcote—Nobel p167-172 (por.240)
Weber—College p302 (por.302)

Starley, James (1831-1881). Eng. inventor.
Hammerton p1247

Starling, Ernest Henry (1866-1927). Eng. physiologist.
Chambers—Dict. col.419
Hammerton p1247
Major—History (2) p961,1048-1049
Rowntree—Amid p435-438 (por.437)
*Snyder—Biology p375-379 (por.377)

Starr, Chauncey (1912-   ). Amer. physicist, aero. pioneer.
Curr. Biog. '54 p586-588 (por.587)

Stas, Jean Servais (1813-1891). Belg. chemist.
Chambers—Dict. col.419
Partington—Short p343-344,353
   (por.343)
Smith—Torch. p236 (por.236)

Stastny, Olga Frances (1878-1952). Amer. physician.
Mead—Medical p67 (por.,appendix)

Statz, Hermann (1928-   ). Ger. physicist.
Curr. Biog. '58 p411-413 (por.412)

Staudinger, Hermann (1881-   ). Ger. chemist.
Chambers—Dict. Supp.
Curr. Biog. '54 p588-589 (por.588)

Staudt, Karl Georg Christian von (1798-1867). Ger. mathematician.
Ball—Short p484   Smith—Hist. I p505
Cajori—Hist. p294

Stauffer, John (n.d.). Ger.-Amer. chemist.
Chem. Ind. p132-133 (por.132)

Steacie, Edgar William Richard (1900-   ). Can. phys. chemist.
Curr. Biog. '53 p584-586 (por.585)

Stebinger, Eugene (1883-1951). Amer. geologist.
G.S.A.—Proc. '52 p153-154 (por.153)

Steell, Graham (1851-1942). Scot. physician.
Major—History (2) p912-913

Steenbock, Harry (1886-   ). Amer. biochemist.
*Darrow—Builders p217-222   Progress—Science '41 p366-367
*DeKruif—Hunger p301-331   (por.367)
  (por.300)

Steenstrup, (Johann) Japetus Smith (1813-1897). Dan. zoologist.
Chambers—Dict. col.419-420
Copen.—Prom. p115-119

Stefan, Josef (1835-1893). Aust. physicist.
Chambers—Dict. col.420   Magie—Source p377-378
Lenard—Great p350-358 (por.349

Stefanini, Giuseppe (1882-1938). It. geologist.
G.S.A.—Proc. '39 p229-232 (por.229)

Stefansson, Vilhjalmur (1879-   ). Can. sci. explorer, anthropologist, geographer.
Curr. Biog. '42 p801-804 (por.801)   Progress —Science '41 p367-368
Hammerton p1249 (por.1249)   (por.367)

Steidtmann, Edward (1881-1948). Amer. geologist.
G.S.A.—Proc. '48 p229-230 (por.229)

Stein, Sir Mark Aurel (b.1862). Brit. archaeologist.
Hammerton p1249 (por.1249)

Steinach, Adelrich (1826-1892). Swiss physician, naturalist.
Swiss—Prom. p134-135

Steinbach, Erwin von (c.1244-1318). Ger. engineer.
Matschoss—Great p25-26

Steincrohn, Peter Joseph (1899-   ). Amer. physician.
Curr. Biog. '57 p525-527 (por.526)

Steiner, Jacob (1796-1863). Swiss mathematician.
Ball—Short p483-484
Cajori—Hist. p290-292
*Miller—Hist. p245-247
Smith—Hist. I p524-525 (por.524)
Woodruff—Devel. p292 (por.30)

Steiner, Walter Ralph (1870-1942). Amer. physician.
Curr. Biog. '43 p735

Steinhaus, Edward Arthur (1914-   ). Amer. microbiologist.
Curr. Biog. '55 p575-577 (por.576)

Steinheil, Carl August von (1801-1870). Ger. physicist.
Hawks—Wireless p64-66 (por.64)

Steinman, David Barnard (1886-1960). Amer. engineer.
Curr. Biog. '57 p527-529 (por.528)
'60 p399
*Waton—Engineers p145-150 (por.144)

Steinmetz, Charles Proteus (1865-1923). Ger. elec. engineer, inventor.
*Beard—Foreign p253-258 (por.256)
*Book—Pop. Sci. (15) p5025-5027 (por.5025)
*Cooper—Twenty p161-178 (por.160)
Hammerton p1249
Radio's 100 p132-137 (por.140)
*Shippen—Design p84-92
Thomas—50 Amer. p358-367
Thomas—Scien. p247-262 (por.245)
Van Wagenen—Beacon p423-426
Year—Pic. p180 (por.180)

Stejneger, Leonhard Hess (1851-1943). Norw.-Amer. ornithologist, zoologist.
N.A.S.—Biog. '47 p145-170 (por.145)

Stekel, Wilhelm (1866-1940). Aust. psychiatrist.
Curr. Biog. '40 p761

Stella, Erasmus (1450?-1521). Ger. physician.
Adams—Birth p147-149

Steller, Georg (1709-1746). Ger. naturalist.
Alden—Early p4-7

Steno, Nicolaus (or Stensen, Niels) (1631-1686). Dan. anatomist, geologist, physiologist, physician.

Adams—Birth p358-364
Chambers—Dict. col.420
Copen.—Prom. p36-43
Fenton—Giants p22-25

Major—History (1) p559
Sigerist—Great p170
Woodruff—Devel. p198,292
Year—Pic. p91 (por.91)

Stensen.   See **Steno, Nicolaus**

Stephens, George (1813-1895). Dan. archaeologist.
Hammerton p1250

Stephens, John Lloyd (1805-1852). Amer. archaeologist.
Ceram—Gods p337-353

Stephenson, George (1781-1848). Eng. engineer, inventor.

*Bachman—Great p50-71 (por.50)
*Book—Pop. Sci. (15) p5027-5028 (por.5028)
Chambers—Dict. col.421
*Crother—Inventors p49-85 (por.65)
*Darrow—Masters p106-110 (por.33)
*Darrow—Thinkers p76-82 (por.77)
*Eberle—Invent. p47-55 (por.46)
Fitzhugh—Concise p652-653
*Glenister—Stories p171-192 (por.171)
Goddard—Eminent p206-215 (por.206)
Gregory—British p30-31 (por.21)
Hammerton p1250-1251 (por.1250)

*Hartman—Mach. p73-78
*Hathaway—Partners p135-151
*Hodgkins—Behemoth p144-153, 154-160
*Larsen—Prentice p26-33
Law—Civiliz p27-33
Matschoss—Great p171-189 (por.171)
*Montgomery—Invent. p195-199
*Nida—Makers p33-40 (por.35)
*Nisenson—More p137 (por.137)
*Parkman—Conq. p242-274
*Pratt—Famous p30-33
Year—Pic. p148-151 (por.151)

Stephenson, H. Kirk (1913-1956). Amer. geologist.
G.S.A.—Proc. '56 p189

Stephenson, Robert (1803-1859). Eng. engineer, inventor.

*Book—Pop. Sci. (15) p5028-5030 (por.5029)
Gregory—British p30-31 (por.21)

Hammerton p1251 (por.1251)
Matschoss—Great p171-189 (por.188)
*Watson—Engineers p81-89 (por.80)

Stern, Arthur Cecil (1909-   ). Amer. engineer.
Curr. Biog. '56 p605-607 (por.606)

Stern, Otto (1888-   ). Ger.-Amer. physicist.

Chambers—Dict. col.421
Heathcote—Nobel p389-397 (por.240)

Weber—College p690 (por.690)

Sternberg, George Miller (1838-1915). Amer. bacteriologist, hygienist.
Bulloch—Hist. p398   Major—History (2) p901
Grainger—Guide p174

Stetson, Henry Crosby (1900-1955). Amer. geologist.
G.S.A.—Proc. '56 p171-173 (por.171)

Stevens family (18th, 19th cent.). Amer. engineers, inventors.
Wilson—Amer. p59-63,154 (por.59)

Stevens, Albert William (1886-   ). Amer. aero. pioneer.
Heinmuller—Man's p349 (por.349)
Holland—Arch. p94-112 (por.54)

Stevens, John (1749-1838). Amer. engineer, inventor.
Abbot—Great p183-185   Hodgins—Behemoth p193-194
*Burlingame—Inv. p59-63   *Hylander—Invent. p35-41 (por.35)
*Epstein—Real p68-69,84   Iles—Leading p3-39 (por.,front.)
Goddard—Eminent p57-58 (por.50)   Law—Civiliz. p34-36
Hammerton p1252   *Watson—Engineers p25-31 (por.24)

Stevens, Robert Livingston (1787-1856). Amer. engineer, inventor.
Goddard—Eminent p57-58 (por.54)   Iles—Leading p3-39 (por.28)
*Hylander—Invent. p41-44 (por.35)

Stevenson, George Salvatore (1892-   ). Amer. psychiatrist, neurologist.
Curr. Biog. '46 p568-570 (por.569)

Stevenson, John J. (1841-1924). Amer. geologist.
Merrill—First p469,585 (por.546)

Stevenson, Robert (1772-1850). Scot. engineer.
Hammerton p1252

Stevenson, Sarah Yorke (1847-1921). Amer. archaeologist.
Mozans—Woman p322

Stevinus (or Stevin), **Simon** (1548-1620). Dutch mathematician.
Ball—Short p244-247   Magie—Source p22-23
Cajori—Hist. p147-148   Sarton—Six p49-53,105,161 (por.24)
Chambers—Dict. col.421-422   Sedgwick—Short p252-254
Hammerton—1253   Smith—Hist. 1 p342-343
Hofman—History p102-104   Van Wagenen—Beacon p82-83
Lenard—Great p20-24 (por.21)   Woodruff—Devel. p292

Stewart, Balfour (1828-1887). Scot. physicist.
Hammerton p1253 (por.1253)

Stewart, George David (1862-1933). Can. physician, surgeon.
Leonardo—Lives (Supp.1) p511-512

Stewart, George W. (1876-1956). Amer. physicist.
N.A.S.—Biog. (32) p379-391 (por.379)

Stewart, Matthew (1717-1785). Scot. mathematician.
Ball—Short p388
Smith—Hist. 1 p456-457

Stiebeling, Hazel Katherine (1896-   ). Amer. phys. chemist.
Curr. Biog. '50 p548-550 (por.549)
Yost—Women Sci. p158-176

Stieglitz, Julius (1867-1937). Amer. chemist.
Browne—Hist. p482-483 (por.103)   N.A.S. Biog. (21) p275-298
Killeffer—Eminent p25 (por.25)

Stifel (or Stiffelius, Styfel, Stieffel), **Michael** (1486/1487-1567).
Ball—Short p215-217   Smith—Hist. 1 p327-328
Cajori—Hist. p140

Stiles, Charles Wardell (1867-1941). Amer. zoologist, physician, surgeon.
Curr. Biog. '41 p829   *Snyder—Biology p243-250 (por.252)
Osborn—Fragments p181 (por.357)

Still, Andrew T. (1828-1917). Amer. physician.
Hammerton p1254

Still, William Joseph (b.1870). Eng. engineer.
Hammerton p1254

Stillé, Alfred (1813-1900). Amer. physician.
Major—History (2) p770

Stillman, John Maxson (1852-1923). Amer. chemist.
A.A.A.S.—Proc. (11) p88-90

Stillwell, Lewis Buckley (1863-1941). Amer. elec. engineer.
Curr. Biog. '41 p830
N.A.S.—Biog. (34) p320-323 (por.320)

Stimpson, William (1832-1872). Amer. zoologist.
N.A.S.—Biog. (8) p419-429 (por.419)

Stimson, Barbara Bartlett (1898-   ). Amer. physician.
Knapp—Women p151-164 (por.151)

Stimson, Lewis Atterbury (1844-1917). Amer. surgeon.
Leonardo—Lives p406-407

Stine, Charles Milton Atland (1882-1954). Amer. chemist.
Curr. Biog. '40 p769-770 (por.769)   Progress—Science '40 p389 (por.389)
'54 p589

Stine, Wilbur Morris (1863-1934). Amer. engineer.
Hammerton p1254

Stinson family (19th-20th cent.). Amer. aero. pioneers.
Maitland—Knights p163-164

Stinson, Katherine (1896-   ). Amer. aero. pioneer.
*Adams—Heroines p29-45 (por.56)   Maitland—Knights p163-164
Heinmuller—Man's p295 (por.295)

Stirling, James (1692-1770). Scot. mathematician.
Smith—Hist. 1 p449-450

Stock, Alfred E. (1876-1946). Ger. chemist.
Partington—Short p355
Weeks—Discovery p463 (por.463)

Stock, Chester (1892-1950). Amer. paleontologist, geologist.
G.S.A.—Proc. '51 p149-152 (por.149)
N.A.S.—Biog. (27) p335-352 (por.335)

Stockberger, Warner W. (1872-1944). Amer. botanist.
Curr. Biog. '41 p831-832 (por.831)

Stöffler, Johann (1452-1531). Ger. astronomer, mathematician.
Smith—Hist. 1 p327

Stokes, Adrian (1887-1927). Irish bacteriologist, physician.
*Shippen—Men p195-196
Williams-Ellis p241-242

Stokes, Sir Frederick Wilfred Scott (1860-1927). Eng. engineer.
Hammerton p1255

Stokes, Sir George Gabriel, Bart. (1819-1903). Irish mathematician,
physicist.
Cajori—Hist. p460-462   Magie—Source p344-345
Chambers—Dict. col.422   Van Wagenen—Beacon p311-313
Hammerton p1255 (por.1255)   Woodruff—Devel. p292
MacFarlane—Ten p94-105
(por.,front.)

Stokes, William (1804-1878). Irish mathematician, physicist, physician.

Castiglioni—Hist. p707 (por.710)
Gordon—Romance p147 (por.147)
Hale-White—Great p124-142
Lambert—Medical p217
Lambert—Minute p217
Major—History (2) p683-685
Walsh—Makers p185-200

Stoll, Maximilian (1742-1788). Aust. physician.

Sigerist—Great p217

Stone, Abraham (1890-1959). Rus.-Amer. physician.

Curr. Biog. '52 p560-562 (por.561)

Stone, Edward James (1831-1897). Eng. astronomer.

Hammerton p1255

Stone, George Edward (1860-1941). Amer. botanist.

Progress—Science '41 p368 (por.368)

Stone, Hannah Mayer (1893?-   ). Amer. physician.

Curr. Biog. '41 p835

Stone, John Stone (1869-1942). Amer. physicist.

Radio's 100 p149-153 (por.140)

Stone, Warren (1808-1872). Amer. surgeon.

Leonardo—Lives p407-408

Stone, William Sebastian (1910-   ). Amer. meteorologist, aero. pioneer.

Curr. Biog. '60 p401-403 (por.402)

Stoney, George Johnstone (1826-1911). Irish math, physicist, astronomer.

Armitage—Cent. p35
Chambers—Dict. col.422

Stopes, Marie Carmichael (1880-   ). Eng. paleobotanist.

Hammerton p1255 (por. 1255)

Störck, Anton Baron von (1731-1803). Aust. physician.

Sigerist—Great p217

Storey-Maskelyne, (or Story) **Mervyn Herbert Nevil** (1823-1911). Brit. mineralogist.

Chambers—Dict. col. 423
Gunther—Early XI p270-271
  (por.270)

Störmer, Fredrik Carl Mulertz (1874-1957). Norw. mathematician, geophysicist.
Chambers—Dict. col. 422-423
R.S.L.—Biog. (4) p257-276 (por.257)

Stout, William Bushnell (1880-1956). Amer. inventor, engineer.
*Cooper—Twenty p257-274 (por.256)   Holland—Arch. p127-144 (por.54)
Curr. Biog. '41 p839-841 (por.840),
  '56 p608

Stovall, John Willis (1891-1953). Amer. geologist.
G.S.A.—Proc. '52 p155-157 (por.155)

Stow, Marcellus (1902-1957). Amer. geologist.
G.S.A.—Proc. '57 p165-166 (por.165)

Stowe, Emily Jennings (1831-1903). Can. physician.
Lovejoy—Women p111-114 (por.112)

Strabo (63 B.C.?-24?A.D.). Gr. geographer, geologist.
Adams—Birth p25-27   Hammerton p1256
Fenton—Giants p11-12   Sedgwick—Short p145-146

Stradonitz.   See **Kekulé von Stradonitz, Friedrich August**

Strassburger, Eduard (1844-1912). Ger. biologist, botanist.
Bodenheimer—Hist. p419
Reed—Short p179-180

Stratemeyer, George Edward (1890-   ). Amer. aero. pioneer.
Curr. Biog. '51 p612-614

Straten, Florence (1913-   ). Amer. meteorologist.
Yost—Women Mod. p124-139
  (por.,front.)

Strato (or Straton of Lampsacus) (fl.287 B.C.). Gr. nat. philosopher.
Clagett—Greek p68-72
Gordon—Medicine p577-578

Stratton, George Malcolm (1865-1957). Amer. psychologist.
N.A.S.—Biog. (35) p292 (por.292)

Stratton, Samuel Wesley (1861-1931). Amer. elec. engineer, physicist.
N.A.S.—Biog. (17) p253-259
  (por.253)

Straus, Isidore (1845-1912). Ger.-Amer. bacteriologist.
Bulloch—Hist. p398-399

Strauss, Joseph Baermann (1870-1938). Amer. engineer.
*Watson—Engineers p131-136
(por.130)

Streeter, George Linius (1873-1943). Amer. physician.
N.A.S.—Biog. (28) p261-278 (por.261)

Stretch, Richard Harper (1837-1926). Eng.-Amer. entomologist.
Essig—Hist. p767-770 (por.768)
Osborn—Fragments p222

Strike, Clufford Stewart (1902-   ). Amer. engineer.
Curr. Biog. '49 p593-595 (por.594)

Stringfellow, John (1799-1883). Eng. aero. pioneer, inventor.
*Bishop—Kite p87-98   Heinmuller—Man's p242 (por.242)
Burge—Ency. p640

Stringham, Washington Irving (1847-1909). Amer. mathematician.
Smith—Math. p134-135

Stromayer, Casper (fl.c.1559). Ger. surgeon.
Gordon—Medieval p685

Stromeyer (or Strohmeyer), **Friedrich** (1776-1835). Ger. chemist.
Chambers—Dict. col.423
Weeks—Discovery p308-312 (por.308)

Stromeyer, Georg Friedrich Louis (1804-1876). Ger. surgeon.
Leonardo—Lives p408-412
Rosen—Four p3-4

Strong, John Donovan (1905-   ). Amer. physicist.
Progress—Science '41 p368-369

Strong, Richard Pearson (1872-1948). Amer. physician.
Major—History (2) p1049

Strong, Theodore (1790-1869). Amer. mathematician.
N.A.S.—Biog. (2) p1-28
Smith—Math. p97-98

Strümpel, Adolf (1853-1925). Rus. physician.
Major—History (2) p1049-1050

Strutt, Jedediah (1726-1797). Eng. inventor.
Hammerton p1260

Strutt, John William.   See **Rayleigh, John William Strutt, Lord**

Struve, von, Family (18th-20th cent.). Ger., Rus., Amer. astronomers.
Hammerton p1260

Struve, Friedrich Georg Wilhelm (1793-1864). Ger. astronomer.
Abetti—History p180-182   Vaucouleurs—Disc. p115-117
Chambers—Dict. col.423   Williams—Great p288,294 (por.289)
MacPherson—Makers p138-140   Woodruff—Devel. p292
Shapley—Astron. p208 (por.209)

Struve, Otto (1897-   ). Rus.-Amer. astronomer.
Curr. Biog. '49 p597-599 (por.598)
Progress—Science '41 p369-370
  (por.369)

Struve, Otto Wilhelm (1819-1905). Ger.-Rus. astronomer.
*Book—Pop. Sci. (15) p5175-5176   MacPherson—Astron. p1-7
Chambers—Dict. col.424

Stubbes, Henry (1632-1676). Eng. physician.
Gunther—Early XI p211-212

Stuckey, Henry Perkins (1880-   ). Amer. horticulturist.
Progress—Science '41 p370 (por.370)

Stuhlinger, Ernst (1913-   ). Ger.-Amer. physicist.
Curr. Biog. '57 p535-536 (por.535)

Stump, Felix Budwell (1894-   ). Amer. aero. pioneer, engineer.
Curr. Biog. '53 p605-606 (por.605)

Sturgeon, William (1783-1850). Eng. inventor.
Chalmers—Historic p272-273   Hawks—Wireless p36-40 (por.34)
Chambers—Dict. col.424

Sturgis, Samuel D., Jr. (1897-   ). Amer. engineer.
Curr. Biog. '56 p610-612 (por.611)

Sturm, Jacques Charles François (1803-1855). Fr. mathematician.
Chambers—Dict. col.424
Hammerton p1261

Suarez, Francisco (1548-1617). Sp. nat. philosopher.
Osborn—Greeks p127-130

Sudhoff, Karl (1853-1938). Ger. physician.
Castiglioni—Hist. p1107 (por.1107)
Major—History (2) p924-925
(por.925)

Suess, Eduard (1831-1914). Aust. geologist.
*Book—Pop. Sci. (1) p3303-3304   Hammerton p1262
Davison—Founders p134-135

Suetonius, Gaius Tranquillus (70/72-123/140). Rom. naturalist.
Adams—Birth p48
Hammerton p1262

Sugden, Samuel (1892-1950). Eng. chemist.
Chambers—Dict. col.425

Suits, Chauncey Guy (1905-   ). Amer. engineer, physicist.
Curr. Biog. '50 p554-556 (por.555)

Sujkowski, Zvigniew L. (1899-1954). Pol.-Brit. geologist.
G.S.A.—Proc. '54 p153

Sullivan, Eugene Cornelius (b.1872). Amer. chemist, inventor.
*Darrow—Builders p127-130
Holland—Ind. p240-253 (por.240)

Sullivan, Harry Stack (1892-   ). Amer. psychiatrist.
Curr. Biog. '42 p812-814 (por.813)
'49 p599

Sullivan, William Starling (1803-1873). Amer. botanist.
N.A.S.—Biog. (1) p277-285
Youmans—Pioneers p394-401
(por.394)

Sultan, Daniel Isom (1885-   ). Amer. engineer.
Curr. Biog. '45 p577-578 (por.577)

Suman, John Robert (1890-   ). Amer. engineer.
*Yost—Engineers p122-139

Summers, Henry Elijah (1863-1949). Amer. entomologist, zoologist.
Osborn—Fragments p220

Summerskill, Edith Clara (1901-   ). Eng. physician, gynecologist.
Curr. Biog. '43 p749-751 (por.749)
Knapp—Women p33-45 (por.33)

Sumner, Francis Bertody (1874-1945). Amer. biologist.
N.A.S. '49 p147-163 (por.147)

Sumner, James Batcheller (1887-1955). Amer. biochemist.
Chambers—Dict. col.425
Curr. Biog. '47 p620-622 (por.621)
   '55 p589
Farber—Nobel p182-184 (por.118)
N.A.S.—Biog. (31) p376-386
   (por.376)

Sundquist, Alma (d.1940). Swed. physician.
Lovejoy—Women p177 (por.177)

Susruta (c100?) Ind. surgeon.
Leonardo—Lives p412-413

Sussmilch, Carl Adolph (1875-1946). Austral. geologist.
G.S.A.—Proc. '48 p233-239 (por.233)

Sutherland, James (d.1719). Scot. botanist.
Oliver—Makers p281-284

Sutton, George Paul (1920-   ). Amer. engineer.
Curr. Biog. '58 p423-424 (por.424)

Sutton, John.   See **Bland-Sutton, Sir John**

Suzuki, Umetaro (1874?-1943). Japan. nutritionist.
Curr. Biog. '43 p751

Sveda, Michael (1912-   ). Amer. chemist.
Curr. Biog. '54 p593-594 (por.593)

Svedberg, Theodor (1884-   ). Swed. chemist.
Chambers—Dict. col.425
Farber—Nobel p99-102 (por.118)
Hammerton p1266
Lindroth—Swedish p271-279

Swain, Clara A. (1834-1910). Amer. physician.
Lovejoy—Women p220-221
Mead—Medical p70

Swain, George Fillmore (1857-1931). Amer. engineer.
N.A.S.—Biog. (17) p331-347
  (por.331)

Swallow, George Clinton (1817-1899). Amer. geologist.
Merrill—First p425-426 (por.426)

Swammerdam, Jan (1637-1680). Dutch naturalist.
Bodenheimer—Hist. p278
Chambers—Dict. col.425-426
Gumpert—Trail p101-104
Locy—Biology p67-77 (por.69)
Major—History (1) p558
Miall—Early p174-199
Oliver—Stalkers p96-97
Peattie—Green p45-52 (por.38)
Schwartz—Moments (2) p539-540
*Shippen—Micro. p75-78
Woodruff—Devel. p228,292
Year—Pic. p90-91 (por.91)

Swan, Sir Joseph Wilson (1828-1914). Eng. physicist, inventor.
Chambers—Dict. col.426
Hammerton p1266 (por.1266)

Swann, William Francis Gray (1884-1962). Eng.-Amer. physicist.
Curr. Biog. '41 p846-847 (por.847)
  '60 p417-419 (por.418)
Progress—Science '40 p392-393
  (por.393)

Swanton, John Reed (1873-1958). Amer. anthropologist.
N.A.S.—Biog. (34) p329-338
  (por.329)

Swartz, Charles Kephart (1861-1949). Amer. geologist.
G.S.A.—Proc. '50 p131-134 (por.131)

Swasey, Ambrose (1846-1937). Amer. engineer, inventor.
N.A.S.—Biog. ('22) p1-29 (por.1)
*Yost—Science p85-99

Swendenborg (or Svedberg), **Emanuel** (1688-1772).
Fitzhugh—Concise p661-662
Hammerton p1267 (por.1267)
Lindroth—Swedish p50-58
Sewell—Brief p75-76

Sweet, John Edson (1832-1916). Amer. min. engineer.
John Fritz p81-82 (por.80)

Swieten, Gerhard van (1700-1772). Dutch physician.

Castiglioni—Hist. p617-618
Major—History (2) p578-581
(por.578)

Sigerist—Great p205-210 (por.208)

Swinburne, James (1858-1958). Eng. elec. engineer.

R.S.L.—Biog. (5) p253-264 (por.253)

Swings, Polidore F. F. (1906-   ). Belg. astrophysicist.

Curr. Biog. '54 p594-596 (por.595)

Swinton, Ernest Dunlop (1868-1951). Eng. engineer.

*Pratt—Famous p121-123

Swirbul, Leon A. (1898-1960). Amer. aero. pioneer.

Curr. Biog. '53 p609-610 (por.609)
'60 p421

Swope, Gerard (1872-1957). Amer. elec. engineer.

Fisher—Amer. p103-105 (por.102)
*White—Famous (3d) p273-282

Sydenham, Thomas (1624-1689). Eng. physician.

Castiglioni—Hist. p546-548 (por.546)
Chambers—Dict. col.426-427
Gordon—Romance p125 (por.125)
Gunther—Early XI p159,256-257
(por.256)
Hammerton p1270
*Hathaway—Partners p17-19
Lambert—Medical p161-166
(por.162)
Lambert—Minute p160-166 (por.145)

Major—History (1) p524-527
(por.525)
Newman—Interp. p39-71
Oliver—Stalkers p107-112
Sedgwick—Short p264
Sigerist—Great p175-183 (por.177)
Tobey—Riders p53
Walker—Pioneers p1-12 (por.1)

Sylvester, James Joseph (1814-1897). Eng. mathematician.

Ball—Short p476-477
Bell—Men p378-380,383-405
(por.,front.)
Cajori—Hist. p343-345
Hammerton p1270

MacFarlane—Lectures p107-121
(por.,front.)
Miller—Hist. p253-255
Smith—Hist. I p463-465 (por.464)
Smith—Math. p124-128 (por.125)
Smith—Portraits (1) xii, unp. (por.)

Sylvester II (or Gerbert of Aquitaine) (999-1003). Fr. mathematician.

Ball—Short p136-139
Cajori—Hist. p115-116

Sedgwick—Short p155

Sylvius, Franciscus (or Boë, Franz de la; Du Bois, François) (1614-1672). Flem. anatomist, physician, physiologist, chemist.

Castiglioni—Hist. p540-541 (por.549)
Chambers—Dict. col.427-428
Gordon—Medieval p668-669 (por.146)
Gordon—Romance p85,117 (por.85)
Major—History (1) p503-504 (por.504)

Oliver—Stalkers p104-106
Partington—Short p54
Sigerist—Great p163-167 (por.161)
Woodruff—Devel. p292

Sylvius, Jacques Dubois (1478-1555). Fr. physician.

Gordon—Medieval p625 (por.242)
Leonardo—Lives p143-145

Major—History (1) p417-419 (por.418)
Woodruff—Devel. p292-293

Syme, James S. (1799-1870). Scot. surgeon.

Hammerton p1270
Leonardo—Lives p413-415

Major—History (2) p879
Thorwald—Century p42-44,244-245, 260-263 (por.80)

Symington, Stuart (1901-   ). Amer. space pioneer.

Thomas—Men p.xvii-xviii
Thomas—Men (2) p.xix

Thomas—Men (3) p.xvii

Symington, William (1763-1831). Scot. engineer, inventor.

Goddard—Eminent p182-188 (por.182)
Hammerton p1270

Symons, George James (1838-1900). Eng. meteorologist.

Hammerton p1270

Synge, Richard Laurence Millinton (1914-   ). Eng. biochemist.

Chambers (Supp.)
Curr. Biog. '53 p611-612 (por.611)

Szent-Györgi, Albert von Nagyrapolt (1893-   ). Hung. biochemist.

Chambers—Dict. col.428
Curr. Biog. '55 p596-599 (por.597)

Stevenson—Nobel p196-203 (por.150)
Year—Pic. p229 (por.229)

Szilard, Leo (1898-   ). Hung. physicist.

Curr. Biog. '47 p622-625 (por.623)
Jaffe—Crucibles p385-386

T

Tabit ibn Korra (or Thabit ibn Qurra; Kurra) (836-901). Arab. mathematician.

Ball—Short p158-159
Cajori—Hist. p104

Gordon—Medieval p1461
Hammerton p1282

Tabuteau, Maurice (1884-   ). Fr. aero. pioneer.
Heinmuller—Man's p283 (por.283)

Tacchini, Pietro (1838-1905). It. astronomer.
Abetti—History p206-207   MacPherson—Astron. p77-83
Davison—Founders p113-116   (por.77)

Tachenius, Otto (d.1670). Ger. chemist, physician.
Partington—Short p60-61

Taff, Joseph Alexander (1862-1944). Amer. geologist.
G.S.A.—Proc. '49 p227-232 (por.227)

Tagault, Jean (or Tagautius, Joannes) (c.1475-1545). Fr. physician,
   surgeon.
Leonardo—Lives p415
Major—History (1) p423,425

Tagliacozzi, Gasparo (1546-1599). It. surgeon.
Castiglioni—Hist. p473-474   Leonardo—Lives p416
Chambers—Dict. col.429   Major—History (1) p445-446
                                         (por.445)

Tainter, Charles Sumner (1854-1940). Amer. physicist, inventor.
Curr. Biog. '40 p789

Tait, Lawson (1845-1899). Scot. gynecologist, surgeon.
Leonardo—Lives p416-420

Tait, Peter Guthrie (1831-1901). Scot. physicist, mathematician.
Cajori—Hist. p459-460   Hammerton p1272 (por.1272)
Chambers—Dict. col.429   MacFarlane—Ten p38-54 (por.,front.)

Taka Kazu.   See **Seki, Kowa**

Talamon, Charles (1850-1929). Fr. physician, bacteriologist.
Bulloch—Hist. p399

Talbot, Arthur Newell (1857-1942). Amer. engineer.
Curr. Biog. '42 p816

Talbot, Mignon (1869-1950). Amer. geologist.
G.S.A.—Proc. '51 p157-158 (por.157)

Talbot, William Henry Fox (1800-1877). Eng. physicist, inventor.
A.A.A.S.—Proc. (78) p8-9
Chambers—Dict. col.429-430
Hammerton p1272
Law—Civiliz. p167-170
People p392 (por.417)
Weeks—Discovery p362,364
(por.362)

Talbott, Harold Elstner (1888-   ). Amer. engineer, aero. pioneer.
Curr. Biog. '53 p613-614 (por.614)

Tallamy, Bertram D. (1901-   ). Amer. engineer.
Curr. Biog. '57 p547-549 (por.548)

Talley, James Ely (1864-1941). Amer. physician.
Curr. Biog. '41 p850

Talmage, James Edward (1862-1933). Eng.-Amer. geologist.
G.S.A.—Proc. '33 p259-263 (por.259)

Tanner, John Henry (1861-1940). Amer. mathematician.
Curr. Biog. '40 p789-790 (por.789)

Tansini, Igino (1855-1943). It. surgeon.
Leonardo—Lives p420-421

Tansley, Sir Arthur George (1871-1955). Eng. botanist.
Chambers—Dict. col.430
R.S.L.—Biog. (3) p227

Tarassevitch, Lyov Aleksandrovich (1868-1927). Rus. bacteriologist.
Bulloch—Hist. p399

Tarr, William Arthur (1862-1944). Amer. geologist.
G.S.A.—Proc. '39 p241-243 (por.241)

Tartaglia, Niccolò (or Fonto, Nicola) (1500?-1557/1559). It.
mathematician.
Ball—Short p217-221
Cajori—Hist. p133-134
Hammerton p1274
Hooper—Makers p88-90
Sarton—Six p29-32 (por.31)
Sedgwick—Short p237-239
Smith—Hist. I p297-299 (por.298)
Van Wagenen—Beacon p67-68
Woodruff—Devel. p293
Year—Pic. p84 (por.84)

Tatin, Victor (1843-1913). Fr. aero. pioneer.
Heinmuller—Man's p249 (por.249)

Tatum, Edward L. (1909-   ). Amer. biochemist, geneticist.
Curr. Biog. '59 p437-439 (por.438)

Taussig, Helen Brooke (1898-   ). Amer. physician.
*Clymer—Modern p91-98 (por.82)   Rowntree—Amid p470-474
Curr. Biog. '46 p50-53 (por.52)   *Truax—Doctors p184-188
Lovejoy—Women p386 (por.386)

Tavel, Ernest (1858-1912). Swiss bacteriologist, surgeon.
Bulloch—Hist. p399

Taylor, (Albert) Hoyt (1879-1961). Amer. physicist, engineer.
Curr. Biog. '45 p592-594 (por.593)
Radio's 100 p194-196 (por.140)

Taylor, Brook (1685-1731). Eng. mathematician.
Ball—Short p380-382   Magie—Source p133
Cajori—Hist. p226-228   Smith—Hist. I p451-452 (por.452)
Chambers—Dict. col.430   Woodruff—Devel. p293
Hammerton p1276

Taylor, Charles Vincent (1885-1946). Amer. biologist, zoologist.
N.A.S.—Biog. '49 p205-221 (por.205)

Taylor, David Watson (1864-1940). Amer. engineer.
N.A.S.—Biog. (22) p135-150
  (por.135)

Taylor, Frank Bursley (1860-1938). Amer. geologist.
G.S.A.—Proc. '38 p191-194 (por.191)

Taylor, Harden F. (1890-   ). Amer. biologist.
Holland—Ind. p186-206 (por.186)

Taylor, William J. (1833-1864). Amer. chemist.
Smith—Chem. p230-231

Ta Yü.   See **Yü**

Tchebichev (or Chebishef), **Pafnutiy Lvovich** (1821-1894). Rus.
  mathematician.
Hammerton p1277
Smith—Portraits (2) xii, unp. (por.)

Tchernichovsky, Saul (1875?-1943). Ger.-Palest. physician.
Curr. Biog. '43 p756
Kagan—Modern p205 (por.205)

Tchlenov, Yehiel (1863-1918). Rus. physician.
Kagan—Modern p204 (por.204)

Teague, Oscar (1878-1924). Amer. bacteriologist.
Bulloch—Hist. p399

Teale, Edwin Way (1899-   ). Amer. naturalist.
Curr. Biog. '61 (Dec.) (por.)
*Milne—Natur. p173-174

Tedder, Sir Arthur William (1890-   ). Eng. aero. pioneer.
Curr. Biog. '43 p756-758 (por.757)

Teeple, John E. (1874-1931). Amer. chemist.
Browne—Hist. p501 (por.133)

Teilhard de Chardin, Pierre (1881-1955). Fr. geologist, paleontologist.
G.S.A.—Proc. '55 p169-171 (por.169)

Teisserenc de Bort, Léon Philippe (1855-1913). Fr. meteorologist.
Chambers—Dict. col.430-431
Hammerton p1278

Telford, Thomas (1757-1834). Scot. engineer.
Hammerton p1278 (por.1278)
*Watson—Engineers p35-44 (por.34)

Telkes, Maria de (1900-   ). Hung. phys. chemist, engineer.
Curr. Biog. '50 p563-564 (por.563)

Teller, Edward (1908-   ). Hung. physicist.
Curr. Biog. '54 p598-600 (por.599)   Thomas—Men (2) p155-178
Year—Pic. p217 (por.217)   (por.106)

Tennant, Smithson (1761-1815). Eng. chemist.
Chambers—Dict. col.431
Weeks—Discovery p256-259

Tennent, David Hilt (1873-1941). Amer. biologist.
Curr. Biog. '41 p854   Progress—Science '41 p376
N.A.S.—Biog. (26) p99-115 (por.99)

Terman, Lewis Madison (1877-1956). Amer. psychologist.
Chambers—Dict. col.431
N.A.S.—Biog. (33) p414-440
  (por.414)

Terrell, Daniel Voiers (1886-   ). Amer. engineer.
Curr. Biog. '54 p601-602 (por.601)

Terry, Luther Leonidas (1911-   ). Amer. physician, surgeon.
Curr. Biog. '61 (Oct.) (por.)

Terzian, Harutyun G. (1888?-1941). Turk.-Armen.-Amer. engineer.
Curr. Biog. '41 p856

Teschner, Jacob (1858-1927). Amer. surgeon.
Kagan—Modern p99 (por.99)

Tesla, Nikola (1856/1857-1943). Yugoslav.-Amer. inventor.
Beard—Foreign p284-288 (por.284)
Curr. Biog. '43 p758
*Darrow—Masters p341
Hammerton p1282 (por.1282)
Hawks—Wireless p205-219 (por.200)
*Hodgins—Behemoth p247-249
Montgomery—Invent. p139-142
Morris—Ency. p722
*Patterson—Amer. p136-147
Radio's 100 p117-123 (por.140)

Tetrick, Paul Roderick (1920-1956). Amer. geologist.
G.S.A.—Proc. '56 p191

Thabit.   See **Tabit ibn Korra**

Thaden, Louise McPhetridge (1906-   ). Amer. aero. pioneer.
*Adams—Heroines p117-133 (por.128)
Heinmuller—Man's p331 (por.331)

Thalen, Tobias Robert (1827-1905). Swed. physicist, astronomer.
Chambers—Dict. col.431
Weeks—Discovery p407 (por.407)

Thaler, William John (1925-   ). Amer. physicist.
Curr. Biog. '60 p427-428 (por.427)

Thales of Miletus (c.640-c.546 B.C.). Gr. mathematician, astronomer.
Ball—Short p14-19
Cajori—Hist. p15-16
Chambers—Dict. col.431-432
Fenton—Giants p2-3
Gordon—Medicine p459-461 (por.460)
Hart—Physicists p3-5
Hooper—Makers p32-34
Radio's 100 p11-12 (por.140)
Sedgwick—Short p42-47
Smith—Hist. I p65-68 (por.64)
Turnbull—Great p4-6
Van Wagenen—Beacon p3-4
Williams—Great p51-52
Wilson—Human p1-5
Year—Pic. p27 (por.27)

Thaxter, Roland (1858-1932). Amer. botanist.
N.A.S.—Biog. (17) p55-64 (por.55)

Thayer, William Sidney (1846-1932). Amer. physician.
Major—History (2) p1050

Theaetus of Athens (fl.c375-368 B.C.). Gr. mathematician.
Smith—Hist. I p86

Thebesius, Adrian Christian (1686-1732). Dutch physician.
Major—History (2) p632

Theiler, Max (1899-   ). S. Afr. bacteriologist, physician.
Chambers—Dict. Supp.
Curr. Biog. '52 p586-587 (por.586)

Thelberg, Elizabeth Burr (1860-1935). Amer. physician.
Lovejoy—Women phys. p52-53
   (por.8,52)

Themison of Laodidea (123-43 B.C.). Rom. physician.
Castiglioni—Hist. p201   Oliver—Stalkers p37,38
Gordon—Medicine p645-648   Sigerist—Great p61-62

Thenard, Baron Louis Jacques (1777-1857). Fr. chemist.
Chambers—Dict. col.432   Smith—Torch. p237 (por.237)
Hammerton p1284   Weeks—Discovery p336-341
Partington—Short p212,223   (por.336)
   (por.225)

Theodoric, Friar (or Borgognoni, Theodoric) (1205-1298). It. physician.
Castiglioni—Hist. p365   Leonardo—Lives (supp.1) p473-474
Gordon—Medieval p330-331   Major—History (1) p293-294

Theodoric the Great (or Theodoricus) (454?-536). It. physician.
Castiglioni—Hist. p290-292   Smith—Hist. I p86
Hammerton p1285

Theodosius (fl.1st cent., B.C.) Gr. astronomer, mathematician, inventor.
Hammerton p1286
Smith—Hist. I p125

Theon of Smyrna (fl.c128-183). Gr. mathematician.
Smith—Hist. I p129

Theophrastus (c.372-c.287 B.C.). Gr. naturalist, botanist.
Adams—Birth p19-21   Gordon—Medicine p576-577
Arber—Herbals p2,3,163,165,166   Hammerton p1286 (por.1286)
Bodenheimer—Hist. p170   Hawks—Pioneers p60-65
Castiglioni—Hist. p181-182 (por.182) Lambert—Medical p29-30
Clagett—Greek p51-52 (por.52)   Lambert—Minute p29-30
Fenton—Giants p11   Major—History (1) p140
                        (*Continued*)

Theophrastus—*Continued*
  Reed—Short p35-39
  Schwartz—Moments (1) p138-139
  Sedgwick—Short p84
  Van Wagenen—Beacon p17-18

Woodruff—Devel. p217-218,293
  (por.224)
Year—Pic. p33

Theorell, (Axel) Hugo Theodor (1903-   ). Swed. biochemist.
  Chambers—Dict. Supp.
  Curr. Biog. '56 p622-624 (por.623)

Thessalus (fl.375 B.C.). Gr. physician.
  Gordon—Medicine p648-649

Thessalus of Lydia (fl.c.60). Rom. physician.
  Oliver—Stalkers p37-39
    Sigerist—Great p62-63

Thibaut, Pierre (fl.c.1674). Fr. chemist.
  Chymia (2) p111-113

Thiele, Friedrich Karl Johannes (1865-1918). Ger. chemist.
  Partington—Short p320

Thiersch, Carl (1822-1895). Ger. surgeon.
  Major—History (2) p888

Thiéry, François (1719-?1775). Fr. physician.
  Major—History (2) p634

Thimonnier, Barthelemy (1793-1859). Fr. inventor.
  Abbot—Great p247-248
  Law—Civiliz. p103-106

Thiselton-Dyer, William Turner (1843-1928). Eng. botanist.
  Gilmour—British p44
  Hammerton p1287 (por.1287)

Thomas, Charles Allen (1900-   ). Amer. chemist.
  Browne—Hist. p493 (por.183)
  Curr. Biog. '50 p566-568 (por.567)

Thomas, Cyrus (1825-1910). Amer. entomologist.
  Essig.—Hist. p770-772 (por.771)

Thomas, George Holt (1869-1929). Eng. aero. pioneer.
  Burge—Ency. p640-641

Thomas, Hugh Owen (1834-1891). Eng. physician, surgeon.
Castiglioni—Hist. p879   Leonardo—Lives p421-423
Chambers—Dict. col.432-433

Thomas, Mary Frame (1816-1888). Amer. physician.
Mead—Medical p27 (por., append.)

Thomas, Miles.   See Thomas, Sir (William) Miles Webster

Thomas, Sidney Gilchrist (1850-1885). Eng. inventor, metallurgist.
Chambers—Dict. col.433   Matschoss—Great p260-261
Hammerton p1288   (por.253)

Thomas, Theodore Gaillard (1831-1903). Amer. physician, surgeon,
gynecologist.
Leonardo—Lives (Supp.1) p512-513
Marr—Pioneer p121-139 (por.122)

Thomas, William L., Jr. (1920-   ). Amer. anthropologist.
Curr. Biog. '58 p431-433 (por.432)

Thomas, Sir (William) Miles Webster (1897-   ). Welsh engineer, aero.
pioneer.
Curr. Biog. '52 p590-592 (por.591)

Thomas, William Sturgis (1871-1941). Amer. physician.
Curr. Biog. '42 p834

Thompson, Benjamin.   See Rumford, Sir Benjamin Thompson, Count

Thompson, Browder Julian (1904-1944). Amer. engineer.
Radio's 100 p278-280 (por.140)

Thompson, David Grosh (1888-1943). Amer. geologist.
G.S.A.—Proc. '43 p235-238 (por.235)

Thompson, Edward Herbert (1860-1935). Amer. archaeologist.
Ceram—Gods p375-390

Thompson, Sir Henry (1820-1904). Eng. surgeon.
Hammerton p1289
Thorwald—Century p42-46,50-51
(por.80)

Thompson, Homer Armstrong (1906-   ). Can. archaeologist.
Curr. Biog. '48 p618-619 (por.619)

Thompson, (James) Maurice (1844-1901). Amer. naturalist.
Tracy—Amer. Nat. p130-137

Thompson, John Vaughan (1779-1847). Eng. surgeon.
Chambers—Dict. col.433

Thompson, Mary Harris (1829-1895). Amer. physician.
Lovejoy—Women p88-91 (por.89)
Mead—Medical p53-54
(por.,append.)

Thompson, Maurice. See **Thompson, (James) Maurice**

Thompson, Paul Williams (1906-   ). Amer. engineer.
Curr. Biog. '42 p834-835 (por.835)

Thompson, Reginald Campbell (1876-1941). Eng. archaeologist.
Curr. Biog. '41 p857   Hammerton p1289
Gordon—Medicine p188 (por.188)

Thompson, Silvanus Phillips (1851-1916). Eng. physicist, elec. engineer.
A.A.A.S.—Proc. (79) p39-40
Hammerton p1289

Thompson, Zadoc (or Zadock) (1796-1856). Amer. geologist, naturalist.
Merrill—First p248-249 (por.248)
Youmans—Pioneers p319-326
(por.319)

Thomsen, Christian Jurgensen (1788-1865). Dan. archaeologist.
People p397

Thomsen, (Hans Peter Jürgen) Julius (1826-1909). Dan. chemist.
Copen.—Prom. p143-147   Smith—Torch. p238 (por.238)
Findlay—Hundred p335   Woodruff—Devel. p121,293
Hammerton p1289

Thomson, Sir Arthur (1861-1933). Brit. biologist, zoologist.
*Bridges—Masters p259-267 (por.260)

Thomson, Sir Charles Wyville (1830-1882). Scot. biologist, naturalist.
Bodenheimer—Hist. p421
Chambers—Dict. col.433-434

Thomson, Elihu (1853-1937). Eng.-Amer. inventor, elec. engineer.
Abbot—Great p25-31 (por.28)   Hammerton p1289-1290
(Continued)

Thomson, Elihu—*Continued*
John Fritz p91-93 (por.90)
*Montgomery—Invent. p143-145

N.A.S.—Biog. (21) p143-162
(por.143)
Radio's 100 p106-109 (por.140)

Thomson, Sir George Paget (1892-   ). Eng. physicist.
Chambers—Dict. col.434
Curr. Biog. '47 p635-637 (por.636)
Heathcote—Nobel p353,362-368
(por.240)

Weber—College p640 (por.640)
Year—Pic. p211 (por.211)

Thomson, James (1822-1892). Irish physicist.
Chambers—Dict. col.434
Hammerton p1290

Thomson, Sir John Arthur (1861-1933). Scot. naturalist, biologist.
Chambers—Dict. col.434
Hammerton p1290 (por.1290)

Thomson, Sir Joseph John (1856-1940). Eng. physicist.
*Book—Pop. Sci. (15) p5137-5138
(por.5138)
Chalmers—Historic p273
Chambers—Dict. col.434-436
(por.435)
Curr. Biog. '40 p801
*Darrow—Masters p341
G.S.A.—Proc. '45 p271-272 (por.271)
Gregory—British p29,41 (por.33)
Hammerton p1290 (por.1290)
Heathcote—Nobel p41-51 (por.240)
Holmyard—British p74-76 (por.74)
*Jaffe—Crucibles p265-288
*Larsen—Scrap. p140,143,180
(por.145)
Magie—Source p583

Morgan—Men p85-111 (por.93)
Moulton—Auto. p502-503
People p397-398 (por.414)
Radio's 100 p109-113 (por.140)
Riedman—Men p46-64
Schwartz—Moments (2) p913-915
*Science Miles p242 (por.242)
*Shippen—Design p107-111
Smith—Torch. p239 (por.239)
Van Wagenen—Beacon p414-416
Weber—College p105 (por.105)
Woodruff—Devel. p293 (por.66)
Year—Pic. p207 (por.207)

Thomson, Thomas (1773-1852). Ger. chemist.
A.A.A.S.—Proc. (81) p90-92
Chambers—Dict. col.436
Chymia (1) p37-51 (por.44)

Hammerton p1290
Partington—Short p214 (por.173)
Weeks—Discovery p191 (por.191)

Thomson, William.   See Kelvin, William Thomson, Lord

Thoreau, Henry David (1817-1862). Amer. naturalist.
Hammerton p1290 (por.1290)
*Milne—Natur. p99-104 (por.98)
Peattie—Gather p321-325

People p398
Tracy—Amer. Nat. p67-85
Welker—Birds p91-114

Thorek, Max (1886-1960). Hung.-Amer. physician, surgeon.
Curr. Biog. '51 p621-623 (por.622)
'60 p432

Thorndike, Edward Lee (1874-1949). Amer. psychologist.
Chambers—Dict. col.436
Curr. Biog. '41 p857-859 (por.857)
  '49 p602
Hammerton p1290
N.A.S.—Biog. (27) p209-222 (por.209)
Progress—Science '41 p377 (por.377)

Thorne, Charles Embree (1846-1936). Amer. agriculturist.
*Ivins—Fifty p275-284 (por.274)

Thorpe, Jocelyn Field (1872-1940). Eng. chemist.
Findlay—British p369-401 (por.369)
Partington—Short p321

Thorpe, Sir (Thomas) Edward (1845-1925). Eng. chemist.
Chambers—Dict. col.436-437
Hammerton p1291
Partington—Short p353
Smith—Torch. p240 (por.246)
Weeks—Discovery p198 (por.198)

Thuillier, Louis (Ferdinand) (1856-1883). Fr. bacteriologist.
Bulloch—Hist. p399

Thunberg, Carl Peter (1743-1828). Swed. botanist.
Lindroth—Swedish p151-159

Thuret, Gustave Adolphe (1817-1875). Fr. biologist.
Hammerton p1293

Thurneisser zum Thurn (or Thurneyser), **Leonhardt** (1530-1595). Swiss botanist.
Arber—Herbals p258-260,261
Major—History (1) p474

Thurstone, Louis Leon (1887-1955). Amer. psychologist.
N.A.S.—Biog. (30) p349-382 (por.349)

Tiegs, Oscar Werner (1897-1956). Austral. biologist.
R.S.L.—Biog. (3) p247-253 (por.247)

Tiemann, (Johann Karl) Ferdinand (1848-1899). Ger. chemist.
Chambers—Dict. col.437

Tigerstedt, Robert (1853-1923). Fin. physiologist.
Major—History (2) p1050

Tilden, Sir William Augustus (1842-1926). Eng. chemist.
Chambers—Dict. col.437
Findlay—Hundred p335-336
Smith—Torch. p241 (por.241)

Tilghman, Benjamin Chew (1821-1901). Amer. inventor.
Iles—Leading p369-392 (por.369)
*Montgomery—Invent. p170-173

Timby, Theodore Ruggles (1819-1909). Amer. inventor.
Hammerton p1296

Tinker, Clarence Leonard (1887-1942). Amer. aero. pioneer.
Curr. Biog. '42 p835-836 (por.836)

Tiselius, Arne Wilhelm Kaurin (1902-   ). Swed. chemist.
Chambers—Dict. col.437-438   Farber—Nobel p194-198 (por.118)
Curr. Biog. '49 p603-604 (por.603)

Tishler, Max (1907-   ). Amer. chemist.
Curr. Biog. '52 p593-595 (por.594)

Tissandier, Albert (1839-1906). Fr. aero. pioneer.
Heinmuller—Man's p250 (por.250)

Tissandier, Gaston (1843-1899). Fr. aero. pioneer.
Heinmuller—Man's p250 (por.250)

Tisserand, (François) Félix (1845-1896). Fr. astronomer.
*Book—Pop. Sci. (15) p5176-5177
Hammerton p1297-1298

Titchener, Edward Bradford (1867-1927). Eng.-Amer. psychologist.
Hammerton p1298

Titus Lucretius Carus.   See **Lucretius**

Tizard, Sir Henry Thomas (1885-   ). Eng. physicist.
Chambers—Dict. col.438
Curr. Biog. '49 p604-606 (por.605)

Tizzoni, Guido (1853-1932). It. bacteriologist, pathologist.
Bulloch—Hist. p399

Toch, Maximilian (1864-1946). Amer. chemist.
Curr. Biog. '46 p603

Todd, Sir Alexander Robertus (1907-   ). Scot. chemist.
Chambers—Dict. col.438
Curr. Biog. '58 p437-439 (por.437)

Todd, Charles (1869-1957). Eng. physician.
R.S.L.—Biog. (4) p281-288
(por.281)

Todhunter, Isaac (1820-1884). Eng. mathematician.
Hammerton p1299   Smith—Hist. I p468-469
MacFarlane—Lectures p134-146
(por.,front.)

Toftpy, Holger Nelson (1902-   ). Amer. space pioneer.
Thomas—Men p.xiii-xiv   Thomas—Men (3) p208-236 (por.74)
Thomas—Men (2) p.xiii-xiv

Toldt, Carl (1840-1920). Aust. physician.
Major—History (2) p1050

Tollens, Bernard Christian Gottfried (1841-1918). Ger. chemist.
Chambers—Dict. col.348
Smith—Torch. p242 (por.242)

Tolles, Robert B. (1824-1883). Amer. optician.
Three—Amer. p35-51 (por.36)

Tolman, Richard Chace (1881-1948). Amer. math. physicist, phys.
chemist.
Jaffe—Outposts p506-514 (por.491)
N.A.S.—Biog. (27) p139-144 (por.139)

Tombaugh, Clyde William (1906-   ). Amer. astronomer.
Chambers—Dict. col.438

Tomlinson, Henry Major (1873-1958). Eng. naturalist.
Von Hagen—Green p312

Tonstall.   See **Tunstall, Cuthbert**

Topping, Norman (1908-   ). Amer. physician.
Curr. Biog. '59 p451-452 (por.451)

Topsell, Edward (d.1638?). Eng. naturalist.
Raven—English p217-226

Torella, Gaspar (fl.1500). Sp. physician.
Major—History (1) p464

Torre   See **Della Torre, Giacomo of Forli**

Torres, Hermión Larios (1886-   ). Mex. geologist.
G.S.A.—Proc. '52 p175

Torrey, John (1796-1873). Amer. botanist, chemist.
*Book—Pop. Sci. (14) p4942-4943   Smith—Chem. p220-221
*Hylander—Scien. p56-59 (por.53)   Youmans—Pioneers p327-335
N.A.S.—Biog. (1) p265-276   (por.327)

Torricelli, Evangelista (1608-1647). It. mathematician, physicist.
*Book—Pop. Sci. (15) p5138-5139   Meyer—World p233-234
  (por.5139)   Schwartz—Moments (1) p346-347
Chambers—Dict. col.439   Sedgwick—Short p256-258
Hammerton p1303   Smith—Hist. I p366
Hart—Physicists p54-56   Van Wagenen—Beacon p112-114
Lenard—Great p48-49 (por.52)   Year—Pic. p84 (por.84)
Magie—Source p70

Toscanelli, Paolo dal Pozzo (1397-1482). It. physician, astronomer.
Abetti—History p54-62

Tossignano.   See **Pietro Curialti da Tossignano**

Totten, Joseph Gilbert (1788-1864). Amer. engineer.
N.A.S.—Biog. (1) p35-97

Tour, Cagniard de la (1777-1859). Fr. physicist.
Magie—Source p181

Tournachon, Felix.   See **Nadar, A.**

Tournefort, Joseph Pitton de (1656-1708). Fr. botanist, biologist.
Bodenheimer—Hist. p286   Miall—Early p230-231
Hawks—Pioneers p240-241 (por.242) Woodruff—Devel. p293

Toussaint, H. (1847-1890). Fr. bacteriologist.
Bulloch—Hist. p400

Toussaint, Manuel (1860-1927). Mex. surgeon.
Leonardo—Lives p423-424

Tower, Beauchamp (1845-1904). Eng. inventor, engineer.
Chalmers—Historic p274

Townsend, Charles Henry Tyler (1863-1944). Amer. entomologist, biologist, physicist.
Osborn—Fragments p212 (por.344)

Townsend, John Kirk (1809-1851). Amer. naturalist, ornithologist.
Alden—Early p40-42

Townsend, Sir John Sealy Edward (1868-1957). Irish physicist.
Chambers—Dict. col.439
R.S.L.—Biog. (3) p257-270 (por.257)

Tozzer, Alfred Marston (1877-1954). Amer. anthropologist.
N.A.S.—Biog. (30) p383-397 (por.383)

Tracy, Martha (1876-1942). Amer. physician.
*Fleischman—Careers p334

Traill, William Acheson (1844-1933). Irish geologist.
Hammerton p1305

Tranum, John (1902-1935). Dan.-Amer. aero. pioneer.
Burge—Ency. p641

Trask, James D. (1890-1942). Amer. pediatrician.
Curr. Biog. '42 p843

Traube, Ludwig (1818-1876). Ger. physician, pathologist.
Chambers—Dict. col.439   Major—Hist. (2) p884
Kagan—Modern p10 (por.10)

Traube, Moritz (1826-1894). Ger. chemist.
Bulloch—Hist. p400
Chambers—Dict. col.439-440

Travell, Janet Graeme (1901-   ) Amer. physician.
Curr. Biog. '61 (Dec.) (por.)

Travers, Benjamin (1783-1858). Eng. surgeon.
Leonardo—Lives p424-425

Travers, Morris William (b.1872). Eng. chemist.
Chambers—Dict. col.440
Weeks—Discovery p478-481 (por.480)

Treherne, Reginald Charles (1886-1924). Eng.-Can. entomologist.
Osborn—Fragments p210-211

Trelease, William (1857-1945). Amer. botanist.
N.A.S.—Biog. (35) p307-316
  (por.307)

Trembley, Abraham (1700-1784). Swiss naturalist, biologist.
Bodenheimer—Hist. p293
Miall—Early p279-284

Trendelenburg, Friedrich (1844-1924). Ger. physician, surgeon.
Leonardo—Lives p425-428   Rosen—Four p40-42,97-101
Major—History (2) p1050-1051

Trevan, John William (1887-1956). Eng. physiologist.
R.S.L.—Biog. (3) p273-287
(por.273)

Treves, Sir Frederick (1853-1923). Eng. surgeon.
Chambers—Dict. col.440   Major—History (2) p960,1051
Hammerton p1308 (por.1308)

Treviranus, Gottfried Reinhold (1776-1837). Ger. naturalist, physician.
Chambers—Dict. col.440   Osborn—Greeks p283-291
Hammerton p1308   Woodruff—Devel. p293

Treviranus, Ludolf Christian (1779-1864). Ger. naturalist, physician,
  botanist.
Chambers—Dict. col.441

Trevisan, Bernard (1406-1490). It. chemist.
*Jaffe—Crucibles p1-17
*Men—Scien. p10-12

Trevithick, Richard (1771-1833). Eng. engineer, inventor.
*Book—Pop. Sci. (15) p5155-5156   *Larsen—Prentice p24-26
  (por.5156)   Law—Civiliz. p18-26
Chambers—Dict. col.441   Matchoss—Great p154-171 (por.170)
*Epstein—Real p65-66   People p400-402 (por.407)
Goddard—Eminent p190-196   Year—Pic. p115,148,149,150
  (por.190)   (por.115)
Hammerton p1308 (por.1308)

Trippe, Juan Terry (1899-   ). Amer. aero. pioneer.
Curr. Biog. '42 p843-845 (por.843)   Daniel—Pioneer. p73-77 (por.72)
  '55 p613-616 (por.614)   Holland—Arch. p175-191

Troja, Michele (1747-1827). It. surgeon.
Leonardo—Lives p428

Troost, Gerard (1776-1850). Dutch-Amer. geologist, mineralogist.
Merrill—First p111-112 (por.112)   Youmans—Pioneers p119-127
Smith—Chem. p222   (por.119)

Troost, Louis J. (1825-1911). Fr. chemist.
Smith—Torch. p243 (por.243)

Trotula of Salerno (or Dame Trott) (c.1000). It. physician, surgeon.
Castiglioni—Hist. p303   Major—History (1) p275
Lambert—Medical p75   Mozans—Woman p284-286
Leonardo—Lives (Supp.1) p513

Trousseau, Armand (1801-1867). Fr. physician.
Major—History p772-773

Trout, "Bobby" (1906-   ). Amer. aero. pioneer.
Heinmuller—Man's p341 (por.341)

Trowbridge, Augustus (1870-1934). Amer. physicist.
N.A.S.—Biog. (18) p219-241,244
 (por.219)

Trowbridge, John (1843-1923). Amer. physicist.
Hawks—Wireless p121-128   *Towers—Beacon p190-194
N.A.S.—Biog. (14) p185-200
 (por.185)

Trowbridge, William Petit. (1825-1892). Amer. engineer.
N.A.S.—Biog. (3) p363-367

Truax, Robert C. (1917-   ). Amer. space pioneer.
Thomas—Men (2) p179-201

Trudeau, Arthur G. (1902-   ). Amer. engineer.
Curr. Biog. '58 p442-443 (por.442)

Trudeau, Edward Livingstone (1848-1915). Amer. physician.
Major—History (2) p1051   *Shippen—Men p163-173 (por.163)
Rowntree—Amid p47-54 (por.47)   Tobey—Riders p201-220 (por.214)
Rosen—Four p104-108,265-269

True, Alfred Charles (1853-1929). Amer. agriculturist.
*Ivins—Fifty p315-320 (por.317)

True, Rodney Howard (1866-1940). Amer. botanist, physiologist.
Curr. Biog. '40 p815

Trueman, Arthur Elijah (1894-1956). Eng. paleontologist.
R.S.L.—Biog. (4) p291-302 (por.291)

Trumbull, James Hammond (1821-1897). Amer. philologist.
N.A.S.—Biog. (7) p143-161 (por.143)

Truog, Emil (1884-   ). Amer. agriculturist.
*Yost—Science p254-270

Tryon, Lewis R. (1872-1951). Amer. physician.
Fabricant—Why p19-22

Tschirnaus (or Tschirnhausen), **Ehrenfried Walter von** (1651-1708). Ger. mathematician.
Cajori—Hist. p225-226
Smith—Hist. I p417

Tsiolkovskii (or Ziolkovsky), **Konstantin Edouardovich** (1857-1935). Rus. rocket engineer, physicist, inventor.
Gartmann—Men p26-34 (por.32)   *Williams—Rocket p52-69 (por.114)
Thomas—Men p90-110
   (por.140,folio)

Tsung-Dao.   See **Lee, Tsung-Dao**

Tswett (or Tsvett), **Mikhail Semenovich** (1872-1919). Rus. botanist.
Chambers—Dict. col.441

Tuckerman, Edward (1817-1886). Amer. botanist.
N.A.S.—Biog. (3) p15-25

Tuckwell, Henry Matthews (1834-1906). Eng. physician.
Gunther—Early XI p151

Tuffier, Théodore (1857-1929). Fr. surgeon.
Major—History (2) p1051

Tulasne, Louis-René (1815-1885). Eng. agriculturist, inventor.
Reed—Short p271-272

Tull, Jethro (1674-1741). Eng. agriculturist.
Hammerton p1312 (por.1312)

Tulp, Nicholas (1593-1674). Dutch physician.
Major—History (1) p538-539

Tunstall (or Tonstall), **Cuthbert** (1474-1559). Eng. mathematician.
Smith—Hist. I p316-317

Tuomey, Michael (1808-1857). Irish-Amer. geologist.
Merrill—First p266-269 (por.268)

Tupolev, André Nickolaevich (1888-   ). Rus. engineer, aero. pioneer.
Curr. Biog. '57 p560-562 (por.561)

Turing, Alan Mathison (1912-1954). Eng. mathematician.
R.S.L.—Biog. (1) p253-263 (por.253)

Turnbull, Hubert Maitland (1875-1955). Scot. pathologist.
R.S.L.—Biog. (3) p289-301 (por.289)

Turner, Charles Cyril (1870-1920). Brit. aero. pioneer.
Burge—Ency. p641

Turner, Charles Henry (1867-1923). Amer. entomologist.
Osborn—Fragments p202 (por.349)

Turner, Edward (1798-1837). Eng. chemist.
Chambers—Dict. col.442

Turner, Sir George (1836-1915). Brit. bacteriologist.
Hammerton p1314

Turner, Henry Ward (1857-1937). Amer. geologist.
G.S.A.—Proc. '38 p201-203 (por.201)

Turner, Roscoe (1895-   ). Amer. aero. pioneer.
Heinmuller—Man's p166-167,335
   (por.171,335)

Turner, Scott (1880-   ). Amer. min. engineer.
*Yost—Engineers p60-76

Turner, William (1510/1520-1568). Eng. botanist, physician, naturalist.
Arber—Herbals p119-124,153,155   Major—History (1) p472-473
Chambers—Dict. col.442   Miall—Early p76-78
Gilmour—British p8-10   Raven—English p48-137
Hammerton p1315   Reed—Short p69-70
Hawks—Pioneers p144-150   Woodruff—Devel. p293

Twining, Louise (1820-1912). Eng. archaeologist.
Mozans—Woman p316

Twining, Nathan Faragut (1897-   ). Amer. aero. pioneer.
Curr. Biog. '53 p629-631 (por.630)

Twort, Frederick William (1877-1950). Eng. bacteriologist.
Bulloch—Hist. p400
Chambers—Dict. col.442
Grainger—Guide p175

Twyman, Frank (1876-1959). Eng. elec. engineer.
R.S.L.—Biog. (5) p269-275 (por.269)

Tye, Mrs. H. H.   See **South, Lillian H.**

Tylor, Sir Edward Burnett (1832-1917). Eng. anthropologist.
Gunther—Early XI p75
Hammerton p1317
People p405
Van Wagenen—Beacon p358-360

Tyndall, John (1820-1893). Irish physicist.
*Book—Pop. Sci. (15) p5139-5140
  (por.5140)
Bulloch—Hist. p400
Chambers—Dict. col.443-444
*Darrow—Masters p341
Grainger—Guide p175-176
Gregory—British p19-20
Hammerton p1317 (por.1317)
Hubbard—Scientists (2) p59-84
  (por.59)
Lenard—Great p282 (por.282)
Locy—Biology p289-293
Van Wagenen—Beacon p313-315
World's Great p359-378 (por.362)

Tyrrell, George Gerrard (1831-1895). Amer. physician.
Jones—Memories p353-357 (por.353)

Tyrrell, Joseph Burr (1858-1957). Can. geologist, engineer, sci. explorer.
G.S.A.—Proc. '57 p167-168 (por.167)

Tyson, Edward (1650-1708). Eng. physician.
Woodruff—Devel. p234,294

Tyson, Philip T. (1799-1877). Amer. geologist.
Merrill—First p290-292 (por.291)

Tytler, James (1747-1805). Eng. aero. pioneer.
Burge—Ency. p641

U

Udet, Ernst (1896-1941). Ger. aero. pioneer.
Heinmuller—Man's p301 (por.301)

Uffreduzzi, Ottorino (1881-1943). It. surgeon.
Leonardo—Lives p428

Ugo Borgognasi.   See **Hugh of Lucca**

Uhlenhuth, Paul Theodore (1870-1954). Ger. bacteriologist.
Bulloch—Hist. p400-401

Uhler, Philip Reese (1835-1913). Amer. entomologist.
Essig—Hist. p773-775 (por.774)
Osborn—Fragments p168-170
(por.346)

Uhlworm, Oskar (1849-1929). Ger. bacteriologist.
Bulloch—Hist. p401

Ulloa, Don Antonio de (1716-1795). Sp. sci. explorer.
Von Hagen—Green p111-112
Weeks—Discovery p237 (por.237)

Ulm, Charles T. P. (1892-1934). Austral. aero. pioneer.
Burge—Ency. p641
Heinmuller—Man's p329 (por.329)

Ulrich, Edward Oscar (1857-1944). Amer. geologist.
G.S.A.—Proc. '44 p331-349 (por.331)
N.A.S.—Biog. (24) p259-275 (por.259)

Ulugh-Beg, Mirza Mahommed ben Shah Rok (1394-1449). Arab.
mathematician, astronomer.
Hammerton p1319
Smith—Hist. I p289

Ulyanof, Dmitri Ilyich (1874-1943). Rus. physician.
Curr. Biog. '43 p779

Umbgrove, Johannes Herman Frederik (1899-1954). Dutch geologist.
G.S.A.—Proc. '56 p175-178 (por.175)

Underhill, Henry Michael John (1855-1920). Eng. naturalist.
Gunther—Early XI p321-322

Underhill, Ruth Murray (1884-   ). Amer. anthropologist.
Curr. Biog. '54 p617-619 (por.618)

Unger, Franz (1800-1870). Aust. botanist.
Hammerton p1319

Unna, Paul Gerson (1850-1929). Ger. dermatologist.
Bulloch—Hist. p401
Kagan—Modern p78 (por.78)

Unverdorben, Otto (1806-1873). Ger. chemist.
Chambers—Dict. col.445

Unwin, William Cawthorne (1838-1933). Eng. engineer.
Hammerton p1319

Upham, Warren (1850-1934). Amer. geologist, archaeologist.
G.S.A.—Proc. '34 p281-282 (por.281)

Urbain, Georges (1872-1939). Fr. chemist.
Chambers—Dict. col.445   Weeks—Discovery p432-433 (por.432)
Smith—Torch. p244 (por.244)

Urban, Charles (b.1867). Brit. inventor.
Hammerton p1320

Ure, Andrew (1778-1857). Scot. chemist.
Hammerton p1320

Urey, Harold Clayton (1893-   ). Amer. chemist.
*Bolton—Famous p299-308 (por.298)   Hammerton p1452
Chambers—Dict. col.445-446   Hylander—Scien. p169-170
  (por.446)   Morris—Ency. p725
Curr. Biog. '41 p877-878 (por.877)   Progress—Science '40 p413-414
  '60 p441-442 (por.441)   (por.414)
Farber—Nobel p138-142 (por.118)   Ratcliffe—Modern p112-114 (por.112)
Fisher—Amer. p267-272   Riedman—Men p172-178
Fitzhugh—Concise p825   Year—Pic. p212 (por.212)

Usaybi'a   See **Ibn abt Usaybi'a**

V

Vacca-Berlinghieri, Andrea (1772-1826). It. surgeon.
Leonardo—Lives p429

Vahl, Martin (1749-1804). Dan. botanist.
Copen.—Prom. p85-88

Vail, Alfred (1807-1859). Amer. inventor.
*Burlingame—Inv. p86-89
Iles—Leading p147-148,151-152,
158-159,164-165 (por.158)

Vail, Theodore Newton (1845-1920). Amer. inventor.
*Forbes—Men p375-382 (por.1)
*Wildman—Famous (2d) p321-328
(por.321)

Vaillard, Louis (1850-1935). Fr. surgeon, bacteriologist.
Bulloch—Hist. p401

Valentin, Gabriel Gustave (1810-1883). Ger. physiologist.
Kagan—Modern p183 (por.183)

Valentine, Basil. See **Basil Valentine**

Valescus de Taranta (or Balsecon) (1382-1417). Port. physician.
Major—History (1) p354

Valier, Max (1895-1930). Aust. engineer, inventor.
Gartmann—Men p74-98 (por.65)

Valleriola, François (1504-1583). Fr. physician.
Major—History (1) p469

Vallisnieri, Antonio (1661-1730). It. physician, naturalist.
Bulloch—Hist. p401
Chambers—Dict. col.447

Valsalva, Antonio Maria (1666-1723). It. surgeon.
Castiglioni—Hist. p525-526 (por.526)   Major—History (2) p629
Leonardo—Lives p429-430

Van.   For other names containing **van,** see part of name following **van**

Van Allen, James A. (1914-   ). Amer. physicist.
Curr. Biog. '59 p461-463 (por.461)
Thomas—Men p111-132
(por.140,folio)

Van Amringe, John Howard (1835-1915). Amer. mathematician.
Smith—Math. p138-139

Van Bibber, Armfield F. (fl. 20th cent.). Amer. physician.
*Logie—Careers p260-274

Van Buren, William Holmes (1819-1883). Amer. surgeon.
Leonardo—Lives p430-431

Vandercock, John Womack (1902-   ). Eng.-Amer. sci. explorer, anthropologist.
Curr. Biog. '42 p850-851 (por.851)

Vandermonde, Alexandre-Théophile (1735-1796). Fr. mathematician.
Cajori—Hist. p266

Van der Veer, Albert (1841-1929). Amer. surgeon.
Leonardo—Lives p432-433

Van Duzee, Edward Payson (1861-1940). Amer. entomologist.
Osborne—Fragments p234 (por.341)

Van Duzee, Millard C. (d.1934). Amer. entomologist.
Osborn—Fragments p229

Vanghetti, Giuliano (1861-1940). It. surgeon.
Leonardo—Lives p433-434

Van Hise, Charles Richard (1857-1918). Amer. geologist.
N.A.S.—Biog. ('10). p145-149

Van Hoosen, Bertha (1863-1952). Amer. physician, surgeon.
Lovejoy—Women p96-98
Lovejoy—Women Phys. p33-34
   (por.32)

Van Horn, Frank Robertson (1872-1933). Amer. geologist, mineralogist.
G.S.A.—Proc. '33 p273-283 (por.273)

Van Roonhuysen, Hendrik (1625-1672). Dutch physician, surgeon.
Leonardo—Lives (Supp 1) p513-515

Van Slyke, Donald Dexter (1883-   ). Amer. chemist, physician.
Curr. Biog. '43 p781-782 (por.781)
Killeffer—Eminent p33 (por.33)
Progress—Science '41 p378-379
   (por.378)
Rowntree—Amid p369-374 (por.370)

Van't Hoff, Jacobus Henricus (1852-1911). Dutch chemist.

A.A.A.S.—Proc. (81) p62-67
*Book—Pop. Sci. (15) p5140-5142
Chambers—Dict. col.224
*Darrow—Masters p341-342
Farber—Nobel p3-6 (por.118)
Findlay—Hundred p326-327
Hammerton p1325-1326
Harrow—Chemists p79-109 (por.79)

Holmyard—Makers p286 (por.285)
*Kendall—Young p146-161,169-172
  (por.115)
Moulton—Auto. p287
Partington—Short p302-306,340
  (por.303)
Smith—Torch. p247 (por.247)
Van Wagenen—Beacon p412-414
Woodruff—Devel. p278 (por.110)

Vanuxem, Lardner (1792-1848). Amer. geologist.

Merrill—First p122-123 (por.188)
Smith—Chem. p220

Youmans—Pioneers p270-278
  (por.270)

Vaquez, (Louis) Henri (1860-1936). Fr. physician.

Major—History (2) p919

Varahamihira (fl.c.505). Ind. astronomer.

Smith—Hist. I p156-157

Varenius, Bernhardus (1622-1650). Ger. geographer.

Hammerton p1327

Varian, Russell Harrison (1898-   ). Amer. engineer.

Radio's 100 p272-274 (por.140)

Varignon, Pierre (1654-1722). Fr. mathematician.

Ball—Short p370
Magie—Source p46-47

Smith—Hist. I p470-471

Varoli (or Varolio), **Constanzo** (1543?-1575). It. anatomist, surgeon.

Major—History (1) p476

Varro, Marcus Terentius (116-27 B.C.). Rom. nat. philosopher.

Castiglioni—Hist. p203-204
Gordon—Medicine p663-664

Hammerton p1326
Smith—Hist. I p121

Vauban, Sebastien le Preste de (1633-1707). Fr. engineer.

Hammerton p1326-1327

Vaughan, Benjamin (1751-1835). Amer. physician, agriculturist.

Bell—Early p75-76

Vaughan, Guy Warner (1884-   ). Amer. engineer, aero. pioneer.

Curr. Biog. '48 p643-645 (por.644)

Vaughan, John (1756-1841). Amer. physician, agriculturist.
Bell—Early p75-76

Vaughan, Thomas Wayland (1870-1952). Amer. geologist, oceanographer.
N.A.S.—Biog. (32) p399-409 (por.399)

Vaughan, Victor Clarence (1851-1929). Amer. biochemist, bacteriologist.
A.A.A.S.—Proc. (79) p40-42
Bulloch—Hist. p401

Vauquelin, Louis Nicolas (1763-1829). Fr. chemist.
Chambers—Dict. col.447
Hammerton p1327 (por.1327)
Partington—Short p177 (por.218)
Smith—Torch. p248 (por.248)
Weeks—Discovery p133-140 (por.136)

Veatch, Arthur Clifford (1878-1938). Amer. geologist.
G.S.A.—Proc. '41 p201-205 (por.201)

Védrines, Jules (1882-1919). Fr. aero. pioneer.
Hammerton p1327
Heinmuller—Man's p287 (por.287)

Vega, George, Baron von (1754-1802). Aust. mathematician.
Chambers—Dict. col.447

Velikovsky, Immanuel (1895-   ). Rus.-Amer. physician, psychologist.
Curr. Biog. '57 p564-566 (por.565)

Velpeau, Alfred Armand Louis Marie (1795-1865). Fr. physician, surgeon.
Castiglioni—Hist. p714 (por.714)
Leonardo—Lives p434-435
Major—History (2) p773-775 (por.774)

Venable, Francis P. (1856-1934). Amer. chemist.
Browne—Hist. p479 (por.73)

Venel, Jean Andre (1740-1790). Swiss surgeon.
Leonardo—Lives p435-437

Verbez.   See Gerbezius, Marcus

Veresaev, Vikenti (or Smidovich, Vasili Vasilievich). (1867-1944). Rus. physician.
Rosen—Four p113-116,194-196

Vernier, Pierre (1580-1637). Fr. mathematician, inventor.
Chambers—Dict. col.448
Hammerton p1333

Vernon-Harcourt, Augustus George (1834-1919). Eng. chemist.
Chambers—Dict. col.448

Verrier.   See Leverrier, Urbain Jean Joseph

Verrill, Addison Emery (1839-1926). Amer. zoologist, entomologist.
*Book—Pop. Sci. (14) p4943-4944   Osborn—Fragments p172-173
   (por.4944)   (por.349)
N.A.S.—Biog. (14) p19-41 (por.19)

Very, Frank Washington (1852-1927). Amer. astronomer.
Chambers—Dict. col.448-449

Vesalius, Andreas (1514-1564). Flem. anatomist, physician.
Atkinson—Magic p151-155
Bodenheimer—Hist. p227
*Book—Pop. Sci. (15) p5115
Castiglioni—Hist. p418-425 (por.426)
Chambers—Dict. col.449
*Chandler—Medicine p23-27
*Elwell—Sci p27-28
*Fox—Great p3-30 (por.3)
Gordon—Medieval p625-632 (por.147)
Gordon—Romance p65,74,110-111,
   287 (por.65,287)
Gumpert—Trail p31-66
Hammerton p1334
Lambert—Medical p103-110 (por.104)
Lambert—Minute p103-110 (por.97)
Leonardo—Lives p437-438
Locy—Biology p22-23,27-38 (por.29)
Major—History (1) p404-408
   (por.405,407)
Moulton—Auto. p94
Oliver—Stalkers p74-76 (por.75)
People p429-430 (por.440)
Robinson—Path. p83-98 (por.94-95)
Sarton—Six p175-178 (por.176)
Schwartz—Moments (2) p515-517
*Science Miles. p48 (por.48)
Sedgwick—Short p226-227
*Shippen—Men p79-83
*Shippen—Micro. p50-54
Sigerist—Great p125-129 (por.128)
*Snyder—Biology p33-36 (por.35)
*Truax—Doctors p17-30
Van Wagenen—Beacon p68-69
Woodruff—Devel. p223-225,294
   (por.224)
Year—Pic. p80-81 (por.81)
Young—Scalpel p10-27 (por.24)

Viala, Eugène (d.1926). Fr. bacteriologist.
Bulloch—Hist. p401

Vicary, Thomas (c1495-1562). Eng. surgeon.
Gordon—Medieval p679
Major—History (1) p453

Vicq d'Azur, Felix (or d'Azyr, Felix Cicq) (1748-1794). Fr. anatomist, physician.
Locy—Biology p146-148 (por.147)   Woodruff—Devel. p294
Major—History (2) p639

Vidius, Guido (or Vidus Vidius) (1500-1569). It. anatomist, physician, surgeon.
Castiglioni—Hist. p436,472-473   Major—History (1) p425
Leonardo—Lives p191-192

Viereck, H. L. (1881-   ). Amer. entomologist.
Osborn—Fragments p238 (por.349)

Vierordt, Karl von (1818-1884). Ger. physician.
Major—History (2) p801-802
   (por.801)

Vièta, Franciscus (or Viète, Francois, Seigneur de la Bigotière) (1540-1603). Fr. mathematician.
Ball—Short p229-234   Sarton—Six p44-49
Cajori—Hist. p137-139   Smith—Hist. I p310-312 (por.311)
Chambers—Dict. col.449-450   Smith—Portraits (1), iii (unp.)
Hofman—History p92-101   (por.)
Hooper—Makers p101-103   Woodruff—Devel. p294
*Miller—Hist. p226-228   Year—Pic. p84 (por.84)

Vieussens, Raymond (1641-1715). Fr. anatomist, physician.
Major—History (1) p539

Vignal, William (1852-1894). Fr. bacteriologist.
Bulloch—Hist. p401-402

Vigneaud.   See **Du Vigneaud, Vincent**

Vigni, Antoine François Saugrain De (1763-1820). Amer naturalist.
Bell—Early p74

Vigo, Giovanni (or John of Vigo) (1460-1525). It. surgeon.
Gordon—Medieval p677-678

Villa, Amelia Chopitea (d.1942). Bol. physician.
Lovejoy—Women p272-273

Villalobos, Francisco Lopez de (c1473-1549?). Sp. physician.
Gordon—Medieval p708-710
Major—History (1) p463

Villemin, Jean Antoine (1827-1892). Fr. bacteriologist, physician.

Bulloch—Hist. p402
Castiglioni—Hist. p837-838 (por.838)

Major—History (2) p892 (por.840)

Vincent, Jean Hyacinthe (1862-1950). Fr. bacteriologist.

Bulloch—Hist. p402

Vincent of Beauvais (or Bellovacensis, Vicentus) (d.before 1264). Fr. chemist.

Hammerton p1340
Holmyard—Chem. p34

Holmyard—Makers p89-90
Major—History (1) p354

Vinci, Leonardo da (1452-1519). It. anatomist, physician, engineer, aero. pioneer.

Ball—Short p212-213
*Bishop—Kite p9-13
Bodenheimer—Hist. p221
Burge—Ency. p635
Castiglioni—Hist. p410-417 (por.411)
Chambers—Dict. col.450
*Cohen—Men p5-8
Gordon—Medieval p616-619
Gordon—Romance p72,74
Hammerton p897-898
Hart—Engineers p27-44
Hart—Physicists p32-38
Heinmuller—Man's p231 (por.231)
Law—Civiliz. p144-145
Lenard—Great p9-12 (por.12)
*McSpadden—How p61-80 (por.66)
Major—History (1) p359-362 (por.360)
Matschoss—Great p48-60 (por.60)

Moulton—Auto. p42-43
*Nisenson—Illus. p148 (por.148)
Osborn—Greeks p119-121
Peattie—Lives p98-107 (por.98)
People p239 (por.264)
Sarton—Six p219-233 (por.24)
*Science Miles. p29-31 (por.29)
Sedgwick—Short p228,234-235
Sewell—Brief p35-36
*Shippen—Bridle p22-27
Sigerist—Great p122-123
Smith—Hist. p294
Tuska—Invent. p110-112
Van Wagenen—Beacon p56-58
Weeks—Discovery p90 (por.90)
Woodruff—Devel. p47,294
Year—Pic. p73,82,83 (por.73)

Vines, Sydney Howard (1849-1934). Eng. botanist.

Gilmour—British p44-45
Hammerton p1340

Virchow, Rudolf (1821-1902). Ger. pathologist, physician.

*Book—Pop. Sci. (15) p5115-5116 (por.5116)
Castiglioni—Hist. p695-698 (por.695)
Chambers—Dict. col.450-451
*Chandler—Medicine p61-65 (por.60)
*Darrow—Masters p342
Gordon—Romance p49,120 (por.49)
Hammerton p1341 (por.1341)
Kagan—Leaders p22-26

Lambert—Medical p205-208 (por.208)
Lambert—Minute p205-208 (por.224)
Locy—Biology p174-175 (por.174)
Major—History (2) p806-808 (por.807)
Oliver—Stalkers p159-161 (por.160)
Sigerist—Great p335-346 (por.336)
Van Wagenen—Beacon p318-320

Virtanen, Artturi Ilmari (1895-   ). Fin. biochemist.

Chambers—Dict. col.451
Farber—Nobel p178-181 (por.118)

Vishniac, Roman (1897-   ). Rus.-Amer. microbiologist, zoologist.
Kinkead—Spider p157-244

Vitruvius Pollio, Marcus (or Pollio, Marcus Vitruvius) (1st cent. B.C.?).
Rom. engineer.
Adams—Birth p35-36
Clagett—Greek p105-107
Hammerton p1343
Matschoss—Great p16-19

Moulton—Auto. p23-24
*Science Miles. p23-24 (por.23)
Sedgwick—Short p143-144
Smith—Hist. I p123

Vives, Juan Luis (1492-1540). Sp. nat. philosopher.
Gunther—Early XI p190-191
Hammerton p1343

Vivian, William (1728-1801). Brit. physician.
Gunther—Early XI p194

Viviani, Vincenzo (1622-1703). It. mathematician, physicist.
Smith—Hist. I p367

Vleck, Edward Burr van (1863-1943). Amer. mathematician.
N.A.S.—Biog. (3) p399-409 (por.399)

Vogel, Herbert Davis (1900-   ). Amer. engineer.
Curr. Biog. '54 p627-629 (por.628)

Vogel, Hermann Carl (1841-1907). Ger. astrophysicist, astronomer.
Armitage—Cent. p172-173 (por.145)
Chambers—Dict. col.451

MacPherson—Astron. p129-137
(por.129)
MacPherson—Makers p174-176

Vogel, Hermann Wilhelm (1834-1898). Ger. chemist.
Chambers—Dict. col.451-452

Vogt, Charles Jean Melchor (1829-1914). Ger. inventor.
Hammerton p1344

Vogt, Karl Christoph (1817-1895). Ger. naturalist, geologist, zoologist.
Woodruff—Devel. p294

Vogt, William (1902-   ). Amer. ornithologist, ecologist.
Curr. Biog. '53 p638-640 (por.639)

Voisin, Charles (1888-   ). Fr. aero. pioneer.
Burge—Ency. p641
Heinmuller—Man's p266 (por.266)

Voisin, Gabriel (1886-   ). Fr. aero. pioneer.
Burge—Ency. p641

Voit, Carl von (1831-1908). Ger. physiologist, chemist.
Major—History (2) p896
*Snyder—Biology p326-327

Volger, Georg Heinrich Otto (1822-1897). Swiss seismologist.
Davison—Founders p123-125

Volhard, Jacob (1834-1910). Ger. chemist.
Partington—Short p318
Smith—Torch. p249 (por.249)

Volkmann, Richard von (1830-1889). Ger. surgeon.
Leonardo—Lives p440-441
Major—History (2) p895

Volney, Constantin François de Chasseboeuf, Comte de (1757-1820). Fr. geologist.
Hammerton p1344
Merrill—First p24-30 (por.26)

Volta, Alessandro, Count (1745-1827). It. physicist, inventor.
Appleyard—Pioneers p55-83 (por.54,81)
*Book—Pop. Sci. (15) p5157-5158
Castiglioni—Hist. p649 (por.648)
Chambers—Dict. col.452
*Darrow—Masters p342
Dibner—Ten p19-22 (por.20)
*Epstein—Real p51-52
Hammerton p1344
Hart—Physicists p101-103
*Hartman—Mach. p87-88
Hawks—Wireless p22-23 (por.20)
*Hodgins—Behemoth p99-104
Law—Civiliz. p197-198
Lenard—Great p163-170 (por.159)
Magie—Source p427
Meyer—World p130-131 (por.130)
Morgan—Men p33-37
100 Great p565-568
Radio's 100 p26-28 (por.140)
Schwartz—Moments (2) p849-850
*Shippen—Design p59-61
*Simmons—Great p27 (por.27)
Smith—Torch. p250 (por.250)
*Sootin—Twelve p47-66
Tuska—Invent. p126-127
Van Wagenen—Beacon p184-185
Woodruff—Devel. p294 (por.52)
Year—Pic. p106 (por.106)

Voltaire, François Marie Arouet (or Arouet, François Marie) (1694-1778). Fr. nat. philosopher.
Hammerton p1345-1346
Smith—Hist. I p477-478

Volwiler, Ernest H. (1893-   ). Amer. chemist.
Browne—Hist. p493-494 (por.227)

Von.   For other names containing **von,** see part of name following **von.**

Von Braun, Wernher (1912-   ). Ger.-Amer. engineer, aero. pioneer, space pioneer.
Curr. Biog. '52 p607-608 (por.607)   Thomas—Men (2) p.xii-xiii
Gartmann—Men p136-159 (por.144)   Williams—Rocket p150,160,205-230
Pringle—Great p152-169   (por.114)
Thomas—Men p133-156
    (por.140, folio)

von Hohenheim.   See Paracelsus, Philippus Aureolus

Von Kármán, Theodore (1881-   ). Hung.-Amer. aerodynamicist, space pioneer.
Curr. Biog. '55 p622-624 (por.623)
Thomas—Men p157-180
    (por.140, folio)

von Lauchen.   See Rheticus, Georg Joachim

von Linné.   See Linnaeus, Carolus

von Nagyrapolt.   See Szent-Györgyi, Albert von Nagyrapolt

Von Neumann, John (1903-1957). Hung.-Amer. mathematician, space pioneer.
Curr. Biog. '55 p624-627 (por.625)   Thomas—Men p181-203
N.A.S.—Biog. (32) p438-446 (por.438)   (por.140,folio)
        Year—Pic. p202 (por.202)

von Reichenstein.   See Müller, Franz Joseph, Baron von Reichenstein

von Stradonitz.   See Kekulé von Stradonitz, Friedrich August

Voronoff, Serge (1866-1951). Rus. physician, physiologist, surgeon.
Chambers—Dict. col.452   Hammerton p1346 (por.1346)
Curr. Biog. '41 p889-890 (por.889),
    '51 p641

Vosler, Everett Jay (1890-1918). Amer. entomologist.
Essig—Hist. p776-777 (por.776)

Vosnesenskv, Ilya Gavrilovich (1816-1871). Rus. naturalist, entomologist.
Essig—Hist. p777-789 (por.780)

Voss, Werner (d.1917). Ger. aero. pioneer.
Burge—Ency. p641

Vries.   See De Vries, Hugo

W

Waage, Peter (1833-1900). Norw. chemist.
Chambers—Dict. col.453
Findlay—Hundred p336
Partington—Short p325-326,339
(por.326)
Woodruff—Devel. p114,295

Waals, Johannes Diderik van der (1837-1923). Dutch physicist.
Chambers—Dict. col.453
Hammerton p1347
Heathcote—Nobel p87-93 (por.240)
Partington—Short p339
Smith—Torch. p245 (por.245)
Weber—College p171 (por.171)

Wacksmuth, Charles (1829-1896). Amer. paleontologist.
Hammerton p1347

Wadhams, Robert Pelton (1879-1940). Amer. physician, surgeon.
Curr. Biog. '41 p892

Wafer, Lionel (1660?-1705?). Eng. physician, surgeon.
Atkinson—Magic p95-98
Von Hagen—Green p79-80

Wagner, Georg (1849-1903). Rus. chemist.
A.A.A.S.—Proc. (77) p53-54

Wagner, Rudolf (1805-1864). Ger. physiologist.
Hammerton p1348

Wagner-Jauregg, Julius von (or Wagner von Jauregg, Julius) (1857-1940).
(1857-1940). Aust. physician, neurologist, psychiatrist.
Castiglioni—Hist. p1048
Chambers—Dict. col.453
Curr. Biog. '40 p833
*DeKruif—Men p249-279 (por.253)
Grainger—Guide p176
Hammerton p1350
Major—History (2) p928-929,1037
Stevenson—Nobel p125-129 (por.150)

Wahlen, Friedrich Traugott (1899-   ). Swiss agric. engineer.
Curr. Biog. '61 (Je.) (por.)

Waite, Henry Matson (1869-1944). Amer. engineer.
Curr. Biog. '44 p709

Waitt, Alden Harry (1892-   ). Amer. chemist.
Curr. Biog. '47 p657-658 (por.657)

Wakley, Thomas (1795-1862). Eng. surgeon.
Hammerton p1351

Waksman, Selman Abraham (1888-   ). Rus.-Amer. biochemist.
Calder—Science p91-92
Chambers—Dict. col.453-454
Curr. Biog. '46 p615-617 (por.616)
*Eberle—Modern p70-72,75-77

Grainger—Guide p176
Robinson—100 p284-286 (por.284)
*Shippen—Men p207

Walcott, Charles Doolittle (1850-1927). Amer. paleontologist, geologist.
Hammerton p1351
Merrill—First p609-611,657 (por.609)

Oehser—Sons p141-166 (por.107)
True—Smiths. p293-298 (por.296)

Wald, Lillian D. (1867-1940). Amer. pub. health nurse.
16 Amer. p61-64

Walden, Paul (1863-1957). Rus. chemist.
Chambers—Dict. col.454
Hammerton p1351

Waldeyer-Hartz, Wilhelm von (1836-1921). Ger. anatomist, physician.
Hammerton p1351
Rosen—Four p264-265

Waldheim.   See Fischer von Waldheim, Gotthelf

Waldo, Frederick Joseph (b.1852). Eng. physician.
Hammerton p1351

Waldren, Percy Talbot (1869-1943). Amer. chemist.
Curr. Biog. '43 p799

Walker, Eric A. (1910-   ). Eng.-Amer. elec. engineer.
Curr. Biog. '59 p468-470 (por.469)

Walker, Francis (1809-1874). Eng. entomologist.
Essig—Hist. p789-790 (por.789)
Osborn—Fragments p28 (por.345)

Walker, Francis Amasa (1840-1897). Amer. economist, statistician.
N.A.S.—Biog. (5) p209-214 (por.209)

Walker, Gertrude A. (d.1928). Amer. physician.
Lovejoy—Women Phys. p38-41,45-46
(por.41)

Walker, Sir James (1863-1935). Scot. chemist.
Chambers—Dict. col.454-455
Partington—Short p341

Walker, James Thomas (1826-1896). Eng. engineer.
Hammerton p1352

Walker, John (1781?-1859). Eng. chemist.
Chambers—Dict. col.455
Hammerton p1352 (por.1352)

Walker, Mary Edwards (1832-1919). Amer. physician.
Mead—Medical p66

Walker, Norma Ford (1893-   ). Can. biologist.
Curr. Biog. '57 p574-575 (por.574)

Walker, Sears Cook (1805-1853). Amer. mathematician, inventor, astronomer.
Youmans—Pioneers p428-435 (por.428)

Walker, Thomas (c.1785-1835). Brit. aero. pioneer.
Burge—Ency. p641

Walker, Thomas Leonard (1867-1942). Can. geologist.
G.S.A.—Proc. '42 p241-243 (por.241)

Wall, John (1708-1776). Eng. physician.
Gunther—Early XI p291 (por.296)

Wallace, Alfred Russel (1823-1913). Eng. biologist, naturalist.
Bodenheimer—Hist. p406
*Book—Pop. Sci. (15) p5117-5118 (por.5117)
Chambers—Dict. col.455
Cutright—Great p23-27
*Darrow—Masters p342
Hammerton p1353 (por.1353)
Hammond—Stories p149-165 (por.161)
Hubbard—Scientists (2) p84-110 (por.84)
Locy—Biology p428,435-437 (por.436)
*Milne—Natur. p89-96 (por.88)
Moulton—Auto. p380-381
Osborn—Impr. p1-32 (por.1)
Peattie—Gather. p247-252
Peattie—Green p298-303 (por.310)
Van Wagenen—Beacon p321-324
Von Hagen—Green p213-214
Williams—Story p309-309 (por.308)
Woodruff—Devel. p295

Wallace, Henry Cantwell (1866-1924). Amer. agriculturist.
*Ivins—Fifty p401-407 (por.400)

Wallace, Robert Charles (1881-1955). Can. geologist.
G.S.A.—Proc. '55 p177-180 (por.177)

Wallach, Otto (1847-1931). Ger. chemist.
Chambers—Dict. col.455-456   Hammerton p1354
Farber—Nobel p42-45 (por.118)   Smith—Torch. p251 (por.251)

Waller, Augustus Volney (1816-1870). Eng. physiologist.
Chambers—Dict. col.456
Hammerton p1355

Waller, Frederic (1886-1954). Amer. inventor.
Curr. Biog. '54 p633

Waller, Kenneth F. J. (1908-   ). Eng. aero. pioneer.
Hammerton p1355

Wallerius, Johan Gottschalk (1709-1785). Swed. agric. chemist, metallurgist, physician.
Lindroth—Swedish p92-97
Weeks—Discovery p54 (por.54)

Wallich, Nathaniel (1786-1854). Dan.-Eng. botanist.
Hammerton p1356

Wallin, Mathilda K. (1858-1955). Swed.-Amer. physician.
Lovejoy—Women Phys. p42,53
  (por.41)

Wallis, John (1616-1703). Eng. mathematician.
Ball—Short p288-293   Hooper—Makers p253-267
Cajori—Hist. p183-187   Magie—Source p117
Chambers—Dict. col.456   Smith—Hist. I p406-409 (por.407)
Hammerton p1356   Year—Pic. p93 (por.93)

Walsh, Benjamin Dann (1808-1869). Eng.-Amer. entomologist.
Osborn—Fragments p29-30 (por.354)
Smiths.—Misc. (84) p50-53
  (por.545,pl.2)

Walsh, James Joseph (1865-1942). Amer. physician.
Curr. Biog. '42 p864
Kagan—Modern p211 (por.211)

Walsingham, Lord Gray, Thomas de (1843-1919). Eng. entomologist.
Essig—Hist. p791-792 (por.791)

Walston, Sir Charles (1856-1927). Brit. archaeologist.
Hammerton p1359

Walter, Philipp (1810-1847). Pol. chemist.
Chambers—Dict. col.456

Walther, Johannes (1860-1937). Ger. geologist.
G.S.A.—Proc. '37 p221-227 (por.221)

Walther, Philipp Franz (1782-1848). Ger. surgeon.
Leonardo—Lives p442

Walton, Ernest Thomas Sinton (1903-   ). Irish physicist.
Chambers—Dict. col.456   Year—Pic. p212 (por.212)
Curr. Biog. '52 p618-620 (por.619)

Wandke, Alfred (1887-1941). Amer. geologist.
G.S.A.—Proc. '41 p211-213 (por.211)

War.   See Dewar, Sir James

Warburg, Otto (b.1859). Ger. botanist.
Hammerton p1360

Warburg, Otto Heinrich (1883-1938). Ger. physiologist, chemist.
Chambers—Dict. col.457   *Snyder—Biology p318-319
Hammerton p1360   Stevenson—Nobel p148-153
      (por.150)

Ward, Freeman (1879-1943). Amer. geologist.
G.S.A.—Proc. '43 p243-246 (por.243)

Ward, Harry Marshall (1854-1906). Eng. botanist.
Bulloch—Hist. p402   Oliver—Makers p261-279 (por.261)
Gilmour—British p45

Ward, James (1843-1925). Eng. psychologist.
Hammerton p1362

Ward, James Benjamin (1915-1952). Amer. geologist.
G.S.A.—Proc. '52 p177

Ward, Seth (1617-1689). Eng. astronomer.
Hammerton p1362

Wardrop, James (1782-1869). Scot. surgeon.
Leonardo—Lives p442-443

Ware, John (1795-1864). Amer. physician.
Farmer—Doctors' p123

Wargentin, Pehr Wilhelm (1717-1783). Swed. astronomer.
Lindroth—Swedish p105-112

Waring, Edward (1734-1798). Eng. mathematician.
Cajori—Hist. p248-249

Warming, Johannes Eugenius Bülow (1841-1924). Dan. botanist.
Copen.—Prom. p156-160

Warner, Edward Pearson (1894-1958). Amer. aero. pioneer, engineer.
Curr. Biog. '49 p620-622 (por.621)   Daniel—Pioneer. p123-129 (por.122)
'58 p456

Warner, John Christian (1897-). Amer. chemist.
Curr. Biog. '50 p595-596 (por.596)

Warner, Lucien C. (1841-1925). Amer. chemist, physician.
Haynes—Chem. (1) p124-142
(por.128,129)

Warner, William Lloyd (1898-). Amer. anthropologist.
Curr. Biog. '59 p474-476 (por.475)

Warnerford, Reginald Alexander John (1892-1915). Eng. aero. pioneer.
Arnold—Airmen p132-133

Warren, Charles Hyde (1876-1950). Amer. mineralogist, petrologist,
geologist.
G.S.A.—Proc. '51 p159-163 (por.159)

Warren, Edward (b.1771?). Amer. aero. pioneer.
Milbank—First p21-23

Warren, Gouverneur Kemble (1830-1882). Amer. engineer.
N.A.S.—Biog. (2) p173-188

Warren, John (1753-1815). Amer. physician.
Farmer—Doctors' p53-54   Major—History (2) p736
Kagan—Modern p84 (por.84)

Warren, John Collins (1778-1856). Amer. surgeon.

Farmer—Doctors' p89,90
Fülöp—Miller p142-158 (por.152)
Kagan—Modern p85 (por.85)
Leonardo—Lives p444-445

Major—History (2) p738
Thorwald—Century p16-23,89-91,
    104-110,151-154 (por.48)
Wilson—Amer. p106-107 (por.107)

Warren, Jonathan Mason (1811-1867). Amer. surgeon.

Leonardo—Lives p445-446

Warren, Shields (1898-   ). Amer. physician, pathologist.

Curr. Biog. '50 p597-598 (por.597)

Washbourn, John Wichenford (1863-1902). Eng. bacteriologist, physician.

Bulloch—Hist. p402

Washburn, Edward Wight (1881-1934). Amer. chemist.

N.A.S.—Biog. (17) p69-77 (por.69)

Washburn, F. L. (1860-1927). Amer. entomologist.

Osborn—Fragments p210 (por.372)

Washburn, Frank S. (1860-1926). Amer. chemist, engineer.

Haynes—Chem. (1) p243-258
    (por.248)

Washburn, Margaret Floy (1871-1939). Amer. psychologist.

N.A.S.—Biog. (25) p275-285 (por.275)

Washington, Henry Stephens (1867-1934). Amer. geologist.

G.S.A.—Proc. '51 p165-168 (por.165)

Wasserman, August von (1866-1925). Ger. bacteriologist.

Bulloch—Hist. p402
Gordon—Romance p338 (por.338)
Hammerton p1366

Kagan—Modern p164 (por.164)
Major—History (2) p932-933

Waterhouse, Benjamin (1754-1846). Amer. physician.

Bell—Early p76-77
Carmer—Caval. p195-197
    (por.195,197)

Farmer—Doctors' p77,78
Major—History (2) p736-737

Waterman, Alan Tower (1892-   ). Amer. physicist.

Curr. Biog. '51 p643-644 (por.643)

Waterston, John James (1811-1883). Scot. physicist.

Chambers—Dict. col.457

Waterton, Charles (1782-1865). Eng. naturalist.
Cutright—Great p12-15   People p437 (por.443)
Hammerton p1367 (por.1367)

Watkins, Thomas James (1863-1925). Amer. gynecologist, surgeon.
Leonardo—Lives p446-447

Watson, Hewett Cottrell (1804-1881). Eng. botanist.
Gilmour—British p42
Hammerton p1367

Watson, James Craig (1838-1880). Can.-Amer. astronomer, mathematician.
N.A.S.—Biog. (3) p43-57
Smith—Math. p133

Watson, John Broadus (1878-1958). Amer. psychologist.
Chambers—Dict. col.457-458   Hammerton p1367
Curr. Biog. '42 p869-871 (por.869)
    '58 p457

Watson, Joseph Ralph (1874-1946). Amer. entomologist.
Osborn—Fragments p229-230

Watson, Sir Malcolm (1873-1955). Br. chemist.
Hammerton p1367-1368

Watson, Richard (1737-1816). Eng. chemist.
Weeks—Discovery p61 (por.61)

Watson, Sereno (1820/1826-1892). Amer. botanist.
N.A.S.—Biog. (5) p267-285 (por.267)

Watson, Thomas Augustus (1854-1934). Amer. inventor.
*Darrow—Thinkers p237-247 (por.240)

Watson, Sir William (1715-1787). Eng. physician.
Chambers—Dict. col.458
Weeks—Discovery p237 (por.237)

Watson-Watt, Sir Robert Alexander (1892-   ). Scot. physicist.
Calder—Science p77   *Larsen—Prentice p166-169
Chambers—Dict. col.458-459   People p438
   (por.458)   Pringle—Great p55-70 (por.65)
Curr. Biog. '45 p656-657 (por.657)   Radio's 100 p256-257 (por.140)
*Larsen—Men p211-221 (por.81)

Watt, James (1736-1819). Scot. inventor, engineer.

Abbot—Great p159-162 (por.160)
Arago—Biog. p351-480
*Bachman—Great p7-24 (por.6)
*Book—Pop. Sci. (15) p5158-5159 (por.5159)
Chambers—Dict. col.459
Chymia (1) p123-137 (por.126)
*Compton—Conquests p150-168
*Cottler—Heroes p138-145
*Crowther—Inventors p11-47 (por.64)
*Darrow—Masters p99-103 (por.289)
*Darrow—Thinkers p57-67 (por.58)
*Eberle—Invent. p13-18
*Epstein—Real p44-46
Fitzhugh—Concise p717-718
Glenister—Stories p153-170 (por.153)
Goddard—Eminent p160-166 (por.160)
Gregory—British p29-30 (por.20)
Hammerton p1368 (por.1368)
Hart—Engineers p79-91
*Hartman—Mach. p59-62
*Hodgins—Behemoth p42-67
*Larsen—Prentice p17-21
Law—Civiliz. p10-17
Lenard—Great p130-136 (por.131)
*McSpadden—How p115-124
Matschoss—Great p84-110 (por.100)
Meyer—World p92-93
*Montgomery —Invent. p105-109
*Nida—Makers p26-32
100 Great p575-581 (por.56)
*Parkman—Conq. p191-213
*Science Miles p104 (por.104)
Sewell—Brief p84-85
Suter—Gallery p114-120
Tuska—Invent. p107-108
Van Wagenen—Beacon p171-172
Wilson—Amer. p48-51 (por.49)
Year—Pic. p145 (por.145)

Watts, James Winston (1904-   ). Amer. neuro-surgeon.

Chambers—Dict. col.459-460

Watts, Lyle Ford (1890-   ). Amer. agriculturist.

Curr. Biog. '46 p628-629 (por.629)

Watts, William Whitehead (b.1860). Eng. geologist.

Hammerton p1370

Way Sung New (1892-1937). Chin. surgeon.

Leonardo—Lives p447-448

Weagant, Roy Alexander (1881-1942). Can. engineer.

Curr. Biog. '42 p871
Radio's 100 p204-207 (por.140)

Weaver, Walter Reed (1885-1944). Amer. aero. pioneer.

Curr. Biog. '44 p722

Weaver, Warren (1894-   ). Amer. mathematician.

Curr. Biog. '52 p625-627 (por.625)

Webb, Philip Barker (1793-1854). Eng. botanist.

Hammerton p1371

Webb, Walter Loring (1863-1941). Amer. engineer.

Curr. Biog. '41 p902

Weber, Eduard Friedrich (1806-1871). Ger. physician.
Major—History (2) p712

Weber, Ernst Heinrich (1795-1878). Ger. physiologist, anatomist.
Chambers—Dict. col. 460   Van Wagenen—Beacon p259-261
Hammerton p1372   Woodruff—Devel. p295
Major—History (2) p711-712

Weber, Max (b.1852). Ger. zoologist.
Hammerton p1372

Weber, Max Maria von (1822-1881). Ger. engineer.
Hammerton p1372

Weber, Wilhelm Eduard (1804-1891). Ger. physicist.
Chambers—Dict. col. 460   Lenard—Great p263-270 (por.263)
Law—Civiliz. p206-207

Webster, Arthur Gordon (1863-1923). Amer. physicist.
N.A.S.—Biog. (18) p337-341 (por.337)

Webster, William (1900-   ). Amer. engineer.
Curr. Biog. '50 p606-608 (por.607)

Wedgewood, Josiah (1730-1795). Eng. chemist.
Chymia (5) p180-192

Wedgewood, Thomas (1771-1805). Eng. inventor, physicist, chemist.
*Epstein—Real p123-124   Law—Civiliz. p152-154
Hammerton p1373

Weed, Clarence Moores (1864-1947). Amer. entomologist, naturalist.
Osborn—Fragments p188 (por.340)

Weems, Philip Van Horn (1889-   ). Amer. aero. pioneer.
Heinmuller—Man's p316 (por.316)

Wegener, Alfred Lothar (1880-1930). Ger. meteorologist, geophysicist,
geologist.
Chambers—Dict. col.460-461
Hammerton p1374

Wehner, Joseph (d.1918). Amer. aero. pioneer.
Maitland—Knights p207-210

Weichselbaum, Anton (1845-1920). Aust. bacteriologist, pathologist.
Bulloch—Hist. p402-403
Kagan—Modern p152 (por.152)

Weidlein, Edward Ray (1887-   ). Amer. chem. engineer, metallurgist, chemist.
Browne—Hist. p488-489 (por.149)
Curr. Biog. '48 p661-663 (por.662)
Progress—Science '41 p382-383 (por.382)

Weidman, Samuel (1870-1945). Amer. geologist.
G.S.A.—Proc. '45 p275-277 (por.275)

Weierstrass, Karl Theodor (1815-1897). Ger. mathematician.
Ball—Short p466
Bell—Men p408-423,429-432 (por.,front.)
Cajori—Hist. p423-431
Chambers—Dict. col.461
*Miller—Hist. p255-257
Smith—Hist. I p509
Woodruff—Devel. p295

Weigall, Arthur Edward (1880-1934). Brit. archaeologist.
Hammerton p1374

Weigert, Carl (1845-1904). Ger. pathologist, bacteriologist.
Bulloch—Hist. p403
Grainger—Guide p177
Kagan—Leaders p87-95
Kagan—Modern p153 (por.153)
Major—History (2) p906

Weil, Richard (1876-1917). Amer. pathologist.
Kagan—Modern p171 (por.171)

Weir, Robert F. (1838-1927). Amer. physician, surgeon.
Leonardo—Lives (Supp.1) p515-516

Weir, William Weir, 1st Baron (1877-1959). Scot. engineer.
Hammerton p1374 (por.1374)

Weirstrass, Karl (1815-1897). Ger. mathematician.
Year—Pic. p117 (por.117)

Weis.   See **Weiss**

Weisbach, Albin (1833-1901). Ger. mineralogist, physicist.
Weeks—Discovery p410 (por.410)

Weismann, August (1834-1914). Ger. biologist.
*Book—Pop. Sci. (15) p5118-5120
Chambers—Dict. col.461
Hammerton p1374 (por.1374)
Locy—Biology p398-408 (por.406)
*Shippen—Micro. p174-178
*Snyder—Biology p144-147 (por.143)
Thomson—Great p151-158
Van Wagenen—Beacon p365-367
*Shippen—Micro. p174-178
Woodruff—Devel. p248,295

Weiss, José (d.1919). Fr. aero. pioneer.
Burge—Ency. p641

Weiss, Soma (1899-1942). Amer. physician.
Curr. Biog. '42 p877
Kagan—Modern p46

Weizmann, Chaim (1874-1952). Rus. biochemist.
Curr. Biog. '42 p877-880 (por.878)
  '48 p663-666 (por.664), '52 p627
*Nisenson—Illus. p152

Welch Family (19th, 20th cent.). Amer. physicians.
Cushing—Medical p204-205

Welch, William Addams (1868-1941). Amer. engineer.
Curr. Biog. '41 p909

Welch, William Henry (1850-1934). Amer. pathologist, bacteriologist, physician.
A.A.A.S.—Proc. (78) p15-17
*Book—Pop. Sci. (15) p5142-5143
Bulloch—Hist. p403
Castiglioni—Hist. p986 (por.985)
Cushing—Medical p199-205
Grainger—Guide p177-178
Hammerton p1375
Jaffe—Outposts p82-128 (por.90)
Kagan—Leaders p127-161 (por.126)
Kagan—Modern p155 (por.155)
Major—History (2) p853-854,911-912, 990 (por.854)
N.A.S.—Biog. (22) p215-224 (por.215)
Rowntree—Amid p57,60 (por.59)
16 Amer. p13-16

Welch, William Wickham (1818-1892). Amer. physician.
Cushing—Medical p204-205

Weldon, Walter (1832-1885). Eng. chemist.
Hammerton p1375

Wellcome, Sir Henry (1854-1936). Amer.-Eng. chemist.
Hammerton p1375

Weller, Thomas H. (1915-   ). Amer. bacteriologist.
Curr. Biog. '55 p183-184 (por.184)

Wellman, Frederick Creighton (or Kay-Scott, Cyril) (1871-1960). Amer. sci. explorer, physician, entomologist.

Curr. Biog. '44 p724-726 (por.725)

Wellman, Walter (1858-1934). Amer. aero. pioneer, sci. explorer.

*Cohen—Men p52-55
Hammerton p1377
Heinmuller—Man's p267 (por.267)
La Croix—They p5-18 (por.98)

Wells, Agnes Ermina (1876-1959). Amer. mathematician, astronomer.

Curr. Biog. '49 p632-634 (por.633)
    '59 p480

Wells, Harry Gideon (1875-1943). Amer. pathologist, biol. chemist.

Curr. Biog. p811
Major—History (2) p1051
N.A.S.—Biog. (26) p233-249 (por.233)

Wells, Horace (1815-1848). Amer. dental surgeon.

Chambers—Dict. col.461-462
*Elwell—Sci. p119-120
Fülöp-Miller p105-110,170-183
    (por.104)
Hammerton p1379
*Morris—Heroes p184-188,191
N.A.S.—Biog. (12) p273-282 (por.273)
Robinson—Victory p93-107 (por.83)
Rosen—Four p178-179,254-256
Thorwald—Century p90-98,100-108,
    140-148,150-155,157-163 (por.80)
*Truax—Doctors p70-73
Year—Pic. p132 (por.132)
Young—Scalpel p138-140,147,148-
    149,151,154,155 (por.154)

Wells, Roger Clark (1877-1944). Amer. chemist.

Chambers—Dict. col.462
G.S.A.—Proc. '45 p279-281 (por.279)

Wells, Sir Thomas Spencer (1818-1897). Eng. physician.

Castiglioni—Hist. p729 (por.729)
Leonardo—Lives p448-450

Wells, William Charles (1757-1817). Amer. physician.

Major—History (2) p702

Welsbach, Carl Auer, Baron von (or Wellsbach, Karl; Auer, Karl) (1858-1929). Aust. chemist.

Chambers—Dict. col.462
Smith—Torch. p252 (por.252)
Weeks—Discovery p426,428-430
    (por.426)

Welsh, Edward Cristy (1909-   ). Amer. space pioneer.

Thomas—Men (3) p.xvii-xviii

Weltzin, Carl (1813-1870). Rus.-Ger. chemist.

Chymia (1) p-153-169 (por.154)

Wenckebach, Karel Friedrich (1864-1940). Aust. physician.
Curr. Biog. '40 p851
Major—History (2) p1051-1052

Wendt, Gerald Louis (1891-   ). Amer. chemist.
Browne—Hist. p502 (por.399)
Curr. Biog. '40 p851-852 (por.851)

Wenham, Francis Herbert (1824-1908). Brit. aero. pioneer, engineer.
Burge—Ency. p641-642
Heinmuller—Man's p247

Wen-Hao.   See **Wong Wen-Hao**

Wenzel, Carl Friedrich (1740-1793). Ger. chemist, metallurgist.
Chambers—Dict. col.462
Partington—Short p160,178

Wepfer, Johann Jacob (1620-1695). Swiss physician.
Major—History (1) p556

Werlhof, Paul Gottlieb (1699-1767). Ger. physician.
Major—History (2) p633-634

Werner, Abraham Gottlob (1749/1750-1817). Ger. geologist, mineralogist.
Adams—Birth p200-205,211-227,
    316-318 (por.210)
*Book—Pop. Sci. (10) p3304
Chambers—Dict. col.462-463
Fenton—Giants p39-48 (por.14)
Geikie—Founders p102-137
Hammerton p1380
Murray—Science p40-42
Van Wagenen—Beacon p192-193
Weeks—Discovery p146 (por.146)
Woodruff—Devel. p175-176,206-207,
    295 (por.176)

Werner, Alfred (1866-1919). Swiss chemist.
Chambers—Dict. col.463
Farber—Nobel p57-60 (por.118)
Hammerton p1380
Partington—Short p355
Smith—Torch. p253 (por.253)

Wernicke, Erich Arthur Emmanuel (1859-1929). Ger. bacteriologist, hygienist.
Bulloch—Hist. p403

Wertham, Fredric (1895-   ). Ger. psychiatrist, neurologist.
Curr. Biog. '49 p634-635 (por.634)

Wertheim, Ernst (1864-1920). Aust. bacteriologist, gynecologist.
Bulloch—Hist. p403

Wertheimer, Max (1880-1943). Ger. psychologist.
Curr. Biog. '43 p816

Wesbrook, Frank Fairchild (1868-1918). Can. bacteriologist, hygienist.
Bulloch—Hist. p403-404

Wessel, Caspar (1745-1818). Dan. mathematician.
Copen.—Prom. p81-84

Westermarck, Edward Alexander (1862-1939). Fin. anthropologist.
Hammerton p1382-1383 (por.1383)

Westgate, Lewis Gardner (1868-1948). Amer. geologist.
G.S.A.—Proc. '48 p243-246 (por.243)

Westinghouse, George (1846-1914). Amer. inventor, engineer.
Abbot—Great p33-36 (por.36)
Chambers—Dict. col.463
*Darrow—Builders p144-153 (por.145)
*Darrow—Masters p253-264 (por.321)
*Darrow—Thinkers p213-223 (por.214)
*Epstein—Real p73-74
*Everett—When p30-37 (por.30)
*Faris—Men p69-74
Hammerton p1383
*Hylander—Invent. p117-125 (por.117)
John Fritz p39-41 (por.38)
*Larsen—Scrap. p104-108 (por.112)
Law—Civiliz. p39
Matschoss—Great p333-343 (por.315)
*Montgomery—Invent. p205-208
Morris—Ency. p728
*Parkman—Conq. p275-289 (por.288)
*Patterson—Amer. p96-109
*Science Miles p211-216 (por.211)
*Wildman—Famous (1st) p285-294
  (por.283)
Wilson—Amer. p256-263 (por.260)
Year—Pic. p156 (por.156)

Weston, Edward (1850-1936). Eng. chemist, inventor.
A.A.A.S.—Proc. (78) p17-18

Weston, William (1752/1753-1833). Eng.-Amer. engineer.
Gunther—Early XI p313-314

Westwood, John Obadiah (1805-1893). Eng. entomologist.
Gunther—Early XI p177 (por.177)

Wetherill, Charles M. (1825-1871). Amer. chemist.
Smith—Chem. p235

Wetmore, (Frank) Alexander (1886-   ). Amer. ornithologist, biologist.
Curr. Biog. '48 p668-670 (por.669)
Oehser—Sons p181-186 (por.154)
Progress—Science '40 p428-429
  (por.428)
True—Smiths. p29 (por.8)

Weyer (or Wierus), **Johann** (1555-1588). Belg. physician.
Castiglioni—Hist. p498-499 (por.502)
Major—History (1) p471

Weyl, Hermann (1885-1955). Ger. mathematician.
R.S.L.—Biog. (3) p305-323 (por.305)

Weyl, Theodor (1851-1913). Ger. physiol. chemist.
A.A.A.S.—Proc. (79) p42-43

Weymouth, Frank Elwin (1874-1941). Amer. engineer.
Curr. Biog. '41 p912

Weyprecht, Karl (1838-1881). Ger. sci. explorer.
Hammerton p1384

Wharton, Thomas (1614-1673). Eng. physician.
Gunther—Early XI p231
Major—History (1) p555

Wheaton, Charles Augustus (1853-1916). Amer. surgeon.
Leonardo—Lives p450-451

Wheatstone, Sir Charles (1802-1875). Eng. inventor, physicist.
A.A.A.S.—Proc. (81) p92-96
Appleyard—Pioneers p85-106 (por.84)
*Book—Pop. Sci. (15) p1560
Chambers—Dict. col.463-464
*Darrow—Masters p342-343
*Darrow—Thinkers p134-135
Hammerton p1385 (por.1385)
*Towers—Beacon p45-54
Van Wagenen—Beacon p277-278

Wheeler, Harold Alden (1903-   ). Amer. engineer.
*Yost—Engineers p168-182

Wheeler, Sir Mortimer (1890-   ). Scot. archaeologist.
Curr. Biog. '56 p648-650 (por.648)

Wheeler, Raymond A. (1885-   ). Amer. engineer.
Curr. Biog. '57 p586-588 (por.587)

Wheeler, Schuyler Skaats (1860-1923). Amer. engineer.
Hammerton p1385

Wheeler, William Morton (1865-1937). Amer. entomologist.
Essig—Hist. p793-796 (por.793)
Hammerton p1385
N.A.S.—Biog. (19) p203-221 (por.203)
Osborn—Fragments p236-237
(por.357)

Whewell, William (1794-1866). Eng. mathematician.
   MacFarlane—Ten p84-93 (por.,front.)

Whipple, Fred Lawrence (1906-   ). Amer. astronomer.
   Curr. Biog. '52 p628-630 (por.629)
   Thomas—Men (2) p202-227
      (por.106)

Whipple, George Hoyt (1878-   ). Amer. pathologist, physician.
   Chambers—Dict. col.464   Rowntree—Amid p389-395 (por.392)
   Hammerton p1452   Stevenson—Nobel p171-172,173-175
   Progress—Science '40 p429 (por.429)   (por.150)

Whipple, Ralph Wheaton (1890-1954). Amer. geologist.
   G.S.A.—Proc. '55 p195

Whistler, Daniel (1619-1684). Eng. physician.
   Major—History (1) p555-556

Whiston, William (1667-1752). Eng. astronomer, mathematician.
   Hammerton p1386
   Smith—Hist. I p451

Whitaker, Douglas Merritt (1904-   ). Amer. biologist.
   Curr. Biog. '51 p651-652 (por.651)

Whitaker, Milton C. (1870-   ). Amer. chemist, chem. engineer.
   Browne—Hist. p502 (por.371)

Whitby, Lionel Ernest Howard (1895-1956). Eng. pathologist, physician.
   Ratcliffe—Modern p38-41

Whitcomb, Richard T. (1921-   ). Amer. aero. pioneer, engineer.
   Curr. Biog. '56 p650-652 (por.651)

White, Canvass (1790-1834). Amer. engineer.
   Wilson—Amer. p74-75 (por.72)

White, Charles (1728-1813). Eng. surgeon.
   Hammerton p1387
   Leonardo—Lives p451-453

White, Charles Abiathar (1826-1910). Amer. geologist.
   Merrill—First p435-436 (por.434)
   N.A.S.—Biog. (7) p223-230 (por.223)

White, Charles McElroy (1891-   ). Amer. engineer.
Curr. Biog. '50 p610-612 (por.611)

White, David (1862-1935). Amer. geologist, paleontologist.
G.S.A.—Proc. '36 p271-280 (por.271)
N.A.S.—Biog. (17) p189-209 (por.189)

White, George Amos (1848-1918). Amer. physician.
Jones—Memories p438-442
    (por.438,439)

White, Gilbert (1720-1793). Eng. naturalist.
Bodenheimer—Hist. p331
*Book Pop. Sci. (15) p5120
Gunther—Early XI p113-116
    (por.108)
Hammerton p1387 (por.1387)
*Milne—Natur. p35-39 (por.35)
Moulton—Auto. p257
Peattie—Gather. p47-51
People p438
Thomson—Great p41-45
Year—Pic. p107

White, Henry Seely (1861-1943). Amer. mathematician.
N.A.S.—Biog. '49 p17-30 (por.17)

White, James William (1850-1916). Amer. surgeon.
Leonardo—Lives p453-454

White, John Rigsby (1908-   ). Can. engineer.
Curr. Biog. '56 p652-653 (por.652)

White, Paul Dudley (1886-   ). Amer. physician.
Curr. Biog. '55 p645-647 (por.646)
Rowntree—Amid p549-552 (por.550)

White, Robert Prosser (1855-1933). Eng. physician.
Hammerton p1388

White, Thomas Dresser (1901-   ). Amer. aero. pioneer.
Arnold—Airmen p130
Curr. Biog. '57 p588-590 (por.589)

White, William Alanson (1870-1937). Amer. neurologist, psychiatrist, physician.
*Hathaway—Partners p71-87 (por.73).

White, Sir William Henry (1845-1913). Eng. engineer.
Hammerton —p1388 (por.1388)
John Fritz p69-71 (por.68)

Whiteaves, Joseph Frederick (1835-1909). Eng. paleontologist.
Hammerton p1388

Whitehead, Alfred North (1861-1947). Eng. mathematician.
Chambers—Dict. col.464-465
Year—Pic. p202 (por.202)

Whitehead, Robert (1823-1905). Eng. inventor.
Chambers—Dict. col.465
Hammerton p1389 (por.1389)

Whitehouse, Sir Harold Beckwith (1882-1943). Brit. surgeon,
gynecologist.
Curr. Biog. '43 p818-819

Whitla, Sir William (1851-1933). Irish physician.
Hammerton p1390

Whitlock, Herbert Percy (1868-1948). Amer. geologist.
G.S.A.—Proc. '48 p249-250 (por.249)

Whitman, Alfred Russell (1882-1940). Amer. geologist.
G.S.A.—Proc. '40 p243-244 (por.243)

Whitman, Charles Otis (1842-1910). Amer. zoologist.
N.A.S.—Biog. (7) p269-286 (por.269)

Whitman, Walter Gordon (1895-   ). Amer. chem. engineer.
Curr. Biog. '52 p630-632 (por.631)

Whitmore, Frank Clifford (1887-1947). Amer. chemist.
Browne—Hist. p489 (por.149)   Progress—Science '41 p383-384
N.A.S.—Biog. (28) p289-295 (por.289)   (por.383)

Whitney, Eli (1765-1825). Amer. inventor.
Abbot—Great p301-302 (por.302)   Goddard—Eminent p60-69 (por.60)
*Bachman—Great p105-120   Hammerton p1390-1391
*Book—Pop. Sci. (15) p5162   *Hartman—Mach. p14-23
*Burlingame—Inv. p122-130   *Hylander—Invent. p27-34 (por.34)
*Burlingame—Mach. p50-68   Iles—Leading p75-103 (por.75)
Carmer—Caval. p223-227   *Ives—Fifty p35-39 (por.37)
   (por.225,226)   *Larsen—Shaped p11-38 (por.32)
Chambers—Dict. col.465   Law—Civiliz. p99-102
*Darrow—Masters p53-57 (por.320)   Meyer—World p238-239
*Darrow—Thinkers p97-103 (por.98)   *Montgomery—Invent. p115-120
*Eberle—Invent. p39-43 (por.38)   Morris—Ency. p730
*Epstein—Real p157-163   *Morris—Heroes p91-95
                    (*Continued*)

Whitney, Eli—*Continued*
  *Nida—Makers p50-55
  *Nisenson—Illus. p157 (por.157)
  *Parkman—Conq. p63-79
  *Patterson—Amer. p1-16
  *Perry—Four p73-130 (por.72)
  *Pratt—Famous p45-50

  *Science Miles. p125-131 (por.125)
  Sewell—Brief p113
  *Tuska—Invent. p79
  Wilson—Amer. p78-83 (por.78)
  Year—Pic. p140-141 (por.140)

Whitney, Mary Watson (1847-1920). Amer. astronomer.
  *Book—Pop. Sci. (15) p5177-5178
    (por.5178)

Whitney, Willis Rodney (1868-1958). Amer. chemist.
  Browne—Hist. p480 (por.87)
  *Darrow—Builders p171-177
  Holland—Ind. p13-32 (por.13)
  Killeffer—Eminent p28 (por.28)

  N.A.S.—Biog. (34) p350-360
    (por.350)
  Progress—Science '41 p384
  Radio's 100 p146-149 (por.140)

Whittaker, Sir Edmund Taylor (1873-1956). Eng. mathematician.
  Newman—What p20-23
  R.S.L.—Biog. (2) p299-321 (por.299)

Whitten-Brown, Sir Arthur (1886-   ). Brit. aero. pioneer.
  Heinmuller—Man's p307 (por.307)

Whittle, Sir Frank (1907-   ). Eng. inventor.
  Chambers—Dict. col.465 (por.466)
  Crowther—Inventors p203-235
    (por.193)
  Curr. Biog. '45 p677-679 (por.678)
  Daniel—Pioneer p105-109 (por.104)

  Larsen—Men p198-210 (por.80)
  *Larsen—Prentice p117-118
  Pringle—Great p136-151 (por.160)

Whitworth, Sir Joseph, bart. (1803-1887). Eng. engineer, inventor.
  Chambers—Dict. col.466
  Goddard—Eminent p254-260
    (por.256)

  Hammerton p1391 (por.1391)

Whymper, Edward (1840-1911). Eng. naturalist.
  Von Hagen—Green p264-265

Whytlaw-Gray, Robert (1877-1958). Eng. chemist.
  R.S.L.—Biog. (4) p327-336 (por.327)

Wick, Frances Gertrude (1875-1941). Amer. physicist.
  Curr. Biog. '41 p916

Wickham, H. F. (1866-1933). Eng.-Amer. entomologist.
  Osborn—Fragments p195-197
    (por.348)

Widal, (Georges) Fernand Isidore (1862-1929). Fr. bacteriologist, pathologist, physician.

Bulloch—Hist. p404
Castiglioni—Hist. p825,826 (por.825)

Kagan—Modern p158 (por.158)
Major—History (2) p966-967,1052 (por.966)

Widman (or Widmann), **Johann** (b.c.1460). Ger. mathematician.

Smith—Hist. I p257-258

Wiedemann, Christian Rudolph Wilhelm (1770-1840). Ger. zoologist, entomologist.

Essig—Hist. p693-694

Wiedemann, Eilhard Ernst Gustav (1852-1928). Ger. physicist.

A.A.A.S.—Proc. (81) p96-97

Wiedersheim, Robert Ernst (1848-1923). Ger. anatomist.

Hammerton p1392-1393

Wieland, Heinrich Otto (1877-1957). Ger. chemist.

Chambers—Dict. col.466
Farber—Nobel p103-106 (por.118)

Hammerton p1452
R.S.L.—Biog. (4) p341-349 (por.341)

Wien, Max Carl (1866-1938). Ger. physicist.

Chambers—Dict. col.467

Wien, Noel (1899-   ). Amer. aero. pioneers.

Potter—Flying p81-92 (por.82)

Wien, Sigurd (1903-   ). Amer. aero. pioneer.

Potter—Flying p190-199 (por.210)

Wien, Wilhelm (1864-1928). Ger. physicist.

Chambers—Dict. col.467
Hammerton p1393
Heathcote—Nobel p94-101 (por.240)

Magie—Source p597-598
Weber—College p182 (por.182)
Year—Pic. p208 (por.208)

Wiener, Alexander Solomon (1907-   ). Amer. physician, hematologist.

Curr. Biog. '47 p673-675 (por.674)
*Eberle—Modern p113-118

Wiener, Norbert (1894-   ). Amer. mathematician.

Curr. Biog. '50 p614-617

Wier (or Wierus.)   See **Weyer, Johann**

Wiesner, Jerome Bert (1915-   ). Amer. engineer.
Curr. Biog. '61 (Dec.) (por.)

Wiggam, Albert (1871-1957). Amer. psychologist.
Curr. Biog. '42 p890-892
   '57 p592

Wigner, Eugene Paul (1902-   ). Hung. physicist.
Curr. Biog. '53 p657-659 (por.658)

Wilbert, Louis Joseph (1919-1953). Amer. geologist.
G.S.A.—Proc. '52 p179

Wilbur, Ray Lyman (1875-1949). Amer. physician.
Curr. Biog. '47 p675-678 (por.676)
   '49 p636

Wilcke, Johan Carl (1732-1796). Swed. physicist.
Lindroth—Swedish p122-130

Wilczynski, Ernest Julius (1876-1932). Ger.-Amer. mathematician,
   astronomer.
N.A.S.—Biog. (16) p295-319 (por.295)

Wild, Frank (1874-1939). Eng. sci. explorer.
Hammerton p1394 (por. 1394)

Wild, Heinrich von (1833-1902). Swiss meteorologist.
Hammerton p1394

Wild, Horace B. (1868-1940). Amer. aero. pioneer.
Heinmuller—Man's p268 (por.268)

Wilde, Sir William Robert Wills (1815-1876). Irish surgeon.
Hammerton p1395

Wildenow.   See **Willdenow, Carl Ludwig**

Wilder, Russell Morse (1885-   ). Amer. physician.
Progress—Science '41 p384-385
   (por.385)

Wile, Ira Solomon (1877-1943). Amer. psychiatrist.
Curr. Biog. '43 p824

Wiley, Harvey Washington (1844-1930). Amer. agric. chemist.
Browne—Hist. p475-476 (por.45)   *Montgomery—Story p228-231
Hammerton p1395-1396   *Yost—Science p117-133
Killeffer—Eminent p14 (por.14)

Wilgus, Sidney Dean (1872-1940). Amer. psychiatrist.
Curr. Biog. '40 p868

Wilkes, Charles (1798-1877). Amer. sci. explorer.
Morris—Ency. p731
True—Smiths. p30-31 (por.34)

Wilkie, Sir David Percival Dalbreck (1882-1939). Scot. surgeon.
Leonardo—Lives p454-456

Wilkins, Sir George Hubert (1888-1958). Austral. sci. explorer, aero.
pioneer, geographer.
Curr. Biog. '57 p592-594 (por.593)   Heinmuller—Man's p329 (por.329)
   '59 p487   Hammerton p1397 (por.1397)
*Fraser—Heroes p541-543   Maitland—Knights p292-293

Wilkins, John (1614-1672). Eng. nat. philosopher.
Crowther—Founders p46-50
  (por.,front.)

Wilkins, John Walker (1827-1913). Eng. wireless pioneer.
Hawks—Wireless p114-119 (por.114)

Wilkins, Robert Wallace (1906-   ). Amer. physician.
Curr. Biog. '58 p471-473 (por.472)

Wilkins, Thomas Russell (1891-1940). Amer. physicist.
Curr. Biog. '41 p917

Wilkinson, John (1728-1808). Eng. inventor.
Hammerton p1397

Wilks, Sir Samuel (1824-1911). Eng. physician.
Hale-White—Great p227-245
Major—History (2) p889

Willan, Robert (1757-1812). Eng. physician.
Hammerton p1398

Willard, DeForest (1846-1910). Amer. surgeon.
Leonardo—Lives p456-457

Willard, Frederic W. (1881-1947). Amer. chemist.
Browne—Hist. p502 (por.399)

Willcocks, Sir William (1852-1932). Brit. engineer.
Hammerton p1398

Willcox, Sir William Henry (1870-1941). Eng. physician.
Hammerton p1398

Willdenow (or Wildenow), **Carl Ludwig** (1765-1812). Ger. naturalist, botanist.
Hawks—Pioneers p268-269
Reed—Short p126-127

William of Saliceto (or Saliceti, Guglielmo; Guilelmus de Saliceto) (c.1210-1275). It. physician, surgeon.
Castiglioni—Hist. p336-337
Gordon—Medieval p328-330 (por.82)
Leonardo—Lives p374-377
Major—History (1) p295-300 (por.298)

Williams, Alford Joseph, Jr. (1896-   ). Amer. aero. pioneer.
Curr. Biog. '40 p870-872 (por.871)
Heinmuller—Man's p313 (por.313)
Maitland—Knights p265-266

Williams, Clyde Elmer (1893-   ). Amer. metallurgist.
Curr. Biog. '47 p683-685 (por.683)

Williams, Daniel Hale (1858-1931). Amer. physician, surgeon.
*Hughes—Negroes p57-60 (por.56)

Williams, Edward Higginson, Jr. (1849-1933). Amer. geologist, min. engineer.
G.S.A.—Proc. '33 p289-293 (por.289)

Williams, Edwin Gantt (1902-   ). Amer. physician, physiologist.
Curr. Biog. '50 p618-620

Williams, Ira A. (1876-1934). Amer. geologist.
G.S.A.—Proc. '34 p295-305 (por.295)

Williams, James Steele (1896-1957). Amer. geologist.
G.S.A.—Proc. '57 p171-173 (por.171)

Williams, John H. (1908-   ). Amer. physicist.
Curr. Biog. p465-466 (por.465)

Williams, John Whitbridge (1866-1931). Amer. physician.
Major—History (2) p1052

Williams, Robert Rampatnam (1886-   ). Amer. chemist.
Curr. Biog. '51 p659-661 (por.660)   Ratcliffe—Modern p91-100
Progress—Science '41 p385-386   *Yost—Science p224-239
(por.385)

Williams, Roger John (1893-   ). Amer. biochemist.
Curr. Biog. '57 p594-596 (por.595)

Williams, Roger Quincy (1894-   ). Amer. aero. pioneer.
Heinmuller—Man's p333 (por.333)

Williams, William Carlos (1883-   ). Amer. physician, pediatrician.
Fabricant—Why p72-74
Rosen—Four p233-234

Williams, William Robert (1867-1940). Amer. physician.
Curr. Biog. '41 p922

Williamson, Alexander William (1824-1904). Eng. chemist.
Chambers—Dict. col.467   Roberts—Chem. p185-192
Findlay—Hundred p336   Smith—Torch. p254 (por.254)
Hammerton p1404   Tilden—Famous p228-240 (por.228)
Partington—Short p262-266,271   Woodruff—Devel. p295
(por.263)

Williamson, Edward Bruce (1877-1933). Amer. entomologist.
Osborn—Fragments p219 (por.342)

Williamson, Hugh (1735-1819). Amer. physician.
Bell—Early p77-78

Williamson, William Crawford (1816-1895). Eng. naturalist, botanist.
Chambers—Dict. col.467-468   Oliver—Makers p247-260 (por.246)
Hammerton p1405

Willis, Bailey (1857-1949). Amer. sci. explorer, geologist, engineer.
N.A.S.—Biog. (35) p333-342 (por.333)

Willis, John Christopher (1868-1958). Eng. botanist.
R.S.L.—Biog. (4) p353-357 (por.353)

Willis, Thomas (1621-1675). Eng. anatomist, physician.
Bulloch—Hist. p404   Hammerton p1405 (por.1405)
Chambers—Dict. col.468   Major—History (1) p522-524 (por.523)
Gunther—Early XI p208-209   Oliver—Stalkers p112
(por.208)

Williston, Samuel Wendell (1852-1918). Amer. entomologist.

Essig—Hist. p796-800 (por.797)   Osborn—Fragments p189 (por.350)
N.A.S.—Biog. (10) p115-135

Willoughby, Charles Clark (1857-1943). Amer. anthropologist.

Curr. Biog. '43 p827

Willoughby, Hugh L. (1856-1939). Amer. aero. pioneer.

Heinmuller—Man's p258 (por.258)

Willows, E. T. (d.1926). Brit. aero. pioneer.

Burge—Ency. p642

Wills, C. Harold (1878-1940). Amer. engineer.

Curr. Biog. '41 p922

Willstätter, Richard (1872-1942). Ger. chemist.

Chambers—Dict. col.468-469   Partington—Short p320-321
Curr. Biog. '42 p892   Smith—Torch. p255 (por.255)
Farber—Nobel p65-69 (por.118)   *Snyder—Biology p315-319 (por.317)
Hammerton p1406

Willughby, Francis (1635-1672). Eng. naturalist.

Hammerton p1406
Miall—Early p102-130

Wilmer, William Holland (1863-1936). Amer. physician.

Major—History (2) p1052

Wilson, Alexander (1766-1813). Amer. ornithologist, biologist.

Bodenheimer—Hist. p350   Peattie—Green p219-224,226-239
*Book—Pop. Sci. (15) p5120-5121   (por.230)
  (por.5121)   Tracy—Amer. nat. p40-51
*Hylander—Scien. p29-35 (por.29)   Welker—Birds p18-57
Jordan—Leading p51-69 (por.51)   Young—Biology p22-25 (por.21)
Peattie—Gather. p221-225   Youmans—Pioneers p90-99 (por.90)

Wilson, Alfred G. W. (1873-1954). Can. geologist, min. engineer.

G.S.A.—Proc. '54 p143-145 (por.143)

Wilson, Charles Branch (1861-1941). Amer. biologist.

Progress—Science '41 p386

Wilson, Charles Edward (1886-   ). Amer. engineer.

Forbes—50 p431-437 (por.430)

Wilson, Charles Erwin (1890-   ). Amer. elec. engineer.
Curr. Biog. '50 p620-622 (por.621)

Wilson, Charles Thomson Rees (1869-1859). Scot. physicist.
Chambers—Dict. col.469   Riedman—Men p106-108
Hammerton p1406   Weber—College p461 (por.461)
Heathcote—Nobel p259-277 (por.240)

Wilson, Sir Charles William (1836-1905). Eng. archaeologist.
Hammerton p1406 (por.1406)

Wilson, Edmund Beecher (1856-1939). Amer. zoologist, biologist.
N.A.S.—Biog. (21) p315-335 (por.315)
*Snyder—Biology p147-148 (por.148)

Wilson, Edward Adrian (1872-1912). Eng. sci. explorer, physician.
Hammerton p1406

Wilson, Ernest Henry (or "Chinese") (1876-1930). Eng.-Amer. botanist.
*Jewett—Plant p26-46

Wilson, Eugene Edward (1887-   ). Amer. aero. pioneer.
Curr. Biog. '45 p687-690 (por.688)

Wilson, George (1818-1859). Scot. physician, chemist.
*Faris—Men p163-172

Wilson, Henry Jan Peters (1863-1939). Amer. biologist.
N.A.S.—Biog. (35) p351-374
   (por.351)

Wilson, James (1836-1920). Scot.-Amer. agriculturist.
*Ivins—Fifty p379-385 (por.378)

Wilson, Leroy August (1901-1951). Amer. engineer.
Curr. Biog. '48 p684-685 (por.685)
   '51 p667

Wilson, Robert McNair (1882-   ). Scot. surgeon.
Hammerton p1407

Wilson, Volney Colvin (1910-   ). Amer. physicist.
Curr. Biog. '58 p474-476 (por.475)

Wilson, Walter Byron (1885-1951). Amer. geologist.
G.S.A.—Proc. '51 p175-176 (por.175)

Wilson, Walter Gordon (1874-1957). Irish inventor.
Hammerton p1409

Wilson, Sir William James Erasmus (1809-1884). Eng. surgeon.
Hammerton p1409
Major—History (2) p881

Winchell, Alexander (1824-1891). Amer. geologist, paleontologist.
*Book—Pop. Sci. (10) p3305
Merrill—First p394-396 (por.450)

Winchell, Newton Horace (1839-1914). Amer. geologist.
*Book—Pop. Sci. (10) p3305-3306
Merrill—First p481-482 (por.434)

Winckelmann, Johann Joachim (1717-1768). Ger. archaeologist.
Ceram—Gods p11-17
Hammerton p1409-1410 (por.1410)

Windaus, Adolf (1876-1959). Ger. chemist.
Chambers—Dict. col.469   Hammerton p1410
Farber—Nobel p107-110 (por.118)

Windle, Sir Bertram Coghill Alan (1858-1929). Eng. anatomist.
Hammerton p1410 (por.1410)

Wing, Joseph E. (1861-1915). Amer. agriculturist.
*Ivins—Fifty p95-104 (por.94)

Wingate, Edmund (1596-1656). Eng. mathematician.
Smith—Hist. II p414

Winge, Emanuel Fredrik Hagbarth (1827-1894). Norw. pathologist.
Major—History (2) p890

Winkler, Clemens Alexander (1838-1904). Ger. chemist.
Chambers—Dict. col.469-470   Smith—Torch. p256 (por.256)
Findlay—Hundred p336-337   Weeks—Discovery p407-412 (por.408)

Winkler, Johannes (1703-1770). Ger. rocket engineer.
Gartmann—Men p90-92
*Williams—Rocket p145-146,152,
  158-159,167-168 (por.146)

Winlock, Joseph (1826-1875). Amer. astronomer.
N.A.S.—Biog. (1) p329-343

Winogradsky, Serge Nicolajewitsch (or Winogradski, Sergei) (1856-1953). Rus. bacteriologist, naturalist.
Bulloch—Hist. p404
Grainger—Guide p178-179
Reed—Short p212,221,227-228

Winslow, Arthur (1860-1938). Amer. geologist.
G.S.A.—Proc. '38 p209-215 (por.209)

Winslow, Jacob Benignus (or Jacques Benigne) (1669-1760). Dan. anatomist, naturalist, physician.
Copen.—Prom. p53-55
Major—History (2) p629

Winslow, Lyttleton Stewart Forbes (1844-1913). Eng. physician.
Hammerton p1410-1411 (por.1411)

Winstanley, Henry (1644-1703). Eng. engineer.
Hammerton p1411

Winster, Reginald Thomas Herbert Fletcher, 1st baron (n.d.). Eng. aero. pioneer.
Curr. Biog. '46 p653-655 (por.653)

Winterbottom, Thomas (1766-1859). Eng. physician.
Major—History (2) p705

Winthrop, John (1714-1779). Amer. astronomer, physicist.
Bell—Early p78-79
Smith—Math. p52-55 (por.53)
Youmans—Pioneers p40-46 (por.40)

Winthrop, John Jr. (1606-1676). Eng.-Amer. chemist, physician.
Bell—Early p78
Chem. Ind. p5-9 (por., front., 5)
Haynes—Chem. (1) p13-25 (por.16)
Weeks—Discovery p184,209-215 (por.184)

Winton, Will McClain (1885-). Amer. geologist.
Chambers—Dict. col.469-470

Wirsung, Johann Georg (d.1643). Ger. physician.
Major—History (1) p552-553

Wirtz, Felix (1500/1510-1575). Ger. surgeon.
Major—History (1) p437

Wise, John (1808-1879). Amer. aero. pioneer.
Arnold—Airmen p82   Milbank—First p97-104 (por.126)
Heinmuller—Man's p240 (por.240)

Wiseman, Richard (1622-1676). Eng. physician, surgeon.
Hammerton p1411   Major—History (1) p527-529
Leonardo—Lives p457-461   (por.528)

Wislicenus, Johannes Adolf (1835-1902). Ger. chemist.
Chambers—Dict. col. 470   Partington—Short p317
Findlay—Hundred p337   Smith—Torch. p257 (por.257)

Wislizenus, Friedrich A. (1810-1885). Ger.-Amer. geologist, physician.
Merrill—First p256-257 (por.257)

Wissler, Clark (1870-1947). Amer. anthropologist.
Hammerton p1411

Wistar, Casper (1760/1761-1818). Amer. physician.
Bell—Early p79
Major—History (2) p730-731

Witham, Henry of Lurtington (or Silvertop, Henry) (d.1844). Eng. botanist.
Oliver—Makers p243-245 (por.243)

Withering, William (1741-1799). Eng. physician.
Castiglioni—Hist. p620-621 (por.609)   Major—History (2) p598-600,638
Chambers—Dict. col.470   Woglom—Discov. p49-60
Gordon—Romance p389,391
 (por.389)

Withington, Alfreda (1860-1951). Amer. physician.
Fabricant—Why p146-147

Witt, Otto Nikolaus (1853-1915). Eng. chemist.
Smith—Torch. p258 (por.258)

Wodehouse, Roger Philip (1889-   ). Can. botanist, biochemist.
Progress—Science '41 p386-387

Wöhler, Friedrich (1800-1882). Ger. chemist.
A.A.A.S.—Proc. (72) p25-26   *Jaffe—Crucibles p175-198
Bodenheimer—Hist. p373   Major—History (2) p793
*Book—Pop. Sci. (15) p4981-4982   Moulton—Auto. p286
Chambers—Dict. col.470-471   Partington—Short p230-232,238
Findlay—Hundred p337-338   (por.231)
Hammerton p1413 (por.1413)   Roberts—Chem. p121-125
                      (*Continued*)

Wöhler, Friedrich—*Continued*
Schwartz—Moments (2) p837-839
*Science Miles p156-159 (por.156)
Smith—Torch. p259 (por.259)
*Snyder—Biology p313-314
Van Wagenen—Beacon p271-273

Weeks—Discovery p346-353
(por.347,348,352)
Woodruff—Devel. p99,295
Year—Pic. p124 (por.124)

Wolcott, Robert H. (1868-1934). Amer. entomologist.
Osborn—Fragments p229

Wolf, Christian (1679-1754). Ger. mathematician.
Smith—Hist. 1 p501-502 (por.501)

Wolf, Maximilian Franz Joseph Cornelius (1863-1932). Ger. astronomer.
Chambers—Dict. col.471
Hammerton p1413 (por.1413)

MacPherson—Astron. p246-252
(por.246)
MacPherson—Makers p208-211
(por.210)

Wolfe, Hugh Campbell (1905-   ). Amer. physicist.
Cuprr. Biog. '50 p622-624 (por.623)

Wolfe-Barry, Sir John Wolfe (1836-1918). Eng. engineer.
Hammerton p1414

Wölfert, Hans (1855-1897). Ger. aero. pioneer.
Heinmuller—Man's p255 (por.255)

Wolff, Irving (1894-   ). Amer. physicist.
Radio's 100 p261-263 (por.140)

Wolff, John Eliot (1857-1940). Can. geologist.
G.S.A.—Proc. '40 p247-250
(por.247)

Wolff, Kaspar Friedrich (1733-1794). Ger. anatomist, physiologist.
Castiglioni—Hist. p581
Gumpert—Trail p135-159
Hammerton p1414

Locy—Biology p210-214,240-241
Major—History (2) p637
Woodruff—Devel. p242,243,295

Wolffhügel, Gustav (1854-1899). Ger. bacteriologist.
Bulloch—Hist. p404

Wolfler, Anton (1850-1917). Bohem. surgeon.
Leonardo—Lives p461-462

Wollaston, William Hyde (1766-1828). Eng. chemist, physicist.

Chambers—Dict. col.472 (por.471)
Hammerton p1414 (por.1414)
Partington—Short p178 (por.158)
Smith—Torch. p260
Van Wagenen—Beacon p209-211

Weeks—Discovery p247-251,254
 (por.254)
Williams—Great p337-338 (por.338)
Williams—Story p325-327 (por.326)
Woodruff—Devel. p295

Wolman, Abel (1892-   ). Amer. engineer.

Curr. Biog. '57 p597-598 (por.597)

Wong Wen-Hao (1889-   ). Chin. geologist.

Curr. Biog. '48 p689-691 (por.690)

Wood, Horatio C. (1841-1920). Amer. physician, entomologist.

N.A.S.—Biog. (33) p462-474
 (por.462)
Osborn—Fragments p227

Wood, James Rushmore (1813/1816-1882). Amer. surgeon.

Leonardo—Lives p462-463

Wood, Jethro (1774-1834). Amer. inventor.

*Epstein—Real p169

Wood, John George (1827-1889). Eng. naturalist.

Hammerton p1417

Wood, Robert Williams (1868-1955). Amer. physicist.

Chambers—Dict. col.472
Progress—Science '41 p387-388
 (por.387)

R.S.L.—Biog. (2) p327-338 (por.327)

Woodall, John (c.1556-1643). Eng. surgeon.

Leonardo—Lives p463-465

Woodhead, German Sims (1855-1921). Eng. pathologist, bacteriologist.

Bulloch—Hist. p404

Woodhouse, James (1770-1809). Amer. chemist.

Bell—Early p79-80
*Kendall—Young p231-233 (por.240)

Smith—Chem. p76-108 (por.76)

Woodhouse, Robert (1773-1827). Eng. mathematician, astronomer.

Ball—Short p440-441

Woodman, Joseph Edmund (1873-1939). Amer. geologist.

G.S.A.—Proc. '39 p249-252
 (por.249)

Woodruff, Louis Bartolomew (1868-1925). Amer. entomologist.
Osborn—Fragments p211

Woodruff, Theodore Tuttle (1811-1892). Amer. inventor.
Wilson—Amer. p223

Woodward, Sir Arthur (1864-1944). Eng. geologist.
*Bridges—Master p268-278 (por.269)   G.S.A.—Proc. '45 p285-291 (por.285)
Curr. Biog. '44 p744   Hammerton p1418

Woodward, Henry (1832-1921). Eng. geologist.
Hammerton p1418

Woodward, John (1665-1728). Eng. geologist, paleontologist.
Woodruff—Devel. p296

Woodward, Joseph Janvier (1833-1884). Amer. physician, pathologist.
N.A.S.—Biog. (2)   p295-299
Three—Amer. p45-46 (por.46)

Woodward, Robert Burns (1917-   ). Amer. chemist.
Curr. Biog. '52 p647-649 (por.648)

Woodward, Robert Simpson (1849-1924). Amer. astronomer,
  mathematician, physicist.
N.A.S.—Biog. (19) p1-15 (por.1)
Smith—Math. p135

Woodworth, Charles William (1865-1940). Amer. entomologist.
Essig—Hist. p800-802 (por.800)

Wooldridge, Dean Everett (1913-   ). Amer. engineer, physicist.
Curr. Biog. '58 p348-350 (por.349)

Woolley, Sir (Charles) Leonard (1880-1960). Eng. archaeologist.
Ceram—Gods p309-313,319-320   Hammerton p1419 (por.1419)
Curr. Biog. '54 p662-664 (por.663)
  '60 p467

Worcester, Joseph Ruggles (1860-1943). Amer. engineer.
Curr. Biog. '43 p845

Worden, Edward Chauncey (1875-1940). Amer. chemist.
Curr. Biog. '40 p884-885

Work, Hubert (1860-1942). Amer. physician.
Curr. Biog. '43 p845

Worsley, Frank Arthur (1872-1943). New Zeal. sci. explorer.
Curr. Biog. '43 p845

Worthen, Amos Henry (1813-1888). Amer. geologist.
Merrill—First p382-383 (por.380)
N.A.S.—Biog. (3) p339-347

Wotton, Edward (1492-1555). Eng. zoologist, naturalist, physician.
Gunther—Early XI p166

Wrangel (or Wrangell), **Ferdinand Petrovich, Baron von** (1794-1870). Rus.
sci. explorer.
Essig—Hist. p802
Hammerton p1422 (por.1422)

Wray. See **Ray, John**

Wren, Sir Christopher (1632-1723). Eng. mathematician.
Ball—Short p314-315
Crowther—Founders p131-180
(por.144)
Gregory—British p22
Gunther—Early XI p159-161
Hammerton p1423-1424 (por.1423)
Major—History (1) p515-516
Smith—Hist. 1 p412-413

Wright, Sir Almroth Edward (1861-1947). Brit. bacteriologist, physician,
pathologist.
Bulloch—Hist. p404
*Book—Pop. Sci. (15) p5121-5123
(por.5122)
Chambers—Dict. col.473
Grainger—Guide p179
Hammerton p1024 (por.1024)
Major—History (2) p1052-1053
Rowntree—Amid p420-422,424-426
(por.422)

Wright, Arthur Williams (1836-1915). Amer. physicist.
N.A.S.—Biog. (15) p241-253
(por.241)

Wright, Berlin Hart (1851-1940). Amer. astronomer, geologist.
Curr. Biog. '41 p938

Wright, Charles (1811-1885). Amer. naturalist.
Geiser—Natural. p172-198

Wright, Edward (1560-1615). Eng. mathematician.
Ball—Short p253-254

Wright, Frank James (1888-1954). Amer. geologist.
G.S.A.—Proc. '55 p183-185 (por.183)

Wright, Frederick Eugene (1877-1953). Amer. geologist.
  G.S.A.—Proc. '52 p159-164 (por.159)
  N.A.S.—Biog. (29) p317-340
    (por.317)

Wright, Helen (1914-   ). Amer. astronomer.
  Curr. Biog. '56 p655-657 (por.656)

Wright, James Homer (1870-1928). Amer. bacteriologist, pathologist.
  Bulloch—Hist. p404-405

Wright, Louis Tompkins (1891-1952). Amer. physician, surgeon.
  Downs—Meet p60-61 (por.60)

Wright, Orville (1871-1948) & **Wright, Wilbur** (1867-1912). Amer. aero. pioneers, inventors.
  Abbot—Great p225,230-233
    (por.224)
  Arnold—Airmen p9-11
  *Bishop—Kite p161-174
  *Book—Pop. Sci. (15) p4982-4983
    (por.Wilbur,p4983)
  Burge—Ency. p642
  Carmer—Caval. p236-239 (por.236)
  Chambers—Dict. col.473 (Wilbur)
  Cohen—Men p35-38,115-135
  *Compton—Conquests p169-182
  *Cottler—Heroes p239-248
  *Crowther—Inventors p163-201
    (por. 192)
  Curr. Biog. '46 p663-665 (por.663)
    (Orville)
  Daniel—Gugg.. p3-9 (por.2)
    (Orville)
  Daniel—Pioneer p1-7 (por.1)
  *Darrow—Builders p85-90
    (por., Orville,p.97)
  *Darrow—Masters p315-325
    (por.,Orville,p32)
  *Eberle—Invent. p113-118 (por.112)
  *Everett—When p38-44 (por.38)
  Fitzhugh—Concise p748-750
  *Fraser—Famous p1-45
  Hammerton p1425 (por.1425)
  *Hartman—Mach. p237-242
  *Hathaway—Partners p163-183
    (por.164)
  Heinmuller—Man's p260 (por.260)
  *Hylander—Invent. p204-205

  John Fritz p113-116 (por.112)
  *Larsen—Men p121-143 (por.80)
  *Larsen—Prentice p114-117
  Law—Civiliz. p67-73
  *Law—Modern p275-286
  *McSpadden—How p265-279
    (por.274)
  Maitland—Knights p10-83
    (por.35,66)
  *Men—Science p28-30
  *Montgomery—Invent. p241-244
  Morris—Ency. p734
  N.A.S. '49 p257-273 (por.257)
  *Nida—Makers p106-113
  *Nisenson—Illus. p160 (por.160)
  100 Great p674-680
    (por.Wilbur,p56)
  *Parkman—Conq. p330-343 (por.337)
  *Patterson—Amer. p174-188
  People p464 (por.Wilbur,p.452)
  *Pratt—Famous p40-43
  *Science Miles. p270-275 (por.270)
  Sewell—Brief p207-209
  *Shippen—Bridle p101-107
  Thomas—50 Amer. p368-375
  Tuska—Invent. p96-97
  Untermeyer—Makers p360-367
  *Webb—Famous p571-580 (por.570)
  Wilson—Amer. p340-351 (por.351)
  Wildman—Famous (1st) p327-338
    (por.325,334)
  *Wright—Great p229-231

Wright, Sewall (1889-   ). Amer. zoologist.
  Progress—Science '41 p388-389

Wright, Theodore Paul (1895-   ). Amer. engineer, aero. pioneer.
Curr. Biog. '45 p694-696 (por.695)
Daniel—Pioneer p99-103 (por.98)

Wright, Thomas (1711-1786). Eng. astronomer.
Shapley—Astron. p113
Williams—Great p239-242

Wright, Wilbur.   See under **Wright, Orville**

Wright, William Greenwood (1830-1912). Amer. entomologist.
Essig—Hist. p802-804 (por.803)

Wrinch, Dorothy M. (1894-   ). Eng. biochemist, mathematician.
Curr. Biog. '47 p693-695 (por.694)
Progress—Science p388-389
(por.388)

Wroblewski, Zygmunt Florenty von (1845-1888). Pol. physicist.
Chambers—Dict. col.473-474   Woodruff—Devel. p296
Van Wagenen—Beacon p397-399

Wronski, Józef Maria (or Hoëne-Wronski) (1778-1853). Pol.
mathematician.
Smith—Hist. 1 p531 (por.531)

Wu, Chien Shiung (1912?-   ). Chin. physicist.
Curr. Biog. '59 p491-492 (por.491)   Yost—Women Mod. p80-93
Year—Pic. p215,217 (por.217)   (por., front.)

Wunderlich, Carl (Reinhold) August (1815-1877). Ger. physician.
Chambers—Dict. col.474   Sigerist—Great p329-334 (por.329)
Major—History (2) p883

Wundt, Wilhelm (Max) (1832-1920). Ger. physiologist, psychologist.
Chambers—Dict. col.474

Wurtz, Charles Adolphe (1817-1884). Fr. chemist.
Chambers—Dict. col.474   Partington—Short p281-283,295
Chymia (1) p157 (por.158)   (por.282)
Findlay—Hundred p338   Smith—Torch. p261 (por.261)
Hammerton p1426   Weeks—Discovery p400 (por.400)

Würtz, Felix (c.1518-c.1574). Ger. physician, surgeon.
Castiglioni—Hist. p479-480   Leonardo—Lives p465-467
Gordon—Medieval p684

Wurtz, Robert-Théodore (1858-1919). Fr. bacteriologist.
Bulloch—Hist. p405

Wu-Ts'ao Suan-king (fl.c.206 B.C.). Chin. mathematician.
Smith—Hist. 1 p141-142

Wyatt, Michael (1929-1956). Eng. geologist.
G.S.A.—Proc. '56 p193

Wyman, Jeffries (1814-1874). Amer. anatomist, naturalist.
*Book—Pop. Sci. (15) p5123-5124   Jordan—Leading p171-209 (por.171)
(por.5123)   Major—History (2) p770-771
Bulloch—Hist. p405   N.A.S.—Biog. (2) p75-117
Hammerton p1428

Wyssokowitsch, Vladimir Constantinovich (d.1912). Rus. pathologist,
bacteriologist.
Bulloch—Hist. p405

X

Xantus de Vesey, Louis John (or Xantus, John) (1894-   ). Hung.-
Amer. entomologist.
Essig—Hist. p804-808

Xenocrates (c396-314 B.C.). Gr. nat. philosopher, mathematician.
Hammerton p1429
Smith—Hist. 1 p92-93

Xenophanes (570-480 B.C.). Gr. nat. philosopher.
Gordon—Medicine p468-469   Osborn—Greeks p50-51
Hammerton p1429

Xenophon (c.430-c.354 B.C). Gr. nat. philosopher.
Bodenheimer—Hist. p160-161
Hammerton p1429-1430

Y

Yahya ibn Serabi (or Yahya isa ibn).   See **Isa ibn Yahya ibn Ibrahim**

Yakawa.   See **Yukawa, Hideki**

Yancey, Lewis Q. Alonzo (1896-1940). Amer. aero. pioneer.
Curr. Biog. '40 p889
Heinmuller—Man's p333 (por.333)

Yang, Chen Ning (1922-   ). Chin. physicist.
Curr. Biog. '58 p484-486 (por.485)

Yang Hui (c.1261). Chin. mathematician.
Smith—Hist. 1 p271

Yang, You Chan (1897-   ). Kor. physician.
Curr. Biog. '53 p663-664 (por.664)

Yankauer, Sidney (1872-1932). Amer. physician.
Kagan—Modern p134 (por.134)

Yarchanai.   See **Samuel, Mar**

Yarrow, Sir Alfred Fernandez (1842-1932). Eng. engineer.
Hammerton p1431

Yates, Donald Norton (1909-   ). Amer. aero. pioneer, meteorologist.
Curr. Biog. '58 p486-487 (por.487)

Yeager, Charles E. (1923-   ). Amer. aero. pioneer.
Curr. Biog. '54 p666-668 (por.667)
Thomas—Men p204-225
  (por.140, folio)

Yeh.   See **Li Yeh**

Yerkes, Robert Mearns (1876-1956). Amer. psychologist.
Progress—Science '41 p390 (por.390)

Yersin, Alexandre Émile John (1863-1943). Swiss-Fr. bacteriologist.
Bulloch—Hist. p405   Grainger—Guide p179
Chambers—Dict. col.475   Hammerton p1432

Yerushalmy, Jacob (1904-   ). Aust. mathematician.
Curr. Biog. '58 p489-490 (por.490)

York, Herbert (1921-   ). Amer. physicist.
Curr. Biog. '58 p491-492 (por.492)

Young, Charles Augustus (1834-1908). Amer. astronomer.

Abetti—History p204-205
Armitage—Cent. p59
Hammerton p1434
MacPherson—Astron. p33-39
   (por.33)

N.A.S.—Biog. (7) p89-108 (por.89)
Shapley—Astron. p318
Williams—Great p279-280,412
   (por.413)

Young, Charles Jacob (1899-   ). Amer. elec. engineer.

Radio's 100 p274-275 (por.140)

Young, Hugh Hampton (1870-1945). Amer. physician, surgeon.

Curr. Biog. '45 p701
Fabricant—Why p178-179

Leonardo—Lives (supp.1) p516-518
Major—History (2) p1053

Young, James (1811-1883). Scot. chemist.

Hammerton p1434

Young, Thomas (1773-1829). Eng. physicist, physician.

Arago—Biog. p280-349
Ball—Short p430-431
*Book—Pop. Sci. (15) p5143-5144
   (por.5144)
Castiglioni—Hist. p632-633 (por.687)
Chalmers—History p274
Chambers—Dict. col.475-476
*Darrow—Masters p343
Gordon—Romance p471 (por.471)
Hammerton p1434
Hart—Physicists p113-117

Lenard—Great p198 (por.198)
Magie—Source p59
Major—History (2) p706
Murray—Science p324-325
People p469
*Shippen—Design p149-153
Van Wagenen—Beacon p221-222
Williams—Story p27,192,204,225,
   231-232 (por.195)
Woodruff—Devel. p58,59,296
Year—Pic. p119,120 (por.120)

Younghusband, Sir Francis Edward (1863-1942). Brit. sci. explorer.

Curr. Biog. '42 p899
Hammerton p1435 (por.1435)

Yperman, Jan (or Jehan) (c.1275/1295-c.1350). Belg. surgeon.

Castiglioni—Hist. p347-348
Leonardo—Lives p467-469

Major—History (1) p318-319

Yü ("The Great Yü" or Ta Yu) (c.2283 B.C.). Chin. engineer.

Matschoss—Great p5

Yuhanna ibn Masawaih.   See **Mesuë, Senior**

Yuhanna ibn Sarabiun.   See **Serapione, Senior**

Yukawa, Hideki (1907-   ). Japan. physicist.

Chambers—Dict. col.476
Curr. Biog. '50 p636-637 (por.636)

Heathcote—Nobel p446-451
   (por.240)

(Continued)

Yukawa,Hideki—*Continued*
Heinmuller—Man's p352 (por.352)
Progress—Science '40 p433
  (por.433)

Weber—College p786 (por.786)
Year—Pic. p215-217 (por.217)

Z

Zacutus, Abraham (or Lusitanus) (1575-1642). Port. physician.
Gordon—Medieval p755-757

Zakrzewska, Marie E. (1829-1902). Ger.-Amer. physician.
Lovejoy—Women p54,62,71-82,84-86,
  172 (por.85)
Mead—Medical p31-33

Zambra, Joseph Warren (1822-1897). It.-Eng. meteorologist.
Hammerton p1437 (por.1437)

Zammit, Themistocles (1864-1935). Maltese bacteriologist, chemist.
Bulloch—Hist. p405

Zander, Arnold S. (1901-   ). Amer. engineer.
Curr. Biog. '47 p703-705 (por.704)

Zborowski, Helmut Philip von (1905-1943). Bohem. rocket engineer.
Gartmann—Men p114-135 (por.128)

Zeeman, Pieter (1865-1943). Dutch physicist.
Chambers—Dict. col.477
Curr. Biog. '43 p852
Hammerton p1438
Heathcote—Nobel p9-17 (por.240)
Magie—Source p384
Van Wagenen—Beacon p422-423
Weber—College p12 (por.12)
Year—Pic. p208,210 (por.208)

Zeise, William Christopher (1789-1847). Dan. chemist.
Copen.—Prom. p104-106

Zeiss, Carl (1816-1888). Ger. optician.
Hammerton p1438

Zeitlin, Nathaniel S. (1898-   ). Amer. physician.
Fabricant—Why p132-134

Zeller, Philipp Christoph (1808-1883). Ger. entomologist.
Essig—Hist. p808-810 (por.809)

Zeno of Elea (c.450 B.C.). Gr. nat. philosopher.

Bell—Men p24-25
Cajori—Hist. p23-24
Chambers—Dict. col.477-478
Gordon—Medicine p470
Hammerton p1439
Hooper—Makers p235-239
Sedgwick—Short p66-67
Smith—Hist. 1 p78

Zeppelin, Ferdinand, Count von (1838-1917). Ger. aero. pioneer, inventor.

Burge—Ency. p642
*Cohen—Men p38-39,77-80
Hammerton p1439-1440 (por.1439)
Heinmuller—Man's p257 (por.257)

Zerbi, Gabrielle (1468-1505). It. anatomist.

Castiglioni—Hist. p369

Zerbi, Rodrigo Ruiz (1462-1542). Port. physician.

Major—History (1) p463

Zernicke, Fritz (or Zernike, Frits) (1888-   ). Dutch physicist.

Chambers—Dict. Supp.
Curr. Biog. '55 p670-672 (por.671)

Zettnow, Hugh Oscar Emil (1842-1927). Ger. bacteriologist.

Bulloch—Hist. p405

Ziegler, David (1804-1876). Amer. entomologist.

Osborn—Fragments p27

Ziehl, Franz (Heinrich Paul) (1857-1926). Ger. bacteriologist.

Bulloch—Hist. p405-406

Ziemssen, Hugo Wilhelm von (1829-1902). Ger. physician.

Major—History (2) p893-894

Zilboorg, Gregory (1890-1959). Rus.-Amer. psychiatrist.

Curr. Biog. '41 p944-946 (por.945)
     59 p497

Zingher, Abraham (1885-1927). Rom.-Amer. bacteriologist.

Bulloch—Hist. p406
Kagan—Modern p171 (por.171)

Zinn, Walter H. (1906-   ). Can. physicist.

Curr. Biog. '55 p674-676 (por.675)

Zinsser, Hans (1878-1940). Amer. bacteriologist.

Bulloch—Hist. p406   Chambers—Dict. col.478
(Continued)

Zinsser, Hans—*Continued*
  Chandler—Medicine p125-129
    (por.124)
  Curr. Biog. '40 p894 (por.894)
  Fabricant—Why p158-159
  Grainger—Guide p180
  N.A.S.—Biog. (24) p323-346
    (por.323)

  Progress—Science '40 p434-435
    (por.434)
  Rosen—Four p209-211,281-287
  16 Amer. p29-32

Ziolkovsky.   See **Tsiolkovskii, Konstantin Eduardovitch**

Zirkel, Ferdinand (1838-1912). Ger. geologist, mineralogist.
  Woodruff—Devel. p296 (por.206)

Zittel, Karl Alfred von (1839-1904). Ger. paleontologist, geologist.
  *Book—Pop. Sci. (10) p3306   Locy—Biology p340 (por.341)
  Hammerton p1441

Zöllner, Johann Carl Friedrich (1834-1882). Ger. astrophysicist,
    astronomer.
  Armitage—Cent. p148-149 (por.144)   MacPherson—Makers p173-174
  Hammerton p1443

Zoph, Wilhelm (1846-1909). Ger. bacteriologist.
  Bulloch—Hist. p406

Zosimos of Panopolis (c.300). Egypt. chemist.
  Holmyard—Makers p35-39
  Partington—Short p20

Zsigmondy, Richard Adolf (1865-1929). Aust. chemist.
  Chambers—Dict. col.478   Hammerton p1443
  Farber—Nobel p95-98 (por.118)   Smith—Torch. p262

Zuelzer, Georg (1870-1949). Ger. physician.
  Major—History (2) p1053

Zwicky, Fritz (1898-   ). Bulg. astronomer, physicist.
  Armitage—Cent. p190   Progress—Science '40 p441-442
  Curr. Biog. '53 p677-678 (por.677)

Zworykin, Vladimir (1889-   ). Rus.-Amer. inventor, physicist, engineer.
  Bachman—Great p294-296 (por.295)   Progress—Science '40 p442 (por.442)
  Curr. Biog. '49 p654-656 (por.655)   Radio's 100 p241-244 (por.140)
  Meyer—World p203-204   Wilson—Amer. p401 (por.400)
  Morris—Ency. p735   *Yost—Science p240-253